Regime and Periphery in Northern Yemen

The Huthi Phenomenon

Barak A. Salmoni, Bryce Loidolt, Madeleine Wells

Prepared for the Defense Intelligence Agency
Approved for public release; distribution unlimited

NATIONAL DEFENSE RESEARCH INSTITUTE

The research described in this report was prepared for the Defense Intelligence Agency. The research was conducted in the RAND National Defense Research Institute, a federally funded research and development center sponsored by the Office of the Secretary of Defense, the Joint Staff, the Unified Combatant Commands, the Department of the Navy, the Marine Corps, the defense agencies, and the defense Intelligence Community under Contract W74V8H-06-C-0002.

Library of Congress Cataloging-in-Publication Data

Salmoni, Barak A.
  Regime and periphery in Northern Yemen : the Huthi phenomenon / Barak A.
  Salmoni, Bryce Loidolt, Madeleine Wells.
    p. cm.
  Includes bibliographical references.
  ISBN 978-0-8330-4933-9 (pbk. : alk. paper)
  1. Yemen (Republic)--History--1990- 2. Civil war--Yemen (Republic)--History--
  21st century. 3. Yemen (Republic)--Politics and government--21st century. 4. Yemen
  (Republic)--Politics and government--20th century. I. Loidolt, Bryce. II. Wells,
  Madeleine. III. Title.

  DS247.Y48S236 2010
  953.305'3--dc22

                                                                    2010003956

Cover photo: Yemeni Huthi rebels supervise the reopening of a road in Sa'da, north of San'a, on February 16, 2010, following a truce between the rebels and government forces that ended six months of fighting. AFP/Getty Images.

Published 2010 by the RAND Corporation
1776 Main Street, P.O. Box 2138, Santa Monica, CA 90407-2138
1200 South Hayes Street, Arlington, VA 22202-5050
4570 Fifth Avenue, Suite 600, Pittsburgh, PA 15213-2665
RAND URL: http://www.rand.org/
To order RAND documents or to obtain additional information, contact
Distribution Services: Telephone: (310) 451-7002;
Fax: (310) 451-6915; Email: order@rand.org

Preface

The RAND National Defense Research Institute was asked to study the conflict between the Government of Yemen and the Huthis of northern Yemen, in all of its sociocultural, political, and military aspects. This study should be of interest to intelligence analysts and military planners concerned with the security of the Arabian Peninsula, Yemen, and the Horn of Africa.

This research was sponsored by the Defense Intelligence Agency's Middle East and North Africa branch and conducted within the Intelligence Policy Center of the RAND National Defense Research Institute, a federally funded research and development center sponsored by the Office of the Secretary of Defense, the Joint Staff, the Unified Combatant Commands, the Navy, the Marine Corps, the defense agencies, and the defense Intelligence Community.

For more information on RAND's Intelligence Policy Center, contact the Director, John Parachini. He can be reached by email at John_Parachini@rand.org; by phone at 703-413-1100, extension 5579; or by mail at the RAND Corporation, 1200 South Hayes Street, Arlington, Virginia 22202-5050. More information about RAND is available at www.rand.org.

Contents

CHAPTER TWO

The Sociocultural Ecology of the Huthi Conflict: Tribalism and Religion...............45

Part II: From Tension to Conflict: Social Change and Huthi Emergence, 1980s–2004

CHAPTER THREE

Run-Up to the Regime-Huthi Conflict, 1980s–2001 81

Figures

Tables

Figure S.1
Map of Yemen

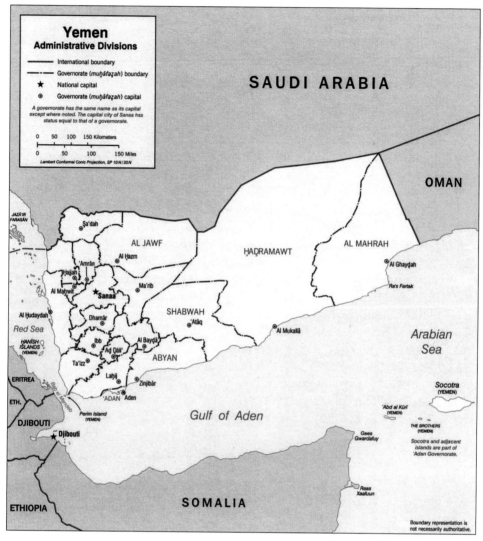

SOURCE: Perry-Castañeda Library Map Collection at the University of Texas, produced by the U.S. Central Intelligence Agency.

RAND *MG962-S.1*

Summary

For nearly six years, the Government of Yemen (GoY) has conducted military operations north of the capital against groups of its citizens known as "Huthis." In spite of using all means at its disposal, as of the beginning of 2010, the GoY has been unable to subdue the Huthi movement. Along with southern discontent and al-Qaʻida–inspired terrorism, the Huthi conflict presents an enduring threat to the regime of President ʻAli ʻAbdullah Saleh and the stability of Yemen. As Huthi-GoY warfare began again in the fall of 2009, Saudi Arabia intervened as well, bringing a major U.S. ally into a regionalized conflict. The recent ceasefire of February 2010 by no means signals an end to conflict, as several such ceasefires have proven short-lived since 2004.

The Huthi movement is based on the family of the same name, which is native to the Saʻda governorate. The Huthi family is part of the Zaydi branch of Islam, theologically situated between Sunnism and Shiʻism. Armed conflict commenced in the summer of 2004, after Huthi supporters started chanting anti-U.S. and anti-Israel slogans in the capital, Sanʻa. Since then, the separate phases of warfare have become continuous conflict with short lulls. In spite of the full force of the GoY military and regional states' attempts at mediation, fighting continues in the north. Clashes have occurred primarily in the Saʻda governorate but have recently been migrating southward.

The Huthi-GoY conflict pits a conventional military using heavy weapons against an unconventional opponent made up of small groups of temporary fighters. The costs to the north of the country have been significant. Casualty estimates range from hundreds to more than 20,000. Estimates of displaced persons reach up to 150,000 people throughout the country, and an estimated 3,000 people have been arrested for supporting the Huthis. At the same time, a news blackout obscures the ongoing destruction in the conflict zone.

At its base, the confrontation between the Huthi family and the Saleh regime is not a conflict among different tribal groupings. Likewise, at its origins, although the Huthi rebellion was inspired by Zaydi revival and led by charismatic Zaydi elites, it is not a confessional opposition movement challenging the legitimacy of the GoY—nor is it a local manifestation of the transnational "Shiʻite Crescent." Rather, it is a conflict in which local material discontent and Zaydi identity claims have intersected with the state center's methods of rule and self-legitimation. As the conflict has proceeded, however, differences between the Huthis and the GoY have taken on the hues of both tribal and confessional strife, rendering a near-term resolution unlikely. Throughout, the Huthi family has been the spearhead of northern Yemeni opposition to the Saleh regime's domestic and foreign policies. The GoY has thus sought to eliminate the family as an influence in Yemen and has targeted sympathetic individuals, groups, and institutions.

The GoY has failed to eliminate the Huthi threat because it emerges from a much more richly textured sociocultural fabric than the government appears to have appreciated. It is this complex fabric that furnishes the multiple dimensions on which to fully understand the Huthi-GoY conflict:

- The first dimension is that of context—the dual context of regime governance techniques and local conditions.
- The second dimension on which to understand the conflict involves the roots of discord, emerging from the 1970s to the late 1990s.
- The post–September 11, 2001, conjuncture provides the third dimension. In this phase, regime calculations and Huthi actions resulted in mutual provocations, furnishing the proximate causes of armed conflict north of San'a.
- The context, roots, and proximate causes act as the drivers of conflict between the regime and the northern periphery in Yemen. In attempting to subdue the Huthis, however, the GoY has pursued policies that can be considered a form of counterinsurgency (COIN) that has had an effect far beyond Huthi strongholds. GoY COIN has sustained the initial drivers of conflict, provoking a widening rebellion that shares the characteristics of insurgency. GoY COIN, therefore, is the fourth dimension illuminating the enduring nature of the Huthi issue.

In responding to GoY COIN, the Huthis have relied on the locally legitimate social bonds of kin networks (tribes) and religion (Zaydism). They have also benefited from the cultural tendency toward collective action in the context of group autonomy. Therefore, after five years of conflict as a combatant entity, the Huthis still exhibit the characteristics of a loosely connected organism—although the leaders of the rebellion are beginning to act in ways that suggest the coalescence of an organization, capable of prosecuting a sustained insurgency. The Huthi journey from resistance organism to insurgent organization will be shaped by enduring GoY approaches and regional conditions surrounding the conflict in 2010–2011.

The February 2010 ceasefire is a welcome development. Yet, over the six-year conflict, ceasefires have broken down several times, due either to the inability of the protagonists to resist targeting each other or to the GoY's tactical use of them as breathing spaces before launching a new offensive. Therefore, it is a reasonable proposition that in the absence of a fundamental restructuring of center-periphery relations, a change of calculations among the protagonists, or a geometric increase of GoY force, this conflict will persist into the next decade in one of two principal forms. In the first form, the GoY will confront a smoldering level of violence that prevents unfettered access to the region, absorbs significant military attention, and results in a progressive destruction of the local means of existence. The GoY may perceive this situation as tolerable: The regime could appeal for support in countering "Shi'ite terror," could justify ongoing military aggrandizement, and could engage in traditionally divisive and cooptative policies in the tribal region. Finally, as Saleh prepares to transition rule to his son at a time when his tribal elite allies are now represented by younger, less-tested leaders, a persistent Huthi insurrection could provide an element of unity. This scenario might be called *smoldering violence and GoY-benefiting chaos.*

In the second scenario, GoY COIN fails to counter the core enablers of Huthi insurgency while widening the geographic and social base of opposition to the regime. Over time, Huthi elements acquire more-sophisticated weapons and coordination capabilities, as well as transnational legitimacy. Here, a progressively contracting Yemeni economy—as oil prices falter and domestic oil production lags—reduces the coercive and cooptative resources at the GoY's disposal, while foreign sponsors call more attention to San'a's stalled democratization, disregard for human rights, and excessive accommodation of extremist Salafism. External powers might then push the GoY to accept more international mediation. Although more high-intensity GoY operations or a peaceful resolution based on reconstruction are also possible, this second scenario, *Huthi persistence and exhaustion of GoY capacity,* currently appears most likely. Combined with lingering discontent in the south and threats from al-Qa'ida, this conjuncture of events would cast a new light on the conflict in Sa'da—aiding the Huthi evolution from organism to organization—and could materially threaten the long-term viability of the Saleh regime.

Acknowledgments

This study has benefited from the insights of several individuals in the United States and abroad that were provided on condition of anonymity. We wish to acknowledge the extensive assistance of academicians in the United States with whom we consulted, who provided published and unpublished documents for our use. International academicians and nongovernmental organization (NGO) workers also proved quite helpful through interviews and suggestions for sources to contact. Several NGOs themselves provided assistance, contacts, and documents, in the United States and Europe, as well as through their Yemen offices.

The authors also wish to thank the staff of U.S. research centers focusing on Yemen for their generosity of time and insights into the finer points of Yemeni political culture and Zaydi religion. In addition, along with Yemeni journalists in Yemen, several Yemeni nationals resident in the U.S. or Canada shared their understanding of the regime-Huthi conflict, in some cases based on first-hand experience. We recognize the danger they face and thank them for their openness. We also wish to thank an American citizen journalist, who has followed Yemen very closely since 2001, for her generosity of spirit and for the access she provided us to these Yemenis as well as to documents in her possession.

At RAND, the authors are particularly grateful for the assistance of Rena Rudavsky, whose ability to mine statistical data and geospatial imaging resources permitted us an interpretive capability grounded in qualitative and quantitative detail. We are indebted to her for her hours of labor and innovative approaches. We also thank our colleague Alireza Nader for his insights on Iranian regional interests and attitudes to the ongoing conflict.

Finally, we acknowledge the enthusiastic assistance of elements of the U.S. special operations community, whose reflections on the capabilities of the Yemeni military were of great value.

Arabic Terms and Definitions

ahkam al-aslaf	tribal law and norms
ahl-al-bid'a	"people of innovation"; derogatory Wahhabi term for Zaydis
ahl al-sunna	people of well-trodden path; Sunni community
al-hirs al-jumhuri	Republican Guard
'alim; pl. *'ulama'*	religious scholar
'allama	noted religious scholar
al-Mawlid al-Nabawi	Birthday of Prophet Muhammad
al-Mawt li Amrika al-Mawt li Isra'il al-La'na 'ala-l-Yahud, al-Nasr li-l-Islam	Huthi slogan: "Death to America, Death to Israel, Curse Upon the Jews, Victory to Islam."
amir al-mu'minin	Commander of the Faithful
anashid; sing. *nashid*	anthem, ballad
'aqil; pl. *'uqqal*	tribal elder
asl	purity and nobility of tribal background
asliha; sing. *silah*	weapons
asliha khafifa	light weapons
asliha mutawassita	medium weapons
asliha thaqila	heavy weapons
awqaf; sing. *waqf*	pious Islamic endowments
'ayb	shame brought on oneself and others by violating honor
bani khums	nontribal, inferior, protected classes of people in northern Yemen
bayt	house, family

bilad al-qaba'il	"the land of the tribes"
bilad Hashid wa al-Bakil	"the land of Hashid and Bakil tribes"
damin; pl. *dumana'*	guarantor in tribal mediation
dayf	guest of tribal member, deserving of protection
diwan	guest parlor of house in northern Yemen
diya	blood money: material compensation for injury or loss of life
faqih; pl. *fuqaha'*	expert in Islamic jurisprudence and legal sources
fatwa; pl. *fatawa*	Islamic legal ruling
fiqh	Islamic jurisprudence
fitna	discord, disorder; conflict in Islamic world
hayba	cultural prestige
hijra	lit. "emigration"; in Yemen, a location protected for religious or economic reasons
hirs al-hudud	Border Guard
'Id al-Ghadir	Ghadir Day, holiday when Muhammad is said to have appointed 'Ali as his successor
ijma'	scholarly consensus; one of the principles of Islamic jurisprudence
Imam	legitimate heir of political rule
ijtihad	scholarly efforts to interpret Qur'an and hadith, to derive legal rulings or an understanding of theology
infisali, pl. *infisaliyin*	separatist; term recalling 1994 Yemeni civil war
'ird	honor; of vulnerable items or people
jambiya (janbiya)	traditional Yemeni dagger in tribal men's waistband
jang-e tahmili	"imposed war" (Persian); refers to 1980–1988 Iraq-launched war with Iran
jar	neighbor of a tribal member, deserving protection
junud mustajaddin	volunteer forces; used by GoY in Sa'da conflict
kafil; pl. *kufala'*	one's representative in a tribal mediation setting
khandaq; pl. *khanadiq*	trench
khayrat	material bounty that a tribal leader can provide to tribesmen

khuruj	departure or going out; Zaydi theological term referring to the claim to imamate
khusma	antagonism between individuals or groups that requires combat or reconciliation
khutba; pl. *khutab*	mosque sermon at Friday prayers
kuffar ta'wil	infidels in interpretation; some Sunnis feel that Zaydis use the term to denote them
ma'ahad 'ilmiya	scientific institutes; Salafi-supported schools in northern Yemen
madaris 'ilmiya	scientific schools; Zaydi-supported schools in northern Yemen
madfa' hawun	mortar
madhhab	school of Islamic jurisprudence
madhhabiya	parochialism based on adherence to a jurisprudential school; term used to criticize excessive attachment to Zaydism
madih	praiseful speech or prose
majlis	sitting room; parlor, gathering in home, council
mahsubiya	patronage used by GoY and tribal leaders
Mahdi	messianic savior
majlis mahalliya	local council
marja'; pl. *maraji'*	reference point for Islamic rulings, practices, and beliefs; term used for most prominent Shi'ite and Zaydi religious leaders
masdar; pl. *masadir*	source used by a journalist
mawqa'; pl. *mawaqi'*	point, position, military location
mudayyif	host and protector of guest
mudhif	tribal guest house maintained by leading tribal family
mudiriya; pl. *mudiriyat*	district, in Yemeni administrative parlance
muhafaza; pl. *muhafazat*	governorate or province, in Yemeni administrative parlance
muhafiz	governor
muhakkam	tribal mediator or arbitrator
mujahidin	freedom fighters

mujawwir	protector of neighbor
muraffiq	host and protector of fellow traveler
mutakhallif	backwards; term used by urban or southern Yemenis to condemn tribal or Zaydi northerners
muzayana	nontribal townsfolk of lower social stratum; café workers, cleaners, musicians, etc.
namus	chastity, modesty, moral honor; an element of *'ird*
naqa'	clean, pure, good name
nasab	affine-based relationship; connotes obligations emerging from marriage ties
nuqtat taftish	checkpoint
qabila; pl. *qaba'il*	tribe
qabili	tribal person
qabyala	ethical code of tribalism in northern Yemen
qadi; pl. *quda*	Islamic judge; in courts or in tribal adjudication
qasida; pl. *qasa'id*	oral poetry traditionally used in tribal Yemen to articulate social concerns and claims of supremacy, or to rhetorically conduct or resolve conflict
qat	mild narcotic cultivated and sold in northern Yemen
rafiq	fellow-traveler of tribal member, deserving protection
sayyid; pl. *sada*	descendent of Prophet Muhammad; in Zaydi Yemen, descendent of Muhammad through line of 'Ali; thus in socially elevated stratum eligible for imamate
shahid; pl. *shuhada'*	martyr
sharaf	tribal honor; individual or collective
shari'a	Islamic law
shaykh; pl. *mashayikh*	tribal leader
shi'ar	slogan or saying; refers to the Huthi anti-U.S., anti-Israel chants
shi'at 'Ali	party of 'Ali, hence Shi'ites
silf al-qaba'il	loyalty to tribal customary practices
sulh wa tahkim	tribal mediation and arbitration
suq	market

ta'addudiya	political pluralism in post-1990 Yemen
taba'ud	distancing of tribal members from their shaykhs
taghut	arbitrary tyranny with non-Islamic tinge; used to refer to tribal law by those who prefer Islamic literalism
ta'ifiya	religious sectarianism; term used by GOY to criticize Huthis
takhalluf	backwardness, underdevelopment; term used by urban or southern Yemenis to condemn tribal or Zaydi northerners
tamarrud	rebellion; term used by Yemeni regime to describe Huthi phenomenon
taqarub	rapprochement, confluence of political interests
taqim	team; small military unit
tawhid	doctrine of unity of God as preached by Salafis
tha'r	tribal revenge
'ulama'; sing. *'alim*	religious scholarly stratum
umma	the Islamic (or Arab) collective
'urf qabali	tribal custom
'uyun	tribal elders who assist the shaykh
'uzla	subdistrict, in Yemeni administrative parlance
wadi	riverbed or canyon in rural Yemen
wahda	unity
wajh	face, prestige, good name
wasata	mediation
watan	nation state
wazn	standing, prominence, prestige in community
wilayat al-faqih	leadership of a righteous jurisconsult; doctrine of religiopolitical authority originated by Ayatollah Khomeini forming the basis of rule in Iran today
wujaha'	people of prestige in the community

Abbreviations

APC	armored personnel carrier
AQAP	al-Qaʿida in the Arabian Peninsula
BY	Believing Youth
C3	command, control, and communcations
COIN	counterinsurgency
CSO	central security organization
DCS	direct commercial sales
DIME	diplomatic/political, information, military, and economic
EDA	excess defense articles
FMF	foreign military financing
FMS	foreign military sales
GCC	Gulf Cooperation Council
GDP	gross domestic product
GoY	Government of Yemen
GPC	General People's Congress
GWoT	Global War on Terror
HMMWV	high mobility multipurpose wheeled vehicle
HRW	Human Rights Watch
IDP	internal displaced person
IED	improvised explosive device
IMET	International Military Education and Training program
IRIN	Integrated Regional Information Networks
JCET	Joint Combined Exchange Training
LAL	local area leader
LDA	local development association

LOO	line of operation
MP	member of parliament
MSF	Médecins Sans Frontières (Doctors Without Borders)
NDI	National Democratic Institute
NGO	nongovernmental organization
PDRY	People's Democratic Republic of Yemen
PKK	Kurdistan Workers' Party
PSO	Political Security Organization
RPG	rocket-propelled grenade
SOF	special operations forces
UN	United Nations
USAID	U.S. Agency for International Development
YAR	Yemen Arab Republic
YR	Yemeni riyal
YRC	Yemeni Red Crescent
YSOF	Yemeni Special Operations Forces
YSP	Yemeni Socialist Party

Introduction

For nearly six years, the Government of Yemen (GoY) has conducted military operations against groups of its citizens north of San'a, known as "Huthis" or Believing Youth (BY). In spite of using all coercive and ideological means at its disposal, the GoY has been unable to fully subdue the Huthi movement, which has sustained a material and popular base over successive phases of armed conflict into the winter of 2010. At the same time, the regime has confronted mounting southern discontent and al-Qa'ida–inspired terrorism, as well as severely contracting economic prospects. The war against the Huthis, however, has of late absorbed more of the GoY's political attention and coercive resources than these other issues, weakening the state's ability to deal with the multiple challenges it faces. The Huthi conflict thus presents an enduring threat both to the regime of President 'Ali 'Abdullah Saleh and to the stability of Yemen as a unitary state. It also fundamentally impairs the GoY's ability to function as a U.S. partner for regional security, stability, and counterterrorism. Furthermore, armed confrontation between the Kingdom of Saudi Arabia and Huthi fighters beginning in November–December 2009 has added a transnational dimension to the conflict and risks pulling in other regional countries, such as Iran. Such an eventuality would fundamentally undermine security in the Arabian Peninsula and Gulf, harming the regional interests of the United States while it is engaged in Iraq, Afghanistan, and nuclear negotiations with Iran.

The Huthi movement is based on the family of the same name, native to the Sa'da governorate north of San'a. The Huthi family is part of the Zaydi branch of Islam, which considers political legitimacy to derive from descent from the family of the Prophet Muhammad. Armed conflict commenced in the summer of 2004, when Sa'da-based charismatic leader Husayn al-Huthi was deemed a threat by the GoY after his followers chanted anti-U.S. and anti-Israel slogans in San'a. Husayn al-Huthi was killed by the government in September 2004 and was succeeded by his brother, 'Abd al-Malik. There have been six GoY-recognized phases of war, ranging from one to eleven months in duration, and the intermittent violence has increasingly evolved into rolling conflict. The latest "Sa'da war" was launched in August 2009 and continued until February 2010. Clashes have occurred primarily in the mountainous areas of the Sa'da governorate. Likewise, along with southward migration of the Huthi-GoY fighting, Saudi forces have engaged Huthi fighters along the Saudi-Yemeni border while bombing Huthi positions in Yemen from the air.

The conflict pits a conventional military using heavy weapons against an unconventional opponent made up of small groups of temporary fighters. The costs to the north have been significant. Casualty estimates range from hundreds or thousands, according to humanitarian organizations, to nearly 25,000, according to Huthi sources. There are an estimated 150,000 displaced persons throughout the country, many of whom lack adequate food, water, or medicine. A further estimated 3,000 people have been arrested so far for allegedly supporting the Huthis, while a news blackout in the conflict zone obscures much ongoing human and material loss.

Through its patriarch, Badr al-Din al-Huthi, and his sons Husayn, Muhammad, Yahya, and 'Abd al-Malik, the Huthi family has spearheaded northern Yemeni opposition to the Saleh regime's political, economic, religious, and foreign policies. The GoY has thus sought to eliminate the family as an influence in Yemen and has targeted all individuals, groups, and institutions considered sympathetic to them.

In this introduction, we provide a broad overview of the background and progress of the Huthi-regime conflict. We also elucidate the study's analytical approach and chapter structure, briefly discussing the source-based challenges to the study of Yemen and the Huthis. For students of Yemen and the Middle East, this introduction thus provides an orientation to the study. It is also a brief survey of the conflict as a whole, guiding policymakers and analysts to chapters and topics of direct concern to them.

Analytical Dimensions of the Conflict

In over five years of combat operations, the GoY has failed in its efforts to eradicate the Huthi opposition. This is because the Huthi family emerges from a much more richly textured and evolving sociocultural fabric than the government appears to have appreciated. It is this complex fabric that furnishes the multiple dimensions on which the Huthi-regime conflict can be fully understood. The first dimension is that of context—the dual context of regime governance techniques and local conditions in a geographic, socioeconomic, political, and ideological periphery.[1] The second dimension involves the roots of discord, visible as early as the 1970s but fully emergent by the late 1990s. The post–September 11, 2001, conjuncture provides the third dimension. In

---

[1]   Our consideration of the GoY-Huthi conflict in the context of "regime" and "periphery" follows social science approaches to center and periphery as regards the domestic economics, political relationships, and ideology structures internal to a single country. For similar usage, see Metin Heper, "Center and Periphery in the Ottoman Empire," *International Political Science Review* 1:1 (1980), 81–104; Serif Mardin, "Center-Periphery Relations: A Key to Turkish Politics?" *Daedalus* 102:1 (1973), 169–191; Steven Solnick, "Will Russia Survive?" in Barnett R. Rubin and Jack Snyder, eds., *Post-Soviet Political Order: Conflict and State Building* (London: Routledge, 1998); and Bernt Glatzer, "Center and Periphery in Afghanistan: New Identities in a Broken State," *Sociologus* 52:1 (2002), 107–125.

this phase, regime calculations and Huthi actions resulted in mutual provocation, furnishing the proximate causes of armed conflict north of San'a. In attempting to subdue the Huthis, however, the GoY has undertaken measures that have an effect far beyond Huthi strongholds, thus prolonging a widening resistance that shares many characteristics with insurgency and over time may evolve into one. An insurgency-provoking GoY campaign, therefore, is the fourth dimension illuminating the enduring nature of the Huthi issue in Yemen.

Context

Perhaps more than any other Arab country, Yemen has a central government that possesses an extremely attenuated degree of control over its peripheries—and the north is the least responsive to San'a. Furthermore, the post-1978 regime led by 'Ali 'Abdullah Saleh has not sought to exert direct control over the north. Rather, Saleh's political method is based on the material cooptation of local tribal leaders, thus permitting GoY sovereignty in the absence of substantive control. As such, the relative historic autonomy of the north continued into the 2000s, including methods of economic exchange, political activity, and conflict mediation that remain only marginally influenced by the republican state.

The physical context of the north symbolizes this autonomy. Scarce resources are allocated across a harsh geographical environment. Population concentrations are scattered and relatively small, separated by deserts, mountains, and other natural obstacles to movement—or external penetration. Material survival has thus required a certain amount of local self-sufficiency, as well as the maintenance of interregion trade routes. Further, environmental constraints have traditionally limited the kind of wealth accumulation that creates large socioeconomic gaps.

This physical context has strengthened hyper-local identities based on place and kin networks, driving a particular kind of social value system known as *qabyala*, or tribalism, in which individual autonomy and collective honor take precedence over other ideas of law and legitimacy. According to *qabyala*, honor (*sharaf*) inheres in solidarity with kinsmen, protection of a kin group's women and other subordinate allies, and the inviolability of an individual or group's territory and possessions.[2]

---

[2] A note on transliteration of Arabic words: In this study, we follow the transliteration guidelines of the *International Journal of Middle East Studies*, though we omit macrons for long vowels. The letter *'ayin* (ع) is represented by " ' " and the *hamza* (ء) is represented by " ' ". We do not indicate " ' " with a doubled a: We use Sa'da, not Saada. In cases where the Arabic name or term is frequently used in English sources, we have followed the conventional Western spelling: President Saleh, not Salih. However, in spite of the usage of "Houthi" in European and Western press for حوثي, this study uses "Huthi," following usage in the U.S. national security community. It should be noted that, in Yemen, the short vowels in names of places and people are often pronounced in locally specific ways or vary according to local dialectical nuances. There is also inconsistent usage in English-language maps and geographic information system (GIS) data. In cases where we did not encounter these terms in the Modern Standard Arabic (MSA) of Arabic books and media, we assimilated the short vowel pronunciations to the voweling suggested by MSA grammatical rules.

Along with providing a complex of interpretive values, *qabyala* also furnishes a social structure for a group of nested tribes that reaches across northern Yemen—from confederations comprising thousands of Yemenis down to subtribes encompassing tens of people. At each level, leaders, or *shaykhs* (Arabic pl. *mashayikh)*, possess a legitimacy based on their ability to provide access to material goods; to ensure common defense of collective property and territory; and to mediate conflict at the individual, collective, and tribe-regime level. Therefore, *qabyala*—as both a value system and a way of structuring sociopolitics—has often rendered the state peripheral to local concerns.

The potential for entropy and conflict produced by *qabyala* in a land of physical scarcity has traditionally been held in check by trade networks and mechanisms of conflict mediation. In the traditional local context, religion has also played a mellowing role as a social bond based on commonality of beliefs and practices. Northern Yemen is the historical heartland of Zaydi Islam—and Sa'da is its epicenter. Distinct from Sunnism, the Zaydi school of Islamic theology and jurisprudence (*madhhab*) venerates 'Ali and the House of the Prophet as the legitimate heirs of political rule (the *Imam*) in the Islamic world (*umma*). Yet, Zaydism is also distinct from the Shi'ism associated with Iran, Iraq, and Lebanon, because it differs from them over the imamate succession in the fifth generation after 'Ali. Although Zaydis are a minority of all Yemenis, they have historically dominated the north, with the current governorate of Sa'da being their sacred historical center. Sa'da was also the geographical basis of the Zaydi imamate, which ruled most of Yemen until the 1960s.

In the traditional context of northern Yemen, Zaydism—including a learned hierarchy and a stratum of socioreligious elites descended from the Prophet's family known as *sayyids* (Arabic pl. *sada*) or Hashimis—coexisted peacefully with Sunni Islam of the relatively permissive Shafi'i school. Further, as a bond transcending tribal or geographic differences, Zaydism provided commonality to diverse groups. In contrast, although the post-1962 Yemen Arab Republic (YAR) featured leaders with tribal backgrounds from among the Zaydis, its perception of a legitimacy challenge drove it to denigrate both Zaydi communalism and tribalism as atavistic and backwards. This perception gained greater weight after the 1990 unification with the previously socialist People's Democratic Republic of Yemen (PDRY)—and, along with Saleh's political approach of neopatrimonial cooptation, has worked against the integration of the Zaydi heartland with the rest of the state. Thus, local dynamics and regime approaches have rendered the Sa'da region problematic at base.

Roots

The second dimension of the Huthi-regime conflict involves the roots of regime-local tension. These roots go back to the 1970s. Like other Arab states, the YAR focused most of its energy on the capital region and those areas with economic resources—and leaders coming from the tribal hinterlands tended to focus energy on the center after they came to power. The rest of the YAR was comparatively marginalized in material and development terms. The Saʿda– ʿAmran–Hajja area, in particular, was neglected by the republican regime in terms of infrastructure, social welfare, education, and security presence.

This comparative deprivation became much more significant in the 1980s and beyond, when the first post-imamate, republican generation of Zaydis reached maturity. Young Zaydi males—including those later entangled in the Huthi conflict—gained dual exposure to the wider world.

First, tribespeople from hitherto isolated parts of the Saʿda governorate came to know each other at regional boarding schools or through trade. Thus, while tribal identity retained significance, these Yemenis began to see common predicaments confronting Saʿdans as a whole, northern Yemenis as a whole, or Zaydis as a whole. An "imagined community" of sorts thus emerged, transcending village, district, and governorate.[3] Second, Saʿda Yemenis began to travel outside of their governorate, to the capital, as well as to Gulf States or the Levant, for advanced schooling and work.

This generational evolution and increased exposure drove several changes that would destabilize the region and plant roots for later discord. First, increased literacy, travel, and exposure gave northern Yemenis a sense of the sociopolitical trends influencing the rest of the Muslim Middle East. These included the revolution of rising material expectations, disappointment with secular political rulers, and a revival of various expressions of Islam. In terms of the latter, the revival of Zaydism in Saʿda from the late 1980s was fraught with tension. This is because, in addition to reflecting the emergence of a new generation of sociopolitically aware males, Zaydi revivalism was also a reaction to the infiltration of Wahhabi-influenced Salafism into the region. Assisted by Yemenis returning from work in the Gulf, Salafism was supported by many tribes of a Sunni Shafiʿi background and aggressively propagated by converted Wahhabis in the Saʿda environs. Local Wahhabism, in turn, derived support after the 1990 Yemeni unification from the quasi-Islamist Islah Party, through which the GoY at times channeled funds, both to increase its patronage-based leverage in the region and to appease otherwise troublesome Sunni Islamists in Sanʿa. Zaydi revivalism was thus a reaction to local ideological challenges as well as to perceived regime opposition to Zaydism as a *madhhab*.

A second way in which generational change destabilized the region relates to traditional social hierarchies. Younger, nonelite Zaydis began to acquire enough education to excel in religious learning, thus challenging the traditional *sayyid* elite. Scions of tribal (*qabili*) families also chafed at the social precedence of Hashimis. Further, local nontribal elements—hitherto on the lowest rungs of the social ladder—began to acquire the education and wealth that merited higher status. Some of them found in Wahhabism a vehicle to counter the social and religious dominance of the Hashimi class; others wished to undermine the preeminence of the tribe or the shaykhs. Still

---

3   See Benedict Anderson, *Imagined Communities*, new ed. (London: Verso, 2006).

others, both *qabili* and nontribal people, rose in defense of Zaydi doctrines and practices in the face of a Wahhabi assault. In the mid-1990s, these socioeconomic-cum-ideological tensions ultimately produced violence between tribes and sects. Although they receded in the late 1990s, the core drivers of violence were never addressed.

A third manifestation of social change, seemingly contradicting the above, involved increased intermixing among social strata. Hashimi males began marrying women from prestigious *qabili* families at higher rates; wealthy nontribals began to acquire positions in local economics and governance, creating alliances with tribal leaders or Hashimis. As a result, social networks diversified and became more interlaced at the same time as Wahhabi-Zaydi conflict ebbed and flowed. In effect, these networks became the vehicles for expressing such conflict.

Finally, generational change and ideological conflict manifested itself sociopolitically in the mid-1990s. Hashimi grandees established the al-Haqq party as early as 1990 as an expression of Zaydi interests in the face of Yemeni unification and Wahhabi encroachment. Of a more enduring legacy, those same young Zaydis of both *qabili* and Hashimi descent, who had gained broader exposure to different regions in Saʿda and also beyond the governorate, began to establish a network of associations, sports clubs, and summer camps in local boarding schools. This network began to be called the Believing Youth (BY). Its founders included the sons of Badr al-Din al-Huthi, themselves *sayyids* of prestigious pedigree. Both al-Haqq and the more popular BY movement embodied the reassertion of Zaydi identity and learning. They also advocated an agenda focused on Saʿda's material, political, and ideological needs. Until the late 1990s, the GoY provided some political space to al-Haqq and funding to the BY, as part of measures intended to balance Wahhabi/Islah influence.

The BY began to peter out by 2000. By that time, however, several factors had combined to inhibit the GoY's control over the region. These included religious conflict accompanied by Zaydi suspicion of GoY support for Salafis, displeasure with Sanʿa's material inattention to Saʿda, generational change and the decreasing sway of tribal shaykhs over their flock, and the post-1994 occlusion of Yemen's democratic opening. At the same time, these developments diminished the effectiveness of traditional GoY levers of cooptative influence. Additionally, elements of the Zaydi population—who would go on to resuscitate the BY and become the initial Huthi core—felt targeted by the regime. Just as social change and broader Middle Eastern trends likely determined the Zaydi revival by the late 1980s, the state of affairs by the late 1990s strongly hinted at subsequent regime-periphery conflict.

Proximate Causes

The proximate causes of the conflict were produced not only by regime and local actions but also by perceptions of the post-2001 global conjuncture. Efforts after 2000 by Badr al-Din al-Huthi's sons to revive the BY's social welfare and educational activities in Saʿda were not condoned by the GoY, whose leaders now viewed Husayn al-

Huthi, in particular, as a political threat—a plausible prospect, since the latter's local prestige exceeded that of GoY representatives in the governorate. One expression of this prestige was the popularity of Husayn al-Huthi's lecture sessions in his home and nearby mosques after Friday prayers, during which he spoke about Zaydi Islamic practice, doctrine, and ethics—as well as local GoY inadequacies. Supported by his brothers Muhammad and Yahya and endowed with the moral weight of his father, a leading Zaydi scholar of his generation, Husayn continued these activities over the next years, hinting at desires for a larger national role.

Global events after September 11, 2001, elicited new calculations both in San'a and Sa'da that drove the Huthis and the GoY to open conflict. At the GoY level, 'Ali 'Abdullah Saleh presented Yemen as a U.S. partner in the global war on terror, particularly with respect to al-Qa'ida. Augmented U.S. military aid and training support increased Saleh's confidence and his perception of coercive preeminence, perhaps causing him to aspire to more direct control of the north and forcing submission of the periphery. At the same time, closer cooperation with the United States exposed him to criticism from Salafi elements inside the regime and the military. He sought to coopt these elements through largesse—and military budgets.

More offensive to Saleh was the reaction in Sa'da. There, Husayn al-Huthi's criticism of the Saleh regime began to target the latter's readiness to close ranks with the United States. Husayn focused in particular on the U.S. campaigns in Afghanistan and Iraq, which were extremely unpopular among the Yemeni masses. His lectures—recorded and distributed in Sa'da and adjoining governorates on cassette tapes—angered the regime, implying collusion in a crusade to kill Muslims. By late 2003, Husayn's lectures were accompanied by crowds chanting outside Zaydi mosques in Sa'da and the capital, as well as in front of the American embassy. These chants condemned the United States, Israel, and Jews and would become the Huthi slogan.

Beyond embarrassing the regime, Huthi actions challenged Saleh's legitimacy, principally because the Huthi family knits together powerful strands of northern Yemen's sociocultural fabric. Badr al-Din al-Huthi, now in his eighties, is among the most prestigious Zaydi religious scholars in Yemen. His age and learned pedigree act as a bridge to the imamate period. Furthermore, the Huthis are a *sayyid* family. While the preeminence of the Hashimi stratum has been challenged, the prestige of a lineage traced back to the Prophet Muhammad is unquestioned. Beyond that, the marriage choices of Badr al-Din, his sons, and his grandchildren have been ecumenical—they have married into several *qabili* and Hashimi families, producing networks of mutual support that cut across different strata and geographical centers in the governorate and beyond. Previous leadership of the BY broadened this network of tribal and *sayyid* networks, also allowing the Huthi family to access nontribal economic actors in the region. Finally, by their work in parliament, as well as in social welfare and educational activities during the 1990s, the Huthi brothers and their associates gained a unique credibility in Sa'da. This authenticity has allowed them to act as a local focus for complaints about the regime's socioeconomic neglect of the Zaydi north, its support of local Salafism, and its post-1994 de-democratization of politics.

Though a Zaydi tribesman himself, President Saleh's origins and sociocultural influence levers are much more modest. The Huthis thus likely appeared an ominous threat to him, also raising the spectre of an imamate resurgence from its historical heartland. This threat perception was combined with a self-perception of greater coercive strength after September 2001. Given his understanding of both threat and opportunity, Saleh eschewed previous approaches of cooptation and mediation, instead electing to send in government forces and arrest Husayn al-Huthi in June 2004.

The GoY Anti-Huthi Campaign: Prolonging Resistance, Provoking Insurgency?

Sending military forces into traditionally autonomous tribal lands was an uncharacteristically aggressive action, given past GoY practices in the north. It also violated local cultural norms whereby mediation and violent rhetoric had traditionally served as a means to preempt violent action. GoY actions and Huthi supporters' armed resistance thus sparked a military conflict. In the initial phases of the conflict, GoY moves against Huthi enclaves further aggravated tensions with the Huthi group, activating wider circles of opposition to the regime—over time, more Zaydis in the north, representing several tribes, began to call themselves Huthis. Subsequent GoY military actions led to levels of material destruction, loss of human life, and violation of core ideas of *qabyala* that produced more conflict. Further, as the GoY sought to enlist local tribes as auxiliaries, it not only reignited latent intertribal differences but also further distanced regime-coopted shaykhs from less obedient tribal members. Therefore, by 2006, the insurrection took on a logic and momentum of its own, transcending initial regime or Huthi family motives.

Since the beginning of the conflict in 2004, it has been described by protagonists as well as outside analysts in various terms. The GoY has called it a "rebellion" and has described Huthi fighters variously as "rebels or "terrorists."[4] In the latter case, the GoY has portrayed the uprising as a variety of terrorism reminiscent of other Global War on Terror (GWoT) challenges. Additionally, the GoY has referred to Huthi-initiated violence as a "discord" threatening Islamic unity. GoY sources, as well as Yemeni and pan-Arab media, have also portrayed the fighting as guerilla warfare. Significantly, outside observers referred to the "Huthi insurgency" from the start, while the GoY itself has also come to use this term for Western consumption.[5] Given recent Western experi-

---

[4] See "18 Houthi Terrorists Killed in Separate Areas," *Almotamar.net*, September 28, 2009. It mentions "Thirteen of the elements of Terrorism and Rebellion . . . ." Also see "Masra' Arba'a min Qiyadat 'Anasir al-Irhab wa-l-Tamarrud," *26 September*, September 28, 2009.

[5] See, for example, Andrew McGregor, "Shi'ite Insurgency in Yemen: Iranian Intervention or Mountain Revolt?" *Jamestown Foundation Terrorism Monitor* 2:16 (May 10, 2005); "Three of the Insurgency Leaders Killed," *Almotamar.net*, September 4, 2009; "Yemeni Public Opinion Pressure Forced Government to End Saada Insurgency," *Almotamar.net*, August 20, 2009. Yemeni usage with respect to these terms follows Modern Standard Arabic.

ences with insurgency in Iraq and Afghanistan, it is tempting to consider the Huthi phenomenon a similar case. This remains a problematic approach, however, from two perspectives: the nature of the Huthi entity and the substance of Huthi goals.

U.S. military doctrine defines *insurgency* as "an organized movement aimed at the violent overthrow of a constituted government through the use of subversion and armed conflict."[6] As an entity, however, the Huthis have yet to demonstrate an organizational cohesion moving significantly beyond a resistance organism based on broadly aligned, though autonomous, local tribal and social networks. Organizationally, therefore, the Huthis cannot yet be considered an insurgency. Second, Huthi ideological communication has yet to articulate specific goals representing a consensus among parts of its organism. Furthermore, as of early 2010, Huthi spokesmen had yet to state that their goals might include the overthrow of the GoY, establishment of a "liberated" area tantamount to a "Huthistan," or the subversion of Yemen's overall political order—all goals associated with insurgencies in the Middle East and beyond.

Although the Huthis as an entity and in terms of goals may not yet be considered an insurgency, it remains useful to analyze post-2004 GoY responses to the Huthis in terms of counterinsurgency lines of operation (COIN LOOs)—although what we refer to in this book as "GoY COIN" has aggravated an increasingly confused insurrection that may tend toward insurgency.[7] Diplomatically, the GoY has sought both to tar the Huthis as a Shi'ite Iranian cat's-paw in the southern Arabian Peninsula and to have them listed as a terrorist organization by Western governments. It has also permitted international mediation by Gulf countries—although as an operational pause in order to reassesses kinetic options. Domestically, the GoY has sought to manipulate different tribal elements to cultivate animosities and amass proxy forces.

The GoY has also operated in the information domain. It has closed down Zaydi schools and outlets associated with the BY and the Huthis, while opening up government schools and summer camps in Zaydi areas. It has also closed Zaydi mosques and coordinated a campaign of mosque sermons and judicial pronouncements permitting the shedding of Huthi blood. More broadly, this is part of an effort to portray the Huthis internally as an anti-republican movement to restore the pre-1962 imamate as well as Hashimite socioreligious preeminence. Another element of GoY information operations has been denial of access to the region, as well as efforts to shut down printed and electronic Huthi (as well as independent) media sources.

"Rebellion" is *tamarrud*, "rebel" is *mutamarrid*, "terrorist" is *irhabi*, and "guerrilla warfare" is *harb al-'isabat*. "Discord," aligned with Islamic historical usage, is *fitna*. Arabic does not have a term for "insurgency," so English-language Yemeni organs use this term.

[6] See Headquarters, Department of the Army, *FM 3-24: Counterinsurgency* (Washington, D.C.: December 2006), Glossary-5.

[7] These generic lines of operation include Diplomatic, Information, Military, and Economic (DIME).

Militarily, GoY forces appear focused on the physical elimination of Huthi principals and on the destruction of regions of Sa'da associated with the Huthi family and supporters. GoY forces have also attacked areas of Zaydi sacred geography, including mosques and Hashimi tombs. Likewise, over time, GoY forces have targeted mountainous areas serving as Huthi strongholds. As elements opposing the regime in the name of the Huthis have spread to the adjoining governorates of 'Amran, Hajja, and San'a itself, GoY forces have broadened the geographic application of kinetic means. In these efforts, GoY has relied on tools attuned to conventional operations, including armor and mechanized assets as well as air-delivered nonprecision munitions. Although it remains premature to evaluate the military effect of Saudi fighting against Huthis, it has added a new political dimension to the conflict, rendering mediation or conflict abatement more difficult.

The degradation of material bases for survival in the region has been a principal economic by-product of kinetic efforts. The military has been billeted in area homes and has requisitioned supplies from markets. Further, its movement through areas has interrupted intraregion and intertribal trade routes, while the GoY has blockaded the conflict zone—interdicting the movement of commodities as well as humanitarian aid. Part of this is a by-product of military operations in general; there is also an element of intentionality because the GoY works to suffocate the material basis of the Huthis and their sympathizers. This was particularly the case in the sixth phase of the war, dubbed a "scorched earth" (*al-ard al-mahruqa*) operation by the GoY. Both conflict and economic destruction have therefore produced large-scale flows of internally displaced persons reaching to the outskirts of San'a. Apart from these "sticks," the GoY has offered the "carrot" of material reconstruction of conflict-affected areas as a means to draw passive support away from the Huthis.

Through its diplomatic, information, military, and economic activities, the GoY has perpetuated Huthi resistance and may provoke an insurgency as the Huthis evolve from organism to organization. The conflict that began in June 2004 has endured into 2010 with no apparent diminution of Huthi capabilities. Instead, ever-widening circles of Zaydi (or even Sunni) Yemenis have been driven into conflict with the regime through violence and the affront to cultural and religious norms. At the same time, the conflict has become increasingly confessional and tribal, due to regional demography, rhetoric, and alliance-making on both sides. Yet, GoY actions, Huthi reprisals, and the effect of over five years of human and societal destruction have all substantially distorted local cultural norms and mechanisms that in other circumstances might have worked toward conflict abatement and compromise. While they persist as the prism through which GoY and Huthi actions are judged by northern Yemenis, these norms and mechanisms may no longer serve as bridges to conflict resolution. Unless the regime either changes its goals and strategies or successfully employs overwhelming coercive force, the conflict will persist.

Chapter Structure and Major Analytical Questions

To provide an understanding of the regime-periphery conflict in northern Yemen, this study seeks to answer several questions, with a focus on the region's sociocultural fabric. Our approach to answering these questions orders the structure of the book.

Part I: The Context of Regime-Periphery Relations in Northern Yemen

Part I, which consists of Chapters One and Two, addresses questions related to the overarching context of the conflict. First, what aspects of the region's local dynamics have prolonged the incomplete incorporation of the north into the Yemeni state since the 1970s?

- How has the dominant mode of social organization—tribalism—facilitated human survival while limiting effective state presence in areas of current Huthi activity? What are the major tribal groupings in northern Yemen, and how do they inform identity and mobilization? How has the tribal distribution influenced the Huthi conflict?
- As a values continuum, how has the ethical code of tribalism (*qabyala*) ensured collective identity while encouraging northern Yemeni autonomy? What norms does *qabyala* cultivate regarding individual loyalty, sanctity of territory, and legitimate modes of conflict or mediation?

Second, what GoY techniques of rule over the past three decades have interacted with local sociocultural norms?

- How has San'a traditionally sought to exercise leverage over regional peripheries? How has Saleh's use of social cooptation, conflict through proxy, porous borders, and nonstate conflict mediation influenced the center's attitude to the periphery and local norms about legitimate interaction with the GoY?

Third, because Zaydism has been a recurrent topic in explaining the Huthi-GoY conflict, we examine the role of religion in the region:

- How is Zaydism unique among other forms of Islam, and what are commonly held views among Zaydis regarding religious and political legitimacy? What has been the historical relationship between Zaydism and Yemen, and how have Zaydis traditionally interacted with Shafi'i Sunnism?
- How has Zaydism evolved as a social structure over the past few generations, and what has been the republican regime's perception of it?

Part II: From Tension to Conflict: Social Change and Huthi Emergence, 1980s–2004
The Huthi family has been in northern Yemen for several generations, Saleh has been in power for 30 years, and a unified Yemen has existed since 1990. Part II therefore investigates why Huthi-regime conflict emerged only in 2004.

Chapter Three explores the main categories and results of recent sociocultural changes among northern Yemenis, also examining relationships among the sociocultural factors that later catalyzed political trends and associational responses. In particular, Zaydi mobilization began after the 1990 unification as a response to local generational change, the opening of political space, and the Salafi challenge. One manifestation of mobilization was the Zaydi al-Haqq political party; the BY was another manifestation. Both prominently featured the Huthi family.

- How did increased access to communications and travel to other Arab states influence attitudes and expectations among northern Yemeni young adults?
- What was the impact of exposure to Sunni Salafism in the Gulf States, and what tensions did that produce among Yemenis returning to Saʿda?
- How did Salafi-Zaydi conflict emerge in the Saʿda region after the late 1980s? What were the GoY's interests?
- What were significant Zaydi religious responses to Salafi infiltration, and how did subsequent Huthi personalities figure in them?
- Who did al-Haqq represent, and what was its contribution to activating Zaydi identities? How did the GoY seek to use it?
- How and why did the BY emerge? Whose concerns did it seek to answer? How did the BY relate to broader generational change and Hashimi-tribal relationships?
- What was the role of the Huthi family in the BY? How did Husayn al-Huthi seek to reinvigorate initiatives reminiscent of the BY in the new millennium?

Chapter Four examines developments among the Huthis and the GoY between 2001 and 2004. We focus on three sets of questions.

- What was the nature of the persistent discontent in Saʿda from the late 1990s to 2004?
- What was Husayn al-Huthi's agenda? How did he seek to mobilize his supporters? What were his major messages regarding Islam and Yemen's relationship with the United States and the region? How did this resonate with local Zaydi and larger Yemeni attitudes?
- How did President Saleh evaluate his new relationship with the United States in terms of his ability to alter center-periphery relations? How did this relationship expose the GoY to domestic criticism? How did the GoY perceive the Huthi threat?

Part III: The Six Sa'da Wars

Open Huthi-regime conflict began in June 2004. Six "Sa'da wars" since then have been characterized by increasingly rolling conflict. Part III concentrates on the armed conflict itself. Chapter Five examines the conflict's time line and progression.

- What led the regime to move against the Huthi family in 2004? Why did the GoY abjure traditional conflict mediation techniques? How did regime actions in 2004 result in expanding armed conflict rather than decisive resolution?
- What has been the geographical progression of the conflict over time? How does conflict geography relate to traditional Huthi family areas, concentrations of armed Huthi supporters, and sacred Zaydi locales?
- What is the relationship between the geography of the conflict and tribal geography? Which tribal groups may have adopted Huthi or GoY sympathies?

Chapter Six moves to aims and operations and considers the GoY's campaign through the lens of counterinsurgency (COIN).

- What appear to be the overall GoY goals and methods in the conflict?
- How has the GoY sought to coopt local members of society, and how has it enlisted elements beyond the immediate area as proxies, intensifying the tribal and sectarian nature of the conflict and thus prolonging it?

Turning to local opposition to the GoY, Chapter Seven concerns the concept of "the Huthis" and examines their response to the state.

- What constitutes the Huthi core, as well as the demographic clusters from which Huthi fighters are drawn? How does this demography relate to earlier BY constituencies?
- Beyond the Huthi core, what are the concentric circles of affiliation—including active supporters, those who condone Huthi actions, and sympathetic Zaydis in the community—driven to greater affiliation with the Huthis? How do we interpret the readiness of groups unrelated to the Huthis to act against the regime or local rivals in the name of the Huthis?
- What has been the substance of Huthi response to GoY COIN? Who speaks for the Huthis, what have been the evolving Huthi goals—and how have they communicated them at home and abroad?
- How have the Huthis evolved militarily? What have been the quality and sources of their weapons and means of movement? How do we evaluate engagements with GoY forces with respect to magnitude and outcomes? How are notions of command, control, and communications interwoven with the local sociocultural fabric?

- How does the organizational consolidation of the Huthis today compare with that of other Middle Eastern armed groups—such as Hizbullah, Hamas, etc.—at different points along their developmental trajectories?

Chapter Eight focuses on the wrenching socioeconomic and human impacts of the Huthi-regime conflict:

- What has been the human, economic, and environmental toll of mass destruction and loss of life in the conflict zone?
- What have been recurrent GoY and Huthi abuses of human rights and local cultural values, and how have these combined with the conflict's duration and magnitude to erode traditional modes of conflict mediation?

Conclusion

Our investigation concludes with a consideration of both the prolongers of conflict in northern Yemen and the significance of the Huthi uprising for Yemeni state stability.

- What are possible scenarios for conflict continuation or resolution?
- What is the significance of the Huthi-regime conflict in the context of the GoY's difficulties with al-Qaʻida, southern discontent, and economic contraction? How might the conflict in the north influence succession from Saleh to his sons or other leadership candidates?
- What is the significance of the Huthi conflict in the larger regional context involving border tensions with Saudi Arabia, Sunni-Shiʻite tensions in the Gulf, and instability in the Horn of Africa?
- How do this conflict and its possible trajectories affect the political, military, and economic interests of local powers and the United States?

Sources Consulted

In preparing this book, the authors consulted Western-language material and Arabic sources.[8] These materials presented both strengths and ultimately instructive shortcomings. The Western material relevant to understanding the Huthi conflict is both academic and policy-oriented. Academic literature in English provides a quite in-depth background. This is particularly true of literature examining kin networks, governance, and religion. The most recent relevant text in this field is Shelagh Weir's *A Tribal Order*, which concentrates on the politics and law of one particular *mudiriya* (dis-

---

[8] For an extended discussion of the uses and challenges of available sources in analyzing the Huthi-regime conflict, see Appendix H.

trict) in Saʿda.[9] This ethnographic study illuminates the hyper-local variability within Saʿda province and its surroundings, as well as the broader regional divides informing tribesmen's understanding of themselves and their relationships to their environment. Recent political science literature has also examined the nature of governance in today's Yemen.[10]

While academic studies are crucial to understanding the roots and context of the Huthi conflict, they avoid policy prescriptions and were thus supplemented by policy-relevant sources. The majority of policy sources and journalism on Yemen concentrate on the multiple stresses facing the Yemeni regime. Such literature is generally produced with U.S. or Western interests in mind and does not link up with the sociohistorical and cultural drivers of conflict. That said, a 2007 National Democratic Institute (NDI) report on Tribal Conflict Management Program, although not focused on the Huthi conflict or Saʿda, reveals some overall trends in the north with respect to tribal mediation, emphasizing the effect of tribal conflict on impairing the government's reach in underdeveloped areas.[11] Additionally, a concise May 2009 International Crisis Group report, "Yemen: Defusing the Saada Time Bomb," skillfully brings these themes together in the context of regime-Huthi conflict and reconciliation efforts.[12] It is important to mention that a media blackout of the north since 2007 has likely contributed to the lack of acuity among Western writers on the conflict. Some writing on the more palpable humanitarian aspects of the conflict has filled this void but cannot account for substantive gaps in knowledge.

Since the media in Yemen are heavily monitored and at times directly controlled by the GoY, the most useful Arabic sources come from more independent media sources. These include dailies such as *al-Ayyam* and the news Web site *Mareb Press*, which offer the most comprehensive coverage of daily events and developments, including casualties on both sides of the conflict. Still, journalists employed by Yemen's "independent" media often simultaneously work for state-run newspapers or receive subsidies from the GoY, leading to clear conflicts of interest and a certain amount of self-censorship. Additionally, the GoY's frequent attempts to shut down independent Web sites impede analysis of the conflict's daily evolution.[13]

---

[9] Shelagh Weir, *A Tribal Order: Politics and Law in the Mountains of Yemen* (Austin: University of Texas Press, 2007).

[10] See Lisa Wedeen, *Peripheral Visions: Publics, Power and Performance in Yemen* (Chicago: University of Chicago Press, 2008); Sarah Phillips, *Yemen's Democracy Experiment in Regional Perspective: Patronage & Pluralized Authoritarianism* (New York: Palgrave McMillan, 2008).

[11] National Democratic Institute (NDI), *Yemen: Tribal Conflict Management Program Research Report* (Washington, D.C., NDI, March 2007).

[12] International Crisis Group, "Yemen: Defusing the Saada Time Bomb," *Middle East Report* 86:13, 2009.

[13] See Daniel Corstange, "Drawing Dissent: Political Cartoons in Yemen," *PS: Political Science and Politics* 40:2 (2007), 293–296.

We therefore also carefully reviewed both Huthi-affiliated and pro-government Web sites. Although the Huthis lack an official press, they electronically distribute their narratives via the *al-Menpar* Web page and, more recently, via the Web site *Sa'da Online*. Huthi propaganda is ubiquitous, popular, and growing on several YouTube channels (including *Sa'da Online*) as an alternative means of exploiting violence despite the information blackout. Such sites and videos offer an important way to survey the group's ideological propagation and conflict narrative. Additionally, reporting from the Ministry of Defense–affiliated *26 September* newspaper illuminates the official narrative of the conflict. Since the sixth Sa'da war, which began in August 2009, government propaganda has become more sophisticated, perhaps in response to Huthi advances in the media war (see Chapters Six and Seven). Note that all transliterations of Arabic in this book were made by the authors.

Finally, the larger pan-Arab media convey a bias broadly reflective of their Sunni and Arab ethnic background. While major news outlets, such as *al-Jazeera* and *al-Sharq al-Awsat,* have broadcast interviews with Huthi leaders, they frequently cast the insurrection as an Iranian proxy. Still, in some cases, pan-Arab coverage of particular issues is extensive and deep, allowing a window into the conflict's background and evolving course. Ultimately, however, the GoY's efforts to control media access to the conflict region and influence news content combine with the hyper-local and fluid dynamics of the conflict to render international media perspectives problematic, requiring a critical eye. As the Huthi-regime conflict continues, the international community is likely to continue to view it through the prism of Yemen's instability and the threefold al-Qa'ida–Huthi–Southern separatist threat to the GoY.

Conclusion

Since the GoY-Huthi conflict began in 2004, the protagonists have deployed various narratives to justify their actions and obtain domestic and international support. Representations of the conflict have therefore become part of the protagonists' strategies for conducting the conflict itself. According to the Yemeni government, Huthis are a foreign-supported imamist threat to Yemen's republican nature and internal tranquility. Internationalizing the issue, GoY-affiliated outlets also portray the Huthis as dangerous to regional Arab (Sunni) interests and thus consider anti-Huthi actions to be part of the global war on terror. For their part, Huthi-friendly sources assert that their movement originated merely in a cultural effort to rejuvenate Zaydism. Huthis thus fight today as true Yemenis, in defense of Zaydism against Wahhabi infiltration, military encroachment, and a GoY campaign against the community of Zaydis. We will return to these GoY and Huthi narratives in Part III.

Part I: The Context of Regime-Periphery Relations in Northern Yemen

Part I examines the context for contemporary politics and violence within the Sa'da governorate. This context exhibits three principal components: physical, human, and conceptual. The physical component is related to the challenges of surviving in the environment of northern Yemen. The human component concerns social organization, economic relationships, and political arrangements. Finally, the conceptual component relates to ideas—cultural norms, religious ideas and practices, and historical memories.

Chapter One begins the exploration of the northern Yemeni context. After delineating the basic themes of recent Yemeni history, it explores the physical bases of life north of San'a that produce particular socioeconomic relationships. Local means for dealing with environmental conditions in the region also provide outside actors, such as the GoY, potential levers for influence. That same environment has implications for military operations.

Chapter Two rounds out our inquiry into the northern Yemeni context by examining tribalism and religion. In northern Yemen, tribalism (*qabyala*) is significant not only as a means of organizing groups of people but also as a values system. Therefore, *qabyala* furnishes the social fabric from which current networks of resistance to the GoY have emerged and forms the interpretive lens through which Yemenis in the conflict area view regime and Huthi actions. As a belief system and social organism, Zaydism unites people but also sets them in latent opposition to other religious approaches in the region—such as the marginal Zaydism or Shafi'i Sunnism of the regime elite and the Wahhabi-inspired Salafism of local groups. Both tribalism and religion have therefore been prominent aspects of the Huthi-regime conflict.

CHAPTER ONE

Sa'da in the North Yemeni Context

After delineating basic themes of recent Yemeni history—and historical memory—referred to by claimants in the current conflict, this chapter explores the physical, geographic, demographic, and economic bases of life north of San'a. We focus on the Sa'da governorate, the predominant region in the current struggle between the GoY and Huthi fighters. We will see that the conditions of life confronting Yemenis in this region force particular coping mechanisms that result in certain kinds of communities and particular norms. We will also see that local means for dealing with environmental conditions allow outside actors, such as the GoY, potential levers for influence. That same environment, however, greatly complicates the conduct of military operations.

A "United" Yemen's Many Divides

The post-2004 Huthi-regime conflict emerges from a particular sociopolitical context in which an enduring sense of "Yemeniness" has not been accompanied by a continuous post–World War I Yemeni state. Rather, until 1990, southern Arabia exhibited distinct and competitive polities. These included a dynastic state in the north and a colonial administration in the south up to the 1960s; the northern Yemen Arab Republic (YAR) and southern People's Democratic Republic of Yemen (PDRY) in the 1960s–1980s; and the "united" Republic of Yemen, born on May 22, 1990.[1] Today's Yemen thus reflects a series of nested divides—geographic, demographic, political, and ideological. These nested divides predate the Huthi phenomenon, giving both the GoY and Huthis a discursive framework within which to portray regime-periphery conflict.

Geographic and Material Divides
Prior to the 1990 unification, the distinct societies of the north and south produced different political systems. After the British colonial departure in 1965–1967, the Marxist regime in the south sought to form a state-centered society through the army, bureau-

---

[1] Sheila Carapico, *Civil Society in Yemen: The Political Economy of Activism in Modern Arabia* (London: Cambridge University Press, 1998).

cracy, and a planned economy. The PDRY's agricultural sector was largely removed from shaykhs and absentee landholders, and its focus was redirected to governmental regulation. This eroded the importance of the tribes, creating a relatively unmediated state-citizen relationship.

The abolition of the imamate in the north did not result in a strong regime presence throughout the YAR. Geographic difficulties, instability in San'a, and YAR leaders' cooptation of tribes as a means of access to the periphery led to northern society's marginal incorporation into the polity—and the persistence of tribalism. While shaykhs obtained patronage from San'a, the northern highlands evolved as a largely self-regulating environment beyond the central government's direct control. Likewise, small-scale agriculture with land ownership consolidated in small households meant that geography, politics, and economy perpetuated the northern sense of autonomy.[2]

The 1990 unification did not produce full integration of the northern periphery and southern constituencies. When the YAR and PDRY joined, "unity" proved elusive. Demography favored the north,[3] while President 'Ali 'Abdullah Saleh ensured northern control of the executive and strategic ministries through kin and protégés. The dominance of the San'a-controlled military in the south added tension. This, in addition to political inequity and contested oil discoveries, led to a short civil war in May 1994, with fighting mostly in the south. The war left a bad impression on southerners, who considered the northern invasion akin to colonialism.[4] This impression persists today, as kinsmen from Saleh's Hashidi tribal confederation dominate southern administration.[5] Recent southern opposition thus results from persistent divisions and grievances that predate the civil war.[6]

Nested within the larger north-south divide is the divide in the YAR areas between the center-north (i.e. San'a) and the areas toward the Saudi border. Decades-old material neglect of the highlands and of those tribes not associated with Saleh's regime, as well as continued Saudi interest, has perpetuated this divide. Furthermore, geographi-

---

[2] For an accessible narrative of recent Yemeni history by a Yemeni national, see Ahmed Abdelkareem Saif, "Yemen: State Weakness and Society Alienation," *al-Masar Journal* 1:2 (2000), 1–15.

[3] Paul Dresch, *A History of Modern Yemen* (Cambridge: Cambridge University Press, 2001), 186. The roughly 11 million people in the North far outnumbered the South's roughly 2.5 million.

[4] Dresch, *A History of Modern Yemen*, 197.

[5] Stephen Day, "Updating Yemeni National Unity: Could Lingering Regional Divisions Bring Down the Regime?" *Middle East Journal* 62:3 (Summer 2008), 422.

[6] The proximate cause of the protests included grievances related to the lack of benefits for South Yemen army veterans. However, analysts note a wider disenchantment with policies of the ruling General People's Congress (GPC).

cal and terrain challenges contribute to the difficulties of government access to far northern areas,[7] which remain among the least developed provinces in the country.[8]

The Sa'da governorate, or *muhafaza,* exemplifies this geographic, socioeconomic, and political peripherality, producing more than one effect. It has suffered from its location and non-Hashidi complexion. Sa'da tribes, largely from Khawlan bin 'Amr and Bakil, have not contributed markedly to San'a-based politics. The central government has also failed to assert its political or developmental presence effectively. For example, with 22 governors since 1962, Sa'da has the largest turnover rate for governors in Yemen.[9] At the same time, Sa'da has traditionally been relatively unaffected by the capital city, symbolized by the continuity of nonstate, customary law in the area. Its proximity to the border with Saudi Arabia and its dependence on expatriate remittances prior to the 1990s also allowed Sa'da residents to develop local economic initiatives, which increased self-reliance. Sa'da remained nonintegrated after the economy worsened quickly in the 1990s.

Along with focusing north-south and center-northern divides, Sa'da also exemplifies a larger division between urban and rural in Yemen. In 1979, the population in the north was estimated to be 90 percent rural.[10] Following unification, the largely rural "tribes of north and east complained that their own world was invaded by urban forces."[11] Still, at the end of the last century, Yemen's population was still more than 70 percent rural, perpetuating the consciousness of rural-urban discontinuity grafted onto the geographic divides.

Social Divides and Distinctions in the Center and North

Geographical divides coexist semicongruently with social divides. These social divides are related to tribes and tribalism and manifest themselves in multiple forms: between a tribal (*qabili*) north and a nontribal south, between the politically dominant Hashidi tribal confederation and other tribes, and between tribes and nontribal people in the north itself.

Subsequent to the establishment of the PDRY, diminution of tribes was accompanied by a negative portrayal of tribalism itself (and by extension the YAR) as socially reactionary. Supported by the regime, modernist intellectuals equated tribalism with

---

[7] For example, the citizens of al-Jawf threatened to request humanitarian asylum in Saudi Arabia following severe floods in April 2009, to which the Yemeni government has not responded. See Abdul-Aziz Oudah, "Al-Jawf Citizens Prepare to Resort to KSA," *Yemen Observer,* April 7, 2009.

[8] It must be noted that grievances about piecemeal development have been a constant in both the north and the south since the economy began to deteriorate in the late 1990s. However, we choose here to focus on those associated with Sa'da.

[9] "Muhafiz Sa'da al-Jadid Yubashir Muhamihu fi Aqqal min 24 Sa'a," *al-Ayyam,* April 21, 2007.

[10] Dresch, *A History of Modern Yemen,* 139.

[11] Dresch, *A History of Modern Yemen,* 139.

the lack of "civilization."[12] At the same time, the San'a-based elite of the YAR also portrayed the northern tribes as ignorant and violent, requiring patrimonial stewardship. Both regimes thus bequeathed to the post-1990 era the idea of the north as tribal and backwards (*mutakhallif*), thus delegitimating northern grievances (the GoY delegitimates southern grievances as *infisali*—separatist).

The north itself, however, is not entirely *qabili*. Nontribal strata include *sayyids*, a hereditary Zaydi elite afforded tribal protection. By contrast, Jews are "protected" as a function of their inferior social status. Other Muslims who are not *qabili*, such as butchers, traders, café workers, singers, etc., are considered socially weak, though protected by virtue of their economic roles. At a more micro level, divides persist within tribes. While tribes in the Yemeni northern highlands share a political culture, they vary regionally and subregionally in terms of their size, identity, and organizational structures.[13] Furthermore, government patronage (*mahsubiya*) can serve to alienate shaykhs from their tribes.

Sect and Society

Beyond geography and kin networks, religion also acts as a force for internal cohesion and intergroup division. As the center of the pre-1962 imamate, the northern Yemeni highlands are largely Zaydi—and the Sa'da governorate itself is the epicenter of Zaydism. Parts of the center-north, however, as well as the entirety of the south, are historically Shafi'i Sunni. While Zaydi-Shafi'i relations are by no means always strained, sectarian tensions have emerged at several points over the past two centuries. From the 1960s, the majority Shafi'i PDRY's Marxist rhetoric portrayed Zaydism and the imamate as reactionary, feudalistic, and irrational.[14] This portrayal resonated with ingrained social stereotypes among southern Shafi'is regarding the Zaydi north.

In the north itself, the YAR disassociated itself from the Zaydi elite of *sayyids* (see below), and the nominally Zaydi regime gradually affected more of a "mainstream" Sunnism aligned with pan-Arab currents.[15] During the 1970s–1990s, the YAR regime and then the united GoY persisted in their tactical rapprochement with Sunni elements, thus adding a sectarian sensibility to the existing Zaydi-Shafi'i divide. Because the GoY supported Salafi ideological propagation in the northern highlands and Sa'da

---

[12] Dresch, *A History of Modern Yemen*, 139.

[13] Shelagh Weir, *A Tribal Order: Politics and Law in the Mountains of Yemen* (Austin: University of Texas Press, 2007), 2.

[14] For the PDRY, see Tareq Y. Ismael and Jacqueline Ismael, *The People's Democratic Republic of Yemen: Politics, Economics, and Society* (Boulder, Colo.: Lynne Rienner Publishers, 1984).

[15] For the YAR, see Robert Burrowes, *The Yemen Arab Republic: The Politics of Development, 1962–1986* (Boulder, Colo.: Westview Press, 1987); for religion in the YAR, see Gabriele vom Bruck, "Being a Zaydi in the Absence of an Imam: Doctrinal Revisions, Religious Instruction, and the (Re-)Invention of Ritual," in Remy Leveau, Franck Mermier, and Udo Steinbach, eds., *Le Yemen Contemporain*, (Paris: Editions Karthala, 1999), 185–187.

itself, it tapped "hitherto dormant resentment of key tenets of Zaydi doctrine still manifest there," as also producing the Zaydi defensive response illuminating the roots of the Huthi phenomenon.[16]

Nested within a north-south divide, the fissure along religious and ideological lines thus presents San'a itself as a new south in opposition to the northern highlands around Sa'da. The distinction between Zaydi and non-Zaydi (or marginally Zaydi) is thus a crucial identity claim in the Huthi conflict, emerging from the divided nature of Yemeni society. The Zaydis' consciousness of earlier political and cultural domination and their awareness of social and (after 1990) increased demographic marginalization can activate resentment under the right conditions, thus evoking highly politicized interpretations of what it means to be a Zaydi.

As with geographical and social differences, religion in Yemen exhibits a series of nested divisions. While one can oppose Sunnism to Zaydism, Zaydism itself is not monolithic as a social system. Rather, it exhibits a social stratum divide, between the general community and those families claiming descent from the Prophet Muhammad through the lineage of 'Ali. Referred to as *Hashimis,* traditional Zaydi theology entitles them to political rule in the form of the imamate. Historically they were a privileged and educated class, referred to with the honorific title of *sayyid* (pl. *sada*). Yet their social aloofness from "regular" Zaydis was condemned by post-1962 regimes. Within the context of Zaydi displacement, condemnation of Hashimis activated latent resentment toward them among some Zaydis in the north itself who desired greater social, economic, and political prominence.

In the 1980s, Salafis and the state took advantage of this internal Zaydi divide, each for its own purposes. Zaydi revivalists responded by taking up Hashimi rehabilitation as part of efforts to resuscitate Zaydism in the face of Sunni encroachment in the north. Furthermore, the religious divide-within-a-divide persists rhetorically today. While the Huthis accuse the GoY of targeting Zaydism as a whole, GoY rhetoric has emphasized the Hashimi background of the Huthis, accusing them of wanting to overthrow the government and reinstate the imamate. The GoY seeks here to activate historical stereotypes about the Hashimis as a politically atavistic and thus dangerous social stratum.

Rendering northern Yemeni society and the Huthi conflict more complex than the binary oppositions implied above, numerous overlapping identities create intergroup social bonds. As noted in reference to the far northwestern areas of Sa'da, "an important factor in the deescalation of sectarian tension was that many of those divided by religion are closely linked in other ways. Leading Wahhabis are related by marriage to leading *sayyids* . . . those rent by religious belief in one situation therefore re-combines in others under different, overriding imperatives including duty to kin, neighbors, and fellow

---

[16] Weir, *A Tribal Order,* 296.

tribesmen—whatever their status category."[17] While distinctions related to sect or social stratum have been activated by both sides of the conflict to mobilize their bases, the conduct of the conflict itself has at times activated these other "overriding imperatives."

The Rhetorical Activation of Yemen's Divides

The nested geographical, social, and religious divides within Yemeni society possess variable significance in peoples' conceptions as circumstances change. To avoid the tendency of "fall[ing] back into classificatory schemes"[18] when referring to Yemen, it is essential to recognize that Yemeni regimes have appropriated these usually latent divides in order to activate them politically, thus intensifying them. For instance, the YAR long accused the socialist south of threatening the cultural and religious identity of the wider Arab Muslim Middle East. Likewise, the GoY today rhetorically activates social divisions. Just as returning "Afghan Arabs" were encouraged to fight "irreligious" southerners in 1994, Saleh seeks today to incite southern Islamists against the Yemeni Socialist Party (YSP).[19]

The rhetorical activation of latent societal divides features in the Huthi conflict as well. The GoY portrays far northerners as rough, *qabilis* as having a propensity toward fighting, and Hashimis as a feudal fifth column wishing to restore the imamate. Likewise, Saleh has used religion as ammunition by subsidizing Wahhabi institutes in the north and has used connections with hardcore Sunni elements to arm tribal mercenaries to go into the north to fight while encouraging sectarian animosity against the Huthis among the latter.

The Huthis and tribes involved in conflict with the state also gain mileage from Yemeni schisms. The enmity between Wahhabis/Salafis and Zaydis can be activated by the Huthis to claim attacks on the Zaydi sect and mobilize their base—energizing it further by accusations of a GoY onslaught against *sada*. The Huthis also claim that the government has destroyed the north without rebuilding it, thereby capitalizing on long-standing geographic imbalances in development while emphasizing the GoY's violation of wholesome northern tribal norms, such as respect for protected places and mediation.[20]

Social divides along the axes of geography, social organization, and religion thus provide both a context for the conflict and mental frames through which protagonists can understand, portray, and perpetuate it. After this basic introduction to Yemen's sociopolitical history, it is therefore important to gain a detailed understanding of the Saʿda governorate's physical, human, and economic geography, which is the purpose of the following sections.

---

[17] Weir, *A Tribal Order*, 303.

[18] Claude Deffarge and Gordian Troeller, *Yémen 62-69: De La Révolution Sauvage à La Trêve Des Guerriers* (Paris: Robert Laffont, 1969), 264.

[19] Day, "Updating Yemeni National Unity," 435.

[20] "YEMEN: Rebel Leader Warns of More Conflict in Saada," *IRIN*, February 10, 2008.

Physical, Human, and Economic Geography North of San'a

Physical Characteristics

The Huthi uprising has taken place within the context of a unique geographical environment that shapes societal parameters particularly vulnerable to the effects of armed conflict. The physical terrain pushes Sa'da residents toward self-sufficiency as well as individual and group autonomy from the Yemeni state. Adaptation methods and coping mechanisms are thus established independent of state authority or control. In this context, the scarcity of economic resources provides the impetus for economic cooperation as well as competition and conflict. It also provides a window of opportunity for external influences to manipulate actors by distributing economic goods and services. Indeed, given the complex social and physical terrain of the Sa'da governorate, the Yemeni state must resort to "neopatrimonial" methods of rule. We will analyze this phenomenon in more detail in Chapter Two, but it is important to note here that it connotes a sociopolitical environment in which patronage networks and cooptation methods can neutralize potential threats and contain indigenous social mobilization, often at the expense of effective governance. Such methods have limited reach, however, yielding a geopolitical context for a particularly durable, resilient brand of political opposition.

Figure 1.1 depicts the physical features of the Sa'da governorate. Located 240 km northwest of San'a, the governorate is roughly 11,375 square kilometers.[21] North from the capital, on what is known as the San'a–Sa'da road, the environment varies from urban settings to farmland and mountainous surroundings. Northwest from the governorate's capital, Sa'da city, the terrain becomes increasingly mountainous, reaching as high as 2,050 meters in the far west. Between the capital and these mountains, the terrain is peppered with basins and *wadis* (valleys), ultimately dropping to form arid plains in the east.

These physical features create natural boundaries for Sa'da residents, separating them from both one another and the central Yemeni state. The varied terrain engenders a sense of detachment among the social groupings of Sa'da. As a result, autonomy and food self-sufficiency have become dominant among its inhabitants. For example, Sa'da residents are known to store supplies of wheat in preparation for times of drought or political instability. Furthermore, residents must also innovate and adapt in order to ensure that crops remain irrigated and that they can continue to sustain themselves. Notably absent from their calculations is substantial government presence, because the Yemeni state is constrained by both the physical and social geography from being an actor with direct, unmediated influence in the area.

---

[21] See "Nabdha Ta'rifiya 'an Muhafazat Sa'da" (Informative Section about the Sa'da Governorate), *Yemeni National Information Center*, undated.

Figure 1.1
Map of the Sa'da Governorate

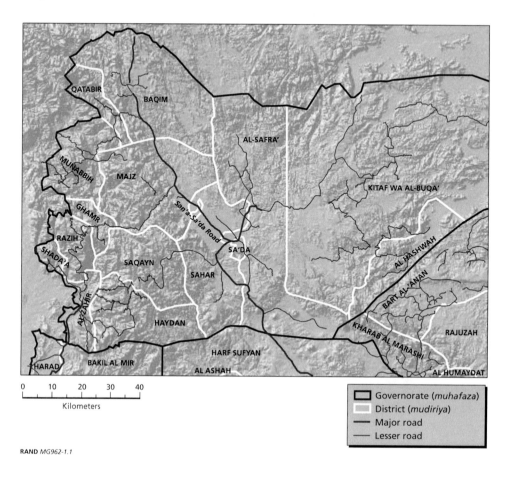

Table 1.1 demonstrates the sources of agricultural irrigation in northern Yemen, focusing on San'a and Sa'da. It also indicates the amounts of cultivated and arable land. We see that Sa'da is deficient in both sources of irrigation and arable land relative to San'a. Despite the fact that the San'a *muhafaza* is only roughly 500 km² larger than

Table 1.1
Irrigation Sources and Arable Land of the San'a and Sa'da Governorates

Governorate	Dams/ Barriers	Floods	Springs	Wells	Cultivated Area (hectares)	Arable Land (hectares)
San'a	405	505	3,303	46,705	132,568	136,596
Sa'da	283	122	1,219	12,201	37,642	40,721

SOURCE: Adapted from Yemeni National Information Council 2004 statistics.

Sa'da, it has more than triple the arable land. Furthermore, within the Sa'da governorate, rainfall varies greatly according to location. The western mountains of Razih, for example, receive as much as 1,000 mm per year, while arid regions east of the governorate capital (Sa'da city) can get as little as 50 mm.[22] This variance in rainfall yields scarce amounts of arable land, in which certain mountain *wadis* and basins are more preferable than others for agriculture. Consequently, terraced farming occurs in the governorate as a method of preserving precious rainfall runoff. The climate is also varied, with relatively mild summers reaching 26 degrees Celsius and winters reaching as cold as –16 degrees Celsius—which can significantly exacerbate already harsh living conditions.[23] Such geographical limitations on arable land and the relatively severe climate further restrict the available resources and complicate the living environment for Sa'da residents.

This suggests that arable land in the Sa'da governorate is dependent on climate but is also particularly vulnerable to physical damage that could result from conflict. Indeed, techniques used to compensate for limited rainfall and arable land could easily be damaged by military confrontations.

Population Dispersion in the Sa'da Governorate

Figure 1.2 depicts the population density of the Sa'da governorate, illustrating the districts with the greatest concentrations of Sa'da's nearly 700,000 residents. The map illustrates that the most densely populated areas in the governorate are west of Sa'da city. The reasons for this are likely related to the fact that most of the governorate's arable land is west of its capital. Population density figures thus demonstrate the extent to which Sa'da's residents have concentrated in areas of economic opportunity, tying them to the land and to one another. The most highly populated areas in the governorate include Sahar (133,056), Razih (62,895), Majz (68,603), and Haydan (60,329), each of which becomes a location of repeated GoY-Huthi kinetic confrontation,[24] causing civilian casualties and damaging economic interests.

Figure 1.2 further highlights a number of locations that are significant to the Sa'da conflict. These include Huthi gathering areas, such as Matra, al-Naqa'a, Razzamat, and Dahyan. Because of both topography and local support, these areas offer an environment in which the Huthis can regroup and possibly train. Other locations, such as al-Salim, Bani Mua'dh, al-Nazir, and Al Sayfi, are locations of repeated, intense conflict.

---

[22] For a detailed breakdown of rainfall distribution, see Gerhard Lichtenthäler, *Political Ecology and the Role of Water: Environment, Society and Economy in Northern Yemen* (Surrey, UK: Ashgate Publishing, 2003), 36.

[23] See "Northern Yemen: Population Faces Increasingly Cold Winter," International Committee of the Red Cross, February 2, 2009.

[24] For a detailed breakdown of each district's size and population, see Appendix A. All data are available from Republic of Yemen Central Statistics Organization, 2004 Census Data Release. Unless otherwise stated, all population data are from this source.

Figure 1.2
Population Density of the Sa'da Governorate by District

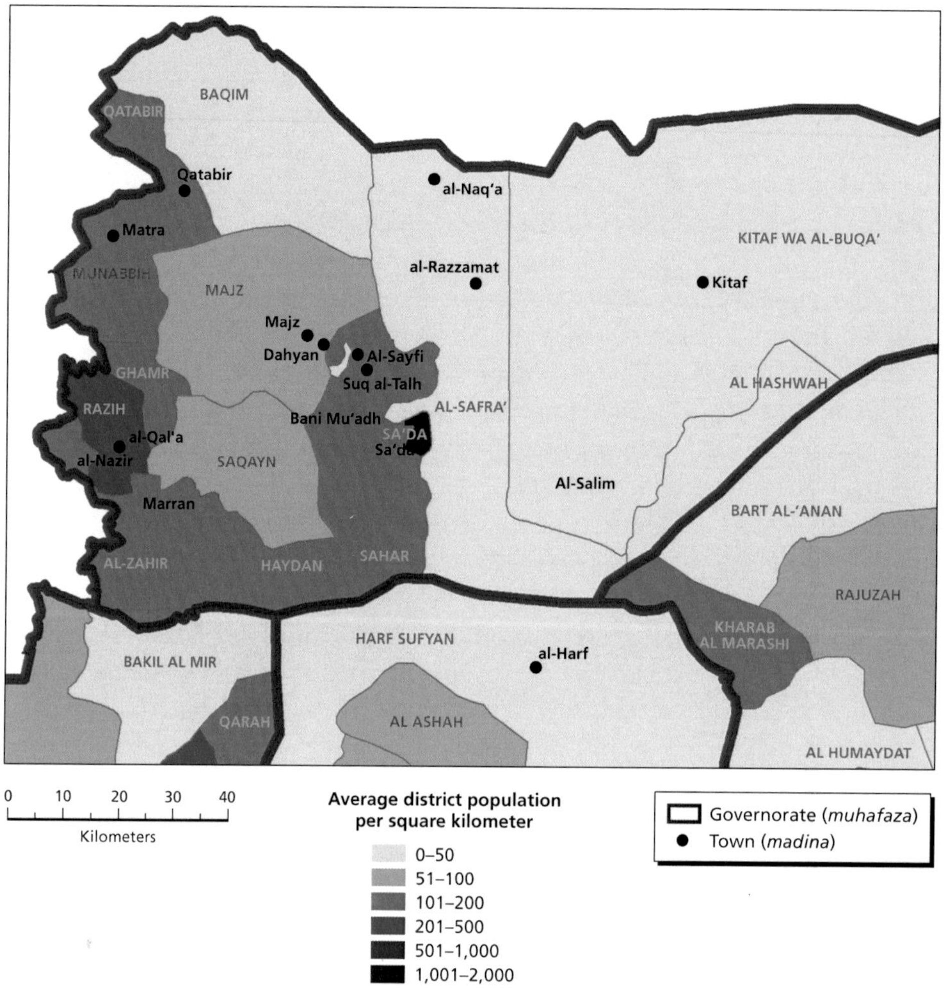

BAQIM

QATABIR

Qatabir

al-Naq'a

Matra

KITAF WA AL-BUQA'

MUNABBIH

al-Razzamat

Kitaf

MAJZ

Majz

Dahyan

Al-Sayfi

GHAMR

Suq al-Talh

AL HASHWAH

RAZIH

Bani Mu'adh

AL-SAFRA'

al-Qal'a

SA'DA

al-Nazir

SAQAYN

Sa'da

Marran

Al-Salim

BART AL-'ANAN

AL-ZAHIR

HAYDAN

SAHAR

RAJUZAH

HARF SUFYAN

al-Harf

KHARAB AL MARASHI

BAKIL AL MIR

QARAH

AL ASHAH

AL HUMAYDAT

0   10   20   30   40
Kilometers

Average district population per square kilometer
- 0–50
- 51–100
- 101–200
- 201–500
- 501–1,000
- 1,001–2,000

☐ Governorate (*muhafaza*)
● Town (*madina*)

RAND *MG962-1.2*

Finally, locations such as Sa'da city, Suq al-Talh, Kitaf, and Majz are important to local residents as capitals of districts and home to significant markets.

Figures 1.3 and 1.4 compare the locations of towns with greater than 1,500 individuals with those possessing populations less than 50. While major population centers appear to be concentrated in and around the Sa'da basin, smaller villages line the governorate's major and lesser roads and are largely located in the governorate's western peripheries. Further noteworthy is the fact that the governorate also has 1,126 villages with

Figure 1.3
Sa'da Locales with 1,500 or More Residents

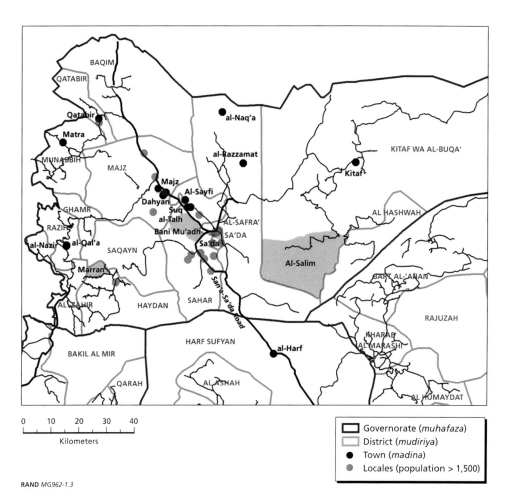

RAND *MG962-1.3*

populations of fewer than 30 individuals. This characteristic is further confirmed by Shelagh Weir's description of the population of Razih district as "dispersed in hundreds of tiny hamlets of up to twenty or so houses."[25] This has implications for social organization—residents define themselves based on their immediate surroundings rather than by their district or governorate. We will return to this idea in our discussion of north Yemeni tribalism. Finally, the location of human settlements along transportation routes indicates the importance of exchange to survival and social identities.

Further aspects of population distribution are important. The greatest number of villages have a population of less than 50. This encourages both autonomy from

---

[25] Weir, *A Tribal Order*, 24.

Figure 1.4
Sa'da Locales with 50 or Fewer Residents

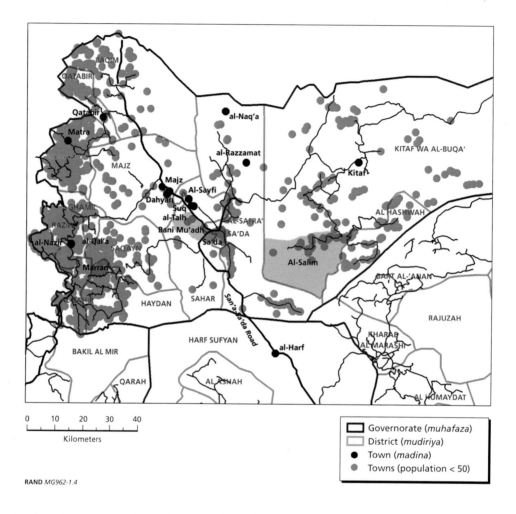

other locales and interdependence within a locale for physical survival. These small population clusters also furnish many discrete areas from which potential Huthi recruits can come. Additionally, Huthi fighters or supporters may conceal themselves from GoY forces in these areas and undoubtedly know their micro-locales better than outside military forces. The largest percentage of Sa'da's population resides in villages of 200–500 individuals. These are often agglomerations of smaller micro-locales, which permit fighters concealment while permitting an adequate material and demographic base for armed activity—Huthi or tribal. Likewise, such areas are large enough and possess enough physical structures to complicate conventional military movement in vehicles or on foot. Finally, the age demographics of the Sa'da district are such that the largest population group is the cohort between ages 16 and 44, giving Huthi insurgents a large demographic pool from which they could recruit. See Tables 1.2 and 1.3.[26]

Economy

While Sa'da's physical geography and climate create a harsh environment driving residents toward self-sufficiency and autonomy, economic needs incentivize cooperation in commerce and trade. Yet one must also consider the social value of economic pursuits. Certain agricultural commodities possess social significance, and, with stalled development and reinvestment in the governorate, farming remains the main vocation of most Sa'dans. Additionally, arid land is often used for raising livestock, which remains a viable profession for some, as does trading. Sa'da is also home to Suq al-Talh, the largest weapons market in Yemen.

Table 1.4 depicts the primary crops of the Sa'da governorate and the incentives and constraints to producing them. Agricultural commodities vary both in their value—economic and social—and their consumption of water resources. Highly

Table 1.2
Village Size in Sa'da

Population	No. of Villages	Percentage of Villages	Percentage of Population
0–50	2,279	43.0	8
50–100	1,101	21.0	11
100–200	953	18.0	19
200–500	712	14.0	31
500–1,500	202	4.0	23
1500 +	24	0.5	8

Table 1.3
Age Groups as a Percentage of Sa'da Population

Age Group	Number	Percentage of Sa'da Population	Males as Percentage of Sa'da Population
5–15	220,964	32	16.4
16–44	279,404	40	21
45–59	46,675	7	3

---

[26] For more on the demographic weight of different Sa'da areas, see Appendix A.

Table 1.4

Incentives and Water Consumption for Primary Saʻda Crops

Crop	Incentive	Constraint	Water Consumption
Grapes	High quality and reputation Cash and subsistence crop High social value	Labor intensive	Drought resistant
Pomegranates	High quality and reputation Exports to Saudi Arabia Storage capacity	Needs expertise Easily damaged from over-irrigation	Water intensive
Citrus fruits	High social, religious, and economic value	Disease Lack of experience Market saturation	Water intensive
Apples	High economic and social value	Disease Lack of experience	Water intensive
Qat	High demand and price Flexible irrigation Dry-season demand Demand in Saudi Arabia	Changing religious value Fear of disease Theft	Drought resistant
Alfalfa	Livestock (social value) Livestock (economic value)	Water scarcity Lack of livestock Daily labor	Water intensive
Sorghum	Social value (breakfast) Fodder Food self-sufficiency	—	Drought resistant

SOURCE: Lichtenthäler, *Political Ecology*, 144–145.

drought-resistant sorghum, a staple used for making bread and rearing livestock, is grown by 90 percent of farmers, with many allocating up to 30 percent of their land to it.[27] With wheat being primarily imported and imports of fruit banned since 1984, Saʻda farmers increasingly dedicated their resources toward the production of highly valued cash crops, including oranges, apples, and pomegranates, as well as grapes and *qat*, which can withstand droughts. Indeed, government figures indicate that cash crops, fruit, and vegetables comprised a combined 13,860 hectares of the governorate's arable land in 2004, roughly 35 percent of the total arable land in the region.[28] These goods are sold at *suqs* within the governorate and in Sanʻa, as well as traded or smuggled into Saudi Arabia.

The production of fruit, which typically requires a large amount of water to grow and is thus sensitive to droughts, illustrates the necessity of analyzing these goods in terms of both their social and economic value. While the economic value of fruit in the

---

[27]   Weir, *A Tribal Order*, 13.

[28]   See "Al-Nashat al-Iqtisadiya li Muhafazat Saʻda" (Economic Activity for the Saʻda Governorate), undated.

governorate peaked in the mid-1980s,[29] citrus orchards continue to carry a great deal of social prestige because having a well-irrigated, green orchard gives the owner respect among Sa'da residents. Furthermore, the oranges themselves are often used as "gifts" to government officials by those hoping to remain in good favor and receive government patronage.[30] Because agricultural commodities and the land itself have both a monetary and social value, replacing their value would be virtually impossible subsequent to destruction. The impact of the latter would be multifold, straitening the economy while assuming a symbolic—and thus political—meaning.

These commodities are produced within a sociopolitical context. As previously mentioned, arable land is to some extent limited to local *wadis* and terraces. Expanding arable land through irrigation methods utilizing terracing or ground wells has considerable limits, involving advanced techniques requiring technology not indigenous to the area. This technology is limited to an elite few.[31] The input requirement and restrictions of irrigation technology therefore provide a lever for outside actors to coopt locals. Although residents certainly strive for self-sufficiency, outside patronage permits improved irrigation and greater wealth accumulation. The prestige associated with these material factors could lead individuals to accept such patronage, putting them under at least partial control of an outside actor—be it the state, patrons from neighboring regions (including Saudi Arabia), or a larger local landowner. This further constructs an environment in which the less powerful must find ways to accommodate or resist encroachments on their economic and territorial sovereignty.

Avenues of Transportation and Networks of Economic Exchange. Figure 1.5 depicts the different types of trade routes in the Sa'da governorate as they relate to Huthi conflict areas. The building of paved roads in the Sa'da governorate has permitted goods to move more efficiently, thus creating bonds within and beyond Sa'da's districts. In the western Sa'da district of Razih, for example, the automobile and paved roads have allowed export of the easily perishable *qat* plant to other markets, creating significant income for the district.[32] Similarly, the San'a–Sa'da road, completed in 1979, allowed fruit from Sa'da to be sold in San'a markets for a profit.[33] These examples illustrate the way in which improved means of transportation have increased ties between Sa'da residents, as well as between Sa'da and other governorates. Such roads are vital to the local economy and thus are guarded and monitored by local tribes.

Other transportation routes include lesser roads—such as dirt or damaged paved routes—and *wadis*. Lesser roads, while more difficult for automobiles or tracked vehi-

---

[29] Lichtenthäler, *Political Ecology*, 144–145.

[30] Lichtenthäler, *Political Ecology*, 144–145.

[31] Lichtenthäler, *Political Ecology*, 21. For a full analysis of these limitations, see Chapter 4 of that book.

[32] Weir, *A Tribal Order*, 22.

[33] Lichtenthäler, *Political Ecology*, 132.

Figure 1.5
Lanes of Transportation and Movement in the Sa'da Governorate

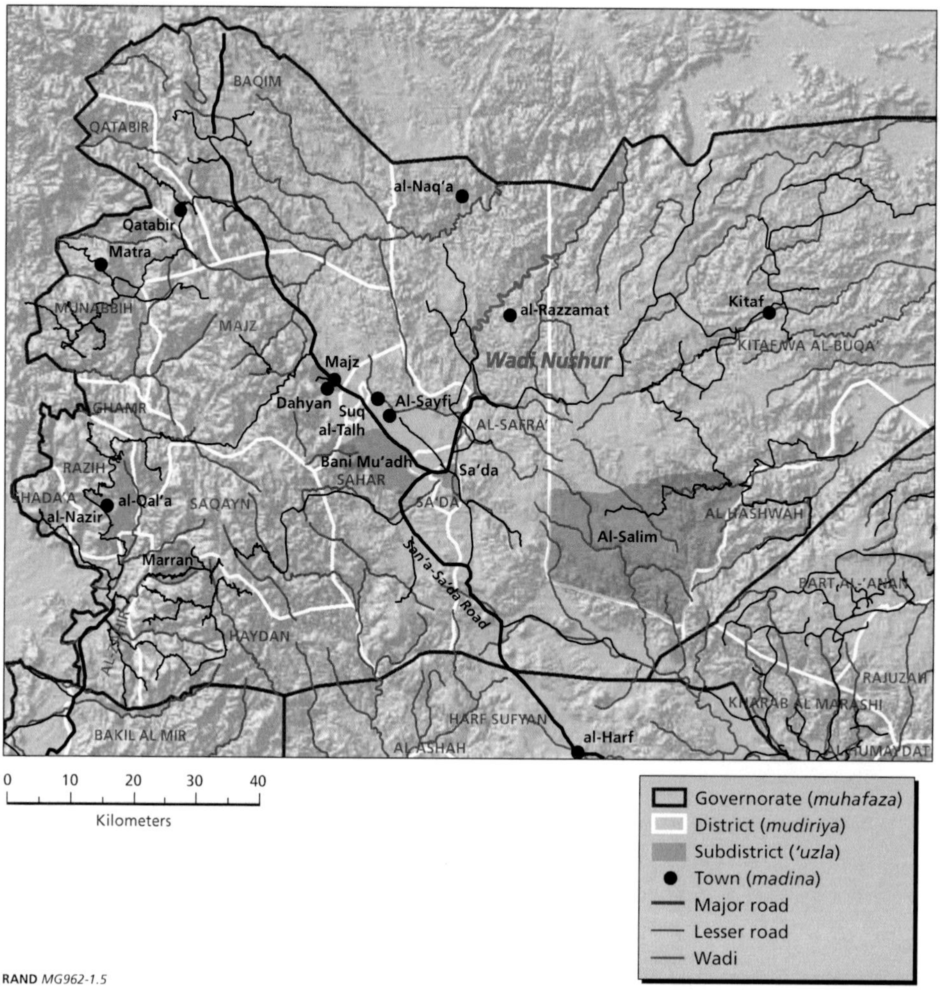

cles to traverse, could further aid in the movement of goods within and beyond the governorate. Such routes are likely still monitored and controlled by locals. Conversely, *wadis* provide a less optimal method of transporting goods, although they are much more difficult to control and monitor. With the exception of *wadis*, these routes of movement also become commodities themselves because movement requires local permission and can be subject to a tax. As we will see presently, the movement of goods within and beyond the governorate serves to tie Sa'dans to each other and those outside its borders.

Figure 1.6 depicts the import and export patterns of the Sa'da governorate. Partnerships and exchanges are made at the local and international levels to permit wealth

Figure 1.6
Networks of Economic Exchange in the Sa'da Governorate

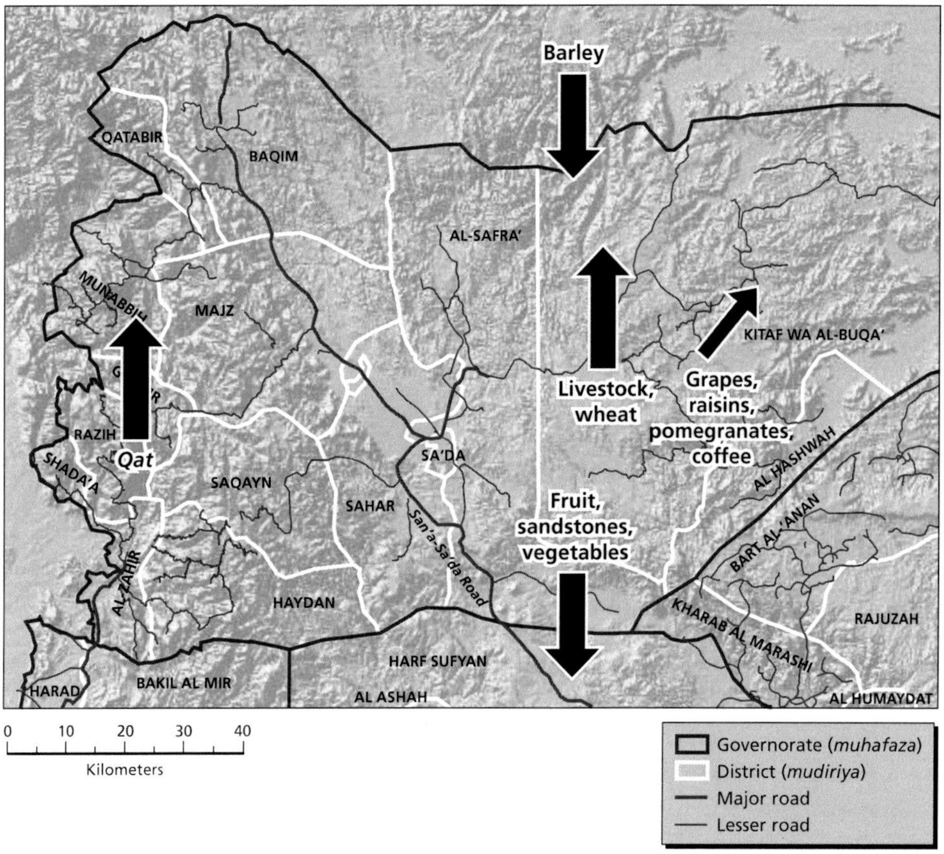

Barley

QATABIR
BAQIM
AL-SAFRA'
MUNABBIH
MAJZ
KITAF WA AL-BUQA'
RAZIH
Qat
Grapes,
raisins,
pomegranates,
coffee
SHADA'A
SAQAYN
SA'DA
AL-ZAHIR
SAHAR
Livestock,
wheat
AL HASHWAH
San'a-Sa'da Road
Fruit,
sandstones,
vegetables
BART AL-'ANAN
HAYDAN
KHARAB AL MARASHI
RAJUZAH
HARF SUFYAN
HARAD
BAKIL AL MIR
AL ASHAH
AL HUMAYDAT

0   10   20   30   40
Kilometers

Governorate (*muhafaza*)
District (*mudiriya*)
Major road
Lesser road

RAND *MG962-1.6*

accumulation in times of calm and survival in times of crises. That being said, the need for self-sufficiency drives residents away from economic specialization. Indeed, specializing in certain goods without compensating or storing goods for times of political instability would leave residents unable to sustain themselves should exchange networks break down. Both the geographical context and nature of these exchanges is such that they are virtually impossible for the authorities to regulate. Goods are exchanged through networks of weekly markets that span Sa'da's districts. The commodities sold and exchanged in them can come from outside the immediate districts, while the limited roads in the governorate delineate specific trade routes known by locals. Given the governorate's proximity to Saudi Arabia, goods also move across the border.

Some of this cross-border trade is illicit. Indeed, *qat*, while illegal in Saudi Arabia, is imported from Sa'da's western districts, while wheat and livestock (raised on barley imported from Saudi Arabia) are also exported to the kingdom. Weapons also easily circulate in Sa'da and are both imported from southern ports and exported across the Saudi border. This further reinforces the lack of government control over the means of transportation and creates cross-border relationships. Such transnational relationships create natural material and physical havens for Sa'da residents across the border. These relationships also provide the kingdom with some leverage in dealing with individuals and groups in the governorate through its own patronage networks. Saudi Arabia thus enjoys a sphere of influence that allows it to affect events in the area to an equal or greater degree than that of the GoY itself. The way in which Saudi Arabia exercises this influence can affect conflict and local development.

At the local level, goods are exchanged through weekly markets (*suqs*). While *suqs* specialize in certain goods to varying degrees, each *suq* features the primary staples of trade—*qat*, sorghum, and grapes.[34] Weekly markets are organized in such a way that each area's *suq* functions on a specific day. These day "assignments" remain static, allowing traders to rotate through multiple markets in a week. Local *suqs* thus serve a purpose beyond economic exchange. Used by residents to exchange news and consult local leaders, *suqs* tie residents together socially and economically. Disrupting commodity exchange, or shutting *suqs* down altogether, will thus erode social and economic bonds between locals, provoking disquiet.

Although improved methods and means of transportation have helped create bonds between Sa'da residents and other governorates, they remain vulnerable to commodity scarcity. Furthermore, economic interdependence contradicts local notions of self- and group autonomy, perpetuating conceptual friction and suspicion of outsiders. Still, the scarcity of resources magnifies the extent to which the provision of commodities or services can yield influence. Indeed, services as simple as drilling a well to building a dam can shift the power and prestige scales toward certain actors—such as the state—leaving locals indebted to the provider of these services.

Finally, reliance on delicate trade routes yields a precarious situation in which their destruction could significantly impact the lives of Sa'da residents, jeopardizing group survival and individual accumulation of wealth and prestige. Furthermore, the interdistrict socioeconomic ties between residents would also be compromised by the physical effects of armed conflict. This could lead communities to simultaneously reassert economic autonomy by relying on local means of production while potentially creating new bonds of solidarity with others affected by the destruction of routes.

Weapons Availability in Sa'da and Northern Yemen. Along with agriculture, weapons are an important part of the local economy—and cultural assertion of manhood, as we will see in our discussion of *qabyala*. For many generations, tribal Yemenis have acquired weapons as symbols of individual and collective autonomy, given them as gifts or mementos of alliances, sold them as largely unregulated commodities at markets throughout the region, and smuggled them to other countries as part of a

---

34   Weir, *A Tribal Order*, 21.

commercial tradition considered licit by its Yemeni practitioners. It has thus become an analytical truism that Yemen is a highly weaponized society, and several reports speak of the country being "awash with weapons."[35] Yet it remains extremely difficult to quantitatively fix numbers of weapons in the country. Estimates often glibly reiterated by shaykhs, government officials, and Western writers put the number of serviceable weapons in Yemen at 40 million to 60 million, a number repeated by international organizations such as the United Nations (UN).[36] Attempts to study the problem of weapons presence in Yemen systematically have relied on visits to San'a, interviews of shopkeepers and officials, and use of internationally recognized calculation methodologies. These efforts have yielded results that suggest fewer weapons in the country, between 7 million and 15 million.[37] Notably, such studies were completed before the increase of al-Qa'ida-associated violence—and prior to the commencement of hostilities between the GoY and the Huthis.

In the present context, the overall number of weapons in Yemen is less important than the availability of combat-worthy weapons and ordnance in those regions where there is violence between the GoY and the Huthis. In this respect, it is worthy of note that the Sa'da governorate itself features one of the largest arms markets in the country, in Suq al-Talh, with other markets in Jawf and San'a. Further, while possession and visible display of weapons has long been associated with tribalism in those parts of Yemen that became the YAR, it had not been evident in the PDRY to nearly the same degree. As such, weapons and the weapons trade are concentrated in San'a and more northern parts of the country—the very areas of the Huthi conflict.

Discussions of weapons in Yemen often focus on the aggregate numbers of weapons per person. Out of a 2004 population of 19.5 million, this means somewhere between just under one to two-and-a-half weapons per Yemeni citizen, based on an estimate of either 15 million or 50 million weapons in the country. Again, this is misleading because it exaggerates the distribution of weapons nationally and understates the presence of weapons in specific areas and among certain segments of the population.

As a corrective, we must focus on the population in the areas of concern to the Huthi-regime conflict, such as Sa'da, 'Amran, and Jawf. In those areas, the relevant numbers relate to the segment of the population most likely to possess weapons and prove susceptible to Huthi or GoY recruitment. These are likely males roughly between the ages of 15 and their mid-40s. Then we can begin to understand the prevalence of weapons among the age group currently engaged in conflict. In doing so, we need to bear in mind that the north is the area of greatest concentration of weapons. Work

---

[35] See "Yemen Clashes: Northern Mountain Rebellion," *Alertnet*, Thomson Reuters Foundation, May 30, 2008.

[36] See "Weapons in Yemen," *IRIN Films* (United Nations), November 8, 2007.

[37] See Derek B. Miller, "Demand, Stockpiles, and Social Controls: Small Arms in Yemen," *Small Arms Survey,* Occasional Paper No. 9, May 2003.

completed just prior to the outbreak of hostilities, in 2003, relied on interviews and the consensus of local Yemenis to suggest that in the governorates of concern—Saʿda, Jawf, ʿAmran, and northern Sanʿa—men possessed an average of 2–3 serviceable weapons in the small arms category.[38]

Table 1.5 tabulates data and estimates among the most conflict-prone age group for small-arms density in the Huthi conflict areas. We should also include those districts of Sanʿa governorate adjacent to ʿAmran and Jawf, where Huthi presence has been reported (Table 1.6).

The numbers in Tables 1.5 and 1.6 show over 1 million small arms outside government control by 2004 in those areas subsequently associated with the GoY-Huthi conflict. It should be noted that this number represents a conservative estimate. Not only does it hinge on the assessment of 2–3 weapons per male in these areas, but it also does not account for men between the ages of 45 and 60. Males in this category likely possess weapons but are not combatants, thus freeing up their weapons for younger Yemeni

Table 1.5
Weapons Estimates for Conflict Governorates, 2004

Governorate	Population	Males Age 16–44	Weapons per Male	Weapons in Governorate
Saʿda	695,091	146,095	2	292,190
ʿAmran	885,601	179,525	2	359,050
Jawf	450,030	109,768	3	329,304
Total	2,030,722	435,388		980,544

SOURCE: Republic of Yemen Central Statistics Organization 2004 Census Data Release; Derek Miller, "Demand, Stockpiles, and Social Controls: Small Arms in Yemen."

Table 1.6
Weapons in Sanʿa *Mudiriyat* in or near Conflict Areas

Sanʿa District	Population	Males Age 16–44	Weapons per Male	Weapons in District
Arhab	90,040	18,097	2	36,194
Nihm	41,507	8,390	2	16,780
Hamdan	85,370	17,004	2	34,008
Bani Hushaysh	73,955	14,629	2	29,258
Total	290,872	58,120		116,240

SOURCE: Derek Miller, "Demand, Stockpiles, and Social Controls: Small Arms in Yemen."

---

[38] Miller, "Demand, Stockpiles, and Social Controls: Small Arms in Yemen."

male users. Based upon 2004 census data and weapons-per-person estimates, this yields a further 152,000 weapons in the three governorates, as well as 21,000 for the relevant districts of San'a governorate.[39] Furthermore, these numbers do not include weapons circulating into the conflict area from a point of origin in the capital city district itself. More significantly, they do not account for large stockpiles in the hands of subtribe and tribal shaykhs, who have been assessed to own between tens and a hundred weapons each. Some of these are sold to weapons retailers. Alternatively, shaykhs deliver both fighters and weapons to the Huthis or GoY, based on alliance formation and coercion. Lastly, these numbers cannot account for massive stocks of weapons in regional arms markets.

Ultimately, what emerges is a picture of the northern Yemen conflict areas—from the northern outskirts of San'a governorate to the Saudi border—featuring large numbers of weapons prior to the commencement of hostilities in 2004, likely more than 1.5 million. The overall number of weapons in Yemen outside GoY control has likely increased since the last studies were completed—and that increase is likely represented most in Huthi conflict areas.

In terms of the sources of weapons found in northern Yemen prior to the beginning of hostilities, shipments come to Yemen's largest ports, including the Aden complex in the south and al-Hudayda along the Red Sea coast. Al-Mukalla in the east and al-Mukha and al-Salif along the Red Sea are also destinations for smaller-scale weapons shipments. From these Yemeni ports of entry, weapons proceed both through GoY hands into tribal possession and directly into the stocks of tribes in the north. Observers have noted that some Soviet-era assault rifles, pistols, and small-caliber mortars go back to the period of Egyptian military presence in the country during the 1960s.[40] Likewise, YAR leaders in the 1970s and 1980s gave portions of Eastern Bloc and Chinese arms imports to tribal leaders to purchase their loyalty. This continued in the 1990s after Yemeni unification. It has further been reported that during and after the 1994 civil war, the GoY permitted northern-based tribal elements to loot weapons stocks in the old PDRY depots, which added to unregulated tribal holdings of small and medium arms and munitions.[41]

In addition to government holdings that the GoY has allowed into private Yemeni hands, the GoY itself has permitted well-connected Yemeni merchants and tribal representatives to engage in large-scale weapons importation from former Eastern Bloc countries, as well as China, east Asia, and even some Western European dealers. These weapons arrive through Yemen's major ports on the Red Sea and Gulf of Aden. The GoY has often stipulated that a percentage of the imported weapons go to San'a's stock-

---

[39] See Appendix A for populations in this cohort.

[40] See Paul Dresch, *Tribes, Government, and History in Yemen* (New York: Oxford University Press, 1989).

[41] Miller, "Demand, Stockpiles, and Social Controls: Small Arms in Yemen," 11.

piles. Of late, officials have made efforts to ensure that the "tax" imposed on private weapons shipments includes the heaviest weapons.[42]

In these areas, and in Hudayda in particular, Yemenis suggest that weapons shipments destined in their entirety for GoY stockpiles are often pilfered by dockworkers connected to weapons dealers in the country's interior, often with the connivance of GoY officials who receive payment in return.[43] Observers have also commented that poor record-keeping in military stockpiles permits Yemeni officers to transfer weapons to relatives for tribal possession or for profit.[44]

Weapons coming into private Yemeni hands at ports or near military bases then move to small-size arms shops, often open storefronts in major cities, including San'a and other northern areas. Larger numbers proceed to regional arms "bazaars," associated with markets selling other goods as well. As mentioned above, al-Talh, about 10 km north of Sa'da city along the road to Majz and the Saudi border, has traditionally been the largest arms market in the country. Al-Bayda in the southeast and al-Jihanah, 40 km southeast of San'a city, are other large markets and transit points.

Movement to small shops and large markets is both overland or, if illicit, on small boats along the Red Sea coast. Strictly speaking, weapons smuggling, at least prior to 2004, did not occur from one Yemeni area to another because such movements were considered licit. Rather, smuggling routes went northwards toward Saudi Arabia. As such, in addition to water routes toward the environs of Jizzan, Sa'da governorate's road to the border and its *wadis* were major lanes of weapons smuggling. Often, Yemeni tribes with brethren on the Saudi side of the border were the major conduit. After 2003, the Saudi and Yemeni governments increased their cooperation and surveillance in order to interdict such smuggling into the kingdom.[45] While the border is now far from hermetically sealed, it is likely that weapons once intended for transfer to Saudi customers now remain in Yemen in the Sa'da governorate.

Among weapons types in the core conflict areas in 2004, the largest portion consisted of 7.62-mm Kalashnikov automatic assault rifles of various classes. Modern Russian and Eastern European models with bipods and lengthened barrels are accompanied by more-inexpensive Chinese variants of 1960s AK-47s. Eastern Bloc semiautomatic pistols are prevalent as well but carry less prestige, since rifles possess greater cultural demonstration value. Additionally, rocket-propelled grenade (RPG) launchers and projectiles are relatively widespread, having been seen in shops in San'a and northern areas. Likewise, photographs in 2003 depicted hand grenades in the arms markets, while 85-mm artillery rockets were reported in Sa'da market areas. In that year, a UN

---

[42] See Integrated Regional Information Network (IRIN), *Guns Out of Control: The Continuing Threat of Small Arms* (New York: United Nations, 2006), 30–32.

[43] Interview, Yemeni national residing in the United States, October 29, 2008.

[44] Interview, international human rights worker from Sa'da, March 20, 2009.

[45] See Ahmed al-Haj, "Yemen, Saudis Join to Stem Weapons Trade," *Yemen Times* 13:679 (October 23, 2003).

report indicated Yemen as the point of origin of surface-to-air missiles found at that time in Somalia, although the GoY subsequently sought to collect such munitions from the markets.[46]

Official Saudi reports of arms seized along the border with Yemen provide a sense of the kinds of weapons circulating in Sa'da at the very time the armed conflict with the GoY was beginning. Between February 2004 and February 2005, Saudi authorities seized nearly 600 Kalashnikov automatic rifles in this area, along with 170 pistols and 80 other heavy-caliber rifles, likely to include FNFAL and G-3 rifles originating in Europe whose range is greater than the AK models the GoY forces possess. Further, eight machine guns of the 12.7-mm variety were seized, along with one mortar tube and 30 mortar rounds. Saudi forces also seized over 100 light cannons. In Yemeni arms markets, weapons are supplemented by explosives. The 2004–2005 Saudi haul thus included two mines, 14 kg of explosive material, 149 assembled bombs, and over 28,000 sticks of dynamite.[47]

Since the beginning of the conflict, news reports, as well as still and video imagery, demonstrate that Huthi fighters have taken advantage of tribal stockpiles that include these weapons and munitions. Further, weapons originating in Yemen and seized in Somalia suggest that Huthi fighters have access to large numbers of RPG rounds, as well as antipersonnel and antitank mines.[48] GoY media and Western aid workers report the existence of small workshops used by the Huthis to manufacture grenades, incendiary devices, and improvised explosive devices (IEDs).[49]

Some analysts feel that there is not a great amount of illicit weapons movement into Huthi areas, given their ubiquity there even before 2004.[50] Likewise, GoY reports and other sources suggest that the Huthi family had begun to stockpile arms prior to the outbreak of hostilities in 2004—though, if true, it is not clear whether this was

---

[46] See United Nations Security Council, "Report of the Panel of Experts on Somalia Pursuant to Security Council Resolution 1474 (2003)," S/2003/1035, November 4, 2003, 29–30.

[47] See Nicole Stracke, "Counter-Terrorism and Weapon Smuggling: Success and Failure of Yemeni-Saudi Collaboration," Gulf Research Center Security and Terrorism Research Bulletin, Issue 4, November 2006, 10.

[48] See United Nations Security Council, "Report of the Monitoring Group on Somalia Pursuant to Security Council Resolution 1811 (2008)," S/2008/768, December 10, 2008. It states, ". . . the Monitoring Group inspected a shipment of ammunition seized by the Somaliland authorities on 15 April 2008 in Burao. The ammunition came from Yemen and was destined to ONLF in Ethiopia. It consisted of 101 anti-tank mines, 100 hand grenades, 170 rocket-propelled grenade-7 rounds, and 170 boxes of 7.62 mm ammunition, each containing 440 rounds. The anti-tank mines were packed in sacks originally for rice from a company based in Sana'a and an investigation by the Somaliland authorities determined that the weapons had been shipped from Yemen." See p. 27 in particular.

[49] Interview, international human rights worker from Sa'da area, April 2009.

[50] Interview, international human rights worker from Sa'da area, April 2009.

an aspect of sociocultural assertion or preparation for warfare against the regime.[51] Still, other means of acquiring weapons have emerged since 2004 as a function of the conflict. The Huthis have taken advantage of them to acquire more and different arms through methods particularly attuned to insurgency in a tribal environment with transnational linkages. We will return to this issue in Chapter Seven.

Government Presence in the Governorate

Today the Sa'da governorate is divided into fifteen *mudiriyat* (districts), which are then further divided into *'uzla* (subdistricts). Administratively, local residents can run for local district councils, while President Saleh appoints the heads of governorates and council directors. There have been 22 governors of Sa'da since 1962, the greatest turnover of any province, demonstrating the inherent difficulties of establishing government control over such a naturally ungovernable territory.[52] Sa'da also fields parliamentary representatives in the 301-seat National Assembly. The introduction of local and national participatory political mechanisms to the north provides yet another channel through which the San'a government can funnel patronage, as we will see in Chapter Three. Indeed, partisan competition between residents allows the government to empower some at the expense of others, creating new divides and exploiting old ones. This competition has also allowed the government to monitor and weaken emerging threats by placing them under the patronage and control of state institutions.

While the government must use patronage networks to maintain influence, it does possess an infrastructural presence in the governorate. Although official figures on the exact numbers of state institutions in the governorate are unreliable or nonexistent, recent scholarship and media reporting does give some insight into the matter. Each district capital city appears to have a local police station, a government bureau, a number of schools, and a hospital or clinic. Furthermore, limited electricity is available in the governorate, as are running water and landline telecommunications. Government figures claim that there are six Internet cafes and 127 telephone centers in the Sa'da governorate,[53] while two cellular telephone providers cover the region: Saba Phone and MTN.[54] It is also likely that GoY troops were garrisoned in certain cities north of San'a prior to the 2004 conflict.

---

[51] 'Abd al-Hamid al-Lisani, "Mudakhala Hadi'a Ma'a 'Zayd' . . . 'An al-Huthiya wa-l-Zaydiya wa-l-Hashimiya wa-l-Futun al-Ukhra," *al-Mithaq.net,* July 16, 2007.

[52] See "Muhafiz Sa'da al-Jadid Yubashir Muhamihu fi Aqqal min 24 Sa'a," *al-Ayyam*, April 21, 2007.

[53] See "Ahamm al-Mu'shirat fi Muhafazat Sa'da," undated.

[54] Yahya al-Thulaya, "Harf Sufyan: Kayf Ahtaraqat Maqqarat al-Ahzab wa Hallat Mahalha al-Huthiya!? Al-Shabab al-Mu'min, min Awwal al-Ghadir Ila Akhir Talaqa . . . Wafa' wa Salsabil wa Haykal . . . Yudhakirun Bila Aml fi Akhtabarat!!" *al-Ahale*, undated.

The increasing GoY presence in the governorate has led to the state's cooptation of initially organic, parallel institutions of governance and service. A salient example of the GoY's integration of organic, informal, social institutions in the Sa'da governorate is the regime's response to local development associations (LDAs). This locally based form of cooperation, which highlighted the state's deficiencies, prompted the GoY to begin incorporating them into the state and to use budgetary funds to begin building both a physical and patrimonial presence in the various districts of the Sa'da governorate. LDAs were eventually formally integrated into the nationwide Confederation of Yemeni Development Associations, which President Saleh was elected to head.[55] This body was essentially a conduit for government patronage. Local councils were created (to replace those of the LDAs), and other development work was integrated under the auspices of state-controlled charitable associations. Ultimately, this led to the deterioration of service efficiency.[56] The net effect of this incorporation was to accentuate variances in wealth among residents, forcing competition for patronage and creating points of friction. The case of the LDAs demonstrates how the broader GoY methods of control and cooptation, which we will see later, were used in an attempt to neutralize Hizb al-Haqq and the Believing Youth in the 1990s.

Sa'da as Geographic Periphery: Implications for the Huthi Conflict

The social and physical geography of the Sa'da governorate creates a context of resource scarcity that drives residents to be both autonomous and interdependent. People must be self-sufficient enough to weather political instability but must reach outside their immediate surroundings to accumulate wealth, prestige, or influence. Therefore, although economic exchange networks are particularly vulnerable to armed conflict, autonomy as a value-in-action allows the population to sustain itself during conflict and endure the crumbling of intercommunity ties. By primarily relying on selective patronage to coopt local elites, the GoY has created further schisms among Sa'da residents, perpetuating its sociopolitical peripherality. The divisive tactics used by the GoY in dealing with Sa'da residents ensure that opposition and resentment of state intrusion will persist. While emerging threats to the government may be further coopted and divided, this high-risk strategy requires striking a delicate balance vulnerable to changes in society and norms.

The social and physical geography of the Sa'da governorate also complicates military operations. For example, transportation routes are limited, and a comprehensive knowledge of both their locations and the local notions of ownership attached to them is likely confined to the governorate's residents. As a result, the GoY would find it dif-

---

[55] Weir, *A Tribal Order*, 290.

[56] Carapico, *Civil Society*, 132.

ficult to effectively regulate the movement of goods and personnel within and beyond the governorate and could obliviously violate local norms associated with permission and ownership of transportation routes. The mountainous terrain further impedes maneuverability of multiton tracked vehicles and mechanized units, leaving them open both to ambush and, due to the limited transport routes, IEDs and land mines (see Figure 1.7). Even knowledge of sustenance locations, such as markets or water supplies, is confined to locals, forcing troops to rely on food convoys that may not reach their destinations. Cross-border trade networks and (as we will see later) social ties could also easily allow for the continued smuggling of material goods, effectively fueling the conflict. Further, these cross-border relationships could provide safe havens for combatants. Ultimately, the geography of the Sa'da governorate helps create networks and means of survival that are vulnerable to armed conflict but that allow for local opposition forces to endure for long periods of time and exploit the local environmental factors to their advantage.

Figure 1.7
Geographic Challenges to Military Operations in Sa'da

SOURCE: Adapted from Huthi video, "Fa Amkana Minhum," *Qism al-I'lam al-Harbi*, June 2008.
RAND *MG962-1.7*

CHAPTER TWO

The Sociocultural Ecology of the Huthi Conflict: Tribalism and Religion

The physical environment of northern Yemen influences not only its economy but its social structure as well. Areas north of San'a have been referred to as *bilad al-qaba'il*, or the land of tribes, with ancestral regions associated with particular tribal segments. *Qabyala*, or tribalism, is an enduring way of organizing society in these areas. Beyond an area on a map, however, *qabyala* functions as both a method of social organization and a complex of values informing the way people evaluate their actions and those of others. Likewise, religion plays a role in creating and sustaining beliefs and social values in Yemen. In the north, Zaydism is not only a belief system; it also contributes along with *qabyala* to social hierarchies and norms of interaction. In Yemen as a whole, however, religion is a domain of contested identity. In addition to multiple interpretations of Zaydism, Yemen has featured a slight majority of Sunnis of the Shafi'i school of jurisprudence since 1990. In the past several decades, Salafism of a Wahhabi bent has also entered the country, both culturally and politically. Therefore, both tribalism and religion create the sociocultural context and predominant norms of northern Yemen. Yet, since Huthi and the GoY efforts to gain supporters or condemn each other often appeal to *qabyala* and religion, they have become dimensions of the Huthi-regime conflict itself.

Qabyala North of San'a: Geography

While Yemenis typically refer to areas north of the capital as the land of the Hashid and Bakil tribes (*bilad Hashid wa al-Bakil*), the Sa'da governorate is home to a unique cross-section of tribal confederations, none of which maintain absolute territorial, political, or material hegemony. While the Hashid have typically been the most dominant tribal confederation in terms of their influence in GoY institutions and Yemeni tribal society, the Sa'da governorate exists as the fringe of Hashid territorial sovereignty. Indeed, Sa'da is primarily home to two other less-powerful tribal confederations: Khawlan bin 'Amr and Bakil, both of which have a significant presence in the governorate. Although Khawlan bin 'Amr is a smaller, less politically prominent tribal grouping, Sa'da, as well as parts of 'Amran and Hajja, constitutes its area of greatest demographic concentration.

Geographic depiction of the tribes of *muhafazat* Sa'da presents challenges, particularly because northern Yemeni tribes exhibit certain peculiarities in terms of how local social imaginations structure them. Two tribes in particular are worth exploring in this section, as they relate to the meaning of tribes and territoriality. First, "tribes" are of all different sizes. That is to say that in northern Yemeni usage, the word for tribe—*qabila* (pl. *qaba'il*)—is applied to kin networks of drastically different demographic magnitudes. A Yemeni, therefore, can refer to a cluster of extended families amounting to 50 people as a *qabila*—and also refer to a grouping of 1,000 people as a *qabila*. Both of these groupings are considered tribes according to perspective and circumstance, and this indeterminacy of usage is even greater when Yemenis from other regions speak of the "tribal north."

Further, in certain Arab tribal environments, local residents use specific terms to refer to kin groups of varying size. These are lineage segments, each of which combines to create a larger, aggregated kin segment. In this way, several "houses" make up an extended family, several extended families make up a subclan, several subclans make up a clan, several clans make up a tribe, and so on—while, at each level, segmentary lineage groups are of roughly the same size. In northern Yemen, however, *qaba'il* are inconsistent in their awareness of the gradations of segmentary aggregation and do not use the same terms for them across the region. Additionally, segments at any given level of aggregation—clan, subtribe, etc.—often exhibit a great diversity in size. For example, a tribe (*qabila*) can break into three, four—or ten—"subtribes" (*fakhdh, lahm*); a tribe (*qabila*) can also break into two tribes (*qaba'il*); or even into three unequally sized "seconds," "thirds," "fourths," etc.

Therefore, the social significance of segmentary gradation is variable across the region. While an author writing about far western Sa'da *muhafaza* could say that local tribes "can be regarded as sovereign polities… like micro states" with "political borders and internal administrative divisions,"[1] an ethnographer covering areas in 'Amran—a governorate just south of Sa'da—in the same period concluded that "the vocabulary denoting sections and subsections varies from place to place . . . [with] no privileged level of organization that stands out in all circumstances, nor any standard distinction of terminology between one level and the next." As such, "the classification of tribal divisions sometimes involves ambiguities that neat diagrams . . . disguise," and "the outsider's attempts . . . to talk about the system in abstract terms" through such

---

[1]   Shelagh Weir, *A Tribal Order: Politics and Law in the Mountains of Yemen* (Austin: University of Texas Press, 2007), 211.

diagrams "easily produce confusion and false classifications that are artifacts of one's questions."[2]

In the context of the current Huthi conflict, this means that what some local or external commentators refer to as a tribe may be considered by others to be merely an extended family—but the opposite is also true. Likewise, tribes that have been named by interlocutors as allied to either the Huthis or the GoY are often not listed in established tribal hierarchies associated with regional confederations. This allows generalizations in terms of Hashid, Bakil, and occasionally Khawlan bin 'Amr—although alliances and differences exist to a great degree within, rather than between, those groups.

A second characteristic relatively unique to Yemeni tribalism is the strong identification of tribe with place. Unlike tribes in parts of Africa or other areas in the Middle East, north Yemeni tribes do not have a tradition of transhumance, nor is a Bedouin nomadism a social value in tribal collective memories.[3] As sedentary agriculturalists, therefore, Yemeni *qaba'il* exhibit a particularly strong attachment to and identification with "their" territories. This identification is illustrated by the Yemeni highlands proverb, *'izz al-qabili biladah*—"the pride/prestige of a *qabila* is [in] his land"—and informs the local geographic imagination.[4] Place names and tribe names become nearly identical, such that even people of unrelated families living in an area are often assimilated to the same tribe over a few generations and named in terms of the preexisting local place name or the demographically dominant grouping in the area.[5]

The GoY has frequently taken up this usage as much as it understands local place-group dynamics, so that *'uzla* names correspond to tribal segment names (although the territorial correspondence is more imperfect). GoY naming conventions reinforce another geocultural tendency. Since we have just seen that some *qaba'il* can be very small, territorial distinctions combine with notions of what a tribe is to create a hyper-local geographic awareness, as well as a relative opacity to outsiders. Most significantly for the current Huthi-GoY conflict, territorial attachments and hyper-local geographies are embedded in local interpretations of tribal values and interpersonal obligations, to be discussed later in this chapter.

Figures 2.1, 2.2, and 2.3 depict the subtribal groupings of the Hashid, Bakil, and Khawlan bin 'Amr confederations. The Hashid tribal confederation comprises the largest in Yemen, having been led by the influential shaykh 'Abdullah al-Ahmar until his death in December 2007. Hashid has been historically well connected in the political

---

[2] Paul Dresch, *Tribes, Government, and History in Yemen* (New York: Oxford University Press, 1989), 78, 77, 111.

[3] Charles F. Swagman, "Tribe and Politics: An Example from Highland Yemen," *Journal of Anthropological Research* 44:3 (1988), 252–253.

[4] Najwa Adra, "Qabyala: the Tribal Concept in the Central Highlands of the Yemen," unpublished Ph.D. dissertation, Temple University, 1982, 145.

[5] Adra, "Qabyala," 117, 121.

realm because President Saleh's tribe is part of the Hashid confederation. The Bakil, while traditionally less powerful than the Hashid, have a much more significant presence in the Sa'da governorate. The Bakil confederation is made up of approximately 31 tribes, some of which exist under the subconfederations of Dahm (eight subtribes) and Wa'ila (seven subtribes). The majority of Bakil tribes relevant to the conflict in the north are locally known as Hamdan al-Sham (northern Hamdan), a categorization that overlays the Dahm and Wa'ila subconfederations themselves, at times replacing these names in local parlance. Finally, Khawlan bin 'Amr, while broadly less powerful than both Hashid and Bakil, is made up of eight tribes, three of which were incorporated into Saudi Arabia in 1934.

Figures 2.1–2.3 therefore illustrate the varied nature of northern Yemen's tribal confederations. Indeed, each is made up of loosely affiliated constituencies that are likely more loyal to their immediate tribesmen than to their overarching confederation. While government patronage likely causes Hashid tribal elements to be more cohesive, Bakil and Khawlan bin 'Amr are much more loosely organized entities, which in turn makes considering them collective units problematic. Indeed, as we will see later, tribes do not have formalized, coercive authority mechanisms ensuring allegiance. Simply put, tribes are far from unitary actors.

Figure 2.4 depicts the general geographical location of the Sa'da governorate's two largest tribal confederations, as well as their subtribes. Khawlan bin 'Amr has traditionally controlled much of the Sa'da basin, leaving Bakil tribes in the more-arid periphery. Over the past 25 years, some Bakil tribes have moved into the Sa'da basin, establishing villages and gaining land holdings. Additionally, territorial control of the governorate's eastern roads gives Hamdan al-Sham tribes considerable leverage over other tribes in the governorate. Generally, then, Hamdan al-Sham tribes cover the eastern plains and areas of the Sa'da basin, while Khawlan bin 'Amr tribes cover the more-fertile areas to the west. This includes the tribes of Razih and Munabbih, which occupy the isolated regions to the west, as well as the Sahar tribes that occupy most of the Sa'da basin.

Depicting tribal locations simply in terms of broad geographic areas would be misleading. Figure 2.5 illustrates the mosaic of confederations and subtribes that occupy the regions surrounding Sa'da city. This includes a wide range of tribes affiliated with both Bakil and Khawlan bin 'Amr, which have considerable material interests in the area. Furthermore, while this fact is not depicted in the map, scholars who have recently conducted fieldwork in the area have observed that Hashid tribesmen have obtained significant landholdings in the basin.[6] Although the basin thus features natural friction among Khawlan bin 'Amr, Bakil, and Hashid, tribal conflicts

---

[6]   Gerhard Lichtenthäler, *Political Ecology and the Role of Water: Environment, Society and Economy in Northern Yemen* (Surrey, UK: Ashgate Publishing, 2003), 4.

Figure 2.1
Khawlan bin 'Amr Tribal Groups

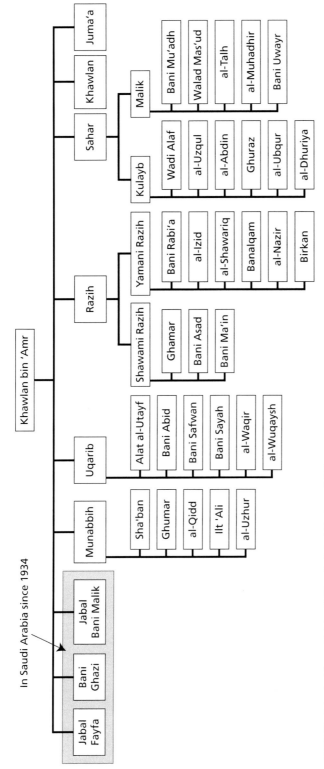

SOURCE: Adapted from Lichtenthäler, *Political Ecology*, 2003.
RAND *MG962-2.1*

Figure 2.2
Bakil Tribal Groups

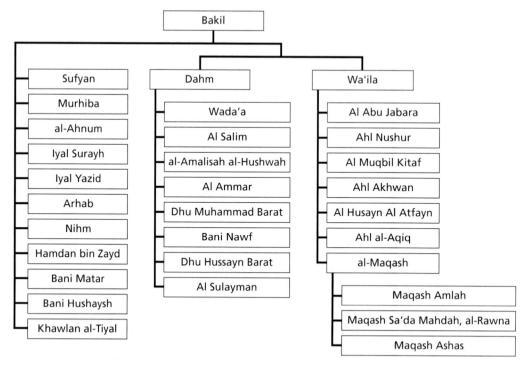

SOURCE: Adapted from Lichtenthäler, *Political Ecology*, 2003.
RAND *MG962-2.2*

Figure 2.3
Hashid Tribal Groups

SOURCE: Adapted from Lichtenthäler, *Political Ecology*, 2003.
RAND *MG962-2.3*

Figure 2.4
Geographic Location of Key Tribes in the Sa'da Governorate

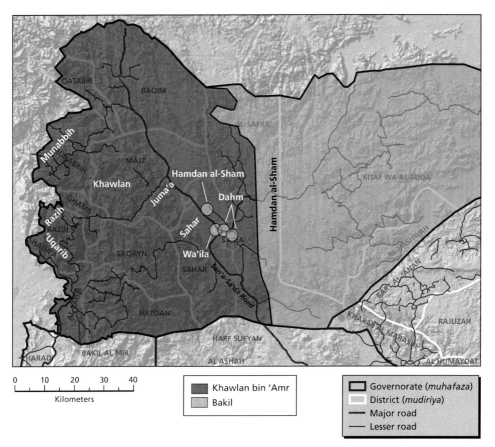

SOURCES: Lichtenthäler, *Political Ecology*, 2003; Weir, *A Tribal Order*, 2007; Yemeni national.
RAND *MG962-2.4*

also emerge within, rather than between, these confederations. Thus, the Sa'da basin exists as a fault line for the three main tribal confederations, as well as for intertribal fissures, which are relatively common.

The preceding discussion of northern Yemen's tribal geography is significant for understanding the regime-Huthi conflict after 2004. In broadest terms, we have seen that the Sa'da governorate is a zone of territorial transition among three tribal confederations—the Hashid, Bakil, and Khawlan bin 'Amr. Although the Hashid are sociopolitically dominant in the north as a whole and are heavily represented among the GoY's elite, northwest Yemen constitutes the edge of Hashidi presence and exhibits a sizable Bakili population. At the same time, though Khawlan bin 'Amr is a smaller, less politically prominent, tribal grouping, Sa'da and parts of 'Amran and Hajja

Figure 2.5
Tribal Map of Sa'da Basin and Environs

constitute its area of greatest demographic weight. The Huthi conflict zone, therefore, is a transitional region featuring three tribal confederations, none of whose influence is hegemonic.

Qabyala North of San'a: Aspects of Social Organization

This geographical introduction to tribalism begins to suggest certain aspects of tribes as social organizations. Tribalism in the Middle East has been examined in detail by several authors and is beyond the scope of this study. In most basic terms, a tribe is a collection of extended family kin networks claiming descent from shared male ances-

tors. Though shared descent may in fact be fictive, this claim cultivates notions of reciprocal social, economic, and political commitments. The idiom of extended family thus
links smaller kin groups that would otherwise be autonomous and potentially conflicting. As such, tribes constitute nested, multigenerational kin networks that combine
in hierarchies based on both size and social prominence, from the extended nuclear
family to the confederation level. Finally, the sociopolitical unity of tribes is not a constant. In many cases, "tribalness" is contingency-based, and tribes become explicitly
relevant to their members and to outsiders when challenges of resource management
and individual or group protection require collective identities. At other times, divergent identities—ideological, geographical, or social class—are more prominent among
tribespeople.[7]

It is also important to remember that the "tribal" north contains nontribal strata.
These include groups of people who perform socioeconomic tasks that *qabilis* historically have disdained but which are necessary for society to function. Referred to as
muzayana, bani khums, or *bayya'* and predominantly urban, they receive tribal protection. They are able to intermix with *qabilis* socially but are considered of degraded,
"client" status by *qabilis* themselves.[8] Conversely, because of their traditionally elevated social status, *sayyids* have been apportioned particular protected locations (*hijra*)
throughout the tribal areas. Likewise, residence areas of religious scholars of *qabili*
background (*fuqaha', quda*) are also considered *hijra*. While we will return to the place
of *sayyids* and *hijras* in Zaydism later in this chapter, it is important to note here that
the association of particular *hijras* with particular tribes creates strengthened bonds of
territoriality through the obligation of protection, while also creating sacred spaces. As
the Huthi conflict involves the Hashimi stratum and has progressed through several
tribes' territories, it impinges upon protected spaces and strata, thus prolonging conflict in the local cultural idiom.

Qabila and Shaykhs

It is important to consider the status of shaykhs within northern Yemeni tribes. Just
as there are tribes of widely varying size, shaykhs possess extremely varying degrees
of power, influence, and wealth and are usually not "chiefs" who can "lead" their fol-

---

[7]   For a few examples, see Philip Carl Salzman, *Culture and Conflict in the Middle East* (New York: Humanity
Books, 2008). See also Lawrence Rosen, *The Culture of Islam: Changing Aspects of Contemporary Muslim Life* (Chicago: University of Chicago Press, 2002), 39–74; David Ronfeldt, *In Search of How Societies Work: Tribes—The
First and Forever Form*, Santa Monica, Calif.: RAND, WR-433-RPC (December 2006); David M. Hart, *Tribe
and Society in Rural Morocco* (London: Routledge, 2000); Madawi al-Rasheed, *Politics in an Arabian Oasis: The
Rashidis of Saudi Arabia* (London: IB Tauris, 1997); Mai Yamani, "The Two Faces of Saudi Arabia," *Survival*
50:1 (2008), 143–156; Glenn E. Robinson, "Palestinian Tribes, Clans, and Notable Families," *Strategic Insights*
(Fall 2008); Gary S. Gregg, *The Middle East: A Cultural Psychology* (New York: Oxford University Press, 2005);
and Michael Eisenstadt, "Tribal Engagement Lessons Learned," *U.S. Army Military Review*, September–October
2007, 16–31.

[8]   Adra, "Qabyala," 47–55.

lowers. Rather, a *shaykh* (pl. *mashayikh*) is the corporate face of the tribal section, both within it and to outsiders. There are multiple routes to becoming a shaykh. A family may have been—or is remembered as having been—among the first to settle in an area that became identified with a tribal segment. This family may have gained prominence among the settlement group, either due to actions or its own pedigree. A charismatic elder from such a "shaykhly family" then becomes the shaykh. In other instances, a shaykhly family may have been remembered as coming from afar and settling among members of a tribal section for the sake for bringing a certain amount of order and stability. Alternatively, an extended kin grouping might break off from a tribal section due to conflict, and, if that fissure passes intergenerationally, that group will become known as its own tribal segment with its own shaykhly family. Further, one tribal section itself may possess two shaykhly families, due either to a division of labor or an enduring competition for influence between them. It is also relatively common for *qabilis* of a given tribal segment to withdraw their consent from a shaykh, electing another in his place.

Finally, within a tribal section's shaykhly family, the status of shaykh by no means passes automatically from father to oldest son, nor is a passing shaykh's preference for succession always respected by his *qabila*—or by outside political forces, be they the state or other tribes. Ultimately, who the shaykh is, how he becomes one, how many *qabilis* choose to consider him "their" shaykh, and how shaykhhood passes intergenerationally are all contested matters, reflecting evolving popular judgments of a shaykh or shaykhly family's reputation and utility to the community. As Dresch put it, "the influence of such men can rise and fall freely without changes in the tribes' formal structure and without major changes in group alignments, while their own position is made more difficult by the fact that in all but the smallest unit there are numerous *shaykhs*, not arranged in a hierarchy or even in order of precedence. Indeed, the number of *shaykhly* families is indeterminately large."[9]

This begins to suggest something of the role of a shaykh in traditional northern Yemeni society. Given the premium *qabilis* place on autonomy (see below), the shaykh is not accorded authority (*sulta*) within his tribe or tribal segment. Rather, a combination of wisdom and discernment permits him to understand the interests of his tribal members, thus allowing him to head off internal conflict while representing the kin group as a corporate entity among others. This wisdom and "ability to solve problems"[10] is most often and laudably articulated through persuasion and influence—as opposed to the kind of raw power whose use would demean *qabilis* subject to it.[11] Therefore, resolving disputes and safeguarding interests without resort to coercion

---

[9]   Dresch, *Tribes, Government, and History*, 102.

[10] Dresch, *Tribes, Government, and History*, 100.

[11] See Steven C. Caton, "Power, Persuasion, and Language: A Critique of the Segmentary Model in the Middle East," *International Journal of Middle East Studies* 19 (1987), 77–102.

render a shaykh worthy of his position—although the ability to resist coercion and rally *qabilis* to armed defense of interests against other *qaba'il* or external powers is indeed a valued quality among shaykhs.

The idiom for a shaykh's moral suasion and influence within his group are weight (*wazn*) and prestige (*hayba*)—or the ability to inspire loyalty among followers and respect among outsiders. As such, a shaykh's *wazn* and *hayba* both aid him in solving problems and stand as the collective articulation of his tribe's honor (*sharaf*)—a concept to which we will return shortly. Put differently, a shaykh considers his *personal* conduct among others as reflecting on the *collective* standing of his tribe or tribal segment. Internally, one way to preserve *wazn* and *hayba* is to credibly mediate conflicts. This is part of tribal justice, to which we return below. Just as important in retaining the loyalty of tribe members is material patronage. Though often not the wealthiest members of the community, shaykhs require sufficient means to either provide material benefits (such as land, vehicles, and weapons) to tribal members or advocate for access to them among external powers, such as the state.[12] A successful shaykh is thus regarded as generous and open-handed, incurring debts, if necessary, for the sake of his tribe's material survival.[13]

Externally, the corporate generosity of the tribe is demonstrated through the shaykh's role as "official host." It is he who must maintain a proper sitting room (*majlis*) and guest house (*mudhif*), and see to it that esteemed visitors, and even foreign strangers, are properly hosted at his expense. This hosting function extends to ensuring the protection of markets, *bani khums*, and Hashimis living in the tribe's area.[14] All the same, shaykhs do not "rule" their tribes. Restrained by their responsibilities and the traditional *qabili* abhorrence of external control, shaykhly power is also moderated by tribal elders, whose counsel is prominent in significant collective dealings.[15] Further, in the realm of arbitration, successful shaykhs are forced to account for the interests of other tribes and embrace nontribal elements—such as *sayyids* or *qadis* (tribal judges)—in the judgment process. Ultimately, shaykhs who retain *wazn* are "accountable to their constituents. A shaykh who forgets that he is among equals and behaves in an authoritarian manner is quickly deposed. . . . Neither shaykh nor any other human being is granted the power to coerce."[16]

This description implies that, rather than knowing who leads a tribe at any time or to which protagonist in a conflict a tribe feels temporary loyalty, it is much more important to understand the meaning of "leading" and "loyalty." Since leadership is

---

[12] Adra, "Qabyala," 60.

[13] Paul Dresch, "The Position of Shaykhs Among the Northern Tribes of Yemen," *Man* (NS) 19:1 (March 1984), 42. The local idiom for "open-handed" is *mabsut al-yadayn*.

[14] Adra, "Qabyala," 58.

[15] In local parlance, these elders are referred to as *'uqqal*, loosely translated as "wisemen," or *'uyun*, "seers."

[16] Adra, "Qabyala," 77.

a matter of influence and persuasion and a tribe is rarely a monolithic collective in its evolving loyalties, a government seeking to use shaykhs as a way to deliver tribes or hold tribesmen's loyalties to account is likely to be disappointed by the basic political dynamics underlying the northern Yemeni manifestation of shaykh-tribe relations.[17] In most cases, "the position of shaykh generally gives little or no authority over tribesmen." Signifying "less a rank than a function," shaykhs are "simply notable figures who have been entrusted with certain authorities on specific occasions and in limited ways."[18] Additionally, although "outright patronage" of *qabilis* is important to sustaining shaykhhood, "the idea of quid pro quo is poorly developed, and without solid personal abilities a shaykh could spend a fortune in largesse which bought him nothing" in terms of tribal loyalties.[19]

Furthermore, as we will see in the next chapter, the nature of tribal relationships has evolved considerably over the past generation. The Hashidi tribal confederation has been able to retain greater cohesion and discipline because of the prominence, prestige, and government integration of its leading al-Ahmar house—Shaykh al-Ahmar has reinforced the GoY since the 1960s, and the GoY has reinforced al-Ahmar preeminence in Hashid. This is distinct from Bakil or Khawlan bin 'Amr, which have never been as close to the regime, and whose internal coherence has always been less, due to the absence of a shaykhly hegemon. In these tribal segments—predominant in the Sa'da area—attitudes to *mashayikh* in particular have changed. As they have pursued greater patronage from a GoY seeking to control the tribal periphery through blandishment and cooptation, shaykhs have sacrificed a fair amount of status and moral suasion among *qabilis* themselves. As shaykhs may view their *sharaf* as coming more from state patronage and less from their ability to mediate for and represent their kinsmen, their ability to influence the latter to the degree the GoY imagines possible has declined. In the current conflict, therefore, *qabili* affinities have not been in lockstep with those of their shaykhs—which themselves change according to perceived patronage opportunities—and it has been reported that loyalties have split down to the extended family level.[20] At the same time, tribes have retained vitality as foci of social organization, and tribalism as a values complex has endured. We turn to this idea next.

Qabyala as a Value System

In spite of differences of tribal power or personal pedigree, tribalism as a value system—*qabyala*—has traditionally been shared by northern Yemenis as a whole. In this respect,

---

[17] Interview with UK ethnographer of northern Yemen, September 8 and October 23, 2008.

[18] J. E. Peterson, "Tribes and Politics in Yemen," *Arabian Peninsula Background Note* APBN-007, December 2008, 2, 3.

[19] Paul Dresch, "The Position of Shaykhs," 42.

[20] Interview with UK ethnographer, October 23, 2008; interview with human rights worker from Sa'da, March 20, 2009.

"tribalism is not so much a mechanism like so much clockwork but a way of perceiving the world."[21] This way of perceiving the world has persisted even as social interactions have changed (see Chapter Three) and informs how Yemenis in the Huthi conflict zone react to the actions of conflict protagonists. In addition to a mode of social organization, it is therefore essential to grasp *qabyala* as a value system. We will focus here on its aspects that bear upon the conflict today.

A good entry point for considering *qabyala* as a complex of values in northern Yemen emerges from the terms that Yemenis use to describe it. Foremost among them are *sharaf, wajh, adab, 'ird ('ard), naqa', asl,* and *'ayb*. In the values complex of *qabyala*, these terms are all contingent upon each other. As ideas, some terms are extensions of others: Some are *qualities*, whereas others refer to *objects* of a certain character; others still are *actions* taken toward these objects that influence the extent to which *qabilis* are perceived to possess these qualities.

As we saw previously in our discussion of the role of the shaykh, *sharaf* can be translated literally as "honor," though it connotes a complex of associations, including status, standing, prestige, appearance, and reputation.[22] *Wajh*, literally meaning "face," is thus synonymous with *sharaf* in parts of northern Yemen and conveys the extent to which one's self-esteem is a function of others' estimation of one's status. That external estimation of one's status amounts to the honor (*sharaf*) and reputation (*wajh*) one possesses, distinguishing someone as an individual, with individual worth, from others. In the same vein, one's *adab*, or "good manners," comes from the public reputation for behaviors that connote *sharaf*.

Two other ideas are directly related to *sharaf*. *Naqa'*, meaning clean or good name, comes from individuals and groups taking measures to ensure no external harm comes to their reputation for *sharaf*—here meaning both honor and inviolability—or responding appropriately to infractions upon individual *wajh* and group *sharaf*. Finally, *asl*, referring to distinctive authenticity of descent, is a quality inhering in *qabilis* as well as Hashimis generically. The latter have distinguished lineages because of religious associations; central to the *qabili* ethos is the notion of pure, authentic (*asli*) lineage going back to noble (*sharif*) ancestors, regardless of genealogical realities. *Asl*, therefore, is a "genetic" quality. However, recurrent, unanswered injuries to *wajh* and *sharaf* chip away at *asl* in society's eyes.

If *sharaf* encapsulates all that is praiseworthy in the northern Yemeni tribal cultural eye, *'ayb* symbolizes all that is condemnable. *'Ayb* can be translated as a "contemptible, blameworthy act" committed or suffered. It also means a "demeaning disgrace" and thus an "insult" resulting from one's own or another's publicly visible conduct. *'Ayb* is not a quality, but a kind of action—and also a status. And like all

---

[21] Paul Dresch, "Tribal Relations and Political History in Upper Yemen," in Brian Pridham, ed., *Contemporary Yemen: Politics and Historical Background* (London: Croom Helm, 1984), 171.

[22] Terms in Arabic parlance include *sum'a* (reputation), *wus'a* (gravitas), *ism* (name).

qabyala concepts, *'ayb* applies to both individuals and collectives, from the family to tribal level. Therefore, *'ayb*-disgrace is like a contamination or contaminated status that must be cleansed from the victim—or the culprit's group. In the local idiom, "*yu'ayyib/ yata'yyib*," to disgrace someone or oneself, is to "break one's honor" (*yaksir sharafah*), tainting the culprit in the eyes of the community. Both the victim of *'ayb* and the offender have their reputations dirtied and thus must restore their *naqa'-sharaf*—clean name and reputation for honor.

Sharaf and *'ayb* are thus polar opposites and have meaning only in the public domain of reputations contested and defended. Standing between *sharaf* and *'ayb* as the key element of contestation is *'ird* (*'ard* in local dialect). Also translatable as "honor," *'ird* refers to people and objects that are vulnerable to outsiders, and whose protection is required in order to preserve *sharaf*—and the violation of which causes *'ayb* upon victim and culprit. In classical Arabic and traditional cultural usage, *'ird* is most frequently equated with women, in two ways. First, there is the *'ird* of women's chastity and modesty, glossed also as *namus*, or sexual honor. Second, and an extension of *namus*, is the physical inviolability of women and their reputation. Women themselves can violate *'ird* in the first sense, while outsiders can violate both kinds of *'ird*. Significantly, in both senses, the *'ird* of a woman is also—or perhaps primarily—that of her menfolk. When one violates or exposes (*hataka*) the ever-vulnerable *'ird* of a woman, one has also violated the *'ird* of the family's menfolk, thus committing an *'ayb* against widening circles of extended family. As we have seen above, this *'ayb* damages *sharaf* in a way that demands a retaliatory response on the part of the victim.

In northern Yemen, items associated with *'ird* go beyond women to include other vulnerable humans whose self-protection would call into question the *sharaf* of a *qabili*. These include children and lower-status nontribal *bani khums* and non-Muslims, as well as the high-status though nontribal Hashimis. Additionally, among tribesmen, certain objects are in the category of *'ird*. Prime among these is one's land and associated property. Sayings in the local dialect affirm the importance to notions of proper *qabili* manhood of protecting one's land: *al-ard 'ard* (land is honor), and *man aqdam li-arduk aqdam li-'arduk* (he who transgresses against [seizes] your land [also] transgresses against [violates] your honor). Taking another's land, property, livestock, or crops—or committing an *'ayb* while on one's land—is a disgraceful attack not only on an individual's or family's *sharaf*, but on that of his tribal segment as a whole: The "honor of the tribe or section depends on maintaining the 'inviolability' of its territory (*hurmat al-watan*)."[23]

The epicenter of one's land is one's home (*bayt*). The home, as well as the family in it, are considered *amin fi aman allah*—safe in the secure trusteeship of God. In tribal norms, a family in its house is to be *amin damin*, safe, and with guaranteed security. Therefore, to attack a house unprovoked, or to steal from it, or to fire on a house

---

[23] Dresch, *Tribes, Government, and History*, 80.

without a reason judged by outsiders to be valid are all *'ayb*, a violation of *'ird* disgracing the culprit and the victims. By extension, attacking or stealing from the lands or property associated with protected kinds of people also violates *'ird*. *Qabilis* are thus *sharaf*-bound to protect the *hijras* and markets associated with their tribal areas. Finally, actions that make it impossible for someone to defend his *sharaf* also expose his *'ird* and are considered disgraceful. Enforced disarmament, or separation of men from their families, are both violations of *'ird*.

As these comments suggest, abstract concepts such as *'ird* receive concrete meaning and consequence through the actions of individual people and groups. These actions result in *sharaf* or *'ayb* and require certain kinds of responses from *qabilis*. We have already seen that certain classes of people—women, *sayyids, bani khums,* non-Muslims—are to be protected because of who they are, joining land and property in the category of *'ird*. Aggression against them is to be answered firmly, for the sake of individual and group *sharaf*. We can begin to see that the concrete actualization of these norms in daily life bears implications for the GoY's conduct of military operations in the Sa'da region. As a conventional military that has sought out Huthi sympathizers in villages, markets, and Hashimi enclaves, it cannot avoid violating *qabili 'ird* in the region, thus provoking aggressive local responses for the sake of protecting both family members and *sharaf*.

The implications of GoY military operations in Sa'da that target families for sheltering Huthi fighters emerge also in consideration of an additional tribal value. This is the obligation to provide hospitality and protection to categories of people who, as it were, become a *qabili's* temporary *'ird*. These include the categories of guest, companion, and protégé,[24] to whom the *qabili* and his *qabila* are obliged to become host, escort, and protector.[25] These terms are used variously in the northern highlands and refer to people traveling through one's area or temporarily residing on one's land or in one's domicile. They also refer to people who have sought refuge in one's tribal area, either because they are being pursued in a conflict or because their own areas have been destroyed. Additionally, the escort-companion relationship includes people traveling together.

In all these cases, the host, escort, or protector becomes the guarantor of the protégé's safety, security, and *sharaf*, as well as the temporary provider of hospitality. Any injury to the protégé's honor is considered an injury to that of the protector, and physical assault—to include violent attack, murder, kidnapping, arrest, etc.—is not just a disgrace, but *'ayb aswad* (a black shame). It is thus particularly disgraceful for the host himself to commit aggression against the guest or to abdicate the responsibility to seek compensation on behalf of his guest if the latter's *sharaf* is harmed. Further, it is significant to note that these ties of hospitality and protection linking protégé and

---

[24] Referred to as *dayf, rafiq,* and *jar*.

[25] Referred to as *mudayyif, muraffiq, mujawwir*.

protector explicitly extend beyond one's tribal segment to people from other segments and tribes—or even to those beyond the tribal system. Symbolic of this category are protégés such as those with whom one shares bread and salt ('aysh wa milh).

Crucially, protection and alliance relationships are established with affines as well, who are people from differing descent groups or villages linked by ties of marriage. This affinity (nasab) extends not only to the married people themselves but to men- and womenfolk of contracted families. In this case, webs of obligation among multiple families from more than one kin network can become very large, connecting to other nasab networks as well. In Chapter Three, we will see this with the Huthi family, and, while these webs of support can sustain resistance to GoY coercion, they also increase the chances that the latter's security operations will activate widening circles of opposition to the regime, based on reasons that have little to do with ideological affinity to the Huthi cause.[26]

Individual and Collective Autonomy as Expressed Through Weapons

As we explained above, a basic understanding of qabyala as a whole involves the relationship between autonomy and collective responsibility. To be a qabili is to be ruled by no other person, including a shaykh. Extended outwards, to be a true shaykhly household is to hold one's own among other households and to prevent mashayikh of larger sections from exerting a demeaning influence over one's people that calls into question individual and group asl and sharaf. Asl, or distinction, in this respect means autonomy, and the lack of asl among bani khums or non-Muslims is attributed in part to their inability to assert their autonomous existence.

For traditional qabilis, possession of weapons communicates this autonomy and asl. As adolescents pass into manhood, they wear a dagger (janbiya; also jambiya) as part of their daily costume. Not meant to be used in anger, the janbiya is fundamental to many men's dress, symbolizing individuality, freedom, and the credibility of one's word. Carrying the janbiya can also be understood as symbolizing the capability for violence—but this demonstration of capacity is customarily intended to excuse qabilis from having to resort to violence frequently. As a young shaykh from among the Rada'a asserted recently, "to this day, a number of people would rather die than be seen in public without their jambiyas."[27]

Just as ubiquitous as part of qabili men's attire in northern Yemen are small arms, spanning from early 20th-century European rifles to modern assault rifles. The free possession and carriage of weapons are integral both to one's identity as a tribesman

---

[26] Adra, in "Qabyala," 188, notes cases where prorepublican qaba'il fought with the royalists due to Egyptian aggression against their communities.

[27] See Abdul Rahim al-Shawthabi, "Jambiya: Deep-Rooted Tradition," Yemen Post, March 12, 2009. Also see Schuyler V.R. Cammann, "The Cult of the Jambiya: Dagger Wearing in Yemen," Expedition 19:2 (1977).

and to articulations of male adulthood.[28] We saw in Chapter One that weapons are part of the economy. Weapons therefore also illustrate a symbiosis between economy and cultural assertion. In this respect, a Yemeni academician noted to a western reporter in 2002 that "just as you have your tie, the Yemeni will carry his gun."[29] Further, firearms are used at several communal ritual events, including tribal dances, weddings, and summonses. Likewise, surrendering a number of one's weapons to shaykhs is an integral part of the process of conflict mediation, symbolizing both parties' cessation of aggression during the mediation period.[30] Ultimately, weapons in northern Yemen are "linked to the norms and traditions, more than being a means of violence and killing."[31]

As mentioned above, however, the effort to deny a *qabili* his weapons touches upon his *'ird,* and can be interpreted as a violation of *sharaf.* Conversely, entering into mediation without surrendering a portion of one's weapons to a neutral arbitrator is considered insincere—even if one of the parties is the state. These points have implications for the GoY's efforts to disarm northern Yemenis imbued with the *qabyala* ethos, who are likely to perceive efforts to reduce the prevalence of weapons in *qabili* areas as emerging from a GoY desire "to destroy the tribes' independence" rather than from a desire to counter Huthi violence.[32] Likewise, the GoY's nonsurrender of weapons in a context of mediation could, in cultural terms, undermine the attempt at mediation. We will return to this matter in Chapter Five.[33]

Along with autonomy comes collective responsibility and obligation. Injury to an individual *qabili'*s honor is injury to that of his group, which must come together to cleanse the collective of the *'ayb.* Likewise, the obligation to protect people or places is traditionally shared among a group, even if that group's demonstration of collective responsibility is only an a posteriori reaction to aggression against one of its individual members who seeks to carry out that obligation. In this respect, collective defense— referred to in historical accounts as tribal wars or the tribal proclivity to revenge—is not simply a matter of survival but also a way to uphold the name of the group and thus deter future aggression.

---

[28] See Gavin Hales, "Guns in Yemen: Culture, Violence and Realpolitik," paper presented at *Guns, Crime, and Social Order: An International Workshop,* York University, May 14, 2008.

[29] Richard Engel, "Yemen's Weapon Culture," *BBC News,* January 22, 2002.

[30] Dresch, "The Position of Shaykhs Among the Northern Tribes of Yemen."

[31] Essedine Saeed al-Asbahi, "Arms in Yemen: A Source of Pride or Instability?" (Part I), *Yemen Times,* December 8, 2009.

[32] James Brandon, "Yemen Attempts to Rein in Outlaw Tribes," *Christian Science Monitor,* January 24, 2006.

[33] For more on this, see Hassan al-Haifi, "Standing Up to the Culture of Violence," *Yemen Times* 13:747 (June 17, 2004); Arafat Madayash, "The Arms Trade in Yemen," *al-Sharq al-Awsat English,* January 9, 2007.

Tribal Law and Conflict Containment

The combination of commitment to autonomy and collective support in a weaponized environment lacking impartial external governance can lead to chronic violence as a symptom of unending social entropy. Indeed, official Yemeni spokesmen at times have dismissed conflict or antistate violence in northern Yemen as reflecting a tribal predisposition to crime, corruption, and fighting.[34] This is a simplistic view. To avoid unending conflicts and feuds, Yemeni tribal society has evolved an important embodiment of collective obligations in the formal of customary, nonstate law. In different parts of northern Yemen, several terms have been used to describe a method of conflict control that is distinct from state law and *shari'a* (Islamic law) but that has been legitimated by both. Referred to as *'urf qabali, ahkam al-aslaf,* or *silf al-qaba'il* (tribal custom, rules of forefathers, or tribal tradition), customary law seeks to reconcile the premium put on individual and collective *sharaf* with the need to prevent violent conflict or segmentary social isolation. Therefore, *'urf qabali* focuses on justice as the restoration of *sharaf* and balance among social groups through material restitution, rather than as a punitive tool.[35]

Given these norms, although an individual or group may signal the ability to prosecute armed retribution after sustaining an offense, custom favors mediation and arbitration (*sulh wa tahkim*) as the first resort in the resolution of either civil differences or criminal offenses. First, a mediator or arbitrator will be chosen. This is usually someone who is convincingly removed from both parties to conflict. While this can be a notable (*'aqil* or shaykh) from one of the aggrieved parties' tribes, it is often a third party, such as a shaykh from an uninvolved tribal section, a *qadi* (religious judge, pl. *quda*), or a *sayyid*. Crucially, the mediator must be someone who is not only impartial but who also possesses high levels of prestige and influence. This is because, after settling on a mediator, the parties to the dispute foreswear a resort to violence during the period of mediation, signaling their rejection of aggression during mediation by turning a portion of their weapons over to the arbitrator (*muhakkam*). The mediator

---

[34] Interview, senior official in Embassy of Republic of Yemen in Washington, D.C., 11 September 2008.

[35] In addition to Dresch, *Tribes, Government, and History,* and Adra, "Qabyala," this section draws on Laila al-Zwaini, "Mediating between Custom and Code: Dar al-Salam, an NGO for Tribal Arbitration in San'a," in Baudouin Dupret and Francois Burgat, eds., *Le cheikh et le procureur: Systèmes coutumiers et practiques juridiques au Yémen et en Égypte* (Cairo: CEDEJ, Egypte-Monde arab series 1:3, 2005), 323–335; Centre Français d'Archéologie et de Sciences Sociales de Sanaa (CEFAS), "Le règlement des conflits tribaux au Yémen," *Les Cahiers du CEFAS* (4:2003); Laila al-Zwaini, "State and Non-State Justice in Yemen," paper for Conference on the Relationship between State and Non-State Justice Systems in Afghanistan, December 10–14, 2006, United States Institute for Peace; Najwa Adra, "Dance and Glance: Visualizing Tribal Identity in Highland Yemen," *Visual Anthropology* 11 (1998), 55–103; Steven Caton, *"Peaks of Yemen I Summon": Poetry as Cultural Practice in a North Yemeni Tribe* (Berkeley, Calif.: University of California Press, 1992); Rashad al-Alimi and Baudoin Dupret, "Le droit coutumier dans la société yéménite: nature et développement," *Chroniques Yéménites* 9 (2001); National Democratic Institute for International Affairs, "Yemen: Tribal Conflict Management Program Research Report," (Washington, D.C.: NDI, March 2007).

must therefore be the kind of person who, in the local social milieu, possesses adequate *wazn* and *hayba* that a violation of the peace by disputants during the period of arbitration would be considered an insult to the mediator's own *sharaf,* thus bringing *'ayb* upon that disputant and his larger kin network.

In many cases, a respected mediator can then make a decision on a case involving material compensation for damages, injury, or death, the latter known in the West as blood money (*diya*). Again, the mediator's status must be impartial and prestigious enough to make a judgment last—and parties must refrain from violence or preparations for violence during the mediation period. In cases where the antagonism has grown particularly great or where the parties to disagreement consist of large groups, each may appoint a guarantor (*damin*; *kafil*), who represents them in meetings with the mediator, thus ensuring that the parties to the dispute do not interact in an unmediated fashion. Like the *muhakkam*, a *damin* also must possess enough *wajh* to exert moral compulsion on the disputants so that they persevere through the mediation process and respect its results. Likewise, failure to abide by the commitments made through guarantors as part of a conflict resolution injures the reputation of that guarantor, so that the defaulting party is disgraced and, by implication, considered guilty.

As customary law, *'urf qabali* is largely unwritten. However, particularly when the mediators or guarantors—or disputants—are prominent or highly educated people or when the case at hand has far-reaching implications, the proceedings will be recorded as precedents and then archived by the arbitrator. Additionally, judgments, even those including large material restitution, usually include an element of reconciliation between disputants, encouraging a social bond as a normative guarantor of amicable relations. Furthermore, *'urf qabali* reinforces not only notions of what a shaykh should be but provides a socially prestigious role to *sayyids* and *qadis* within the tribal ethos. Thus, even though *'ulama'* (religious scholars) have been known to refer to tribal justice as *taghut*, or arbitrary tyranny, the social enactment of *shari'a*—i.e., the way *shari'a* is thought of and understood by members of society, and its melding with tribal law during daily interactions in northern Yemen—legitimates *'urf qabali* by validating its decisions and being a part of its processes. As we will see below, Zaydism as a *madhhab*—as well as Shafi'ism—permits the inclusion of *'urf* into local interpretations of *shari'a*. As such, the significance of customary law lies not so much in the jurisprudential body of "statutes" emerging from it but in the norms it cultivates among *qabilis* of how disputes are to be treated and how different segments of society are to act within the continuum of customs. These norms then condition how northern Yemenis will weigh their own actions and evaluate those of others, including those of the state.

Indeed, as regards notions and symbols of autonomy, collective commitment, and customary justice, the state itself is not considered exempt from respecting *qabyala*. During the Imamate, for example, the state's coercive behavior was often considered a hostile act rather than a punishment for infractions. This view continues today in many areas beyond the GoY's direct control, where the state itself is considered an element within the cosmos of *qabyala*. The current regime has reinforced this view. Saleh's rule is based, in part, on Hashidi tribal connections, and he has continued to practice *mahsubiya* in efforts to selectively coopt and punish different kin groups. This includes regime validation of tribal legal rulings, agreement to extralegal mediation of state-society disputes, the payment of blood money, and so forth.[36]

In this way, the GoY has brought the tribal moral calculus into state-citizen dealings. Thus, in spite of the sociocultural changes in northern Yemen that we will encounter in the next chapter, northern Yemenis likely view the republican regime's actions vis-à-vis the Huthis through the lens of *qabyala*. In the Huthi case, however, the GoY is not an arbitrator, mediator, or an ex post facto validator of *qabyala* legal norms—rather, it may be considered a disputant, with all the social expectations that go along with such a status.

Zaydism as a Religious and Social Phenomenon

Zaydism emerged in the 8th century among those early Muslims who felt that 'Ali should have followed the Prophet Muhammad as his first successor (caliph) in the spiritual and temporal leadership of Muslims. When Abu Bakr had become the first caliph in 632 CE, the partisans of 'Ali (*shi'at 'Ali*, hence Shi'a) felt the latter's claim was more legitimate because of his reputed nomination by Muhammad and his family ties to the Prophet ('Ali was Muhammad's cousin and son-in-law). Sunnis (or *ahl al-Sunna*, meaning people of accepted tradition) recognized Abu Bakr and his successors as legitimate, whereas partisans of 'Ali considered only those from the family of the Prophet, in the form of 'Ali's male descendants, to be worthy of rule. These male descendents became imams, one in each generation—although on a few occasions, disagreement emerged over which descendent of 'Ali was to be considered imam. This explains the emergence of Zaydism.

Zayd bin 'Ali, a grandson of 'Ali's son Husayn, was killed leading an unsuccessful rebellion against the Umayyads in 740. Whereas most Shi'ites regard his brother, Muhammad al-Baqir, as the Fifth Imam, some considered Zayd to be the Fifth Imam, and became known as "Fivers" or Zaydis. Zaydism as a doctrine has emphasized philosophy and rationalism rather than textual literalism.[37] In practice, the later Zaydi Imamates demonstrated tolerance for Shafi'is, the dominant Sunni school of thought in Yemen, which is said to make up slightly over half the population.

---

[36] See Elham M. Manea, "La tribu et l'Etat au Yemen," in Mondher Kilani, ed., *Islam et changement social* (Lausanne: Editions Payot, 1998), 205–218.

[37] See Moojan Momen, *An Introduction to Shi'i Islam* (New Haven: Yale University Press, 1987).

Zaydi Political History in Yemen to 1962

The first Zaydi state was established in Yemen in 893 by Yahya bin al-Husayn (d. 911), who had originally been invited to Yemen to mediate between quarrelling tribes.[38] Remembered as *al Hadi ila al-Haqq* (the guide to the truth), his theology (*al-Hadawiya*) forms the basis of the Zaydi *madhhab* in north Yemen.[39] Its central tenet is that the spiritual leader of the Muslims should be a *sayyid*, a descendent of the Prophet through the lineage of 'Ali and Fatima. That spiritual leader—known as the imam—should also be the leader of the state. Notably, his respect for *'urf* and use of tribal mediation practices facilitated a religiocultural melding between Hadawis and the tribes of the highlands. Enabling successive Zaydi imamates until 1962, this melding persists today.

Theology

Zaydi-Hadawi theology differs from other Shi'a branches regarding who is qualified to rule as imam and how the imamate may be established. Zaydis accept the Shi'a consensus that 'Ali, Hasan, and Husayn were the first three rightful imams. Most Zaydis are less vehement than other Shi'ites in their condemnation of the early Sunni caliphs, believing that while the latter were erroneous in their rejection of 'Ali, they were not essentially sinful. This belief permits tolerance of other interpretations of Islam.

The Zaydi-Hadawi doctrine stipulates that the spiritual leader of the Muslim community should also be supreme ruler (*imam*) of the Muslim state, emphasizing the importance of an imam's scholarly credentials and descent. After the first three imams, Zaydis believe that the imamate is open to any learned and pious descendant (*sayyid*) who asserts his claim to the imamate publicly. While succession was theoretically based on acquired characteristics rather than birthright,[40] the imam was, of necessity, a *sayyid*, and all Zaydi imams have come from the *sayyid* social stratum. Yet, this is a broader pool than in other versions of Shi'ism.[41]

---

[38] Ira Lapidus, *A History of Islamic Societies*, 2nd ed. (Cambridge: Cambridge University Press, 2002), 53, 178, 565–572.

[39] The term *maddhab* refers to an Islamic school of thought or religious jurisprudence. While it is generally agreed that they do not constitute separate sects, the four Sunni *madhhabs* differ with respect to finer judgments and jurisprudence stemming from the various imams and scholars affiliated with them over time.

[40] Dresch, *Tribes, Government, and History,* 161.

[41] The Jarudi branch of Zaydism is a notable exception with respect to its views on the imamate. Emerging from one of the earliest Zaydi groups, they vehemently rejected the first Sunni caliphs. Highlighting Jarudi Zaydism's doctrinaire approaches to political legitimacy, Arab and Yemeni sources at times refer to Husayn al-Huthi and his father Badr al-Din as Jarudis. See Anwar al-Khidri, "al-Huthi wa-l-Waraqa al-Ta'ifiya al-Khasira," *Al-Bayyina,* May 6, 2006; Hassan abu Talib, "al-Huthiyun wa al-Ma'raka ma Qabl al-Akhir fi-l-Yaman," al-Ahram Center for Strategic Studies, July 9, 2008.

Practice and Interpretation

Zaydi practices are only marginally distinct from those of Sunnis. Zaydis are theologically permitted to pray with Sunnis, and this has been the social reality in many parts of Yemen up to today (though likely not among hardcore Huthis). Zaydis also observe publicly recognized Muslim holidays in Yemen. A significant, distinctive celebration for Zaydis has been 'Id al-Ghadir (Ghadir Day), the holiday commemorating the Prophet's designation of 'Ali as his successor. Officially recognized as a holiday prior to the 1962 revolution, 'Id al-Ghadir has become highly politicized in northwest Yemen. Zaydi revivalist ceremonies commemorating the date became contentious in the early 1990s. Most recently, regime-Huthi conflict has provided an added impetus for tension on this matter.[42] Prohibited between 2004 and 2008, 'Id al-Ghadir was illicitly celebrated in Huthi areas and, after its 2008 relegalization, has provided a venue for Huthi mobilization. Additionally, in the past several decades, Zaydis have begun to revive other festivals abandoned after the revolution and invent rituals commemorating religious figures. This trend has benefited the Huthis, as we will see in Chapter Seven.[43]

Zaydi Self-Definition

Zaydi informants often invoke the history of the imamate to illustrate their doctrinal flexibility and tolerance for other forms of Islam, and in particular, their differences from other manifestations of Shi'ism. Some speak of a reliance on philosophy more than jurisprudence.[44] This understanding of religion as a personal experience facilitates public acquiescence to the modern state.[45] Of course, Zaydi self-definition in post-Imamate Yemen continues to evolve in relation to political power and as the Huthi rebellion continues. For instance, many prominent *sayyids* in the post-Imamate period have attempted to accommodate republican political realities by rejecting the Hadawi stipulation that the imam must be a *sayyid*. We will return to this accommodation in Chapter Three, also examining its pitfalls for the al-Haqq party.[46]

---

[42] Shelagh Weir, "A Clash of Fundamentalisms: Wahhabism in Yemen," *Middle East Report* 204 (July–September 1997), 23. In 2008, 'Id al-Ghadir was celebrated by Shafi'is, Isma'ilis, and Zaydis in San'a, al-Jawf, Marib, 'Amran, Lahj, and Dhamar, in addition to Sa'da.

[43] Gabriele vom Bruck, "Being a Zaydi in the Absence of an Imam: Doctrinal Revisions, Religious Instruction, and the (Re-)Invention of Ritual," in *Le Yemen Contemporain*, Remy Leveau, Frannck Mermier, and Udo Steinbach, eds. (Paris: Editions Karthala, 1999), 185–187.

[44] Vom Bruck, "Being a Zaydi in the Absence of an Imam," 188.

[45] Bernard Haykel, "Rebellion, Migration, or Consultative Democracy? The Zaydis and Their detractors in Yemen," in Remy Leveau, Frannck Mermier, and Udo Steinbach, eds., *Le Yemen Contemporain* (Paris: Editions Karthala, 1999). For example, a number of important Zaydi scholars publicly rejected the doctrine of *khuruj* in 1990 in an effort to show their deference to the state.

[46] See vom Bruck, "Being a Zaydi in the Absence of an Imam."

Significantly, Zaydis represent themselves as a fifth *madhhab* rather than a sect of Shi'ism,[47] and there are significant Zaydi distinctions from the better-known Iraqi and Iranian version of Shi'ism ("Twelver Shi'ism"), both in doctrine and in practice. In light of GoY and other Arab assertions of Huthi loyalty to the Islamic Republic of Iran, it is important to note one distinction in particular. Unlike Iran's policy of exporting its revolution since 1979, Zaydis traditionally have not been interested in propagating their beliefs or proselytizing. Likewise, neither Zaydi doctrine nor most Zaydis today are sympathetic to the theory of state called *wilayat al-faqih* (rule of the jurisconsult) championed by Khomeini during the Islamic revolution, which holds that only Islamic jurists, as the embodiment of the hidden Twelfth Imam, are qualified to guard over the state and interpret its laws. While Zaydism long had a political imamate (and never felt the imam to have occulted), it was not called *wilayat al-faqih*—nor was it tied to the Zayd family, much less to the imams of Twelver Shi'ism. And Zaydism has moved *away* from the idea of a political imam as proper ruler of Yemen, whereas Twelver Shi'ism gradually moved *toward* it in Iran during the 1970s. Finally, Zaydis today are not subordinate to a clerical hierarchy or its jurists, as are Iranian Twelvers. For a more in-depth discussion of Zaydi history, doctrines, and practice, see Appendix B.

Zaydi Religious Strata: *Sada, Fuqaha'*, and *Quda*

In the previous discussion of *qabyala,* we saw how enduring social strata in the tribal northwest often had strategic societal roles and common interests that facilitated their cooperation. The same is true with Zaydi religious strata. Over the course of Zaydi history, *sayyids* (Arabic pl. *sada*) generally remained the most powerful socioreligious stratum. They were accompanied by the other elite non-*sayyid fuqaha'* (scholars of religion) who made important contributions to Zaydi legal and political developments and held privileged positions above *qabilis* in everyday society. While both scholarly strata—interwoven and at times intermarried—functioned as '*ulama*' in interpreting Zaydi law, theology, and imamate governance, *fuqaha'* remained largely subordinate to *sayyids* prior to the demise of the Imamate.

   Sada (sing. *sayyid). Sada* or Hashimis form an elite social stratum claiming descent from the Prophet Muhammad through 'Ali and Fatima.[48] *Sada*, who are by definition not tribal, formed the core of the religious aristocracy during the Zaydi

---

[47] Interview, Tarek and Zayd al-Wazir, November 18, 2008. Also see the comment by Sayyid Muhammad al-Mansur in vom Bruck, "Being a Zaydi in the Absence of an Imam," 183.

[48] The honorific term *sayyid* is often used interchangeably with the term Hashemite/Hashemi/Hashimi in the literature dealing with Zaydism and other branches of Shi'ism. In this book, we use the form Hashimi. Hashimi refers to those belonging to the Banu Hashim, a subclan of the larger Quraysh tribe, the tribe of the Prophet Muhammad. The term can also be applied more generally to all descendants of Hashim bin 'Abd al-Mutalib, grandfather of the Prophet Muhammad. However, the terms are used interchangeably here (as other scholars and informants have done) and are intended to invoke the particular lineage of 'Ali and Fatima, progenitors of the *sayyid* social strata in Yemen.

Imamate because they were the only Zaydis eligible to rule. Imams frequently drew upon them to form the majority of government administrators. Indeed, due to the *sayyid* background of imams and the spoils associated with power, *sada* were in many respects socially superior up until the 1962 revolution. In addition to their politicore-ligious role, *sada* were generally an educated, politically connected, and land-owning elite, with the prestige to intervene and mediate tribal conflicts. As a social stratum, *sada* usually practice endogamy, contributing to the incorrect perception by many Yemenis that they are an exclusive ethnic group. However, despite the popular perception of them as such, we will see that *sada* are not a homogenously influential community.[49]

Although status as a *sayyid* is hereditary, *sada's* status as religious scholars ('*ulama*') must be acquired, and they are not revered as saints. Though a few great *sayyid* families were conspicuous in the history of Yemen, their more-distant relatives were further from the nucleus of power and "did not occupy any fixed place in political structures or in relations of production. . . . Some taught, some farmed, and some, at particular junctures, governed, although intermittently. They cannot safely be spoken of en bloc as having been a ruling class."[50]

Additionally, there has long been tension as well as codependence between *sayyids* and *qaba'il*, both of whom gain legitimacy and status within their respective communities from their lineage. *Sada* traditionally consider themselves more learned and pious than *qaba'il*, and *qaba'il* have long attempted to maintain their autonomy in the presence of successive *sayyid* rulers. Furthermore, the abuse of power by some imams and *sada* toward the end of the imamate tended to diminish tribal respect for *sayyids*. Nevertheless, *sada* tended to be confirmed in their elite status because of their functional roles as mediators. Likewise, tribes have a reciprocal role in protecting *sada*. The defense of *sayyids* against outsiders was long important to tribes.

As a protected class outside of the tribal system, *sada* are associated with *hijra* (sanctuary; pl. *hujar*) areas, which have been used as safe havens during wars. *Qabi-lis* are traditionally bound to protect the *hujar* associated with their tribal areas as an aspect of '*ird*. Breach of *hijra* thus violates tribal terms of honor and is "paid for by heavy amends; the blood money might have to be paid not just once but eleven-fold."[51] *Hujar* also took on significance as places for Zaydi religious learning and power. In spite of their importance, however, there has yet to emerge a rigorous, focused carto-graphic study of *hujar* in northern Yemen that accounts for locations, size, population, and the evolution of their uses over the past half-century. Additionally, as with much else related to place, name, and social use in northern Yemen, knowledge about the location, status, and size of *hujar* is hyper-local, possessed only imprecisely by people foreign to the relevant '*uzla* or even *mudiriya*.

---

[49] Dresch, *Tribes, Government, and History*, 141.

[50] Dresch, *Tribes, Government, and History*, 141.

[51] Dresch, *Tribes, Government, and History*, 141, 143, 146, 150.

Figure 2.6 was therefore developed based on a combination of interviews of Yemenis and ethnographers who have visited the region, published literature in English and Arabic, and GoY-produced data sets providing names of populated areas in the region. The figure depicts the location of some hujar in areas touched by the GoY-Huthi conflict, while Tables 2.1 and 2.2 indicate the consensus of interviews, texts,

Figure 2.6
Likely Hijra Locations in Conflict Areas of Sa'da and Adjoining Governorates

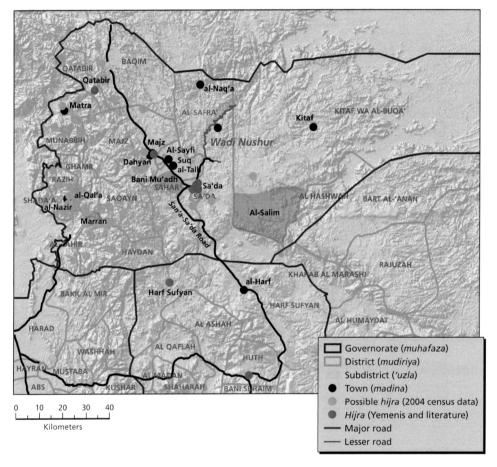

SOURCES: Interviews with Yemenis, references in secondary literature, and ARC-GIS data from the Republic of Yemen Central Statistics Organization 2004 Census Data Release.
NOTES: For the census, we drew on areas noted for Sa'da *muhafaza* with the root h-j-r (and occasionally h-j-l, accounting for census-taker error). Areas depicted in dark green on the map reflect results of interviews and examination of secondary literature. GIS data validated interviews and literature in many cases, generating additional possible *hijra* locations (see Tables 2.1 and 2.2). The latter are depicted in bright green. The map is thus intended to be illustrative of the multiple areas of *sayyid* presence and protection in Sa'da, rather than suggesting precise *hijra* locations.
RAND *MG962-2.6*

Table 2.1
Sa'da (S) and 'Amran (A) Hujar, Identified in Literature and Interviews

	District	Subdistrict/City
S	Haydan	Marran
S	Majz	Dahyan
S	Majz	Wadi Fulah
S	Sahar	Hamazat
S	Razih	Nadir
S	Qatabir	Location unknown
S	Safra and Sahar	Sa'da City—multiple
A	Harf Sufyan	Sufyan
A	Huth	Al-Huth

Table 2.2
Likely Hujar in Sa'da Muhafaza as Identified in GoY GIS Database

District	Subdistrict	Name
Haydan	Dhuwib 'Aliya	Dhuwib Safli
		Marran Sanwan
		M. Walad Ja'shan
		M. Walid Yahya
		Walad 'Aish
		Zabid al-Wadi
Saqayn	Al-Khawalah	Naw'a
		Aqish
		Ala al-Ifnijad
		Bani Was
		Sharq 'Arama
	Al-Azhur	Nazir
		Shuwareq
		Bakil
		Bani Sabah
		Sha'ban
Majz	Bani 'Abad	Bani Hadhifah
		Majz
		Sarah
		Wadi Falah
Munabbih	Al-Qaqishin	Yazid (2)
		Bani 'Ayash
		Batsin
Kitaf wa al Buq'a	Al-Muqbil	
Sahar	Farwah wa al- Mahadhir	
Al-Dhahir	Ghafrah	
Al-Safra'	Wadi'a	

and data sets. The historically most prominent *hijra* was in Saʿda city itself, accompanied by individual or multiple hujar in Haydan-Marran, Majz-Dahyan and Wadi Fulah, Sahar-Hamazat, Razih-Nazir, and Qatabir.

After 1962, many *sada* relinquished their *hijra* status and left the rural centers for cities. Still, the *hijra* areas remain historically significant from a Zaydi theological and social standpoint, representing a sacred geography of protected learning spaces for an elite social stratum. As knowledge of their location is often possessed by locals in relative terms (i.e., "there is a *hijra* in Baqim, midway to the Saudi border . . ."), not only is mapping *hujar* difficult—but they complicate the conduct of military operations by forces not native to the area. Accidental targeting of *hujar* might violate local norms, raising opposition to the GoY. Conversely, purposeful conduct of operations in areas known to be *hijra*, or possessing high concentrations of *sada* and *fuqaha'*, might undermine the legitimacy of GoY actions or the morale of Zaydi troops—even if these areas are also known Huthi centers. We return to this topic in Chapter Eight.

Fuqaha' (sing. Faqih). Non-*sayyid* *'ulama'*—known as *fuqaha'* and *quda*—are traditionally members of the judicial aristocracy, the social category immediately underneath *sada*.[52] Historically, *fuqaha'* (scholars of Islamic law) were scribes, fashioners of talismans, or merely learned men. The Zaydi religious view of the *faqih* is that he should be skilled in classical jurisprudence (*fiqh)* and thus be able to arbitrate the validity of local customs in terms of *shari'a*. Local customs or *'urf* that were not deemed contrary to *fiqh* and *shari'a* by *fuqaha'* were essentially harmonized with religious law, creating a composite legal system. Thus, while tribal custom has often been condemned in Zaydi histories as *taghut* (idolatrous), the role of the *fuqaha'* gives evidence of the flexible practice of Zaydi law because it conferred Zaydi/Hadawi Islamic legitimacy on tribal law and mediation.

Fuqaha' engaged in state administration are known as *qadis* (judges). While in theory any tribesman can become a *qadi*, the practice has proven largely hereditary in Yemen, and certain *qadi* lineages have played crucial political roles inYemen for centuries. *Qadis*, like *sayyids*, are granted the ability to "intervene," having historically been called on to mediate tribal disputes and opine on issues of inheritance and marriage. Their education and literacy made them prime administrative candidates, and they became a privileged stratum beginning in the 19th century because of their position in government, which was largely seen as legitimating the Qasimi regime.

Despite their status as *'ulama'*, *fuqaha'* were ultimately subservient to *sayyids* in Zaydi religious life. For example, although *sayyids* needed *qadis* to legitimate their rule following *khuruj*, the latter required *sayyids* to appoint them as ministers. And although *sayyids* and *qadis* shared a protected environment, *sayyids* were referred to in documents as "*hijra*" but *qadis* were referred to as their "*shi'a*," or party. Thus, the perception of inequality has caused tensions between the groups over time. For just as *sada*

---

[52] This section follows Dresch, *Tribes, Government, and History,* 137–141, 182.

feel superior to *fuqaha'* because of their lineage, *fuqaha'* have been willing to question the relevance of the *sayyids'* claims to preeminence based on lineage.

The Latent Nature of Socioreligious Tension

As shown above, there have been tensions between *sayyids* and non-*sayyids* throughout Yemeni history, as well as significant reasons for cooperation among them. There are two methods by which one could attain elite status in Zaydi religious society; one is hereditary, whereas the other is acquired and learned. In reality, there has been significant overlap between the two groups. For example, not all *sayyids* are necessarily learned. Likewise, *quda* and *fuqaha'* could theoretically rise from the tribal stratum and acquire elite status by studying. Furthermore, social mixing and intermarriage between *sayyids* and non-*sayyids* has become more common in the past two decades.

Nevertheless, the underlying tensions between social strata have been aggravated over time by various political regimes' patronage of elements advantageous to their rule, creating a type of enduring political technology still utilized by the GoY today. One historical example of this is how the imams in power under the Qasimi Imamate supported *qadis* who advocated a nonconfrontational form of Islamic law. A shift to dynastic, hereditary rule under the shaky political conditions of the mid-18th century meant that the Qasimis no longer fulfilled the merit-based qualifications necessary to be imams aligned with Zaydi law. During this time, therefore, ruling imams patronized "Sunni-oriented" scholars who forbade *khuruj* (the Zaydi theological term referring to the claim to imamate). By the end of the 18th century, many traditional Zaydi scholars, including some *sayyids*—eligible for the imamate and thus seen as possible threats to the regime—were excluded from elite state posts in favor of these *quda* who legitimized Qasimi rule.[53] One such *qadi*, Muhammad bin 'Ali al-Shawkani (d. 1834), advocated reforms to Hadawi Islamic law, which, among other aspects, encouraged obedience to the imams in power. Al-Shawkani served nearly 40 years as chief justice.[54] Salafis active in Sa'da in the 1980s and later Zaydi converts to Wahhabism would eventually claim al-Shawkani as an intellectual precursor. Yemeni regimes are also able to invoke the Sunnization of jurisprudence under al-Shawkani as evidence of a more uniform Yemeni pan-Islamic identity over time. As we will see in the next chapter, this strategy has become less useful in the context of a Zaydi religious revival.

---

[53] Haykel, "Rebellion, Migration, or Consultative Democracy?" 194.

[54] See Bernard Haykel, *Revival and Reform in Islam: The Legacy of Muhammad al-Shawkani* (Cambridge: Cambridge University Press, 2003).

The Sunni Spectrum: Implications for GoY-Huthi Conflict

Estimates of the percentage of Sunnis in Yemen range from 50 to 55 percent, the majority of whom associate with the Shafi'i *madhhab*.[55] Shafi'is dominate the south and the Red Sea coast but have long constituted a sizable population in the north as well. They are considered the most intellectually open of the four Sunni *madhhabs*, allowing for integration of inoffensive local traditions.[56] Additionally, while relying on the Qur'an and *hadith* (sayings of Muhammad or reports about something he did) as preeminent sources of law, Shafi'i scholars also supported the concept of consensus (*ijma'*) for interpreting ambiguous Qur'anic passages. If no consensus was found, then *qiyas* (reasoning by analogy) was invoked. The philosophy allows for some scholarly interpretation (*ijtihad*) and local variation as opposed to textual literalism. While Shafi'is differ from Zaydis in sources of law, modern Zaydism is considered close to Shafi'i Islam in its current practice, particularly in its emphasis on acquiescence to authority.[57]

Among Yemen's divides, the one between Zaydis and Shafi'is is often more latent than explicit and is described by Yemenis as more an issue of lineage than of religion. By the early 20th century, the Zaydi theory of the state had approached the Shafi'i theory, with the exception that the ruler had to be a *sayyid*—thus legitimating imamate dynasticism.[58] In this respect, from the late 19th century, Zaydi imams were aided by embracing Sunni approaches to political rule, which emphasized loyalty to the existing regime. Demonstrating the increasing Shafi'i tinge to the imamate, Imam Yahya celebrated the first day of Rajjab, a typically Shafi'i festival, in addition to the Shi'a holiday of 'Id al-Ghadir. Nevertheless, Shafi'is at times spoke of Imam Yahya's rule as "sectarian," asserting that they were treated as "infidels in interpretation" (*kuffar ta'wil*).[59]

Although the Shafi'i population expressed feelings of marginalization, the imamate often integrated them—by no means were all Shafi'is republicans and all Zaydis royalists by the late 1950s. Socially prominent Shafi'i shaykhs were plentiful in the 1930s, and Shafi'i conscripts formed a likely majority of the so-called "Zaydi army" through the 1940s. By the 1950s and 1960s, the difference between sects was "seldom doctrine"—Shafi'is were nearly universally loyal to the imam.[60] Ultimately, despite being typecast as having discrete political identities following "sect" lines,[61] it was not

---

[55] Yemen does include small numbers from the Maliki and Hanbali *madhhabs*, in addition to Salafis.

[56] The other three Sunni *madhhabs* are Hanifi, Maliki, and Hanbali. Each is named after the founder of the school of jurisprudence. The Shi'a *madhhab* is called the Ja'fari school, after the sixth Shi'a Imam, Ja'far as-Sadiq.

[57] Haykel, "Rebellion, Migration, or Consultative Democracy?"

[58] Paul Dresch, *A History of Modern Yemen* (Cambridge: Cambridge University Press, 2001), 46–47.

[59] Dresch, *A History*, 47.

[60] Dresch, *A History*, 68–69.

[61] Dresch, *A History*, 117: "Political categories were also problematic as well. When Sallal, a Zaydi soldier who was oppressive both south and north of San'a, was deposed in November 1967, the crowds of Shafi'i Ta'izz rioted

until the rise of Salafism in the 1970s and 1980s that sectarian tensions could be politicized by the government. Part of this was due to the emergence of Saudi-inspired Salafism among Yemenis, with which we will deal in detail in the next chapter. The most prominent organizational manifestation of Salafism working within the Republic of Yemen's political framework, however, is the Yemeni Islah Party (*al-Tajammu' al-Yamani li-l-Islah*), which emerged from initiatives encouraged by both the YAR and the Saudis in the 1970s and 1980s to counter leftist regional tendencies (the PDRY). Yet Islah itself espouses no consistent Sunni Islamist ideology, serving instead as a wide coalition for Sunnis of the Muslim Brotherhood and apolitical backgrounds, Wahhabi Salafis, and tribals seeking patronage, some from Zaydi backgrounds.

Islah has thus been described as a "tribal-Islamist force" made up of multiple political tendencies, each affiliated with leading figures that exemplify the diversity of Sunni political practice in Yemen. It "continues to elude black-and-white definitions, and it is a party of ongoing negotiations between competing ideological tendencies."[62] Among northern tribes, for example, the broad influence of Shaykh 'Abdullah al-Ahmar induced loyalty to Islah. Rather than Islamist zeal, Hashid tribe members nurtured expectations of patronage and regime connections because of Ahmar's close relationship with President Saleh.[63] At times, Zaydis from the north have worked with Islah, either hoping to benefit from kin network affiliations or out of grievance with the General People's Congress (GPC), Saleh's party. Around San'a as well, Islah has represented a counterweight to the GPC rather than a distinctly Sunni political party.

Since Islah is a "wide tent" with personalities closely associated with the GoY elite, it has often been open to political cooptation and use by the regime. Though nurturing the appearance of opposition, Islah has sided with the GPC on many occasions. For instance, in the 1990s, Islahi ideologues condemned the Zaydi doctrine of *khuruj* while issuing *fatwas* calling socialism and the YSP un-Islamic in the run-up to the 1994 civil war.[64] At the same time, it does shelter a more-extreme Salafi contingent that is open to politicization and deployment by the GoY as the latter seeks to counter

---

in favor of him."

[62] Sarah Phillips, *Yemen's Democracy Experiment in Regional Perspective* (London: Palgrave McMillan, 2008), 151.

[63] Phillips, *Yemen's Democracy Experiment*, 166. The negotiated nature of Islah is symbolized by its significant public individuals. Founders 'Abdullah al-Majid al-Zindani and Shaykh 'Abdullah al-Ahmar (d. 2007), were a hard-line extremist and a tribal leader, respectively. Other key figures, such as 'Abd al-Wahhab al-Daylimi, former Minister of Justice in the 1990s, represent the more pragmatic views of Sunni traditionalists. Islah thus has distinct political meanings and uses for Yemenis. Toward the end of Shaykh 'Abdullah's life, however, his relationship with Saleh soured as the GPC marginalized and criticized him in public. According to Phillips, "Ultimately Islah's actions have been guided more by elite relationships than by consideration of its grassroots constituents. The fraying of Shaykh Abdullah's relationship with President Saleh and its impact on Islah's political style demonstrates the constraints that surround political participation in Yemen."

[64] Phillips, *Yemen's Democracy Experiment*, 140.

rebellion in Saʿda. The Huthi phenomenon itself has seen Salafis in the north reiterating the anti-Hashimi line of the GoY, reinforcing sectarian aspects of GoY propaganda. As the GoY has turned to tribal (Hashidi) proxies in its anti-Huthi campaign, the Islah, as a patronage machine and shelter to Salafis, provides a source of combatants—who themselves might frustrate conflict containment and resolution.[65] All the same, Shafiʿis in Yemen do not play a singular role with respect to the Huthi conflict. In the north, many Shafiʿi tribes have treated the conflict opportunistically, pursuing patronage from the state and increased power locally. Other Shafiʿi tribes have allied with Huthis as revenge for a range of complaints they have with the GoY.[66] More broadly, local Yemenis—be they Zaydi or Shafiʿi—have used the current instability as a vehicle to voice their grievances over development and other matters.

Conclusion

This chapter has focused on sociocultural dynamics in the context of the country's divides as explored in Chapter One. Throughout, we have alluded to how northern Yemen's complexion has constrained central GoY control and influenced the practice of politics as well as war. As seen in the Introduction, political scientists have referred to the political technologies deployed by the Saleh regime managing Yemeni society as "neopatrimonialism." Patrimonialism itself is a form of personalized politics whereby one's right to rule emerges more from individual charisma, webs of connections, and so forth—than from the legitimacy bestowed by the office. As such, loyalty is acquired through patronage and cooptation. To reign is not to rule throughout the realm, and the regime's sovereignty is continually negotiated between the patron, in the person of the ruler, and clients who seek to maintain both autonomy and connection to the political center. Decisive use of coercive force is both rare and difficult, so violence serves a more communicative than punitive function. Further, given the weaknesses of the political center and the preference for personalized relations of patronage and loyalty, institutions inhabited by patrimonial actors lose their freestanding significance and become effective due to the interventions—and whims—of the people who inhabit

---

[65] It must be noted in another context, however, that despite recent concern about the increasing ideological and material threat of al-Qaʿida in the Arabian Peninsula (AQAP) in Yemen, Laurent Bonnefoy argues that the main Salafi trend is characterized by its apolitical, nonconfrontational stance. An example of this is the school of thought of Saudi-educated Shaykh Muqbil bin Hadi al-Wadiʿi (d. 2001, to be discussed later). Salafis in Wadiʿi's school of thought aim to prevent *fitna* (strife) by not engaging in politics in any form and do not endorse violence against the Yemeni state or its allies. Because of steps taken to show their disapproval of violence against the state, these Salafis have actually transformed themselves into allies of the Yemeni government, akin to the Saudi ʿulama. They condemn Muslim civilian casualties from terrorist attacks but ultimately remain as vocally anti-imperialist and anti-American as more hardcore groups. Their role has been invigorated in the north as a function of the Huthi conflict. See Laurent Bonnefoy, "Deconstructing Salafism in Yemen," *CTC Sentinel*, 2:2 (February 2009).

[66] Interview with Yemeni national in the United States, October 10, October 29, and November 2, 2008.

them. Where "the customs and patterns of patrimonialism coexist with, and suffuse, rational-legal institutions," neopatrimonialism obtains.[67]

In the Yemeni context, "neopatrimonialism refers to the permeation of these informal patrimonial loyalties into formal political institutions. Political parties, civil society organizations, and parliaments—institutions associated with a modernstate—are used in conjunction with traditional informal organizations by the leaders to expand their patron-client networks."[68] In this respect, today's GoY at times appears to be an extension of the kin networks of its leaders. Hailing from the Sanhan segment of the Hashid tribal confederation, for example, President Saleh has stacked key posts in the central government, military, and commanding heights of the economy with his Sanhani kinsmen.[69] Likewise, the ruling GPC also possesses strong Sanhani and, more broadly, Hashidi representation.[70] Further, it has long been known that Shaykh 'Abdullah al-Ahmar has been the regime's major tribal support, thus preserving Hashidi primacy. Having learned from the mistakes of previous northern Yemeni rulers,[71] Saleh has nurtured these relations not only to surround himself with friendly elements but also to ensure their loyalty. Therefore, the GoY since the mid-1980s has been described as "neotribal," founded on personal relations and the "reinterpretation of traditional tribal mechanisms."[72]

While remaining central to Saleh's political technology, the cooptation of certain tribal shaykhs and the personal patronage animating formal institutions—collectively known as *mahsubiya*—extends beyond the Hashid tribes. To obtain influence and persuasion in the periphery—in short, to fulfill roles associated with a shaykh—Saleh has accepted the overtures of Bakili shaykhs and those from the Khawlan bin 'Amr as well, empowering them economically and politically at home and in San'a. Further, *mahsubiya* extends to cooptative practices vis-à-vis potential rivals, including the Islah party, known Salafi sympathizers—who at times overlap with Saleh's Hashid confederates—and even members of the politically active Zaydi community, as we will see in the next chapter.

Given the geographical, cultural, and broader social barriers the GoY faces, neopatrimonialism allows the regime itself to survive as the arbiter of *mahsubiya* in the

---

[67] Michael Bratton and Nicolas van de Walle, *Democratic Experiments in Africa: Regime Transitions in Comparative Perspective* (Cambridge, UK: Cambridge University Press, 1997), 62. For more on patrimonialism, see Max Weber, *The Theory of Social and Economic Organization* (New York: Free Press, 1947); Joel S. Migdal, *Strong Societies and Weak States: State-Society Relations and State Capabilities in the Third World* (Princeton, NJ: Princeton University Press, 1988).

[68] Phillips, *Yemen's Democracy Experiment*, 4.

[69] See Jane Novak, "Ali Abdullah Saleh Family in Yemen Govt. and Business," in Armies of Liberation.

[70] Abdu H. Sharif, "Weak Institutions and Democracy: The Case of the Yemeni Parliament, 1993–1997," *Middle East Policy,* 9:1 (2002), 82–93.

[71] Rulers such as President Ibrahim al-Hamdi (ruled 1974–1977; assassinated), who is known to have pressed the tribes too hard. See Dresch, *A History,* 126.

[72] Phillips, *Yemen's Democracy Experiment*, 4.

north. This approach, however, elicits ongoing local competition for patronage, which creates rumbling chaos, discord, and conflict. Some have theorized that these conditions are favorable to the regime, sustaining it among weaker contenders.[73] Yet, because of the confluence of cultural norms, geographical conditions, and resultant neopatrimonial practices, the GoY has yet to achieve thoroughgoing legitimacy in many—particularly northwestern—eyes as an impartial, supreme power in Yemeni society. It is in circumstances such as these that challenges to the regime, such as that of the Huthis, can endure for so long—especially since geography, tribalism, and religion also favor the latter.

---

[73] This is the view of Lisa Wedeen in *Peripheral Visions: Publics, Power and Performance in Yemen* (Chicago: University of Chicago Press, 2008).

Part II: From Tension to Conflict: Social Change and Huthi Emergence, 1980s–2004

The physical, human, and conceptual characteristics that we encountered in Part I have remained the foundations of life and sociopolitical organization in Yemen's northwestern governorates. As seen, these characteristics have inhibited the full integration of the periphery into a unified Yemen and its central government structures. After the 1980s, however, Sa'da underwent several social changes. These changes in turn produced the conditions for greater prominence of Huthi family members and like-minded Sa'dans as social activists in the 1990s, just as they drove Sa'da toward internal tensions as well as friction with the Yemeni center. Although this friction waxed and waned, its core drivers were never addressed locally or by the GoY.

In the post–September 11 era, the GoY chose certain international partnerships. These partnerships—with the United States, in particular—exposed it to criticism issuing from the Huthi family while also providing the GoY a sense of increased coercive power relative to the periphery. Chapter Three examines social change in the Sa'da governorate in the 1980s and 1990s, culminating with the activities of the Believing Youth (BY) and the increased prominence of the Huthi family. Chapter Four then examines what developments, both in Sa'da and in terms of San'a's political calculations, drove the GoY and the Huthis toward open armed conflict in 2004.

Run-Up to the Regime-Huthi Conflict, 1980s–2001

Physical conditions, along with tribalism and religion, have remained the foundations of life and sociopolitical organization in Yemen's northwestern governorates. Over the past generation, however, the northern areas, Sa'da in particular, have undergone intense economic, demographic, and sociopolitical changes. These changes increased Sa'da's exposure to the wider world, created tensions within the governorate, and shifted the ways in which people understand and relate to their environment, tribes, and religious identities. These shifts are important to understand, because they informed the emergence of Badr al-Din al-Huthi's sons and Yemenis who later became Believing Youth (BY) or Huthi supporters. By the mid-1990s, these tensions had politicized the Huthi family and led to the formation of the BY. Huthi aspirations and the GoY's failure to exert a more positive influence in the area set the stage for violence in the late 1990s and armed antiregime activity after 2001.

Economic, Social, and Political Ferment

Regional Opening and Economic Changes, 1970s–1990s

The YAR did not arrive in Sa'da until 1969, and some of its outlying areas did not receive GoY officials until 1980.[1] Around this time, the governorate began to gain greater connectivity to the outside world. Hastened by road building, connectivity was manifested through increasing links within the province and to the rest of Yemen, as well as by exposure to trends and ideas from Saudi Arabia and other parts of the region. In 1979, the rocky dirt road connecting San'a to Sa'da was replaced by a paved road funded by the GoY. This reduced the ten-hour journey from the capital to Sa'da city to four hours and permitted a greater variety of vehicles to make the trip. This paved road was later extended to Baqim, and by stages to the border of Saudi Arabia. During the 1980s, Sa'da was also connected to the Red Sea coast by paved roads branching off from Huth in 'Amran governorate. Likewise, in the 1980s, the individual *mudiriyat* of

---

[1] See Shelagh Weir, *A Tribal Order: Politics and Law in the Mountains of Yemen* (Austin: University of Texas Press, 2007), 294.

Sa'da were linked better internally through improved roads, also easing inter-*mudiriya* movement. Along with roads, the provision of telephone exchanges to *mudiriya* centers during the 1980s and early 1990s increased Sa'da peoples' exposure to citizens of other *mudiriyat* in the governorate, to Yemenis beyond Sa'da, and to Arabs beyond Yemen.

The earliest and most visible effect of Sa'da's greater local-to-regional integration was economic. As we saw in Chapter One, Sa'da governorate has traditionally supported wheat, sorghum, and citrus production, in addition to grapes and apples. In the 1970s and 1980s, tribal farmers and nontribal traders expanded production beyond the needs of local consumption, exporting cash crops to other parts of the governorate and other regions of Yemen to the south. Likewise, trade northwards to Saudi Arabia expanded in the 1970s and 1980s, building on existing kin networks. Sections of the Khawlan bin 'Amr tribes have lived north of the Saudi side of the border since its 1934 demarcation; farther to the east, Hamdan Bakil sections are also resident in Saudi Arabia (see Figures 1.5 and 1.6). For several decades, therefore, cross-border trade and smuggling had characterized the region.

Subsequent to road construction, licit trade (as well as weapons smuggling) increased, as demand for agricultural goods in Saudi Arabia remained high. During this time, between one-third and one-half of the Sa'da male population was involved in some way with cross-border trade.[2] This increased the affluence of both *qabili* shaykhs and non-*qabili* traders, driving them to further develop their orchards and bring in heavier machinery for irrigation and cultivation. Likewise, the cross-border trade provided greater income in the late 1970s and 1980s, leading to a comparative flood of consumer goods into the region, including cars, trucks, television sets, radios, and cassette players. When the GoY imposed a ban on fruit imports in 1984, the potential for commercial profit from domestic commerce was even greater for local farm owners and merchants, leading to broader exposure to the ideas and goods of the larger world. It also shaped social inequalities and status challenges, to be discussed below.

Greater than the contribution of Yemeni trade to income and consumerist exposure was the impact of Yemen's chief export from the 1970s until 1990: male labor to the oil-wealthy Gulf States, Saudi Arabia in particular. By 1975, roughly 280,000 YAR citizens were working in Saudi Arabia, with a further 10,000 in other Gulf countries. By the mid-1980s, more than 380,000 northern Yemenis were working abroad, representing about a quarter of the region's adult men. By 1990, about 800,000 of newly united Yemen's citizens were working in the oil-wealthy Gulf States.[3] In the case of the northerners, migrants were agricultural workers, who took up jobs as semiskilled labor-

---

[2]   Gerhard Lichtenthäler, *Political Ecology and the Role of Water: Environment, Society and Economy in Northern Yemen* (Surrey, UK: Ashgate Publishing, 2003), 87.

[3]   Fred Halliday, "Labor Migration in the Middle East," *MERIP Reports* 10:56 (1977); Fred Halliday, "Labor Migration in the Arab World," *MERIP Reports* 14:4 (1984); Thomas Stevenson, "Yemeni Workers Come Home: Reabsorbing One Million Migrants," *Middle East Report* 23:2 (March–April 1993).

ers, builders, service industry laborers, and guards. The bulk of these were aged 20–40; just over 50 percent of them were literate or possessed further education.[4]

The average time abroad in these countries for northern governorate Yemenis during the 1970s and 1980s varied from two to five years, interspersed with long visits home for Muslim holidays or seasonal vacations. It was during these visits home that the migrants brought remittances. In 1975, YAR workers' remittances totaled just over $309.7 million; by 1980, that number had climbed to $1.25 billion, after which it declined to between $700 million and $900 million per year. By the late 1980s, labor migrants' remittances accounted for about 20 percent of the YAR's gross domesic product (GDP).[5] This repatriation of funds spurred a further proliferation of construction, agricultural expansion, and consumer goods in northern Yemen, facilitated by the importation into the region of generators, drills, and water pumps. The economic benefit to the Sa'da basin during these years has been characterized as "disproportionate" to that of the rest of the country, given proximity to the Saudi border.[6]

Social Change and Friction in Sa'da

The social and demographic effects of greater income during the 1980s and early 1990s are of tremendous importance to the subsequent conflict in the governorate. There were four chief effects: greater geographical and social intermixing; exposure to new ideas and ways of communicating them; movement of more-diverse groups of people into parts of Sa'da; and social stratum frictions reflecting these changes. Although all were important on their own, they combined to have even greater effect by the mid-1990s.

First, because of eased communication and transportation, Yemenis from individual *mudiriyat* started to intermix with those from other regions in the governorate. Razihis, for example, came to know Qatabris, and Saharis came to know Safrawis. Not only did such processes increase the awareness of membership in tribal groupings larger than the clan or subtribe, they also aided the emergence of a sense of "Sa'da-ness" alongside preexisting *'uzla-* and local-region-based identities. Travel within the governorate and beyond for commerce and education further exposed certain segments of society to life in the rest of northern Yemen. These segments were made up of the semi- to fully literate group of males between the late teenage years and their late thirties, the same people who traveled to the Gulf States as migrant laborers. Within a very short time, their horizon had expanded multifold compared to that of their forebears.

A second important effect of these years involved the substance of their exposure. Whether in the governorate, Yemen, or the Gulf, Yemenis from the north began to

---

[4] Nicholas Van Hear, "The Socio-Economic Impacts of the Involuntary Mass Return to Yemen in 1990," *Journal of Refugee Studies* 7:1 (1994), 18–38.

[5] Halliday, "Labor Migration in the Middle East," and "Labor Migration in the Arab World"; Stevenson, "Yemeni Workers Come Home."

[6] Lichtenthäler, *Political Ecology,* 5.

interact more and share common experiences with each other, crossing the divides of social hierarchy described in earlier chapters. Yemenis from tribes of differing prestige began to interact, and there was a greater mixing of *qabilis* with non-*qabilis* and Hashimis with non-*sayyid* Zaydis. This mixing occurred in the context of domestic agriculture and commerce, through education in the region's emerging schools, and during labor abroad. It would have important implications for both the creation of the BY and subsequent Huthi popularity.

Beyond more diverse social exposure and interaction was the ideational substance of exposure, particularly for those working or studying abroad. The late 1970s and 1980s witnessed Islamic revivalism throughout the broader Middle East. Muslim Brotherhood activism in Egypt and Syria was paralleled by a greater self-awareness and communal organization among Shi'ites in Lebanon. Much closer, and of possibly greater conceptual impact, was the Islamic Revolution in Iran—along with exposure to Wahhabi Islam during sojourns in Saudi Arabia. Combined with heightened awareness of regional trends and generational change among northern Yemenis, these two influences produced a defensive reaffirmation of Zaydi identity among many Yemenis in the Sa'da governorate, as we will soon see.

Third, broader economic opportunities drove, or coincided with, demographic shifts at home. During the 1970s and 1980s, heightened trade increased wealth in regional markets, including al-Talh to the north of Sa'da, as well as al-Qabil and Suq al-Ammar to the south. In those years, also, the travel of Sa'da men abroad produced labor shortages in the region. Likewise, higher incomes from agricultural goods and importation of irrigation machinery made large-scale investment in commercial agriculture attractive. During those same years, regional tribes privatized ownership of previously collectively held land. At the same time, during the 1980s, areas outside the basin and the governorate were suffering from intermittent droughts.[7]

These factors drew more population to Sa'da from various social backgrounds. Individual laborers, both tribal and otherwise, entered the region. On the other end of the economic spectrum, wealthy shaykhs, Hashimis, or nontribal traders—representing three different social strata—began to acquire more land from tribal farmers who were to cultivate all of their land due to a labor shortage. New landowners focused largely on citrus farming for cash. Further, shaykhs from tribes foreign to the basin began to acquire land historically held by other tribes, while segments of tribes also began to move into the area, either because of their shaykhs' acquisitions or because of droughts in other areas. Local laborers returning from abroad also acquired land with their new wealth—or entered into trading or services, previously the preserve of the non-*qabili* stratum.

By the end of the 1980s, therefore, Sa'da was much more crowded than it had been previously. In addition to traders and Hashimis moving into the area, segments

---

[7] Lichtenthäler, *Political Ecology*, Chapters 2 and 3.

of all three major north Yemeni tribal confederations—Hashid, Bakil, and Khawlan bin 'Amr—had moved into the basin and its surrounding environs, creating the latent three-way tribal fault line seen in Chapter Two. At the same time, Sa'da's economy heated up, with greater competition. This competition expressed itself initially among social strata that had previously been largely separate. For example, *qabilis* and Hashimis were competing with non-*qabili* traders over land, agricultural market share, and commercial trade, and tribes were competing with other tribes over these issues in addition to access to land and irrigation.

Competition also emerged within groups whose solidarity appears to have been diminishing. In this respect, the relationship between tribal leaders and tribal members was beginning to change. Shaykhs, relatively wealthier than their tribes' members and better connected to the government, began to acquire more land than did tribal members, often purchasing it directly from people with whom they used to hold it as collective tribal territory. In the process, shaykhs alienated themselves somewhat from their tribes, who were seeking to retain land—an important tribal value, as we saw previously. This alienation increased because of a perception that shaykhs were concerned more about farms and government connections than about the tribe's collective well-being—shaykhs' eyes were turned more toward the governorate capital or San'a than toward their *qabili* brethren. As such, the prestige of shaykhs among their own tribes began to decline in some places. They could not fulfill the roles of arbitrator and mediator to the same degree as before, since they were no longer perceived as impartial. This would have implications for the Huthi-GoY conflict in later years. As tribal solidarity at the confederation, tribe, and subtribe level diminished, the ability of a shaykh to "deliver" his tribe to the GoY or Huthis would decrease, while loyalties would split down to the extended-family level.

Fourth, as our discussion of intratribal dynamics suggests, another by-product of the new economic circumstances was increased social inequality and a change in the relations among social strata. As certain people or groups acquired more land or more access to regional markets, those that did not were left behind, decreasing the relative socioeconomic equity of the region. Furthermore, some of the new "haves" were from nontribal trader groups, while some of the "have-nots" were from tribes or Hashimi families of respectable pedigree. As we have seen in earlier chapters, however, non-*qabilis* traditionally occupied a lower rung on the social hierarchy ladder. The new economic circumstances thus evoked some resentment in addition to interstratum intermixing—it could be galling to tribesmen, for example, to see their shaykhs collaborate with traders while they themselves went without the largesse. Likewise, heretofore-prominent tribes could see their prestige and wealth decline as the prospects of other, more-subordinate tribes improved. In short, socioeconomic pressures and opportunities were misaligned with traditional social hierarchy norms.

This misalignment featured implications for the Hashimi families of Sa'da. As we have seen, the traditional social hierarchy placed them outside tribal hierarchies, superior to both *qabilis* and traders. Likewise, as we saw previously, this superiority was expressed and reinforced through certain social practices related to marriage, residence, and economic interaction. In the 1980s and 1990s, however, as certain shaykhs and nontribals grew in wealth and government patronage, they began to resent the social discrimination of Hashimi families, particularly because the scions of some of these families did not possess the learning or prestige of their forebears. This resentment was spurred on, as we have seen above, by a GoY portrayal of Hashimis as backwards, anti-republican, and atavistic. Those shaykhs and nontribals in the governorate whose fortunes had risen with those of the republic were particularly receptive to this motif, and some evinced their resentment by refusing to address Hashimis as *sayyid*.

At the same time as resentment toward Hashimis was rising in certain quarters, a countervailing tendency was working to reduce the social distance between them and others in the area. Since the 1970s, certain Hashimi families had begun to drop last names that were identifiably Hashimi, substituting tribal-sounding names or last names associated with locations in Sa'da. Others no longer insisted on being addressed as *sayyid*. Further, some Hashimi families began to disassociate themselves from Zaydi religious leadership, instead pursuing commerce or agriculture in collaboration with *qabilis* or nontribals. Additionally, in some cases, Hashimi fathers consented to marriages whereby their sons married into prominent *qabili* families. Whereas male Hashimi marriage of shaykhs' daughters had been permitted before, it increased somewhat during the 1980s and 1990s. Although these marriages did not eliminate interstratum social friction, they began to create kin network– and interest-based alliances between Hashimi and prominent tribal families.

These changes would prove important during the Huthi conflict. While the GoY could use social resentment to gain local proxies in its armed campaign, the reduced social distance between Hashimis and others made a broader swath of north Yemeni Zaydi society the target of the regime's anti-Hashimi actions than the GoY might have thought. Additionally, by the late 1990s and early 2000s, the Hashimi class retained a fair amount of residual prestige, and the tribal value of protecting them still resonated in the region. As for marriage choices in the Huthi family, those of Badr al-Din and his sons ensured they could benefit from multiple, overlapping alliances, both with local tribes and prominent *sayyid* families. We will return to this later.

The Role of the Pre-Unification Regime, 1980s–1990

Given its limited capacity to govern directly in Sa'da, the YAR leadership under President Saleh used a series of tactics to obtain access to and influence in the region through alliances with local tribal leaders or economically powerful merchants—tactics aligned with the neopatrimonial policies described in Chapter Two. Yet, GoY actions in this regard aggravated the emergent tensions we have just seen. In some cases, the GoY focused on tribal segments that had supported the republicans during the civil war of the 1960s, ignoring other, more traditionally prominent tribes or leaders who had harbored royalist sympathies (these often continued to receive subsidies from the Saudi government). Alternatively, the GoY at times elected to support younger sons of royalist shaykhs, or other families within prominent Sa'da tribes, as a way to gain influence while shifting weight in a kin network.

During the 1980s and into the 1990s, this *mahsubiya* (patronage) took the form of gifts of money, seedlings, irrigation pumps, and vehicles. Additionally, the GoY routed roads through territories of preferred tribes, thus increasing their access to regional and capital-city markets and creating a perceived threat to other, nonfavored tribes. Likewise, preferential access to local governorate jobs, positions within the military,[8] plots of land, and terms of sale were other tactics used by GoY to cultivate influence in the area.

These actions resulted in several effects, in some cases contrary to the regime's intent. As mentioned before, shaykhs whose second homes were in San'a tended to focus less on their governorate, reducing their esteem among tribal members. Instead, shaykh-*qabili* relations become more transactional than before, with *qabilis* concerned less about the status and prestige of their shaykhs than about what the latter could get out of the government for them. These GoY actions also meant that shaykhs no longer had the pulse of their communities and could not slow down or channel social change in a direction benefiting the GoY. They could also not "deliver" tribes, as social solidarity was reduced, and in some cases tribal members came to oppose their shaykhs. This was symbolized by the refusal of individual *qabilis* to sell land to their shaykhs, or in preferences they demonstrated for alternative tribal elders as shaykhs.[9]

Of course, elevating certain kin networks (or nontribals) and, by default, lowering others stirred up conflicts among tribes, expressed through commercial competition or violent feuding. Although this stirring up of competition was at times conscious, the GoY was unaware at other times of the conflicts it had stoked. Alternatively, in certain instances, the GoY was forced to back down in confrontations with locally prestigious shaykhs. While the GoY was able to obtain loyalty through placation in these cases, the lesson to other tribal segments, reinforced by notions of autonomy and collective defense, was that defiance can pay.[10] We will address specific instances of this in Chapter Four.

---

[8] Lichtenthäler, *Political Ecology*, 88.

[9] Gerhard Lichtenthäler and A. R. Turton, *"Water Demand Management, Natural Resource Reconstruction and Traditional Value Systems: A Case Study from Yemen,"* Occasional Paper No. 14, Water Issues Study Group, London: School of Oriental and African Studies (SOAS), University of London, 1999, 8.

[10] Lichtenthäler, *Political Ecology*, 59–60.

From Unification to the Believing Youth

An Overheating Governorate, 1990–2001

The latent tensions in Saʿda society were quite visible by 1990, and they corresponded to major political-economic shifts at the national and regional levels. In 1990, the YAR and the PDRY united to form the Republic of Yemen, with the YAR leadership emerging supreme. At the regional level, Iraq's invasion of Kuwait worked to the newly united Yemen's disadvantage. The GoY's neutrality in the conflict and its failure to endorse Saudi Arabia's invitation of U.S. military support were interpreted by the Saudis and other Gulf Arab powers as pro-Iraqi.

For this and other reasons, nearly one million Yemeni guest workers were sent home. In Saʿda, effects were mixed. On the one hand, given the labor migration patterns described above whereby laborers had retained connections with families and ancestral plots of land, many could return to their native areas and engage in farming or commerce. As the Yemeni riyal was progressively devalued in the 1990s, more put their remittances into land, given its escalating riyal value. On the other hand, returning laborers were coming home to a much more crowded environment. It is estimated that between 1975 and 1994, for example, the population in the Saʿda basin alone had more than quadrupled.[11] This accounts for natural increase as well as the Saʿda portion of the post-1990 returnees from Gulf countries. The latter came into a more competitive land and commercial market, since local traders and shaykhs had amassed larger plots over time, at the expense of small farmers. Thus, while Yemenis in the Saʿda area did not suffer the unemployment, impoverishment, and social dislocation of central and southern Yemen, the socioeconomic conditions meeting them upon return made for an overheating political-economic space.

Identities and ideologies in the Zaydi heartland were also influenced by the changes of the 1980s and 1990s. While the socioeconomic and political trends in place by 1990 gained momentum thereafter, the context had evolved in a more charged direction. On the one hand, the complexion of Saʿda's people had changed from the 1970s and 1980s. Generational change is very important here. Either returning from abroad or engaged in increased commerce and travel in the governorate, Yemenis in their twenties and thirties represented the first generation of semi- to fully literate Saʿda residents. With the expansion of schooling and communications, they were on the whole better educated—and more exposed to the larger world—than were their forebears. In many cases, while remaining committed to *qabyala* as a values system and social structure, they chafed at the older generation's leadership, to which they were now less responsive.

Additionally, the generation of Zaydis coming into sociopolitical maturity during the 1980s and 1990s—the generation of Badr al-Din al-Huthi's sons—were members

---

[11]   Lichtenthäler, *Political Ecology*, 108.

of the first post-imamate generation. They could not remember the negative aspects of life under the imamate and had no mental image of that era resonating with republican narratives. Instead, some among them were aware that Sa'da had been the religiopolitical heartland of the state, and they could thus nurture some nostalgia for the cultural prominence it had entailed for their region and tribes. This generation also saw the relative governmental neglect of Sa'da in infrastructural and social welfare terms, compared with San'a and the Gulf countries in which they had worked or studied. As members of Khawlan bin 'Amr or Bakil tribes, they could also look askance at the Hashidi hue of the GoY and the movement of Hashidis into central Sa'da areas.

Finally, while abroad in Sunni countries during the years of the Iran-Iraq war, some had been exposed to anti-Zaydi sentiment with a racist tinge or a Sunni presumption of their Shi'ites' Iranian leanings.[12] By contrast, others had been exposed to Salafi thinking and practice in Saudi Arabia—or as *mujahidin* (freedom fighters) in Afghanistan—and found it appealing. They returned home inclined to challenge Zaydism as a *madhhab* and social hierarchy. Thus, by the early 1990s, an element of religious friction had been added to the generational changes and social dislocations of Sa'da, a product of which would be the defensive recrudescence of Zaydi identity among the region's young adult males.

Salafism in the Zaydi Heartland

The demographic, socioeconomic, and generational changes converging in the early 1990s were compounded further by events surrounding the first five years of Yemeni unification, including the introduction of Wahhabi Salafism to northern Yemen, the GoY's experiment in political "pluralism," and the 1994 Yemeni Civil War. Wahhabism emerged in the Sa'da governorate due to four chief influences: Yemenis returning from work in Gulf or from stints as *mujahidin* in Afghanistan; Saudi Arabian funding and publications; the Islah Party in Yemen; and local Salafi firebrands.

As mentioned previously, Yemenis circulating between Sa'da and Saudi Arabia from the 1970s to 1990 had been exposed to Salafi beliefs and practices in the kingdom. These included the intellectual tradition of *tawhid*, which focused on the oneness of God as understood through direct encounter with the Qur'an unmediated by centuries of scholarly commentaries or worldly accommodations. Salafism also focused on the equality of all Muslims, considering excessive veneration of 'Ali and his descendents as a derogation from monotheism. Likewise, tombs, shrines, or special locations

---

[12] See Paul Dresch, *A History of Modern Yemen* (Cambridge: Cambridge University Press, 2001), 153, 191, wherein he writes that during these years the term *Zuyud* as a plural for Zaydi took on a racist connotation among Sunni Arabs in the Gulf. Also see Lichtenthäler, *Political Ecology*, 90.

for celebrating "saintly" lineages are considered *bid'a* (nondoctrinal innovation) at best, *shirk* (polytheistic associationism) at worst.[13]

Yemenis encountered these ideas in mosques, schools, and study circles in Gulf countries. In Saudi Arabia in particular, lavishly funded outlets circulated pamphlets, books, and cassettes among the migrant laborers. The literacy of this generation of Yemenis permitted them to absorb these materials and bring them home during visits. From the 1980s into the 1990s, as these Yemeni "converts" to Salafism returned to Sa'da, they established study circles and schools. They also began to infiltrate previously Zaydi-dominated mosques and to attain teaching posts in government schools. In both locations, they propagated ideas about Islam and the social order explicitly at odds with Zaydism, shifting the values of some students and worshipers and attracting adherents. For reasons we will see shortly, there was initially no countervailing Zaydi voice to compete in the Yemeni marketplace of ideologies.

Converted Yemenis in Sa'da could rely on external support for their efforts. Since the late 1970s, prominent Saudi clerics had been preaching against Zaydism from within the kingdom; their recordings had nurtured the "Salafication" of Zaydis working there. In the 1970s and 1980s, Saudi clerics also visited northern Yemen, preaching at study circles or Wahhabi-infiltrated mosques or teaching in newly formed schools. Groups affiliated with the clerics had also funded the importation into Yemen of Salafi publications. Some of those providing financial support were not *'ulama'* per se, but rather wealthy Saudi businessmen who at times would funnel money to Salafism-propagating Saudi clerics or local Yemenis. Likewise, cross-border business links permitted transfer of Saudi funds to pro-Salafi businessmen in the governorate or capital city.[14]

Sources external to Sa'da but within Yemen also contributed to the Salafi-Zaydi conflict. These sources emerged from the Sunni segment of Yemen's population, in the form of the 1970s–1980s Yemeni Muslim Brotherhood offshoot that, by 1990, had become the Islah Party. From 1979, the YAR supported the Islamic Front (the preunification Islah Party)—initially to counter PDRY-supported groups that intermittently attacked the YAR. Religion was seen as a useful antidote to southern Yemeni Marxism. And although Saleh and the ruling elite were marginally Zaydi, support of a Sunni Islamist group earned the approbation of Saudi Arabia and kept presumed pro-imamate Zaydis at a distance.

Starting in the late 1970s, Sunni Islamists associated with Brotherhood leader 'Abdullah al-Majid al-Zindani had begun to relocate some of their activities to the Wadi Nushur region of the Sa'da governorate, which they used as a base for regional initiatives. Reportedly supported by GoY-patronized Qa'id Shawit, shaykh of the Bani

---

[13] One of the best recent examinations of Wahhabism is Natana DeLong-Bas, *Wahhabi Islam: From Revival and Reform to Global Jihad* (London: Oxford University Press, 2004).

[14] Weir, *A Tribal Order*; Lisa Wedeen, *Peripheral Visions: Publics, Power and Performance in Yemen* (Chicago: University of Chicago Press, 2008), 164–165.

'Uwayr subtribe of the Sahar (Khawlan bin 'Amr), Zindani and others embarked on a school- and mosque-building campaign partially subsidized by Saudis.[15] The campaign picked up speed in the 1980s and 1990s, with GoY encouragement through the Ministry of Religious Guidance.[16] The leader of the Hashid tribal confederation, Shaykh 'Abdullah al-Ahmar, also became affiliated with the Islamist camp during these years, retaining and augmenting his influence with the Saleh regime as the paramount tribal shaykh in the north.

In the 1980s and 1990s, therefore, while pursuing positions in state schools, Yemeni Salafis were also able to establish a "parallel and separate institution of education to the national school system,"[17] including local teachers as well as instructors from Egypt, Sudan, and Saudi Arabia who used a Salafi curriculum. Called "scientific institutes" (*ma'ahad 'ilmiya*) these Salafi schools featured numerous branches and satellites in the Sa'da governorate by the mid-1990s. The Dar al-Hadith school, for example, was established in Dammaj, just southeast of Sa'da city. It has had thousands of students at any one time. Local "colleges," associated with Yemeni Salafis, also sprang up in *mudiriya* centers and were patronized by Sunni Islamists of the Muslim Brotherhood as well as GoY.[18]

For a few years after Yemeni unification, the GoY continued to view patronage of Salafi preachers, publications, and schools as a valuable hedge against both the south's Yemen Socialist Party and Zaydi elites, of whom it was still suspicious. By this time, Yemeni Salafism was most broadly incarnated in the *Tajammu' al-Yamani li-l-Islah* (Yemeni Grouping for Reform), or the Islah Party—led nationally by al-Zindani and al-Ahmar, with Qa'id Shawit, among others, representing them locally.[19] Symbolic of its initial support by the GoY, al-Zindani founded al-Iman University in 1993–1994, a San'a-based school for the development of a cadre of Salafi scholars and activists. By the end of the 1990s, graduates would occupy positions in various schools and mosques in the republic, likely including the Sa'da governorate.[20]

Certain local firebrands, with tribal support, also raised the Salafi banner, directly targeting Zaydi tradition and practices. Shaykh Muqbil bin Hadi al-Wadi'i (d. 2001),

---

[15] Yahya al-Thulaya, "Sa'da Ta'rikh Mutamarrid," *al-Ahale*, August 12, 2008.

[16] Weir, *A Tribal Order*.

[17] Bernard Haykel, "Rebellion, Migration, or Consultative Democracy? The Zaydis and Their Detractors in Yemen," in Remy Leveau, Franck Mermier, and Udo Steinbach, eds., *Le Yemen Contemporain* (Paris: Editions Karthala, 1999), 96.

[18] D. Ahmad Muhammad al-Dughshi, "al-Zahira al-Huthiya: Dirasa Manhajiya fi Tab'iyat al-Nash'a wa Jadaliyat al-'Allaqa bi-l-Ta'rikh," *Nashwan News*, April 20, 2009.

[19] Sarah Phillips, *Yemen's Democracy Experiment in Regional Perspective* (London: Palgrave McMillan, 2008), 138; Lichtenthäler, *Political Ecology*, 57, 64.

[20] See Gregory Johnsen, "Yemen's al-Iman University: A Pipeline for Fundamentalists?" *Jamestown Foundation Terrorism Monitor* 4:22 (November 16, 2006).

in particular, is significant. A shaykh among the Wadiʿa tribes of Bakil just east of Saʿda (Hamdan al-Sham), Muqbil al-Wadiʿi had sought to study advanced Zaydism at the historic Saʿda Mosque of al-Hadi Yahya bin al-Husayn during the immediate pre-revolution years. He claimed to have been discriminated against by *sayyids* in the area due to his tribal origins.[21] Frustrated in his studies, he went to Saudi Arabia, where he studied *hadith* according to the Hanbali school associated with Wahhabi Islam. He returned to Yemen in 1979–1980 after the occupation of the Great Mosque in Mecca by Juhayman al-ʾUtaybi.[22] Muqbil al-Wadiʿi was thus a Bakili convert from Zaydism to Salafism, in part because of the stratum-based discrimination he found in the Saʿda of the 1960s and in part because of the proselytizing nature of the Salafism he found abroad.

He returned to Yemen as a "Salafi ideologue par excellence."[23] Having obtained tribal support and protection from the government, he established the Dammaj Institute on Wadiʿa-owned land. Through classes, pamphlets, booklets, and cassette-taped sermons, he denounced the major tenets of Zaydism, including the imamate, *khuruj*, veneration of saintly *sayyids*, and visitation of grave sites and shrines. His materials were used at Dammaj and other Salafi-associated schools in the governorate. By rejecting *madhhabs* as a divisive concept contrary to the principle of *tawhid*, he called upon Zaydis—*ahl-al-bidʿa*, or the people of doctrinal innovation—to return to *ahl al-sunna*—the people of the proper path. During the 1990s, he had "at one point thousands, even tens of thousands, of followers."[24] In lectures and writings, he explicitly called for the destruction of Zaydi shrines and tombs, which his students carried out in the mid-1990s around Saʿda.

Taken together with the Salafication of Yemeni migrant laborers and Salafism entering Saʿda from other parts of Yemen, the story of al-Wadiʿi is important for several reasons that would inform the emergence of the Zaydi counter-revival associated with the Huthi family. First, it shows the energy with which certain former Zaydis sought to propagate Salafism and denounce Zaydi practices in the Saʿda region, galvanizing other Salafi elements in the region.

Second, al-Wadiʿi's Bakili tribal background indicates the limited analytical utility of recent attempts to label the Bakil as Zaydi/pro-Huthi and then oppose this to a Hashidi-Salafi/anti-Huthi alignment. Not only does this ignore the numerically strong Khawlan bin ʿAmr confederation, it also obscures the complex reality of pro-GoY or -Huthi sympathies, which cut across both kin networks and geographical lines.

---

[21] Bernard Haykel, "The Salafis in Yemen at a Crossroads: An Obituary of Shaykh Muqbil al-Wâdiʿi of Dammâj (d. 1422/2001)," *Jemen Report* (October 2002), 28–31.

[22] See Yahya al-Thulaya, "Jamiʿat al-Mutanaqqidat: Dammaj al-Salafiyin, wa Dahyan al-Huthiyin, wa Saʿda al-Muʿtammar al-Shaʿbi," *al-Ahale.net*, n.d.

[23] Bernard Haykel, "A Zaydi Revival?" *Yemen Update* 36 (1995): 21.

[24] Wedeen, *Peripheral Visions*, 162.

Aligning "pro-Huthi Zaydi Bakilis" against "pro-GoY Hashidis" as fixed categories also neglects the changing nature of affinities through time, to which we will return in a subsequent chapter.

Third, al-Wadi'i's case shows that in the 1980s and 1990s, the GoY did not stand apart from intertribal and interconfessional tensions. Al-Wadi'i received protection from the regime, which legitimated his efforts in Dammaj. It has been suggested that during these years, he had links to 'Ali Muhsin al-Ahmar. An elder Sanhani kinsman of President Saleh, Muhsin al-Ahmar has nurtured collaborative relationships with Yemeni Salafis from the 1990s through to the present, in order to counter both southern Marxists and Zaydis connected with Sa'da. He has commanded northern forces fighting the Huthis since 2004. We will return to Muhsin al-Ahmar later, but it is important to note that "al-Wadi'i's own politics, then, could jibe well with the regime's project of divide and rule."[25] This divide-and-rule policy has continued ever since; overall, since the early 1990s, it has contributed to a sense among Huthi loyalists that their religion and culture are under ideological and physical siege instigated by the GoY itself.[26]

Finally, the phenomenon of the attraction to Salafism by a portion of Sa'da governorate's native sons seems paradoxical. One of the reasons Salafism could appeal to segments of the Zaydi population, however, is that its religious messages resonated with social class and generational dissatisfaction among its target populations. This is true of the Wahhabi condemnation of the social and religious superiority of *sayyids* as doctrinally deviant from the Islamic ideal of human equality. It appealed to certain shaykhs, who resented being held at social arms-length by *sayyids* and who perceived that any diminution of Hashimi status would facilitate their own advancement. In political terms, these shaykhs "hoped the pro-shaykh and anti-*sayyid* thrust of Islah would strengthen their position and bring material benefits,"[27] not the least because it would increase the likelihood of patronage from Shaykh 'Abdullah al-Ahmar.

More important than the minority of shaykhs were the younger nonelite *qabili* and traders. In some areas, these were "the most public and active converts to Wahhabism."[28] Younger Yemenis of all backgrounds chafed at the continuing social precedence of *sayyids* and shaykhs, in comparison to whom they were better educated and possessed an unmediated understanding of Islam's scriptures. As such, Wahhabism in the Sa'da governorate fused several conflict-producing vectors: social class frictions, generational change and educational differences, material interests, ideological attractions, and GoY efforts to obtain levers of influence. Ultimately, a Zaydi response to Salafism would

---

[25] Wedeen, *Peripheral Visions*, 165.

[26] Interview, Yemeni living in Europe associated with Huthi leadership, February 2, 2009.

[27] Weir, *A Tribal Order*, 297.

[28] Weir, *A Tribal Order*, 296.

also reflect generational and social change, as a self-consciously defensive reaction to an ideological threat perceived to be supported by the GoY.[29]

Zaydi Defensive Responses

As suggested above, another reason that local Zaydis could be attracted to Salafism was the absence in the 1980s and early 1990s of an opposing Zaydi message. In fact, the Zaydi community initially lacked a cadre analogous to the Salafi activists. After the 1960s civil war, as the elder *sayyids* and Zaydi *'ulama'* receded in prominence and scholarly production, a younger generation of Zaydi religious leaders did not emerge among the *sayyid* families. Likewise, in the absence of government patronage from the imamate, religious schools and publication were curtailed, particularly as the new republican government was ill-disposed toward pro-Hashimi socialization of Zaydis. In the 1980s and early 1990s, therefore, the Zaydi community possessed neither the substance nor mechanisms for a response to Wahhabi Salafism. Most religious scholars were older or detached from Sa'da's sociocultural and religious dynamics, while their sons, in most cases, did not possess the learning or skills to present an opposing religious message.[30]

From the mid-1990s, a specifically Zaydi response did emerge, however, in two forms. The first of these was political, in the form of the al-Haqq Party. The second involved ideology and popular mobilization, in the form of the Believing Youth (*al-Shabab al-Mu'min*) and specifically religious responses to perceived threats. Both kinds of responses featured the Huthi family. The second response, however, focusing on religious revival and social activism in the Sa'da governorate throughout the 1990s until 2004, allowed the Huthi family to harness the social and generational changes of the previous years to create networks of support and action that crossed Hashimi, tribal, and nontribal lines over multiple generations. The GoY attempted to use both responses to its local and national advantage but failed, particularly in the latter case.

Politics at the Center

The al-Haqq Party was formed in 1990 by older-generation Hashimi grandees and the scions of *qadi* families, who observed the post-unification emergence of political parties that did not represent Zaydi interests. These grandees included Majd al-Din al-Mu'ayyidi, the senior Zaydi *marja'* (source of religious authority), as well as Badr al-Din al-Huthi, who had been a student and protégé of *sayyid* al-Mu'ayyidi in the 1950s and 1960s. Hasan Zayd, Saleh Falita, and Muhammad al-Mansur, considered

---

[29] For more on the various and at times divergent strands of Salafism in Yemen, see François Burgoit et Muhammad Sbitli, "Les Salafis au Yémen ou . . . La modernisation malgré tout," *Chroniques Yéménites* 10:2 (2002).

[30] See Gabriele vom Bruck, "Being a Zaydi in the Absence of the Imam: Doctrinal Revisions, Religious Instruction, and the (Re-)Invention of Ritual," in Mermier, Leveau, and Steinbach, eds., *Le Yémen contemporain* (Paris: Karthala, 1999).

the third-ranking Zaydi *marja'* after al-Mu'ayyidi and al-Huthi, were also among the founders, as was Muhammad al-Maqalih, of *qadi* background.[31] Rhetorically, al-Haqq stood against Salafism. According to *sayyid* Ahmad bin Muhammad bin 'Ali al-Shami, the party's general secretary,

> Wahhabism is a child of imperialism . . . we are seeing imperialism in our country in its Islamic guise. . . . Saudi Arabia is pouring lots and lots of money into Yemen to promote its own version of Wahhabi Islam. . . . So, we need to counter these efforts.[32]

Overall, however, al-Haqq was predominantly an effort to obtain political recognition and largesse from the GoY, taking advantage of the Saleh regime's announced policy of pluralism for greater political participation. While some of its younger members saw it as a means to bring greater governmental attention to Sa'da's developmental and infrastructural needs,[33] al-Haqq was an elite party appealing largely to those disinclined to mass mobilization. It therefore possessed little resonance with the younger generation of northern Zaydis who were apt to be more politically active, and it did not develop a grassroots organization. Further, while attempting to portray itself as a Zaydi party safeguarding Zaydi interests, its leadership put itself at odds with historical Zaydi religious views. In order to allay GoY fears about Zaydi politicization, in 1990 al-Haqq leaders declared the imamate defunct as a Zaydi institution, subsequently also renouncing the doctrine of *khuruj*. As a price for political inclusion, al-Haqq therefore relinquished the defining elements of Zaydism. Although it claimed a particularly Yemeni Islamic view, "without the imamate it was difficult for outsiders to understand what that view consisted of other than constantly inveighing against the presence of Wahhabis in Yemen."[34]

Because of these doctrinal compromises, credible Zaydi scholars—such as Badr al-Din al-Huthi and Majd al-Din al-Mu'ayyidi—distanced themselves from the party over time, and the party's lack of popular appeal resulted in a poor showing during the relatively free 1993 parliamentary elections.[35] In Zaydi Sa'da governorate, al-Haqq only earned two seats. These went to Husayn al-Huthi, who represented Haydan/Saqayn, and 'Abdullah al-Razzami, who represented the Razzami tribal areas of Wadi

---

[31] Samy Dorlian, "Zaydisme et modernization: émergence d'un nouvel universel politique?" *Chroniques Yéménites* 13:13 (2006), 93–98.

[32] See *al-'Allama al-Shami: Ara' wa Mawaqif* (Amman, Jordan: Matabi' Sharikat al-Mawarid al-Sina'iya al-Urdiniya, 1994): 89; Paul Dresch and Bernard Haykel, "Stereotypes and Political Styles: Islamists and Tribesfolk in Yemen," *International Journal of Middle East Studies,* 27:4 (November 1995), 412.

[33] Interview, Yemeni living in Europe associated with Huthi leadership, February 2, 2009.

[34] Haykel, "Rebellion, Migration or Consultative Democracy?" 199.

[35] Sheila Carapico, "Elections and Mass Politics in Yemen," *Middle East Report* 26:6 (1993), 2–6; Sheila Carapico, "Mission: Democracy," *Middle East Report* 28:4 (1998), 17–20.

al-Nushur. The two would go on to lead a reemerging BY after 2000, as well as the first phases of armed Huthi opposition to the regime in 2004–2005. Embodying the younger Zaydi generation, their electoral success suggests the centrality of this demographic group in the region.

Al-Haqq was useful to the regime, however, as the GoY sought to leverage potential adversaries against other opponents. During these years, the GoY considered the Islah party a threat to the domination of the GPC and wished to restrain the appeal of the former PDRY's YSP. At the same time, the GoY remained wary of any effervescence of grassroots Zaydi activism. Support for al-Haqq thus implied many local-level benefits for the GoY—including the means to draw northern governorate people away from either Islah or the YSP, to decrease somewhat the Wahhabi-Zaydi tensions, and to obtain greater influence with prominent Zaydis. It also held out the possibility of restraining overzealous younger-generation Zaydi politicization through cooptation of their elders—who also did not want to see alternative channels for Zaydi expression. At the political center, the advent of an additional political actor—though without a mass social base—could permit the Saleh regime to dilute Islah's governmental influence while retaining patronage relationships with such personalities as Zindani and Shaykh al-Ahmar. As an indication of al-Haqq's tactical utility to Saleh, in 1997 the GoY granted it the Ministry of Religious Endowments (*awqaf*), even though al-Haqq had failed to win a single seat in that year's elections. The GoY thus used al-Haqq to remove Islah from the ministry after the breakup of the post-1993 GPC-Islah coalition. Although the al-Haqq leadership justified the action in pragmatic terms, the party lost further legitimacy among politically inclined Zaydis.

By this time, however, the shine was already off al-Haqq. From 1990 to 1993, it is said to have pursued a "tacit" alliance with the YSP as it sought inclusion in GPC governments. Later, during the 1994 civil war, it adopted a position of neutrality against armed conflict.[36] This position was not viewed kindly by the regime, which suspected al-Haqq of supporting the southern forces—and later popularized this as an accusation to tar al-Haqq and the Huthis as *infisaliyin* (separatists). The party itself was suffering from internal splits on matters related to religious doctrine and suspicions of factional alliances with other parties. Before his term as an al-Haqq member of parliament (MP) was over, therefore, Husayn al-Huthi and his father dissociated themselves from the party and, along with their kinsmen and allies, moved to other modes of Zaydi activism.

Religious Revival

By 1995, as al-Haqq was petering out as a Zaydi voice, a more intellectual response to the perils of Yemeni modernity and Salafism was in full force in Saʿda. It combined efforts of Badr al-Din with the activities of much younger, non-*sayyid* Zaydi *ʿulamaʾ* and

---

[36] Dorlian, "Zaydisme et modernization," 97.

teachers. Badr al-Din had taken on Saudi clerics in the late 1970s, rebutting anti-Zaydi sermons and fatwas. During the 1990s, his 1979 text on this topic began to recirculate in Sa'da in new editions, as he reinvigorated his teaching and writing initiatives in the Haydan-Marran region of the governorate.[37] Farther to the east, in a *hijra* just outside Sa'da city, *sayyid* al-Mu'ayyidi also continued to teach. Collectively, they "encouraged a younger generation of Zaydi activists to pursue activities in the fields of education, religious exhortation, and the editing and publication of Zaydi manuscripts."[38]

Around the same time, non-Hashimi Zaydi scholars became active in the Sa'da region. Originating in Razih *mudiriya*, Muhammad 'Izzan is the most well known of these. Having studied with *sayyid* al-Mu'ayyidi, he went on to teach Zaydi jurisprudence and practice from his home during the mid-1990s. Critically, he edited Zaydi texts and pamphlets instructing young Zaydis about their *madhhab's* unique beliefs and practices, also editing newer editions of seminal Zaydi works from the nineteenth century that opposed Salafi influence in the region.[39] He is said to have traveled to Beirut several times in his capacity as Zaydi book editor and purchaser. In San'a, al-Murtada al-Mahatwari engaged in similar activities as prayer leader at the Badr Mosque, publishing books, notable sermons on cassettes, and developing Zaydi curricula for the emerging generation.

Mirroring the Wahhabis, these activists went on to establish schools for Zaydi revival, using materials they and others had written as curricula. To counter the Salafi Scientific Institutes, individuals such as 'Izzan began to establish Scientific Schools (*madaris 'ilmiya*), with financial support from wealthy Zaydis associated with al-Haqq. Schools of this type soon were established in Sa'da, Jawf, and San'a; while in Sa'da city itself, 'Izzan and colleagues established a Zaydi teacher-training institute, named after the nineteenth-century Zaydi martyr Muhammad bin Saleh al-Samawi (d. 1825), who had dealt with a regime-supported Sunni challenge in his own day—the symbolic communication inherent in the naming was intentional. Curricula in these schools were also being used by pro-traditionalist Zaydi teachers in local GoY middle, secondary, and teacher schools, increasing the sense of Zaydi group identity among literate, politically attentive youth.

---

[37] See *al-Ijaz fi al-Radd 'ala Fatawa al-Hijaz* (San'a: Maktabat al-Yaman al-Kubra, 1979); *Man Hum al-Rafida*, ed. Ibrahim ibn Muhammad al-'Ubaydi, (San'a: Mu'assasat al-Imam Zayd ibn 'Ali al-Thaqafiya, 2002); *Miftah Asanid al-Zaydiya* (Amman, Jordan, n.d.); *Tahrir al-Afkar* (Qum, Iran: al-Majma 'al-'Alami li Ahl al-Bayt, 1997)—all by Badr Din ibn Amir al-Din ibn al-Husayn al-Huthi.

[38] Haykel, "Rebellion, Migration or Consultative Democracy?" 200.

[39] See the following works written or edited by Muhammad 'Izzan, *al 'Allama al-Shami: Ara' wa Mawaqif* (Amman, Jordan: Matabi' Sharikat al-Mawarid al-Sina'iya al-Urdiniya, 1994); ed., *Majmu' Kutub wa Rasa'il al-Imam Zayd ibn 'Ali* (San'a: Dar al-Hikma al-Yamaniya, 2001); *al-Imam Zayd ibn 'Ali: Sha'la fi Layl al-Istibdad* (San'a: Dar al-Hikma al-Yamaniya 1999); ed., *al-Ifada fi Ta'rikh A'immat al-Zaydiya*, original author Yahya ibn al-Husayn, d. 1032 (San'a: Dar al-Hikma al-Yamaniya 1996).

The Believing Youth

These doctrinal efforts provided the intellectual basis for the mobilizational activities of the *Muntada al-Shabab al-Mu'min*, or Believing Youth, while the schools of Sa'da provided the initial associational space. In the early 1990s, having studied Zaydi *fiqh* and theology with their father Badr al-Din, Huthi family members Husayn, Yahya, and Hamid became students in the *ma'ahad 'ilmiya*. They and their Zaydi teachers subverted the Salafi curriculum, providing a Zaydi slant and sense of Zaydi community among the students. A few years younger, Muhammad al-Huthi had also studied for a time at a *ma'ahad 'ilmiya*, then transferred in the mid-1990s to the Sa'da city teachers training institute, embracing the new curricula and ideas of people like Muhammad 'Izzan, who became his colleague. Muhammad then proceeded to the Dahyan teachers institute in Majz, working as a teacher, likely inculcating in students—teachers-to-be—a renovated appreciation of Zaydism.[40]

From 1993 to 1997, Husayn al-Huthi was in parliament; from 1994 to 1996, Badr al-Din spent periods in Iran. Within the Huthi family, therefore, Muhammad was most closely identified with BY efforts. As a teacher, he is reported to have started informal groups among students, many of whom had traveled from other localities to board at the institute. These groups focused on such mundane issues as after-school study, sports, and local field trips. They were not avenues for explicit religious indoctrination—and some more literalist teachers and *'ulama'* looked down on the activities as possessing inadequate religious content.[41] Yet, these groups provided the associational setting for a specifically Zaydi identity among Sa'da's adolescent and young adult males. Notably, students had traveled to these schools from many parts of the governorate. Therefore, the clubs (sing. *muntada*; pl. *muntadayat*) that began to emerge at Dahyan and other boarding schools were not associated with one particular tribe and transcended all social strata, including the sons of Hashimis, *qabilis*, and traders. As school *muntadayat* went through a phase of semiformalization in the mid-1990s by issuing identity cards to encourage group solidarity, local-level social networks of Zaydis emerged, crossing over and blurring the social divides that had been important to previous generations.

As the first cohorts of *madaris 'ilmiya* and teachers-institute students began to graduate, the clubs moved beyond schools. Around 1994, BY-affiliated summer camps began to emerge, encapsulating a youth-to-young adult demographic much broader than that in the schools. It is reported that around this time, Hashimi elders, such as Badr al-Din, Ahmad al-Shami, and Salah Falita, took notice of the BY in the schools and sought to support it, potentially in a cooptative fashion that would ensure younger-generation loyalty to them. With their encouragement, the first BY summer camp was

---

[40] Interview, Yemeni newspaper editor, March 22, 2009; interview, Yemeni emigrant living in the United States, October 10 and 29, 2008.

[41] Interview, U.S. scholar of Zaydi religion, September 22, 2008.

reportedly established in Hamazat, a well-known *hijra* north of Sa'da where wealthier landowning Hashimis lived. The Hamazat camp became quite popular, often by word of mouth on the part of Zaydi youths and teachers. In particular, Khawlan bin 'Amr and Hamdan Bakil tribe leaders considered it a matter of prestige to be seen sending their children to these camps in the *hijra* areas, adding to their popularity.[42] By 1994–1995, between 10,000 and 15,000 students from the governorate and adjoining regions had reportedly attended Shabab al-Mu'min camps in Hamazat and other areas of Sa'da. In the next years, local sources indicate that similar camps (centers; *marakiz*) were in action in 'Amran, Hajja, the capital city governorate, Mahwit, and Dhamar, as well as in Ibb and Ta'izz.[43]

These camps combined learning with play. In the morning, Qur'anic study, Zaydi religious lessons, and classes on moral exhortation acquainted youth with their faith; in the afternoon, campers could enjoy sports competitions and drama in a way that explicitly reaffirmed both learning and identity—and attracted more adherents. Teachers or guest lecturers included Muhammad 'Izzan; Muhammad, Husayn, and Yahya al-Huthi; and the *qabilis* Karim Jadban and Salih Habra. With the exception of 'Izzan, all of them would play roles in the Huthi opposition to the regime after 2004. The BY camps thus allowed future Huthi leaders to gain prestige with the youth, in this way preparing networks of mutual support for later years. Although some Zaydis grumbled that there was too much play and not enough religion, the BY camps grew in popularity, expanding in numbers and attendees into the second half of the 1990s. The camps also permitted the proliferation of Zaydi revivalist literature and recorded sermons beyond those in attendance.[44]

As had been the case with al-Haqq, the GoY initially considered the BY an additional lever for influence in the region. Having repented of its unconditional support of the Salafis in the late 1980s and 1990s, the GoY considered the BY a mechanism to counteract Salafi attraction of younger Yemenis in the north. A small amount of regime funding thus found its way into the BY activities in schools and camps, perhaps through the hands of those local shaykhs bound to the GoY through traditional ties of *mahsubiya*, or through al-Haqq funds.[45] Later, as al-Haqq became suspect in GoY's eyes, the regime may have seen the BY as a way to reduce the party's resonance

---

[42] Interview, Yemeni emigrant living in the United States, October 29, 2008.

[43] See al-Dughshi, "al-Zahira al-Huthiya"; Haykel, "A Zaydi Revival?" 21.

[44] Bernard Haykel, "Recent Publishing Activity by the Zaydis in Yemen: A Select Bibliography," *Chroniques Yéménites* 9 (2001), 225–230. See also "Mukhayyamat al-Yaman . . . Furas Badila li-Himayat al-Shabab," *al-Moheet.com*, August 27, 2008.

[45] 'Abd al-Hamid al-Lisani, "Mudakhala Hadi'a Ma'a 'Zayd'. . . 'An al-Huthiya wa-l-Zaydiya wa-l-Hashimiya wa-l-Futun al-Ukhra," *al-Mithaq.net,* July 16, 2007; al-Dughshi, "al-Zahira al-Huthiya."

among the emerging generation of Zaydis.[46] Whatever the case, the emergence of the BY simply provided the GoY with yet another possibility for patronage, cooptation, and control through divisive influence.

In the context of today's regime-Huthi conflict, the BY phenomenon is significant for several reasons. First, it furnished the human and organizational links from the pre-1962 generation of Zaydi scholars to the activists of the 1990s and the Huthi hardcore of today. Majd al-Din al-Mu'ayyidi was already a noted Zaydi scholar prior to 1962, and Badr al-Din al-Huthi was his student during these years. In the 1970s and 1980s, Badr al-Din established himself as among the senior Zaydi *maraji'* through both literature and teaching. Al-Mu'ayyidi, and even more Badr al-Din, therefore, passed Zaydi knowledge, identity, and a belief in the need for Zaydi revival on to the generation of 'Izzan and the Huthi sons, who were very much republican-era Yemenis likely to be sociopolitically inclined.

Second, the BY exhibited a mode of associationism and activism that was particularly modern and different from traditional Zaydi social practices. State schools, as well as the formal schools founded for the express purpose of providing a Zaydi-informed education to the young of the entire community, *sayyid* and otherwise, were an entirely new associational space for young Zaydis to meet under the tutelage of leaders who were younger than and educated differently from their forebears. This holds true also for the school clubs for sports, conscious youth socialization, and collective identity creation. These *muntadayat* emerged at the initiative of teachers and students, not driven by the preferences of the older generation of *'ulama'*, Hashimis, or shaykhs. The dissemination of Zaydi religious ideas in written and audio form among newly literate younger Zaydis was likewise only possible with new communications technologies and understandings of how they could be used. As elsewhere in the Middle East from the 1970s to the 1990s, these new modes of association and communication led to a relative democratization of access to religious ideas, messages, and means of mobilization.[47]

Third, the Zaydi revival and the BY reacquainted adolescent and young adult Zaydis with doctrines of the faith, interpreted in the light of contemporary conditions. They thus brought together the effects of generational and sociocultural change in the service of Zaydi revivalism. Before the 1980s and 1990s, it was nearly unheard of for Hashimis, *qabilis*, and nontribal town dwellers to intermingle meaningfully in a sustained fashion. The post-1962 decentering of the Hashimi stratum, the 1970s–1990s economic opportunities, and the demographic evolution in Sa'da combined to change

---

[46] Charles Schmitz, "Book Review of *Political Ecology and the Role of Water: Environment, Society, and Economy in Northern Yemen*, by Gerhard Lichtenthäler," *Journal of Political Ecology*, Vol 11 (2004), 14–17; Dorlian, "Zaydisme et modernization," 97.

[47] See Barak Salmoni, "Islamization and American Policy," in James A. Russell, ed., *Critical Issues Facing the Middle East* (Palgrave Macmillan, 2006).

that. Likewise, increases in literacy and education, achieved in the course of greater intermixing of young Zaydis from various social strata during travel and schooling, further broke down social barriers and allowed the kind of common identity to emerge that was a precondition for revival and the BY. Although these changes also led to social friction, they meant that phenomena such as the BY would be less susceptible to control on the part of the traditional elite or the GoY.

Fourth, while apolitical in focus during the 1990s, Zaydi revival and the BY emerged to counter implicit threats of Salafi encroachment in the governorate, a diminished young Zaydi attachment to religion, and GoY socioeconomic neglect. In this respect, it resembles the late 1950s emergence of the Da'wa Movement among Shi'ites of Iraq, in which younger clerics, such as Muhammad Baqr al-Sadr, witnessed Sunni governmental neglect and an alarming attraction of young Shi'ites to communism.[48] In both cases, religious revival could not be conceived without a threat referent. For Zaydis like 'Izzan and the Huthi brothers, activism was a necessary defense against the palpable danger of Salafism, and it had an element of rescuing the faith, in the form of its youth, from gradual disappearance. Further, because it began in earnest after 1990 in the context of participatory politics, the younger generation's revival would also come to see the GoY as a potential antagonist because of its material neglect of the region and its tacit support of Wahhabist elements. As these issues were not resolved in subsequent years, they were irritants that produced conflict.

Fifth, like the Salafis and al-Haqq, the BY benefited from certain kinds of support from the GoY that was provided to nurture local influence in the absence of full governmental reach. Because it also provided patronage to GPC and Islah elements, as well as other Salafi activists, the GoY's strategy of patronage as a means of cooptation and control of multiple, conflicting groups engendered latent tensions in the small local society of Sa'da. These tensions were aggravated by the fact that some of those receiving GoY patronage—such as the BY—represented the younger generation, and this was considered a political affront in cultural terms by the older generation of *qabilis* and Hashimis. As we will see, tensions among different groups competing for local prominence and GoY patronage emerged as explicit conflict from the late 1990s until 2004. Thus, an additional by-product of local tensions and the regime's strategies was the perception that the GoY was a negative force in the region.

The Huthi Family

Finally, much more than al-Haqq, it is from the mid-1990s emergence of the BY that the story of ideological, social, and political Zaydi revivalism in Sa'da became the story of the Huthi family. Therefore, as a bridge to the next two chapters' focus on the armed conflict between the GoY and the Huthis, it is important to understand the structure

---

[48] See Yitzhak Nakash, *The Shi'is of Iraq* (Princeton, NJ: Princeton University Press, 1994); Yitzhak Nakash, *Reaching for Power: the Shi'a in the Modern Arab World* (Princeton, NJ: Princeton University Press, 2006).

of the Huthi family. Data regarding the members of the Huthi family and their relationships with other families are very limited. Because these relationships formed prior to the 2000s, this information has not figured prominently in reportage about the conflict. Further, for a researcher, inquiring of Yemeni informants about Huthi family members' ages, marriage patterns, familial relationships, life experiences prior to 2004, and internal conflicts is a very sensitive matter, potentially violating cultural norms about the sanctity and honor of individuals and the family (*sharaf* and *'ird*). Likewise, Yemenis from outside the family—including Sa'da residents—are often simply unaware or imprecise regarding family history details, and may be culturally reluctant to discuss them. Nevertheless, the Huthi family structure is extremely significant for the current conflict. The relationships emerging from that structure help to explain the Huthis' ability both to mobilize a core of adherents and to endure several years of conflict through reliance on a supportive periphery. Conversely, understanding the Huthi extended family structures and relationships in their sociocultural context strongly suggests that GoY COIN measures widen the circles of opposition to the regime.

Considered from the post-2004 vantage point, the Huthi family is—by Western terms—large, with over twenty people. It is also a multigenerational family. Equally significant for family longevity and conflict endurance, the Huthi family exhibits multiple age cohorts within the same generation. That is, while Badr al-Din and his brothers and cousins belong to the same generation, enough years separate their births that they belong to different age cohorts. This is even more the case with Badr al-Din's sons. Though of the same generation, 'Abd al-Malik is likely two decades younger than Husayn, for example, belonging to the same age cohort as Husayn's son. These intragenerational age cohort differences are due to Badr al-Din's four marriages over several decades, so that his family has several branches, although brothers consider each other "whole" siblings. Finally, in his marriage choices, Badr al-Din married both prominent *sharifas*—daughters of *sayyids*—as well as daughters of prominent local *qabili* shaykhs. His sons appear to have continued these marriage patterns. Husayn, for example, married both a *sharifa* and a shaykh's daughter, with the latter issue in turn being married to Yusuf al-Madani, a *qabili* and Huthi field commander.

From Badr al-Din al-Huthi to Husayn's offspring, the Huthis thus illustrate the consummate republican-era north Yemeni hybrid family. Including a representative number of Huthi family members, Table 3.1 demonstrates the degree and category of hybridity. It has been compiled based solely upon data at hand and does not account for male Huthis' marriage alliances or offspring that could not be verified through research. And, with the exception of one of Husayn al-Huthi's daughters, no data have come to light about Huthi family females, given the particularly sensitive nature of this topic. It is thus highly likely that the Huthi family's social hybridity is even broader than reflected here, taking advantage of the greater social intermixing described above.

Table 3.1
Huthi Family Hybridity

Confirmed Families	
Hashimi	**Qabili**
al-Huthi	Bani Bahr
al-'Ijri	Walad Yahya
al-Sittin	Madani
Husayn's first wife	Husayn's second wife
Yahya's wife	

Generations
Badr al-Din, his brother, and his cousins
Husayn, Yahya, Muhammad, Hamid, Ahmad, 'Abd al-Malik, etc.
'Abdullah Husayn, siblings, cousins; 'Abd al-Malik's offspring
Offspring of 'Abdullah Husayn, his sibling, and his cousins

Age Cohorts
Badr al-Din
Badr al-Din's siblings and cousins
Husayn, Yahya, Muhammad, Hamid, Ahmad
'Abd al-Malik, 'Abdullah Husayn
'Abdullah Husayn's and 'Abd al-Malik's offspring

Area of Activity			
Zaydi Marja'iya	**Zaydi Revival**	**Politics**	**Armed Action**
Badr al-Din	Muhammad, Hamid, Husayn, etc.	Husayn, Yahya	Husayn, Yahya, 'Abd al-Malik

The Huthi family therefore is more than just a social network. Rather, it manifests—and can take advantage of—a social network of multiple cross-cutting social networks in the Sa'da governorate. Some of these networks are *organic*—a product of the structures of the families linked to the Huthis—and other networks are *associational*, built on relationships established through travel and schooling in the 1980sand 1990s or through political and armed action in the 1990s and 2000s. And, while the organic social networks bring with them the prestige of prominent Hashimis or shaykhs, the associational networks possess the strength of shared affinities, experiences, and memories.

The ancestral home of the Huthi family is Dahyan, a *hijra* in the Majz *mudiriya*. Badr al-Din was born in Dahyan in 1922. His father, Amir al-Din al-Huthi (d. 1974), and his uncle Husayn al-Huthi (d. 1968) were highly esteemed Zaydi scholars, and

Badr al-Din completed his initial studies with them. Transferring to the *hijra* associated with Sa'da town, Badr al-Din studied with *sayyid* al-Mu'ayyidi and *sayyid* Ahmad bin 'Isa bin Zayd bin 'Ali. Emerging early as a highly qualified *'alim*, therefore, Badr al-Din was associated with the leading late-imamate names in Zaydi scholarship. As he began a career of teaching and writing, their prestige thus became his prestige.[49]

Sometime between his mid-twenties and early thirties, asthma and other respiratory difficulties led Badr al-Din to settle in the Marran area of Haydan, where he married the daughter of a Khawlan bin 'Amr shaykh from Bani Bahr. This marriage produced Husayn, Yahya, Ahmad, and 'Abd al-Qadir—who could thus appeal to tribal as well as *sayyid* prestige. A few years later, Badr al-Din married again, this time taking a wife from among the Dahyan-based al-Sittin *sayyid* family. Two sons, Muhammad and Hamid, were produced from this marriage. Broadly within the same age cohort, the offspring of the Bani Bahr and al-Sittin mothers—Husayn, Yahya, Ahmad, 'Abd al-Qadir, Muhammad, and Hamid—would be the Huthi sons to go to the new state schools and Zaydi revival schools. Active as leaders or teachers in the Shabab al-Mu'min, and intermixing with *qabilis, sayyids,* and traders from all over the *muhafaza*, this would also be the age cohort going on to political activism, providing the Huthi movement with its first "martyrs" (sing. *shahid*; pl. *shuhada'*) after 2004.

Badr al-Din married a third time probably over a decade later, producing two sons, Ibrahim and Amir al-Din, who has been imprisoned by the GoY. Badr al-Din's wife was *qabili*, from a Walad Yahya tribe of the Khawlan tribes in Marran. In his late fifties or early sixties, he then married his fourth wife. She was a member of the al-'Ijri family of *sayyids*. *Sayyid* al-'Ijri was a quite prominent Zaydi *'alim* from the Mashhad *hijra*. He had arbitrated resource disputes in the Sa'da basin, and Badr al-Din had cited him in his own writing.[50] Badr al-Din had at least five sons with this wife. An entirely different age cohort than the Huthis from the Bani Bahr and al-Sittin unions, among these children is 'Abd al-Malik, the current Huthi leader. Given their ages in the pre-teens to late teens during the 1990s, the Walad Yahya and al-'Ijri sons would have been students under BY leader tutelage at the schools and would have attended summer camps. They would not have been pre-2004 sociopolitical activists. 'Abd al-Malik, for example, was known more for his Zaydi religious studiousness than for his engagement with society in this era. Subsequent to 2004, in his late twenties or early thirties, his

---

[49] The background on Badr al-Din al-Huthi was gleaned from interviews with Yemenis, as well as "Huwa al-Sayyid al-'Allama al-Wali al-Wari' al-Zahid al-Sabir al-Mufassir Badr al-Din bin Amir al-Din bin al-Husayn bin Muhammad al-Huthi," undated document provided by Yemeni immigrant; 'Abd al-Karim Salam, "Man Huwwa al-Shaykh Badr al-Din al-Huthi," April 7, 2005; and al-Dughshi, "al-Zahira al-Huthiya"; al-Thulaya, "Sa'da Ta'rikh Mutamarrid." In our analysis of the Huthi family network of networks, we have made every effort to harmonize the often imprecise information culled from documents and informants. In the absence of absolute cetainty, we have nevertheless elected to include details for the sake of illustrating concepts that are reflective of kin and associational network in northern Yemen.

[50] Lichtenthäler, *Political Ecology,* 183.

combined Huthi-'Ijri *sayyid* pedigree has likely lent credibility to his leadership, since he has jumped the age cohort precedence appropriate to Arab culture (see Figures 3.1 and 3.2).

A genealogy-based analysis such as the one above does not account for the associational networks in which the Huthis might obtain tribal support from strong affinity-based relationships with 'Abdullah al-Razzami and 'Abd al-Karim Jadban or with other BY activists. Of course, associational networks can also emerge from shared antipathies, either toward local Sa'da actors or toward the GoY. Likewise, we noted above that the data providing a basis for this discussion do not depict the female Huthi contribution to network formation. Nor do they address the extent to which 'Ijri, Bani

Figure 3.1
Partial al-Huthi Family Picture, 1996

SOURCE: Yemeni national.

Figure 3.2
Al-Huthi Four-Family Network

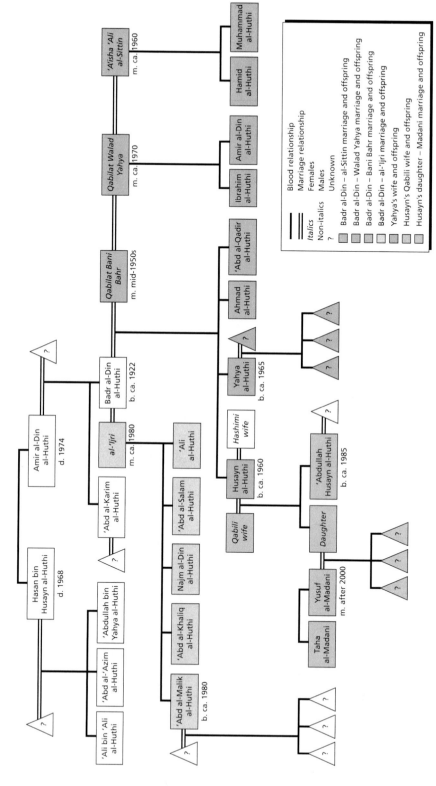

Bahr, and so forth—family members not related to Huthis by marriage—act as nodes, creating bridges to other social networks branching off from the four families from which Badr al-Din took wives.

Closer in, this general understanding of the Huthis' organic network of social networks should include other, more-distant Huthi family branches as latent nodes. In the Nazir *'uzla* of Razih, 'Ali bin 'Ali al-Huthi was active in the 1980s in providing Zaydi education to Razihis concerned about fending off the local Wahhabi threat.[51] Likewise, in the mid-1990s, rather than engaging in Salafi-Zaydi disputes, 'Abdullah bin Yahya al-Huthi, likely a cousin of Badr al-Din, moved to the Takhya *hijra* outside of Sa'da to study in seclusion.[52] Another Huthi *sayyid*, 'Abd al-'Azim, has been located in the Hamazat *hijra*. These "other" Huthis had not been associated with Zaydi revival or with the BY and had either been quietist scholars or less-scholarly *sayyids* living off land-based wealth in the Hamazat. After 2004, the regime frequently targeted them as "Huthis," at other times attempting to coopt them to GoY purposes. This was the case for 'Abd al-Karim al-Huthi, brother of Badr al-Din and uncle of Husayn, whom the GoY used at one point in mediation. Targeting and coopting has generally expanded the circle of anti-regime enmity both socially and geographically.[53]

Conclusion: Toward 2001

Toward the end of the 1990s, the BY began to recede as a dominant social force in northern Yemen. Local informants have suggested that the GoY began to fear the popularity of Somalia's al-Shabab and were reluctant to permit a genuine grassroots movement to grow to the point that it would decisively counter local Salafism, which the GoY wished to retain as an instrument of leverage. Other local observers feel that GPC- and Islah-affiliated local shaykhs resented the growing popularity of Badr al-Din's family. They may have found allies among those Hashimis who were 10–20 years older than Zaydi revival and BY leaders. These Hashimis, mostly from eastern Sa'da, may have felt that greater prestige was due to them rather than to younger upstarts from less-wealthy Hashimi and *qabili* families. These upstarts, such as Husayn al-Huthi and 'Abdullah al-Razzami, had also defeated more established shaykhs, such as 'Abdullah Rawkan and 'Abdullah Hamis al-'Awjari, in parliamentary elections. Those shaykhs—who would later side with the GoY after 2004, may have been receptive to the regime's efforts to reduce BY vitality in the late 1990s.[54]

---

[51] Weir, *A Tribal Order,* 298.

[52] Haykel, "A Zaydi Revival?" 21.

[53] Interview with UK academician studying northern Yemen, October 23, 2008.

[54] See "Al-Yaman al-Kubra . . . Tarwi Fusul al-Qissa al-Kamila li-Khanadiq al-Muwajahat fi Sa'da," *al-Yaman al-Kubra,* n.d.; and interview with Yemeni national from conflict area residing in the United States, October 29,

Another reason for decreased BY activities after 1997 may have also been differences of opinion among its initial leaders. These involved the degree of politicization appropriate for the Shabab. Likewise, given the diverse Hashimi and *qabili* complexion of the BY leaders, there were differences about the extent to which certain Zaydi ideas, such as *khuruj* or *sayyid* precedence in selection for the imam, should be taught to the youth. The GoY is said to have encouraged splits within the BY, offering members jobs in local administration. Muhammad 'Izzan, for example, received a job in the Sa'da municipality, running the government radio station, at the time the Huthi-regime conflict erupted in 2004.[55]

These developments occurred during the same time that increased violence swept through the region. GoY spokespeople have averred that high levels of violence are endemic to the backwards tribal north, where feuding and revenge cause chronic bloodshed.[56] Yet, the decade prior to Huthi-regime conflict appears to have witnessed more violence than usual. Part of this was due to Wahhabi-Zaydi tensions that erupted in bloodshed in parts of the governorate during the early 1990s.[57] By 1995, Wahhabi-related incidents had subsided but were replaced by violence whose substance and motives remain murky today. Some of this violence involved competition over access to economic resources and government patronage. Shaykh 'Awjari of Wa'ila Hamdan, for example, was the target of a land mine attack during this period because of his aggressive land acquisition efforts at the expense of Sahari shaykhs, and other feuds about access to land, control of roads, or political influence have also been noted.[58]

Beyond this, several Huthi-sympathetic sources report that throughout the 1990s the Huthi family itself was harassed by the GoY. This harassment reputedly included the use of criminal gangs to conduct automatic rifle and rocket attacks on Huthi family houses, targeting Husayn or Badr al-Din. These sources suggest that local military units intervened to have the perpetrators released from jail and that such intimidation drove Badr al-Din to flee to Saudi Arabia, Jordan, and then to Iran sometime between 1994 and 1999 before being summoned back to Yemen by President Saleh. External sources do not repeat these statements. Rather, their true value is likely the cultivation of a heroic memory of those years to justify enduring anti-GoY resistance. According to one Huthi personality, "we have, actually, been in an undeclared war [*harb ghayr*

2008; Interview with Yemeni associated with Huthi leadership residing in Germany, February 2, 2009; consultation with American political scientist working on Yemen, September 10, 2008.

[55] Interview with Yemeni associated with Huthi leadership residing in Germany, February 2, 2009; "Yemen: The Conflict in Saada Governorate," Integrated Regional Information Networks (IRIN), July 24, 2008.

[56] Interview with senior GoY official in Yemeni Embassy, Washington, D.C., September 11, 2008.

[57] See Shelagh Weir, "A Clash of Fundamentalisms: Wahhabism in Yemen," *Middle East Report* 204 (July–September 1997).

[58] Lichtenthäler, *Political Ecology,* 60–62.

muʿlana] ever since we formed the al-Haqq party in 1991."[59] Therefore, even if claims of GoY anti-Huthi or anti-Zaydi violence during the late 1990s are untrue or exaggerated, by the time Husayn al-Huthi left for schooling in the Sudan in 1999, events had left the region entirely unsettled—while the BY's "alumni" and its broader demographic base remained available for further mobilization.

---

[59] Interview with Yemeni associated with Huthi leadership residing in Germany, February 2, 2009.

CHAPTER FOUR

From Tension to Confrontation: Triggers of Conflict, 2001–2004

In this chapter, we explore the proximate causes and triggers of the regime-Huthi conflict, in the Sa'da governorate and at the national level in Yemen. This will enable us to examine in detail the course of the "Sa'da wars" (June 2004–mid-2010) through an interpretive lens analyzing GoY measures in terms of counterinsurgency lines of operation. These measures have sustained Huthi resistance, which over time might evolve toward insurgency. In the present chapter, we grapple with the question of why the GoY and Huthis broke from accepted and time-tested modes of regime-periphery relations in 2004 and chose violent and enduring conflict to solve differences. We will approach this question from the vantage point of two vignettes.

In 1986, a disagreement between Hashid and Khawlan bin 'Amr tribesmen in Sa'da resulted in the murder of two of the latter. The Hashidi culprits were jailed, but material compensation was rejected by the deceased men's tribe, the Bani Mu'adh of Sahar. Rather, they opted for blood revenge, or *tha'r*, and requested that the two Hashidi perpetrators be put to death. At this point, Hashidi *shaykh al-mashayikh* 'Abdullah al-Ahmar intervened. Representing both GoY and Hashidi interests, he objected to *tha'r*. Perceiving such an outcome to violate collective Bani Mu'adh *sharaf*, the victims' relatives broke into the prison where the Hashidi offenders were being held and exacted revenge, sheltering there afterwards. Exposed as unable to control its own institutions in the area, the GoY was criticized by Hashidis as impotent. Further, when summoned to the capital to answer for his kin's actions, the shaykh of Bani Mu'adh refused to do so, allegedly saying "we will not answer to the government." The army, responding to this rejection of GoY authority, surrounded the prison with tanks, and both sides vowed to fight to the end. Regime-periphery conflict was averted, however, when the Bani Mu'adh shaykh intervened again and persuaded his kin to give themselves up. Taken to San'a, they were sentenced to death—whereupon the shaykh traveled to San'a, confronted President Saleh, and secured his men's release. Ultimately, then, the state had abjured violence, while the Bani Mu'adh had affirmed *qabili* autonomy and improved relations with the president.[1]

Six years later, in 1992, a group of shaykhs was meeting in Sha'ara town in *mudiriyat* Razih to discuss an unresolved murder when they were surprised by the unannounced appearance of 20 Yemeni Army gun trucks and mechanized vehicles. Since tribes were used to prior government notification of visits or military vehicle passage, "this was a flagrant breach of the usual courtesies" of northern Yemeni *qabyala*. Continuing on to al-Nazir, the vehicles parked near the telephone exchange, and troops took up positions in surrounding buildings. Ostensibly, they had come based on a rumor that a descendent of the last imam had returned from abroad and was receiving shelter from the local shaykh, a known Zaydi loyalist. It is more likely that the GoY wished to flex its muscles as the untrammeled ruler of its periphery in an area of Wahhabi-Zaydi conflict. "Asserting their steadfast adherence to tribal values and leadership," Naziri *qabilis* placed armed men on roofs above the troops, with weapons aimed at the GoY soldiers. Shortly thereafter, the local shaykh returned from Sha'ara in his own convoy of armed kinsmen, joining the tense stalemate. Violence did not ensue, however. Local tribals were "terrified that someone might fire and shed blood," and took pains to enforce discipline on each other, to avoid an escalation of force. Restraint was exercised on both sides, to the extent that Naziris provided food and water to the GoY's soldiers. The military finally broke off its siege but demanded that the shaykh return with the column to Sa'da city. The local tribe rejected this demand: "it would have insulted tribal honor" to be led out in figurative chains by the army. After the army had been totally removed from the area, the shaykh went by himself to Sa'da, met with officials, and returned to Nazir. His—and his tribe's—*sharaf* and *asl* had been preserved, while his *wazn* and *wajh* had grown. Again, regime-periphery conflict had been avoided.[2]

These two vignettes illustrate instances in which the regime and its geopolitical periphery in Sa'da came to the brink of armed conflict but then stepped back, with local-to-national ties strengthened and the prestige of local leaders increased. In particular, there emerged in both cases an awareness of a customary etiquette of state-tribe interaction in Yemen: GoY authority is negotiated and conditional upon respect for autonomy and the appearance of tribal/shaykh inviolability. Furthermore, although both sides affirmed the capability for violence, they took pains to avoid a clash. In this respect, northern Yemeni cultural values that conduce toward violence were tempered by others that prevent or contain conflict. By contrast, in 2004, conflict containment failed. To understand why, we must look to three sets of factors: dynamics internal to

---

[1]   This sequence of events is narrated in Gerhard Lichtenthäler, *Political Ecology and the Role of Water: Environment, Society, and Economy in Northern Yemen* (Surrey, UK: Ashgate Publishing, 2003), 59–60.

[2]   This episode is narrated in Shelagh Weir, *A Tribal Order: Politics and Law in the Mountains of Yemen* (Austin: University of Texas Press, 2007), 301–302. All quotations related to this episode are from this source.

Sa'da society, factors involving the actions and motives of Husayn al-Huthi and his associates, and finally—and perhaps most significantly—the attitude of the GoY leadership to challenges on the periphery in the context of evolving global challenges and opportunities.

Sa'da in the New Millennium

By 2000, the dynamic and liberating aspects of the Zaydi revival had diminished. Though still in existence, al-Haqq was not able to mobilize those rising segments of the Sa'da population discussed in Chapter Three and was no longer a target of GoY blandishments. Furthermore, with the departure from parliament of people like Husayn al-Huthi and 'Abdullah al-Razzami, other status quo candidates among Sa'da's wealthier and Sunni-friendly families had entered parliament, through GPC or Islah, likely exerting less effort toward redressing developmental imbalances in the governorate. Rather, as suggested in Chapter Three, local economic elites and shaykhs tied to the political center through patronage were less concerned about Sa'da matters or the collective well-being of their communities. Likewise, GoY-Saudi efforts to reduce the weapons trade and the export of *qat* also targeted economic pursuits important to the region.[3] The effects of peripheral marginalization in terms of social welfare and governmental development presence were likely felt more strongly in this period as well, because of reduced remittances and less international aid, San'a's privileging of the center, and a perception in Sa'da that it was not receiving its fair share of government attention. [4]

Therefore, while the motive forces for Zaydi revival and the demographic base for social activism persisted in Sa'da, their means for mobilization and expression were occluded by traditional patronage politics, diverting local elites' attention at the same time that the perception of local deprivation continued. Further, because of social changes since the 1980s and the experience with non-elder, non-elite–driven social activism from the BY in the 1990s, it is likely that loyalty to traditional elites, while still present, had been attenuated by 2000. Similarly, the devotion to social norms emphasizing the minimization of conflict and dissent may have weakened among those who

---

[3]   See Ahmed al-Haj, "Yemen, Saudis Join to Stem Weapons Trade," *Yemen Times* 13:679 (October 23, 2003). For *qat*, see, for example, Wafeq Shadhili, "Wheat or Qat!" *Yemen Times* 15:1133 (February 28, 2008).

[4]   In addition to post-1990 reduced remittances due to labor repatriation, the $70 million U.S. aid package was eliminated. By 1996, the U.S. Agency for International Development (USAID) mission had shut down in San'a, and European Union countries' aid also remained low, not increasing markedly until after 2003. See Adel al-Solwi, "Shabakat al-Ta'awun al-Duwali Tuhaqqiq Ziyada Naw'iya fi 'Adad al-Manihin bi-Miqdar al-Du'f khilal Sanawat al-Wahda," *SabaNet*, May 18, 2009; Noman Kassim al-Madaghi, *Yemen and the United States: A Study of a Small Power and Super-State Relationship, 1962–1994* (London: IB Tauris, 1994), 132–135; Alfred B. Prados and Jeremy M. Sharp, *Yemen: Current Conditions and U.S. Relations,* CRS Report for Congress, January 4, 2007, 6.

had reached their teens to late twenties.[5] In the absence of credible leaders among the established elites, reactions to perceived material deprivation and Zaydi political-cultural marginalization would be aggravated by larger regional and global conditions, and would be in search of an outlet. These conditions came to pass after September 11, 2001, and the outlet came in the form of the charismatic personality of Husayn al-Huthi.

Sa'da Dissent and Husayn al-Huthi as Mobilizer and Ideologue

In 2000, Husayn al-Huthi returned to Sa'da, having completed studies toward a master's degree in Qur'anic sciences at a Sudanese university. Perceiving the decline in BY momentum, he probably chose to reinvigorate ideological activities in the Zaydi schools of Marran, Dahyan, and Harf Sufyan. It is also reported that, after returning from Sudan, he and his earlier BY colleagues worked to steer the curricula of Sa'da-area government schools in more of a Zaydi-revivalist direction.[6] Husayn's efforts to collect funds for other educational centers, as well as for local social welfare initiatives, have also been noted during this period, likely increasing his prestige among the area populace and cultivating in him a desire to return to politics, perhaps with the hope of reentering parliament or the local administration.[7]

Shortly thereafter, Husayn found himself in the midst of a shifting regional order. As we shall see below, after 9/11, U.S. policies toward the Middle East and Yemen were driven by the global war on terror (GWoT), and President Saleh, for his own reasons, came out in support of the United States. From late fall 2001, Arab Muslims in Sa'da encountered on television and the Internet images of civilian deaths, U.S. troops violating Islamic values, and Muslims being rounded up en masse and sent to Guantanamo Bay. At this time, the Sa'da governorate was represented in San'a by old-guard shaykhs beholden to Saleh through ties of *mahsubiya*. Yemenis in this region, as elsewhere, thus lacked a participatory outlet through which to channel grievances.[8] However, Sa'da-area marginalization and disappointment with the stalled democratization gained a new dimension in the context of U.S.-Yemeni security cooperation, which was highly unpopular throughout the country. After the U.S. invasion of Iraq, such cooperation became even more odious to many Yemenis, who nurtured fraternal feelings for Iraq and its regime going back to the 1980s and 1990s. Yemeni unhappiness with the GoY's relationship with the United States thus presented Husayn al-Huthi with a lever to agi-

---

[5]   Interview with American political scientist, September 10, 2008.

[6]   See Muhammad al-Ahmadi, "Min Ab'ad Fitnat Husayn al-Huthi–2: al-Huthi, Ara'uhu wa Mu'taqadatuhu," *Ahl al-Bayt*, May 30, 2005.

[7]   Consultations with Yemeni from the Sa'da area residing in the United States, October and November 2008.

[8]   See Jillian Schwedler, "Yemen's Aborted Opening," *Journal of Democracy* 13:4 (2002), 33–44.

tate and motivate his audiences—a lever that cut across tribal and socioeconomic lines, just as the original BY had.

By virtue of his last name, Husayn al-Huthi already had a natural audience within the Sa'da governorate. Indeed, he came from a socially and religiously respected family and was deemed by many to be an *'allama* (learned one).[9] This designation granted Husayn credibility with his audiences, which initially likely consisted of earlier BY members. These audiences had been exposed to original Zaydi awakening literature written by Badr al-Din al-Huthi and his colleagues—although the messages in Husayn's lectures go far beyond the messages of his father's writings. Further, Husayn was able to preach both as a scholar, given his family ties and learning lineage, and as a "warrior," since he could adapt Islamic teachings to real-world scenarios.[10] From this position, Husayn could credibly employ religious discursive forms—historically powerful instruments for Islamic mobilization across the region—to catalyze already-simmering dissent in the governorate.

Methods, Occasions, and Locations

The manner in which Husayn's lectures were delivered, recorded, and circulated meant that his audience transcended local Zaydis inclined to heed a traditional religious *'allama*, allowing those with little formal education to access them. Husayn spoke in a number of settings—from classrooms in religious schools and mosques to sitting rooms in houses—and his lectures and lessons were recorded onto cassette tapes and circulated both within and beyond the confines of the Sa'da governorate. Roughly three years after they had been recorded—after he had been "martyred" at the hands of the GoY in September 2004—a number of his lectures and lessons were both transcribed and also converted to MP3s for electronic distribution. Ultimately, these methods allowed Husayn's teachings to reach individuals beyond his immediate audience and steadfast followers. Husayn's lectures were thus canonized, assisting his growing popularity and local prestige during his lifetime. Further, the continuing preservation and dissemination of his lectures (and interviews) after his death allowed him to reach Zaydis from beyond the grave while also ensuring that the latter would interpret his words in the context of subsequent Huthi ideological communication. In this respect, the Huthi phenomenon connects with other religious revivalist movements in the Middle East, where circulating religious discourse in this manner has been

---

[9]   See, for example, the Hizb al-Haqq Web site, which depicts Husayn as a "symbol of the party" alongside respected Zaydi scholars.

[10]   This distinction is made in Patrick Gaffney, *The Prophet's Pulpit: Islamic Preaching in Contemporary Egypt* (Berkeley, Calif.: University of California Press, 1994).

common since the 1970s to draw attention to sociopolitical grievances and galvanize supporters.[11]

While each of Husayn's lectures was recorded, distributed, and circulated, the occasions on which they were delivered are also significant, because they set the stage for confrontation with state authorities who found themselves in a lose-lose situation. First, many of Husayn's lectures were delivered as *khutab* (sermons; sing. *khutba*) on Fridays (*yawm ʿal-jumʿa,*—literally, day of gathering). A number of these lectures were delivered in his home area of the Marran mountains and the city of Dahyan in the Saʿda governorate. The use of Friday sermons is significant, because they traditionally have served as public forums that could easily be utilized by opinion makers seeking to inspire opposition and mobilize dissent.[12] In addition to Fridays, Husayn could utilize other occasions to set the stage for confrontation with the state—among them, al-Ghadir Day (*ʿId al-Ghadir*), the Prophet Muhammad's Birthday (*al-mawlid al-nabawi*), and International Jerusalem Day (*yawm al-Quds al-ʿalami*).

Husayn al-Huthi's use of these holidays to decry GoY actions and mobilize supporters illustrates his calculations and highlights the local friction between Zaydis and Wahhabis, as well as between Zaydis and the state. Indeed, Husayn built on the work of his father, Badr al-Din al-Huthi, who was a strong proponent of Zaydi revivalism as a response to Wahhabi encroachment. The exaltation of al-Ghadir Day, which marks the day on which the Prophet Muhammad declared ʿAli to be his successor, indicates Husayn's appeal to specifically Shiʿite rituals, creating a natural dichotomy between his followers and those of Wahhabi doctrine. Celebrating the Prophet's Birthday—while not a specifically Shiʿite practice—further highlights the differences with Wahhabis, who declare the celebration to be *haram* (forbidden). Finally, International Jerusalem Day, while not necessarily contested by Wahhabis, provided Husayn with the ideal atmosphere to lambaste American and Israeli policy, allowing him to begin to monopolize oppositionist discourse in the region.

Likely due both to the messages being touted by Husayn and to the significance of these occasions themselves, the Yemeni authorities began to intervene to prevent their celebration. Such intervention on the part of the state had many dimensions. For one, because two of these occasions were also contested by Wahhabis, state intervention made the regime appear to be in line with the Wahhabis and against the Zaydi religion as a whole. Additionally, regime intervention on International Jerusalem Day made the GoY appear motivated to protect American—and by extension Israeli—interests, rather than those of Muslims. Both of these actions played directly into the messages in Husayn's lectures, placing the GoY in a difficult position wherein intervention would be interpreted as symbolizing its alliance with Wahhabis or America, and

---

[11]   See for example, Dale F. Eickelman and James Piscatori, *Muslim Politics* (Princeton, NJ: Princeton University Press, 1996), 125–127.

[12]   See Gaffney, *The Prophet's Pulpit*.

nonintervention would mean sitting idly by while Husayn al-Huthi's local prestige and mobilizational capacity grew. These occasions would continue to be significant throughout the conflict's five phases because they were locally known days during which gatherings could easily be organized, lectures delivered, and masses mobilized.

We here examine Husayn al-Huthi's seminal lectures.[13] They include the following:

- "Imran Chapter, from Verse 33 to Verse 91, the 13th Lesson" (delivered November 7, 2003; transcribed September 6, 2007).
- "God's Knowledge, God's Sublimity" (delivered January 25, 2002; transcribed March 1, 2004).
- "There Is No Excuse for Mankind in Front of God" (delivered March 5, 2002; transcribed March 1, 2004).
- "Qur'anic Culture" (delivered August 4, 2002; transcribed March 1, 2004).
- "The Danger of America's Entering Yemen" (delivered February 3, 2002; transcribed September 23, 2006).
- "A Scream in the Face of the Arrogant" (delivered January 17, 2002; transcribed March 1, 2004).
- "Terrorism and Peace" (delivered March 7, 2002; transcribed September 23, 2006).

Themes, Messages, and Motifs in Husayn al-Huthi's Lectures

Muslim Humiliation, Revivalism, and Unity. Husayn al-Huthi makes regular references to the idea that the Muslim world is in a state of weakness, "under the feet of the Jews and Christians."[14] Indeed, al-Huthi notes that Muslims have "lost the wisdom, and returned to illiteracy . . . despite the existence of the holy Qur'an . . . despite the fact that we can read and write."[15] In Husayn's view, this state of weakness is anathema to historical tradition, since he points out that when the Jews lived under the Arabs, they were "unable . . . to found a state."[16] He further invokes examples from the Qur'an to point out that even in a state of weakness, Muslims can overcome adversity.[17] Being in such a position is unfounded, according to Husayn, because one must

---

[13] The sample used for this study includes lectures recommended by a Yemeni national and touted by Yemeni Web denizens. See post by 'Ali al-Hadirmi, "Jum' Muhadarat wa Durus Husayn Badr al-Din al-Huthi" (A Collection of Husayn Badr al-Din al-Huthi's Lectures), *Majalis al-Muhammad*, posted May 9, 2006. See Appendix C for a description of the lectures.

[14] Husayn Badr al-Din al-Huthi, "La 'Adhr lil Jumi' Amam Allah" (There Is No Excuse for Mankind in Front of God).

[15] Husayn Badr al-Din al-Huthi, "al-Thaqafa al-Qur'aniya" (Qur'anic Culture).

[16] Husayn Badr al-Din al-Huthi, "al-Thaqafa al-Qur'aniya."

[17] Husayn Badr al-Din al-Huthi, "al-Thiqafa al-Qur'aniya."

understand that God "presides over everything," even Western leaders, and thus those leaders should not be feared.[18]

Furthermore, while acknowledging that "It is clear in front of us collectively that Israel is powerful over the Arabs . . . [and] that Jews and Christians are the masters of Muslims," Husayn al-Huthi regularly alludes to the idea that the Shiʻa, rather than the Sunnis or al-Qaʻida, are the true targets of Israeli-American hegemony.[19] Indeed, Husayn al-Huthi argues:

> Usama and the Taliban are not the ones being targeted. The event that occurred in New York is not what motivated America. Who knows, the American intelligence could be the ones who carried out that event, to create justifications and clear the air for them to strike those who really form a danger to them, and they are the Shiʻa, they are the Shiʻa.[20]

Furthermore, Husayn refers specifically to the current weakness of Zaydis in the region, noting, for example, "the Wahhabis were able to call [Salafi military commander and relative of President Saleh] ʻAli Muhsin directly," whereas the Zaydis are left without a government official to support them.[21]

Accordingly, Husayn prescribes a return to Islam—what he refers to as "Qurʼanic Culture"—to bring the Islamic world back to its rightful place. Indeed, Husayn encourages those seeking peace and security to return to religion and derive their power from its teachings. Within this context, Husayn constantly refers to the potential strength of the Muslim world, noting "if the [Arab] leaders united, they would be able to strike Israel."[22] Finally, Husayn argues that Islam is supreme, reciting the verse from the Qurʼan, "If anyone desires a religion other than Islam (submission to Allah), never will it be accepted of him; and in the Hereafter He will be in the ranks of those who have lost (all spiritual good)" (3:85).[23] In Husayn's view, it is not just desirable that Muslims return to their faith; rather, he argues that they have a responsibility to do so and possess the potential to defeat "Islam's enemies."

Husayn's ideas on Islamic unity appear somewhat contradictory. On the one hand, he laments that "Sunnis want to convert the Shiʻa, and the Shiʻa are keen to convert the Sunnis to Shiʻism . . . and Twelvers want to convert Zaydis to Twelverism."[24] On

---

[18] Husayn Badr al-Din al-Huthi, "al-Sarakha fi Wajh al-Mustakbirin" (A Scream in the Face of the Arrogant).

[19] Husayn Badr al-Din al-Huthi, "La ʻAdhr lil Jumiʻ Amam Allah."

[20] Husayn Badr al-Din al-Huthi, "al-Sarakha fi Wajh al-Mustakbirin."

[21] Husayn Badr al-Din al-Huthi, "Khatir Dukhul Amrika al-Yemen" (The Danger of America's Entering Yemen).

[22] Husayn Badr al-Din al-Huthi, "al-Thaqafa al-Qurʼaniya."

[23] Cited in: Husayn Badr al-Din al-Huthi, "Surat al-ʻImran min al-Ayyat 33 Ila al-Ayyat 91 [al-Dars al-Thalith ʻashr]" (Imran Chapter, from Verse 33 to Verse 91, the 13th lesson [Yusuf Ali Translation of Qurʼan]).

[24] Husayn Badr al-Din al-Huthi, "al-Sarakha fi Wajh al-Mustakbirin."

the other hand, Husayn does not avoid drawing attention to past Wahhabi encroachments on Zaydism in Saʿda, claiming that "the true terrorists are the Wahhabis that . . . emanated from this mosque and that village, this school and that institute, to incite . . . enmity and hate . . . to indoctrinate the sons of Muslims."[25] Husayn is careful to balance these past tensions with his current call for Islamic unity, however. He asks, "did we not cheer when we saw them taking Wahhabis into custody in Yemen?"[26] Thus, in the interest of unity and confronting American hegemony, Husayn notes that "we condemn taking anyone into custody, under the accusation that he is a terrorist against America."[27]

America, Israel, and Arab Complicity. As a whole, Husayn al-Huthi's lectures mercilessly denigrate Jewish, Christian, and Zionist "conspiracies" against the Muslim world. Indeed, Husayn refers to the "Zionist entity" as a "cancer," while referring to America as "the Great Satan."[28] The anti-American and anti-Israeli motif in Husayn al-Huthi's lectures is epitomized by the slogan (*shiʿar*) chanted at the end of nearly all of his sermons: "Death to America, Death to Israel, Curse Upon the Jews, Victory for Islam" (*al-Mawt li Amrika al-Mawt li Israʾil al-Laʿna ʿala-l-Yahud, al-Nasr li-l-Islam*). This slogan was first chanted collectively at Imam Hadi school in the Marran mountains on January 17, 2002.[29]

Although the chant would go on to become an emblem of the broader Huthi movement, giving the GoY and policymakers alike warranted alarm, it is important to note the original context and seeming intent behind its use. After highlighting the Muslim world's current weakness vis-à-vis the West, Husayn asks rhetorically, "What do we do?" He answers, "I say to you, oh brothers, yell . . . *God Is Great, Death to America, Death to Israel, Curse Upon the Jews, Victory for Islam*."[30] The hope Husayn expresses, however, is not that this slogan will incite acts of violence per se, but that it will create "discontent that the Jews avoid."[31] Indeed, Husayn notes that such slogans "from Americans'—the Christians' and Jews'—point of view . . . form an extreme danger to them."[32] Finally, Huthi instructs his followers to "act in this way . . . in our meetings, after Friday prayers," and to be "pioneers" of the slogan.[33] Examining the original context of the slogan, it becomes clear that Husayn al-Huthi intended it as a

---

[25] Husayn Badr al-Din al-Huthi, "al-Sarakha fi Wajh al-Mustakbirin."

[26] Husayn Badr al-Din al-Huthi, "al-Sarakha fi Wajh al-Mustakbirin."

[27] Husayn Badr al-Din al-Huthi, "al-Sarakha fi Wajh al-Mustakbirin."

[28] See Husayn Badr al-Din al-Huthi, "Khatir Dukhul Amrika al-Yemen" and "al-Sarakha fi Wajh al-Mustakbirin."

[29] See transcriber's footnote in: Husayn Badr al-Din al-Huthi, "al-Sarakha fi Wajh al-Mustakbirin."

[30] Husayn Badr al-Din al-Huthi, "al-Sarakha fi Wajh al-Mustakbirin."

[31] Husayn Badr al-Din al-Huthi, "al-Sarakha fi Wajh al-Mustakbirin."

[32] Husayn Badr al-Din al-Huthi, "al-Sarakha fi Wajh al-Mustakbirin."

[33] Husayn Badr al-Din al-Huthi, "al-Sarakha fi Wajh al-Mustakbirin."

rallying cry through which he could capitalize on anti-U.S. sentiment while also giving his followers a way of identifying with one another in his absence. This notion is further reflected in another Husayn al-Huthi lecture in which he notes that the goal of the slogan is to "ingrain in the minds of Muslims that America is the criminal terrorist, that America is evil, that Jews and Christians are evil . . ."[34] While the slogan certainly seems incendiary, it is important to note that such sentiment fell, and continues to fall, within the normal discursive parameters of Friday sermons in Yemen and the broader Arab world.[35]

Husayn also alludes to Arab governments throughout a number of his lectures. Indeed, Huthi criticizes Sunni Arab leaders' complicity in America's agenda, noting "Jews know that the Sunnis will not pose any danger to them . . . are the leaders of the Islamic world today not Sunni? Are they not the ones who agreed, who hurried to agree, that America is to lead the world against what is referred to as terrorism?"[36] Husayn rarely calls out President Saleh directly, noting instead that "they [Arab rulers] have become more harmonized with America, with America's policy."[37] He further claims that blind obedience to these rulers is not necessary, given their disconnect from their respective populations.[38] Indeed, as Husayn points out, "if the issue of confronting Israel were brought to a popular referendum . . . [the people] would vote 90 percent in favor of confronting America and Israel."[39]

A Call to Action: Iran, Khomeini, and Hizbullah as Models of Resistance. Husayn al-Huthi uniformly rejects those who look at events for the "sake of analyses, news for the sake of news."[40] Instead, he encourages Muslims to take a stand against Western hegemony in the Arab world and support those who fight America and Israel. He supports this idea by claiming, "Islam is the religion of peace . . . but not in the meaning of closing the files of war with the enemies of God."[41] Indeed, from Husayn's perspective *jihad* is necessary on the part of the Muslims to combat Islam's enemies, because anything less would constitute surrender in the face of American hegemony.

Within this context, it is worth exploring Huthi's references to Iran and Hizbullah, which are made in a number of his lectures. Husayn regularly cites statements

---

34 Husayn Badr al-Din al-Huthi, "al-Irhab wa al-Salam" (Terrorism and Peace).

35 These discursive parameters had been established over a decade before, as Islamists confronted U.S. presence in the region. See, for example, James Piscatori, ed., *Islamic Fundamentalisms and the Gulf Crisis* (Chicago: University of Chicago Press, 1991), 1–28 in particular.

36 Husayn Badr al-Din al-Huthi, "al-Sarakha fi Wajh al-Mustakbirin."

37 Husayn Badr al-Din al-Huthi, "al-Thaqafa al-Qur'aniya."

38 Husayn Badr al-Din al-Huthi, "al-Thaqafa al-Qur'aniya."

39 Husayn Badr al-Din al-Huthi, "al-Thiqafa al-Qur'aniya."

40 Husayn Badr al-Din al-Huthi, "al-Thaqafa al-Qur'aniya."

41 Husayn Badr al-Din al-Huthi, "al-Thaqafa al-Qur'aniya."

made by Imam Khomeini in support of his arguments. For example, Huthi credited Khomeini with referring to the United States as the "Great Satan,"[42] while also quoting his opinion that "America and Israel are planning to take over the holy sites."[43] Thus, he looks to Iran as an example of strength in the Muslim world, compared to its Sunni Arab counterparts. With respect to Hizbullah, he describes them as the "head of *mujahidin* in this world, they are the ones who present martyrs, the ones who truly preserve the water of the face of the *umma*."[44] While Husayn makes reference to Iran and Hizbullah, he does so from the perspective that they stand up to the "enemies of Islam," a view widely held in the Arab world.

As we saw in Chapter Two, and as scholarship examining the trajectory of Islamic fundamentalism has noted,[45] the Iranian revolution inspired both Zaydis and Sunni Islamists in the region. While Husayn does not advocate abiding by the edicts of the Iranian *marja'iya* or condone *wilayat al-faqih*, his references to Iran and Hizbullah are based on the idea that they are currently the pillars of opposition to Western hegemony in the Arab world. Indeed, Iran and Hizbullah represent the rejection of U.S. intervention in the region during a time of perceived Arab regime collaboration and cooperation with the West. As such, it is important to assess Husayn's Iran and Hizbullah references as an affirmation of their anti-U.S. posturing rather than an endorsement of a religious ideology outside of Zaydism.

What Did Husayn Want?

An analysis of Husayn Badr al-Din al-Huthi's speeches that were delivered between 2002 and 2003 indicates that they appear to be typical—albeit somewhat more confrontational—manifestations of anti-U.S. sentiment present throughout the region during this time period. While the Huthi slogan is certainly provocative, it falls into the discursive parameters of *khutab* in mosques across Yemen and the Arab world writ large. In the lectures sampled, Husayn does not make any outlandish claims, such as being the hidden Imam, nor does he call for the return of the Imamate to Northern Yemen. Furthermore, within the sample we surveyed, Husayn's only reference to Twelver Shi'ism is the pejorative claim that Twelvers have attempted to convert Zaydis. While Husayn does reference Zaydism, he does so to point out its relative weakness and the lack of Zaydi cohesion when compared to Wahhabism. In doing so, Husayn does not appear to encourage the return of the pre-1962 Zaydi Imamate. Additionally, Husayn never explicitly calls on his followers to take up arms against the Yemeni state. Rather, he appears to be more concerned with confronting the "Jewish" enemies of Islam. Particularly telling in this regard is Husayn al-Huthi's 2004 open letter to

---

[42] Husayn Badr al-Din al-Huthi, "al-Irhab wa al-Salam."

[43] Husayn Badr al-Din al-Huthi, "al-Sarakha fi Wajh al-Mustakbirin."

[44] Husayn Badr al-Din al-Huthi, "al-Sarakha fi Wajh al-Mustakbirin."

[45] Gilles Kepel, *Jihad: The Trail of Political Islam* (London: I.B. Taurus, 2002).

President Saleh, in which he assures the president that "I do not work against you, I appreciate you and what you do tremendously, but what I do is my solemn national duty against the enemy of Islam . . . America and Israel."[46]

Husayn's approach to criticizing the Saleh regime is also nuanced, reflecting both his sensitivities and his calculations. Indeed, had he directly attacked the republic, he could easily have been accused of seeking to overthrow it, threatening Yemeni unity. Instead, Husayn mentions the Yemeni regime only in conjunction with other Arab rulers. Husayn's discursive habit of portraying Arab rulers as well-meaning leaders unaware of the realities facing the Muslim *umma* gives his words an advisory tone, making them less confrontational and thus more palatable for the GoY. That being said, his vague references to Arab leaders are clearly veiled condemnations of the Saleh regime.

Whether or not Husayn had any motives or goals beyond capitalizing on anti-American sentiment to increase his local prestige and religious identity is difficult to say. While he certainly expresses his support for groups such as Hizbullah, there was no structured "Huthi" organization at the time of these lectures. While government reports claim that Husayn was founding schools and collecting money as early as 1997, it is difficult to know whether he was doing so to lay the foundations for a more formal organization or merely to encourage religious revivalism.[47] Indeed, the establishment of parallel, "popular" religious institutions is a phenomenon that is not particularly new or unique to Yemen or the Arab world.[48] How the resulting networks could be utilized in times of armed conflict, however, became quite apparent once the first war broke out.

Because we do not know what "the Huthis" wanted in 2002–2004, we must speculate about Husayn's interests. Having served in parliament from 1993 to 1997 but now facing incumbents from the GPC with GoY support as well as tribal or mercantile backing, he may have sought to mobilize enough BY alumni and younger voters to support him in elections after 2003, thus countering support for opponents through emotive discourse on hot-button issues. In this respect, it is not known whether he supported his brother Yahya's successful 2003 GPC candidacy as an extension of his own efforts or whether he wanted to join him in parliament. At the same time, Husayn was likely earnestly committed to Zaydi religious revival and the defense of communal interests in Sa'da and perhaps hoped to use the "bully pulpit" and enduring Huthi prestige to galvanize a BY reemergence. In this respect, it is quite possible that beyond

[46] Mohammed bin Sallam, "200 Killed or Wounded: Al-Hothy Appeals," *Yemen Times*, June 30, 2004.

[47] See "Jama'at al-Huthi Shirdhimat Irhabiya Tastahdif al-Wahda wa al-Jumhuriya wa Yajib Hasmha: 26 Sebtember net Tunshir Nass Taqrir al-Aman al-Qawmi al-Muqaddam Ila Majlis al-Nuwwab wa al-Shura Hawl Ahdath al-Fitna fi Sa'da," *26 September*, February 15, 2007.

[48] As an example, see Carrie Rosefsky-Wickham, *Mobilizing Islam: Religion, Activism, and Political Change in Egypt* (New York: Columbia University Press, 2002).

the events after 2001—in particular the U.S. invasion of Afghanistan and Iraq, as well as Israeli military operations in the West Bank during "the Second Intifada"— genuinely disturbed Husayn to the point of inciting his followers. Of course, political opportunism and genuine feeling probably fused for him in this period.

Beyond these mundane goals, more-extensive hopes have been imputed to Husayn. GoY sources have spoken of a conspiracy to reestablish the Zaydi imamate or hoodwink Zaydis into unwitting conversion to Twelver Shi'ism.[49] While we will return to GoY propaganda later, it has also been suggested that Husayn wanted a wider role in Sa'da and San'a and was angling for greater attention and cooptation by Saleh. In this understanding, Husayn's post-Sudan charitable efforts, including collecting funds for schools, local electrification, clean water supplies, and so forth, were not intended in the first instance to build a Huthist insurgent base. Rather, these efforts provided him with a fair amount of material means, local prestige, and social influence, rivaling (at least in Haydan and other Huthi ancestral areas) that of the Sa'da governor and other GoY representatives. Therefore, Husayn may have hoped to garner Saleh's support and enter into a customary neopatrimonial relationship. This would perhaps have resulted in appointment as governor of Sa'da at the same time as his brother was an MP in San'a. *Mahsubiya* for both Husayn and Yahya would have thus permitted both greater momentum to Zaydi revivalism and Sa'da's material uplift and marginalized local shaykhs standing in Huthi's way, potentially facilitating the establishment of a Huthi political machine in the governorate.[50]

If this was the direction of Husayn and his associates' thinking, they may indeed have exaggerated both their own local influence and the prospects for cooptation by Saleh, for reasons we will soon see. After all, Husayn was not a seasoned capital-city politico, nor was he a tribal shaykh with generations of experience at the opportunistic deployment of both brinkmanship and ingratiation with the GoY—and 2003–2004 was not 1986 or 1992. By the spring of 2004, chanting of the Huthi slogan had spread at an alarming rate within Sa'da, while Husayn's lectures began to spread widely among Zaydis in the governorate and beyond. Eventually Huthi-inspired agitation spread down to the capital city, where individuals would take to the streets chanting after Friday prayers. Although anti-U.S. and anti-regime activity was widespread throughout the Arab world in 2002–2004, the GoY took Huthi chanting very seriously, placing a ban on chanting the slogan and suspending the salaries of 60 teachers in the region because they took part in it.[51] More broadly, GoY authorities likely saw Husayn as both a threat to their control of outlying regions and an opportunity to

---

[49] Interview with senior GoY diplomat serving in the United States, September 11, 2008.

[50] These assessments are based on interviews with Yemeni refugees, lawyers, and students residing in the United States and Canada; consultations with U.S. political scientists and anthropologists; and interviews with academicians from the UK, during the fall of 2008 and spring of 2009.

[51] See "al-Qissa al-Kamila li-l-Huthi wa-l-Zaydiya fi-l-Yaman," *al-'Arabiya,* July 10, 2004.

bring a local phenomenon that was vexing the regime into the regional context of the GWoT, thus justifying whatever course of action the regime chose.

The Post–9/11 Environment and Saleh Regime Calculations

Just as post–9/11 conditions galvanized Huthi mobilization, it is highly likely that President Saleh's evolving international relationships subsequent to these events combined with domestic considerations to produce his decision to pursue armed conflict in Sa'da rather than the kind of mediated settlements seen in the 1986 and 1992 cases. Since the late 1990s, but particularly after the 2000 bombing of the USS *Cole*, Yemen had been under U.S. pressure to rein in violent Islamists in the form of al-Qa'ida. Lack of capacity, a concern not to appear excessively solicitous to the United States, and the presence of Salafi sympathizers in the government had assured this would not happen. After 9/11, however, Yemeni policy turned around, for several reasons. First, U.S. officials were aware that a number of the hijackers had been born in Yemen—putting previously lackluster Yemeni pursuit of terror suspects into sharp relief. Second, the GoY retained the memory of the disastrous consequences for U.S.-Yemeni relations of opposing the 1990–1991 Gulf War. Third, President Saleh likely felt that rhetorical support for the United States would yield dividends for authoritarian assertion at home. These factors all led the GoY to side publicly with Washington in the global war on terror.

President Saleh visited Washington in late 2001, shortly after the 9/11 attacks, to voice support for U.S. policies. Meeting President Bush, he pledged assistance in the emerging GWoT and also received assurances of U.S. economic and military support to the GoY, as well as a reduced pressure on matters such as democratization. In March 2002, Vice President Cheney visited San'a—this was the highest-level U.S. visit to Yemen since then–Vice President George H. W. Bush had arrived in 1986. Praising the "very close bilateral relations" developing between the United States and Yemen, Vice President Cheney was reported to have discussed increased economic and military aid with President Saleh, including the dispatch to Yemen of U.S. military advisers to train counterterror and special operations forces. Saleh is likely to have consented in principle to higher levels of intelligence sharing and counterterror cooperation against al-Qa'ida inside Yemen. Indeed, later that year, a Predator attack on a vehicle in Yemen resulted in the death of Yemeni terrorists, with advisers to Saleh suggesting that such attacks would be permitted again in the future.[52]

---

[52] See Robert Collier, "U.S.-Yemen Relationship in Spotlight: Few Answers About Who Did What in Killing of al Qaeda Operative," *San Francisco Chronicle,* Nov 6, 2002; Mark Katz, "U.S.-Yemen Relations and the War on Terror: A Portrait of Yemeni President Ali Abdullah Saleh," *Jamestown Foundation Terrorism Monitor* 2:7 (19 May 2005); Nora Boustany, "Yemeni Proclaims His Nation's Solidarity with US in Fight against Terrorism," *Washington Post,* Nov 27, 2002, A13; Patrick E. Tyler, "Yemen, an Uneasy Ally, Proves Adept at Playing Off Old Rivals," *New York Times,* Dec 19, 2002, A1; Tom Raum, "Cheney Promises Help to Yemen in War on Terror," Seattlepi.com, March 15, 2002; "Cheney Discusses Terror War in Yemen," *BBC News,* March 14, 2002.

Buoyed by rhetorical support from Washington and closer military aid and counterterrorism assistance, Saleh also saw benefits in the material realm. Up through 2001, U.S. military aid to Yemen had been negligible. There was no foreign military financing (FMF), while foreign military sales (FMS) were at 8 percent of what they had been in 1990, after a total interruption in 1992–1998. Likewise, the International Military Education and Training program (IMET) was at a third of 1990 levels after complete cessation in the mid-1990s. Approved direct commercial sales (DCS) of military materiel were also very low, as was provision of excess defense articles (EDA) to Yemen. The U.S. Agency for International Development (USAID) had closed its offices in the middle of the decade, and other civilian aid was very low. As Table 4.1 shows, while modest relative to other countries, the increase in aid to Yemen after 2002 is staggering compared with pre-2001 years.

In addition to providing articles such as high mobility multipurpose wheeled vehicles (HMMWVs), armored personnel carriers (APCs), and other materiel, post-2001 aid was used to support a dramatic increase in training and advisory missions to Yemen. In addition to support for the development of a coast guard, U.S. special operations forces (SOF) sent repeated Joint Combined Exchange Training (JCET) missions to Yemen, focusing on the Republican Guard, Counter-Terrorism Forces, and Yemeni Special Operations Forces (YSOF).[53] Although intended to improve Yemen's ability to counter Islamist terrorism and contraband smuggling in support of U.S. regional and GWoT interests, this greatly augmented material and rhetorical support likely influ-

Table 4.1
U.S. Military Aid to Yemen, 2001–2006, in U.S. Dollars

Year	FMF	FMS	IMET	DCS	EDA
2001	0	54,000	198,000	0	0
2002	20,000,000	307,000	488,000	1,000	0
2003	1,900,000	271,000	638,000	45,000	1,047,960
2004	14,910,000	1,069,000	882,000	1,842,000	35,000
2005	10,420,000	5,893,000	967,000	2,311,000	0
2006	8,415,000	4,123,000	924,000	1,155,000	0

SOURCES: Center for Defense Information, 2007, p. 5; Center for Defense Information Terrorism Project, 2002, pp. 1, 5, 6; Prados and Sharp, 2007, p. 6; Sharp, 2009, pp. 12–13, 15; Lumpe, 2002; Knights, 2008.

---

[53] See Lora Lumpe, "U.S. Foreign Military Training: Global Reach, Global Power, and Oversight Issues," *Foreign Policy in Focus,* Special Report, May 2002, 8–11; "Pre-empting Terrorism in Yemen: U.S. Special Forces are in Osama bin Laden's Home Ground Assisting Local Soldiers to Hunt al Qaeda Terrorists," *Veterans of Foreign Wars Magazine,* August 2002.

enced Saleh's calculations in dealing with domestic competition and opposition in general, including that of the Huthis. Further, as the scales of coercive power seemed to tip ever more in the GoY's favor, U.S. aid to Yemen may have convinced Saleh he could rearrange relations between the GoY and the periphery, welding the latter more firmly to San'a.[54] Thus, while earlier circumstances might have required the GoY to accommodate the Huthis, the post–9/11 conjuncture may have convinced him that this was no longer necessary—he could now afford to use offensive military means and he also had the political cover to do so as an "ally" in the GWoT.

Internal considerations may have also influenced Saleh to approve an aggressive approach to solving the Huthi problem. The first relates to the need to preserve regime cohesion. Although it is difficult to assess the extent of Sunni Islamist influence in the GoY and military, by the early 2000s, several influential people associated with the regime elite were either known propagators of an anti-Western, anti-Zaydi Salafi Islam or were associated with Salafi sympathies. The former included 'Abd al-Majid al-Zindani, discussed in Chapter Two and Three, whose efforts as part of Islah and at the al-Iman University were supported by the Islah party and received government funding. The latter include 'Ali Muhsin al-Ahmar, a Sanhani kinsmen (and half-brother) of President Saleh, who also commands the Army's First Armored Division and has been the regional commander for Sa'da-related operations. Likewise, until about 2005, the Political Security Organization (PSO), one of Yemen's civilian intelligence agencies, possessed a leadership known for its support of Salafism, as did the Ministry of the Interior's Central Security Organization (CSO). Muhsin al-Ahmar and PSO/CSO leaders—as well as many in the senior ranks of the Army's officer corps—had trained *mujahidin* during the 1980s wars in Afghanistan, recycling them for the war against the south in 1994. Inclined to a Sunni view of the world and well disposed toward the Ba'thist regime in Iraq, these elements inside and outside of the security services were suspicious of growing U.S.-Yemeni cooperation and also viewed reemergent Zaydi activism as a threat to both the regime and proper Islam. In this respect, aggressive prosecution of a war against Sa'da—reportedly strongly advocated by Muhsin al-Ahmar—allowed Saleh to deflect Salafi criticism and acted as a hedge against dissent from within his own security services as he sought to prepare the way for the succession of his son Ahmad (currently commander of the Republican Guard and YSOF) sometime in the next decade.[55]

Finally, the nature of the Huthi threat itself would likely have inclined the GoY to treat it differently from previous disagreements with elements in the periphery. In

---

[54] Lisa Wedeen, *Peripheral Visions: Publics, Power and Performance in Yemen* (Chicago: University of Chicago, 2008), 185; interviews with U.S. political scientists and ethnographers working on Yemen, September 9–10, 2008.

[55] See Andrew McGregor, "Yemen and the U.S.: Different Approaches to the War on Terrorism," *Jamestown Foundation Terrorism Monitor* 5:9 (May 10, 2007); Jane Novak, "Yemen's Internal Shia Jihad," *Global Politician*, March 21, 2007.

confronting the Huthis, the GoY was doubtless aware that it was not dealing, in the first instance, with a tribal uprising but with a movement deriving credibility from certain Zaydi religious leaders. On the one hand, this may have led Saleh to feel that the Huthis could not call upon the support of multiple and overlapping kin networks—nor would they be inclined toward *qabyala*-linked modes of conflict resolution, mediation, or material cooptation. In this view, then, not only was the danger of a potential tribal uprising absent, so were the "benefits" of dealing with opportunistic tribal leaders.

On the other hand, the Zaydi revivalist nature of the Huthist agitation, led by a *sayyid* who was the eldest son of one of the most prominent Zaydi *'ulama'*—and who himself had a background of social mobilization and political involvement in Sa'da—presented what was likely perceived as a unique challenge to Saleh's legitimacy. The Sa'da governorate and its surrounding region had been the font of Zaydi spiritual and political leadership several times in the past millennium and was also one of the last royalist holdout regions during the 1960s civil war. In these areas, Saleh could not be perceived as a conscientious Muslim or Zaydi. Husayn and his brothers were perceived as such, and they possessed a fair amount of prestige- and accomplishment-based charisma, which Saleh lacked. The Huthis also had a residual social base from BY days, which Husayn had cultivated again after his return from the Sudan. Further, as *sayyids* in far-off tribal areas beyond Hashidi dominion, it was possible the Huthis could rely on multiple networks of support among Khawlan bin 'Amr as well as Bakili tribesmen, who could be incited to greater anti-regime activity.

Furthermore, as we have seen above, by criticizing Yemen's newfound closeness to a "Christian" America which was prosecuting a new "crusade" against Muslims while supporting "infidel" Israel, Husayn was implicitly accusing Saleh of being a bad Muslim. He was thus censuring the GoY on very sensitive issues, at the same time as other groups within Yemeni society were protesting against GoY support for the GWoT and marching on the U.S. embassy in San'a.[56] What made Huthi's offense greater was that he criticized the regime in specifically Islamic terms and did it as a Zaydi *sayyid* with a politically activated social base from a part of the country that raised the spectre of an imamist revanche as well as snowballing popular opposition to the regime because of its foreign policy. Therefore, in addition to an embarrassment, Husayn's lectures, open letters, and supporters chanting the slogan (*shi'ar*) from Sa'da to San'a were likely perceived as a threat to the survival of the regime—while Saleh now possessed the coercive capability and diplomatic cover to deal with it aggressively, perhaps also changing the balance of state-tribe relations in the region to his advantage.

---

[56] See Tim Golden, "Mideast Turmoil: Demonstrations: At Least 2 Killed in Egypt and Yemen as Protests Mount," *New York Times,* April 10, 2002; "Four Killed in Sanaa Protest," *Yemen Times* 13:627 (March 17, 2003); Gary Leupp, "The 'War on Terrorism' in Yemen," *CounterPunch*, 20 May 2002.

Part III: The Six Sa'da Wars

In June 2004, the Government of Yemen sought to eliminate the Huthi threat by arresting Husayn al-Huthi, the charismatic oldest son of Badr al-Din al-Huthi. This was a break from previous center-periphery approaches. An armed conflict ensued; and even though the GoY declared victory in September 2004, Sa'da and the adjoining governorates have witnessed nearly six years of fighting since then. Although the GoY has recognized six phases of war, the Sa'da region and parts of 'Amran and Hajja have been characterized by nearly continuous conflict since 2005. Considering the heavy toll in military, human, and economic terms, it is likely that the Huthi conflict currently absorbs more GoY energy and resources than any other threat to the regime.

Part III focuses on these six "Sa'da wars," up through the most recent ceasefire of February 2010. Chapter Five examines the evolution of GoY-Huthi fighting in terms of magnitude, geographic migration, GoY goals, and results. Chapter Six then analyzes GoY conduct throughout the conflict. It examines military activities, information operations, GoY diplomatic engagement, and economic measures. Our approach focuses on lines of operation associated with counterinsurgency (COIN). Although the GoY has likely not consciously adopted a COIN strategy, their particular approaches prolong the conflict, potentially driving a loosely interconnected organism-like Huthi resistance toward an organized insurgency.

Chapter Seven turns to the Huthis themselves. Examining them as a combatant entity, we focus in particular on the evolution of command and control, armaments, and preferred tactics. We also examine Huthi ideological communication in terms of methods and substance. The chapter closes with an assessment of the Huthis' ongoing transformation from a resistance organism to a more organized entity in the midst of local fighting.

The conflict in Sa'da has caused large-scale destruction—in economic, environmental, and human terms—and has been accompanied by violations of local cultural mores and human rights. This human impact of the conflict thus is itself likely to prolong local violence between the GoY and Huthis as well as among different local factions and competitors. Chapter Eight catalogues material destruction, refugee flows, and economic hardship, addressing their implications for conflict continuity.

CHAPTER FIVE

From Phases to Rolling Conflict: Time Line, Geography, and Magnitude of Huthi-GoY Fighting

In this chapter, we focus on the multiple phases of armed conflict between the Yemeni regime and those who resist it under the banner of the Huthis. War has continued from June 2004 until now. It remains difficult to determine the goals of either the Huthis or the GoY. Yet from an outside perspective, it is possible to analyze GoY measures as a form of counterinsurgency (COIN). Whether or not this GoY COIN results from policy or unintegrated actions, we can analyze it according to diplomatic/political, information, military, and economic (DIME) lines of operation (LOOs). GoY actions on these LOOs evoked and sustained a particular kind of armed resistance among Huthi fighters, reflecting the geographic-cultural environment as well as responses to GoY measures. In this perspective, six wars' worth of GoY COIN have produced the character of the Huthi phenomenon, to which we will turn in Chapter Seven.

The Six "Sa'da Wars"

By 2004, both Husayn Badr al-Din al-Huthi and the GoY were in positions of perceived power. Husayn had managed to capitalize on anti-U.S. sentiment to mobilize supporters as far as 240 km south of the Sa'da governorate and had created, to some extent, a Huthi rallying call that began to take on an anti-GoY dimension as the government moved to clamp down on it. The GoY considered itself in the American camp with regards to the GWoT and could attempt to encourage increased foreign aid by arguing that Husayn al-Huthi's lectures were inciting terrorism. Domestically, GoY authorities could easily strike a nerve by accusing Husayn of wanting the return of the imamate, which Yemenis in the capital associate with *takhalluf* (backwardness). Within the context of a resurgent Iran and growing activism among Shi'ites in the Gulf, GoY authorities could also easily depict Husayn as a proxy for the Islamic Republic—thus touching a chord among both foreign powers and local Salafis. Finally, chanting of the Huthi *shi'ar* gave the GoY further pretext to paint Husayn as an extremist and attempt to discredit him by accusing him of inciting religious discord. The GoY thus felt empowered enough to begin arresting individuals who chanted the slogan, which—far from deterring others—likely incited further opposition to a GoY that appeared to be doing America's bidding.

Details of the events immediately preceding the first phase of armed conflict remain unclear, but two distinct narratives concerning the run-up to the Sa'da wars have emerged. From the government's perspective, the BY/Huthi supporters had over-stepped the boundaries of permissive discourse and behavior in Yemen. Indeed, government reports claimed that Husayn's followers were stockpiling weapons[1] and argue that while President Saleh had visited a Sa'da mosque in 2003 and witnessed the chanting, the Huthi slogan was not the issue.[2] Instead, the GoY was concerned over a possible rebellion and therefore attempted to engage Husayn in dialogue. When these initiatives failed, however, the GoY was left with no alternative but to pursue legal action to fulfill its "responsibility to protect the constitution and detain those who are outside the laws."[3] The GoY further alleges that it imposed a blockade on Husayn and his followers in the Marran area only after he refused to surrender himself to authorities, who themselves had adhered to legal channels, even obtaining an arrest warrant from the Yemeni attorney general. In this narrative, it was only after meeting armed resistance that the GoY was forced to resort to armed conflict, after dropping leaflets on Sa'da residents warning them against associating with Husayn al-Huthi.

Huthis depict GoY actions in a very different light. From the Huthi perspective, the GoY began arresting students who were repeating the Huthi slogan as early as 2002. This changed, however, after Saleh visited the Imam Hadi mosque that same year, and allegedly ordered Sa'da governor Yahya al-'Amri to release any prisoners accused of chanting the slogan.[4] Given this implicit permission, the Huthis felt enabled to continue their activities, and it was not until the U.S. government pressured Saleh to do so that he began cracking down on Husayn's supporters, who were acting within the boundaries of the laws and constitution. Soon after this crackdown, the Huthis claim the government began waging its "tyrannous acts . . . against Zaydism," with its announcement of the start of conflict on June 18, 2004.[5] Thus, from the Huthi perspective, the GoY never intended to arrest or detain Husayn al-Huthi in a fashion that would preserve his safety; rather, the Saleh regime took deliberate, unprovoked, and devastating military action intended to physically eliminate Husayn and his supporters.

---

[1]   See "Jama'at al-Huthi Shirdhimat Irhabiya Tastahdif al-Wahda wa al-Jumhuriya wa Yajib Hasmha: 26 Sebtember net Tunshir Nass Taqrir al-Aman al-Qawmi al-Muqaddam Ila Majlis al-Nuwwab wa al-Shura Hawl Ahdath al-Fitna fi Sa'da," *26 September*, February 1, 2007.

[2]   International Crisis Group, "Yemen: Defusing the Saada Time Bomb," *Middle East Report*, No. 86, May 27, 2009, 13.

[3]   See "Jama'at al-Huthi Shirdhimat Irhabiya Tastahdif al-Wahda wa al-Jumhuriya wa Yajib Hasmha."

[4]   "Taqrir 'an Harb Sa'da 2004–2005 wa Tabi'atuha," *al-Menpar*, 2006.

[5]   "Taqrir 'an Harb Sa'da 2004–2005 wa Tabi'atuha."

Time Line and Geographic Migration of the Conflict

Figure 5.1 depicts a time line of the conflict. Although it has been divided by analysts and government officials into six discrete phases, the Saʿda wars are best characterized as a "rolling" conflict, with spikes occurring during times of increased GoY retaliation for Huthi ambushes and skirmishes. Indeed, the GoY, not the Huthis, has announced each phase of the war. Each phase, however, does appear to have a "spark" that ignited the ensuing escalation of armed conflict. These sparks have been uniformly disputed by protagonists in the conflict and likely fail to accurately pinpoint the true reason for each successive phase. Such disputation further highlights the polarizing and ambiguous nature of the conflict itself. Below, we explore the contours of each phase. For each, we provide statistics, significant locations, and a summary.[6]

Figure 5.1
Time Line of the Sa'da Wars

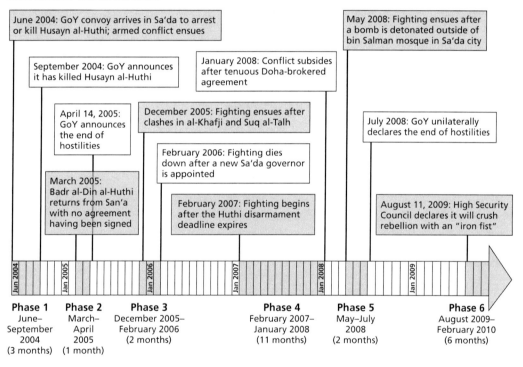

[6]   Our timing of the beginning and end of conflict phases follows the approaches found in other studies, with the exception of Phases 3 and 4. Though recognizing these periods of conflict as "wars," the GoY and Huthis have not indicated what they consider to be their beginning and end points. Our timing—which differs from Human Rights Watch's "Disappearances and Arbitrary Arrests in the Armed Conflict with Huthi Rebels in Yemen" (Report 1-56432-392-7, October 2008), for example—is based on the kinetic incident tracking method applied to the conflict as a whole, for which we used *al-Ayyam* and corroborating sources known to follow the fighting on a daily or near-daily basis (see note below). For Phases 3 and 4, when we found that the frequency and magnitude of conflicts had reached those reminiscent of previous and subsequent phases of recognized "war," we judged that the transition from interim phase to "war" phase had occurred.

Phase 1 (June 2004–September 2004)

As previously mentioned, Phase 1 of the Saʿda conflict began with either a government police or military convoy sent to arrest or kill Husayn al-Huthi in the Marran area. Fighting continued for approximately three and one-half months, with casualties reaching roughly 480 individuals. Most of the fighting took place in the mountainous terrain of Marran, which is located in the Haydan district (see Figure 5.2). It appears that the GoY was primarily concerned with finding and either killing or arresting Husayn al-Huthi. GoY forces employed both rotary and fixed-wing aviation, while Huthi fighters likely used small-to-medium arms. Limited skirmishes also took place in both Saʿda city and Kitaf city, where Huthi fighters detonated hand grenades. The GoY apparently utilized the support of the Hashidi al-ʿUsimat tribe during this first phase, although the tribe was reportedly roundly defeated in the conflict, with their shaykh beheaded by Huthis.[7] Fighting ultimately subsided when the GoY announced that it had killed Husayn al-Huthi, printing images in state-sponsored newspapers of his dead body being dragged through the street.

Interim 1 (September 2004–March 2005)

Data for attacks that took place between Phases 1 and 2 are currently unavailable in open-source reporting. It is likely, however, that the governorate was relatively quiet after the death of Husayn al-Huthi. In the spring of 2005, Badr al-Din al-Huthi made a trip to Sanʿa, allegedly in response to an invitation to negotiate with President Saleh. For one reason or another, however, no deal was made between the two parties. Before leaving, Badr al-Din gave an incendiary interview to *al-Wasat* newspaper in which he argued that the president had not met with him despite the fact that he had been in Sanʿa for two months.[8] It is this perceived GoY recalcitrance that likely led Badr al-Din to return to Saʿda with no deal having been signed.

Phase 2 (March 2005–April 2005)

Phase 2 began in March 2005 upon Badr al-Din's return to the Saʿda governorate, with fighting in al-Khafji market, where Huthis reportedly attempted to assassinate Shaykh

---

[7] "Hudu' Jabhat al-Qital fi Saʿda Naharan wa Ishtiʿaluha Laylan," *al-Ayyam,* March 3, 2007. In gathering data for sections dealing with the time line and characteristics of Huthi-GoY warfare, we utilized the archives of the Yemeni daily *al-Ayyam* and supplemented them with English media reporting, where available. Such data should not be seen as exact, given the media blackout on the Saʿda governorate and the opaque nature of the conflict itself. That being said, until its mid-2009 temporary closure by the GoY, *al-Ayyam* was unparalleled in its daily reporting on incidents of military conflict in the area. Further, it is important to understand the difficulty of assigning responsibility for initiation of a clash to one protagonist or another. In cases where reportage did not—or did not credibly—indicate who initiated an attack, we did not assign it to the Huthis or GoY, though we did record it as a clash. It is likewise challenging to identify some conflict locations. Where available, we utilize GIS data collected in 2004. Otherwise, locations are extrapolated from other publicly available maps and sources.

[8] "Badr al-Din al-Huthi li-l-Wasat: al-Raʾis Khafa An Yaʾkhudh (Husayn) minhu," *al-Wasat,* March 19, 2005.

Figure 5.2
Map and Statistics of the First Phase of the Sa'da Conflict

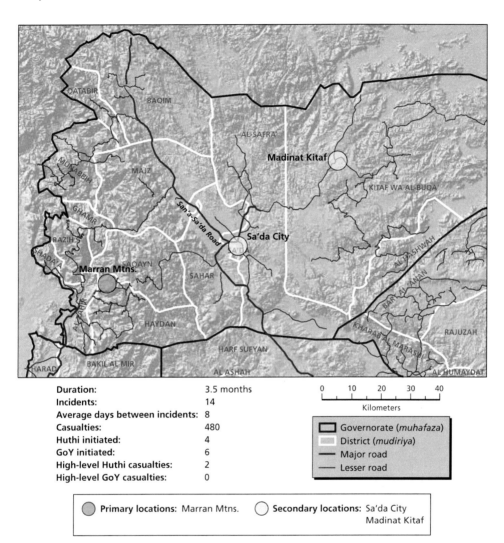

Duration:	3.5 months
Incidents:	14
Average days between incidents:	8
Casualties:	480
Huthi initiated:	4
GoY initiated:	6
High-level Huthi casualties:	2
High-level GoY casualties:	0

0   10   20   30   40
Kilometers

Governorate (*muhafaza*)
District (*mudiriya*)
Major road
Lesser road

Primary locations: Marran Mtns.   Secondary locations: Sa'da City
Madinat Kitaf

RAND *MG962-5.2*

Muhammad Hassan Mana', secretary general for the area's local council.[9] Fighting also occurred in Suq al-Talh, where alleged Huthi supporters were attempting to purchase weapons. Soon thereafter, sustained military engagements occurred in the Wadi Nushur area of the governorate, leading to the death of Huthi commander Ahmad

---

[9] "Na'ib Muhafiz Sa'da wa Mudir Amnuha Yata'arradan li-Kamin Musallah," *al-Ayyam*, April 4, 2005.

al-Daʿi and the wounding of Huthi commander Yusuf al-Madani.[10] The conflict primarily occurred in the regions of Al-Shafiaʿ, Wadi Nushur, and al-Razzamat, which saw the use of GoY heavy artillery, tanks, and attack helicopters (see Figure 5.3). At the time, these were the likely locations of Huthi leadership, since Badr al-Din by his own admission had spent the first phase of the conflict in Wadi Nushur. It appears that the GoY was primarily concerned with dismantling Huthi leadership by targeting such individuals as Yusuf al-Madani, ʿAbdullah al-Razzami, and Badr al-Din al-Huthi. Furthermore, Saʿda city also witnessed a significant amount of conflict during this phase, leaving tens dead and wounded on each side.[11] Fighting in Saʿda city likely prompted the GoY to declare a curfew on Saʿda city residents, in some cases denying the city's traders the right to conduct business.[12]

There were Huthi ambushes in other areas of secondary importance to the conflict, such as Talh and ʿAkwan, clustered near Saʿda city, as well as areas as far west as Dahyan. Fighting also broke out in Bani Muʿadh after the primary areas of conflict had grown quiet. Further significant to the conflict was al-ʿAbdin, roughly three kilometers south of Saʿda city.[13] There, Huthi supporters and/or members of the Hamid tribe clashed with followers of Shaykh ʿUthman Husayn Fayyid Mujalli, an MP from the area. This clash alone left tens dead and wounded. Toward the end of this phase of the conflict, Ahmad Manaʿ requested that the al-Faris, al-Qadami, and al-Abqur tribes take a more proactive role in preventing Huthi movement in their areas.[14]

It was not until ʿAbdullah al-Razzami's body was (falsely) identified that the government announced the end of major combat operations, arguing that it now had established complete control over all Huthi strongholds.[15] GoY security sources did regret, however, that Badr al-Din al-Huthi had managed to "flee from the hole in which he was hiding."[16] The concurrence of the identification of al-Razzami's body with the end of this phase suggests that the GoY was primarily concerned with dismantling what it perceived to be Huthi leadership. Indeed, similar to Phase 1, when GoY forces concentrated on locating and arresting or killing Husayn al-Huthi, throughout Phase 2, the GoY concentrated on areas where members of the Huthi leadership were alleged to be hiding.

---

[10] "48 Saʿa Mahla li-l-Huthi wa Munasirihi li-Taslim Anfusihum," *al-Ayyam*, April 3, 2005.

[11] "Musadamat ʿAnifa bi-Shawariʿ Saʿda bayn al-Aman wa ʿAnasir al-Huthi," *al-Ayyam*, April 9, 2005.

[12] "Hujum ʿAnif li-Marwahiyatin ʿala Atbaʿ al-Huthi bi-Kitaf," *al-Ayyam*, April 21, 2005.

[13] "Muwajihat bayn Qabilatayn Ahadahuma Mawaliya li-l-Hukuma wa Ukhra li-l-Huthi," *al-Ayyam*, April 5, 2005.

[14] "Marwahiya ʿAskariya Tulqi Munasharat Tadʿu ʿAnsar al-Huthi li-l-Istislam," *al-Ayyam*, April 11, 2005.

[15] "Al-Lajna al-Amniya: al-Huthi Najaha fi Farar min al-Juhr aladhi Akhtabaʾa fihi," *al-Ayyam*, April 14, 2005.

[16] "Al-Lajna al-Amniya."

Figure 5.3
Map and Statistics of the Second Phase of the Sa'da Conflict

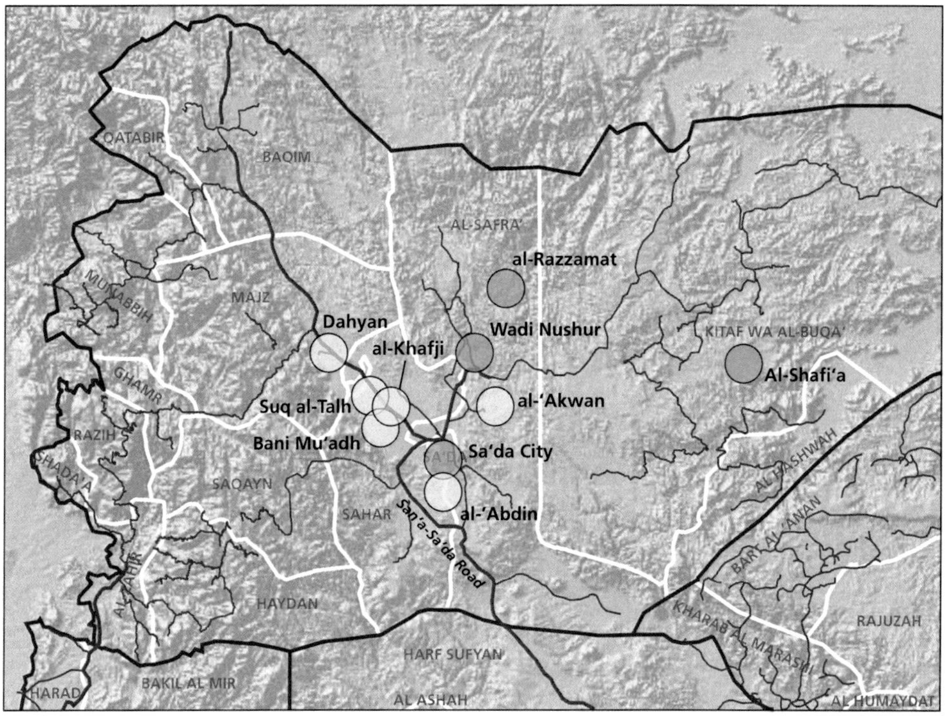

Duration:	2 months
Incidents:	39
Average days between incidents:	1.5
Casualties:	500
Huthi initiated:	12
GoY initiated:	14
High-level Huthi casualties:	3
High-level GoY casualties:	10

0 10 20 30 40
Kilometers

Governorate (*muhafaza*)
District (*mudiriya*)
Major road
Lesser road

Primary locations: Wadi Nushur, al-Razzamat, Al-Shafi'a, Sa'da City

Secondary locations: Suq al-Talh, al-Khafji, Bani Mu'adh, Dahyan, al-'Abdin, al-'Akwan

RAND *MG962-5.3*

Interim 2 (April 2005–December 2005)

Despite the fact that GoY sources announced the end of major combat operations, armed conflict continued to take place from April 16, 2005, to December 2005, albeit on a smaller scale. The government carried out a sweeping arrest campaign against Huthi supporters, blockading roads leading to al-Naq'a, Marran, Dahyan, and al-'Atfin, simultaneously attacking and sweeping these locations for Huthi commanders (see Figure 5.4). For their part, in addition to resisting GoY advances on Huthi strongholds in Nushur and al-Naq'a, the Huthis moved to the Al-Salim region. Huthis attacked GoY military outposts and targeted prominent GoY supporters and military men. This included an attempt to assassinate the head of military intelligence, 'Ali al-Siyani, allegedly carried out by Huthi supporters in San'a city.[17] Multiple attempts were also made to assassinate Deputy Governor Muhammad Hassan Mana', as well as two family members of Sa'da governorate politicians, including the now deceased 'Abdullah al-'Amri, nephew of the one-time Sa'da governor.

Media reporting indicates that during this period local shaykhs, such as Shaykh Shajia' Muhammad Shajia', attempted to negotiate a solution to the conflict. In September 2005 President Saleh announced amnesty for Huthi prisoners and supporters.[18] However, GoY general 'Abd al-'Aziz Dhahab reportedly refused to negotiate with any tribe suspected of being pro-Huthi, a fact that likely hampered mediation efforts in the area.[19]

During the second interim phase, clashes between Huthi fighters and followers of prominent tribesmen were prevalent. Upper echelons of the GoY forces in the area were also from local tribes. For example, Colonel 'Ali Fanis bin Lathala of the Wa'ila tribe was wounded in an ambush, which likely prompted some of his tribal brethren to side with the GoY. In Bani Mu'adh, Shaykh Ja'fir's supporters refused to allow Huthis passage through their territory, leading to fighting between the tribesmen and Huthi supporters. Further confrontations between Huthis and local tribesmen were reported in Nushur, where Shaykh Hamas al-'Awjari clashed with Huthi supporters.[20] Shaykh 'Amr Hindi in Nushur also fought against the Huthis, as did the Naq'a area tribe from al-Lajba. Additionally, a local from the Wa'ila tribe, which controls most of al-Naq'a, permitted GoY forces to conduct searches in his territory.[21] Thus, Huthi fighters were able to continue ambushing and attacking both GoY supporters and military outposts in a number of areas throughout this period, while GoY forces attempted to impede the group's movement and mobilize tribes against them. During this time, Huthi fighters were relocating to both al-Naq'a and areas of Al Salim, suggesting the areas that the GoY forces would focus on throughout the third phase.

Phase 3 (December 2005–February 2006)

In late December 2005, Huthi fighters attacked a military checkpoint in the al-Khafji region, prompting GoY forces to attack civilian homes on the suspicion that Huthis

---

[17] "Naja Ra'is al-Istikhbarat al-'Askariya min Muhawalat al-Ightiyal," *al-Ayyam*, April 27, 2005.

[18] "Al-Ra'is: Sana'rad Usrat Al Hamid al-Din 'an Mumtalakatihum," *al-Ayyam*, September 26, 2005.

[19] "Hujum 'Anif li-Marwahiyatin 'ala Atba' al-Huthi bi-Kitaf."

[20] "Ma'arak Dariya fi 'Iddat Mawaqi' bi-Sa'da," *al-Ayyam*, December 28, 2005.

[21] "Hujum 'Anif li-Marwahiyatin 'ala Atba' al-Huthi bi-Kitaf."

Figure 5.4
Map and Statistics of the Second Interim Phase of the Sa'da Conflict

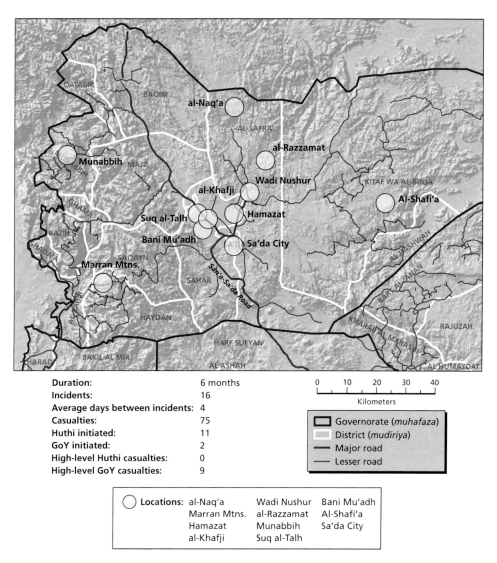

Duration:	6 months
Incidents:	16
Average days between incidents:	4
Casualties:	75
Huthi initiated:	11
GoY initiated:	2
High-level Huthi casualties:	0
High-level GoY casualties:	9

Governorate (*muhafaza*)
District (*mudiriya*)
Major road
Lesser road

Locations:	al-Naq'a	Wadi Nushur	Bani Mu'adh
	Marran Mtns.	al-Razzamat	Al-Shafi'a
	Hamazat	Munabbih	Sa'da City
	al-Khafji	Suq al-Talh	

RAND *MG962-5.4*

were hiding in them.[22] This marked the beginning of the third phase of the Sa'da conflict, during which GoY artillery, air support, and infantry concentrated their attacks on the Al-Salim *'uzla*, Al-Sayfi village, and Talh area mountains (see Figure 5.5). Signi-

---

[22] "Tajaddada al-Ishtibakat bayn Wahdat al-Jaysh wa Atba' al-Huthi bi-Sa'da," *al-Ayyam*, December 21, 2005.

Figure 5.5
Map and Statistics of the Third Phase of the Sa'da Conflict

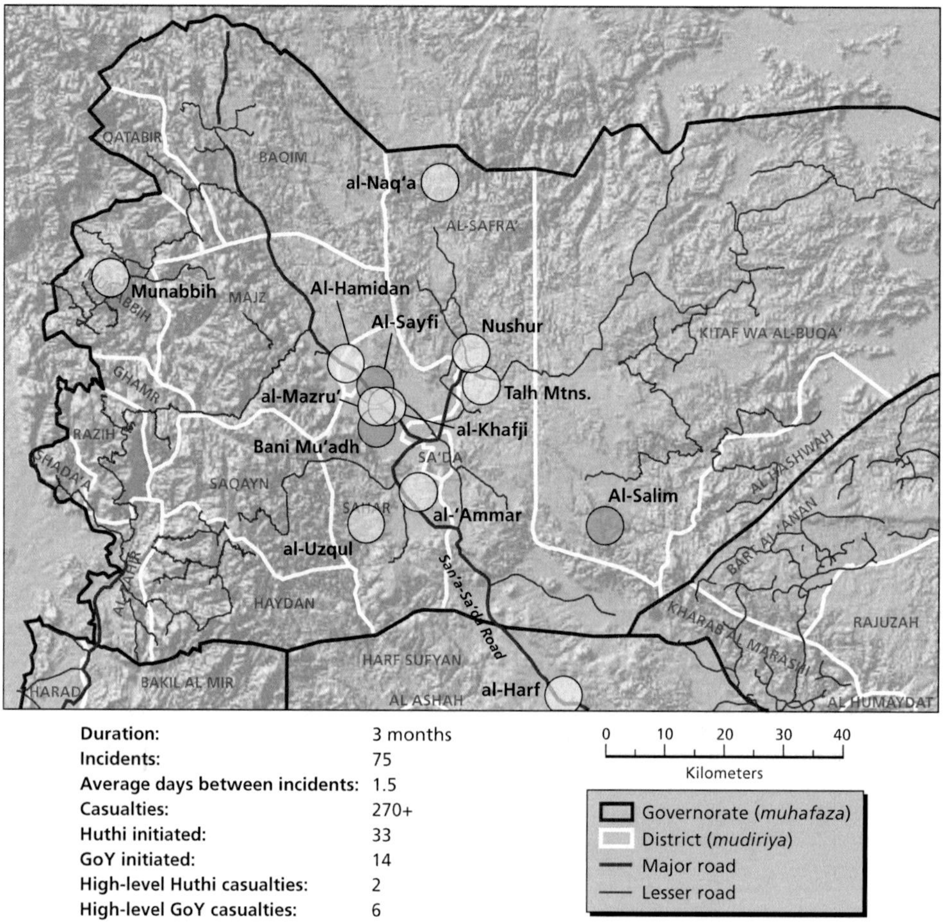

Duration:	3 months	
Incidents:	75	
Average days between incidents:	1.5	
Casualties:	270+	
Huthi initiated:	33	
GoY initiated:	14	
High-level Huthi casualties:	2	
High-level GoY casualties:	6	

Governorate (*muhafaza*)
District (*mudiriya*)
Major road
Lesser road

Primary locations: Al-Sayfi
Al-Salim
Bani Mu'adh

Secondary locations: Munabbih   al-'Ammar   al-Naq'a
al-Mazru'   al-Harf   Al-Hamidan
al-Khafji   Talh Mtns.
al-Uzqul   Nushur

RAND *MG962-5.5*

ficant damage was also reported to have occurred in Bani Mu'adh, although the number of incidents in the area remained relatively low.

In addition to exchanging fire with GoY units in Al Salim, Al Sayfi, and Talh (specifically the Dal'an and Ubqur areas), Huthi fighters launched a number of ambushes on GoY troop and border guard locations, including an attack on troops guarding the entrance to Sa'da city, as well as on a military convoy using the San'a-Dahyan road.

Furthermore, the Huthis continued assassinations, targeting government officials. This included the head of criminal investigations in the Majz province, who was killed in the Al Hamidan region.[23] General Husayn Shawit, head of security in Sahar, was also targeted by the Huthis, who managed to wound him.[24] Reports indicated that a government building in Harf Sufyan was attacked in February, leading to clashes between GoY and Huthi fighters. Huthis also targeted Deputy Governor Hassan al-Mana' in an assassination attempt. Fighting died down, however, when Yahya Muhammad al-Shami, a Hashemi, was appointed governor of Sa'da.[25]

Followers of MP Shaykh al-'Awjari also had a role in fighting both Huthi supporters and rivals from the al-Nimri tribe, who may or may not have supported the Huthis. Bani Mu'adh tribe al-Kabas was also reported to have sided with GoY forces in fighting Huthis in the area, as did tribes in the al-Salah village in Nushur. GoY forces using bulldozers and allied tribesmen (including the aforementioned Yahya Ja'far) also attempted to limit Huthi movement, primarily focusing on the Bani Mu'adh area. Unrest in the Bani Mu'adh area prompted the powerful Shaykh al-Surabi to request that GoY forces vacate the area.[26]

Interim 3 (February 2006–February 2007)

While possible backroom negotiations were taking place, low-intensity conflict continued in the Sa'da governorate. There were clashes in Al-Salim, and areas as far northwest as Qatabir witnessed Huthi ambushes on military convoys (see Figure 5.6). Indeed, the Huthis attacked a number of GoY troop locations and convoys in dispersed locations while also attempting to assassinate GoY notables, among them head of political security in Sa'da, Yahya al-Murani. Huthi supporters also detonated explosives that destroyed the artesian water pump owned by Shaykh Hassan al-Thawra in Baqim, sup-posedly because he had offered support to the GoY.[27] For its part, the GoY did begin attacking the Huthi stronghold in Matra with Katyusha rockets.[28] Finally, further unrest in the Sa'da prison was reported during this period, with the warden of the prison eventually having to cut off the electricity and deny prisoners food and water.[29]

---

[23] "Masra' Mudir li-l-Bahath al-Jina'i wa 3 Murafiqin lahu wa Naja Mas'ul Akhar bi-Sa'da," *al-Ayyam*, January 28, 2006.

[24] "Masra' Mudir li-l-Bahath al-Jina'i wa 3 Murafiqin lahu wa Naja Mas'ul Akhar bi-Sa'da."

[25] "Al-Hudu' Yasud Sa'da ba'd Wusul al-Muhafiz Ila Ma'qil al-Huthi," *al-Ayyam*, February 22, 2006.

[26] "Istimrar Tabadul al-Hajamat bayn Atba' al-Huthi wa Wahdat al-Jaysh," *al-Ayyam*, December 25, 2005.

[27] "Infijar 'Anif Yahazz Madinat Baqim bi-Muhafazat Sa'da," *al-Ayyam*, December 10, 2006.

[28] "al-Jaysh Yuhajim Manatiq Matra bi-l-Sawarikh wa Ta'zizat 'Askariya Satasul Sa'da Qariban," *al-Ayyam*, January 18, 2008.

[29] "Itlaq Nar wa Qanabil Musila al-Dumu' li-Muwajahat 'Isiyan fi Sijin Sa'da," *al-Ayyam*, December 19, 2006.

Figure 5.6
Map and Statistics of the Third Interim Phase of the Sa'da Conflict

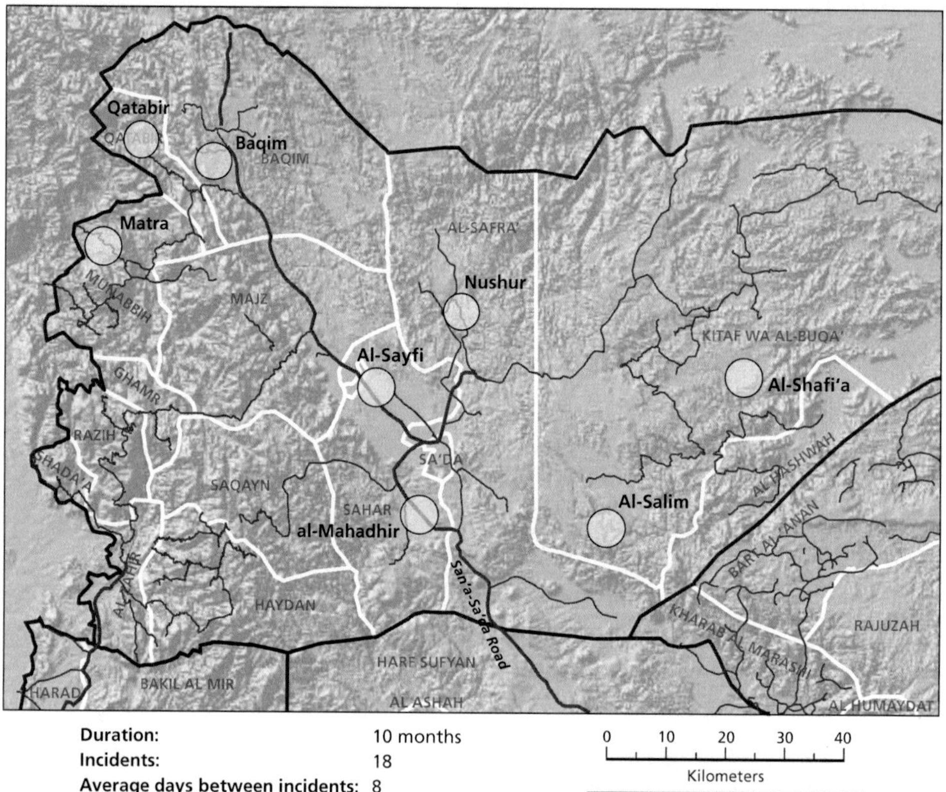

Duration:	10 months	
Incidents:	18	
Average days between incidents:	8	
Casualties:	80+	
Huthi initiated:	12	
GoY initiated:	2	
High-level Huthi casualties:	0	
High-level GoY casualties:	0	

Governorate (*muhafaza*)
District (*mudiriya*)
Major road
Lesser road

Locations:	Al-Sayfi	Qatabir
	Al-Salim	Nushur
	Matra	Al-Shafi'a
	Baqim	al-Mahadhir

RAND *MG962-5.6*

Thus, despite the relative calm in the area, clashes continued, with both sides appearing relatively unrestrained by the opaque mediation process taking place at the time.

A number of tribal issues became prominent during this interim period. For example, the shaykh of the al-'Udham tribe in Shabwa expressed his resentment that his men were being arrested while Huthi supporters were being compensated.[30] Furthermore, clashes near al-Shafiʿa occurred between al-ʿAwjari tribesmen and Huthis in retaliation for the former's involvement in the killing of a BY member. Also, Harf Sufyan tribesmen blocked the ʿAmran-Saʿda road, in order to pressure GoY forces to release their tribal brethren.[31] Both of these instances highlight the notions of revenge and tribal solidarity that have motivated both pro-GoY and pro-Huthi tribal affiliations. The longest and deadliest phase of the conflict commenced in February 2007, after the GoY's deadline for the Huthis to disarm and surrender had expired.[32]

Phase 4 (February 2007–January 2008)

The fourth phase of the Saʿda conflict was the most intense and deadly fighting the Saʿda governorate had ever witnessed. The 11 months of armed conflict included the GoY's sustained use of air support, heavy artillery, and mechanized units conducting continuing bombing campaigns on suspected Huthi locations. Throughout Phase 4, the GoY appeared unrestrained, mercilessly attacking Huthi locations and staying on the offensive throughout the conflict's duration. During this phase, significant reports emerged of the GoY using "volunteer" forces to fight the Huthis. For their part, the Huthis appeared resilient during this period, fighting in both urban and rural environments and managing to surround and trap GoY forces. They also continued to raid military convoys and outposts and ambush suspected GoY supporters. After a lull in the summer of 2007, likely due to Qatari mediation efforts, combat in this phase renewed.

Sustained GoY bombing and ensuing clashes between Huthi fighters and GoY forces took place in a number of locations. These included previous conflict areas of Al-Salim, Al-Sayfi, the Talh mountains, Marran mountains, Bani Muʿadh, Kitaf, and Nushur, as well as new areas of sustained conflict, including Razih and Dahyan (in the Majz district). Other secondary areas that witnessed some GoY bombing, scattered clashes, and/or Huthi ambushes are further noted in Figure 5.7, and include areas just south of Saʿda city such as al-Muhadhir, al-ʿAmar, and Dammaj (home to the Salafi-leaning Dar al-Hadith Institute), as well as more-peripheral areas of the governorate such as Munabbih, Qatabir, and Ghamr.

Fighting began with GoY forces bombing primarily the Bani Muʿadh, the Talh mountains, and Al-Sayfi but also striking al-Khafji, al-'Amar, Nushur, Hamazat, and

[30] "Ihtijaz Majmuʿa min Al-ʿUzam bisabab Mutalabatihum bi-Tariq Farʿi Ila Mintaqatihum," *al-Ayyam*, April 30, 2006.

[31] "Wasata Qabaliya Tatawassal Ila Rafaʿ Nuqta Mustahditha Aqamuha Musallahun bi-Tariq ʿAmran-Saʿda," *al-Ayyam*, July 22, 2006.

[32] "Baʿd Intihaʾ al-Mahla li-Taslim Aslihatihum . . . Istimrar al-Muwajahat bayn al-Jaysh wa Atbaʿ al-Huthi aladhin Yuwasilun Hajamatahum," *al-Ayyam*, February 3, 2007.

Figure 5.7
Map and Statistics of the Fourth Phase of the Sa'da Conflict

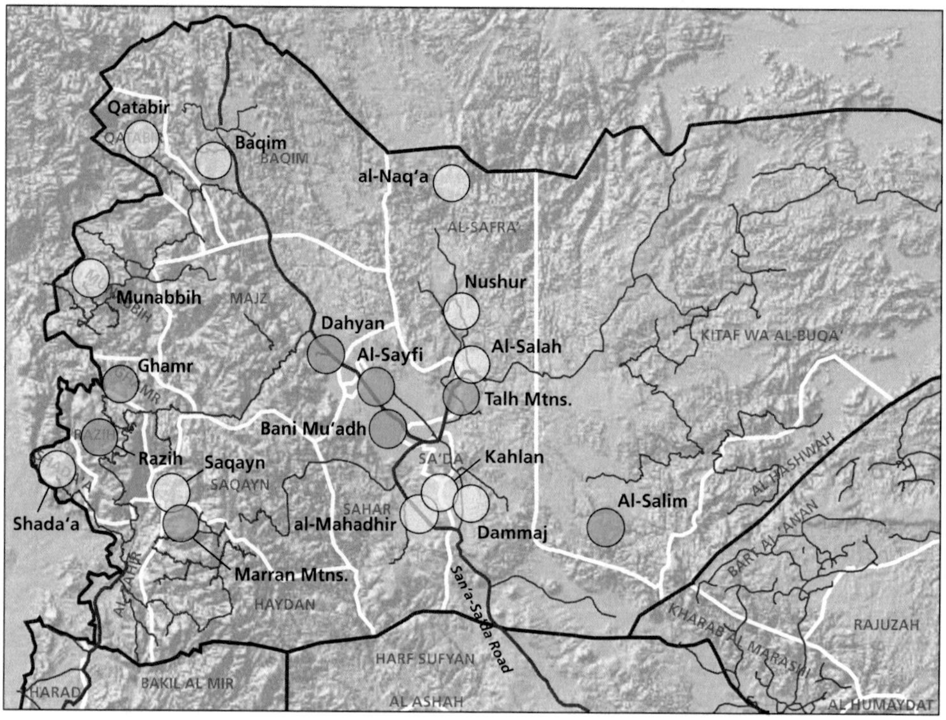

Duration:	11 months
Incidents:	519
Average days between incidents:	1
Casualties:	3,035
Huthi initiated:	140
GoY initiated:	166
High-level Huthi casualties:	10
High-level GoY casualties:	16

Governorate (*muhafaza*)
District (*mudiriya*)
— Major road
— Lesser road

Primary locations:	Dahyan	Bani Mu'adh	Secondary locations:	al-Mahadhir	Ghamr
	Al-Sayfi	Al-Salim		Kahlan	Baqim
	Marran Mtns.			Al-Salah	Qatabir
	Talh Mtns.			Nushur	Munabbih
	Razih			al-Naq'a	Dammaj
	Ghamr			Saqayn	

al-Naq'a. This was probably intended to pave the way for GoY ground forces and/or tribal volunteers to move into and possibly hold these areas. Put on the defensive by this initial GoY show of force, Huthis initially attacked military units and outposts in Talh and al-'Amar, while establishing roadblocks in al-Muhadhir and destroying a bridge on the San'a-Sa'da road. Eventually, however, and much to the chagrin of some of the locals, the Huthis moved into areas in Razih and Dahyan, while simultaneously continuing to ambush GoY convoys and strike GoY outposts. Toward the end of the phase, Huthi fighters were able to successfully surround and trap GoY units in Marran.[33] We first provide a narrative and analysis of the major theaters of combat during Phase 4 and then discuss areas of secondary importance.

The Al Salim district remained a significant area of conflict from March to July 2007. Much of the fighting in the area was initiated by GoY forces, which launched airstrikes, shelled, and made direct contact with Huthi fighters in the area. Huthi fighters, reportedly led by Yusuf al-Madani, launched several attacks on GoY outposts, as well as periodic sniper attacks on idle GoY soldiers. However, based on the number of GoY-initiated attacks, it is apparent that the Huthis found themselves in a defensive posture in the Al-Salim area.

A number of locations in the Sahar district were significant areas of conflict during the fourth phase. For example, the village of Al-Sayfi also saw a significant amount of combat during the fourth phase, beginning mainly in May 2007. As in Al Salim, the GoY remained primarily on the offensive in most combat incidents, utilizing air and ground forces against Huthi locations. For their part, the Huthis put up resistance, leading to a number of sustained armed clashes with GoY forces. Fighting died down in Al-Sayfi in August 2007. The mountainous areas surrounding Talh city saw a large number of clashes and GoY airstrikes, remaining an area of periodic conflict throughout the duration of the fourth phase. Bani Mu'adh also witnessed heavy bombing from GoY forces. Despite this, the Huthis were able to mount a handful of attacks on GoY convoys.

Areas to the far west and northwest of the Sa'da governorate were heavily contested throughout this phase. The Huthis penetrated Razih in late March 2007, despite local tribal resistance.[34] When the Huthis initiated attacks against military outposts in the area, the GoY responded with devastating airstrikes and artillery bombardments, eventually deploying armored units to rid the area of Huthis. The latter attempted to impede GoY troop movement by destroying the asphalt road near the district's capital.[35] Although GoY forces were eventually able to regain control of the district's urban centers by July 2007, press reporting noted that Huthis were still able to maintain a presence in the surrounding mountains.[36] Fighting in the Razih district was likely due to Huthi control of areas in Ghamr, Munabbih, and Qatabir. Indeed, reaching such peripheral areas of the governorate and establishing control required GoY boots on the

---

[33] "Istimrar al-Hisar 'ala Kutibat al-Jaysh bi-Haydan wa Inkhifad al-Hajmat al-Mutabadila bayn al-Janibayn," *al-Ayyam*, January 24, 2008.

[34] "Quwwat al-Jaysh Ta'thur 'ala Makhzan Silah fi Ihda Manatiq Mudiriyat Sahar bi-Sa'da," *al-Ayyam*, March 22, 2007.

[35] "Al-Jaysh Yatamakkan min Dukhul Madinat al-Nazir bi-Sa'da," *al-Ayyam*, May 9, 2007.

[36] "Hushud 'Askariya Kabira li-Ijtiyah Dahyan wa al-Saytara 'alayha," *al-Ayyam*, March 19, 2007.

ground, and, with limited transportation routes, passing through Razih was one of two possible ways to reach these areas. The other would require passing through Dahyan, which, as we will see, GoY forces also found to be quite difficult.

Although the Huthis were able to launch attacks on military convoys traveling via the San'a-Sa'da road from heavily attacked locations, such as Bani Mu'adh, the group was able to offer the stiffest resistance to GoY force movement in the urban environ of Dahyan, commonly referred to as the "Zaydi Najaf."[37] Dahyan was of strategic significance to GoY forces because it straddles the primary transportation route to areas in the northwest of the governorate, where Huthis had established strongholds. In trying to secure Dahyan, however, GoY conventional and volunteer units sustained heavy casualties. Air strikes and shelling likely destroyed a significant amount of the city's infrastructure and sacred religious sites, a situation we explore at the end of this chapter. Despite having been periodically blockaded by GoY forces through this and previous phases, Dahyan was still under Huthi control by the end of the fourth phase.

Engagements between GoY and Huthi forces were first reported in Dahyan in mid-March, with the GoY commencing airstrikes and artillery attacks. The GoY also was beginning to build up forces to sweep and control this Huthi stronghold.[38] Soon, however, after moving troops into the city, GoY forces found themselves trapped in Dahyan.[39] The Huthis also held GoY volunteer forces captive in a school, despite sustained GoY air strikes on the city. By the end of March, it was reported that casualties sustained in Dahyan exceeded those of the 2004 conflict.[40] By mid-April, there were reports that casualties surpassed those sustained in the second phase as well.[41] Heavy clashes continued in the city, despite periodic claims by the GoY that the city was under its control. While clashes in the area had subsided by November 2007, it is unclear whether this was due to GoY control over the area or the Huthis' ability to repel GoY forces.

Tribal dynamics continued to play a role throughout Phase 4, and it is possible that tribal volunteers played a much larger role in this round of fighting. Hundreds of tribesmen were reportedly traveling to Sa'da from the 'Amran and Hajja governorates to fight alongside GoY forces against the Huthis.[42] Local tribes supporting the GoY

---

[37] For this reference, see Yahya al-Thulaya, "Jami'at al-Mutanaqidat . . . Dammaj al-Salafiyin, wa Dahyan al-Huthiyin, wa Sa'da al-Mu'tammar al-Sha'bi," *al-Ahale.net*, n.d.

[38] "Hushud 'Askariya Kabira li-Ijtiyah Dahyan wa al-Saytara 'alayha."

[39] "Al-Jaysh Yatamakkan min Dukhul Suq al-Talh wa Yudammir Mahattat Wuqud bi-Dahyan Yashtabih bi-Tazwidiha al-Huthiyin bi-l-Banzil," *al-Ayyam*, March 24, 2007.

[40] "'Ashirat al-Algham Tanfajir fi al-Huthiyin wa Dahyan Muhawir al-Ma'raka al-Ra'is," *al-Ayyam*, March 31, 2007.

[41] "Khasa'ir al-Ma'rak bi-Dahyan Faqat Khasa'ir Harb 2005," *al-Ayyam*, April 10, 2007.

[42] "Hudu' Jabhat al-Qital fi Sa'da Naharan wa Ishti'aluha Laylan," *al-Ayyam*, March 3, 2007.

included the Jahli,[43] Shaykh 'Abdullah Daris, elements of the Munabbih (under MP Shaykh 'Ali Husayn Salim),[44] and others from Baqim, Ghamr, Majz, and Qatabir.[45] For their part, the Huthis were able to kill a number of GoY-allied tribal shaykhs, including one from Baqim[46] and one from Majz (Ibn Muqayt).[47] The GoY also reportedly dispatched volunteers to secure control of precincts in Talh and Dahyan and sent arms to local tribesmen in Razih and Shadda.[48] Tribal support for the GoY campaign was far from absolute, however. For example, Talh tribes previously armed by the GoY threatened to retreat due to the fact that they had been underequipped by their GoY benefactors.[49]

The Huthis also managed to obtain the overt support of some tribal shaykhs, whereas GoY activities alienated others. For example, tribesmen from the Ibb province south of San'a pressured Shaykh al-'Anisi to confront the authorities for arresting and harassing their tribesmen on the pretext of being Huthi sympathizers.[50] Tribal Shaykh al-'Asar al-Ka'bi reportedly also fought with the Huthis.[51] Shaykh al-'Awfwan, who reportedly had initially sided with the GoY, allegedly changed sides after his land was hit in an air strike during Phase 1.[52] From this we see that a tribe's allegiance to the regime can be short-lived and easily jeopardized by a misstep on the part of the GoY armed forces. Shaykh al-Surabi, reportedly one of the most "prominent shaykhs of the Sa'da governorate," returned to the area in May, requesting that GoY troops allow Bani Mu'adh citizens to return to their homes and salvage their possessions.[53] Similarly, tribal members from Dar Husayn, Khawban, al-Muhtawiya, Ba'ir Hayyan, and Al-Hadyan all complained about the adverse affects of the GoY's military campaign.[54]

---

[43] "al-Jaysh Yuwajjih Darbat li-Kull min Tasul lahu nafsuhu Musa'adat al-Huthiyin," *al-Ayyam*, June 5, 2007.

[44] "Istimrar Tashdid al-Ijra'at al-Amniya bi-Madinat Sa'da Wasat Tasa'ud li-l-Muwajihat," *al-Ayyam*, May 8, 2007.

[45] "Al-Jaysh Yaktashif Nisa' Muqatilat fi Sufuf al-Huthiyin," *al-Ayyam*, June 7, 2007.

[46] "Fima Lajnat al-Ishraf 'ala Tanfidh Ittifaqiyat al-Htkuma wa-l-Huthiyin Tuwasil 'Amalha . . . Maqtal Ahad al-Mashayikh fi Muwajahat 'Anifa ma'a al-Huthiyin," *al-Ayyam*, June 20, 2007.

[47] "Fima Lajnat al-Ishraf 'ala Tanfidh Ittifaqiyat al-Htkuma wa-l-Huthiyin Tuwasil 'Amalha . . . Maqtal Ahad al-Mashayikh fi Muwajahat 'Anifa ma'a al-Huthiyin."

[48] "Masra' 3 'Askariyin fi Ishtibakat Musallaha Wasat San'a," *al-Ayyam*, April 16, 2007.

[49] "Khasa'ir Fadiha li-l-Janibayn fi Sa'da wa Taghyirat 'Askariya wa Amniya Murtaqiba," *al-Ayyam*, April 25, 2007.

[50] "Majmu'a min Shuban Ibb Yutalibun bi-Radd al-I'tibar li-Min Ahtajazahum al-Amn al-Siyasi bi-Tahma Munasirat al-Huthi," *al-Ayyam*, February 28, 2007.

[51] "Al-Jaysh Yuwajjih Darbat li-Kul min Tasul lahu Nafsihu Musa'adat al-Huthiyin," *al-Ayyam*, June 5, 2007.

[52] "Al-Jaysh Yuwajjih Darbat li-Kul min Tasul lahu Nafsihu Musa'adat al-Huthiyin."

[53] "Al-Jaysh Yuzhir Jum' al-Jabal al-Mushrifa 'ala Madinat al-Nazir," *al-Ayyam*, May 27, 2007.

[54] "Harb I'lamiya Maqru'a wa Masmu'a bayn al-Jaysh wa al-Huthiyin bi-Sa'da," *al-Ayyam*, May 29, 2007.

Thus, while the Huthis lacked the resources that the GoY could use to buy tribal allegiance, they were still able to obtain explicit and implicit support from tribes that defected to them for myriad reasons, among them the destructive nature of the GoY's COIN campaign.

Phase 4 ended in January 2008, but GoY objectives were not achieved. Unleashing all its force on Huthi combatants, the GoY launched sustained artillery and airstrikes on Huthi strongholds and deployed conventional and volunteer infantry to occupy urban locations. Despite all this, the GoY seemed unable to dismantle the Huthi leadership or destroy the group's popular base. Thus, although the Huthis probably sustained greater casualties, they essentially emerged victorious from the fourth phase of the conflict. The GoY had used every means at its disposal and, in doing so, probably wreaked untold damage on the governorate's physical and social base—as well as on its own international image. Despite Qatari mediation in June and July of 2007, it was only months later that a negotiated ceasefire seemed to partially restrain both sides from attacking one another. Even so, at the end of this phase the Huthis still had a GoY unit trapped in the mountains of Marran.

Interim 4 (January 2008–May 2008)

Notwithstanding the fact that GoY troops were trapped in the Marran mountains where the Huthis could interdict air-dropped resupply,[55] both GoY and Huthi forces appear to have attempted to limit armed conflict to some extent during this period. Perhaps of greatest significance in this interim period were clashes between the pro-GoY Bukhtan tribe of Al-Salim and Huthi fighters.[56] Indeed, these clashes indicate how, despite the signing of a ceasefire agreement, tribal notions of revenge and honor continued to spur fighting. Further ambushes and clashes were reported in al-Khafji and Dahyan, while Huthi fighters skirmished with GoY troops in Marran (see Figure 5.8). However, a mysterious explosion in the bin Salman mosque of Sa'da city, which left 17 dead and 48 wounded, ultimately shattered the ceasefire and caused fighting to resume.

Phase 5 (May 2008–July 2008)

Phase 5 of the conflict, which began roughly in May 2008 and ended in July of the same year, was much less intense than the previous devastating round. Still, fighting was reported in Marran, Dahyan, and al-Harf in Harf Sufyan, where Huthis allegedly

---

[55] "Infijar Ta'ira 'umudiya wa Suqutuha fi Haydan ba'd Isabatiha bi-Niran al-Huthiyin," *al-Ayyam*, February 4, 2008.

[56] "Isthibakat 'Anifa bayn al-Huthiyin wa Rijal Ihda al-Qaba'il wa Suqut Thamaniyat 'Ashir Qatilan min al-Janibayn," *al-Ayyam*, April 7, 2008.

Figure 5.8
Map and Statistics of the Fourth Interim Phase of the Sa'da Conflict

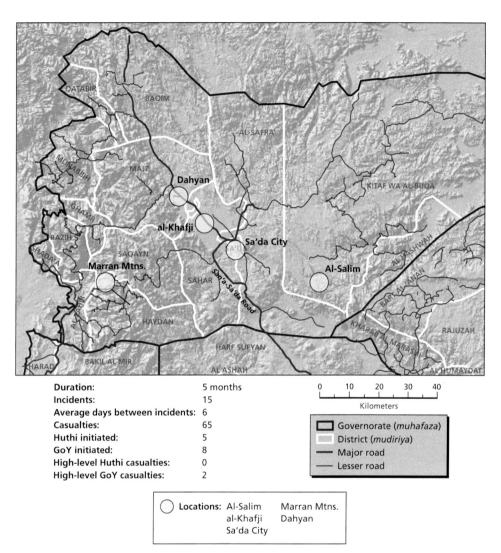

Duration:	5 months
Incidents:	15
Average days between incidents:	6
Casualties:	65
Huthi initiated:	5
GoY initiated:	8
High-level Huthi casualties:	0
High-level GoY casualties:	2

0   10   20   30   40
Kilometers

- Governorate (*muhafaza*)
- District (*mudiriya*)
- Major road
- Lesser road

○ Locations: Al-Salim   Marran Mtns.
al-Khafji   Dahyan
Sa'da City

RAND *MG962-5.8*

had strong tribal support.[57] A number of additional areas also witnessed skirmishes between GoY troops and Huthi supporters, including areas south of the Sa'da governorate, such as Huth in 'Amran and Bani Hushaysh in the San'a governorate. Also, helicopter attacks occurred in Munabbih, where Huthis had previously established

---

[57] "Fima Qaba'il Bakil Tad'u Ila Tahkim al-'Aql wa Iqaf al-Harb . . . Masra' Habish wa Isabat Akharin bi-Harf Sufyan fi 'Amran," *al-Ayyam*, May 17, 2008.

strongholds. Throughout this period, however, GoY forces appeared focused on break-ing the Huthi blockade on their troops in Marran. In an attempt to limit GoY force movement, the Huthis also set up roadblocks in the al-Muhadhir area, as well as on the Kitaf-Sa'da road. On July 16, 2008, President Saleh declared the conflict to be over. Despite this, fighting has continued in a wide range of areas within and beyond the Sa'da governorate, and presently continues unabated (Figure 5.9).

Interim 5 (July 2008–August 2009)

Despite the unilateral ceasefire declared by the GoY on July 17, 2008, both protagonists seemed dissatisfied with the status quo throughout the ensuing interim phase, almost ensuring a sixth phase of the conflict. Still, late 2008 and early 2009 saw a number of good-faith efforts to ease tensions by the GoY and Huthis. Indeed, the GoY released Hizb al-Haqq notable Muhammad al-Muftah[58] and, in a March 2009 interview in the pan-Arab daily *al-Hayat,* President Saleh appeared to at least partially back off from the accusation that the Huthis were completely foreign backed.[59] For their part, the Huthis also reported in a number of instances that they, unlike the Saleh government, were releasing prisoners.[60] Generally, however, several factors drove the GoY and the Huthis toward a sixth war. First, elements supportive of the GoY began to express frus-tration with the embattled Saleh government's capacity to confront Yemen's multiple problems. Second, the Huthis and the GoY continued to exchange accusations regard-ing who was responsible for undermining the peace and reconstruction process. Third, sporadic armed clashes also continued in areas within and beyond the Sa'da governor-ate during these months, further exacerbating existing tensions and catalyzing both rhetorical and kinetic conflict escalation.

In the summer of 2009, a number of salient indicators suggested a weakening of the GoY's support base in the region. Most prominently, four long-standing pro-GoY MPs resigned from the GPC in mid-July, complaining of neglect and destruction in the governorate—but also signaling to President Saleh their displeasure at being treated as mercenaries and of having been sidelined from the process of reconstruc-tion and reconciliation. Notably, resigning MPs included 'Uthman Mujalli and Fa'iz al-'Awjari, whose tribal segments have been GoY mainstays in the *muhafaza* for gen-erations.[61] Further, Islah party member and tribal notable Hamid al-Ahmar—scion

---

[58] "Ba'd al-Ifraj 'anhu . . . Muftah: Sujintu dun Mubarrir wa Utalib bi-Itlaq Jami' al-Sujuna' wa Ta'widihum," *al-Ayyam*, September 8, 2009.

[59] "'Ali 'Abdullah Salih: al-Tansiq al-Yamani—al-Su'udi Mumtaz I'dam Saddam Intiqaman wa Tahawwul al-Bashir Matluban Lidha Ansah al-Akhirin An Yasta'du," *al-Hayat,* March 28, 2008.

[60] "al-Huthi: Itlaq Sirah 24 Asiran min 'Askar al-Nizam Ta'kidan li-Khiyar al-Salam," *al-Menpar*, August 8, 2009.

[61] "Qalu Anna al-Sulta Tata'amal ma'a Shurafa' al-Muhafaza wa kannahum Majami' Murtaziqa: Arba'a min Nuwwab Sa'da 'an al-Mu'tammar al-Hakim Yuqaddimun Istiqalatahum min al-Mu'tammar li-Rai'is al-Jumhuriya," *Mareb Press,* July 12, 2009.

Figure 5.9
Map and Statistics of the Fifth Phase of the Sa'da Conflict (May 2008–July 2008)

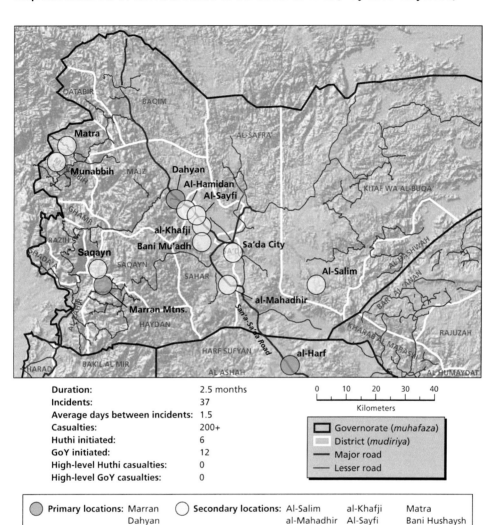

Duration:	2.5 months
Incidents:	37
Average days between incidents:	1.5
Casualties:	200+
Huthi initiated:	6
GoY initiated:	12
High-level Huthi casualties:	0
High-level GoY casualties:	0

0   10   20   30   40
Kilometers

Governorate (*muhafaza*)
District (*mudiriya*)
— Major road
— Lesser road

Primary locations: Marran   Secondary locations: Al-Salim   al-Khafji   Matra
Dahyan   al-Mahadhir   Al-Sayfi   Bani Hushaysh
al-Harf   Sa'da City   Saqayn   (not pictured)
Bani Mu'adh   Munabbih

RAND *MG962-5.9*

of the influential and typically pro-GoY Hashid tribal family—called on President Saleh to step down in an August 5 interview on al-Jazeera.[62] Such statements were powerful indicators that some of the GoY's staunchest allies were beginning to grow

---

[62] "Mashhad al-Siyasi fi al-Yemen," *al-Jazeera*, August 5, 2009.

tired of Saleh's conduct of the Sa'da conflict—even of his methods of rule. Additionally, there were reports of Sa'da war veterans expressing their frustration with the fact that they had not been paid their salaries,[63] while tribal shaykhs in the al-Jawf governorate accused an election official of attempting to stir discord between tribes.[64]

As with previous interim phases, mutual accusations between the protagonists persisted. In a January 2009 interview, for instance, 'Abd al-Malik al-Huthi claimed that the government was continuing to reinforce its military positions, further noting that the GoY was contributing nothing in the way of good-faith efforts toward achieving a peaceful reconciliation.[65] Additionally, during this period 'Abd al-Malik al-Huthi continued to tour the *muhafaza* during contested holidays, delivering incendiary speeches suggesting that a sixth war was "looming on the horizon" because of GoY military buildup in the area.[66] In a March 2009 speech on the Prophet's Birthday, 'Abd al-Malik warned the GoY against launching a sixth war. During the spring and summer of 2009, the GoY countered by accusing 'Abd al-Malik of subverting peace efforts in the area[67] while also hinting that the group was stockpiling weapons in preparation for a new rebel offensive.[68] GoY sources then issued a damning report outlining the amount of material damage the Huthis had inflicted on the Sa'da governorate,[69] later listing the group's various "terrorist acts" during the interim period.[70]

Two instances in particular demonstrated the capacity for rising tensions to catalyze armed conflict during this fifth interim phase: the Bani Hushaysh trial and the European hostage saga. During the Bani Hushaysh trial of June–July 2009, seven Huthi supporters were publicly tried and sentenced to death for their involvement in the Huthi rebellion. The trial and its verdict dramatically increased acrimony in the conflict region.[71] Around the same time, in mid-June 2009, reports emerged of nine

---

[63] "Jundi Yunashid Wazir al-Difa' Inha' Harmanihi Ratibihi Mundhu 17 Shahran," *al-Ayyam*, September 2, 2009.

[64] "Bayyan Sadir min Qibal Mashayikh Muhafazat al-Jawf Yudinun fihi A'mal Khalid al-Sharif," *al-Menpar*, July 30, 2009. Again, note the use of *fitna* for "discord," with its implicit connotation of intraconfessional strife.

[65] "al-Minbar.net Yu'id Nashr Hiwar al-Sayyid 'Abd al-Malik al-Huthi ma'a Sahifat al-Diyyar," *al-Menpar*, January 20, 2009.

[66] Muhammad 'Abd al-Salam, "Sa'da . . . Harban Sadisatan Taluh fi al-Ufuq," *al-Menpar*, January 8, 2009.

[67] "Faris Mana': al-Huthi Yasa'i Ila Ta'zim al-Awda' wa Nasf Juhud al-Salam," *26 September*, May 30, 2009.

[68] "Itihamat Hukumiya Li-l-Huthiyin bi Takdis al-Asliha al-Haditha Isti'dadan li Jawla Jadida," *Al-Ayyam*, April 24, 2009.

[69] "Taqrir al-Hukumi Yukashif Tadmir al-Huthiyin 10 Alf Mansha'a fi 11 Mudiriya," *26 September*, August 16, 2009.

[70] "al-A'mal al-Irhabiyya wa al-Khuruqat Allati Qamat bi-ha al-'Anasir al-Irhabiya al-Safawiya min ba'd I'lan Waqf al-Harb fi 17 July 2008," *26 September*, August 13, 2009.

[71] "Damn al-Majmu'a 4 li-'saba Qatl wa A'mal Takhrib fi Bani Hushaysh, al-Jaza'iya al-Mutakhassisa Tuqadi bi-I'dam Sab'a wa Sijin Sab'a Akhirin min 12 Ila 15 'am," *Mareb Press*, July 6, 2009.

Europeans being kidnapped in the area. Three of these were confirmed dead soon thereafter. While the GoY was eager to pin the kidnapping on the Huthis, the Huthis condemned the abduction in large rallies and marches, arguing that the GoY was responsible for the tourists' fate.[72] The European hostages remained a contentious issue for both protagonists and were included on the Yemeni government's original list of demands.

Within this context, armed clashes were reported in a number of districts within and beyond the Sa'da governorate. Indeed, as early as December 2008 Huthis were reported to have clashed with the Al-Hamati and Munabbih tribes.[73] In the spring of 2009, fighting flared in Ghamr between Huthi supporters on one side and GoY forces and allied tribes fighting under Shaykh 'Ali Zafir on the other.[74] Huthi fighters also engaged Central Security Forces elements in the same *mudiriya* in the summer.[75] Further, the Huthis clashed with the pro-GoY al-Bushr tribe in Saqayn and GoY troops in Marran and Malahiz. Later Razih again saw GoY kinetic action, with Huthis complaining of GoY roadblocks and assaults on civilians. The Jawf governorate also witnessed conflict in late July, in one case between Huthi supporters and local tribesmen/Islah party members who were fighting in a mosque.[76] Two days after these clashes, the Huthis ambushed and killed a military officer and his two bodyguards.[77]

These political, rhetorical, and military factors combined to render the status quo of the initial, unilateral ceasefire unsustainable. From the GoY's perspective, the Huthis had continued to be uncooperative and were refusing to abide by the conditions of the ceasefire. Further, the Saleh regime was facing an increasingly restless southern movement, as well as a resurgent al-Qa'ida presence, both of which likely lowered its patience and highlighted the need to deal with one of these three threats in a decisive manner.[78] Similarly, the Huthis expressed their frustration with what they perceived to be continued GoY aggressions and preparations for a sixth Sa'da war, which seemed to evolve into a self-fulfilling prophecy at a time when Huthi leaders continued to demonstrate mobilizational capacity.

---

[72] "Bayan min Maktab al-Sayyid 'Abd al-Malik al-Huthi Hawl Ikhtitaf 9 Ajanib fi Madinat Sa'da," *al-Menpar*, June 14, 2009.

[73] "23 Qatilan wa 33 Jarihan fi Muwajahat bayn Atba' al-Huthi wa Al al-Hamati," *al-Ayyam*, December 4, 2008.

[74] "al-Jaysh wa 'Anasir al-Huthi Yujriyan Taharukat wa Isti'dadat Kabira bi Sa'da ba'd Ma'rik Ghamr," *al-Ayyam*, April 5, 2009.

[75] "Ishtibakat bayn Junud al-Amn al-Markazi wa al-Huthiyin bi-Sa'da," *al-Ayyam*, February 28, 2009.

[76] "al-Masajid Masrah li-l-Qatl, Sa'at min al-Harb bayn al-Ma'zin wa al-Huthiyin wa al-Islah Hal Yadkhal al-Muwajaha," *Mareb Press*, July 20, 2009.

[77] "Ba'd Yawmayn li-Maqtal 10 Ashkhass bi-Khilaf 'ala Masjid bi-l-Jawf Maqtal al-'Aqid 'Iydrus al-Yafa'i wa Ithnayn min Harasihi, fi Kamin Musallah bi-Mahadhir Sa'da," *Mareb Press*, July 21, 2009.

[78] This argument is made in Gregory Johnsen, "The Sixth War," *The National*, November 12, 2009.

Phase 6 (August 2009–February 2010)

On August 11, 2009, President Saleh convened a meeting of his High Security Committee to review events and developments in Saʿda.[79] The committee concluded the meeting by arguing that, because of those developments, it would strike the rebellion "with an iron fist."[80] These statements came in the wake of a statement by Sadiq al-Ahmar—Hamid's brother and current head shaykh of the Hashid confederation—vowing support for GoY action in Saʿda.[81] Appropriately, GoY reporting indicated that it was again preparing local tribesmen to fight alongside GoY units against the Huthis.[82] The GoY originally laid out six conditions for a ceasefire: returning the European hostages; removing roadblocks and vacating the mountainous terrain; withdrawing from districts and ceasing interference in affairs of local authorities; returning stolen civilian and military property; and adhering to the constitution. The condition concerning the European hostages was later removed by the GoY after the conflict had been reignited.[83] On August 19, President Saleh made a personal visit to ʿAmran to affirm his resolve to uproot the "Satanic rebellion" from Saʿda.[84] In addition, the Yemeni Ministry of Interior released its list of 55 most-wanted Huthi leaders and associates.[85] With these announcements, the GoY initiated the sixth phase of the Saʿda war.

The sixth phase of the Saʿda war touched a number of locales in and around Saʿda, including Harf Sufyan, Tazih, Munabbih, Marran, Malahit, Shadda, Saqayn, Hassama, Talh, and Sahar. Typical to this conflict, both the Huthis and the GoY claimed a number of military successes, with the former claiming control of no less than 63 military locations,[86] and the latter regularly noting the successful targeting of Huthi

---

[79] "Waqfat Amam Tatawwurat bi-Saʿda wa Munashida al-Sulta al-Mahalliya li-l-Dawla Himayat al-Muwatinin: al-Lajna al-Amaniya al-ʿUliya Tujaddid Tahdhiraha li-ʿAnasir al-Tamarrud min Maghbat al-Istimrar fi Aʿmaliha al-Irhabiya wa Tuʾakkid Idtirar al-Dawla li-l-Qiyyam bi-Masʾuliyatiha Tibqan li-l-Dustur wa al-Qawanin," *26 September*, August 11, 2009.

[80] "Waqfat Amam Tatawwurat bi-Saʿda wa Munashida al-Sulta al-Mahalliya li-l-Dawla Himayat al-Muwatinin."

[81] "Akkada Haqq al-Dawla fi Ijtithath min Yakhraj ʿan al-Dustur wa al-Qanun al-Shaykh al-Sadiq al-Ahmar: Qabilat Hashid Satakun Ila Janib al-Quwwat al-Musallaha al-Amn al-Mulahiqqa al-Huthi wa ʿAsabatihi," *26 September*, August 19, 2009.

[82] "Tajawaban maʿa Ruh al-Wataniya li-l-Muwatinin: al-Muʿaskarat Tastaqbil Aʿdad al-Mutatawaʿin min Abnaʾ al-Qabaʾil al-Yamaniya li-l-Tasadi li-Duʿat al-Fitna wa al-Tamarrud," *26 September*, August 19, 2009.

[83] "al-Hukuma Tuʿlin Taʿliq al-ʿAmaliyat al-ʿAskiriya fi al-Mantaqa al-Shamaliya al-Gharbiya bi-Munasibat ʿId al-Fitr," *26 September*, September 19, 2009.

[84] "Akkada al-Taʿamul maʿa al-Fiʾat al-Dala al-Kharija ʿan al-Qanun bi-Masʾuliya Wataniya, Raʾis al-Jumhuriya: Al-Quwwat al-Musallaha wa al-Amn Satuwasil ʿAmaliyatiha Hata al-Qadaʾ Nihaʾiyan ʿala Fitnat al-Tamarrud bi-Saʿda," *26 September*, August 19, 2009.

[85] "Tadman Qaʾima bi-Asmaʾ 55 Shakhsan, al-Dakhiliya Tatlub min al-Niyaba al-ʿAmma Isdar Amr Qahari bi-l-Qabd ʿala Qiyyadat al-Tamarrud wa al-Takhrib min al-Huthiyin bi-Saʿda," *26 September*, August 18, 2009.

[86] "Sudur al-ʿAddad al-Awwal min Nashrat Bashaʾir al-Nasr fi al-Harb al-Sadisa," *al-Menpar*, September 14, 2009.

commanders.[87] Also significant have been Huthi videos and claims of destroying a GoY military communications tower in Jabal al-Ahmar,[88] and the declarations that the Huthis maintain "complete control" (*saytara kamila*) over a number of districts in the Sa'da governorate, including Qatabir[89] and Munabbih.[90] Another notable event was a clash initially reported by the state-run Saba news agency and then picked up by a number of pan-Arab and Western sources as taking place in Sa'da city, where the Huthis allegedly employed 70 "armored vehicles" in an unsuccessful strike on the presidential palace in Sa'da city.[91] For their part, the Huthis denied this particular engagement, underscoring the difficulty of obtaining accurate information on the conflict's daily events.[92]

The sixth phase of fighting has witnessed a significant new development in the Huthi conflict, as the Kingdom of Saudi Arabia employed air assets, artillery, and ground forces against Huthi fighters. The events leading up to Saudi involvement in the current round of conflict remain difficult to determine. From the Huthi perspective, the Saudi military had permitted GoY forces to use a strategic mountain in Saudi Arabia—Jabal Dukhan—to attack Huthi units from the rear.[93] The Huthis claim that they warned the Saudis about allowing GoY forces to attack them from Saudi territory but received no response. Therefore, Huthi units crossed the border on November 4, entering into a skirmish with Saudi border guards, who the Huthis claim fired first. After forcing GoY units to vacate Jabal Dukhan, the Huthis argued that they remained there only to prevent the reemergence of GoY forces. From the Saudi perspective, Huthi fighters had "infiltrated" Saudi territory and fired on border guards, necessitating a response from the country's armed forces.[94]

---

[87] "Masra' Thalatha min Qiyyadat al-Tamarrud al-Matlubin Dimn Qa'ima al-55," *26 September*, September 26, 2009.

[88] "Maktab al-Huthi: Fidiyu li-Qat' al-Ittisalat fi al-Jabal al-Ahmar, wa Fawda Dakhil al-Jaysh wa al-Sulta," *al-Menpar*, September 10, 2009.

[89] "'Ajil: al-Saytara al-Kamila 'ala (Mudiriyat Qatabir) al-Muhadda li-l-Su'udiya," *al-Menpar*, November 10, 2009.

[90] "'Ajil: al-Huthiyun Yu'linun al-Saytara al-Tama 'ala Mudiriyat Munabbih al-Muhadda li-l-Su'udiya," *al-Menpar*, October 7, 2009.

[91] See Mohammed Jamjoom, "State-Run Media: Yemeni Military Kills 150 Rebels," *CNN*, September 21, 2009.

[92] "'An Akhbar al-Yawm al-'Id: al-Huthi Yanafi ma Tud'ihu I'lamiyat al-Sulta min Qittal fi Madinat Sa'da," *al-Menpar*, September 20, 2009.

[93] This narrative was articulated by 'Abd al-Malik al-Huthi in an audio statement released November 10, 2009. See "Tasjil al-Sawti li-l-Sayyid 'Abd al-Malik Badr al-Din al-Huthi Yuwwadih fihi ba'd al-Nuqat al-Muhimma Jidan," *al-Menpar*, November 10, 2009. See also Gregory Johnsen, "The Sixth War."

[94] Saudi military reporting regularly refers to the Huthis as "armed infiltrators." See, for example, "al-Bayyan al-'Askari al-Sadir min al-Quwwat al-Musallaha: Quwwatina al-Musallaha Tu'min al-Qura al-Su'udiya al-Muhita bi-Jabal Dukhan wa-l-Dawd wa-l-Ramih wa Tadhar al-Mutasallilin," *Saudi Ministry of Defense*, undated.

From November 4, 2009, onwards, Saudi air and artillery assets regularly attacked Huthi locations along the Yemeni-Saudi border, including areas near Jabal Dukhan and Jabal Dawd.[95] Saudi border guards also engaged Huthi units on the ground during the sixth phase. Predictably, Huthi fighters and Saudi forces routinely claimed military successes after clashes.[96] Notably, Huthi fighters captured Saudi soldiers and aired videotaped confessions while also pilfering Saudi military equipment.[97] It is unclear whether Saudi-initiated *ground* engagements have in fact occurred on sovereign Yemeni territory, although its military buildup along its southern border reportedly constituted the largest deployment of Saudi ground troops since the 1990–1991 Gulf War.[98] Saudi involvement, which was officially sanctioned by the Wahhabi religious establishment as *jihad*,[99] also prompted a number of ominous condemnations from Iranian officials, to be discussed later.

With the exception of Saudi involvement and some larger-scale GoY air raids reported to have caused high numbers of civilian casualties while seeking high-value targets,[100] the sixth phase of fighting resembled earlier periods in its small skirmishes, large-scale movement of GoY troops, and artillery barrages. In spite of having been advertised as a "scorched earth" campaign, however, at the time of writing it appears to have lasted only about five and one-half months. Although the GoY indeed killed many Huthi fighters, it did not decapitate Huthi leadership. Further, from December on, fighting in the north was accompanied by renewed regional and global concern about the al-Qa'ida presence in Yemen. Such concern turned into pressure on San'a after the December 25, 2009, attempted bombing of a U.S. airliner by a Nigerian Muslim who had obtained training and spiritual guidance from the Yemeni al-Qa'ida in the Arabian Peninsula (AQAP). Confronting this challenge may have led the GoY to call off the northern offensive. Conversely, Huthi leaders may have come to perceive their presence in Saudi territory as a misstep.

Beginning in January 2010, 'Abd al-Malik made a number of overtures suggesting he was ready to accept a peaceful resolution to the sixth phase of fighting. This included announcing a withdrawal from Saudi territory, provided that Saudi troops

---

[95] It is unclear whether Saudi airstrikes have been launched against targets within Yemeni territory.

[96] "Ahdath al-Masa': Inkissar al-Zahf al-Su'udi 'ala Jabal al-Ramih wa Tadmir (3) Malalat wa (18) Ghara Jawiya 'ala Qarya Yamaniya," *al-Menpar*, December 7, 2009; "al-Quwwat al-Musallaha Taqtal 'Adadan min al-Mutamarridin fi Ishtibakat Qaryat al-'Ayn al-Hara," *Saudi Ministry of Defense*, undated.

[97] "Fidiyu min Maktab al-Huthi: Yuzhir fihi al-'Inaya al-Tibbiya wa-l-Sakaniya li-l-Asra al-Su'udiyin," *al-Menpar*, November 9, 2009; "Ba'd al-Ghana'im min al-Jaysh al-Su'udi wa Qasf al-Su'udi 'ala al-Aradi al-Yamaniya, wa Asra min al-Jaysh al-Yamani, wa li-Nazihin Madaniyin," *al-Menpar*, November 13, 2009.

[98] "Saudis Taking Lead in Battling Houthi Rebels," *Peninsula,* December 2, 2009.

[99] Zafir al-Sha'lan, "Mufti al-Su'udiya: al-Mutasallilun Da'at Fasad wa Dalal . . . wa Afrad al-Jaysh 'Mujahidun'," *Elaf,* November 11, 2009.

[100] See "Yemen Army Air Raid Kills 80 Civilians: Witnesses," *al-Arabiya.net,* September 17, 2009.

would no longer fire on Huthi fighters.[101] In February, the Huthis further announced that they would accept the government's conditions, an offer initially rebuffed by the GoY because it did not include a condition concerning firing on Saudi troops.[102] On February 11, 2010, however, the GoY announced the end to its military campaign in Sa'da,[103] with 'Abd al-Malik's press office similarly acknowledging the ceasefire.[104]

A discussion of the geographical migration and time line of the Sa'da fighting reveals its opacity. Indeed, isolating true causes of each phase is extremely difficult. Similarly, delineating the goals of each side through each phase's duration also presents challenges because it runs the risk of assigning intent and forethought to each side that simply may not exist. We can, however, analyze each side's approach to the conflict through the lenses of insurgency and COIN. Additionally, each side's conduct can be evaluated based on the effect on the Sa'da governorate's environment, economy, citizens, and social fabric. We now turn to GoY operations, the Huthis as combatants, and the human effect of the conflict in Sa'da and beyond.

---

[101] Author unknown, "Yemen Rejects Houthi Truce Offer," *al-Jazeera English*, January 31, 2010.

[102] See Robert F. Worth, "Yemen Seems to Reject Cease-Fire with Rebels," *New York Times*, January 31, 2010.

[103] "Ra'is al-Jumhuriya Yar'as Ijtima'an li-l-Lajna al-Wataniya Iqaf al-'Amaliyat al-'Askariya fi al-Mintaqa al-Shamaliya al-Gharbiya" *26 September,* February 11, 2010.

[104] "'Ajil: al-Sayyid 'Abd al-Malik al-Huthi Yuwwajih bi-Iqaf Itlaq al-Nar," *al-Menpar,* February 12, 2010.

CHAPTER SIX

GoY Operations: Goals and Methods

As we have suggested throughout this book, whether by design or result, the GoY has approached the Huthi problem in a fashion that can be analyzed as counterinsurgency (COIN). The GoY has made the military and informational lines of operation (LOOs) a priority, although it has taken tactical-level actions on the economic LOO. It remains unclear whether, in approaching the domestic political LOO and the regional diplomatic LOO, the GoY has chosen tactical opportunism or strategic commitment. Because it appears that GoY COIN has elicited and sustained a Huthi resistance that has much in common with—and perhaps is becoming—an early-stage insurgency, we will examine GoY actions first before moving onto the Huthis as insurgent combatants.

GoY Military Operations

Analysis of GoY military operations presents multiple difficulties. Because Sa'da is a closed military zone, very few western reporters have obtained access to the area since 2004. Likewise, on-site Yemeni media presence has been minimal. Yemeni journalists who report on Huthi or GoY actions often do so from San'a or communicate with Yemenis from the Sa'da governorate but not necessarily from a conflict area. Further, Yemeni media outlets fundamental to a systematic understanding of the progression of fighting and negotiations have at times been closed down by the GoY, particularly in mid-2009.[1] Additionally, infrequent visits to the conflict zone by Yemeni journalists mean that they are not observing engagements but talking after the fact to residents, Huthis, or GoY representatives—all biased parties. In rare cases, Yemeni journalists have gained access to protagonists during the fighting or have seen its immediate aftermath. These reporters, however, encounter great risk, and have in some cases become casualties in the conflict.[2] Further, not being from the Sa'da-'Amran regions, Yemeni reporters—not to mention foreign commentators—are not aware of the cultural

---

[1] *Al-Ayyam*'s Web site, for example, was inaccesible from May to September 2009.

[2] We note with sadness and concern that the perceptive journalist Yahya al-Thulaya was wounded grievously in the fall of 2009. See "Sahwa Net Correspondent Wounded in Sa'da," *al-Sahwa.net*, September 28, 2009.

nuances of the area. In general, reporters do not grasp or report on the lineage relation-ships among tribal sections. While they know the names of the extended family—or confederation—to which people in an area belong, they are not aware of the interme-diate tribal segments related to them or the status of intertribe relations among them. Additionally, in many cases Yemeni observers do not relate geographic place names to districts or significant terrain features.

Finally, neither Western nor Yemeni observers possess a sharp enough under-standing of military affairs to distinguish among the kinds of weapons in use, size of combatant formations involved in an engagement, tactics used, or level of operational sophistication and coordination—either on the Huthi or GoY side.[3] Coverage of clashes is not in chronological order, and at times there are double reports of certain engage-ments while others are missed—particularly since some media outlets are dailies, while others are weekly or occasional. As such, the following discussion covers what open-source reporting suggests are the main contours of the GoY's military approach.

Prior to commencement of hostilities, the GoY already had garrisons in the area—to the east of Sa'da ('Akwan), in the northeast, and in the Suq al-Talh and Walad Mas'ud areas, in addition to border guards (*hirs al-hudud*) stationed in the north near Saudi Arabia—all built up since 2002.[4] In the second phase of the war and onwards, the GoY augmented these garrisons with additional personnel; moved forces from 'Amran, Hajja, and San'a; and established additional camps and firm bases in the region. Open-source reporting indicates that the anti-Huthi campaign fell under the operational command of 'Ali Muhsin al-Ahmar, half-brother of the president and commander of the 1st Armored Division/Northern Command. Over the course of the conflict, other general officers have circulated through the area of operations, although al-Ahmar seems to have retained paramount influence—so much so that some local Yemenis and analysts refer to the Huthi conflict as "'Ali Muhsin's War."[5]

Visits to the Sa'da basin in the 1990s indicated that local shaykhs favored by the regime had obtained positions for their relatives as army officers, also ensuring that they were posted to Sa'da-area duties. They include the Shawit clan and relatives of

---

[3]   For example, reporters at times confuse rockets with missiles (both referred to as *sarukh* in Arabic, though both terms are used in English-language reports), artillery with mortars (*madfa', madfa' hawun*), tanks with other tracked or armored vehicles (both called *dababa*), and small arms with medium machine guns (variously referred to as *asliha, asliha khafifa, asliha thaqila*). Nor is discipline used in distinguishing among temporary checkpoints, bivouacked outposts, firm baselike encampments, and sustained garrisons (variously labeled *nuqta, nuqta 'askariya, nuqtat taftish, mawqa', mu'askar, qa'ida*). Likewise, GoY unit size is variously reported as a team (*taqim*, also used in reference to Huthis), battalion (*katiba*), or brigade (*liwa'*), with no indication of the size or relationship among these formations.

[4]   See "Indila' al-Qital Mujaddadan bayna al-Jaysh wa al-Ansar al-Huthi bi-Sa'da," *al-Ayyam*, March 29, 2005.

[5]   Interview with U.S. analyst who conducted fieldwork in Yemen in 2006, September 22, 2008; interview with U.S. political scientist focusing on Yemen, September 10, 2008. Also see references to this on Yemen Web fora at al-Yemen.org, May 18, 2007; al-Majlis al-Yamani, May 18, 2007.

Shaykh al-'Awjari.[6] Members of these families, who had been opponents of al-Haqq, the BY, and the Huthi family in the late 1990s, were senior officers in the zone, at times targeted by Huthi fighters.[7] Local sources also suggest that the military has transferred other, less dependable northern-origin Zaydi units out of the zone and replaced them with troops of a more Hashidi and/or Shafi'i complexion from the country's center and south.[8] This has raised rumors, reiterated by Western scholars, that at key junctures southern troops have been responsible for Huthi deaths.[9] Whether this is true or not, it stokes the south/Shafi'i versus north/Zaydi divide.

By and large, the GoY has deployed conventional army units into the region— infantry, armor, and artillery units, augmented by "engineer" units, likely of a logistical, motor transport, and road maintenance/demolition nature. Conventional army units consist almost entirely of short-term conscripts in the enlisted ranks, with a combination of short-term conscripts in the company grade ranks and "professional" officers in the field grade/general officer ranks. Local informants suggest that the material conditions of the conscript soldiers—out-of-doors billeting, poor and intermittent food and water, shoddy uniforms, and incomplete gear, as well as interruptions in pay—have negatively influenced morale, resulting in a limited amount of desertion.[10] More frequently, soldiers and junior officers have resorted to *qat,* acquired by "losing" weapons and ammunition to local sources, some of them Huthi.[11] There are only limited open-source reports indicating deployment of higher-quality Republican Guard units or YSOF into the area, mostly in connection with the pursuit of high-value Huthi targets.[12] The GoY elite likely has preferred to retain these assets—commanded by the president's son—close to San'a for the purposes of regime security or interdiction of al-Qa'ida–related threats. Finally, GoY army forces are augmented by local police personnel.

Since 2007, an additional component of the GoY force in the Sa'da conflict zone has been the regime's use of auxiliaries. Referred to as "volunteers" (*junud mustajaddin*)

---

6 Gerhard Lichtenthäler, *Political Ecology and the Role of Water: Environment, Society and Economy in Northern Yemen* (Surrey, UK: Ashgate Publishing, 2003), 64, 88.

7 See "al-Jaysh Yadkhul Madinat al-Nazir li al-Marra al-Thaniya wa 'Awdat ba'd al-Sukkan li Madinat al-Talh," *al-Ayyam*, May 14, 2007.

8 Interview with human rights worker from Sa'da area, March 20, 2009; interview with U.S. Yemen observer, October 2, 2008.

9 Lisa Wedeen, *Peripheral Visions: Publics, Power and Performance in Yemen* (Chicago: University of Chicago Press, 2008), 148.

10 Interview with human rights worker from Sa'da area, March 20, 2009.

11 Interview with human rights worker from Sa'da area, March 20, 2009; interview with Yemeni emigrant from conflict zone, October 10 and 29 and November 2, 2008.

12 See "30 Qatilan wa Jarihan fi Ma'arik bi-Sa'da wa Kamin Akhar Yanju minhu Na'ib al-Muhafiz," *al-Ayyam*, April 7, 2005; "Musadamat 'Anifa bi-Shawari' Sa'da Bayna al-Amn wa 'Anasir al-Huthi," *al-Ayyam*, April 9, 2005; "Masra' 3 'Askariyin fi Ishtibakat Musallaha wast San'a," *al-Ayyam* April 16, 2007.

or "mercenaries" (*murtaziqa*) depending on reporter bias, these include fighters from tribes located near the Saʿda governorate or farther afield from adjoining areas. In the former case, local tribes have been encouraged through money and coercion to supply troops to the GoY. Alternatively, tribal shaykhs, frustrated by continued fighting in their areas, have chosen to throw their lot in with the GoY. Regions that have seen tribal elements supporting the GoY include Abu Ghabr, al-Talh, Bani Muʿadh, Maruna in Sahar, and al-Salim and Wadi Nushur in Safra, as well as limited instances in Haydan and Razih. These local Saʿda alignments do not follow strictly tribal lines. Shaykh Shawit, for example, is of the Bani ʿUwayr, from the Sahar branch of the Khawlan bin ʿAmr, as is Shaykh Faʾid al-Mujalli of the al-ʿAbdin.[13] At different times, Bani Muʿadh tribal segments have associated with the GoY, likely from Khawlan bin ʿAmr groupings. Shaykh al-ʿAwjari, however, is of the Waʾila, a Bakil subtribe—although Ahl Nushur have in many cases supported the Huthi and are also Bakili (Hamdan al-Sham).[14] Furthermore, tribal alliances with the GoY—or Huthis—are short-lived, changing with circumstances or *qabili* assessments of what benefits them at any given time. Changing loyalties in Razih and Qatabir can likely be explained in this fashion.

In the latter case of the GoY employing fighters from farther afield, these have included members of Hashid tribes from governorates adjoining Saʿda with ties to the regime. During its offensive of spring and summer 2007, for example, it is reported that the GoY called upon al-ʿUsaymat and Bani Surim tribesmen from ʿAmran to join the GoY's ranks against the Huthis.[15] In many cases—though not all—these tribal elements are of a Sunni/Salafi persuasion. They have been used extensively during the several engagements in the environs of Dahyan. Additionally, however, it has been reported that the GoY has employed what are referred to as "Salafi tribal irregulars."[16] This is an ambiguous category. In some cases, it includes Hashidi tribesmen of Sunni background, potentially affiliated with Islah. In other cases, writers refer to explicit efforts on the part of the Saleh regime—and in particular by ʿAli Muhsin al-Ahmar— to recruit extremist Salafis directly into the fight, regardless of geographic or tribal background. Sources point to deals with al-Qaʿida sympathizers, as well as southern "Salafi jihaddists [sic]," those with a background in the Afghan Jihad, and veterans

---

[13] "Masraʿ Mudir li-l-Bahth al-Jinaʾi wa 3 Murafiqin lahu wa Najat Masʾul Akhar bi-Saʿda," *al-Ayyam*, January 28, 2006; "Hujum Barri wa Jawwi Wasiʿ ʿala Mawaqiʿ al-Huthiyin wa-l-ʿUthur ʿala Juthath Madaniyin," *al-Ayyam*, May 22, 2007; "Muwajahat bayna Qabilatayn Ahadahuma Mawaliya li-l-Hukuma wa Ukhra li al-Huthi," *al-Ayyam*, April 5, 2005.

[14] See "Kamin Thalith Yanju minhu Naʾib Muhafiz Saʿda wa Rami Qanbulatayn ʿala Taqim ʿAskari," *al-Ayyam*, May 3, 2005.

[15] See "War Continues, Government Warns Media about Coverage," *Yemen Times* 14:1031 (March 11, 2007).

[16] "The Saada War in Yemen," *Jane's Intelligence Digest*, April 27, 2007.

from fighting against the former PDRY in the 1994 civil war. Reports have also suggested that the Aden-Abyan Islamic army have been integrated by the GoY.[17]

There is very little of this in the Yemeni press, since it is likely too sensitive a matter for discussion. Therefore, it is not clear whether groups supporting the GoY are Hashidi, Islahi, or Salafi—nor is it clear what motivates them to side with the GoY (or Huthis). Furthermore, the reported numbers of tribal auxiliaries assisting the GoY have varied widely. Local press reporting notes scores to hundreds at any given location and time, and efforts to recruit up to 3,000 Hashidis at one time.[18] External reporting in the summer of 2007 suggested that 5,000 "Salafi tribal irregulars" were involved in the fighting,[19] while reportage from a year later suggested the GoY was attempting to raise a "popular army" of 27,000 tribal irregulars, to include Sa'da-area tribes frustrated by continued Huthi-instigated fighting.[20]

Still, it remains unknown how many tribals—or jihadists—are being provided to the GoY at any given time, and whether those fighters are in fact in the field. Indeed, even during the 1960s struggle between pro-imamate royalists and the YAR, local tribes often shifted loyalties between the two according to the logic of their own ongoing intertribe competitions for preeminence. Bribes, punishment, or external (Saudi) influence were all used to harness shaykhly opportunism. This fluidity of alliances remains today, with people in some areas being "farmers by day, Huthis by night." Further, anecdotes from local informants indicate that tribes can split on this issue down to the family level, rendering a numerical assessment even more difficult.[21] Likewise, as we have seen above in the case of the Mujalli and al-'Awjari resignations from the GPC, even longtime GoY supporters can break ranks as a form of protest or as interests change. Still, it is certain that the GoY has availed itself of these diverse paramilitary and auxiliary forces that in some cases have a much better awareness of the local environment than the GoY regular units. Of course, by tribalizing the Huthi campaign, the GoY has likely prolonged it, for reasons we discuss below.

In spite of the increase in military assistance to Yemen after 9/11 discussed above, FMS and IMET, in particular, have targeted niche elements in the GoY armed forces, such as the Coast Guard, counterterrorism units, and SOF. The conventional military has yet to benefit markedly from a security cooperation relationship with the United States or the United Kingdom. Therefore, the GoY has sought to prosecute the mili-

---

[17] "The Saada War in Yemen"; also see Jane Novak, "Yemen Strikes Multi-Faceted Deals with al-Qaeda," *The Long War Journal*, February 11, 2009.

[18] See "War Continues, Government Warns Media about Coverage."

[19] See "The Saada War in Yemen."

[20] See "Yemen: The Conflict in Saada Governorate," *Integrated Regional Information Networks* (IRIN), July 24, 2008.

[21] Interview with Yemeni emigrant from conflict region, November 2008; also see Lichtenthäler, *Political Ecology*, 55–57.

tary LOO of anti-Huthi COIN with a force suboptimized to the task. Compared to its opponents, it is a heavy, slow-moving force. Huthi propaganda images of destroyed GoY materiel indicate that forces in the field move about in heavy trucks—or at times buses—as well as in limited numbers of thin-skinned HMMWVs. Additionally, Soviet-era infantry fighting vehicles (BMPs and BTRs) are the basis for mechanized movement, augmented by small numbers of M113-style armored personnel carriers (APCs) likely acquired through EDA sales. None of these possess the up-armoring that affords protection against the rocket-propelled grenades (RPGs) used by Huthi fighters (see below). Armor likely consists mostly of T-55 and T-62 tanks. The GoY has also employed its air force, mostly in the form of Mi-8 transport helicopters and MiG-29s. Though the PDRY had acquired Mi-24 attack helicopters from the Soviet Union, it is not known if they are still serviceable, and imagery of their use in the Huthi conflict has not emerged.[22]

For the reasons delineated above, in-depth analysis of GoY military operations based on open sources remains difficult. In broad terms, however, GoY operations are constrained by the human and material assets it possesses, as well as by the geographic conditions described in Chapter One. In most cases, it has not chosen to use foot-mobile ground forces to pacify regions through a clear-and-hold strategy involving soft entry and policelike operations in urban and village areas, driven by intelligence and an understanding of the local environment. This would expose poorly trained and poorly equipped soldiers, who are unfamiliar with the environment, to fire in areas optimized for local rebel survival. In some cases, GoY forces have engaged in house-to-house searches for Huthi fighters or weapons, although this has sometimes aroused the anger of tribal Saʿdans as an affront to *sharaf*, particularly when females have been searched or roughly handled.[23]

Instead, it appears that in most cases, GoY forces have attempted to isolate Huthi centers from each other, cutting off avenues of transportation and applying kinetic force for purposes that can best be described as attrition, reaction, and punishment. While engaging in mechanized sweeps in the central parts of Saʿda, including the basin and lowlands abutting mountainous areas, the GoY has not regularly taken the fight to the enemy in the sense of committing ground troops to force-on-force assaults on known Huthi strongholds defended by fighters, be they in mountain or desert areas far from the governorate core. It seems that GoY forces invest the environs of locations occupied by Huthis, attempting to blockade and cut off these sectors from resupply. GoY forces then reportedly employ indirect fire—artillery, mortars, Katyushas, and tank munitions—either on suspected Huthi sites or in response to Huthi direct and indirect fire. Engagements thus have the character of reciprocal bombardments or GoY

---

[22] Yemeni press reports of "attack helicopters" (*taʾira ʿumudiya qatila*) may be referring to machine-gun mounted Mi-8s. See "Hajamat li-Marwahiyat Muqatila ʿala Mawaqiʿ al-Huthiyin bi-Saʿda," *al-Ayyam*, May 6, 2008.

[23] Consultations with Yemenis from the conflict zone and U.S./UK researchers with contacts in the area.

punitive reactions to "small-unit" Huthi raids on fixed or mobile GoY elements. Tank and artillery fire is also the means of choice to attack Huthi positions in mountains.

Lacking precision fires and pursuing standoff offensive operations, therefore, the GoY has caused casualties among both Huthi sympathizers and others unrelated to the conflict. Such tactics also ensure damage to noncombatants' means of livelihood, an issue to which we will return at the end of this chapter. Therefore, GoY occupation of areas previously held by Huthis usually results from blockade, bombardment, and Huthi withdrawal to other areas—not liberation through assault or patient patrolling. Likewise, Huthis occupy areas left undefended or recently abandoned by GoY forces. Territorial control thus alternates between the two sides with some frequency.

This is not to suggest an absence of engagements between GoY soldiers and Huthi fighters themselves. These have occurred throughout the conflict, mostly around checkpoints. Engagements tend to be at the squad-through-platoon size. In these situations, there does not appear to be a coordinated use of mechanized or armored assets in a maneuver-and-fire fashion. Rather, the pattern of Huthi-GoY direct confrontation seems to be successive individual small-unit engagements. Likewise, GoY employment of air assets has not been in the context of coordinated air-land operations. Without tactical air controllers embedded in ground elements, individual rotary-wing aircraft mostly resupply static GoY units. Limited reporting further suggests a preference for use of helicopters away from the front lines or in a non–ground attack role, so as to lessen the likelihood of ground-based fire bringing them down.[24] As such, rotary wing assets are not regularly used in air assault or ground attack.

Likewise, fixed-wing attack aircraft are used as flying artillery to hit mountainous areas or rural villages suspected of supporting Huthis. The absence of forward air controllers has also resulted in incidents of attacks causing significant civilian casualties, a trend that continued into the autumn of 2009.[25] Broadly, offensive air operations are not coordinated with ground movements, nor do they appear to consist of more than single aircraft servicing individual static targets and then returning to base. In particular, MiGs, artillery, and Katyushas have been used to hit areas such as Razzamat, Nushur, Matra, and Naq'a—where the strength of GoY ground troops does not permit infiltration, reconnaissance in force, or assault of Huthi regions.

There have been cases departing from this overall pattern. During the 2007 fighting, for example, it appears that a major objective of GoY forces was to assume control of the Huthi stronghold of Dahyan, northwest of Sa'da city, likely because control of Dahyan would both be a great propaganda victory over the Huthis and would open up avenues of advance to areas such as Matra, Razih, Munabbih, and perhaps even Naq'a.

---

[24] See "Taqallus Mawaqi' Atba' al-Huthi wa Masadir Tufid bi-annihum Yuqatilun bi-Sharasa," *al-Ayyam,* January 2, 2006; Mohammed al-Asaadi, "Yemen Strives to Stop Firearms Proliferation," *Yemen Times* 16:1176 (July 30, 2008).

[25] See "Yemen Army Air Raid Kills 80 Civilians: Witnesses," *al-Arabiya.net,* September 17, 2009.

Throughout the spring and into the summer, GoY artillery and air pounded much of the city, with intermittent forays of GoY ground units into the city. They were not able to sustain an assault, however, or follow up temporary advances with enough force to push farther into the city and establish permanent toeholds adequately defended against Huthi counterattack. By the end of the summer, GoY forces had withdrawn.[26]

Likewise, the fifth phase of fighting during the summer of 2008 featured GoY ground forces moving toward Dahyan again, also attacking Marran, the home region of the Huthi family, perhaps seeking to close with and destroy the enemy. In this case, however, GoY army units—reportedly attached to the Seventeenth Division—were surrounded by Huthi fighters in areas the latter knew much better and were cut off from the rest of the GoY. Division commander 'Abd al-'Aziz Shahari was blockaded with his men, and GoY forces suffered severe shortages in ammunition, food, and water, requiring resupply from the air. In at least one case, an Mi-8 was brought down by Huthi small-arms fire as it attempted resupply, leading to reluctance on the part of GoY commanders to send others in—and consequent anger by local troops, who allegedly began telephoning Yemeni press outlets to complain that they had been abandoned. A subsequent attack against Matra by the Tenth Division was called off after its training officer, Muhammad al-Fadli, was killed by a Huthi sniper.[27]

With respect to preferred tactics, the sixth phase of GoY military operations mostly resembled previous phases. Large-scale artillery barrages and use of fixed-wing aircraft against static targets were prominent. Greater numbers of armor and mechanized assets were shown moving into the area of operations—although there have yet to emerge reports of mass employment of these assets, either alone or in coordination with foot-mobile forces.[28] In a relative departure from previous phases, the GoY allegedly referred publicly to its campaign as a "scorched earth" approach (*al-ard al-mahruqa*).[29] Yemeni observers have therefore suggested that in the most-recent phase of fighting, the GoY disposition of forces consisted of several small outposts throughout the 'Amran and Sa'da regions. While perhaps intended to provide a GoY presence in man areas, these posts are susceptible to isolation and attack by Huthi groups, driving the GoY to use more intense air- and ground-based fire to gain logistical resupply

---

[26] See "al-Jaysh Yatamakkan min al-Saytara 'ala Mu'azzam Ajza' Jabal Gharaba bi-Sa'da," *al-Ayyam,* April 24, 2007.

[27] Mohammed bin Sallam, "Dozens Killed as Sa'ada Clashes Become Fierce," *Yemen Times* 16:1167 (June 29, 2008); "Istimrar al-Hisar 'ala Katibat al-Jaysh bi-Haydan wa Inkhifad al-Hajamat al-Mutabadila bayna al-Janibayn," *al-Ayyam,* January 24, 2008.

[28] See "Yemen to Fight Rebels for 'Years,'" *BBC News,* September 26, 2009, which shows a column of Yemeni armored vehicles moving north on the San'a-Sa'da road.

[29] See "Fi al-Ard al-Mahruqa bi-l-Yaman . . . Junud Murhaqun wa Nazihun Ghadibun min al-Huthiyin," *al-Sharq al-Awsat,* September 18, 2009; Sadiq al-Silmi, "al-Yaman Ya'tamidd Siyasat "al-Ard al-Mahruqa" li-l-Qada' 'ala al-Huthiyin," *al-Watan,* August 20, 2009; "al-'Alam: al-Yaman Tuwasil 'Amaliyat 'al-Ard al-Mahruqa' fi Ma'arikiha ma'a al-Huthiyin," *al-Sabah* (Iraqi), September 17, 2009.

access to these posts. Additionally, it has been suggested that the GoY hoped to alienate Huthi fighters from the communities in which they operate by aggressively and repeatedly targeting population centers and local infrastructure, thus cultivating a sense by noncombatants that the Huthis are to blame for incessant violence.[30] Whether this is the thinking behind current GoY operations is unknown, though it would seem to correlate with reports suggesting that individual clashes grew in intensity—greater numbers of casualties, more prisoners taken, more materials confiscated, and so forth.[31] Of course, compared with previous rounds of fighting, the greater regional and global press interest in the Huthi phenomenon during this sixth phase may have resulted in inflated and double reporting, creating an impression of greater conflict magnitude.

Somewhat of a departure during the sixth Sa'da war has been the readiness of the GoY to employ special operations units (*wahdat khassa*; YSOF) in more instances, including night operations against selected high-value targets. The GoY has sought to advertise this, featuring on its Web sites amateur videos allegedly taken by military personnel in the area, which depict Yemeni special operators conducting precombat checks, examining maps, and moving to forward staging areas. In such cases, the intent appears to have been to neutralize points of origin for Huthi indirect fire and sniper attacks or to eliminate Huthi leaders.[32] However, since YSOF and counterterror elements likely operate according to their own chains of command with tactical control originating in San'a, they may not have been well integrated into local-level command-and-control structures. If so, their overall operational impact would have been diminished, unless they came to manage anti-Huthi operations throughout the region. This, of course, bears other risks, because it could commit President Saleh's most skilled forces to the north at a time of persistent southern discontent and a greater need to combat the al-Qa'ida threat.

It is noteworthy that the GoY army has been able to support multiple combat deployments into the 'Amran-Sa'da-Hajja areas for over five years, alternating between defensive and offensive operations even while wars have been declared "over." Aside from isolated cases and rumors,[33] soldiers and officers have not mutinied or defected in large numbers, and the army does not appear to be a political liability to the GoY yet,

---

[30] For this view, see Ahmad Salih al-Faqih, "al-Istratijiya al-'Askariya li-l-Dawla wa-l-Huthiyin fi Harb Sa'da al-Haliya," *al-Taghyir*, October 1, 2009. A Yemeni human/legal rights group, al-Taghyir has been critical of the GoY's conduct of anti-Huthi operations.

[31] See, for example, "Yemen Troops Pound Northern Rebels with Artillery," *al-Arabiya TV,* as featured in *Mosaic News,* September 29, 2009; "Yemeni Forces Kill 28 Houthis in North," *Press TV* (Iran), September 30, 2009.

[32] See "Ghara Jari'a 'ala Awkar al-Huthiyin fi Sa'da," video posted at YouTube on September 16, 2009.

[33] Interview with human rights worker from Sa'da area, March 20, 2009; Abdul Rahim al-Shawthabi, "Government Investigates with 70 Rebel Soldiers," *Yemen Post,* February 9, 2009: "Security source confirmed that investigations are still underway with some (70 military soldiers) belonging to the 127 Infantry Brigade of the First Armored Division on the background of a army rebellion last week against the Brigade Commander Brigadier General Jihad Ali Antar, in the camp known as Airport Camp in Gaflat Ethr District of Amran province. The

although soldiers do complain about pay and provisions.[34] Indeed, Yemeni military forces have been able to respond to Huthi provocation and have not been decisively defeated in set battles. However, the former results in a grinding tit-for-tat that harms noncombatants, while the latter is not the nature of insurgent warfare or northern Yemen tribal combat. Fundamentally, however, the GoY's military actions have yet to provide Saleh with the capability to kinetically shut down the Huthis or to pursue political resolution in a fashion of decisive advantage to the GoY. And, as conflict has continued, the GoY's favored tactics—which include the seemingly indiscriminate use of force that targets civilians, as well as measures that harm the environmental and economic bases of life (see Chapter Eight)—both elicit and sustain the Huthi insurrection.

The Information Dimension

In combating the Huthis, GoY actions along the information LOO have been both punitive-preventative and active-shaping. Punitive actions have included repeatedly "cleansing" schools of suspected Huthist employees and closing down BY-type summer camps in areas under GoY control.[35] Additionally, the regime has removed pro-Huthi Zaydi teachers and prayer leaders from mosques and has ensured wide coverage of trials of certain prominent Zaydi personalities.[36] It has also arrested and sentenced prominent journalists who sought to report on the conflict in a fashion unfavorable to the GoY.[37] Finally, from 2007 onward, the GoY has sought to prevent journalists' access to the conflict region, at times also blocking access of foreign analysts to the country.[38]

We will return to elements of the punitive-preventative campaign in our discussion of human rights issues below. Regarding efforts to shape attitudes toward the conflict through active production of themes and messages, the GoY has used all the means at the disposal of a state and regular army. Therefore, in addition to routinely hammering consistent themes and messages in the army's newspaper (*26 September*), the GPC's organ (*al-Mu'tammar*), and English news sources affiliated with the GoY

---

same source said that the investigation into the incident so far did not show any motives behind the incident other than the rebels' demands of financial sums."

[34] See "Jundi Yunashid Wazir al-Difa' Inha' Harmanihi Ratibihi Mundhu 17 Shahran," *al-Ayyam*, September 2, 2009.

[35] See "Mukhayyamat al-Yaman . . . Furas Badila li-Himayat al-Shabab," *al-Moheet.com*, August 27, 2008.

[36] See "al-Isti'nafiya Kanat qad Qadat bi-Habasihi Khamas Sanawat: al-Ra'is Ya'mur bi-l-Ifraj 'an al-Qadi Luqman fi Itar 'Afuhi 'an Atba' al-Huthi," *26 September*, August 7, 2006.

[37] See "Ra'is al-Jumhuriya Ya'mur bi-Iqaf Tanfidh al-Ahkam al-Qada'iya fi Haqq al-Daylami wa Miftah wa-l-Ifraj 'Anhuma," *26 September*, May 20, 2006; J. E. Peterson, "The al-Huthi Conflict in Yemen," *Arabian Peninsula Background Note*, APBN-006, August 2008, 8.

[38] See Nabil Sabi', "Tard al-Shuhud min al-Yaman wa Ighlaq al-bilad 'ala Hurub Ghayr Mahduda," *al-Nida'*, April 30, 2009.

(*Saba' News*), the GoY leadership, including President Saleh himself, has given televised interviews on the conflict and has taken advantage of "impromptu" appearances before journalists' cameras to talk about the GoY's progress in the conflict. As these interviews are often subsequently transcribed and printed in GoY-affiliated papers as well as semi-independent party organs or English-language outlets, not only do readers encounter reinforcing messages several times, but wider audiences can be reached as well.

Like other Muslim regimes confronting internal opposition, the GoY has deployed additional state-driven means of ideological communication. In schools, curricula and guidance to teachers have been aligned with regime messages—although compliance is impossible to enforce. The GoY has also set up its own summer camps, both in and around the conflict zones.[39] Additionally, the GoY has sought to mobilize Yemen's state-funded and state-monitored hierarchy of Islamic functionaries. It has provided Shafi'i and Zaydi prayer leaders with approved guidance on the subject matter of Friday sermons. Indicating the extent to which it considers the Huthis an ideological threat, the regime has also mobilized GoY-affiliated Shafi'i and Salafi *'ulama'* to publish *fatwas*, or legal rulings, condemning the Huthis in terms aligned with GoY rhetoric. These efforts have been particularly strong in the army.[40] Military chaplains have echoed GoY pronouncements to both Zaydi and Sunni troops, ensuring that soldiers encounter Islamic justification for prosecuting a war against fellow Yemenis.

The GoY has also sought to connect directly with the conflict area and protagonists. Leaflets and handbills have been distributed among the population in Sa'da and other conflict-affected governorates, as have been incriminating pictures of alleged Huthi fighters (see Figure 6.2 on p. 177). Likewise, it has used the Sa'da-area government radio station to broadcast anti-Huthi statements. Finally, the GoY has deployed individuals linked to the Huthi family itself through blood or association, to delegitimize Huthi claims that the Huthis represent authentic Yemeni Zaydism. Using these means, the GoY has communicated several interrelated messages that seek to distance the Huthis from authentic Yemeni society, politics, and even religion. Huthis are thus portrayed as foreign-inspired elements seeking to sunder hard-won republican unity through brutal actions that oppress the Yemeni people in hopes of returning the country to the dark ages of the imamate according to interpretations of Zaydism that are fundamentally incorrect or out of step with the spirit of the times.

Huthis as Foreign

In this approach, GoY spokesmen and regime-sympathetic media have portrayed the Huthis from the first as inspired by "external elements" (*jihat kharijiya*), receiving foreign funding (*tamwil khariji*) as well as weapons and moral support from regional

---

[39] "Mukhayyamat al-Yaman . . . Furas Badila li-Himayat al-Shabab."

[40] Note the *fatwa* by senior Yemeni Mufti Isma'il al-'Amrani justifying the shedding of Huthi blood. See "War Continues, Government Warns About Media Coverage," *Yemen Times* 14:1031, March 11, 2007.

countries.[41] Early in the conflict, Interior Ministry spokesmen assured listeners that "investigations had . . . exposed . . . many details about the support that these rebels against the constitution and the law receive from regional entities [*jihat iqlimiya*], either through intelligence agencies in some countries, or through faith or sect-based groups [*jama'at madhhabiya aw 'aqa'idiya*], or from welfare societies in the region." The goal of such foreign support is "to create a sort of instability, and to spread chaos and destruction in Yemeni society."[42]

GoY sources have repeated this theme throughout the conflict, with increasing emphasis on state roles and transnational Islamic elements. At the beginning of the fourth phase of the war, for example, the GoY Minister of Pious Endowments emphasized that "we must make exceptional efforts . . . to clarify that the nation is exposed to a great conspiracy today, and that there are countries whose hands target Yemen, along with Shi'ite institutions that have a hand in this [Huthi] strife."[43]

In their official public pronouncements, Yemeni officials do not accuse specific countries of external support for the Huthis. However, Yemeni officials have hinted in public as to who they consider involved,[44] and GoY-supportive press outlets have been explicit. Iran, in particular, has been highlighted as a foreign state sponsor of the Huthis. In 2005–2007, the Yemeni press gave wide coverage to visits to Tehran by Yemeni officials to discuss the Huthi rebellion. Although Yemeni Foreign Minister Abu Bakr al-Qurbi frequently averred that relations with Iran were strong and that "the Iranian government has affirmed that it does not intervene in the internal affairs of Yemen," Shi'ite Iranian association with the Huthi revolt was rhetorically established.[45] Indeed, in 2007 Yemen withdrew its ambassador from Tehran for consultations, implying Iranian support for the Huthis as the fourth war intensified.[46] In private, Yemeni officials have been blunt about Iranian support for the Huthis, drawing attention to Badr al-Din al-Huthi's visits to Iran during the 1990s, as well as Tehran's

[41] See Anwar Qasim al-Khidri, "al-Huthi wa-l-Waraqa al-Ta'ifiya al-Khasira," *Al-Bayyina*, May 6, 2006; and Hassan abu Talib, "al-Huthiyun w-l-Ma'raka ma Qabl al-Akhir fi-l-Yaman," *al-Ahram Center for Strategic Studies*, July 9, 2008.

[42] "al-'Uthur 'ala Adilla Tathbut Tawarrut Jihat Iqlimiya wa Mahalliya Fi Da'm al-Tamarrud alladhi Qadahu," *26 September*, September 16, 2004.

[43] See "Qal Inna Tamarrud 'Anasir al-Irhab bi-Sa'da Sina'a Istikhbariya . . . Wazir al-Awqaf Yatahimm Duwal wa Mu'assasat Shi'iya bi-Istihdaf al-Yaman," *26 September*, February 18, 2007.

[44] See Ghassan Sharbil, "'Ali 'Abdullah Salih: al-Tansiq al-Yamani-al-Su'udi Mumtaz," *al-Hayat*, March 28, 2009.

[45] See "Dr Abu Bakr al-Qurbi: Ajhizat al-Amn Mustamirra fi al-Taharri 'an Ay Da'm Khariji Yasl ila Jama'at al-Huthi," *al-Ayyam*, June 11, 2005; "Dr. al-Qurbi, Ziyarati li-Iran li-Sharh Tatawwurat Tamarrud al-Huthi wa Man' Istighlaliha li-l-Waqi'a," *al-Ayyam*, May 26, 2005.

[46] See Mohammed bin Sallam, "Yemen Recalls its Ambassador to Iran and Libya," *Yemen Times* 15:1050, May 16, 2007.

fraternal view of the Huthi family.[47] Additionally, media supportive of the GoY have directly implicated Iran.[48]

When discussing Huthi motives for a linkage with Iran, GoY spokesmen have tarred Badr al-Din al-Huthi and his sons as allied with Iran's agenda to drive a Shi'ite wedge into the Arab heartland. They declare that the Huthi family has duped its followers into becoming the Yemeni component of Iran's regional "Shi'ite crescent" policy, along the way receiving support and encouragement from nonstate Shi'ite groups in Bahrain, Saudi Arabia, and other Gulf countries. As a terrorist organization receiving support and perhaps even orders from Iran, therefore, the Huthis are not just a foreign-supported internal threat. Rather, they are also a threat to Arab (Sunni) interests and U.S. regional interests. While distancing the Huthis from Yemen, therefore, the GoY seeks to internationalize the issue. Not only do the Huthis threaten the regional balance of power, they should be seen as part of the GWoT.[49]

The Huthi-as-foreign idea focuses mostly on Iran and regional Shi'ites. In some cases, however, the GoY has also listed Libya as a Huthi supporter—part of Muammar Qaddafi's efforts to meddle in Yemen in order to threaten Saudi Arabia.[50] Likewise, in a possible effort to tap into enduring anti-American sentiment, the visits of U.S. diplomats to Sa'da and other Zaydi areas, along with public U.S. statements encouraging conciliation on both sides, have been cited as indications that the United States supports the Huthis, either as a way to lessen Salafi power or to increase American leverage on the GoY under the guise of counterterror assistance.[51] In all these cases, the implicit message is that the Huthis have put themselves beyond the pale of the Yemeni national collective (*watan*).

Huthis as Closet Imamis Who Distort Zaydism

Portraying the Huthis as foreign-sustained, the GoY has sought to challenge them on their own terms. GoY narratives assert that the Huthi family seeks to restore the Zaydi imamate, dismissing the notion that ongoing disturbances reflect the Zaydi struggle for religious freedom. In several instances, GoY outlets have accused Husayn al-Huthi of having referred to himself as "Imam" and "Commander of the Faithful" (*amir al-mu'minin*), terms reserved for the Prophet or his successors. In this vein, GoY sources refer to Husayn's extracting pledges of allegiance (*mubaya'a*) "as the imam and amir

---

[47] Interview with senior official in Republic of Yemen embassy, Washington, D.C., September 11, 2008.

[48] See Anwar Qasim al-Khidri, "al-Huthi wa-l-Waraqa al-Ta'ifiya al-Khasira"; Najib Ghallab, "al-Yaman wa 'al-Huthiya' wa-l-Hajis al-Irani," *al-Sharq al-Awsat,* May 15, 2008.

[49] Interview with senior official in Republic of Yemen embassy, Washington, D.C., September 11, 2008.

[50] See Mohammed bin Sallam, "Yemen Recalls its Ambassador"; Nasser Arrabyee, "Yemen's Rebels Undefeated," *al-Ahram Weekly,* No. 838, April 4, 2007; Mohammed bin Sallam, "Houthis Seize Four Sa'ada Districts," *Yemen Times* 15:1045 (April 29, 2007).

[51] See Anwar Qasim al-Khidri, "al-Huthi wa-l-Waraqa al-Ta'ifiya al-Khasira."

al-mu'minin," and issuing *fatwas* requiring payment of taxes in cash and kind "as a legitimate divine right, as he [Husayn] has the right to rule over them in consideration of him being from the Al al-Bayt," or Prophet's house.[52] GoY sources also published alleged lectures of Husayn stipulating that the goals of the Huthis included establishing an imamate and ensuring that Hashimis rule.[53]

Indeed, the GoY has gone to considerable lengths to portray Husayn and his successor 'Abd al-Malik as possessing delusions of grandeur. GoY forces allegedly found Husayn's will, where he considered himself "the second Husayn," whose head should be cut off after he dies, just as was that of Husayn bin 'Ali in Karbala in 680 CE.[54] Additionally, GoY-supportive press outlets have repeated the claim that Husayn and his followers had frequently read the text *'Asr al-Zuhur* (the Age of the Appearance), which allegedly states that an Islamic revolution heralding the arrival of the Mahdi (messianic savior) will be led by a Yemeni named Hasan or Husayn from the Sa'da region.[55] Whether or not the Huthis read or believe this material—or endow their actions with apocalyptic value—the government has used such claims to discredit them.

These portrayals support a broader effort to discredit the Huthis in both Zaydi and Islamic terms. Pro-GoY venues emphasize that Badr al-Din al-Huthi sided with the Jarudi school of thought, which rejected Islam's early rulers and is the closest of Zaydi approaches to Twelver Shi'ism.[56] Pushing Huthis farther to the edge of the Zaydi community, GoY-approved descriptions of the Huthis' background point to Husayn and Badr al-Din's travels to Iran, where they reputedly toured Qum to learn about the success of the Iranian revolution as well Hizbullah's evolution. In the process, Husayn, in particular, absorbed Twelver Shi'ism: "the importation by [Husayn] al-Huthi of the religious and political beliefs of Twelver Shi'ism into his movement was not odd, on the basis of Twelverism's confluence of views with the Jarudi group of Zaydism, for which his father Badr al-Din al-Huthi was its reference point [*marja'*] in Yemen." Such narratives also allude to visits of Lebanese and Iraqi Shi'ites to Yemen to study in "Huthi" centers in the late 1990s, as well as to establish Twelver-style learning centers (*husayniyas*) in the region. These same sources describe a form of Huthi-inspired BY activity from 1999 to 2004 that was much more politically threatening than in previous years. This involved nightly meetings of groups of youths under the stewardship

[52] See "Muwatinin min Haydan: al-Huthi Farada 'ala Atba'ihi Dafa' Nasab min Amwalihim ka Atawat Ba'dama Atlaqa 'ala Nafsihi Siffat Amir al-Mu'minin," *26 September,* June 25, 2004.

[53] "26 Septembernet Tunshir Nass Muhadarat 'al-Huthi' allati Kashafat Ab'ad al-Mukhattat al-Ta'amurri," *26 September*, May 16, 2005.

[54] See "al-Huthi Yuwassi bi-Qat' Ra'sihi idha Mat Hatta La Yu'raf," *26 September*, September 3, 2004.

[55] See Nabil 'Abd al-Rabb, "Fusul Qissat Muntahiya . . . 'al-Shabab al-Mu'min' min Mukhayyamat Dahyan ila 'Fallal' al-Doha," *al-Mithaqnet*, June 25, 2007.

[56] See Anwar Qasim al-Khidri, "al-Huthi wa-l-Waraqa al-Ta'ifiya al-Khasira;" Hassan abu Talib, "al-Huthiyun wa-l-Ma'raka ma Qabl al-Akhir fi-l-Yaman."

of Husayn and his colleagues, which would "follow a Karbal-esque manner in their character." Such practices involved viewing Iranian films about an historically imagined 'Ali and Husayn, as well as films from the Iranian revolution and Hizbullah and the worship of death as a higher value than charitable living.[57]

Indeed, by focusing on these issues—to include claiming that Huthi supporters collected weapons and began military training in these years—the GoY asserts that the Huthi hardcore has departed from the traditional course of Zaydism, and has disgraced the legacy of the BY and 1990s Zaydi scholars who sought to revive a Zaydi religious awareness among the new generation and make the *madhhab* relevant to an era of change, better education, Yemeni unity, and political pluralism. In making this point, the government has relied on BY veterans and Huthi family members who have criticized the Huthis in religious terms. Wide coverage has been given to the statements of Muhammad 'Izzan, as well as 'Abdullah al-Huthi, Husayn's oldest son. The latter, not a known Zaydi scholar but a person possessing credibility due to his name as well as the time he was imprisoned by the regime, has called for the Huthis to lay down their arms and desist from threatening Yemeni unity, religious freedom, and the lives of Zaydis and instead to pursue legitimacy through democratic political activism.[58] 'Izzan, the *qabili 'alim* we encountered in Chapter Three as a founder of the BY, has attacked his erstwhile colleagues on specifically religious grounds. Praising Zaydism's intellectual openness, rejection of sectarianism, and tradition of coexistence among multiple approaches to Islam, 'Izzan has condemned "the plainly evident differences of al-Huthi from the Zaydi school [*madhhab*] of Islam." While Zaydism is a "continually renewing approach able to be in step with the eras and in harmony with changes . . . al-Huthi has adopted a bunch of thoughts that disagree complete with Zaydism, especially those thoughts upon which he has risen his *fitna*." Therefore, in 'Izzan's judgment, the Huthis have "departed from the general path of Zaydism."[59] Worse still, the Huthis have "drawn a repugnant and fear-inspiring picture of the Zaydi *madhhab*."[60]

---

[57] See Nabil 'Abd al-Rabb, "Fusul Qissat Muntahiya . . . 'al-Shabab al-Mu'min' min Mukhayyamat Dahyan ila 'Fallal' al-Doha"; 'Abd al-Hamid al-Lisani, "Mudakhala Hadi'a ma'a 'Zayd' . . . 'An al-Huthiya wa-l-Zaydiya wa-l-Hashimiya wa-l-Futun al-Ukhra," *al-Mithaq.net* July 16, 2007; D. Ahmad Muhammad al-Dughshi, "al-Zahira al-Huthiya: Dirasa Manhajiya fi Tab'iyat al-Nash'a wa Jadaliyat al-'Alaqa bi-l-Ta'rikh," *Nashwan News*, April 20, 2009.

[58] See "Najl Husayn al-Huthi; Ad'u 'Anasir al-Tamarrud fi Sa'da li-Taslim Anfusihim li-l-Dawla Dun Shurut," *26 September.net*, July 13, 2008; see same article at other pro-GoY sites: *al-Mu'tammar*, with English précis at "More al-Houthi Insurgents Surrender," al-Motamar.net, July 16, 2008; also see Husayn Jarbani, "al-Yaman: Najl al-Huthi Yasif al-Huthiyin bi-'al-Kharijin 'an al-Nizam' . . . wa Yarfud Taza "um tamarrudihim," *al-Sharq al-Awsat,* July 14, 2008.

[59] See Ahmad al-Ram'i, "al-Khilafat al-Jalliya li-l-Huthi ma'a Madhhab al-Zaydiya," *al-Mithaq.net*, May 21, 2007.

[60] See "'Izzan Mukhatiban al-Huthiyin: Intum Shawwahatum al-Madhhab al-Zaydi fa-Alqu bi-Aslihatikum wa Salamu Anfusakum li-l-Dawla," *26 September.net*, June 17, 2008.

Therefore, instead of a republican regime ensuring freedom of religion, the Huthi-as-closet-Imamis motif accuses the Huthi family of wishing to bring back the Middle Ages regime under which a socioreligious minority—the Zaydi Hashimis—ruled autocratically, isolating Yemen from progress and religious enlightenment. They wish to do this in spite of the consensus of Zaydi scholars today, who renounce *khuruj* and an imamate dependent on Hashimi preeminence. Here, the GoY has mobilized the *'ulama'* as well. In a May 2007 statement, a gathering of Yemeni religious scholars warned:

> What is going on in Sa'da . . . is a great danger threatening the existence and unity of the nation, and its stability, given what it has in terms of shedding of blood . . . the bringing to life of ignorant clannish fanaticism [*'asabiya jahiliya*], and taking the nation [*umma*] back to fragmentation and perforation. . . . There is no doubt that what is going on in Sa'da is an armed revolt [*tamarrud*] . . . against the state, exceeding all fixed religious and national bounds. . . . They encourage their revolt through ideas strange to our Yemeni Muslim society, which disagree with the book and the *sunna* and the consensus [*ijma'*] of the *umma*, and are hostile to the companions of the Prophet . . . who brought to us this religion, and illuminated the path for us. They [the Huthis] make the leadership of the Muslims the monopolistic prerogative of a particular lineage, and this is a denial of the principle of consultation [*shura*] in Islam, just as in their cause is the incitement of sectarian and ideological chauvinism.[61]

Of course, not all Yemenis in the conflict zone are literate or read GoY-generated media. Therefore, leaflets have been distributed in Sa'da and adjoining areas, bearing summaries of the GoY claims against the Huthis, attributed to "respected *'ulama'* of Yemen" (see Figure 6.1).

Huthis as Cowardly, Oppressing Yemenis in the North

Perhaps mindful of the effect of deploying a conventional army to the region, the GoY seeks to counteract accusations of callousness by focusing attention on Huthi misdeeds. Huthi fighters are portrayed as "using citizens as human shields in an attempt to influence the advance of the government's troops" and routinely destroying infrastructure provided by the GoY, such as schools, electricity, and hospitals. Rather than making common cause with the Huthis, therefore,

> the people [of Sa'da] feel tremendous anxiety due to the practices of the so-called 'al-Huthi' and his followers, who prevent residents from fleeing areas of combat,

---

[61] "al-Ra'is Yufaddil al-Hall al-Silmi Kay La Tuthar al-Na'arat al-Madhhabiya wa-l-'Ulama' Yarfudun Ihtikar al-Wilaya li-Sallala Mu'ayyana," *26 September.net*, June 2, 2007.

Figure 6.1
GoY Tactical Information Operations Leaflet Condemning Huthis in Islamic Terms

[Translation]

The Illustrious Religious
Scholars of Yemen:

Shaykh al-Raymi: All together must stand against those who are working very hard to establish an apostate [Shi'ite; *rafidi*] order.

Shaykh Mahfuz: We must continue the efforts and close ranks to confront this discord and bury it.

Shaykh al-Mu'allim: There is no use to endeavoring with the rebels except for decisively finishing [them] and using force.

Shaykh al-Mahdi: These [Huthis] directed their weapon towards the *umma*; fighting them is legitimate and this is a religious ruling [*hukm shar'i.*]

Shaykh Hasan: Those who revolt against the consensus of the *umma* and the [existing political] order require the leaders to take responsibility and preserve security.

SOURCE: Yemeni national from conflict area.

RAND *MG962-6.1*

thus turning them into hostages in their home areas and trying to provoke the military into harming the people.[62]

Seeking to resonate with local cultural values, the GoY has also pointed to alleged Huthi ethical violations. Along with "torture and savage practices" (*al-ta'dhib wa-l-mumarasat al-wahshiya*) toward captured soldiers and pro-GoY tribespeople,[63] GoY media claim that Huthi fighters have killed men "rejecting the ideas of the group of

---

[62] See "Masra' wa Isaba 75 min Atba'ihi: al-Huthi Yalja' ila Istikhdam al-Muwatinin ka-Duru' Bashariya," *26 September*, July 10, 2004; "Fima Batat Nihayatuhum Qariba fi Zull Tadyiq al-Khinaq 'alayhim: Ajhizat al-Amn Tulqi al-Qibd 'ala Irhabiyin fi Sa'da bi-Sharashif Nisa'iya," *26 September*, March 22, 2007.

[63] See "Al-Irhabiyun Qat'u Atraf Jundi wa Isab'ahu wa Udhunihu: al-Yemen Yanfi Istikhdam al-Tiyran wa al-Aslaha al-Kimawiya Did al-Huthin," *26 September*, February 14, 2007.

terrorist elements" and murdered mothers protecting their children.[64] They are also claimed to have bombed girls' schools, threatened young females, and left them without opportunities for uplift.[65] Furthermore, Huthi funds are said to come from selling drugs, which they also use to ensure the loyalty of their mostly youthful followers, whom they turn into addicts.[66] Additionally, although the GoY at one time blamed the Huthi emergence on Jewish (read perfidious, Zionism-serving) support, even the President himself has brought attention to the plight of Sa'da's Jews since 2007, accusing Huthis of harming these protected Yemeni citizens.[67] Huthis have thus departed from the pale of *qabyala*, violating local *'ird* by aggression against vulnerable people and leaving a trail of orphans. Finally, the GoY press has said that Huthi fighters have donned women's clothing in order to attack soldiers.[68] This is a double transgression—dressing in a way religiously inappropriate as well as culturally dishonorable, they have exploited GoY soldiers' respect for the sanctity of women. This theme has been absorbed into local-level tactical information operations (see Figure 6.2).

Huthis as Anti-Republican

Since the GoY considers Huthis to be foreign-sponsored oppressors of northern Yemenis in the name of a distorted understanding of Zaydism, the movement threatens the foundations of the republic itself. Pointing to the al-Haqq Party's opposition to the use of armed force against the south in the 1994 civil war—and asserting a continuity from al-Haqq to the Huthis—the GoY has labeled the latter as *infisaliyin*, or separatists. In this narrative, the Huthis "have repeated the same position inimical to the republican order and the blessed Yemeni unity."[69] Maintaining contacts with the southern socialists, even receiving arms from them, and stirring up sectarianism (*ta'ifiya*, *madhhabiya*), the Huthis oppose a unified Yemeni state, seeking instead to "rip apart national unity [*al-wahda al-wataniya*] for the sake of selfish interests."[70]

---

[64] See "Isaba Baligha li-Walidatihi wa Hiyya Tuhawil Himayatahu bi-Jasadiha Wa Masdar Mahalli Yu'akkid innaha Tu'akkis Inhiyarihim," *26 September*, June 16, 2008.

[65] "al-Qibd 'ala Majami' Kabira min Atba' al-Huthi," *26 September*, June 19, 2008.

[66] "Muhafiz Sa'da li-26 Sabtambir: al-Ma'raka al-Hasima Lam Tabda' Ba'd min Janib al-Dawla," *26 September*, February 15, 2007.

[67] "al-Huthi Yurid al-Khilafa li-Nafsihi: Sahifat Watan Tunshir (Wajh al-Iman) wa bi-l-Watha'iq Haqiqat Ahdaf al-Fitna fi Sa'da," *26 September*, June 2, 2007; Shaker Khalid, "Yemeni Jews . . . From Creation to the Magic Carpet Operation," *Yemen Post*, No. 67, January 5, 2009.

[68] "Fima Batat Nihayatuhum Qariba fi Zull Tadyiq al-Khinaq 'alayhim: Ajhizat al-Amn Tulqi al-Qibd 'ala Irhabiyin fi Sa'da bi-Sharashif Nisa'iya."

[69] See "Atlaqa 'ala Nafsihi Amir al-Mu'minin wa Za'ama annahu al-Mahdi al-Muntazar," *26 September*, June 24, 2004.

[70] See "Fi Muhadara Muhimma Alqaha bi-l-Kulliya al-Harbiya bi-San'a': Fakhamat Ra'is al-Jumhuriya: Alladhin Yarfa'un Shi'ar al-Mawt li-Amrika al-Mawt li-Isra'il Kidhban wa Zawran Hum Yarfa'un Shi'ar Mawt li-l-Watan," *al-Ayyam*, November 30, 2005.

**Figure 6.2
GoY Leaflet Accusing Huthi Men of Dressing as Women**

SOURCE: Yemeni national from conflict area.

TRANSLATION: "This is a picture from among the Huthis who killed three of [our] greatest heroes. He enters and departs from our lines, and out of respect for women, we did not undertake to search him, until he crept away, escaping, and from his gait, we knew that he really was a male. And we did not want to show this picture, if not for the abundance of lies and deceiving [by the Huthis]. I ask Allah to forgive me [for showing this picture] and make this [effort] sincere in the face of God, and may he have mercy on [the dead soldiers] Majid and his heroic fellows."

RAND *MG962-6.2*

In this respect, the Huthis are held to stand against the aspiration of every republican government since the 1960s, opening the door to *fitna* throughout the country.

As a corollary to the Huthis-as-anti-republican motif, pro-GoY sources emphasize Huthis' rejection of the regime's constitutional right and requirement to exercise its writ all over the state's territory. The Huthi revolt and denial of state access to the region are thus not only illegitimate but also a violation of democratic politics and the constitution, and this should be considered a legal matter. In this way, GoY narratives also tap into existing motifs of the northern tribal areas as chaotic, endemically violent, and backwards (*mutakhallif*), with an inadequate understanding of the benefits of modern politics and republican progressivism. In this respect, GoY sources suggest that Huthis have duped simple folk (*al-busata' min al-nas*) in the north regarding the Huthi *shi'ar*. Although the Huthis have used this slogan to "stir up the enmity of others against the nation, simple folk say that these [supposed] oppressed people only raise the slogan 'death to America' but in fact, they raise the slogan to harm Yemen and to incite others against it."[71] As such, the Huthis take advantage of the well-meaning but *mutakhallif* northerners. Information operations material distributed in the region invites those who have gotten mixed up in the Huthi revolt to value "your nation and your people and your family . . . your family awaits you" (see Figure 6.3).

The GoY as Aligned with the People

The GoY has been careful to portray its own actions as defensive. Its operations in the north reflect its legal obligation to guard its sovereignty and integrity as a law-based republic aspiring to peaceful participatory politics and national reconciliation. In particular, pro-GoY statements emphasize the GoY's use of force as a last resort only after intolerable Huthi provocations, Huthi amassing of weapons, and repeated rejection of the president's own offers of conciliation.[72] As such, the GoY has used armed force to restore proper governance, law and order, and social services to a province that has come under the sway of separatist sectarians. When it does employ force, the GoY presents itself as reacting proportionately. Limited use of offensive airpower is based on a desire to limit collateral damage, and the GoY has refrained from hitting electric

Figure 6.3
GoY Leaflet Advising Yemenis to Disassociate from Huthis

SOURCE: Yemeni national from region.

RAND *MG962-6.3*

---

[71] See "Fi Muhadara Muhimma Alqaha bi-l-Kulliya al-Harbiya bi-San'a'."

[72] See "Jama'at al-Huthi Shirdhima Irhabiya Tastahdif al-Wahda wa-l-Jumhuriya wa Yajib Hasmha," *26 September*, February 15, 2007.

utilities, schools, or water supplies.[73] Further, frequent amnesties prove the GoY's magnanimity—even if it means that Saleh shuts down proceedings of his own court system—while soldiers have been respectful to women, observing segregation of sexes as much as possible.[74] Therefore, in spite of being held hostage in Saʻda by the Huthis, the people of the region support the GoY's efforts to return constitutional rule, republicanism, and freedom of religion. GoY military operations thus embody true patriotism, an idea reinforced by media images from the conflict area.

During the current round of hostilities, most of the GoY's rhetoric remained consistent or has received renewed emphasis. The patriotism of Yemeni forces continued to be featured, though now with greater focus on their martial prowess, including photos and news clips featuring modern weapons and well-ordered Yemeni columns.[75] Likewise, after having softened its accusations of Iranian support for the Huthi rebellion during 2007–2008, Sanʻa resurrected this theme during the sixth phase of fighting, again accusing Iran of funding the Huthis and ideologically influencing their leaders.[76] In this respect, the GoY continued to mobilize regime-supportive *ʻulamaʼ*—both Sunni and Zaydi—in condemning the Huthi *fitna*.[77] Recently, the GoY extended its messages along these lines, accusing Iraqi Shiʻite elements of supporting the Huthis, focusing on groups allied with Muqtada al-Sadr.[78] GoY spokespeople have also alleged that Huthi fighters collude with or offer moral support to both al-Qaʻida terrorists threatening the regime and southern separatists endangering the state itself, although these charges are less plausible, given the Huthi-Salafi animosity described in Chapter Three.[79] These claims, though unsubstantiated in GoY-sanctioned Yemeni sources, reinforce the themes of Huthis as foreign-inspired, closet Twelvers, who harbor desires to undo the republic.

Beyond continuity, the mode and message of GoY information operations during the most recent fighting have demonstrated a certain innovation. As regards mode, the GoY's Web- and video-based communications are now much more sophisticated and visually engaging, also responding more quickly to Huthi claims.[80] The GoY also has

---

[73] See "Muhafiz Saʻda li-26 Sabtambir: al-Maʻraka al-Hasima Lam Tabdaʼ Baʻd min Janib al-Dawla," *26 September*, February 15, 2007; "al-Irhabiyun Qataʻu Atraf Jundi wa Asabiʻahu wa Adhnayahu: al-Yaman Yanfi Istikhdam al-Tayran wa-l-Asliha al-Kaymawiya Didd al-Huthiyin," *26 September*, February 14, 2007.

[74] See "al-Shurta al-Nisaʼiya Tusharik fi Taʻaqqub ʻAnasir al-Fitna wa-l-Irhab," *26 September,* June 22, 2008.

[75] See "Ghara Jariʼa ʻala Awkar al-Huthiyin fi Saʻda," video posted on YouTube on September 16, 2009.

[76] "Yemen Protests to Iran over Shiʻite Rebels," *Reuters,* August 31, 2009.

[77] "al-Irhab al-Huthi Wathaiʼiq Khatira Tunshar li-Awwal Marra": pt. 1 (3:15-7:15), video hosted at *26 September*'s devoted Web page.

[78] "Yemen Blames Sadrists for Rebel Support," September 10, 2009, *UPI.com.*

[79] "al-Shami: al-Silat bayn al-Huthiyin wa-l-Qaʻida wa-l-Infisaliyin Mawjuda mundhu Fitra," *al-Muʼtammar Net*, September 30, 2009.

[80] See "al-Irhab al-Huthi Wathaiʼiq Khatira Tunshar li-Awwal Marra."

proven more adept at publicizing embarrassing images of Huthi prisoners or televising interrogations of Huthi detainees. These segments are probably televised in an effort to expose ideological inconsistencies and brutality, while shaming the movement through exposure of captured fighters. Most notably, the GoY has begun to articulate a new theme—Huthi representatives as liars—by attacking the latter's statements point by point. One adroitly produced video show is featured on *26 September*'s revamped Web site. It features a screen with Yahya al-Huthi giving interviews to international news outlets. Yahya is depicted broadcasting from Germany, with the German flag waving behind him, thus implicitly tarring him as non-Yemeni. Additionally, Yahya most frequently appears angry or even incoherently combative on the screen. After several seconds or a minute of footage featuring Yahya, the show cuts away to GoY-supportive videos or statistics refuting his statements—at times even using other statements by Yahya himself.[81]

Finally, in the summer and fall of 2009, GoY-supportive media outlets began to present the regime's anti-Huthi efforts as receiving international support. Linking up with the earlier theme that this campaign is part of the GWoT, with regional and global implications, pro-GoY sources have highlighted U.S. and Arab diplomatic statements approving of efforts to subdue the Huthis, affirming the importance of Yemeni regime survival, and pledging aid to the government or conflict-affected region.[82] These latest rhetorical developments, in terms of mode and message, can be considered the information line of the "scorched earth" operation.

Considering the GoY's own ideological communication, certain inconsistencies emerge. The Huthis as a threat to U.S. interests would seem to contradict the idea that the United States condones the Huthis. Likewise, the pro-Imamate narrative is not congruent with the Twelver Shi'ite accusation, nor are any of these ideas compatible with tying the Huthis to Salafi al-Qa'idists or to socialist southerners. Yet, when considered as part of the GoY's information LOO to target different audiences both in Sa'da and on the national level, these messages indicate the regime's concern to counter the Huthis' ideological as well as political challenge to its own legitimacy. If the cease-fire ending the sixth phase of fighting is followed by substantive GoY-Huthi dialogue, it will be interesting to track any changes of emphasis in GoY information operations.

Throughout the conflict, the regime has exploited some of the very cultural and rhetorical divides that we noted in Chapter One, which have been persistent in Yemeni political discourse over the decades. The GoY has thus sought to turn the tables on

---

[81]   For example, see "al-Irhab al-Huthi Wathai'iq Khatira Tunshar li-Awwal Marra": pt. 1.

[82]   See "Ra'is al-Jumhuriya Yastaqbal Qa'id al-Qiyada al-'Askariya al-Amrikiya al-Markaziya: Bahatha ma'ahu al-Ta'awun al-'Askari wa Mukafahat al-Irhab," *26 September*, July 26, 2009; "Petraeus: US will Support Yemen anti-Terror Fight," Embassy of the Republic of Yemen Media Office Web site, July 27, 2009; Mohammed al-Kibsi, "US Supports Yemen's Security and Stability: McCain," *Yemen Observer*, August 17, 2009; "GCC and US Support Yemen's Unity and Stability," *Yemen Post*, September 27, 2009; "US Offers Yemen Help in 'Fight Against Terrorism,'" *al-Arabiya*, September 7, 2009.

Huthi claims, using all the information mechanisms at the disposal of a state. Still, as a state, it has not been able to avail itself of other mechanisms that are less moldable from San'a and perhaps more culturally authentic in northern Yemen. The Huthis—neither a state nor a group that controls nationally circulating media organs—have used these other mechanisms to great effect, as we will see below.

Politics, Diplomacy, and Mediation

During various stages of the Huthi-regime conflict, the GoY has worked on the diplomatic plane. This has involved visits to Tehran and Tripoli to ensure that Iran and Libya do not support the Huthis or—in the case of Libya—provide safe haven to Huthi-affiliated personalities out of favor with the GoY.[83] Prime among these is Yahya al-Huthi, Husayn's brother, who had been a GPC MP at the time hostilities began but had his parliamentary immunity lifted and fled. Subsequent to Yahya's departure from Libya for asylum in Germany, the GoY also sought to have Interpol extradite him to Yemen. Although the GoY appeared to have success in this regard, Yahya is still permitted to reside in Bamburg.[84] The GoY has repeatedly attempted to have the Huthis listed as international terrorists by the U.S. and EU governments but has not succeeded.[85] Additional diplomatic engagement has been in the pan-Arab arena. The GoY has sought to incline other Arab states, as well as the Gulf Cooperation Council (GCC), to view the Huthis as terrorists and a common threat to the Arab region, addressing the issue on the margins of GCC accession discussions.[86]

In terms of domestic political measures, the GoY's efforts in Sa'da- and San'a-oriented patronage politics remain murky. As we have seen above, in the Sa'da region, it has worked to preserve and strengthen the loyalties of traditionally pro-GoY local shaykhs and merchants—hence the continued support by the Shawit, 'Awjari, Man'a, Daris, and Bukhtan families, among others. As we have also seen, many of these families were GoY mainstays going back to YAR days and have benefited from ties to the GPC and Islah. Their loyalty has been preserved through continued economic blandishments, including positions in the military as well as payments for auxiliary forces

---

[83] See "al-Qurbi: La Wasata bayn al-Yaman wa Iran wa Milaf al-Huthi Sayughlaq Qariban," *26 September,* August 4, 2007; "al-Yaman Tastad 'I Safiraha bi-Libiya wa-l-Akhira Tanfi Mughadaratahu," *al-Ayyam,* May 12, 2007; "al-Hadath al-'Arabi wa-l-'Alam: San'a Tatlub Rasmiyan Min Libiya Taslimaha al-Huthi," *al-Mada,* n.d.

[84] See "al-Yaman Tatlub al-Interbol al-Duwali bi-Taslimiha al-Irhabi Yahya Badr al-Din al-Huthi," *26 September,* February 10, 2007: 3; Nasser Arrabyee, "Interpol Agrees to Extradite al-Houthi, Government Says," *Yemen Observer,* April 14, 2007.

[85] See "Mutalabi Urubiya li Idraj Tanzim al-Huthi Dimn al-Munazzamat al-Irhabiya," *26 September,* February 7, 2007; "al-Houthi Welcomes America's Refusal to Classify Houthis as Terrorist," *Mareb Press,* July 6, 2008.

[86] See "al-Qurbi Yu'akkid: Yumkin bi-l-Irada al-Siyasiya Tajawuz 'Amil al-Zaman li-Indimam al-Yaman li Majlis al-Ta'awun al-Khaliji," *26 September,* February 10, 2008.

they provide. Likewise, local administration positions have been provided to pro-GoY elements, including the governor's position itself.[87] Further, there is a strong likelihood that the GoY has been able to involve Saudi intelligence agencies in providing payments to regional shaykhs to preserve their loyalty to the Yemeni regime. The Saudis also likely provide payments to anti-regime tribes in order to maintain influence in the region—a practice going back several decades.[88] Cooptation of local actors and funding through extragovernmental sources are likely major issues in the prolongation or resolution of conflict, although they remain difficult to validate.

Along the diplomatic and political LOOs, a recurrent phenomenon has been mediation (*wasata*) between GoY-appointed Yemenis and the Huthis themselves. There have been multiple attempts at mediation, several of which clustered around the opening stages of the conflict in February–June 2004. This was followed by international efforts, led by Qatar. Rather than bringing parties closer together, mediation attempts have temporarily raised expectations on the part of the GoY, Huthis, and local Sa'dans, then led to disappointment as efforts failed or the terms of agreements were not carried out. Thus, it may even be argued that successive mediation experiences have increased mutual distrust and cynicism toward other than violent solutions.

Between the spring of 2004 and 2006, up to six attempts at mediation occurred, either sponsored or condoned by the GoY. Perhaps overly impressed by his own relative popularity and sensing a GoY trap, Husayn al-Huthi was initially unresponsive. Therefore, no conclusive results emerged from early mediation. Around June 2004, political mediation may have then fallen out of sync with the military's own plans. It has been rumored that the Yemeni military under 'Ali Muhsin al-Ahmar hoped to short-circuit peaceful mediation by commencing operations while mediation teams were either with Husayn or traveling to Sa'da—raising the spectre of internal regime schisms linked to Salafi assertion within the military. Subsequently, mediation in July 2004 failed during ongoing fighting in which the Huthis felt they had the upper hand. Mediation during the fighting a year later resulted in a short cessation of violence. Mutual violation of the peace, however, led to abandonment of mediation. Through 2006, frustrated reconciliation efforts were characterized by ongoing fighting as well as mutual accusations of foul play.

Qatar intervened again in the early summer of 2007, hosting rounds of mediation and ceasefire talks in Doha. The result was an agreement signed by both sides in February 2008. Heavy fighting ensued shortly thereafter, in spite of the enthusiasm related to the international nature of the agreement and the possibility of hefty Qatari fund-

---

[87] An example of this includes Hasan al-Man'a, who was elected governor in May 2008. He is a pro-GoY GPC member of the Man'a shaykhly house.

[88] Interview with international human rights worker from Sa'da area, March 20, 2009; interview with Yemeni emigrant from region, November 2, 2008; American academician specializing on Yemen, September 10, 2008; senior GoY diplomat serving in the United States, September 11, 2008. For a Yemeni view, see "Al-Nufudh al-Su'udi Yatasaddir al-Qa'ima . . . al-Yaman Saha Sira'at Jadida," *al-Ahale*, undated.

ing of reconstruction. Although the Doha agreement appears to remain a touchstone, the GoY has declared it a failed venture because of Huthi perfidy—while the Huthis accuse the GoY of failing to live up to its commitments in the realm of reconstruction, prisoner release, and permission for Huthis to engage in nonviolent activities.

Numerous reasons have been adduced for the failure of mediation, ranging from GoY military opposition to Saudi discomfort with Qatar's aspiring to a larger role.[89] Probably, more-fundamental factors caused mediation to fail. First, even though splits within the GoY and army are possible, it is most likely that the GoY as a whole took an instrumentalist approach to reconciliation, at least in 2004 and 2005, but likely throughout. Once *wasata* was found not to be immediately successful in shutting down Huthist agitation, therefore, it was likely perceived by the GoY as a tactic in service of a larger strategy of Huthi elimination—a plausible idea given Saleh's increased confidence in Yemeni security capabilities discussed in Chapter Four. Past 2005, the utility of *wasata* likely shifted—while still tactical in intent, it now could provide the GoY international legitimacy as it pursued military options. It could also allow a breathing space prior to national elections (2006), before the regime could prepare a larger offensive. Although this is speculation, the notion of tactical instrumentality is supported by failure to make good on mass prisoner release announcements, as well as ongoing GoY operations during periods of mediation.

Turning from the GoY, the characteristics of the Huthi entity likely narrowed the prospects for mediation's success. It is unlikely that senior Huthis decisively control subordinate leaders in various areas of Sa'da. Neither Husayn, nor 'Abd al-Malik, nor 'Abdullah al-Razzami is likely able to prevent violations of agreements or to keep local fighting groups from engaging in attacks while talks are going on. It is equally likely that those who speak for Huthis may not be aligned with the changing decisions and priorities of the leaders for whom they speak—this is particularly the case for Yahya al-Huthi, whose alignment with the views of 'Abd al-Malik has been incomplete. As we will shortly see, the lack of cohesion and top-down command and control among Huthi groups makes exercise of discipline and restraint—essential in any mediation process—very difficult to ensure.

If the above points are valid, mediation efforts may have had very little impact past a certain point in the GoY-Huthi confrontation, given the nature of the Huthi movement and the mistrust among protagonists. Still, a fundamental shortcoming of various mediation efforts has been their sociocultural construction. In effect, there appears to have been a mismatch between the methods and personalities involved in mediation, on the one hand, and the *qabyala*-conditioned modes of conflict mediation and resolution encountered in Chapter Two, on the other.

---

[89] Broad coverage of this issue, including interviews with several knowledgeable Yemenis, can be found in International Crisis Group, "Yemen: Defusing the Saada Time Bomb," *Middle East Report*, No. 86, May 27, 2009.

As we saw earlier, during mediation and arbitration (*sulh wa tahkim*), parties to a conflict are treated as being of equal status as much as possible. They are also to abjure violent action for the duration of mediation. Indeed, symbolic relinquishment of at least a portion of weapons to a neutral arbitrator is traditionally considered a substantive element of such a commitment. Likewise, we saw that the arbitrator—*muhakkam*—needs to possess both prestige and separation from the issues at hand. He cannot be, at least explicitly, an interested party. Additionally, it is often the case in *'urf qabali* that contesting parties do not address each other directly. Rather, protagonists each appoint a representative—a *kafil* (pl. *kufala'*)—who also possesses adequate esteem and neutrality. These representatives communicate with each other through the arbitrator, in order to arrive at a restorative, restitutive—rather than a punitive—agreement producing greater bonds of reciprocal trust. In all these cases, the arbitrator and representative must possess distinguishing levels of prestige among parties to a dispute. They must also be viewed as separate enough from the matter of disagreement so that violation of either the process of *sulh wa tahkim* or the terms of an agreement would be considered an *'ayb*, violating the *sharaf* of arbitrator, representative, and protagonists.

If these are the norms of traditional Yemeni mediation, and if the GoY sought to prevent violence as it had in earlier instances as seen in the beginning of Chapter Three, *wasata* since 2004 has in no way reflected these norms. To begin with, the GoY has emphasized throughout the inequality of status between its mediators and the Huthis. Rather than a peer or equal to the state (*nidd li-l-dawla*), the GoY has approached the Huthis as rebels (*mutamarridun*). President Saleh himself has considered the effect of mediation—particularly that by Qatar—negative in this respect, encouraging the Huthis to consider themselves equal to the GoY and thus injuring the Yemeni state's interests.[90] Though it is understandable that a state's government would not want its nonstate internal opposition to be considered an equal partner in any mediation, this attitude not only lessens the chance of successful negotiations, but it also runs contrary to the norms of traditional *sulh wa tahkim*. It thus appears to be distinct from attitudes conveyed by previous actions of the GoY in the tribal north. Likewise, although in previous instances of GoY confrontations with elements in the north tension was defused by scrupulous avoidance of aggressive action during mediation, neither the GoY nor the Huthis have observed this *qabyala*-aligned custom.

Beyond this, a discussion of the concepts of customary tribal law suggests that who performs mediation roles is as important as the agreement itself.[91] In this respect, neither side has employed people with adequate prestige or separation from the dispute.

---

[90] See Ghassan Sharbil, "'Ali 'Abdullah Salih li-l-Hayat: La 'Ilm Li bi-Muhawalat li-Ightiyali wa-l-Safqa al-Iraniya al-Amrikiya Mawjuda," *al-Hayat*, March 28, 2009.

[91] The following section draws on "Jama'at al-Huthi Shirdhima Irhabiya Tastahdif al-Wahda wa-l-Jumhuriya wa Yajib Hasmha: 26 Sebtember net Tunshir Nass Taqrir al-Aman al-Qawmi al-Muqaddam Ila Majlis al-Nuwwab wa al-Shura Hawl Ahdath al-Fitna fi Sa'da," *26 September*, February 15, 2007. This extensive article covers phases of mediation, indicating names of participants and results.

Broadly, rather than roles of *muhakkam, kafil*, etc. being assigned and fulfilled, the GoY has dispatched committees of mediators, akin to negotiating teams. These committees have indeed included prominent personalities. Early on, the well-known Hashimi scholar Muhammad bin Muhammad Mansur was sent to mediate with Husayn al-Huthi and was engaged by the GoY again in 2006. Likewise, Shaykh ʿAbdullah al-Ahmar has been associated with mediation efforts. These are indeed prominent, prestigious personages—but they do not possess enough neutrality. Al-Ahmar, for example, is completely identified with the GoY, al-Islah, and the Hashidi confederation, all suspect in Huthi eyes. Sayyid Mansur might also be suspect in Huthi eyes, given his role in al-Haqq and the potential for intellectual competition between Badr al-Din al-Huthi and Mansur—but his neutrality was also questioned in GoY/military quarters because of his Zaydi Hashimi background and previous associations with Badr al-Din in al-Haqq and elsewhere.

Huthi mediators have included Salih Habra, previous BY member and emerging spokesperson for the Huthis (see below), and ʿAbd al-Karim Jadban, a BY founder and (by 2004) MP from the GPC. In the earlier phases of mediation, as well as in the Qatar mediation, Yahya al-Huthi also represented the Huthis. Although these people possess a certain amount of *wazn* among Huthis, the GoY has consistently been apt to view them as a part of the rebel movement. Likewise, at times the GoY has included on its mediation committees people whom it may have felt were agreeable to the rebels. These have included ʿAbd al-Karim al-Huthi, Husayn's uncle, as well as Ismaʿil al-Huthi, who is from a more distant branch of the family, in addition to Salah Falita, an al-Haqq founder and early supporter of the BY. While Falita could have been suspect in Huthi eyes for reasons similar to those pertaining to Mansur, it may also be argued that Huthi family members are too close to the rebels. This excuses both the GoY's punitive actions against them—at one point the GoY allegedly arrested ʿAbd al-Karim al-Huthi and has pursued Yahya—as well as its desultory follow-through on mediation efforts. Significantly, however, in northern Yemeni cultural terms, their status may also render them inappropriate as representatives or guarantors.

GoY mediation committees over the years have included people who are undeniably protagonists in the conflict: for example, the GoY's Minister of Endowments, as well as serving and retired army generals, some of whom were currently serving in the Saleh-appointed Consultative Council. Further, at various phases of mediation, senior GPC representatives, such as Muhammad Husayn al-ʿAydrusi, and Islah leaders, such as Muhammad Qahtan and ʿAbd al-Wahhab al-Anisi, have been involved. In the context of the conflict, these men could not have been considered neutral by either side. The same is true of the inclusion in mediation committees of the (Sunni) religious scholar Hamud al-Hitar, known for his efforts to deprogram imprisoned Huthi youth.[92] Most egregious in this respect, the Qatar mediation efforts in 2007 included

---

[92] See International Crisis Group, "Yemen: Defusing the Saada Time Bomb," 20.

'Ali Muhsin al-Ahmar. Though President Saleh might have included him in order to obtain military buy-in, his status as commander of operations against the Huthis and as openly pro-Salafi with links to jihadists means that it would be easy for Huthis to dismiss the GoY's sincerity in signing the Doha agreement. In cultural terms, 'Ali Muhsin did not have the status to act as guarantor (*damin*; pl. *dumana'*) for the GoY.

Finally, mediation efforts have included several local tribal leaders. Normally, they would be the best choices, in terms of local cultural norms, to include as representatives or guarantors for the protagonists. Yet, due to GoY *mahsubiya* practices going back to the 1990s and efforts during the conflict to enlist local tribes in alliances, the regime has in effect ensured that there would remain few local personalities who combine *wajh* with an adequate appearance of neutrality. As such, the presence of shaykhs such as 'Uthman Mujalli, 'Ali Husayn al-Munabbihi, 'Abdullah Daris, Husayn al-Surabi, and 'Abd al-Karim Mana' could reduce both sides' trust in the process, by including in it people who have an interest in conflict prolongation or Huthi defeat. Conversely, inclusion of more neutral mediators, such as Shaykh Salih 'Ali al-Wajman, has been marred by their subsequent arrest. As we will discuss later, these tactics have the effect of perpetuating the tribalization of an initially nontribal conflict.

It can therefore be argued that the structure and personalities of mediation efforts, including those of Qatar, have been out of sync with traditional modes of *sulh wa tahkim*, so that the processes and resultant agreement cannot exercise adequate moral compulsion on its participants—or that there is little *'ayb* associated with the Huthis persisting in armed conflict during and after negotiations. Likewise, the content of agreements might also prolong conflict. Although various phases of the war have resulted in agreements—the substance of which has been contested—the Doha agreement is a relatively agreed-to text (see Appendix F). Even here, it can be argued that certain of its stipulations defy the restorative logic of tribal mediation among equals— or simply ensure that the agreement would not be seen as "resolution" by Huthi signatories. For example, while the Huthis were to desist from operations and relinquish their medium weapons and ammunition (*asliha mutawassita wa dhakha'iraha*) under the agreement, no equivalent GoY action was required aside from beginning reconstruction activities. While a government is not likely to relinquish weapons, the Doha agreement does not appear to call for even a symbolic withdrawal of GoY forces from Sa'da but rather stipulates "the extension of the state's general order [*nizam al-dawla al-'amm*] in the region as in all the other regions of the republic."[93] Since the Huthi weapons relinquishment was not to be reciprocated by the GoY in any symbolic or substantive way, it could be interpreted as a violation of *'ird*.

More importantly, the Doha agreement stipulated the "arrival" of Yahya, 'Abd al-Malik, and al-Razzami to Qatar, where they would remain until GoY permission to return to Yemen was given and from whence they would refrain from "political and

---

[93] "Waqf al-Qital fi Sa'da wa-l-I'lan 'an al-'Afu," *al-Ayyam*, June 17, 2007.

press activities hostile to Yemen."[94] By exiling the Huthis' most esteemed leaders, this agreement could very well be viewed as punitive, or at least inequitable in cultural terms—as well as implausible in terms of *realpolitik.* Therefore, by 2006 at least, the conflict may have so aggravated conditions in Sa'da as to acquire a logic of its own that precluded mediation. Still, the way that the GoY has gone about *wasata* has diverged both from culturally normative processes and the GoY's own previous cooptative, neo-tribal practices in the periphery, suggesting that its view of politics and diplomacy is tactical and subordinate to a coercion-focused strategy.

Subsequent to the 2007–2008 Qatari involvement, no notable instances of international mediation have come to light. Some reports of GoY-Huthi negotiations have emerged regarding the ceasefire ending the August 2009–February 2010 sixth phase of fighting, although details have yet to emerge as of the time of writing.[95] It appears that, under pressure from Riyadh, San'a pressured 'Abd al-Malik al-Huthi to accept a greater number of GoY conditions as part of the ceasefire, allowing the latter to justify its military operations.[96]

During the most recent fighting, however, the Huthi conflict may also have become a diplomatic liability for San'a. While the Arab League and GCC early on endorsed Yemen's right to self-defense, it became difficult to justify regime operations in the north after the al-Qa'ida threat emerging from Yemen received much greater attention from December 2009. At a January 27, 2010, international conference in London, diplomats urged President Saleh to swiftly resolve several of Yemen's problems that prevent it from achieving stability. Analysts have taken this admonition to refer to the Huthi conflict, implying that increased economic aid to Yemen would require San'a to demonstrate action on that front.[97] Against the backdrop of the mid-February GoY-Huthi ceasefire, it will remain a challenge for the international community to persistently move Saleh towards reconciliation without seeming to wield the kind of undue influence that either results in a backlash or makes him appear to be a Western lackey.

Economic Actions

Finally, the GoY has employed economic measures during the conflict. On the one hand, since the fall of 2004, the GoY has claimed to have established several committees to assess war damages, provide payments to local noncombatants affected by

---

[94] "Waqf al-Qital fi Sa'da wa-l-I'lan 'an al-'Afu."

[95] See "Yemen's Elusive Peace Deal: A Bloody Blame Game," *The Economist,* February 4, 2010.

[96] See Appendix F for the February 2010 ceasefire conditions.

[97] See "North Yemen Calm After Truce," *al-Jazeera.net,* February 12, 2010; Robert F. Worth, "Yemen's Government Agrees to a Cease-Fire with Rebel Forces," *New York Times,* February 11, 2010.

hostilities, and coordinate efforts at overall reconstruction in the area.[98] Press reports associate Saleh and the provincial administration with these efforts.[99] It is very difficult to validate whether these initiatives have been fully implemented. However, the inefficiencies of a hypercentralized government, functioning in the periphery among the differing agendas of the local population and the military and confronting armed resistance, have likely reduced the effectiveness of measures designed to increase GoY popularity.

More obvious are punitive measures aligned with the military goals of isolating and attriting Huthi fighters and areas sympathetic to the Huthis. These have included blocking roads to interdict the movement of people, goods, water, and fuel, as well as trying to close down markets in the area known for selling and storing weapons.[100] During 2007–2009, blockades became a regular tactic of military operations, as the GoY sought to deny Huthis access to the economic bases of survival.[101] Along with these intentional actions, GoY military operations—as well as Huthi reactions and attacks—have likely had additional, unintentional economic consequences. We will return to this topic in more detail in Chapter Eight, when we discuss the human, environmental, and economic impacts of the Saʻda wars.

---

[98] See "Muʼassasat al-Salih Qaddamat Musaʻadat Ghadhaʼiya li-Khamsat Alaf Usra Mutadarrara min Fitnat al-Huthi," *26 September*, October 31, 2004.

[99] "Muʼassasat al-Salih Qaddamat Musaʻadat Ghadhaʼiya li-Khamsat Alaf Usra Mutadarrara min Fitnat al-Huthi."

[100] See "al-Shami Yuʼakkid anna Fitnat al-Huthi Tamm Muʻalajatuha Nihaʼiyan," *26 September*, October 13, 2006; "Taʻzizat ʻAskariya Dakhma li-Yasl Taʻdad al-Quwwat Nahu 20 Alf Jundi. . . al-Jaysh Yuhasir Thani Akbar Madina bi-Saʻda Istiʻdadan li-Muhajamat al-Huthiyin," *al-Ayyam*, March 8, 2007.

[101] See "al-Jaysh Yamnah Fursa Akhira li-l-Ahali fi-l-Talh li-Ikhraj Atbaʻ al-Huthi min Mintaqatihim," *al-Ayyam*, February 19 2006.

CHAPTER SEVEN

The Huthis as Combatants

Rather than an *organization*, the Huthis are an *organism* that has existed from the first phase of the Sa'da war as a heterogeneous entity having multiple interests and united under a banner that has different meanings for different adherents. The notion of a hierarchical organization, with a clear table of organization or order of battle, does not necessarily apply to the Huthi entity. The various names used to describe the Huthis manifest this fact: The group is referred to by many as the "Huthis" *(al-Huthiyin)*, the "Huthi movement" *(al-Haraka al-Huthiya)*, "Huthist elements" *(al-'anasir al-Huthiya)*, "Huthi supporters" *(Ansar al-Huthi)*, or "Believing Youth Elements" *('Anasir al-Shabab al-Mu'min)*. Huthi supporters refer to themselves by numerous monikers as well, including "Supporters of Truth" *(Ansar al-Haqq)* and "Husaynis" *(Husayniyun)*, not to mention typical nomenclature associated with militant Islamist movements, such as *mujahidin* and "soldiers of Allah" *(Junud Allah)*. These multiple names make it problematic to consider the Huthis a top-down, structured organization with a clear command and control apparatus. The multifarious nature of the Huthi organism is further manifested in the varied themes propagated through its ideological communication, which have evolved significantly since 2004. Most fundamentally, five years of unabated GoY-Huthi conflict have generated common memories, rituals, emblems, and associations that sustain a sense of group solidarity and motivation. The prolongation of the Huthi-GoY conflict has in effect furnished a shared "Huthi narrative." If the conflict continues along its current trajectory, not only might the Huthis move from organism to organization, but their demographic influence will grow apace.

Command, Control, and Communications (C3)

The Huthi entity did not begin combat operations in 2004 with an order of battle and organizational hierarchy that could be analyzed in conventional military terms. Instead, it emerged from the structures, processes, and values that are organic to its mountainous, rural, and tribal environment. It is important to consider the Huthis as an organism that mobilizes, survives, and fights in terms of these norms. Having said that, we can examine members of the Huthi organism and associate them with certain functions and roles. It is likely, however, that these roles have evolved in response to challenges and opportunities, and are not top-down designations.

While both Husayn and 'Abdullah al-Razzami had previously held seats in the Yemeni parliament, the group's political and "diplomatic" functions have partially been carried out in absentia by Husayn's brother Yahya al-Huthi, who currently resides in Germany, as well as by Salih Habra. As mentioned previously, Yahya was involved early in the government's mediation efforts, including an initiative prior to the conflict.[1] Since then, Yahya al-Huthi has been stripped of his parliamentary immunity and, after the end of the first phase of the conflict, has resided in Germany. Yahya has thus served as an international spokesperson for the group, participating in television interviews on pan-Arab news outlets and writing editorials in foreign newspapers.

Yahya's "political" function for the group has been disparaged by some of the Ansar al-Haqq Web denizens, who have argued that he has tried to turn the Sa'da conflict into a "political issue," presumably for his own gain.[2] Interestingly, Yahya al-Huthi is often referred to on the pro-Huthi Web page *al-Menpar* as a "parliamentarian" (*barlamani*), rather than a spokesperson, which is indicative of his standing among Huthi leadership.[3] There has also been alleged criticism of Yahya from 'Abd al-Malik al-Huthi, who is purported to have harangued his older brother for having political ambitions.[4] Yahya al-Huthi does, however, give the group a legitimate face to pan-Arab media outlets and has recently adopted mainstream, pro-republican opinions: arguing, for example, against southern secession.[5]

Salih Habra participated in domestic mediation initiatives and also served as a local spokesperson for the Huthi group before being reported as killed on August 28, 2009.[6] While initially mediating between the GoY and the Huthis, Habra emerged as a harsh critic of the Saleh government's handling of the aftermath of the first phase of the Sa'da conflict.[7] Although Habra was later one of the Huthi signatories to the origi-

---

[1]   See "Jama'at al-Huthi Shirdhima Irhabiya Tastahdif al-Wahda wa-l-Jumhuriya wa Yajib Hasmha: 26 Sebtember net Tunshir Nass Taqrir al-Aman al-Qawmi al-Muqaddam Ila Majlis al-Nuwwab wa al-Shura Hawl Ahdath al-Fitna fi Sa'da," *26 September,* February 15, 2007.

[2]   Forum administrator, "As'ila Muwajjaha li-l-Huthiyin Ansar al-Haqq," *Ansar al-Haqq Forum,* December 27, 2008.

[3]   See, for example, "al-Barlamani Yahya al-Huthi Yuwajjih Risala Ila Ahzab al-Liqa' al-Mushtarik," *al-Menpar,* July 5, 2008.

[4]   Author unknown, "Abd Al Malik Al-Houthi: Yahya Represents the Ruling Party and Wasn't in Our Resistance Movement Against America," *Al-Wasat,* August 2005.

[5]   "Wijhat Nazr al-Akh Yahya al-Huthi Hawla Mawdu' al-Infisal wa Qadiyat al-Junub," *al-Menpar,* May 24, 2009.

[6]   "'Abd al-Malik al-Huthi: La Nurahin 'ala Ayy Quwwa Iqlimiya wa Idha Awqafatal-Sulta Istihdafna, Sanantahi al-Tamtarus," *al-Sharq al-Awsat,* September 20, 2009.

[7]   "Al-Ustadh Salih Habra li-l-Manbar: Nutalib al-Sulta bi-l-Iltizam bi-Ittifaq al-Doha Aw An Tukshif Rafdha lahu 'Alnan," *al-Menpar,* November 22, 2008.

nal Doha agreement, he also provided a running commentary on the GoY's failure to implement it.[8] Habra appeared to have been more attuned to a Yemeni audience, as his open letters to President Saleh have appeared in local Yemeni news outlets and he resided in the country. As such, Habra appears to be Yahya al-Huthi's more-Yemeni counterpart, a fact which is perhaps also indicated by their choice of attire: for Yahya a suit; for Salih Habra, traditional Yemeni garb. Thus, both Yahya al-Huthi and Salih Habra have served as spokesmen for the Huthi group, but do so in different capacities—one as "diplomat," the other as "politician."

While an official Huthi ideology has yet to formally crystallize, the writings and lectures of both Husayn and Badr al-Din contain elements that can be analyzed in terms of a set of principles and beliefs. We have already outlined major motifs and themes that are prevalent in Husayn's lectures, but it is important to note that such themes have taken on new meaning in the context of armed conflict with the GoY. Indeed, in Husayn's vernacular, the GoY becomes the "Enemy of Islam" and is thus synonymous with Israel and America. Husayn's charisma and his father's prestige also imbue 'Abd al-Malik's speeches with religious legitimacy and credibility. As such, 'Abd al-Malik has also begun to emerge as the ideological font of the group, building on the legacy of his father and brother and delivering speeches during contested holidays. Thus, while the Huthi organism has yet to develop a concrete ideology, certain members of the group have at times laid out concepts that could certainly be molded into one, given the right circumstances.

Interestingly, those who established and continue to maintain a sense of group ideology have also been "head commanders" in the group's military activities. Indeed, Husayn al-Huthi served as commander during the first phase, with Badr al-Din taking over during the second. Husayn's much younger brother 'Abd al-Malik has taken over Huthi leadership from the third phase of fighting onwards. While the title of military commander may lead one to believe that the group has a clear command and control structure, this is not the case, as we will soon see. The geographic location of this main commander has varied throughout the conflict and is never known precisely. That being said, we can ascertain that Husayn was based primarily in the Marran mountains, while Badr al-Din resided in Nushur and al-Naq'a. At least until the sixth Sa'da war began, 'Abd al-Malik operated out of al-Naq'a and Matra, though he likely moved among various Huthi safe havens to deter GoY targeting. 'Abdullah 'Ayda al-Razzami has also been mentioned as a commander with equal standing to 'Abd al-Malik. The geographical isolation of the main Huthi commander from his subcommanders has implications that will be discussed soon, but suffice it to say that this significantly limits comprehensive control over day-to-day operations.

---

[8] "Salih Habra Yawajjih Khutabahu Ila al-Ra'is wa Yatasa'al In Kanat Tasrihat al-Jundi Tansalan Rasmiyan min Ittifaq al-Doha," *al-Menpar*, April 15, 2008.

Figure 7.1 depicts the locations and, where available, the names of those we are dubbing local area leaders (LALs), referred to in the Arabic press as *qa'id maydani* or field commander. It also illustrates possible locations of head Huthi commanders throughout the conflict. Regardless of the accuracy of reporting on commander locations and names, press coverage does reveal that the Huthis do in fact have such leaders who operate at the level below 'Abd al-Malik al-Huthi. One reporter's visit to the Huthi and Zaydi stronghold of Dahyan illustrates trends that are likely the norm within the Huthi organism.[9] This account depicts LAL Taha al-Madani—brother of the Huthi LAL Yusuf al-Madani, who is reported to operate from Harf Sufyan—living in a heavily guarded compound. The journalist describes a number of Taha's underlings—many using aliases such as "Abu x"—walking him to the commander's home and, at times, speaking for the commander. Although the LAL has locally recognized authority and a guarded compound, his direct authority over underlings seems vague and based on prestige rather than coercion. The Huthi rank and file thus have a considerable amount of autonomy in their daily actions.

Figure 7.2, which is taken from a September 2009 Huthi video release, clearly reflects the previously mentioned trends. Indeed, one individual appears to be highly regarded—and thus closely guarded—by his local cadres. Further, he addresses the captured GoY troops with an element of authority, further reflecting the fact that the territory is considered his jurisdiction. The LAL in the video also does not carry a firearm, further indicating that he derives his legitimacy among his peers and guests from local prestige rather than coercion.

Examining some of the names of the various Huthi commanders further helps to illustrate the heterogeneous nature of the organism itself. Indeed, some LALs have assumed aliases, such as Abu Nasr or Ramah; others have maintained their tribal names, such as Shaykh al-Nimri. This indicates that the Huthi organism is made up of a number of distinct constituencies with various goals and interests, much like a tribal confederation. It is likely that some of the commanders are diehard followers of Husayn, highly militant, and heavily radicalized. For example, press reports of dissent within the Huthi organism have surfaced, with an LAL in one instance allegedly detonating himself to protest 'Abd al-Malik accepting the Doha-brokered peace deal.[10] Similarly, other reports have noted substantial schisms in the movement, with Huthi follower Ahmad Dughsan allegedly splitting from the movement to form his

---

[9] Yahya al-Tholaya, "Jami'at al-Mutanaqidat: Dammaj al-Salafiyin, wa Dahyan al-Huthiyin, wa Sa'da al-Mu'tammar al-Sha'bi!" *al-Ahale*, undated.

[10] "Astawilu 'ala Qura ba'd Ishtibakat Adat Ila Suqut 12 Qatilan min Ibna' al-Mintaqa . . ." *al-Ayyam*, July 3, 2007.

Figure 7.1
Possible Head Huthi Commander and Local Area Leader (LAL) Locations and Names,
as of March 2009

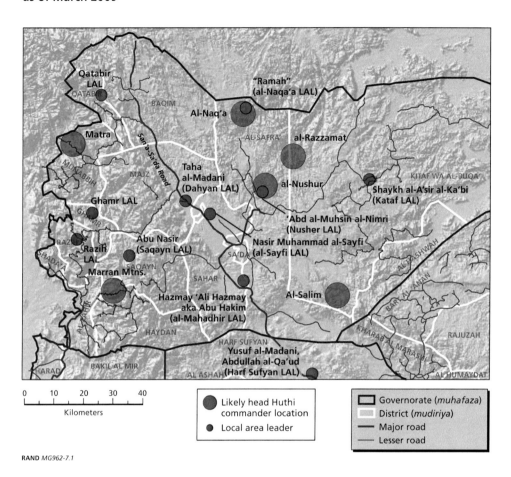

RAND MG962-7.1

own group due to Huthi leadership's agreeing to the Doha peace deal.[11] Furthermore, rifts between al-Razzami and 'Abd al-Malik have been mentioned in the media, with al-Razzami referred to as leading the more radical constituency in the Huthi group.[12] 'Abd al-Malik al-Huthi has emphatically denied any disagreement with al-Razzami, however, arguing that they both "represent one body."[13] Finally, as with GoY tribal auxiliaries, tribal "supporters" of the Huthis, such as 'Abdullah al-Nimri, may merely be utilizing the Huthi banner and the resulting conflict as a vehicle to settle old dis-

---

[11] "Wad'u Shurutan Jadida fi Muqabil Tanfidh Ittifaq Waqf al-Tamarrud: 'Huthiyin' Yushakkilun Qiyadat Jadida Munawwa'a li-l-Ittifaq al-Mawqa' mava al-Yemen," *al-Arabiya*, June 24, 2007.

[12] 'Ali al-Zafiri (host), "Sira' bayn Jama'at al-Huthi wa al-Hukuma al-Yamaniya," *al-Jazeera*, January 2, 2007.

[13] "Al-Manbar net Yu'id Nashr Hiwar al-Sayyid 'Abd al-Malik al-Huthi ma'a Sahifat al-Dayyar," *al-Menpar*, January 20, 2009.

Figure 7.2
Local Area Leader (in Blue) Addressing Captured GoY Troops

SOURCE: "Insihab al-Liwa' 105 al-Mutamarkaz fi Mawaqi' Asfal Marran,"
video posted to YouTube.com, September 2, 2009.
RAND *MG962-7.2*

putes.[14] Indeed, it is likely that old disputes, rather than hard-and-fast Huthi allegiances, fueled the summer 2008 conflict in Bani Hushaysh.[15]

Available data on Huthi leaders further illustrates how local norms of organization permeate the Huthi organism. For one, the fact that the head "commander" of the group has resided in isolated areas during times of sustained armed conflict can inform our assumptions about the group's internal dynamics. With the central leadership removed from the planning and execution of daily combat operations, the LAL retains considerable autonomy in the day-to-day execution of operations. This allows the LAL to initiate engagements independent of the central commander while simultaneously forcing the central Huthi commander to "own" those decisions, relying on personal prestige and nonviolent persuasion to maintain loyalty. This is highly reflective of the norms of tribal leadership and influence that we outlined in Chapter Three.

While defined notions of hierarchy, command and control, and tables of organization are typically associated with effective insurgencies, the Huthi leadership model is the military manifestation of *qabyala*, which favors group and individual autonomy

---

[14] "'Asharat al-Jarha min Ataba' al-Huthi wa Afrad al-Jaysh Yunaqalun Ila Mustashfa al-Salam bi-Sa'da," *al-Ayyam*, January 4, 2006.

[15] Interview with Yemeni national, October 10, 2008.

over stringent group solidarity. Much like the tribal shaykh who relies on soft power to maintain influence over individuals and cannot sustain authoritarian control, both the central commanders and LALs within the Huthi organism must rely on local prestige to mobilize their subordinates. Thus, instead of leading through intimidation, the Huthi commander—whether Husayn or 'Abd al-Malik—must cultivate loyalty and obedience through influence and persuasion. Such methods are congruent with long-enduring local norms according to which authority and prestige do not emanate from authoritarian control or physical coercion. As a result, it is our assessment that Huthi leaders' exercise of physical discipline is improbable and currently undesirable for the group.

The permeation of indigenous social institutions into the Huthi command structure is further reflected in the family networks that span the echelons of the Huthi organism, demonstrating that physical coercion to maintain loyalty is not only improbable and undesirable but also unnecessary. For example, Yusuf al-Madani, who married one of Husayn's daughters (see Figure 7.3), serves as an LAL. This marriage ties him into the Huthi family and the broad network associated with it. It also likely sustains his loyalty to the Huthi "cause." Similarly, Yusuf's brother, Taha al-Madani, also serves as a Huthi commander, likely feeling a loyalty to his brother and, by extension, to the Huthi family. Taha al-Madani probably has at least one wife. She and some of her affines would be tied to the Huthis via Taha. The example of the al-Madani family's role in the Huthi command structure indicates that an authoritarian presence and influence on the part of the primary Huthi commander is not

Figure 7.3
Example of a Possible C2 Network in the Huthi Organism

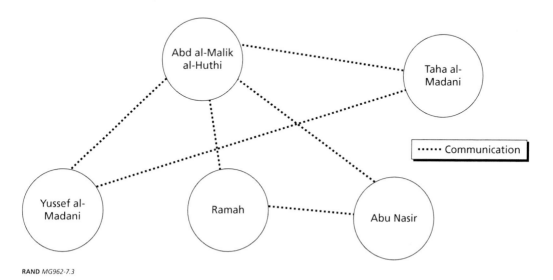

only impossible and unappealing, given physical and social constraints, but also largely unnecessary because local prestige and organic ties are prevalent within the organism. More broadly, these people can take advantage of the Huthi family—a network of multiple social networks, as seen in Chapter Three.

The lack of a need for centralized leadership is further underscored by the way the Huthis have sustained themselves materially. Indeed, the material aspects of this conflict reinforce local autonomy within the rubric of broad allegiance to the Huthi "cause." First, the wide availability of weapons in the Sa'da governorate eliminates the need for a top-down weapons and ammunition procurement and distribution strategy. Similarly, because Sa'da residents have long survived in an environment of material scarcity, foodstuffs can be acquired locally, whether through forced or voluntary donations. The donation aspect is further highlighted by claims made in both GoY reports and international aid workers that Hussein al-Huthi had collected *zakat*, the Islamic tax. The transregional and transnational dimensions of the Sa'da economy that we described in Chapter One open various channels of licit trade and illicit smuggling, so that goods can also be imported to the governorate through outside actors. Such imports, however, are likely unnecessary for Huthi insurgents, given the availability of local storage sites and the Huthi organism's ability to exploit them. The Huthi resistance can therefore sustain itself via local procurement methods rather than a top-down distribution network or hierarchy.

That is not to say, however, that Huthi units act completely independent of one another or any central leadership. According to press reports and interviews with international aid workers who have recently been on the ground in Sa'da, the Huthis have used both cellular and satellite telephones to communicate with one another. One press report noted that, when the government attempted to impose a cell phone blackout on the governorate, the Huthis were able to obtain Yemen Mobile phones that were designated for government-coopted locals.[16] Similarly, other media reports have indicated that the Huthis have utilized Thoraya satellite phones to communicate with one another.[17] Further reporting has revealed that the Huthis utilize these communication tools to relay information on GoY convoy movements from locations near transportation hubs.[18] Finally, journalists' reports of meetings with Huthi LALs also demonstrate that these subcommanders can reach 'Abd al-Malik via cell phone.[19] As Figure 7.3 indicates, the lines of communication within elements of the Huthi organism are unlikely to be standardized.

---

[16] See Yahya al-Thulaya, "Jami'at al-Mutanaqidat: Dammaj al-Salafiyin."

[17] See "Dabt 3 Shahinat Asliha wa-l-Huthiyin Yatahatifun 'Abr al-Aqmar al-Istina'iya," *al-Ayyam*, May 30, 2007.

[18] "al-Jaysh Yatamakkan min al-Saytara 'ala Mu'azzam Ajza' Jabal Gharaba bi-Sa'da," *al-Ayyam,* April 24, 2007.

[19] See Yahya al-Thulaya, "Jami'at al-Mutanaqidat . . . Dammaj al-Salafiyin, wa Dahyan al-Huthiyin, wa Sa'da al-Mu'tammar al-Sha'bi!" *al-Ahale*, undated.

Indeed, given their familial ties, Yusuf and Taha al-Madani likely maintain contact. Additionally, Ramah and Abu Nasir might communicate to alert one another about certain occurrences in their respective areas, but ongoing "cross-talk" by LALs at similar "echelons of command" is not necessarily the rule. As we will see, while regional units do not currently have the capacity to execute coordinated operations, the Huthi communications network can alert regional units to the advance of military convoys and the location of local leaders deemed enemies of the Huthis.

The composition of the Huthi C3 system has important implications for possible resolutions to the conflict. Because of its decentralized nature and lack of internal coercive capacity, expecting the group to immediately and uniformly abide by a ceasefire would be unrealistic. This is further emphasized by the possibility of different factions within the organism itself. Indeed, more-militant, diehard constituents in the group likely find virtually any peace deal unpalatable, especially in the wake of six conflicts that have resulted in widespread human and material damage. Additionally, the group's tribal "supporters," who are likely more focused on goals only partially overlapping with those of 'Abd al-Malik, could still continue fighting no matter what peace deal is officially signed by the Huthi "leadership." This internal structure (or lack thereof) also significantly affects what the group can and cannot accomplish in terms of military operations, as we will soon see.

Huthi Armaments

As discussed in previous chapters, one of the distinguishing features of *qabyala* is the association of manhood with the possession of weapons. Likewise, weapons of various varieties have been easily available in the region. The three major sources for Huthi leaders to obtain weapons since the beginning of the conflict have therefore been arms dealers, tribal allies, and the Yemeni military itself. As for weapons dealers, the arms trade in Suq al-Talh and other markets, such as that in Ma'rib, were said by the GoY to have been closed down in early 2004. Reports indicate, however, that merchants there continued to sell to the Huthis just before and in the opening stages of conflict.[20] In the first two phases of the war, in particular, many of them supported the Huthi family by providing arms. Part of this might have been out of ideological motivation in support of a prominent Zaydi family or due to a cultural disapprobation of the GoY for penetrating the region with armed force. Suq al-Talh, for example, is in the al-Talh subtribal area, part of the Sahar tribe of the Khawlan bin 'Amir confederation. Many of the arms dealers were thus Zaydi and tribally related to members of the BY. It is also

---

[20] See Shaun Overton, "The Yemeni Arms Trade: Still a Concern for Terrorism and Regional Security," *Jamestown Foundation Terrorism Monitor* 3:9, May 6, 2005.

rumored that prominent arms dealers in the area originated from Marran in Haydan, which is the traditional family area of the Huthis.[21]

Even more important than such motives, selling arms to the Huthis was lucrative, particularly when new restrictions on smuggling weapons (as well as *qat*) to Saudi Arabia rendered a new outlet all the more attractive. Additionally, bans on the carrying of weapons in major cities, as well as on-again, off-again efforts to remove certain classes of weapons from markets in San'a, would have made the Huthi interest in acquiring weapons welcome to dealers.[22] Further, dealers seem to have felt that the confrontation would be short-lived, making it worthwhile to sell weapons early on in great quantities.[23]

As the conflict has continued, the ability of arms dealers in Sa'da and beyond to provide large numbers of diverse weapons is likely to have contracted somewhat. Movement of military forces has resulted in interdiction of trade and smuggling routes, and GoY forces have likely confiscated weapons, though leaving other stocks concealed. Further, post-2006 GoY efforts to crack down on unmonitored arms sales outside of Sa'da have increased, with stores being closed and weapons confiscated.[24] Along with this, improved cooperation with Saudi authorities on the border and development of a Yemeni Coast Guard with U.S. assistance have likely tightened the availability of weapons through traditional merchants—but only to a limited degree.[25] Efforts to interdict the arms trade run up against strong tribal and mercantile interests throughout the country, and some of these interests are represented in the parliament and among the president's confidants.[26]

Although the availability of weapons through arms markets has thus been somewhat reduced, the Huthis have been able to turn to tribal connections. To begin with, those tribes with whom the Huthis were allied possessed their own stocks, which are beyond enumeration—though a recent estimate suggested that, countrywide, tribal holdings exceeded 5 million small arms.[27] Furthermore, the GoY has distributed added weapons to tribal leaders as a means to recruit proxy fighters against the Huthis. Since

---

[21]   Interview with Yemeni national from conflict zone, November 2, 2008.

[22]   "Yemen: Weapons Ban Declared in Capital," *Almotamar.net*, August 24, 2007; "Yemen: Despite Ban on Arms, Activists Warn of Increasing Violence," *IRIN News*, July 8, 2007.

[23]   Interview with Yemeni national from conflict zone, October 29, 2008.

[24]   "About 140,000 Weapons Confiscated in Yemen," *Bernama.com*, June 30, 2008.

[25]   See "Yemen to Establish Coast Guard with U.S. Assistance," *MarineLink.com*, October 18, 2002; Sue A. Lackey, "Yemen After the *Cole:* Volatile Nation Remains a Strategically Important Ally, But Experts Worry About its Intrinsic Vulnerabilities," *Seapower Magazine*, March 2005.

[26]   See Mohammed al-Asaadi, "Yemen Strives to Stop Firearms Proliferation," *Yemen Times* 16:1176 (July 30, 2008).

[27]   See Nicole Stracke, "Counter-Terrorism and Weapon Smuggling: Success and Failure of Yemeni-Saudi Collaboration," Gulf Research Center Security and Terrorism Research Bulletin, Issue 4, November 2006.

the consensus among those familiar with the conflict is that tribes have not remained consistent in their loyalties, it is likely that weapons provided by the GoY to regime-friendly tribes can later be used against the GoY when tribes or subgroups switch loyalties. As tribal alliances have both deepened over time and shifted, Huthi leaders are thus able to bring into their ambit new stores of weapons.

Alternatively, Huthi commanders apply coercion to obtain weapons, reminiscent of other insurrections or insurgencies. Local sources and Western aid workers suggest that Huthi leaders—as well as GoY commanders—approach villages, asking tribal leaders to join with them out of ideological affinity and threatening reprisals if they do not.[28] In this case, joining with the Huthis means providing fighters and weapons. Over the past three years, therefore, tribal supplies of weapons have likely prevented Huthis from encountering shortages. A further new source of weapons, providing both diversity and quantity, is the GoY military itself. GoY forces have been operating in the Sa'da governorate for nearly five years. As discussed earlier, conventional conscript-based forces—among them Zaydi soldiers—encounter material challenges and receive poor pay. Their straitened material conditions and limited ideological commitment to the fight has led many to "lose" weapons and gear during patrols or engagements with the Huthis. Alternatively, soldiers have sold military hardware to Huthi fighters in return for cash or *qat*.

Beyond individual illicit transfers from GoY forces, larger weapons sets come through GoY hands into the Huthi arsenal. In this case, commanders in the field or supply officers along transport routes have pilfered GoY stockpiles, providing weapons to intermediaries who then convey a portion of them to Huthi commanders. GoY officers have also notified Huthi sympathizers about the time line and routes of supply convoy movements, facilitating Huthi raids on them. Sources suggest that GoY military officers have engaged in this pilfering and informing, either to supplement paltry incomes or out of a discomfort with Salafi influence in the military and among the GoY's proxies in the region.[29] Of course, with or without the help of information leaked from GoY sources, Huthi fighters have ambushed convoys passing through the Sa'da governorate. In this case, they remove the weapons and take possession of vehicles, or destroy the vehicles in place after stripping them of arms and gear.

Finally, particularly at the end of the fifth Sa'da war and during the opening phases of the sixth, the difficult geography and overextended deployment of GoY forces have enabled Huthi fighting groups to isolate entire units, interdicting their resupply and detaining many soldiers. This practice serves many purposes, which we describe below. Regarding armaments, in one particular instance from late August 2009 that was captured on video, Huthi fighters detained a company-sized GoY element and

---

[28] Interview with human rights worker from Sa'da region, March 20, 2009.

[29] Interview with Yemeni emigrant, October 2008; interview with human rights worker in region, March 20, 2009.

stripped it of all its gear, sizable numbers of AK-47s, RPK medium machine guns (along with full ammunition boxes), and RPG launchers as well as projectiles—including the more modern, slender munitions with significant penetration capabilities.[30] Notably, available video imagery depicts munitions wrapped in plastic coating, with Huthi fighters engaging in some sort of inventory process (see Figure 7.4). This suggests either that the Huthis seized unopened munitions boxes or that they have developed an appreciation for the storage of weapons and munitions that allows for preservation and transportation. Beyond this, the seizure of such large numbers of weapons from intact GoY units suggests that Huthi LALs, if they are inclined to do so, might generate fighting groups having increasingly standardized size and weapon sets, with associated small-unit tactical implications.

With every new phase of intensive GoY military activity in the area, therefore, it is reasonable to conclude that Huthi fighters acquire more weapons and vehicles. Along with assault rifles, medium machine guns, and RPGs with diverse munitions, armaments have included 12.7-mm heavy machine guns, 90-mm recoilless rifles, and light (23-mm) antiaircraft cannons converted for antipersonnel or antivehicle use. In some cases, Huthi fighters have acquired GoY vehicles mounted with these weapons; at other times, they have fashioned their own "technical vehicles" with these weapons. Additionally, videos of Huthi fighters show troop transport trucks similar to those used by the GoY, suggesting acquisition through pilfering or ambush, while on two separate occasions, pro-Huthi videos have depicted Huthi fighters operating an M-113 armored personnel carrier (APC) taken from GoY stocks (see Figure 7.5). Other pro-Huthi videos have depicted fighters using a European-built armored car taken from GoY stocks, as well as Eastern Bloc models, in addition to a single T-55/62 series tank.

In addition to hunting rifles with long ranges, Huthis have also fashioned their own sniper rifles (see Figure 7.6), while the easy availability of small digital camcorders permits reconnaissance of routes, surveillance of GoY vehicles, and procedures for weak points and, potentially, training. There have also been unsubstantiated rumors of Huthi fighters using light shoulder-launched surface-to-air missiles (SAMs) in a ground-to-ground capacity, though these have not been corroborated through imagery analysis. In this case, since local informants tend not to be military experts, it is possible that what they are seeing is a class of RPG. Still, the weapons described here, along with dynamite, homemade explosives, and retooled mortar and artillery ammunition, have allowed Huthi fighters to engage GoY forces' T-55s and T-62s, as well as BTRs, HMMWVs, lightly armored jeeps, and trucks (see Figure 7.7). Isolated destruction of GoY Mi-18s is likely due to small arms fire rather than SAMs.

---

[30] This unit may have been either from the 105th or 82nd Infantry Brigade, both reputedly isolated in Huthi areas during summer 2009. See below for more details.

Figure 7.4
Weapons Seized by Huthis from GoY Forces

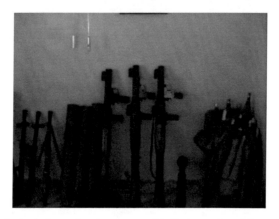

SOURCES: "Insihab al-Liwa' 105 al-Mutamarrkiz fi Muwaqi' Asfal Marran," video posted to YouTube.com, September 2, 2009; "Ba'd al-Ghana'im min al-Dhakha'ir wa-l-Asliha allati Tamm al-Saytara 'alayha khilal Shahr Wahid," video posted to 4shared.com, October 17, 2009.
RAND *MG962-7.4*

Figure 7.5
GoY Armor, Trucks, Heavy Weapons, and Technical Vehicle Taken by Huthis

SOURCES: "Fa Amkana Minhum," Huthi video, *Qism al-I'lam al-Harbi,* June 2008; Yemeni national; "Anshuda Hajim al-'Askariya li-Ansar al-Huthi," video posted to Youtube.com, December 30, 2009.
RAND *MG962-7.5*

Figure 7.6
Improvised Huthi Weapons

SOURCE: "Fa Amkana Minhum," Huthi video, *Qism al-I'lam al-Harbi,* June 2008.
RAND *MG962-7.6*

Figure 7.7
Huthi Engagement of GoY Army Assets

SOURCE: Yemeni national.
RAND *MG962-7.7*

Since every new phase of fighting presents Huthis with additional opportunities to acquire arms, Huthi engagement of Saudi ground forces is likely to do the same. Subsequent to the November 2009 fighting with well-armed but apparently poorly trained Saudi units, Huthi fighters collected moderate numbers of NATO-class weapons (see Figure 7.8). These included American 50-caliber heavy machine guns, 81-mm mortars and munitions, 7.62-mm G-3 rifles, a smattering of Heckler and Koch assault rifles and submachine guns, and 9-mm Beretta-style sidearms—as well as several ammunition belts and spare magazines. Notably, while earlier imagery depicts Huthi use of improvised sniper rifles based on AK variants, the arms acquired subsequent to engagement with Saudi forces included dedicated sniper rifles with advanced scopes. Additionally, at least in this instance, Huthi fighters acquired several sets of advanced American-style body armor and helmets, along with 40-mm grenade rounds and squad-level voice communications gear, along with two more M-113 APCs and a tank recovery vehicle. While some of these arms and gear may exceed current Huthi technical competencies, their presence in Huthi hands could permit new tactical options for enterprising LALs as well as senior Huthi leaders. At base, introduction of NATO-class weapons and gear into the Saʿda area is a potentially significant development, and individual GoY units may find themselves outgunned in force-on-force engagements.

Huthi Tactics

Analysis of Huthi combat operations presents the same difficulties as that described above for GoY military operations. Thus, examination of Huthi actions can only be impressionistic and illustrative rather than exhaustive and systematic. Additionally, as the sixth phase of war, which began in August 2009, had just entered its second month at the time of writing, it remains premature to derive conclusions about evolving tactical preferences or emerging operational priorities. Still, analysis of available reports suggests that the kinds of operations conducted by Huthi fighters benefit from the organism-like nature of the movement. Over the phases of conflict, certain actions have persisted, while additional operations have gradually become more regular. The following are examples of persistent or increasingly regular operations:

- Throughout, 7.62–12.7-mm harassing fire has been directed against military camps, police checkpoints, and convoys moving through towns or along roads ringed by elevated terrain. The likely addition of 23-mm cannons to Huthi arsenals in 2008–2009 has had a withering effect when used for these purposes. A

Figure 7.8
Weapons Acquired by Huthi Fighters Subsequent to
Engagement with Saudi Forces, November 2009

SOURCES: Pro-Huthi videos posted to YouTube: "Ghana'im Su'udiya
min Mawqa' al-Ramih," November 27, 2009; "Mudarra'at Su'udiya
Tamma al-Istila' 'alayha Khilal al-Muwajahat," November 29, 2009;
and "Ghana'im Su 'udiya Khilal al-Zahf al-Akhir," November 30, 2009.

RAND *MG962-7.8*

similar purpose has been achieved by occasional use of indirect fire from mortars, likely of the 61–81-mm variety.[31]

- Huthi fire has at times gone unanswered by GoY forces; at other times, skirmishes (*ishtibakat*) have resulted in the death or injury of team-to-squad size elements on either side.

- Throughout the conflict, Huthi fighters have employed IEDs to attack military convoys or the vehicles of prominent military or civil administration officials. These devices include antipersonnel mines as well as homemade grenades, bombs, and incendiary devices based on stocks of dynamite likely acquired prior to the beginning of hostilities. Employed intermittently and not in coordinated campaigns, Huthi IEDs do not yet exhibit levels of sophistication approaching those found in Iraq since 2004.[32]

- Since 2005, Huthi fighters have targeted senior GoY personnel or local supporters in the conflict area, including specific targeting of field-grade and general officers[33] or local civilian administrators of the GoY.[34] Methods for attacking the former have included ambushes with small arms fire, grenades, and, in a minority of cases, dedicated sniper rifles. As for local supporters, Huthis have attacked shaykhs in league with the government or their family members.[35] In addition to their persons, their houses, agricultural plots, and other property have also been targeted. In some cases, local GoY supporters have been gruesomely murdered, violating local cultural norms while seemingly intending to send a message to local tribesmen to reject GoY entreaties.[36]

- From 2005, Huthi fighters have attacked military checkpoints, and—increasingly from late 2006—have established temporary checkpoints along roads to

---

[31] See "al-Jaysh Yudammir Manzilayn Tabi'ayn li Qa'id Jumu' al-Huthi wa Marwahiya Taqsif Mawaqi' fi Bani Mu'adh," *al-Ayyam*, March 1, 2006; "al-Jaysh Yuahqqiq Saytara Shibha Kamila 'ala Bani Mu'adh wa Al 'Ammar Ba'd Khaluha min al-Huthiyin," *al-Ayyam*, March 20, 2007.

[32] See "al-Haraka Tashall bi-Sa'da Ba'd Ghurub al-Shams wa Raqaba Mafruda 'ala Madakhil al-Madina," *al-Ayyam*, April 10, 2005; "Istimrar al-Muwajahat fi Sa'da wa Maqtal Arba'a min al-Mutatawwa'in," *al-Ayyam*, February 3, 2008.

[33] "Marwahiya 'Askariya Tulqi Manshurat Tad'u Ansar al-Huthi li-l-Istislam," *al-Ayyam*, April 12 2005: "Silah al-Iududu bi-Sa'da wa Masra' Najlihi wa Shaqiqihi fi Kamin Musallah," *al-Ayyam*, May 14, 2005; "Masra' Mudir li-l-Bahth al-Jina'i wa 3 Murafiqin lahu wa Naja Mas'ul Akhir bi-Sa'da," *al-Ayyam*, January 28, 2006; "Istishhad Qa'id Katiba wa Masra' 6 min Atba' al-Huthi bi-Sa'da," *al-Ayyam*, February 13, 2007; "Ittisa' Ruq'at al-Muwajahat bayn al-Jaysh wa-l-Huthiyin," *al-Ayyam*, April 17, 2007.

[34] "Na'ib Muhafiz Sa'da wa Mudir Amnuha Yata'arradan li-Kamin Musallah," *al-Ayyam*, April 4, 2005.

[35] See "Al-Jaysh Yuhaqqiq Ba'd Tadmir 5 Manazil li-l-Muwatinin bi-Qadhai'ifihi," *al-Ayyam*, May 31, 2007.

[36] See "Hudu' Jabhat al-Qital fi Sa'da Naharan wa Isht'aluha Laylan," *al-Ayyam,* March 3, 2007.

prevent GoY military movement or the transport of people sympathetic to the GoY cause.[37]

- From 2006, Huthi fighters have fired on or destroyed local administration buildings in several of Sa'da's *mudiriyat*.[38]
- During this same period, but increasingly from 2007 into 2009, Huthi fighters, or those operating under the Huthi banner, have either closed roads in parts of the region or have taken measures to physically destroy sections of roads, including the Sa'da-San'a road and routes between Razih and Shada'a, Baqim and Majz, and Sa'da and Dahyan.[39] Huthis have on occasion demonstrated the ability to cut roads south of Sa'da governorate, in Harf Sufyan—a major area of combat in the beginning stages of the 2009 fighting.[40] In a few cases, Huthis have destroyed strategic infrastructure, such as bridges and electricity stations. These actions appear to result from tactical opportunism rather than a consistent strategy.[41]
- Throughout the conflict, but particularly from 2007, Huthi attacks on static positions or convoys have resulted in acquisition of GoY weapons, including mortars, artillery, and wheeled and tracked vehicles—although it is not known whether Huthis have subsequently used the latter offensively.[42]

Beyond this, Huthi fighters have been capable of a range of more aggressive actions in different areas of the *muhafaza*, carried out over a few days by multiple, usually autonomous and uncoordinated, armed groups. A few examples highlight this capability from mid-April 2007, during the yearlong fourth phase of the Sa'da conflict. In the first week of April 2007, a Huthi-GoY skirmish resulted in seven soldiers being taken prisoner by Huthis in the Bani Mu'adh and Dahyan districts. A few days later, on April 4, 2007, persistent Huthi harassment fire on GoY forces surrounding Dahyan led to a portion of those forces withdrawing to reorder their ranks. That night, in the 'uzlas along the border of Sahar and Safra', Huthi groups attacked multiple static army

---

[37] See "Ishtibakat Musallaha ma'a Ansar al-Huthi wast Madinat Sa'da," *al-Ayyam*, March 20, 2005; "Tajaddadat al-Ishtibakat bayn Wahdat al-Jaysh wa Atba' al-Huthi bi-Sa'da," *al-Ayyam*, December 21, 2005; "Masra' 3 'Askariyin fi Ishtibakat Musallaha wast San'a," *al-Ayyam*, April 16, 2007.

[38] See "'Anasir al-Huthi Yufajjirun Mabna Mahattat Kahraba' Qatabir bi-Sa'da," *al-Ayyam*, April 19, 2007.

[39] See "Darba Qawwiya Murtaqiba li-Hasm al-Ma'raka fi Sa'da bi-Aqqal Waqt," *al-Ayyam*, February 12, 2007; "Mudiriyat Ghamar fi Sa'da Tashhad Ma'arik 'Anifa," *al-Ayyam*, April 12, 2007; "al-Jaysh Yataqqadam fi 'Iddat Mawaqi' wa Yahkum al-Saytara 'ala Dahyan," *al-Ayyam*, April 22, 2007; "Musadamat 'Anifa bi-Sa'da wa-l-Huthiyin Yaqta'un Tariq Sa'da-San'a," *al-Ayyam*, May 10, 2008.

[40] See "Ma'arik bayn al-Jaysh wa-l-Huthiyin bi-Harf Sufyan wa 'Ummal a-Nazafa Yantashilun al-Juthath min al-Shawari'," *al-Ayyam*, May 29, 2008.

[41] See "al-Silah al-Jawwi Yughayr 'ala Mawaqi' al-Huthiyin fi-l-Talh wa-l-Madfa'iya Taqsuf Tahsinatahum fi Nushur," *al-Ayyam*, February 28, 2007; "'Anasir al-Huthi Tantaqil fi Manatiq Bani Mu'adh wa Sahar wa-l-Safra' 'abr al-Mazari' al-Kabira," *al-Ayyam*, April 18, 2007.

[42] See "Istimrar al-Qital al-'Anif fi Dahyan wa Ta'zizat 'Askariya Murtaqiba li-l-Jaysh," *al-Ayyam*, April 7, 2007.

outposts (*mawaqi'*), while overnight and into the morning of April 5, running squad-to-platoon-size engagements in the al-Ghabir region of al-Talh *'uzla* resulted in Huthis occupying a GoY position, allegedly also taking control of Yemeni army mortars and a tracked vehicle.

Throughout April 5, Huthi groups fought against members of the local Daris tribe, who were supporting the GoY and were reinforced by Yemeni border troops, using small arms, medium machine guns, and mortars. Throughout the same day, Huthi elements cut off roads and transportation corridors through Wadi Badr in Ghamr district, preventing local volunteers (*junud mustajaddin*) originating in Munabbih from moving to Sa'da to join regime forces. In the late afternoon of April 5, Huthi fighters also attacked a GoY weapons and ammunition convoy in the Dahyan area, setting it alight with RPG fire and causing more than a squad's worth of GoY casualties. Local observers suggested that in this engagement Huthis used larger-caliber rockets, potentially of the RPG-29 variety. On the afternoon of April 6, Huthis followed up previous actions by attacking a GoY position in western Kahlan in Sahar with small arms and rockets. That night, Huthis again engaged the GoY in Kahlan, this time attacking what was likely a larger military camp (*mu'askar li-l-jaysh*). In an engagement lasting a few hours, Huthi mortars were detonated near the camp's command post.[43]

Thus, in nearly ten incidents in just over 48 hours, Huthis had engaged GoY forces in multiple parts of central Sa'da governorate, some more than once, also demonstrating an ability to at least occupy GoY positions temporarily. This frequency and intensity was perhaps the impetus for the movement into Sa'da of a platoon's worth of Republican Guards by the end of April 6. Further, while interrupting GoY logistics and resupply as well as local lanes of communication, Huthis devoted attention to attacking tribal supporters of the GoY and interdicting the flow of local volunteers to GoY lines. The concern to prevent locals from supporting the GoY has grown in particular since 2006–2007, with Huthi fighters targeting GoY-supportive shaykhs multiple times.[44]

This sequence of events was not a one-off. According to local Yemeni news sources, almost two weeks later, on April 15, 2007, Huthi elements ambushed a military convoy on the Sa'da–San'a road in Mahadhir *'uzla*, south of Sa'da city itself. Using small arms and possibly grenades and RPGs, Huthi fighters caused around 20 GoY casualties. The following day, they attacked a GoY *mawqa'* in Katfa, northeast of Sa'da city, eventually taking over the position. That evening in the mountainous areas of Sahar, a military encampment came under Huthi direct fire. In this instance, exchanges of fire were followed by an explosion that killed two GoY soldiers—however, it is not clear whether this was a complex attack involving direct fire and an IED or whether ordnance in the soldiers' possession ignited due to munitions striking it. Later that night, repetitive

---

[43] "Istimrar al-Qital al-'Anif fi Dahyan wa Ta'zizat 'Askariya Murtaqiba li-l-Jaysh."

[44] See "Masra' 3 'Askariyin fi Ishtibakat Musallaha wast San'a," *al-Ayyam*, April 16, 2007.

exchanges of 7.62-mm and 12.7-mm fire occurred between Huthis and GoY forces in the Dahyan environs, while into the morning of April 17, farmlands and orchards in Bani Mu'adh, Safra', and Sahar were points of origin for indirect and sniper fire on GoY positions and vehicles.

Also on the morning of April 17, direct fire exchanges in Dahyan resulted in 15 casualties among both Huthis and GoY forces. Around the same time, Huthi fighters ambushed a battalion commander's vehicle in the Harf Sufyan district of 'Amran governorate, killing the driver. That same morning, in the district capital of Qatabir, Huthis attacked the local municipal offices, eventually occupying them and the district security office, and forcing the evacuation of the district governor, head of local council, and the director of district security. Later in the day, they also attacked a government school in al-Qal'a, the capital of *mudiriyat* Razih.

Over a 48-hour period, therefore, nine Huthi-GoY kinetic incidents occurred, from Harf Sufyan in the south all the way to al-Qal'a in the northwest.[45] Ranging from harassing fire to attacks on mobile GoY units and static positions, as well as the temporary occupation of government buildings, the cumulative effect was to force the GoY to attempt to coordinate defense, reinforcement, and relief of assets over distances and diverse terrain. These attacks also drew the GoY into a response highlighting the limitations of a conventional conscript force, targeting civilian areas with indirect fire. Yet, Huthi fighters were able to raise the pressure on GoY forces without focusing their efforts on coordinated planning, operating, or reinforcement of their brethren in other sectors. In fact, the relative autonomy of armed groupings under LALs has permitted a temporary increase of attack frequency in multiple areas. In a sense, the informal, incomplete, or notional C3 relationships among fighting groups assist the sustainability of Huthi kinetic actions.

Broadly speaking, therefore, the nature of Huthi armed activity has taken the form of small-unit raids, where groups ranging in size from squads to platoons attack similar-sized GoY forces in static positions. Along with direct and indirect harassing fire—whose value is both kinetic and rhetorical—ambushes of military convoys and significant officials are accompanied by temporary occupation of GoY positions. In some cases, Huthi elements have established control (*saytara, haymana*) over areas for extended periods of time—for example, in Matra, Naq'a, and Dahyan. While the Arabic press does not refer to these locations as "liberated areas," reports point to Huthi takeover of schools, establishment of Huthi courts judging according to *shari'a* and mediating disagreements among locals, and forced purchase of foodstuffs from local farmers.[46]

---

[45] See "'Anasir al-Huthi Tantaqil fi Manatiq Bani Mu'adh wa Sahar wa Safra' 'abr al-Mazari' al-Kabira," *al-Ayyam*, April 18, 2007.

[46] See "Istimrar Tabadul Itlaq al-Nar bayn al-Huthiyin wa Junud al-Jaysh," *al-Ayyam*, August 8, 2007; interview with Western human rights worker from the conflict region, March 20, 2009.

Rather than signifying a strategic effort to establish a "Huthistan," Matra, Naqʻa, and Dahyan are unique cases. Although the latter is not an example of a Huthi assault into an urban environment, by early 2007 Dahyan possessed local Huthi fighting groups under a regional *qaʻid*. A pro-Hashimi area at times referred to as the "Najaf of the Zaydis,"[47] it likely was taken over by groups of Huthi combatants in the spring of 2007. Taking refuge in local homes and schools, Huthis used Dahyan as a logistical support base, obtaining food and fuel and probably storing weapons. Dahyan thus became a major strategic focus for the GoY during the fourth phase of their anti-Huthi operations. Into the fall of 2007, Huthis withstood repetitive aerial bombing, as well as artillery and tank fire into the city. They also withstood and repelled foot soldiers' assaults into the city on multiple occasions. Temporarily relinquishing ground, Huthi fighters were able to draw in GoY and volunteer units, at times cutting them off from larger formations. At the same time, other Huthi fighters in the rest of the governorate, not concerned with reinforcing Dahyan, maintained pressure on GoY forces. On at least one occasion, however, Huthi fighters attacked a GoY battalion attempting to move into the Dahyan region from another area, causing at least 30 casualties and raising the possibility of coordination among Huthi elements in different sectors. Ultimately, the GoY was unable to establish full control of Dahyan and pulled back, having failed to open routes to Matra and other Huthi areas to the north.[48]

Thus, in friendly built-up areas, Huthi fighters can demonstrate tactical endurance through defense, while unrelated Huthi groups can persist in offensive raids. Naqʻa and Matra are similar instances in less-urban, mountainous areas distant from the governorate center. These regions can be considered Huthi safe havens. Since 2006, fighters, sympathizers, and elements of the Huthi leadership have found refuge there. Fortifying the area with trenches (*khanadiq*), weapons, and food stores, Huthis in this area have withstood repetitive GoY airstrikes, threatened GoY helicopters, and denied GoY forces the secure avenues of movement into the region required in order to mount an assault.

The above cases refer to defense in urban and mountainous environments. Given their small size and autonomous nature, Huthi fighting groups have not regularly gone on the offensive against large GoY units—although in some cases they have been able to slow GoY military advances. For example, in 2006 Huthi fighters attacked the lead element of a company-sized GoY force in Al Shafiʻa east of Saʻda city, advancing to dislodge them from the area. Killing five soldiers in addition to the local commander, they halted the advance while taking the GoY soldiers' weapons.[49] Likewise, in Sep-

---

[47] See Yahya al-Thulaya, "Jamiʻat al-Mutanaqidat . . . Dammaj al-Salafiyin, wa Dahyan al-Huthiyin, wa Saʻda al-Muʻtammar al-Shaʻbi," *al-Ahale.net*, n.d.

[48] See "al-Jaysh Yatamakkan min al-Saytara ʻala Muʻazzam Ajzaʼ Jabal Gharaba bi-Saʻda," *al-Ayyam*, April 24, 2007.

[49] See "Tajaddud al-Ishtibakat bayn Quwwat al-Amn wa-l-Jaysh wa-l-Huthi," *al-Ayyam*, June 7, 2006.

tember 2009 Huthi spokesman Muhammad 'Abd al-Sallam claimed that rebel forces had ambushed a Yemeni army battalion in the Ghula locale of Harf Sufyan ('Amran), "killing all the troops of it." Though likely an exaggeration, 'Abd al-Sallam spoke of attacking a full regular army unit in a complex ambush employing landmines and small and medium arms. This would be a potentially notable advance.[50] Still, the autonomous nature of Huthi fighting groups, which answer to LALs notionally allied with other Huthi groups in other 'uzlas or mudiriyat, has meant that Huthi operations are not characterized by coordinated reinforcement by other "friendly" units in adjoining sectors. However, on certain occasions, Huthis have been able to reinforce fighters under pressure, particularly through the use of cellular and satellite communication.[51]

Finally, in line with their preference for squad- to platoon-sized raids, Huthi fighters have not regularly conducted large-scale assaults into urban areas. However, the few occasions when this has happened have been on Huthi initiative. In April 2005, for example, a platoon-sized group of Huthis moved into the northern and western environs of Sa'da City, spurring a day's worth of street-to-street fighting with GoY forces that flared again over the next few days. Judging from the divergent press reports, between 90 and 150 Huthi and GoY casualties resulted from about four days of fighting, suggesting repetitive platoon- to company-sized engagements where more than 100 Huthi fighters reinforced each other based on several local fighting groups. While this fighting did not result in Huthi occupation of significant portions of the city, it was a strong show of force that greatly diminished local confidence in GoY capabilities.[52]

As mentioned above, Yemeni reporting on military aspects of the Huthi-regime conflict has always been imprecise. Yemeni reporters are not military correspondents and are not familiar with operational aspects of their military. Likewise, Yemeni journalists function with the awareness of GoY censorship, which encourages self-censorship. Since late 2007 in particular, reporting on GoY or Huthi operations has been increasingly intermittent, given the press blackout the GoY has imposed on the area. Additionally, the sixth phase of fighting has so far been characterized by one side's reports on combat—including magnitude, location, casualties, and outcomes—which either are not corroborated or are rejected by the other side. Indications suggest, however, that over the past year and a half, Huthi operating methods have remained consistent with earlier trends, with a few noticeable developments. First, as the conflict has broadened both demographically and geographically since 2007, more fighting has involved intertribal conflicts as opposed to strictly Huthi-GoY engagements. In some cases, tribal segments have risen against each other or against the GoY without direct connection to the Huthi conflict.

---

[50] "Rebels Kill Battalion in Harf Sufyan, Spokesman Claims," *Yemen Post*, September 27, 2009.

[51] "Dabt 3 Shahinat Asliha wa-l-Huthiyun Yatahatifun 'abr al-Aqmar al-Istina'iya."

[52] See "Musadamat 'Anifa bi-Shawari' Sa'da bayn al-Amn wa 'Anasir al-Huthi," *al-Ayyam*, April 9, 2005.

Second, in some areas of strong Huthi loyalty, such as Maran in Haydan, Huthi fighters have been able to take advantage of terrain unfavorable to conventional forces to cut GoY units off from ground reinforcement, isolating them and laying siege to GoY positions.[53] Huthi isolation of GoY units has at times resulted in detention of individual officers—including field-grade or general officers—or even entire units at the squad, platoon, or company size (see Figure 7.9). We have seen previously that this practice provides weapons to Huthi groups. It may also be a source of (somewhat trained) fighters or supporters if it leads to desertion of GoY soldiers. In one particularly noteworthy case during the opening phases of the sixth war, it was reported that the Yemeni Army's 105th Infantry Brigade was cut off from other GoY forces and isolated in the Marran region. After a 17-day siege (*hisar*) the brigade commander, Muhammad Saleh 'Amir, pulled the unit back in full retreat on August 31, 2009, allegedly leaving behind most of the brigade's armaments, which fell into Huthi hands. According to GoY sources, a Yemeni colonel was killed during the retreat.[54] Finally, in some instances, GoY resupply of isolated and materially depleted units has relied on helicopters, which are not immune to Huthi small arms fire and have been brought down on a few occasions (see Figure 7.10).[55] Huthi sources also claim to have brought down a GoY MiG-21 in early October 2009. Though official sources assert that the fighter went down because of technical problems, Huthi sources subsequently claimed to have downed a second Yemeni fighter plane, complete with video showing smoldering wreckage.

Third, while the sixth phase of fighting was in general characterized by heavy GoY assaults and bombardments of conflict areas, Huthi fighters themselves may be demonstrating greater tactical boldness. Reports have emerged of Huthi fighters not only attacking roads at key points but also taking control of strategic points

---

[53] See "al-Jaysh Yatamakkan min Dukhul Suq al-Talh wa Yudammir Mahattat Wuqud bi-Dahyan Yashtabih bi-Tazwidiha al-Huthiyin bi-l-Banzin," *al-Ayyam*, March 24, 2007.

[54] See Tayyib Mahjub, "al-Tamarrud al-Zaydi fi Shimal al-Yamanj: Haraka Siyasiya wa 'Askariya," *al-Sabah al-Jadid* (Iraq), October 2, 2009; "al-Yaman min Janubihi ila Shimalihi Ma'raka Maftuha 'ala Kull al-Ihtimalat," *Ilaf*, October 1, 2009. Significantly, the brigade commander in question is now subject to court-martial for allegedly abandoning his post and aiding the Huthis by permitting them access to weapons. 'Amir, however, is a member of the Khawlan tribe, and this case has led several Khawlani shaykhs, such as Husayn Ahmad al-Qadi and Muhammad bin Naji al-Ghadir, to protest the GoY's actions, calling for a dismissal of the case or for prosecution of all officers involved in the operation. It has also been reported that the 82nd Infantry Brigade was broken up by Huthi fighters on August 6, 2009, just prior to the GoY's announcement of a sixth phase of fighting. In this instance, the brigade commander is reported to have fled to Saudi Arabia with several officers, leaving large stocks of cannon, rockets, and even armored vehicles to the Huthis. See "Anba' 'an Saytarat al-Huthiyin 'ala Liwa' Yamani fi Sa'da," *Ilaf*, August 6, 2009. Continued such instances, along with GoY reprisal, could potentially harm the cohesion of army units, as well as Saleh's tribal support base.

[55] See "Istimrar al-Hisar 'ala Katibat al-Jaysh bi-Haydan wa Inkhifadh al-Hajamat al-Mutabadila bayn al-Janibayn," *al-Ay yam*, January 24, 2008; "al-Huthiyun Yudammirun Manzalan Yatamarkaz bi-Dakhilihi Junud al-Jaysh," *al-Ayyam,* January 14, 2008; Yahya al-Thulaya, "Harf Sufyan, Kayfa Ihtaraqat Maqarrat al-Al-Ahzab wa Hallat Mahallha al-Huthiya!" *al-Ahali*, undated.

Figure 7.9
GoY Officers and Units Detained by Huthis

SOURCES: "Junud Tamm Asirhum min Qabl al-Muqatilin al-Huthiyin," posted to Youtube.com, August 31, 2009; "Dubat Asra Yansahun al-Sulta bi-Iqaf al-Harb," posted to Youtube.com, September 2, 2009; "Insihab al-Liwa' 105 al-Mutamarrkiz fi Muwaqi' Asfal Marran" (The Withdrawal of Batallion 105 Based in Lower Marran), video posted to YouTube.com, September 2, 2009.
RAND *MG962-7.9*

of passage, such as the Khaniq bridge on the Sa'da–San'a road in Harf Sufyan. In this case, sources reported that hours of fighting preceded the Huthi occupation of the bridge, entailing many Huthi casualties. Though these reports may reflect inflated numbers, they also suggest a greater readiness to stand and fight for the sake of tactical objectives—as does the assault on a communications tower in Jabal al-Ahmar (see Chapter Five).[56]

---

[56] See "Mubarak Yu'lin Da'mahu li-l-Yaman wa-l-Su'udiya Tanfi Qasf Mawaqi' li-l-Huthiyin," *al-Akhbar* (Lebanon), October 3, 2009; "Masadir Mahalliya Tu'akkid Tamakkun al-Huthiyin min al-Saytara 'ala Jisr Khaniq al-Wasil bayna Harf Sufyan wa San'a," *al-Hadath,* October 3, 2009; "At Least 34 Killed in North Yemen Clashes," *AFP,* October 3, 2009; "Shiite Fighters 'Capture Another Gov't Position,'" *PressTV* (Iran), October 3, 2009.

Figure 7.10
GoY Helicopter and Fighter Aircraft Downed by
Huthi Fighters

SOURCES: "Fa Amkana Minhum," Huthi video,
Qism al-I'lam al-Harbi, June 2008; "Ihtiraq al-Ta'ira,"
posted to 4shared.com, October 5, 2009.

RAND *MG962-7.10*

One particularly striking incident was reported by GoY authorities in mid-September 2009. In this case, the GoY claimed that Huthi fighters attacked the presidential palace in Sa'da City from multiple directions with more than 60 "armored vehicles." Reports suggested that over 150 Huthi fighters were involved, requiring the GoY to call in helicopter support. Around the same time, reportedly on the same day, Huthi fighters attacked three checkpoints in the area. The veracity of these reports is suspect, because Huthi sources have not corroborated them in spite of having every reason to showcase another "heroic" exploit against the regime. Likewise, this clash—although reported by the GoY as a victory—would seem to highlight advances in Huthi capabilities if it did occur. The simultaneous use of several armed vehicles (likely mostly technical vehicles with a smattering of ex-GoY transports, jeeps, and gun-trucks) to converge on the same target in a sustained assault—in the face of fire from the air and large casualty numbers—implies a certain aggressiveness, endurance, and nascent tactical coordination. Given the logic of insurrection or insurgency, therefore, more significant than the state's ability to rebuff the assault is that it may have occurred in the first place.[57]

Still, as a combatant entity, the Huthis have not moved substantially beyond semi-autonomous, mostly territorially bound fighting groups with LALs paying notional allegiance to 'Abd al-Malik al-Huthi. While they are able to communicate better both within and among groups, consistent reporting does not yet indicate that Huthi forces are capable of complex operations requiring the coordination of mounted and dismounted personnel from multiple groups. To get this capability, Huthi fighters would require some standardization of group size and materiel. Of late, pro-Huthi imagery has depicted fighters arranged in marching columns of uniform size with similar clothing, just as Huthi Web sites feature efforts to practice fighting skills (see Figure 7.11). Likewise, acquisition of weapons sets from GoY units could permit standardization.

Beyond indicating a desire to use ideological communication to create an impression of progressively advancing Huthi military prowess, such images do not prove standardization or professionalization of Huthi groups. Nor do they indicate a desire to transcend a fighting organism based on the kinds of small, locally focused forces characteristic of northern Yemeni tribalism—which have served Huthi purposes well up to this point. Greater tactical capabilities would also require an amount of training and assistance from Yemenis or foreigners with regular military experience, as well as improved C3 both across groups and up a solidifying chain of command. Although these changes would help Huthis become more combat-effective in conventional terms, the shift from Huthi combatant organism to paramilitary-like formation would sacrifice the benefits of the former that we have discussed above, perhaps also allowing a conventional GoY force to target them better.

---

[57] See "State-Run Media: Yemeni Military Kills 150 Rebels," *CNN.com*, September 21, 2009; "Hundreds of Rebels Killed in North Yemen," *UPI.com*, September 21, 2009.

Figure 7.11
Huthi "Units" at Attention and in Training

SOURCE: "Anshuda Hajim al-'Askariya li-Ansar al-Huthi" video posted to Youtube.com, December 30, 2009.
RAND *MG962-7.11*

Huthi Information Operations: Mechanisms, Modes, Messages, and Audiences

As we demonstrated in Chapters Three and Four, by 2004 the Huthi family had produced a considerable amount of written and audio material containing messages that resonated with the Sa'da population. These motifs included a revival of Zaydi identity and practice, Arab humiliation, Arab regime complicity in American/Israeli agendas, and a call to action against Islam's enemies (America and Israel). Within the context of armed conflict, these lectures would continue to circulate, taking on new meaning and providing a point of departure for subsequent Huthi propaganda material. Understood in the context of past Huthi ideological propagation, these materials are endowed with the authenticity of historical messages communicated throughout the 1980s and into the 21st century in the governorate. These earlier materials exist in a recursive relationship with post-2004 Huthi ideological communications: Earlier ideological communication endows later Huthi messages with its pedigree and aura of religio-ideological authenticity, while newer Huthi messages help to craft the interpretive framework through which their supporters understand Husayn or Badr al-Din's words of the past.

In disseminating its messages, the Huthi organism has utilized culturally legitimate mechanisms such as poems (*qasa'id*), lectures (*muhadarat*), and anthems (*anashid*) while also exploiting cutting-edge tools such as Web pages, videos, and Web forums. This spectrum of mechanisms and modes ensures that the group can connect with multiple audiences and also demonstrates ways in which the Huthi organism's information operations have shifted and evolved throughout the duration of the conflict.

Indeed, as a nonstate entity, the Huthi organism has been able to astutely utilize both time-tested and cutting-edge mechanisms and modes of ideological dissemination in a much more effective and quickly evolving manner than the GoY itself.

Figure 7.12 illustrates the operational evolution of the mechanisms employed by the Huthi organism in the dissemination of their propaganda. It clearly demonstrates a conscious effort on the part of the Huthis to expand their informational capabilities and, by extension, the scope of their audience. Pinpointing when the group began using certain mechanisms is particularly difficult, given the fact that they are delivered orally and rarely reprinted. But we know, for instance, that Huthi supporters have championed their cause through the use of poems (*qasa'id*), which are likely exchanged during group meetings. Similarly, it is difficult to ascertain the particular point at which Huthi leaders other than Husayn al-Huthi began delivering speeches or their impetus for doing so, though Zaydi commemorations feature them. These settings, revalorized as specifically Huthi holidays, are now joined by celebrations innovated by the Huthis themselves, which we discuss below. These are all arenas for distribution of pro-Huthi pamphlets such as *Nashirat al-Haqiqa*.

Figure 7.12
Evolution of Huthi Ideological Mechanisms over Phases of Conflict

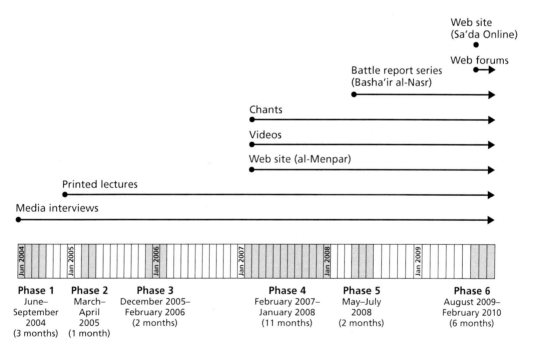

More broadly, the development of Huthi informational capabilities illustrates a conscious effort to combine both culturally resonant modes of propagation with cutting-edge mechanisms that have become commonplace among various militant Islamist organizations. In this regard, and most visible to Arab and Western audiences, Huthi leaders have taken part in a number of interviews within a wide range of media outlets both in the West and the Arab world. These have included live phone interviews with the BBC and *al-Jazeera*, as well as printed interviews in Yemeni newspapers. The interviews typically are conducted during times of relative calm in the governorate and rarely include a face-to-face meeting between a main Huthi commander and his interviewer. While primarily agreeing to interviews with independent newspapers, Huthi leaders do not currently appear to prefer any one of them exclusively. Interviews provide Huthi leaders the opportunity to reach out to the broader Yemeni and Arab audience and allow them to shape their message in a clear, unmediated manner. They can thus legitimate their actions to the Yemeni and Arab public and portray themselves in a more positive light.

The Huthis have also utilized a number of culturally acceptable methods of ideological propagation that perform a number of functions for the Huthi organism. For one, distributing printed and audio recordings of Husayn al-Huthi's speeches while also referencing them in videos and imagery gives the group religious authenticity. It was Husayn, after all, who had initially mobilized the Sa'da population against GoY forces in 2004 and who built on the religious prestige of Badr al-Din. *Qasa'id* serve a similar purpose. By employing a well-established and acceptable method of ideological transmission, Huthi communication achieves a level of cultural authenticity that GoY information operations cannot.

Further, Huthi leaders have appropriated a number of preexisting holidays (al-Ghadir Day, National Jerusalem Day, and the Prophet's Birthday (see Figure 7.13) to deliver speeches, rally support, and likely distribute Husayn's lectures. It is also likely that *qasa'id* are exchanged at such public gatherings. Speeches—which often resemble religious *khutab*, or sermons—as well as *qasa'id* imbue the Huthi organism with both the prestige of Husayn and Badr al-Din al-Huthi and cultural legitimacy, appealing to traditional mores and modes of expression. As we will shortly see, Huthis have also established their own holidays. This adds a new dimension to the Huthi information strategy, providing the group a commemorative holiday directly associated with the conflict in a religious idiom.

The significance of these holidays cannot be overstated. Indeed, based on video footage, it appears that thousands of supporters travel to specified locations to listen to 'Abd al-Malik speak. This indicates the Huthi leader's growing popularity as well his ability to use preexisting holidays to mobilize and indoctrinate his supporters. These events require a certain amount of preparation, since the stage, loudspeakers, and seating must be arranged ahead of time. Further, they demonstrate a certain amount of discipline among the Huthi supporters themselves, who sit in an organized fashion,

Figure 7.13
Huthi Supporters Chanting at Prophet's Birthday Celebration, 2009

SOURCE: "Maqati' min Khutab al-Sayyid 'Abd al-Malik Badr al-Din al-Huthi
Hafazuhu Allah," posted to Youtube.com, August 31, 2009.

RAND *MG962-7.13*

remain silent during the speech, and chant in unison. The immense number of supporters who show up to these events should be seen as an indicator of the growing
mobilizational capacity of the Huthi organism.

The sixth phase of the war has shown another form of Huthi indoctrination that
could allow the Huthis to expand their influence beyond the Sa'da governorate itself:
the capturing, indoctrination, and release of GoY soldiers (see Figure 7.14). Indeed, the
Huthis have released video footage of company-sized regiments of captured GoY forces
receiving water and lectures from Huthi commanders. This method of indoctrination
indicates the ways in which the Huthis can erode the morale of GoY troops while
simultaneously appearing to be adopting the moral high ground in the conflict. Most
important, however, it illustrates a form of propaganda that could earn the Huthis support or sympathy within the GoY armed forces and broader Yemeni and Arab public.

Just as the Huthi organism employs long-accepted cultural modes in its information operations, so too does it utilize new technology to deliver its messages. *Al-
Menpar* is the Huthis' primary Web page. It hosts press releases, editorials, speeches,
and images, all of which directly relate to the Sa'da conflict. The group's small Web
following has moved from Yemeni Web forums to the Ansar al-Haqq Web page and

Figure 7.14
GoY Soldiers Receiving Lecture from Huthi LAL

SOURCE: "Insihab al-Liwa' 105 al-Mutamarkaz fi Muwaqi' Asfal Marran,"
video posted to YouTube.com, September 2, 2009.
RAND *MG962-7.14*

forum (shown in Figure 7.15), which, while far less sleek than *al-Menpar*, hosts discussions and allows the exchange of files ranging from Huthi videos and Zaydi jurisprudential works to videos created by militant Shi'a groups in Iraq. Further, the Sa'da
Online Web site, also pictured in Figure 7.15, serves a similar function to *al-Menpar*
and also contains active forums.

Similarly, Huthi members directly involved in the conflict have captured footage
depicting combat operations, training, and Huthi gatherings. These videos, possibly
distributed in local *suqs* and shops, are likely intended to be disseminated electronically via the Huthis' YouTube channels and other video-sharing Web sites and forums.
The length and production quality of the videos has steadily improved, with the group
producing an hourlong video during the fifth phase of the conflict. Since the start of
the sixth phase, the group has demonstrated a growing capability in its media releases.
The number of video releases advertised on its Web page has grown significantly, as
have the group's daily conflict updates. Further, the Huthis have often immediately

Figure 7.15
Huthi Web-Based Communication: al-Menpar, Ansar al-Haqq, and Sa'da Online

SOURCES: al-Menpar Web site; Ansar al-Haqq Web site; Sa'da Online Web site.

responded to charges and accusations leveled by the GoY, sometimes providing video evidence to support their case. These Web pages and videos, likely banned in Yemen, also indicate the group's attempt to expand its audience beyond Yemen's borders and appeal to the broader Shi'ite Web community. This could allow the group to depict itself as genuine Shi'ite *muqawama* (resistance) a la Hizbullah.

The various modes of dissemination the Huthis have used throughout the duration of the conflict highlight both the evolution of its capabilities and an acute awareness of the local, regional, and international stages on which the group must have a presence. Indeed, while it draws on old works and modes to confirm its cultural, social, and religious credentials, it also uses new mechanisms to reach an audience beyond Yemen's borders. Next we explore the way in which these various mechanisms have been used to convey new messages and motifs while redefining old ones. Through such portrayals, however, the Huthis have propagated messages that are in some cases contradictory and in other cases inconsistent.

The GoY as Foreign Proxy ('Amil)

While Husayn al-Huthi rarely criticized the Saleh government's close relationship with the United States directly, Huthi propaganda has attempted to portray the government as an agent ('amil) of the United States. Figure 7.16, taken from a Huthi video production, serves as an ideal propaganda tool for the Huthis. Crucially, it depicts President Saleh with his hand on his heart—a cultural sign of sincerity. The audio accompanying the image is taken from a speech presumably made by 'Abd al-Malik al-Huthi, which declares "The Arab leaders, the Yemeni leader himself and the Yemeni government itself . . . have become dirty, despicable tools, to execute the American agenda, and the American-Israeli plans in the Arab world and Yemen."[58]

Similarly, increasing criticism has been directed at the Kingdom of Saudi Arabia's involvement in inciting the conflict and urging the GoY to take action against the Huthis. In a 2007 interview, 'Abd al-Malik al-Huthi pleaded with the Saudis to "correct their stance . . . to use their money for building, not destruction; life, not death; supporting the Yemeni people who are their neighbors, not to support the imposition of power over them."[59] More explicit in its accusation of Saudi meddling was an April 2009 editorial posted on *al-Menpar*, which accused the kingdom of "participating with the government in launching a sixth war with large financial support, this time—according to sources—more than 400,000,000 Saudi Riyals."[60] Similarly,

---

[58] "Fa-Amkana Minhum," *Qism al-'Alam al-Harbi,* June 2008.

[59] "'Abd al-Malik al-Huthi: Lam Nabda' al-Harb al-Fi'liya Ba'd," *al-Akhbar,* July 3, 2008.

[60] 'Ali al-Yamani, "Al-Tahaluf al-Thulayi fi Mu'amarat al-'Adwan al-Sadis . . . Da'm Mali Su'udi . . . wa Lujisti wa Fini Amriki. Wa Tanfidh Yamani," *al-Menpar,* April 20, 2009.

**Figure 7.16
President Saleh Meeting with President Bush**

SOURCE: "Fa Amkana Minhum," Huthi video, *Qism al-I'lam al-Harbi,* June 2008.
NOTE: The Arabic text reads: "The American Initiative and the Manipulation
of the [Yemeni] Government."
RAND *MG962-7.16*

another Huthi editorial declared "the two sides reached, with Qatari mediation, a solution, concluding an agreement and peace between them, except that the Saudis refused
this, and forced their *'amil* 'Ali Saleh to launch a fifth war."[61]

Throughout the first few weeks of the sixth phase, accusations of Saudi meddling
initially increased. Indeed, in September 2009 the group released a video of Saudi
mortars presumably supplied by the kingdom to Yemeni forces (Figure 7.17).[62] Also,
a number of other pro-Huthi editorials have argued that the Saleh government is, in
fact, aligned with Yemeni Salafi-jihadi groups, and is thus carrying out their agenda.[63]
Direct Saudi military involvement in the conflict has further given the Huthis ample
material to depict the GoY as acting at the behest of the kingdom. Indeed, in an audio
statement, 'Abd al-Malik al-Huthi argued that the Yemeni army's complacency in the

---

[61] 'Amar Husayn al-'Arjli, "Al-Su'udiya Taz'az 'a Amn al-Yaman wa Tantahik Siyadatihi, wa Qara' Tabul al-
Harub fi al-Yaman Tabda' Duma min al-Riyad," *al-Menpar*, April 3, 2009.

[62] "Maqta' Fiydiyu Yuwwadih Haqiqat al-Tamwin al-'Aaskari al-Su'udi Did al-Huthiyin," *al-Menpar*, September 3, 2009.

[63] Jamal Na'man, "Al-Tahaluf al-Jadid bayn 'Ali Salih wa al-Qa'ida fi-l-Yaman," *al-Menpar*, January 28, 2009.

Figure 7.17
Saudi Mortar Allegedly Found by Huthi Militants

SOURCE: Huthi "Maqta' Fiydiyu Yuwwadih Haqiqat al-Tamwin al-'askari
al-Su'udi Did al-Huthiyin," *al-Menpar*, September 3, 2009.
RAND *MG962-7.17*

face of Saudi "aggression" indicates that it "is not an army for the people or country."[64]
As we will see in the following section, the Huthis take this theme a step further by
portraying their operations against Saudi targets as being spurred by the need to preserve Yemeni territorial integrity.

Declaring the Saleh government to be a U.S., Israeli, and/or Saudi proxy has
a number of implications. For one, it paints the Saleh government as explicitly non-
Yemeni and far removed from the will of its people. This lack of popular support has
also been emphasized in editorials by Yahya al-Huthi.[65] Perhaps more significantly,
however, such accusations imbue Husayn al-Huthi's anti-American tracts with new
meaning. In the context of an alleged proxy relationship between the United States
and Yemen, Husayn's calls for action against America are revalorized as a call to action
against the GoY itself.

---

[64] "Tasjil al-Sawti li-l-Sayyid 'Abd al-Malik Badr al-Din al-Huthi Yuwwadih fihi ba'd al-Nuqat al-Muhimma
Jidan," *al-Menpar*, November 10, 2009.

[65] Yahya al-Huthi, "Al-Quwwat al-Duwaliya fi al-Yaman min Ajl Himayat al-Diktaturiya," *al-Menpar*, March
10, 2009.

The Huthis as *Mujahidin*

Much of the Huthis' propaganda output has portrayed the group as religious warriors or *mujahidin*, capable of launching spectacularly devastating, preplanned attacks on GoY forces. Such a depiction inflates the Huthis' military capabilities and in some cases conflicts with statements made by the upper echelons of Huthi leadership, suggesting their awareness of different audiences and different tastes. These materials depict the group as highly adept and organized military units, who are, at the very least, capable of expanding the Saʿda war and, at the most, ready, willing, and able to assassinate GoY leaders.

The images in Figure 7.18 are clearly intended to depict the Huthis as a paramilitary organization. Its clear green and white emblem bears the group's slogan (*God is Great, Death to America, Death to Israel, Curse upon the Jews, Victory to Islam*) and often appears in its more militant propaganda outputs, either as a figurative or literal emblem on weaponry or a flag.[66] In the panel at the top (meant for distribution as a handbill), Huthi fighters are seen waving their banner while moving in GoY vehicles. This implies a number of messages, not the least of which is that the group can attack mechanized units and has the expertise to effectively operate the assets shown. As well as speaking to Huthis or uncommitted Yemenis, this is also a none-too-implicit challenge to GoY personnel, suggesting that Huthis can move around freely. The images of destroyed GoY vehicles with accompanying Huthi fighters further depicts the group as uniquely capable of destroying heavy mechanized GoY units, as does the Huthi battle report series, *Basha'ir al-Nasr* (Prophecies of Victory). Just what the group intends to do with that mobilizational capacity is partially illustrated by the crosshairs image in the panel on the bottom right, which is accompanies by a voiceover criticizing President Saleh's alliance with the United States.

On top of this, the group's use of militant *anashid* (anthems; sing. *nashid*) in its videos further portrays it as more in line with Hizbullah models of resistance. Images like the one in Figure 7.18 depicting Huthi fighters with the sun as a background further draw a parallel to other Shiʿite jihadi groups. Sun imagery, which is prevalent in jihadi media,[67] gives the Huthis spiritual legitimacy within the context of a Shiʿite jihadi—not necessarily cultural—organization. Propaganda pamphlets distributed in the conflict zone touting the importance of jihad further render the group as a more militant organization, again hinting at the desire to connect with audiences of different backgrounds and tastes.

Exaltation of Martyrs

With some pamphlets and videos portraying current Huthi fighters as *mujahidin*, the group has simultaneously sought to lionize casualties of the conflict—civilian or oth-

---

[66] See, for example: "Mahrajan al-Intisar," n.d., likely Autumn 2009.

[67] See "The Islamic Imagery Project," Combating Terrorism Center at West Point, March 2006.

Figure 7.18
Huthi Pamphlet (top) Identifying Stolen and Destroyed GoY Vehicles; Huthi Video (bottom) Depicting Huthi Fighters Wielding AK-47s with President Saleh in the Crosshairs

SOURCES: (Top) Yemeni national; (bottom) "Fa Amkana Minhum," Huthi video, *Qism al-I'lam al-Harbi*, June 2008.

RAND *MG962-7.18*

erwise—as martyrs (*shuhada'*; sing. *shahid*). Husayn al-Huthi is by far the most cel-ebrated martyr of the group. As we demonstrated in Chapter Four, prior to his death Husayn al-Huthi had amassed much local prestige based on his speeches and per-sonal charisma. Indeed, his speeches existed on a continuum, conceptually following his father's lengthy Zaydi revivalist tracts. Upon becoming a *shahid*, however, Husayn al-Huthi has simultaneously been portrayed by his followers as a religious scholar (*'allama*) and warrior (*mujahid*), as Figure 7.19 indicates. Similarly, Husayn's works are referenced in Huthi propaganda videos and continue to circulate on the Internet.

Husayn is not the only *shahid* honored by the Huthis. In fact, the group com-memorated the first martyr of the conflict in a weeklong holiday in mid-May 2009 that featured tents lined with images of the group's dead cadres. The commemorations also featured speeches and appearances by 'Abd al-Malik himself, who met martyrs' families and posed for pictures with them (see Figure 7.20). These commemorations took place within and beyond the Sa'da governorate, with celebrations taking place in the 'Amran, Jawf, and San'a governorates.[68] While this week of martyr exhibits eerily mirrors the memorial erected by Hizbullah for leader 'Imad Mughniyeh,[69] more sig-nificant is the sense of group solidarity such commemorations engender within the Huthi organism.

Indeed, with the continued grind of the conflict come new commemorations, more unrest, and an increasingly permissive environment in which the Huthis can

Figure 7.19
Husayn in the Center of Huthi Family "Universe," Including Badr al-Din (left); Husayn Behind an Assault Rifle (right)

SOURCES: (Left) "Min Isdarat Atba' al-Sayyid Husayn al-Huthi, Muzahir Intisaratihum," video posted to Youtube.com, March 17, 2008; (right) Ansar al-Haqq Web site: ansaar.yoo7.com.
RAND *MG962-7.19*

[68] "Al-Taqrir al-Khitami li-l-Dhikra al-Sanawiya al-Ula li-l-Shuhada' wa-l-Mafqudin," *al-Menpar*, May 14, 2009.

[69] See Ulrike Putz, "Hezbollah Exhibit Celebrates War and 'Martyrs,'" *Spiegel Online*, September 4, 2008.

Figure 7.20
Commemoration of Huthi Martyrs

SOURCE: al-Menpar.com.

NOTE: Upper left: Huthi supporters viewing images of Huthi martyrs; upper right: Huthi supporters viewing video biographies of Huthi martyrs; lower left: commemoration of a child slain in the conflict; lower right: 'Abd Al-Malik Al-Huthi posing with children whose father was killed in the Sa'da war.

evolve and develop as an organization. Based on these commemorations, one can certainly argue that a "cult of martyrdom" is beginning to take root within the Huthi organism. Huthi leaders could at some point employ such a cult to encourage more "offensive" tactics, such as suicide bombing. Such tactics, however, would conflict with another theme propagated in the group's materials.

The Huthis as Defenders of Faith and Yemen

As mentioned earlier, the Huthis have depicted themselves as warriors, *mujahidin* who are uniquely capable of defeating well-supplied GoY forces. Simultaneously, however, members of the Huthi organism have characterized their conflict with the GoY and Saudi forces as being *defensive* in nature. Indeed, much of the group's materials portray the Huthis as individuals who are protecting the Zaydi *madhhab*, Islamic religion, and even their constitutional rights from being decimated by the sinister and materially superior GoY forces. In this self-portrayal, the Huthis are less a militant organization and more a dedicated group of locals who are merely defending their rights. In a 2009 interview, ʿAbd al-Malik depicted the Huthi organism as being in a defensive posture, fighting for its very existence. When asked by the interviewer what gains the group has made in the wake of the conflict, the Huthi leader argued:

> We didn't launch a war from the very beginning to realize any political or other gains. Our stance was only defensive. It is not true, and not logical to say to he who is defending himself and his existence 'what did you achieve [in terms of] gains?' . . . . [T]he matter is clear, the existence of our luminous view. Our Islamic culture, and our social existence has remained.[70]

Similarly, in a July 4, 2007, interview with a Lebanese weekly, ʿAbd al-Malik took care to stress the defensive nature of the conflict. Indeed, the Huthi commander noted "the war, from our perspective, is not with the goal of overthrowing the government from ruling, it is solely self-defense in the face of aggression that the government initiated."[71] In such depictions, ʿAbd al-Malik portrays the Huthis as fighting for survival and lacking other motives that may appear less honorable, or anti-republican. Somewhat conversely, ʿAbd al-Malik has at other times stressed the group's dispute with the government, arguing in a speech during the Prophet's Birthday,

> We have presented many martyrs, and faced many hardships . . . our problem is with the regime, our problem is with the government. It has not been like [what] the government propagates [about our motives] . . . we have been, and are still keen on sparing the blood of our countrymen . . . they are the ones who, each time, aggressed upon us.[72]

Saudi-Huthi military engagements have also prompted the Huthis to portray themselves as defenders of Yemen soil. After the Huthis entered Saudi territory to attack Yemeni forces stationed in Jabal Dukhan, ʿAbd al-Malik stressed that the "mountain is not the target," arguing instead that it was only after Yemeni forces attacked them from Saudi soil that they needed to respond.[73] Saudi attacks on Huthi targets have further

---

[70] See "al-Manbar Yuʿid Nashr Hiwar al-Sayyid ʿAbd al-Malik al-Huthi maʿa Sahifat al-Diyar," *al-Menpar*, January 20, 2009.

[71] "ʿAbd al-Malik al-Huthi: Lam Nabdaʾ al-Harb al-Fiʿliya Baʿd," *al-Akhbar*, July 3, 2008.

[72] Quote taken from Huthi video "Fa Amkana Minhum," from 5:20 to 6:15. This video is also hosted at the Internet Archive as "The Islamic Shia Revolution in Yemen: New Realise."

[73] "Tasjil al-Sawti li-l-Sayyid ʿAbd al-Malik Badr al-Din al-Huthi Yuwwadih fihi baʿd al-Nuqat al-Muhimma Jidan," *al-Menpar*, November 10, 2009.

been depicted by the group as "aggression" on Yemeni soil, with one Huthi commentator referring to it as an occupation (*ihtilal*).[74] 'Abd al-Malik has similarly referred to Saudi attacks as "unjustified" and an affront to the "sovereignty of the country."[75] Such statements seek to portray Huthi actions and reactions to Saudi military engagements as defensive and motivated by the need to preserve Yemeni sovereignty and lives.

In this vein, throughout the sixth phase, the Huthis have distributed video "confessions" of captured soldiers, as well as footage of the Huthis capturing, lecturing, and then releasing GoY prisoners (see Figure 7.21). Such footage is significant because it portrays the Huthis taking a number of measures to ensure that Yemeni lives are preserved. Indeed, in one case the Huthis showed an LAL lecturing a group of GoY soldiers, noting, "150,000 American, Italian soldiers, all of them Western forces, that is the enemy." As such, the Huthis appear to be compassionate captors, in one case referring to the captured soldiers as "guests" and pointing out that the Huthis "feed them and treat them." While this portrayal contradicts many of its operations—which have,

Figure 7.21
Captured GoY Soldiers in Huthi Custody

SOURCE: "Junud Tamm Asruhum min qabl al-Muqatilin al-Huthiyin," video posted to Youtube.com, August 31, 2009.

RAND *MG962-7.21*

---

[74] Yassir Abu Shusha', "al-Su'udiya Ihtilal al-Yaman wa Tadlil I'lami," *al-Menpar*, November 25, 2009.

[75] 'Abdullah Abu Bakr, "'Abd al-Malik al-Huthi li-l-'Nahar': al-Nizaman al-Su'udi wa al-Yamani Tajawwaza Masalih Sha'biha Ila Hissabat Ukhra," *al-Menpar*, November 11, 2009.

of course, regularly targeted GoY personnel and infrastructure—it further characterizes the group's posture as defensive.

Interestingly, Huthi leaders have also sought to portray the group as grossly out-
matched militarily. With respect to his own organizational capabilities, 'Abd al-Malik
admitted in an interview, "We are not an organized army, and the Yemeni army perhaps is able, after using combat equipment such as airplanes, tanks, and thousands of
soldiers, to advance on the ground in some areas."[76] Having said that, the leader went
on to argue that "this doesn't mean the [Yemeni army] has won, that it controls the
situation, or is able to stop our operations."[77] Such an approach portrays the Huthis
as being primarily in a defensive position with regard to GoY troops but still able to
wage, in 'Abd al-Malik's words, an effective "guerilla war" (*harb al-'isabat*).[78] 'Abd al-
Malik later sums up this position by arguing, "We didn't start the war, rather they are
the ones who imposed war upon us."[79] While perhaps implicitly recalling the Iraqis'
"imposed war" on Iran during the 1980s,[80] this approach also has the merit of excusing
the Huthi leadership from articulating positive goals or a sociopolitical agenda through
a united platform. Such an effort might alienate elements of the Huthi base because
such an agenda would have to make choices among priorities.

Indeed, simultaneous Huthi use of the offensive *mujahid* and defensive guerilla
themes appears contradictory. On the one hand, this reflects the divergent discursive styles and thematic interests of Huthi speakers—Yahya, for example, is not 'Abd
al-Malik. On the other hand, in an already saturated Islamist communication environment, Huthi message makers have been able to learn from other examples. Their
seemingly contradictory themes likely also emerge from an awareness that different
messages and modes connect with different audiences. Interviews with al-Jazeera, al-
'Arabiya, and so forth, are encountered by more educated Yemenis at home or abroad,
as well as by the pan-Arab audience and the GoY, before being translated into English.
They are thus appropriate venues for striking a more defensive stance that emphasizes
protection of religious freedoms, cultural heritage, and constitutional rights against an
oppressive, violent regime.

These messages are not likely, however, to sustain an emotionally engaged base
made up of adolescents and young adult males in Sa'da and its environs. This group
is also less subject to socialization through the media outlets just mentioned; they
undergo a daily experience of violence and deprivation and likely know the casual-

---

[76] "'Abd al-Malik al-Huthi: Lam Nabda' al-Harb al-Fi'liya Ba'd."

[77] "'Abd al-Malik al-Huthi: Lam Nabda' al-Harb al-Fi'liya Ba'd."

[78] "'Abd al-Malik al-Huthi: Lam Nabda' al-Harb al-Fi'liya Ba'd."

[79] "Muqabilat al-Sayyid 'Abd al-Malik al-Huthi ma'a Sahifat al-Nas," originally printed in *Al-Naas*, April 26,
2006.

[80] See 'Shūrā-yi 'Ālá Difā', *The Imposed War: Defence vs. Aggression* (Tehran: Supreme Iran Defense Council.
1983–1987). "Imposed war" in Persian is *jang-e tahmili*.

ties of the wars. Therefore, for this group, images of aggressive, courageous military operations inspired by a young, charismatic scion of the Huthi family living up to his brother's legacy are likely much more appealing—to their religious imagination, political aspirations, and desire to assert adult masculinity in a fashion aligned with cultural mores (see Chapter Two). To a great extent then, audience and mode influence the various messages produced.

Differing messages may also hint at conceptual tensions. The Huthis do appear aware of their potential niche in the broader Shi'ite jihadi community, which would expand their audience and possible circle of supporters. Yet, it pushes them toward becoming more militant in message and action. Conversely, the group appears simultaneously concerned with being associated too closely with Middle Eastern jihadis that attack both regimes and civilian communities, such as al-Qa'ida, Hizbullah, or the more apposite Algerian Salafist Group for Preaching and Combat (GSPC), now known as al-Qa'ida in the Islamic Maghreb. Thus, when the group's main figurehead admits that the Huthis do not wish to overthrow the Saleh government, the Huthis appear as a defensive group struggling to guard against and deter GoY attacks, rather than pursuing its own offensive. Along with mujahid-oriented messages intended to sustain a hard core, such an admission likely reflects awareness of a constituency within the group that seeks to remain loyal to the "republican" spirit of the Yemeni state, which leads us to another theme in the Huthi information strategy.

The Huthis as Republican and Yemeni

While the GoY information campaign has sought to portray the Huthis as operating outside the system (*kharij al-nizam*), the Huthis have consistently highlighted their allegiance to the Yemeni state and constitution. First, the Huthis have had to distance themselves from Iran, emphatically denying any connections to the Islamic Republic. Indeed, when asked about possible connections between Iran and the Huthis, 'Abd al-Malik claimed in an interview "the government surely knows that it is a false and fake claim that does not contain any evidence."[81] When pushed on the matter, he has noted that there is no need for outside provision of weapons, arguing in a September 2009 interview, for example, "The Yemeni people are armed people . . . weapons markets are scattered across numerous governorates."[82]

The Huthis furthermore argue that they are not operating as a "state within a state" but rather simply abiding by traditions of autonomy in northern Yemen. The group has denied establishing parallel systems of governance, noting instead that they, "as is the norm in Yemen, help in solving some of the problems and issues as others

---

[81] "Al-Sayyid 'Abd al-Malik al-Huthi fi Hiwar Jadid ma'a Sahifat al-Nas," *al-Menpar*, June 21, 2008.

[82] "'Abd al-Malik al-Huthi: La Nurahin 'ala Ayy Quwwa Iqlimiya wa Idha Awqafat al-Sulta Istihdafna, Sanantahi al-Tamtarus."

do."[83] Similarly, Yahya al-Huthi argued in a recent article on the southern secession movement, "We [the Huthis] have adhered to the unity of the country . . . and refused completely the idea of separatism," clearly attempting to highlight the Huthis' loyalty to the unified Yemeni republic while countering GoY accusations of *infisali* inclinations.[84] More recently, the Huthis have had to respond to direct charges that they are cooperating with the movement in the south. Addressing this accusation, 'Abd al-Malik argued in an interview with *al-Khalij* that the "link is the government's manner of dealing with the country's problems, wherein it deals [with them] with excessive aggression."[85]

The Huthis as a Cultural and Opposition Movement

Within the rubric of loyalty to the Yemeni republic, the Huthis have depicted themselves as a cultural movement with peaceful intentions. In a 2006 interview, 'Abd al-Malik al-Huthi stressed that the group sought to undertake only "cultural, peaceful activities" as opposed to armed rebellion.[86] Similarly, when asked in a January 2009 interview about the group's "future plan," 'Abd al-Malik declared that the group had a plan only "to reform the reality of our Muslim community (*umma*)."[87]

Also, in a 2008 interview 'Abd al-Malik argued, "The Huthi current is an expression of popular solidarity mobilizing peacefully to oppose the American-Israeli attack on the Islamic world and spreading the Qu'ranic culture in the face of intellectual assault."[88] The peaceful nature of the Huthi "movement" was further highlighted in a January 2008 interview in which 'Abd al-Malik claimed that his first demand was "freedom of thought, expression, and religious occasions," going on to argue that the group aims to "educate our Islamic community [about] the culture of the Qur'an."[89] In this light, the Huthi leaders have attempted to portray the group as a peaceful movement rather than a violent militia or insurgency.

The multiple modes and messages employed by the Huthi organism in its information strategy highlight its multifaceted nature. Indeed, utilizing multiple mechanisms to distribute their message(s), the Huthis have been able to reach a wide audience

---

[83] See "al-Manbar Yu'id Nashr Hiwar al-Sayyid 'Abd al-Malik al-Huthi ma'a Sahifat al-Diyar."

[84] See "Wijhat Nazar al-Akh Yaha al-Huthi Hawl Mawdu' al-Infisal wa Qadiyat al-Janub," *al-Menpar*, May 24, 2009.

[85] "al-Sayyid 'Abd al-Malik al-Huthi li-l-Kahlij: La Natallaqi al-Da'm min Iyran, wa al-Azma al-Siyasiya bi-Imtiyyaz wa la Nurid 'Awda al-Imama," originally printed in *al-Khalij*, September 29, 2009.

[86] "Muqabilat al-Sayyid 'Abd al-Malik al-Huthi ma'a Sahifat al-Nas," originally printed in *al-Naas*, April 26, 2006.

[87] "al-Manbar Yu'id Nashr Hiwar al-Sayyid 'Abd al-Malik al-Huthi ma'a Sahifat al-Diyar."

[88] "Abd al-Malik al-Huthi: Lam Nabda' al-Harb al-Fi'liya Ba'd."

[89] "'Abd al-Malik al-Huthi min Ma'qilihi fi Matra li 'al-Ahali': Lan Nakun Hizban Siyasiyan, wa Walayat al-Batanin 'ala Hukam al-Yawm," *al-Ahale*, n.d.

of local and possibly international supporters. The group appeals to these audiences through varied and sometimes contradictory messages. While hardcore Huthi support-ers would likely find the group's militant anthems and videos appealing, its less loyal tribal supporters are likely attracted to the idea of defending the Zaydi heartland from GoY aggression. Furthermore, more politically inclined supporters—whether mem-bers of the Zaydi Hizb al-Haqq or journalists from the Zaydi-oriented *al-Balagh*—are likely attracted to the pro-republican trend within the group. This varied audience reflects the Huthis' own internal constituencies, which could hinder the organism's possible evolution into a more formal organization.

Huthi Transformation: From Resistance Organism to Insurgent Organization?

As discussed in the Introduction and mentioned elsewhere in this book, it is difficult to determine precisely the category into which the GoY-Huthi conflict falls. Yemeni and other Arabic sources have described the conflict as a rebellion (*tamarrud*), also referring to guerrilla warfare (*harb al-'isabat*). Official GoY spokesmen have called the Huthi conflict a rebellion, referring to the Huthis as terrorists. The same sources point to a "Huthi insurgency," a term also used by Western analysts.[90] This usage likely reflects the GoY's attentiveness to Western hot-button issues, as well as an undisciplined use of the term "insurgency" by Western writers since the invasion of Iraq. As we discussed at the outset of this book, however, if defined as "an organized movement aimed at the violent overthrow of a constituted government through the use of subversion and armed conflict,"[91] insurgency connotes both a phenomenon linked to a political agenda and an organized entity with a certain coherence and commonality. In both senses, the Huthi phenomenon is not yet an insurgency. It may develop in this direction, however, just as it could move toward activities within legitimate Yemeni politics, however con-strained the latter may be. At this point, however, the Huthi phenomenon remains an *organism* in the midst of tentative transformation into an *organization*.

Considering the Huthis from the perspective of an organization, it clearly remains in its infancy compared to other resistance movements. Organizations such as the Irish

---

[90] See "18 Houthi Terrorists Killed in Separate Areas," *Almotamar.net*, September 28, 2009. The article mentions "Thirteen of the elements of terrorism and rebellion . . ." Also see "Masra' Arba'a min Qiyadat 'Anasir al-Irhab wa-l-Tamarrud," *26 September*, September 28, 2009; Andrew McGregor, "Shi'ite Insurgency in Yemen: Iranian Intervention or Mountain Revolt," *Jamestown Foundation Terrorism Monitor* 2:16 (May 10, 2005); Peter Kenyon, "Yemen Tries to Shut Down Shiite Insurgency," "Morning Edition," National Public Radio, August 26, 2009; Robert Worth, "Yemen's Instability Grows as One of 3 Insurgencies Heats Up," *New York Times*, August 10, 2009; "Three of the Insurgency Leaders Killed," *Almotamar.net*, September 4, 2009; "Yemeni Public Opinion Pressure Forced Government to End Saada Insurgency," *Almotamar.net*, August 20, 2009.

[91] See Headquarters, Department of the Army, *FM 3-24: Counterinsurgency* (Washington, D.C.: December 2006), Glossary–5.

Republican Army, Hizbullah, Hamas, the Kurdistan Workers' Party (PKK), and the recently defeated Tamil Tigers, for example, exhibit, to varying degrees, particular characteristics that have allowed them to be self-sustaining organizations with a purpose for existence transcending the initial grievances or causes that permitted their emergence. Initially these groups needed to thrash out an identity, defeat rivals, and establish rudimentary social services.[92] Eventually, however, many of them evolved into "para-statal" entities. Such entities feature internal political competition and negotiation among different stakeholders, participate in the external political process, and offer parallel governance and substantial social services—often while carrying out politically motivated violence against the state or other opposition groups. All these actions serve to grow and maintain an identifiable base, attract constituencies, and make their claims to detractors.[93] Just as important from the perspective of legitimation and sustainability, some of these organizations now have a national and international political presence, clear ideologies and rituals endowed with an unquestioned religious (or nationalist) pedigree, and increasingly regularized military units operating with relatively standardized C3 structures. Ultimately, many such groups—be they insurgencies, rebellions, or resistance to occupation—gain an organizational immortality, with charismatic leaders who have been able to sustain their respective organizations, legitimating them on bases going beyond a specific conflict or issue.

By contrast, nearly every aspect of the Huthi organism suggests a loosely defined group with multiple, sometimes autonomous, elements. For one, it has yet to choose an official name that is identifiable as representing something more than a family. Further, currently absent from the organism is a clear ideology or reason for being that transcends responding to GoY aggression or opposing American foreign policy in the region. In this sense, the Huthi organism has yet to identify itself or act in terms of what it *seeks* rather than solely what it *opposes*. The group's ambiguous organization and command relationships reflect the physical environment of northern Yemen and are congruent with the cultural expectations of *qabyala* in the Sa'da governorate. Also, whereas Hizbullah and its spiritual leaders such as Husayn Nasrallah possess an unquestioned religious pedigree, the Huthis' adherence to the Zaydi school (*madhhab*) is constantly called into question by local and outside analysts. As suggested above, relationships between units and subcommanders are based on persuasion rather than coercion. Local leaders retain significant latitude in daily operations, permitting the group's subunits to launch attacks independent from one another on multiple fronts in a small period of time. The varied mechanisms and messages the organism utilizes in its information operations further reflect its multiple audiences and internal con-

---

[92] For discussion of this in the context of emerging insurgencies, see Daniel Byman, "Understanding Proto-Insurgencies" (Santa Monica, Calif.: RAND Corporation, OP-178, 2007).

[93] Yezid Sayigh, *Armed Struggle and the Search for State: The Palestinian National Movement 1949–1993* (Oxford: Clarendon Press, 1997).

stituencies. These limitations could threaten the longevity of the Huthi organism and jeopardize its ability to transform into a more uniform, self-sustaining organization.

There are some indications, however, that the Huthi organism may have the capacity to shift to a more robust and self-perpetuating organizational model. The group exhibits a rudimentary ideology that has begun to solidify a sense of identity among its followers through group rituals. The future impact of these rituals could be enhanced by charismatic Huthi leaders, should any emerge beside 'Abd al-Malik. Further, while 'Abd al-Malik has criticized political participation amid rumors suggesting the group was going to form a political party,[94] the family does have a legacy of participatory politics and, since 2004, a basis for foreign representation. Finally, there are slight indications that the Huthis may eventually move to a more standardized organizational structure, although such a transformation is likely in its infancy. What remains to be seen, however, is whether or not the group can begin to offer concrete social services that fill the void of—and thus highlight—government neglect of the area. This would ultimately allow the Huthi leadership to prove that it can do more than emphasize government failures and instead offer real solutions. We will now treat these issues individually.

First, perhaps most salient in forming a sense of "groupness" among its constituencies are the rituals now associated with the Huthi organism in Yemen. As we have mentioned, these include al-Ghadir Day, the Prophet's Birthday, International Jerusalem Day, and the Commemoration of Martyrs Day. These occasions, during which the Huthi slogan is repeatedly chanted, engender a sense of group solidarity among what would otherwise be disparate elements aggrieved by GoY policies or Yemen's socioreligious order. Just as significant is the Huthi emblem now associated with these rituals. It provides a literal and figurative banner under which Huthi constituencies can congregate and with which they can identify. Such rituals and emblems have the potential to transcend local identities and thus create new associational links within the Huthi orbit—much as the BY did on the cultural plane in the mid-1990s.

The mobilizational capacity demonstrated by the Huthi organism's rituals and the Huthi family's parliamentary legacy could provide the necessary components for future Huthi political participation. A political grouping of Zaydis functioning in secular politics as a Zaydi religious party departs from pre-1990 tenets of the *madhhab*. Indeed, as previously mentioned, participation in politics as a civilianized party has been ruled out by 'Abd al-Malik al-Huthi. That is not to say, however, that Huthi political reengagement is completely out of the question. Indeed, as we have mentioned, the Huthi organism is composed of multiple elements, some of which likely still see value in having a political presence. Thus, while 'Abd al-Malik is unlikely to endorse transforming the organism completely into a political party, he may eventually con-

---

[94] See "Nass Hiwar Sahifat al-'Arab al-Qatariya ma'a al-Sayyid 'Abd al-Malik al-Huthi," *al-Menpar*, June 2, 2008; "Hal Yushakkil al-Huthiyun Tanziman Siyasiyan bi Ism 'Hizb al-Shuhada?" *al-Ayyam*, August 4, 2007.

cede that having a political wing within the group could legitimate it as a force within Yemen. This would be similar to moves by Hizbullah in the 1990s and Hamas after 2000. Furthermore, Yahya al-Huthi has set the precedent of providing the group with foreign representation. While not as robust as the representation boasted by groups like Hamas, it could provide the model for future Huthi engagement with foreign actors.

Transition from organism to organization is also a matter of leadership. In 'Abd al-Malik, the Huthis possess a charismatic figurehead whose popularity is growing—but who has yet to demonstrate firm overall leadership and control. On the one hand, 'Abd al-Malik's local popularity and visibility appears to be on an upward trajectory. Indeed, in a few years Husayn's brother has gone from being a youngster tentatively acting as a Huthi commander in the shadow of a martyr to being the most identifiable "leader" of the Huthis. He maintains a press office, sends email news updates to followers, and, most importantly, delivers rousing speeches during contested holidays. The shift in 'Abd al-Malik's position within the Huthi organism is perhaps best illustrated by Figure 7.22, which compares older and newer images of him. He has also increased his local visibility by visiting war-affected areas during contested holidays, posing for pictures with children. Indeed, the Huthi leader appears to be quite charismatic and, crucially, has picked up where his brother left off. In this capacity, 'Abd al-Malik al-Huthi has become much more than just a military leader for the group, and his local prestige is further enhanced by the negative impact of the conflict on Sa'da and the surrounding governorates.

On the other hand, however, given norms of authority and leadership in northern Yemen, it is not certain that 'Abd al-Malik—after all, a younger person—is able or inclined to exert decisive control over his near-peers or subordinates. Further, beyond 'Abd al-Malik, the group lacks *depth* with respect to charismatic leaders who are rec-

Figure 7.22
Old and New Pictures of 'Abd al-Malik al-Huthi from *al-Menpar* Web Site

SOURCE: *al-Menpar.*
RAND *MG962-7.22*

ognized across the region as having adequate prestige and influence. 'Abd al-Malik's co-leader al-Razammi, for example, prefers to avoid press appearances.[95] That is not to say that elimination of 'Abd al-Malik or other Huthi family members can decapitate the movement. Indeed, in their respective communities, LALs likely possess adequate charisma or social network connections. These LALs, however, have not yet exhibited the trappings of broader movement leadership. They do not give extensive interviews or make speeches during holidays, nor are they likely able to exercise influence or call for operations beyond their local areas. Notably, LALs themselves are rarely identified by name to reporters. This lack of by-name identification may be due to fears of reprisals from the GoY or local rivals. Still, the current shortage of charismatic Huthi leadership further inhibits the group from transitioning to a structured organization, as does the limited functional differentiation evident among Huthi organism members.

Of equal significance to organizational maturation and the development of a broadened support base is the notable absence of a Huthi social-welfare plank, as is an identifiable parallel Huthi sector outperforming state institutions. For one, socio-economic self-help, both as a cultural value and in reaction to GoY marginalization, would not be a deviation from the norms of the Sa'da governorate, where autonomy from state authority typifies tribal existence in the northern periphery. Presently, the Huthi organism does not have the fiscal engine needed to provide social services to Sa'da residents. This is perhaps the organism's most striking deficiency in comparison to other resistance or insurgent groups. As such, the movement's future trajectory partially hinges on its ability to develop a social-welfare network in and beyond its geographical center. Such a network would require substantial and sustained material input, as well as methods of procurement and distribution. While this does not appear to be a current priority of the Huthi organism, such a capacity would amplify its durability and increase its chances of showing up the GoY and local elites on issues of enduring socioeconomic concern. Ultimately, a social-welfare plank could aid the Huthis in becoming a more organized, self-sustaining entity able to retain a social base mobilized for both ideological and material interests, and defined both in opposition to the GoY as well as in support of a cause. If this circumstance should evolve, the resilience of the threat to the GoY would be much greater, chipping away at the comparative advantage of the latter's resources.

One more organizational aspect of the Huthi organism is worthy of consideration. We have discussed above the Huthis' military shortcomings and the barriers they face in evolving from 'isabat—unconnected fighting groups—to a coordinated, synchronized fighting force. We also noted that such a transformation sacrifices the asymmetric advantages of current operational modes over the GoY's regular military. Fundamentally, however, in the politicized environment of violence in the Middle

---

[95] "al-Manbar Yu'id Nashr Hiwar al-Sayyid 'Abd al-Malik al-Huthi ma'a Sahifat al-Diyar," *al-Menpar*, January 20, 2009.

East, such a transformation might not be necessary for Huthi endurance as a resistance movement. Huthi fighting groups do not need to improve or become better coordinated—they need only to persist. And while these fighting groups appear more tactically adept than do GoY units, the track records of the Palestine Liberation Organization, Hizbullah, and the PKK, for example, suggest that even while sustaining tactical defeats, armed opposition groups earn political advantage against regimes both at home and internationally. The burden then falls on the GoY to decisively defeat or eradicate the Huthis—or to manifestly coopt both their cause and social base.

Turning to the issue of political agendas associated with insurgencies, this discussion suggests an additional, important aspect of the Huthi-GoY conflict. Given the loosely connected character of different operational elements in the Huthi organism and the movement's incomplete progress on the path from organism to organization, it is imprecise to speak of a unitary entity—"the" Huthis. These factors also render it misleading to speak of what "the" Huthis want in monolithic terms. As we have seen above, Huthi leaders, including 'Abd al-Malik and Salih Habra, have often cast their goals in entirely defensive terms, characterizing Huthi efforts as focused on removing the threat to life and property presented by GoY forces. An equally enduring theme has been the portrayal of Huthi goals as aligned with those of the earlier BY: opening up a greater, more legitimized space for the cultural and religious assertion of Zaydism, coupled with the defensive goal of reducing the GoY-supported Sunni threat to the region and to Zaydi youth, in particular. Alternatively, these and other speakers have pointed to the related, yet grander, goal of realizing true constitutional republicanism, including equitable northern (Zaydi) access to political participation and socioeconomic benefits. Some Huthi personalities have in private spoken of the goal of removing the current regime in the service of such true republicanism—but this approach is out of character with leaders' pronouncements, likely reflecting the frustrations of the individual interlocutor.[96] Also, although rare examples of information operations imagery may imply that the central GoY is a target or suggest an ability to eject the GoY from Huthi territory, neither the themes emphasized by the Huthis in public statements nor their favored tactics and operational modes suggest a desire to take down the Yemeni state, establish an imamate centered on Sa'da, or liberate territory for the purpose of declaring a sustainable "Huthistan" within Yemen. As such, as of early 2010, it remains difficult to credibly refer to the Huthis as insurgents.

Indeed, as late as October 2009, the document most closely resembling a manifesto or group charter was an August 17, 2009, statement released by the Huthis explaining their stance on peace, society, and the regime.[97] Notably, this document does not present broad goals or general stances that differ from what has been repeat-

---

[96] Interview with Yemeni affiliated with Huthi leadership, February 2, 2009.

[97] "Thamaniya Bunud Tudhakkir bi-Mawqif al-Huthiyin min al-Harb wa al-Salam wa al-Mujtama' wa al-Nizam," al-Menpar, August 17, 2009.

edly put forth by 'Abd al-Malik in his media interviews. While putting these "goals" into a single document is certainly significant, the group has yet to formally introduce a "Huthi program"—reminiscent of the Hamas 1988 charter, for example—that elaborates on its future goals and objectives.[98]

At base, then, it is probably the case that different parts of the Huthi organism want different things or could be dissuaded from armed opposition to the GoY if a number of their needs were met. For example, some LALs likely have goals motivated by Zaydi religious zeal and are galvanized by a particular reading of Zaydi texts and Huthi information operations products. In other cases, LALs are motivated by tribal imperatives of *sharaf* and *'ird*, desiring either to protect their areas from GoY encroachment or to demonstrate an ability to respond to GoY aggression. Many LALs may also have opportunistic goals, either seeking Huthi financial support or hoping to be coopted by the GoY through material blandishment and support in quarrels with other local kin networks. Indeed, LALs and their fighting groups, or even smaller groupings calling themselves "Huthis," may have goals completely unrelated to the conflict. Instead, in their desire to undermine their neighbors, they may have chosen the moniker "Huthi" in intertribal fights in which the opposing kin network is known or presumed to be pro-GoY. Additionally, those northern Yemenis whose interests are purely financial—weapons dealers, smugglers of assorted goods, and so forth—may cloak their activities in Huthi garb. For these people, a short-term goal would include perpetuation of the conflict for pecuniary reasons. And, as suggested throughout this book, the mode of operations of the GoY may often have created motives and goals for resistance to it.

Moving beyond the fighting core, peripheral Huthi supporters—or those who endorse some of the Huthis' claims—would likely want to see elimination of the GoY's pressure on Hashimis and Zaydi scholars, accompanied by recognition of Zaydism and the north as legitimate, integral components of the Yemeni cultural, religious, and political arena. Some of them, along with certain fighting groups, might also want to see a lessening of Hashidi dominance in the politics of state-tribal bargaining. Additionally, for those youth who attend Huthist gatherings but are not yet fighters, an implicit motive or goal likely involves young adult assertion of manhood and identity in an environment where other means of doing so are less readily available. Finally, returning to the Huthi family core, goals may include the use of resistance to force the Yemeni government to recognize al-Huthi as the paramount political family in the governorate, including patronage locally and parliamentary representation nationally. Although 'Abd al-Malik has discounted this path, such statements do not foreclose it as a goal. Likewise, for the Huthi core as well as for those thinking in terms of Yemen's place within the Islamic *umma*, discomfort with the GoY's closeness to the United

---

[98]   See Appendix C for the Huthi "Press Office's" latest statement of movement goals.

States as the latter supports Israel and pursues the GWoT may result in a hope to coerce Saleh into distancing San'a from Washington.

The above suggests that, while the Huthis still have a ways to travel along the road to organizational unity, the very diversity of motives and goals has ensured the enduring resonance of the Huthi cause among various social strata. Likewise, this diversity permits the current Huthi leadership to alter public pronouncements of what it wants in response to GoY actions. Additionally, in this still proto-organizational phase, 'Abd al-Malik and Salih Habra can be more accommodating or more extreme in their articulations of goals, sensing attitudes of diverse "Huthi" groups. This makes it easier to declare success in the absence of the fixed metrics that clear goals would impose. Conversely, if the GoY were to better disaggregate the Huthi movement in terms of social strata, motives, and needs, it might be able to wean greater numbers of Yemenis in the region away from supporting or participating in the Huthi rebellion. Until now, however, the GoY's cooptative efforts have produced enmity among both kin networks and confessional groups. Actions taken in the aftermath of the February 2010 ceasefire will thus be instrumental in shaping the Huthi organism's evolution, as well as local responses to both the movement and the GoY.

Conflict Prolongers: The Environmental, Human, and Economic Consequences of Huthi-GoY Fighting

As we have emphasized throughout this study, northern Yemen is a place of resilient, resourceful people who live in an environment characterized by scarcity and the delicate balance of competition and mutual reliance among communities. On the rural-to-arid margins of a semi-industrialized society, northern Yemen and the Sa'da governorate are particularly vulnerable to processes that damage the physical environment and interrupt networks of production and exchange. The multiple phases of fighting among Huthis, the GoY, and both parties' local supporters have indeed damaged the environment. This is because, rather than solely targeting each other, GoY and Huthi actions have affected entire communities and local economies, approaching "unlawful collective punishment."[1] These measures have had both first-order effects in the realm of human security and possible negative consequences for the resilience of cultural norms that might, in other cases, diminish conflict. As such, the environmental, human, and economic consequences of the Huthi-GoY confrontation now act as enablers of persistent conflict. Ultimately, as the human and environmental aspects of the conflict rend the fabric of northern Yemeni society, the conflict-reducing norms of tribalism will be less helpful in any reconciliation process.

Environment and Infrastructure: Agriculture and Its Inputs

In areas not damaged through direct combat or reprisals for supporting one side or the other, Huthi and GoY interdiction of agricultural commerce presents obstacles to getting perishable goods to market. Diesel fuel, for example, is traditionally needed for vehicles and for generators that power wells to irrigate staple crops. Beginning in mid-May 2008, the government interrupted the movement of commercial goods, food, and fuel into the conflict area. After the Huthi conflict reached Ban Hushaysh near San'a itself in June 2008, the GoY's blockade of diesel fuel and food expanded to sectors

---

[1] Human Rights Watch, "Invisible Civilians: The Challenge of Humanitarian Access in Yemen's Forgotten War," *Human Rights Watch*, Report 1-56432-396-X, November 2008, 34.

of the population heretofore unrelated to the conflict.[2] Since no new diesel reached Sa'da during this period, the price of all fuel doubled, and the city went without electricity for over two months.[3] Given the recent shortage of basic necessities in a now-overcrowded Sa'da City, the prices of propane gas have increased over three times in only the first month of the sixth war.[4] Movement of local goods to markets in Sa'da and other governorates—not to mention Saudi Arabia—has been greatly reduced, with some products left rotting at home.[5] Such interruptions harm both the economy and day-to-day life. A final obstacle with effects in the economic realm and beyond involves the closure or destruction of roads. Using a common means of tribal defiance, Huthis have destroyed asphalt roads during attacks on the military in an effort to stop the advance of government troops.[6] The GoY has also acted similarly, using bulldozers and other methods to block traffic to high-priority areas, such as Bani Mu'adh and along the San'a-Sa'da road in the summer of 2008.[7]

Water scarcity has not been caused by the Sa'da wars, but it is seriously aggravated by several factors related to the conflict.[8] Aerial bombardment in the hardest-hit areas, such as Dahyan, Sa'da, and Razih, has partially destroyed local water networks and damaged generators.[9] *Birkets* (reservoirs) in Marran, already low due to lack of summer rain in 2008, were also damaged. Additionally, in Sa'da and other conflict-affected areas, diesel shortages mean that many water pumps are not operating. The alternative of transporting water into hard-to-access regions is both difficult and expensive, rendering safe drinking water unaffordable for many and forcing recourse to less-healthful

---

[2]   Human Rights Watch, "Invisible Civilians," 34.

[3]   For example, a Sa'da hospital employee claimed in July 2008, "The price for a 200 liter container of diesel reached YR 22,000 from [its previous price of] YR 7,500." See Maryam Al-Yemeni and Nadia Al-Sakkaf, "Relative Optimism As Humanitarian Aid Slowly Finds Its Way to Sa'da," *Yemen Times,* July 30, 2008, 33.

[4]   For example, in mid-September 2009, a supply officer from the NGO Islamic Relief (IR) in Yemen noted that in Sa'da Cty ". . . the price of propane gas increased threefold over the past month—from YR 700 ($3.50) to YR 2,000 ($10) per cylinder." See "YEMEN: Saada City Residents Most Affected by Fighting," IRIN, September 24, 2009.

[5]   Interview with senior Human Rights Watch official, March 20, 2009.

[6]   See "al-Jaysh Yatamakkan min Dukhul Madinat al-Nazir bi-Sa'da," *al-Ayyam*, May 9, 2007; "Musadamat 'Anifa bi-Sa'da wa-l-Huthiyun Yaqta'un Tariq Sa'da-San'a," *al-Ayyam*, May 10, 2008; "Darba Qawiya Murtaqiba li-Hasm al-Ma'raka fi Sa'da bi-Aqall Waqtin," *al-Ayyam*, February 12, 2007.

[7]   See "Marwahiya 'Askariya Tuhajim Ma'qalan Jabaliyan Yushakkil Khuturatan 'ala Tanaqqulat Wahdat al-Jaysh," *al-Ayyam*, January 1, 2006.

[8]   The water table in Sa'da has been falling by 4–6 meters a year of late. See Johannes Bruwer, "Yemen: War and Water Woes," International Committee of the Red Cross interview, December 9, 2008. See also Gerhard Lichtenthäler, *Political Ecology and the Role of Water: Environment, Society and Economy in Northern Yemen* (Surrey, UK: Ashgate Publishing, 2003); Gerhard Lichtenthäler and A. R. Turton, "Water Demand Management, Natural Resource Reconstruction and Traditional Value Systems: A Case Study from Yemen," Occasional Paper No. 14, Water Issues Study Group, School of Oriental and African Studies, University of London, 1999.

[9]   Bruwer, "Yemen: War and Water Woes."

supplies. Finally, large refugee flows into Saʻda City and its environs at the height of conflict have further drained the local water table. The lack of access to clean water during conflict can increase the prevalence of waterborne diseases, reduce immune-system resilience, and threaten overall health and nutrition of longtime residents and refugees. Furthermore, over time, this situation risks transforming water into a strategic commodity manipulated by conflict protagonists to secure the loyalty of Saʻda residents.

Demographic Impacts: Urban Destruction and Refugee Flows

As the foregoing implies, physical destruction has touched the urban environment as well. Combat and physical damage to settlement areas have resulted in refugee flows of thousands of Saʻdans.[10] With respect to urban destruction, aerial bombardment has damaged areas of Bani Hushaysh (*muhafazat* Sanʻa) and Harf Sufyan (ʻAmran), as well as towns linked to Bani Muʻadh, Al-Salim, Haydan Dahyan, Razih, and Saʻda. Areas in the governorates of Jawf and Hajja have also been damaged through combat and movement of GoY forces. Official numbers released by the GoY in August 2008 after the fifth war claimed that 6,000 houses, 900 farms, 90 mosques, 80 schools, and five health facilities had been damaged in Saʻda. An additional 1,120 facilities, houses, and farms were damaged in Harf Sufyan and the *hijra* of Bani Hushaysh, worth an estimated 1.9 billion riyals.[11]

Destruction of urban areas aggravates preexisting inadequacies of infrastructure and social welfare—thus connecting the current conflict to old grievances. As a GPC member of the Consultative Council remarked, "The Huthis seem to have a lot of followers, not for religious reasons, but because the population feels discriminated against and excluded from development policies. Unfortunately, the destruction of villages has not helped fight that impression."[12] For example more than one-quarter of Dahyan town (a *hijra*) was destroyed by mid-2008.[13] Indeed, many of the consistently hit areas are historical *hijras*, thus increasing the sense that Zaydis and Hashimis are being targeting purposefully and producing a feeling of violation of tribal honor by invoking notions of collective tribal responsibility (see Figure 8.1). The destruction of mosques may also be perceived as a violation of Zaydi religious sanctity.

---

[10] Human Rights Watch, "Invisible Civilians," 2.

[11] "YEMEN: Government Calls for International Support to Reconstruct War-Affected Areas," *IRIN*, September 18, 2008.

[12] International Crisis Group, "Yemen: Defusing the Saada Time Bomb," *Middle East Report*, No. 86, May 27, 2009, p. 13.

[13] Human Rights Watch, "Invisible Civilians," 16.

Figure 8.1
Regions of Conflict Overlaid on Hijra Areas, as of the Fifth War

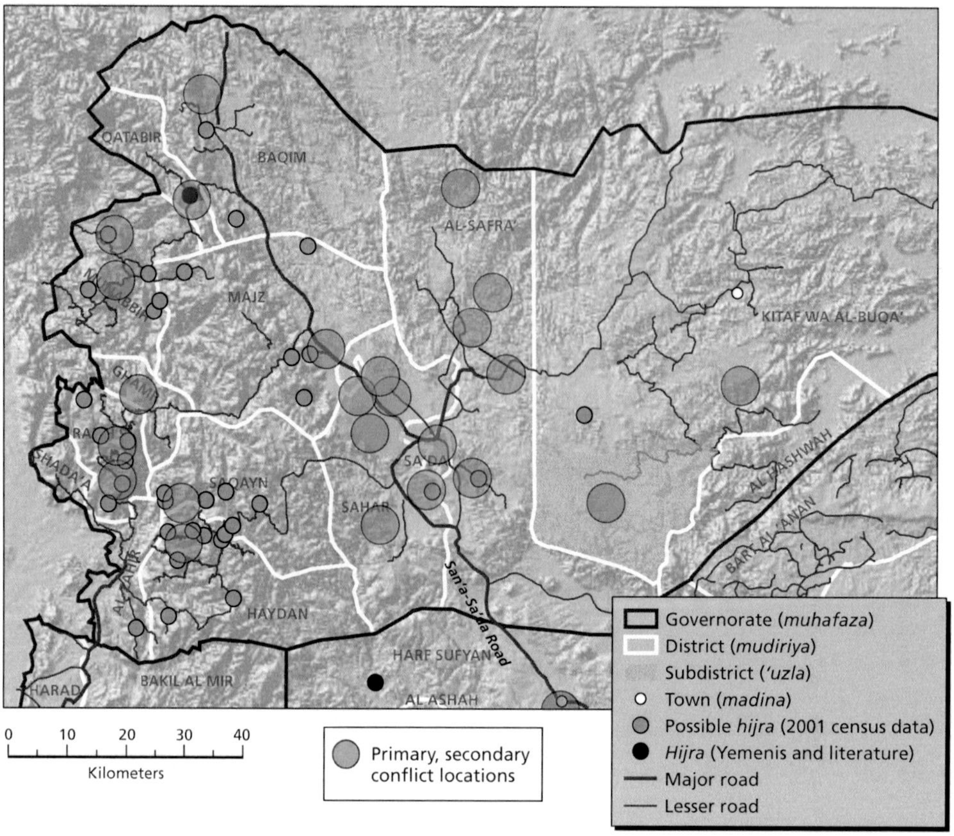
QATABIR
BAQIM
AL-SAFRA'
MAJZ
KITAF WA AL-BUQA'
SA'DA
SAHAR
SAQAYN
HAYDAN
HARF SUFYAN
AL ASHAH
BAKIL AL MIR
San'a-Sa'da Road
0 10 20 30 40
Kilometers
Primary, secondary conflict locations
Governorate (*muhafaza*)
District (*mudiriya*)
Subdistrict (*'uzla*)
Town (*madina*)
Possible *hijra* (2001 census data)
Hijra (Yemenis and literature)
Major road
Lesser road

RAND *MG962-8.1*

Refugee flows have proceeded apace with destruction of the urban bases of life. Movement of internally displaced persons (IDPs) has been within Sa'da governorate—extending all the way to the Saudi border—as well as to locations farther afield, such as parts of San'a city and the neighboring governorate of Hajjah. Significantly, while many IDPs fled their homes because of GoY destruction, some fled in opposition to the local Huthi cause, or due to the latter's intimidation.[14] As of June 2008, there were an estimated 130,000 IDPs throughout the governorate of Sa'da. During the fifth phase of fighting (May–July 2008) an estimated 17,000–20,000 IDPs were living in seven camps around Sa'da City managed by the Yemeni Red Crescent (YRC). Of these IDPs, 80 percent were women and children. This is a particularly vulnerable group—in human as well as cultural terms—and their honor and safety are among the top

[14] Interview with senior Human Rights Watch official, March 20, 2009; interview with academic Yemen specialist, September 22, 2008.

priorities for tribes to protect.[15] As of mid-September 2009, the UN estimates that the number displaced since August 12 brings the current total to around 150,000. Most IDPs are located in Harf Sufyan and 'Amran, with women and children still constituting the majority of those displaced.

Because of continuing violence, IDPs remain both unsettled and increasingly likely parties to the conflict. For example, on September 16, 2009, at least 87 people were killed (mostly women, children, and the elderly) in a government air raid on an IDP camp in 'Adi, east of Harf Sufyan.[16] Yemeni officials denied knowledge of the refugee camp's existence and suggested that the rebels had fired on troops and used IDPs as human shields.[17] Uncharacteristically, the GoY claims that the bombing was unintended and has launched an investigation into the incident.

If it is true that over 150,000 Yemenis have relocated due to the Sa'da conflict, their displacement represents nearly one-quarter of the governorate's population. Furthermore, IDP concentrations remain in regions of displacement between phases of fighting, putting tremendous pressure on already limited resources of food, clean water, clothing, and medical supplies. For example, in the lead-up to the sixth war, the price of wheat doubled. The increased displacement during the sixth war has decreased the prospects for near-term IDP resettlement and widened the areas of the camps to include Hajjah, particularly the Mazraq camp.[18] New IDP camps aside, even those Sa'da and 'Amran areas free from the first-order effects of conflict (destruction) will confront the second-order effects (resource pressure, effects on public health, and concomitant social friction) for years to come, frustrating reconciliation.[19]

Post-2004 fighting has also furthered preexisting public health inadequacies in the north. The Sa'da governorate initially had only seven significant health facilities. During the 2007 and 2008 blockades, the regime aggravated this problem by disrupting nongovernmental organization (NGO) access to the area. By 2007, the region had witnessed a 20 percent reduction in USAID health activities, and the work of Médecins Sans Frontières (MSF) and other basic health providers had also been interrupted.[20] Ongoing fighting further complicated the health crisis caused by the blockade, and no health supplies reached Sa'da's 30-bed Republican Hospital between early May

---

[15] Human Rights Watch, "Invisible Civilians," 21; United Nations Children's Fund, UNICEF Humanitarian Action Report 2009 (New York: UNICEF, 2009), 154.

[16] "Yemen: Investigate Aerial Bomb Attacks," *Human Rights Watch*, September 16, 2009.

[17] "'Many Killed' in Yemen Air Raid," *BBC News*, September 17, 2009.

[18] "YEMEN: Saada City Residents Most Affected by Fighting," *IRIN*, September 24, 2009.

[19] "YEMEN: Saada City Residents Most Affected by Fighting." The estimated 20,000 who have fled to Sa'da in the first month of the sixth war have put pressure on the city's infrastructure because the city's population has increased by one-third.

[20] Abdul-Aziz Oudah, "BHS Works to Secure Health Care for Poorest Areas," *Yemen Observer*, March 31, 2007; Human Rights Watch, "Invisible Civilians," 21, 34–35.

and late July 2008—a time of peak casualties. Because the second hospital in the city was devoted to military use, the Republican Hospital was over capacity and had to turn people away.[21]

There have been repeated GoY and outsider attempts to assess reconstruction needs in the north during the "non-war" and mediation phases of the conflict. Persistent hostilities, however, interrupt such efforts. For example, the Qatar mediation document, signed in February 2008, came with Qatar's pledge to finance development projects costing $300–$500 million. Renewed fighting, however, superseded the terms of the peace accord.[22] The GoY itself has pursued intermittent reconstruction initiatives. According to the Embassy of Yemen in Washington, D.C., the Sa'da Reconstruction Fund (known as the Sa'da High Committee for War Damages and Assessments from 2004 to 2008) was reconstituted in the summer of 2007 to inventory damage; the fund has had mixed results thus far.[23] In September 2008, the GoY appealed for $190 million from international donors to rehabilitate infrastructure and to support IDPs.[24] It claims to have spent $55 million already and has presented a $500 million development plan for 2009–2012. In March 2009, the GoY approved an estimated 10.7 billion Yemeni riyal (YR) to rebuild houses, farms, and 200 public institutions in Sa'da.[25] Nevertheless, incidents in the fifth interim and sixth phases of the war have led to a halt of all on-the-ground reconstruction because the area has once again become an official conflict zone and an inhospitable environment even for third-party public works employees. Most recently, the U.S. government donated $121 million to Yemen, but it is unclear where and how the funds will be distributed.[26]

The GoY initiatives discussed above, however, are not synchronized with kinetic operations. This suggests that rather than supporting a *strategic* choice for conflict abatement and resolution, the GoY's rhetoric and proposals for reconstruction are intended to be *tactics* along information and economic LOOs to support a largely coercive, kinetic COIN strategy. That this is the case is hinted at by the fate of the Sa'da Reconstruction Fund. Its workers faced difficulties entering the region in August 2008, when they were stopped by progovernment tribes. According to an informant, mem-

---

[21] Human Rights Watch, "Invisible Civilians," 34.

[22] International Crisis Group, "Yemen: Defusing the Saada Time Bomb," 22.

[23] According to the GoY, among its accomplishments before August 2009, the fund restored 12 schools, worked on over half of its projected water projects to conserve and rehabilitate water infrastructure, and implemented a "self-construction" method for housing damage in which affected beneficiaries work with construction workers on a phased payment plan of installments to rehabilitate the homes. Official comments from the Embassy of Yemen in Washington, D.C., October 1, 2009.

[24] "YEMEN: Government Calls for International Support to Reconstruct War-Affected Areas."

[25] "PM Approves Saada Reconstruction Fund's 2009 Budget," *Saba News Agency*, March 23, 2009.

[26] Yemen Post Staff, "United States Provided 121 Million Dollars as Assistance to Yemen; Yahya Al-Houthi Rejects," *Yemen Post*, September 17, 2009.

bers of the committee were subsequently arrested after releasing their damage assessments.[27] For their part, the Huthis claimed in late 2008 that they deserved YR 300 billion for war-related damages.[28] They are unlikely to receive it in any mediation context.

Since the fall of 2008, the GoY-created Sa'da Committee for Peace and Reconstruction has surveyed reconstruction needs. NGOs and international NGOs (INGOs), including the Qatari Red Crescent Society and the president's Saleh Foundation, have distributed some goods to refugees, while Oxfam, MSF, Medecins du Monde, the International Committee of the Red Cross, and Islamic Relief launched a drive after the fifth war, in Huthi-controlled zones as well as others.[29] Even good-faith efforts by NGOs and INGOs, however, confront several challenges. Funding—both domestic and international—has become particularly hard to secure in the global economic downturn. Moreover, donors may want better guarantees that the GoY will not destroy rebuilt property. Efforts are also complicated by unrelenting instability due to the increasingly tribal nature of fighting between pro-Huthi and pro-government camps in the region, particularly during the sixth war. Huthi leaders themselves have also been distrustful of reconstruction organizations. Indeed, major Yemeni NGOs have been implicated as corrupt and pro-government by Huthis,[30] while tense relations with INGOs pose obstacles to reconstruction workers. Ultimately, the actions of both sides prevent baseline assessments of damages, as well as meaningful provision of aid and reconstruction, thus lessening local trust.

Regime Human Rights Violations: Detainees, Freedom of Religion, and Press Restrictions

We have suggested that GoY COIN has both sustained Huthi armed opposition and aggravated the humanitarian situation, complicating prospects for postconflict reconciliation. Other regime actions, such as the enforced disappearance and detention of civilians, should also be considered in the context of human rights violations.[31] Additional abuses include restricting Zaydi freedom of religion and preventing NGO and press access to the north. Various reports and articles detail the disappearances and arbitrary arrests of civilians presumed to be in collusion with the Huthis. Human

---

[27] International Crisis Group, "Yemen: Defusing the Saada Time Bomb," 20–21.

[28] Mohammed Bin Sallam, "Blaming The Government for Only Being Interested in Upcoming Election Houthis Claim YR 300 Billion in Compensation for War-Related Damage," *Yemen Times,* September 24, 2008.

[29] International Crisis Group, "Yemen: Defusing the Saada Timebomb," 23.

[30] Phone interview with citizen journalist, October 22, 2008.

[31] According to Human Rights Watch, under international law, an enforced disappearance refers to "a government's refusal to acknowledge the detention of an individual or their whereabouts." Human Rights Watch, "Disappearances and Arbitrary Arrests," 15.

Rights Watch investigated 62 cases linked to the Huthi rebellion, describing a number of categories of those detained by the regime.[32] These include relatives of alleged combatants or human rights advocates, Hashemite preachers and scholars in Zaydi religious institutions, suspected Huthi supporters returning from conflict areas, and those publishing information about the conflict.

Civilians with alleged relationships to the Huthis were arrested as early as 2004. Particularly in late 2008, disappearances and arrests expanded.[33] According the UN Office for the Coordination of Humanitarian Affairs, 3,000 people were arrested for supporting the Huthis during the fifth Sa'da war.[34] GoY officials themselves admitted to holding 1,200 political detainees in jail in August 2008.[35] Various human rights organizations in Yemen have reacted by issuing lists of missing persons and organizing rallies to urge the government to release prisoners.[36] When the GoY does release detainees, the numbers are often far below what it announces.[37]

Linking Zaydi revival with armed Huthi rebellion and exploiting anti-Hashimi sentiment, the GoY has violated religious freedom as well. Documented arrests of Zaydi scholars accompany anecdotal and numerical evidence of Hashemite repression. One well-documented example is the September 2004 arrest of Muhammad Miftah, the prayer leader of San'a's Rawda Mosque—where Huthi supporters chanted their slogans in 2003 and 2004.[38] Miftah's public opposition to GoY actions in Sa'da led him to form the San'a Youth Organization, a Zaydi group supporting the Huthis. Originally convicted of establishing contacts with Iran in order to harm the country, Miftah was sentenced to eight years. This sentence was eventually commuted by Saleh in May 2006, but he is now prohibited from lecturing in public.[39] Finally, although the GoY does not declare its intent to target Hashemites specifically, many former detainees of Hashemite background have told Western researchers that they felt targeted due to

---

[32] Human Rights Watch, "Disappearances and Arbitrary Arrests in the Armed Conflict with Huthi Rebels in Yemen," Report 1-56432-392-7, October 2008.

[33] Human Rights Watch, "Disappearances and Arbitrary Arrests," 2.

[34] "Yemen: The Conflict in Saada Governorate—Analysis," *IRIN*, July 24, 2008.

[35] See Mohammed Bin Sallam, "Sa'ada Security Situation Relatively Calm," *Yemen Times*, August 17, 2008.

[36] On October 5, 2008, the Arab Sisters Forum headquarters hosted meetings in solidarity with prisoners of the Sa'da war coordinated with YDRF, National Rights Department (a.k.a. HOOD), the Hewaar Forum, Political Development Forum, Yemen Observatory for HR, Al-Tagheer Rights and Freedom Defence Org., Female Journalists Without Chains, the Social Democratic Forum, and the Committee on Torture Fighting. E-mail correspondence with human rights activist: "Statements of the prisoners and announcement [*Kashufat almu'taqalin wa bayan*]," October 9, 2008; Human Rights Watch, "Disappearances and Arbitrary Arrests," 2.

[37] For example, only 70 prisoners of the 500 whose release was announced in September 2007 appear to have been freed. See International Crisis Group, 20.

[38] Human Rights Watch, "Disappearances and Arbitrary Arrests," 30.

[39] "Yemen: International Religious Freedom Report 2007," U.S. State Department Bureau of Democracy, Human Rights and Labor, 2007.

their *sayyid* lineage. Thus, whatever the basis for these arrests, the GoY practices turn the narrative motif of Hashimi-republican tension into a reality of enmity.[40]

General violations of religious freedom occur in the context of a larger government campaign against public expressions of Zaydi identity. Not only did the regime shut down Zaydi schools in the run-up to the conflict, it also posted Sunni preachers to Zaydi mosques, and sources have observed signs reading "Sunni Mosque" in Zaydi areas.[41] Further, under the pretext that Yemeni Zaydis were imitating Twelver Shi'ite rituals, the government banned al-Ghadir Day celebrations between 2004 and 2008. Ironically, it thus gave Zaydi rituals an element of political resistance that indeed characterizes Twelver Shi'ite celebrations in Lebanon, Iraq, and elsewhere.[42] In December 2008, al-Ghadir Day observance was allowed for the first time since the war began. The holiday was accompanied by acts of violence as well as unprecedented celebrations by the Huthis, affirming group identity in resistance to the state.

As the GoY seeks to restrict outsider access north of San'a, the press has been literally unable to reach the north. Papers were shut down if they wrote about the war, and observers ranging from professional journalists to regular citizens with videos or photos of the region were arrested. Few of the journalist arrests related to the Huthi conflict have resulted in charges, with the exception of Yemeni journalist Abdulkarim al-Khaiwani, whose case has been widely publicized and internationalized. The former editor in chief of the now closed *Al-Shoura* newspaper, al-Khaiwani was arrested in June 2004 after publishing a series of articles on human rights violations against Zaydis.[43] He was sentenced to six years' imprisonment for allegedly conspiring with the Huthi rebels. Though later pardoned by President Saleh, a special criminal court on terrorism reimposed the sentence in January 2009. He has since been released. Al-Khaiwani's case demonstrates the violations of freedom of speech perpetrated by the regime in its effort to control information about the conflict. Despite the internationalization of al-Khaiwani's case, journalist detentions have continued into the sixth war. In mid-September 2009, the editor of the Al-Ishtiraki Web site, which is affiliated with the opposition Socialist Party, disappeared from San'a shortly after criticizing the government's role in clashes in Sa'da.[44] It should also be noted that Western journalists and

---

[40] Human Rights Watch, "Disappearances and Arbitrary Arrests," 24, 29; interview with academic Yemen specialist, September 22, 2008; interview with Yemeni citizen journalist, October 2, 2008.

[41] Human Rights Watch, "Disappearances and Arbitrary Arrests," 30.

[42] As noted previoiusly, al-Ghadir Day has no particular sectarian background and has become a widely popular practice in Yemen. Mohammed bin Sallam, "Four Killed, Six Injured in Shia Ghadir Day Celebrations," *Yemen Times*, December 17, 2008.

[43] See "Yemen: Human Rights Defender and Journalist Abdul-Karim al-Khaiwani Sentenced to Six Years Imprisonment," *Front Line*, posted on June 10, 2008; Roy Greenslade, "Al-Khaiwani a 'Very Special Journalist,'" *Guardian, Greenslade Blog*, May 18, 2009.

[44] The southern opposition movement has heated up again in parallel to the run-up of the sixth Sa'da war. Al-Ishtiraki, like the southern daily *al-Ayyam,* is frequently blocked in Yemen. Amel al-Ariqi, "Editor disappears

scholars have been prevented from traveling to the region, with some even turned away at the San'a airport.[45] All this has a chilling effect on Yemenis. Some refuse to communicate directly with Western analysts, and others practice self-censorship.

A Shared Responsibility

Although we contend that Huthi armed resistance can be described as defensive and reactive to GoY methods, the Huthis share with the GoY responsibility for damaging the economic and environmental bases for survival in Sa'da. Likewise, violation of human rights has been increasingly mutual—although Huthi violations are harder to substantiate because they are either anecdotal or based on GoY propaganda. Still, examples of Huthi contribution to conflict prolongation are worthy of consideration. Some of these are acts of Huthi "resistance." Huthis have raided soldiers inside their camps and have also conducted targeted killings and attempted assassinations of GoY representatives and military figures—thus provoking reprisals that are often collective in nature.[46] Furthermore, Huthi fighters have killed, at times in gruesome, demonstrative fashion, pro-GoY Sa'dans, including tribal shaykhs whose prestige and standing far outweigh that of the killers. It is notable in this respect that, as time has progressed, local Huthi leaders are increasingly intolerant of tribes' efforts to remain neutral. Finally, to the extent that the GoY itself takes mediation seriously, the Huthis also undermine reconciliation efforts by launching attacks during negotiations.[47]

With respect to local violations of human rights, Sa'da citizen freedoms, and tribal norms, sources speak of Huthis hiding in and firing from farms and croplands, thus provoking GoY responses.[48] They also discuss Huthi looting. It is reported that Huthi leaders moving into villages assess the stock of local traders, demanding half up front and half after significant engagement with the GoY—or prior to departure for other conflict areas. Though Huthi leaders do pay for goods thus "purchased," locals are forced into complicity—if they do not provide sustenance to the Huthis, they face revenge killings; if they do, they become Huthi sympathizers in GoY eyes.[49] Huthis

---

after publishing critical material," *Yemen Times*, September 27, 2009.

[45] For example, French Yemen specialist Laurent Bonnefoy was turned away at the San'a airport even though his spouse resides in Yemen. See Nabil Sabi', "Tard al-Shuhud min al-Yaman wa Ighlaq al-bilad 'ala Hurub Ghayr Mahduda," *al-Nida'*, April 30, 2009.

[46] As examples, see "Na'ib Muhafiz Sa'da wa Mudir Amnuha Yata'arradan li-Kamin Musallah," *al-Ayyam*, April 4, 2005; "Naja Ra'is al-Istikhbarat al-'Askariya min Muhawalat al-Ightiyal," *al-Ayyam*, April 27, 2005; "Kamin Thalith Yanju minhu Na'ib Muhafiz Sa'da wa Rami Qanbulatayn 'ala Taqim 'Askari," *al-Ayyam*, May 3, 2005.

[47] "YEMEN: Humanitarian Situation Worsens after Short-Lived Truce," *IRIN*, September 6, 2008.

[48] See "'Anasir al-Huthi Tantaqil fi Manatiq Bani Mu'adh wa Sahar wa-l-Safra' 'abr al-Mazari' al-Kabira."

[49] Interview with senior HRW official, March 20, 2009.

have also taken weapons from defeated GoY soldiers and, according to the government, have looted property from potential reconstruction projects.[50] These requisitioning tactics—practiced by the GoY as well—also deplete the stores of wheat, sorghum, and so forth that have customarily allowed extended families to weather conflicts or interruptions in supply. [51] In their operations targeted against GoY forces, Huthis have allegedly used child warriors and human shields in order to further involve tribals in the conflict.

We have discussed cases in which GoY actions have targeted Sa'da infrastructure, just as we have indicated that the GoY has yet to permit full access to the region for purposes of reconstruction needs assessment. The Huthis, as well, have destroyed infrastructure and thwarted reconstruction attempts. Huthis have severed electricity lines in contested regions, either as an offensive tactic or a rear-guard action.[52] Likewise, Huthis have cut roads to prevent the movement of GoY forces and those they consider to be GoY sympathizers. Along with requisitioning supplies of diesel fuel headed for towns, the Huthis are also responsible for preventing the flow of aid to the region by means of roadblocks. While these kinds of actions mirror GoY measures, Huthi fighters at times exceed the regime's actions. In May 2008, for example, the Huthis attacked a YRC convoy heading for IDPs in Harf Sufyan.[53]

Two other GoY and Huthi practices in this conflict recall phenomena seen both in Middle Eastern conflicts and African civil strife. As in the Middle East, the Huthi conflict—emerging from the social bases of Zaydi revivalism and rhetorically identified by the GoY as conspiring toward restoration of the imamate—has become increasingly sectarian in its actions. Since 2006–2007, the GoY has employed tribal volunteers as auxiliaries (*junud mustajaddin; murtaziqa*). In addition to locals susceptible to GoY material offers, these volunteers have also included Sunnis from Hashidi areas—and reputed former Afghan Salafi mercenaries that the GoY had previously used in the south.[54] For their part, Huthi spokesmen and sympathizers have attacked such practices as a Wahhabi effort to divide Yemenis against themselves.[55] A March 2007 Huthi attack on students studying at the Salafi Dammaj institute, however, as well as sub-

---

[50] According to the GoY, the government built a medical center in one of the rural areas in the district of Saqayn in 2009, but the building was occupied and looted by Huthis. Official comments from the Embassy of Yemen in Washington, D.C., October 1, 2009.

[51] It was noted in the interview that the Huthi method of taking half of local goods as preferable to the GoY method, in which they move into an area, take provisions, and do not pay at all. Interview with senior HRW official, March 20, 2009; Human Rights Watch, "Invisible Civilians," 20.

[52] See "'Anasir al-Huthi Tantaqil fi Manatiq Bani Mu'adh wa Sahar wa-l-Safra' 'abr al-Mazari' al-Kabira."

[53] "Yemen: Spotlight on IDPs in Amran," *IRIN News*, August 18, 2008.

[54] See Jane Novak, "Yemen's Internal Shia Jihad," *Global Politician*, March 21, 2007; Ginny Hill, "Yemen: Fear of Failure," Chatham House Briefing Paper, Middle East Programme, MEP BP 08/03, November 2008.

[55] See Appendix C for Huthi statements to this effect.

sequent assaults on its property, suggest that Huthi fighters have taken the sectarian bait and are now departing from the traditional Zaydi approach of being open to other expressions of Islam sharing the same geographical space.[56]

As to the latter, reports as well as video imagery also suggest that both Huthis and the GoY recruit and employ what are considered child soldiers in the West.[57] Huthi leaders are reported to stipulate that supporting tribes provide fighters. Some of those provided by shaykhs are minors, reportedly as young as 13–15 years old. Likewise, a portion of the GoY's tribal auxiliaries are teenage minors.[58] In the Yemeni tribal context, this is a complex matter. On the one hand, the employment of minors as fighters is indeed problematic in international law—and Yemen is in fact a member of the UN. On the other hand, as we have seen earlier, the public carriage of weapons is considered a part of manhood in many tribal cultures, and *qabyala* is no different in this respect, with adolescents aspiring to demonstrate adulthood in this fashion. Likewise, in Arab societies less exposed to the post-industrial West's norms, "adulthood" begins somewhat earlier, given traditional needs for labor, defense, alliance-making through marriage, procreation, and so forth.[59] Therefore, what external observers consider child soldiers may not be considered so in Yemen by the protagonists, tribes, or the combatant youths. Further, it must be remembered that for the Huthis, one of their original social bases was the Believing Youth, and that demographic base—or their younger siblings—went on to provide a recruitable hard core, susceptible (or vulnerable) to the masculine assertion furnished by resistance and armed activity. Additionally, the rituals or gatherings appropriated by the Huthis discussed above—where adolescents and young adults congregate together with "adult" fighters—make ideal environments for socialization and recruitment of youth.

What makes the presence of youthful fighters similar to that in Africa is that some are required to join either the Huthis or the GoY—raising the possibility of coercion and duress. Yet the situation is different because these young fighters do not sever ties with their families but likely become part of kin-network-based fighting teams, as seen in Chapter Seven. They are not permanently removed from their native areas; they return seasonally or fight in the area. Additionally, reports have not yet emerged of local area Huthi leaders ensnaring child fighters by addicting them to drugs. Still, the presence of youthful combatants does constitute a violation of human rights by both sides. Additionally, it distorts and exaggerates certain aspects of *qabyala*, decreasing the appeal among the younger generation of other ideas, such as mediation and con-

---

[56] "British, French Killed and Algerian Wounded in Saada," *Al-Sahwa*, March 26, 2007.

[57] Interviews: human rights worker from area, March 20, 2009; American citizen journalist in fall 2008 and spring 2009; Yemeni emigrant from conflict area, October 29, 2008; official from the Embassy of Yemen in Washington, D.C., fall 2009.

[58] Interview with senior Human Rights Watch official, March 20, 2009.

[59] See Gary S. Gregg, *The Middle East: A Cultural Psychology* (New York: Oxford University Press, 2005).

flict avoidance. More ominously, however, it creates a younger generation of Yemenis socialized to violence who perceive violent opportunism to be a normal aspect of life.

The presence of youthful combatants is merely part of a larger complex of socio-psychological issues that are the consequence of continuing violence in Sa'da. While malnutrition, disease, and routine exposure to violence and brutality hurt all people involved, they have a greater developmental effect on certain populations.[60] In this respect, it is important to note the UNICEF psychosocial assessment survey of Sa'da province in August–October 2006. Out of 1,400 respondents, 630 children and adolescents (92.4 percent of children and adolescent respondents) had been exposed to armed conflict; nearly 6 percent had been evacuated temporarily during conflict; 44 percent had been forced to hide for their lives; 15 percent had been injured in the conflict; and nearly 14 percent had had a family member killed. Additionally, nearly half had witnessed destruction of homes and property, and 10 percent had family members who were missing. Conflict also led to chronic fear among over 25 percent of the sample. These numbers are likely to have grown over the past three years. Additional UNICEF assessments in early 2008 also highlighted "severe acute malnutrition" as increasing the prevalence of anemia, wasting, and stunted growth among youths.[61] If the Sa'da conflict continues on its current trajectory, its negative effects on all aspects of the emerging generation's physiological, psychological, and social development will themselves act as drivers of conflict and rend the social fabric of the region.

Conclusion

Since the summer of 2004, low-intensity conflict to high-intensity war has ranged over the Sa'da governorate, into 'Amran, Hajja, and sometimes Jawf, reaching all the way to the Sa'da *muhafaza* and the capital city environs. Armed conflict has also spilled over the border into southern Saudi Arabia, and the latter's air force has bombed locations in northern Yemen. In Sa'da itself, warfare has touched all heavily populated areas, particularly in the form of artillery and air bombardments from the GoY, as well as Huthi reponses ranging from raids to indirect fire. Destruction has been great, and none of the customarily protected people or sites have been able to avoid the conflict. For its part, the GoY military has been able to sustain a field presence and operations conducted by its mostly conscript force. Yet, it has not been able to decisively eliminate or degrade the Huthi threat, and—crucially in a proto-COIN context—the army's accomplishments in the field have not secured a political space for the GoY to engage

---

[60] See "YEMEN: Children in Clash-Prone North Highly Traumatized—Aid Workers," *IRIN News*, February 18, 2008; interview, U.S. administrator of post-trauma child-health programs, May 20, 2009.

[61] Almigdad Mojalli, "Rehabilitation Program for Young Victims of Sa'ada War," *Yemen Times*, March 30, 2008; United Nations Children's Fund, *UNICEF Humanitarian Action Report 2009*, 154–156.

in substantial reconstruction in the economic LOO or engage in diplomacy from a position of advantage.

The Huthis have been able to develop over time. Surviving the loss of senior leaders and LALs, they have sustained operations in the absence of a hierarchical or fully differentiated organization. As parts of an organism, fighting groups have engaged the GoY often on their own terms and have been able to maintain persistent pressure on the regime's military forces—at times establishing control over an area, at other times focusing on remote, safer areas. There are no indications of recruitment problems, and fighting techniques do not appear to have altered markedly over the past five years. At the same time, there are hints that the Huthi organism is beginning to evolve into a true organization, particularly in the realm of ideological communication. Circumstances in the governorate, as well as at the national level of Yemeni policy, will influence whether and how the Huthis continue to evolve.

The biggest losers in the Huthi-regime conflict have been the physical environment, economic base, and human communities in Sa'da and surrounding locations. Given the precarious existence of the people in the area, which requires group autonomy and intercommunity ties, the Sa'da wars have done the kind of damage that will require concentrated GoY and local—as well as international—focus to fix. And these efforts will likely have to take place in the midst of ongoing fighting and internal GoY factionalism. Unfortunately, the GoY has yet to engage in mediation and negotiation for more than tactical purposes, and regional powers have not provided mechanisms and terms that could secure a mediated breathing space for all protagonists as well as suffering Sa'dans. Finally, it is not certain how the Huthis want to approach Sa'da and Yemen's future, whether they wish to engage seriously in credible negotiations—and what their relationship to broader Zaydism and Yemeni Islam will be.

Beyond these results of the ongoing conflict lie the uncertain, but particularly significant, effects on local norms and values-in-action. We have repeatedly emphasized the importance of *qabyala* in northern Yemen. Its social enactment by *qabilis* and others articulates values, norms, and modes of existence. Yet, just as the way *qabilis* express *qabyala* changes, so might the complex of values change. In Chapter Three we saw the ways that sociogenerational changes catalyzed attitudinal changes toward *sada*, *mashayikh*, and the gravitational pull of tribal loyalty. We also saw that these loyalties have remained, yet in an altered, enervated form. The Huthi conflict may have an effect on norms and values as socially enacted through the choices of the GoY, Huthis, tribal leaders, and *qabilis* themselves.

Changing Tribal Norms

The Huthi conflict can be said to have emerged from the domain of religion into the field of tribes. The kinds of alliances the Huthis and the GoY have made, as well as the interpretation of offenses and the enactment of responses to them, have used tribes as the means of mobilization and action. Yet, it is a distorted, weakened kind of tribalism that does not have the moral suasion of shaykhs and room for individual and group autonomy, because the GoY and the Huthis no longer permit these luxuries. Thus, alongside reports of increased tribalization, one can detect the erosion of tribal values and mediation of conflict in traditional ways. Those in the BY generation and later seem to be less knowledgeable about the enduring principles and social enactment of tribal norms. In addition, the collusion of local shaykhs with a neopatrimonial GoY has lessened the calming influence of traditional principles.[62] Of course, the broad structural features of tribe-government interaction remain constant in Yemen and Saʻda, because citizens have become accustomed to living without a central state presence and because there have been no outside invasions as in Iraq or Afghanistan. At the same time, violence in the north associated with the Huthi conflict differs in both magnitude and kind from what scholars have described as the organized chaos of tribal revenge and conflict mediation in the country. Thus, today's conflict, when evaluated by protagonists through the lens of *qabyala*, threatens a "total breakdown [in tribal rules] . . . you haven't seen this in years."[63]

It is therefore important to consider the Saʻda wars and their human effects in terms of the local grammar of violence and mediated conflict. In this respect, the Huthi-regime confrontation may go beyond damaging physical infrastructure to distorting the ideational infrastructure of tribalism that has prevented social disintegration in northern Yemen over several centuries. As we have previously seen, notions of *sharaf* apply to protecting a tribe's houses, villages, and weaker classes. With respect to the conflict, GoY COIN and Huthi responses have violated *ʻird* (honor) by damaging property and violating traditionally weak members of society.[64] Likewise, from both a

---

[62] See NDI, "Yemen: Tribal Conflict Management Program Research Report," *National Democratic Institute for International Affairs,* March 2007; also see Almigdad Mojali, "Tribal Norms Protecting Women Are Diminishing," *Yemen Times,* September 2, 2007. The comments of Shaykh al-Nini, tribal leader of Bani Siham, a tribe in Khawlan with the largest population, are useful in this regard. He noted in 2007 that tribes all have the same norms, which he likened to constitutions in Yemen's northern and eastern governorates. At the same time, he recognized that norms have weakened, commenting, "There's a big change in norms and traditions, both for individual tribes as well as for all tribes, as a result of civilization and the spread of education." See al-Miqdad Dahesh Mojalli, "When Cultural Norms Undermine Tribal Rules," *Yemen Times,* 15:1099 (November 1–3, 2007).

[63] Interview with academic Yemen specialist, September 22, 2008.

[64] Regarding protection of weaker members of society, the Jewish community in Yemen has been described as pawns of both sides in the conflict. It also demonstrates how the issue of violating protected groups may be deployed rhetorically by both sides of the conflict. There was consensus among our Yemeni informants and several academics that, despite their anti-Israel, anti-Jewish chanting, Huthis are not anti-Semitic. GoY sympathizers even accused the Huthis of receiving Jewish support early on. Nevertheless, certain violations have been committed against the small community of Jews residing in Saʻda, and the fourth Saʻda war became a turning point for the Jews. Displacement related to the conflict and accusations traded by the Huthis and GoY about who had treated this minority worse have resulted in politicizing the community's status. In January 2007, some members of the residual Saʻda Jewish community were relocated to Sanʻa following Huthi threats. Over a year later, in April 2008, men allegedly associated with the Huthis destroyed a house belonging to a member of the Jewish community. The sensitivity of the issue has been heightened by Saleh's intermittent efforts to protect the Jewish community, in addition to unrelated incidents in the north. The November 2008 killing of Yaish Nahari by an

religious and tribal perspective, targeting historical *hijra* territories violates a community's *'ird*. Such measures also perpetuate violence because violations of *sharaf* should be "paid for by heavy amends."[65] These cultural provocations mean that local Sa'dans will respond to destruction with disobedience and violence—potentially, long after the initial cause of the conflict has receded.

As mentioned above, this GoY-Huthi conflict has not removed traditional norms. Sa'dans still function within a *qabyala* social milieu, justify their own actions according to their understandings of *qabyala* as a complex of values, and evaluate others' conduct in the same terms. But social structures and belief systems are dynamic, responding to external stimuli and daily exigencies. Therefore, continuous GoY-Huthi warfare has likely altered interpretations of long-standing local norms and diminished the durability of traditional social ties. One example in particular demonstrates the potential distortion of traditional *qabyala* norms. Blockades of roads or fuel fit into tribal warfare norms as a way to target specific opponents.[66] Yet, GoY blockades have affected an entire region rather than a specific tribe, exceeding cultural norms of warfare. Instead of tribes working with tribes within an established albeit chaotic framework of give-and-take animated by group autonomy, the government may appear to tribes to be collectively punishing them. This changes the entire dynamic of the tribe-state relations—but it also changes the meaning of "tribal norms" and the content of northern Yemeni "culture," particularly among the younger generation of Sa'dans who are most exposed to conflict but least socialized to traditional mores.

This raises the question of whether tribal mediation or the broad equilibrium-preserving elements of the northern Yemeni social structure will survive the conflict. Ethnographers who have worked in the area suggest that northern Yemen has always been relatively insulated from the larger world and that not enough time has elapsed since 2004 for its social structures to no longer function as they did. Political scientists and scholars of religion are less sanguine. Tribal violence—and tribalization of conflict—may be becoming more prevalent in the north at the same time as traditional proclivities toward tribal conflict management and resolution are failing. A 2007 National Democratic Institute (NDI) report on tribal mediation in Ma'rib, al-Jawf,

---

unrelated Sunni extremist was followed by a mid-December explosion at Jewish homes. Following the incident, Saleh responded to complaints by having authorities allocate land and YR 2 million for each Jewish family in San'a after they sold their properties in 'Amran. But the government has allegedly not followed through with the proposal. Allegedly, fewer than 500 Jews remain in Yemen, with many of them headed to Israel and the United States to seek safety because havens provided by the government in San'a have not been fully funded. See Shaker Khalid, "Yemeni Jews . . . From Creation to the Magic Carpet Operation," *Yemen Post*, January 5, 2009; "Yemen's Jews Uneasy as Muslim Hostility Grows," *Jerusalem Post*, April 27, 2009. Also see interview with Israeli academic Yemen experts, December 23, 2008, in Tel Aviv, and December 24, 2008, in Haifa.

[65] Paul Dresch, *Tribes, Government, and History in Yemen* (New York: Oxford University Press, 1989), 143, 146, 150.

[66] Hasan Al-Zaidi, "Interior Ministry Orders Lifting Tribal Road Blockade; Diesel Still Unavailable in Some Gas Stations," *Yemen Post*, July 21, 2008.

and Shabwa highlighted security concerns in the north resulting from tribal conflict. It also described how violence associated with revenge killings is considered a growing problem in Yemen by the tribes themselves.[67] Indeed, blood feuds stem from the failure, inability, or unwillingness to engage in tribal resolution.[68]

We have seen that in the Huthi conflict itself, *tha'r* (revenge) seems to have superseded *sulh wa tahkim* (mediation and arbitration), at both the local level and between the GoY and Huthis generally. At the same time as mediations are failing, attacks

> driven by group solidarity and the growing involvement of tribal militias alongside government or rebel forces have further inflamed the conflict and contributed to its endurance. By some accounts, the war has turned into a tribal conflict between the pro-government Hashid and pro-rebel Bakil confederations.[69]

As one local journalist opined, in recruiting tribes to fight the rebels in the north, "the government made the mistake of recruiting Zaydi Hashid tribes that were traditional rivals of the Sa'ada-based Bakil. This led to talk of the conflict being tribal in nature, with the Sa'ada tribes backing al-Houthi."[70] This development suggests that the conflict may spread beyond its initial scope and geography, even without overt GoY military interference. Over time, regardless of the initial *casus belli*, protagonists—Hashimis and *qaba'il* from all three of the major tribal confederations mentioned in this study—may develop fresh enmities with each other and the GoY that can sustain conflict regardless of the Huthis. Relationships based on kin networks will continue to be important, and ideas associated with *qabyala* will remain the lens through which people evaluate actions and calculate responses. Both will thus remain analytically significant for the conflict. These same relationships and ideas, however, will possess a diminished ability to moderate tendencies toward violence.

---

[67] See National Democratic Institute for International Affairs, *Yemen: Tribal Conflict Management Program Research Report,* March 2007.

[68] Laila al-Zwaini, "State and Non-State Justice in Yemen," paper for Conference on the Relationship between State and Non-State Justice Systems in Afghanistan, United States Institute for Peace, December 2006, 8.

[69] International Crisis Group, "Defusing the Saada Timebomb," 14.

[70] Muhammad 'Aysh, *al-Sharei* editor, as quoted in *IRIN,* "Yemen: The Conflict in Saada Governorate: Analysis."

Conclusion

In this book, we have treated the Huthi-GoY conflict as emerging from regime-periphery tension aggravated by new social conditions and mobilizational strategies in the periphery during the 1990s. Some of this tension is structural, related to the conditions of existence in northern Yemen and the resultant norms and social structures that have arisen under those conditions—tribalism and Zaydism. Together, these physical conditions and social structures present challenges to the periphery's integration with all of Yemen. In seeking to influence Yemen's periphery for its own benefit, the GoY has had recourse to a form of politics known as neopatrimonialism. Accessing aspects of the norms and practices associated with tribalism, the GoY has relied on cooptation, patronage, and divide-and-weaken measures in the absence of its ability to fully rule all its territory. Thus, northern Yemen presents a context of tension and potential conflict with the center.

Socioeconomic evolution in northern Yemen, Sa'da in particular, began to disturb the status quo from the 1980s on, leading to local tensions within and among strata and hopes for greater GoY attention to economic and infrastructural uplift. Yet, GoY measures on the political and religious plane aggravated emergent tensions, causing overt strife between Salafis and Zaydis as well as over political representation and economic patronage. In the process, local Sa'dan Zaydis galvanized a religious revival expressed through politics, scholarship, and a novel form of associationalism in the form of the Believing Youth. Although Salafi-Wahhabi tensions had abated by the middle of the 1990s and the BY had gone into hiatus by the decade's end, the basic drivers of discontent were not addressed and became the roots of the post-2004 regime-Huthi conflict.

The global conjuncture after September 11, 2001, had a particular regional impact. Although the GoY was materially empowered in the security realm and felt more cofident about its ability to control the periphery directly, Yemenis, and those around Husayn al-Huthi in particular, were repelled by the close security and counterterror relationship between San'a and Washington. At the same time, none of Sa'da's material grievances had been addressed, while the political enfranchisement of the younger generation of Zaydis—the BY-age cohorts—had stalled, just as political liberalization had stalled throughout Yemen. Husayn al-Huthi reentered the arena at a time when there were few potential alternative Zaydi leaders. Using family prestige and capitalizing on welfare and educational activities, he catalyzed a movement of ideological opposition to the GoY's policies toward Zaydis and the United States. In the context of growing al-Qa'ida threats and overall regional instability in the wake of the U.S. invasions of Afghanistan and Iraq, the regime perceived the Huthi movement, led by the son of one of Yemen's most prestigious Zaydi *marji'*, as a fundamental threat to its legitimacy. Conversely, it felt unusually capable of directly confronting the Huthi followers rather than coopting some of them. These elements furnished the triggers for armed conflict between the regime and the northern periphery.

In seeking to eliminate the Huthi threat, the GoY has availed itself of military, ideological, and diplomatic resources and has attempted to use local political alliances and economic "sticks" to undermine the Huthis. Thus, the GoY's actions can be analyzed according to counterinsurgency lines of operation. Though it is unlikely that the GoY consciously implemented a COIN strategy, counterinsurgency-like lines of operation have not diminished the Huthi challenge. Rather, regime operations have elicited a particular form of armed opposition arising from the cultural landscape of Sa'da and the social phenomenon that is the Huthi family. Likewise, over successive conflict phases of war, ceasefire, and war-during-ceasefire, GoY COIN has sustained a Huthi insurrection tending toward insurgency, while Huthi resistance drives the GoY to continue operations in the governorate. The aggressive approach of the GoY may reflect splits in the regime between Salafis and marginal Zaydis or may be a function of President Saleh's efforts to retain military loyalty. But GoY COIN and Huthi tactics both prolong the conflict. Further, even in the shadow of the February 2010 ceasefire, the progressive damage to the environment, economy, and sociocultural fabric of Sa'da renders containment, abatement, and reconciliation exceedingly difficult.

Analytical Implications of the Conflict

Given this background of the conflict's context, roots, triggers, and prolongers, the continuing Huthi-GoY confrontation has implications for near-term analysis on three levels. The first level is that of Yemen itself. The next level involves surrounding regional countries, while the third level consists of U.S. considerations regarding Yemen and the larger Gulf and Horn of Africa region. We will address the conflict's implications for each of these levels.

Yemen State Level

Yemen is a country whose challenges—security, political, economic, ideational—sorely tax the capabilities of the regime. The Huthi conflict complicates matters in each domain. As long as the military is engaged in Sa'da, it cannot defend its frontiers against incursions. It also cannot devote adequate attention to interdicting the trafficking of people, weapons, or contraband goods. With a military otherwise occupied with internal defense, Yemen may thus become a (more) porous gateway for illicit movement throughout Arabia and the Horn of Africa. Further, pressing current security concerns will mean that—aside from niche entities such as the Republican Guard, the Central Security Force Counter Terrorism Unit, or the YSOF—the Yemeni security forces will not be able to get better at what they do. The post-2001 increase in international aid will not have improved the GoY's overall institutional security and defense capabilities to a transformative degree. Ironically, the Yemeni security apparatus will suffer as the Egyptian military did in the years before the 1967 war with Israel, due to its engagement in the Yemeni civil war. Ongoing combat operations will also attrite stores of weapons and equipment, making it more difficult to recapitalize assets and modernize forces.

Ultimately, then, ongoing operations in the north degrade the effectiveness of GoY responses to security challenges across the threat spectrum—in particular, the Huthi distraction inhibits the GoY from dealing conclusively with al-Qa'ida and the potential of armed discontent in the south. An armed Sa'da conflict persisting into the next decade may also have implications for continued cohesion of the army itself at the enlisted and junior officer levels, particularly because it may become economically difficult to support operations. Additionally, though cases of senior officer disaffection have been limited until now (see Chapter Six, "GoY Operations"), continuing fighting without definitive GoY victories could yield more instances of commanders failing to implement orders or coming to temporary local accommodations with Huthi fighters in order to protect troops and lines of communication. All these concerns may be partly responsible for driving the GoY toward a ceasefire in February 2010, a mere six months into its "scorched earth" campaign. At the least, recent events suggest that the GoY's political leadership may lose confidence in some of its field commanders and rely on punitive action enforce discipline. Such measures themselves may undermine *esprit de corps* and loyalty.[1]

On the economic plane, Yemen is already a country beset with problems. As just one indicator, per capita gross domestic product (GDP) for 2008 was less than half that of Egypt, about a third lower than that of Iraq—approximately that of Djibouti, Timor Leste, and Pakistan.[2] These countries have either very large populations and well-known economic challenges, ongoing internal instability, or a postconflict dependency on foreign support. Yemen is thus in dire economic straits—and, simply put, combat operations are expensive, be they low- or high-intensity. The Huthi conflict

---

[1]   See "al-Yaman: al-Huthiyun Yaksibun al-Ma'raka al-I'lamiya wa Ihkam bi-I'dam Dubat Muwatinin ma'a shari'a al-Huthiyin," *al-Quds al-Arabi*, November 18, 2009. This piece refers to the GoY's recent decision to sentence three Yemeni army officers to death for collusion with Huthi fighters, along with sending 27 others to prison for 10–12 years. This event may be related to the isolation and retreat of the 105th Brigade from Marran without its weapons and equipment. See Chapter Six for coverage of this incident.

[2]   See International Monetary Fund, World Economic Outlook Database, October 2009.

will therefore complicate Yemeni efforts to address economic problems throughout the country. These problems include an imbalance of wealth distribution across strata and regions and poor indicators for the human inputs to economic development, such as health, education, and vocational training.

Yemen's economic resources themselves will likely be straitened over the next years. Remittances have never approached a fraction of their pre-1990 levels. While export of Yemeni oil from the mid 1990s partially made up for the lack of remittances, Yemen's production capacity is shrinking. The end of its reserves is reputedly in sight ,and natural gas production is only partially compensating for oil. Likewise, the current downturn in oil prices means that near-term benefits of oil—for the purposes of guns or butter—are diminished.[3] Therefore, just as the Huthi conflict pressures Yemen's vulnerable economy, that economy itself constrains robust kinetic continuation of the conflict, while also reducing the GoY's capacity to pursue political reconciliation and economic reconstruction without international support.

Of course, such decisions are political. In the realm of politics, along with the al-Qa'ida threat and southern discontent, the Huthi conflict complicates matters during the likely twilight of 'Ali 'Abdullah Saleh's rule. Having been in power for over 30 years, he is said to be hoping to transition power to his son Ahmad by the next presidential election. Yet his political coalition may be less cohesive now than it might have once been. Saleh's Hashidi pillar 'Abdullah al-Ahmar died in 2007, and his sons have yet to establish absolute primacy—either among themselves or over the Hashid confederation. In this light, continuing conflict raises the possibility that Saleh may not be able to count on Hashidi political or military support unless he accommodates demands for more Hashidi influence or autonomy—which would rankle with other tribes in the north, as well as in the restive south.

Thus, Saleh may bequeath an undesirable political field to his son. Or he may choose—or be cornered into accepting—succession by someone else. An alternative successor might be more Salafi-identified, or more attractive in the eyes of Saleh's Sanhani military relatives. That alternative could be 'Ali Muhsin al-Ahmar, although the Sa'da conflict has not aided him in this respect. Overall, however, at a time of occluded economic potential and a rising Salafi element in the military, security forces, and other GoY domains, a continuing or aggravated Huthi conflict might undermine elite political cohesion, endanger a smooth transition, or result in Saleh retaining power. All these possibilities would further retard the stalled process of political liberalization in Yemen while having the additional effect of ensuring that political mobilization is oppositional, frustrated, and based on subnational identities and ideologies—be they Salafi, Zaydi, Marxist, or other.

---

[3]   Ginny Hill treats this issue well. See "Yemen: Fear of Failure," Chatham House Briefing Paper, Middle East Programme, MEP BP 08/03, November 2008, 8–9.

This raises the issue of ideas. The Huthi conflict brings into focus all the divides—geographical, social, ideological, and religious—discussed in Part I. These divides have been rhetorically activated by the regime in its information operations and have also been taken up by the Huthis. Thus, these divides become the interpretive lenses through which Yemenis understand the conflict. In the process, they obtain renewed relevance, though perhaps altered content. Therefore, a key implication of the conflict is the reenergization of divides—between fervent Zaydis and marginal Zaydis, Zaydis and Sunnis, northerners and southerners, tribals and nontribals, San'a and the rest of Yemen, and so forth. By labeling the Huthis as provoking separatist discord in the north, the GoY may have reopened the question of Yemen as a unified society and polity. In a related fashion, by permitting Saudi involvement in the conflict on its side of the border, the GoY may communicate an inability to protect its sovereignty, confirming suspicions of a subordinate client relationship with its northern neighbor. Putting the genie back in the bottle will require a resolution of the conflict that legitimates the political participation of Huthi affiliates, is not punitive, and validates diversity of cultural and political attitudes. This resolution may be all the more difficult in 2010, given the larger Yemeni context of reenergized al-Qa'ida violence, increasingly aggravated southern discontent, a troubled local and global economic conjuncture, and a just-suspended sixth war in the north.[4]

Concerns of Regional Powers

Over the past three years, regional states have become increasingly involved in the GoY-Huthi conflict. While San'a has often referred to foreign (Libyan, Iranian) involvement as a way to explain Huthi persistence, neighboring governments are concerned that the Huthi challenge aggravates the mounting threats to Yemen's internal security. In this respect, the lack of adequate security along Yemen's land and maritime borders increases the likelihood that terrorism, illicit trade, and weapons smuggling will persist throughout the region, raising the possibility that combatants in numerous substate conflicts will circulate transnationally, contributing to other simmering conflicts.[5] These issues pose a problem for Gulf Cooperation Council (GCC) countries as well as Iran, while increasing the dangers in the ungoverned spaces in the Horn of Africa

---

[4] For a well-researched, judicious treatment of the many challenges Yemen faces, see Christopher Boucek, "Yemen: Avoiding a Downward Spiral," Carnegie Papers No. 102, Carnegie Endowment for International Peace, Middle East Program, September 2009.

[5] GoY reports of Somalis arrested in Harf Sufyan for fighting with Huthis during the sixth war may be imprecise or may be an element of regime propaganda focusing on the Huthis' supposed foreign support. Still, such reports do suggest a Somali presence in areas of Huthi-GoY conflict, a worrying development in its own right. See "Ba'd Usbu' min Iktishaf Muqatilin Sumaliyin fi Sufuf al-Tamarrud bi-Sa'da . . . al-Jiza'iya Tabda' al-Yawm Jalsataha bi-Muhakamat 12 Qursanan Sumaliyan," *Akhbar al-Yawm*, September 29, 2009; Husayn al-Jarbani, "al-Yaman: Al-Qabdh 'ala 7 Sumaliyin Yuqatilun ma'a al-Huthiyin wa-Tawaqqu'at bi-Silatihum bi-Jama'at Jihadiya," *al-Sharq al-Awsat*, September 27, 2009.

and the Red Sea littoral. The regional threat perception caused by the conflict may also increase Sunni sentiment against alleged Iranian-Shi'a encroachment in the Gulf.

Huthi violence in northern Yemen directly increases the threat to Saudi Arabian border regions. Although Yemen is not yet officially a part of the GCC, instability in a region that shares borders and security concerns requires a *regional* focus on boosting Yemeni security capabilities. Part of the security problem stems from the fact that much of Yemen's border has never been satisfactorily delineated, despite recently heightened security coordination. Without consistent border security, the frequent frontier crossings by Yemeni tribesmen pose a concern to both states, in light of the Huthi challenge to the GoY. Additionally, tribal populations in the Saudi provinces of 'Asir, Jizzan, and Najran (which has a large Isma'ili and a small Zaydi minority) may identify with their Yemeni cousins.[6] Specifically, although the Khawlan bin 'Amr subtribes of Jabal Fayfa, Bani Ghazi, and Jabal Bani Malik have been on the Saudi side of the border since 1934, their members often travel back and forth for purposes of commerce. Given the geographical extent of GoY-Huthi clashes, these tribal sections may include some pro-Huthi members or may host small numbers of refugees from the conflict in Sa'da. As we have seen, at different times the GoY has alluded to cross-border tribal support for Huthi fighters, while Huthi sources have alleged Saudi provision of funding and arms to the GoY, as well as cooperation in armed attacks on Huthi supporters.[7] In the 2009–2010 round of fighting, this became a regular theme of Huthi statements. More basically, unmonitored movement of population permits the proliferation of the enablers of regional strife, including weapons, funds, contraband goods, and ideas.

As seen in Chapter Five, the sixth phase of the war in Sa'da has highlighted the conflict's regional aspects and its potential for further transnationalization. Saudi Arabia has become directly entangled in fighting with Huthi forces on both sides of its border with Yemen and could persist in anti-Huthi operations. According to local analysts, Saudi involvement reflects frustration with GoY failures as well as a fear that a border open to Huthi movement could also permit the reinfiltration of al-Qa'ida in the Arabian Peninsula (AQAP) into Saudi territory, from which it had been mostly eradicated in 2003–2006.[8] Toward the end of 2009, regional Arab fora, such as the

---

[6]   Subsequent to the 1934 qaba'il Treaty of Ta'if, these regions were ceded to Saudi Arabia. Although Saudi Arabia renegotiated the 1934 treaty with Yemen in 2003, the Saudis have been unsuccessful in building a border fence because of the original terms of the treaty, as well as GoY and local tribal objections. Article 5 of the Treaty of Taif states that "no wall or fortified building shall be built along the frontier line." See Ibrahim Al-Hajjri, "The New Middle East Security Threat: The Case of Yemen and the GCC," master's thesis, Naval Postgraduate School, Monterey, California, June 2007, 12; J. E. Peterson, "Tribes and Politics in Yemen," *Arabian Peninsula Background Note*, No. APBN-007, December 2008.

[7]   See "'Ajil: al-Su'udiya Taqsif Mantaqat al-Malahit bi-l-Tiran," *al-Menpar.net*, August 27, 2009.

[8]   See "Saudis Taking Lead in Battling Houthi Rebels," *Peninsula*, December 2, 2009. For more on Saudi responses to al-Qa'ida in the kingdom, see Mai Yamani, "The Two Faces of Saudi Arabia," Survival 50:1 (February–March 2008), 143–156; also see Thomas Hegghammer, "Terrorist Recruitment and Radicalization in Saudi

GCC and Arab League, came out in support of Saudi actions to prevent "encroachment on Saudi and Yemeni sovereignty," considering Yemeni security integral to that of surrounding Arab Gulf States.[9] While Arab League and GCC states maintained the appearance of a united Arab front, their support for Saudi Arabia and the GoY lessens their ability to act as impartial mediators in any future conflict abatement process that might begin where the Qatar process ended.

Iran declined to endorse renewed GoY actions and Saudi involvement in the sixth phase of fighting. While it has been careful not to articulate explicit support for the Huthi movement,[10] Iran began to address the ongoing violence in Saʿda in its official statements in late 2009. In an implicit signal to Saudi Arabia, the Islamic Republic's foreign minister cautioned all states to respect Yemen's sovereignty and indicated Iranian willingness to participate in conflict resolution. Iran's defense minister echoed his colleague, implicitly criticizing both Yemen and Saudi Arabia by affirming that there is no military solution to the conflict.[11] Beyond the executive branch, Iranian statements have been more direct. Ali Larijani, speaker of the Iranian parliament (Majles-e Shura), explicitly condemned Saudi intervention in the conflict, and parliament members prepared an anti-Saudi resolution in relation to the conflict.[12] In December 2009, the national security and foreign affairs committee chairman appealed for the mobilization of "Islamic organizations" to deal with the plight of northern Yemen. He also criticized "Salafi currents" for harming Islamic unity in Yemen and accused Saudi Arabia of prolonging conflict through its intervention.[13] In an exception to the regime elite's preference for implied criticism, the Iranian Joint Armed Forces Chief of Staff Major General Hassan Firouzabadi referred to the Saudi involvement as "state Wahhabi terrorism."[14] In a further departure, the state-sanctioned Iranian press has focused much more attention on the conflict since the November 2009 Saudi intervention,

---

Arabia," *Middle East Policy* 13:4 (2006), 39–60; Hegghammer, "Islamist Violence and Regime Stability in Saudi Arabia," *International Affairs* 84:4 (2008).

[9]   See Prasanta Kumar Pradhan, "Houthis and External Intervention in Yemen," *IDSA Comment*, Institute for Defence Studies and Analyses, November 25, 2009; "Musa Yuʾakkid Rafdahu al-Massas bi-Siyadat al-Suʿudiya wa-l-Yaman," League of Arab States Web site, November 10, 2009; Habib Toumi, "Yemen Security High on the GCC Agenda Summit," *Gulf News*, November 17, 2009.

[10]   In this respect, it is notable that official Iranian sources rejected claims that Iran had appealed to Hamas to aid the Huthis. See "Dar Khwast-e Tehran az Hamas Baraye Komak beh al-Huthiha Tekdhib Shod," *FarsNews*, December 1, 2009.

[11]   See "FM: Tehran Concerned about Shiites Condition in Yemen," *FarsNews*, August 27, 2009; "Iran Ready to Solve Crisis in Yemen," *FarsNews*, October 29, 2009.

[12]   See "Yemen Conflict Inflaming Saudi-Iranian Rivalry," *CBS News*, November 24, 2009.

[13]   See "Dowlat-e Iran Bayed Sazemanha-ye Mokhtallef-e Islami-ra Darbareh Havadeth-e Yaman Foʾal Konad," *FarsNews*, November 23, 2009.

[14]   See "Iran Points to Saudi Terrorism in Yemen," *UPI*, November 18, 2009; Hashem Kalantari, Fredrik Dahl, and Samia Nakhoul, "Iran Military Denounces Saudi 'Killing' in Yemen," *Reuters*, November 17, 2009.

mentioning Saudi use of proscribed munitions against Yemeni civilians, meddling among northern Yemeni tribes, Saudi/Yemeni "cooperation" with al-Qa'ida against the "al-Huthi Shi'ites," and Huthi defeats of Saudi forces.[15]

Though condoned by regime elites, these statements probably signal Iran's dissatisfaction with Saudi Arabia's power projection and influence in the region rather than suggesting Tehran's intent to intervene directly in the conflict or to confront Saudi Arabia. At least by the beginning of 2010, the Huthi conflict and Yemeni stability have not yet become a priority for Tehran, beyond being an additional element in the enduring rivalry with Saudi Arabia for regional prominence.[16] Iran and Yemen have had proper political and economic bilateral relations over the past two decades. Still, Tehran is perceived as a destabilizing force in the Gulf, and the GoY has been vociferous in its allegations of Iranian inspiration and backing to the Huthis. This motif, also espoused by Sunni Arab analysts and diplomats, resonates with Arab fear-mongering about increasing Iranian influence on Shi'a minority populations within Gulf states. Indeed, it has been suggested that Saudi Arabia's long-standing concerns in this regard partially explain its recent decision to engage Huthi fighters in combat, and to maintain a military presense in the south in the absence of a credible GoY ability to contain what is presumed to be a an Iranian-backed insurrection along their shared border.[17]

Broadly speaking, the Huthi conflict provides several opportunities to Iran that could result either in cooperation with Yemen and the Gulf or in increasing friction. First and foremost, failed mediation has left a vacuum in which another international third party may attempt to assert its role in the conflict abatement process. Here, there is an opening for Iran to increase its leverage in the Gulf by mediating and stabilizing the conflict or funding reconstruction. If executed deftly, such an initiative would be a positive and welcome gesture after the most recent ceasefire, possibly diminishing fears of a harmful Iranian spectre in northern Yemen and the Arab Gulf.

Another option for Iran is to demonstrate good behavior through transparent disengagement from the issue. Indeed, the Iranians have thus far made rhetorical reference to events in Sa'da but have largely steered away from policies directly inserting themselves into the conflict. At the same time, it is clear that security forces in the region will be highly sensitive to Iranian financial or other ties to the Huthi conflict,

---

[15] See "Artesh-e 'Arabistan az Bambha-ye Khushe'i 'alayhi Mardom-e Yaman Estefade mi-Konad," *FarsNews*, December 7, 2009; "Mobarezan–e al-Huthi Seh Dastegah-e Tank-e Artesh-e 'Arabistan-ra Monheddem Kardand," *FarsNews*, December 4, 2009; "Hamdasti-ye Niruha-ye al-Qa'ida ba Dowlat-e San'a dar Sarkub-e Shi'iyan-e al-Huthi," *FarsNews*, December 2, 2009; "'Arabistan Qabayil-o-'Ashayir-e Yaman-ra Baraye Moqabele ba Huthiha Bassij Mi-Konad," *FarsNews*, December 7, 2009; "Marhale-ye Jadid-e Hamlat-e 'Arabistan-o-Yaman beh Shi'iyan-e Huthi," *Hamshahri*, December 10, 2009.

[16] For a recent historical view of this rivalry, see F. Gregory Gause, "Gulf Regional Politics, Revolution, War, and Rivalry," in William Howard Wiggins, T. P. Lyons, and F. Gregory Gause, *Dynamics of Regional Politics: Four Systems on the Indian Ocean Rim* (New York: Columbia University Press, 1992), 23–88.

[17] See "Saudis Taking Lead in Battling Houthi Rebels."

tenuous as they might be. The delicate relations between Saudi Arabia and Iran could deteriorate rapidly if concrete evidence emerges of Tehran's relationship to the Huthis. Therefore, both constructive engagement in mediation and studious avoidance of the Huthi issue are welcome policy options. Yet, even such positive approaches will leave much suspicion of Iran, which has a well-earned reputation for involvement in the internal affairs of countries with religious groups it seeks to patronize for the sake of regional influence. Further, in the aftermath of the June 2009 Iranian elections, Tehran does not appear predisposed toward the deft diplomatic treatment of regional issues, particularly because the Ahmedinejad regime perceives these through the prism of rivalry with the United States.[18]

Ultimately, Iran's leverage in the region is highly contingent on the evolution of the Huthis as a movement. If the conflict continues and the Huthis evolve from an organism into an organization that provides social services or exhibits more standardized C3 arrangements, it may be more tempting for regional security officials to view the group as approaching the Hizbullah/Hamas model. This could intensify speculation about Iranian contacts with the group, increasing anti-Iranian and anti-Shi'a sentiment in the Gulf. In this case, the GCC states, already sensitive about sectarian activism and the presence of Shi'a within their borders, could take further actions to prevent Iran from meddling—thus legitimating such involvement in Tehran's eyes. When paired with the GoY-approved tendency of analysts to refer to the Huthis as Shi'ite rebels[19] and the increasing readiness of Iranian speakers to speak of Zaydis as "al-Huthi Shi'ites," the sectarian motif of the GoY information operations could become the dominant conceptual paradigm through which the conflict comes to be understood—not only by outsiders, but by regional protagonists themselves. This would harm prospects of conflict abatement.

Of perhaps greater immediate security concern to regional Arab states and the United States is the growing global reach of AQAP based in Yemen. As suggested above, the Huthi rebellion in Sa'da has likely distracted Yemeni forces from focusing adequate resources on counterterrorism. Notably, as the Huthi conflict heated up in later 2009, so did the operational and propaganda activity of AQAP, whose visibility has grown

---

[18] For discussion of Iran's foreign policy orientations and evolving regime dynamics, see Ray Takeyh, *Guardians of the Revolution: Iran and the World in the Age of the Ayatollahs* (New York: Oxford University Press, 2009). Also see Mohsen Milani, "Tehran's Take: Understanding Iran's U.S. Policy," *Foreign Affairs,* July/August 2009. For an examination of this issue subsequent to the June 2009 elections, see Henri Barkey, "Why America Should Play the Long Game in Iran," *The National,* August 13, 2009; Haleh Esfandiari, "Tehran's Self-Fulfilling Paranoia," *Washington Post*, August 21, 2009.

[19] For recent coverage portraying Huthis as belonging to the "Shia branch of Islam" and Zaydism as "a Yemeni branch of the Shia faith," see "Pity Those Caught in the Middle," *The Economist,* November 19, 2009; "Saudis and Yemenis Versus Jihadists: A Bloody Border," *The Economist*, November 5, 2009.

since January 2009.[20] AQAP's professed interest in Yemen lies in the exploitation of its territory for the use of safe havens, and as a launching point for attacks against Saudi Arabia and targets in the West.[21] As Yemen grapples with AQAP's growth within its borders and its appeal to extremist Saudis as a shelter, Yemen's lack of effective counterterrorism legislation to criminalize AQAP activities further increases its appeal as a Sunni jihadist safe haven. At the same time, in an effort to contain the perceived threat of the Huthis, the GoY may have clogged its judicial system with detainees related to that conflict—rather than prosecuting AQAP members.

In conjunction with the Huthi movement, the longer the southern protest/separatist issue remains unresolved and the longer AQAP persists in using and destabilizing Yemen, the greater the seeming potential for links among these ideologically disparate groups. This prospect would certainly interest regional powers assessing Yemen's ability to maintain stability within its borders. Still, links between the various anti-regime forces are unlikely at this point. Despite recent statements by AQAP in support of the southern movement, southerners would likely not consent to the imposition of Islamic law in the south.[22] Collusion between the Huthis and southerners is also unlikely because geographical separation would complicate their collaboration, and these links would legitimate GoY accusations of Huthi separatism. However, similarities between Huthi and southern grievances—particularly their roots in historical and material

---

[20] Originally a Saudi affiliate of the al-Qaʿida movement, the most recent organized manifestation of AQAP (*Al-Qaʿida fi Jazirat al-Arab*) increased its presence in Yemen after the Saudi security apparatus dealt the organization several major blows in 2004 and 2006. Elements affiliated with al-Qaʿida had access to Yemen prior to 2006, as evidenced by the 2000 bombing of the USS *Cole* and the 2002 bombing of the French oil tanker *Limburg*. However, it was not until the last several years that the group settled operationally on Yemen. Roundups executed by the Saudi Ministry of Interior harmed the movement inside the kingdom, leading to Salafi jihadis promoting Yemen as a more hospitable strategic environment for their activities in the Gulf.

[21] For example, the eighth edition of AQAP's Arabic language jihadi magazine, *Sada al-Malahim,* was released on March 22, 2009, and contained a reprinted excerpt from an Abu Musʿab al-Suri article entitled "The Responsibility of the People of Yemen Toward the Holy Sites of the Muslims." The article is part of a longer document, originally printed in 1999, that outlines the significance of Yemen as a safe haven, as well as its centrality to the overall al-Qaʿida strategy. This document points to Yemen's population density, mountainous topography, weapons availability, and the tribal proclivity toward fighting. See Abu Musʿab al-Suri, "Masʾuliya Ahl al-Yaman Tujah Muqaddasat al-Muslimin wa-Tharwatihim," *Sada al-Malahim*, AQAP, Year 2, Issue 8, 21.

[22] However, the southern protest movement's rhetoric against the government has appealed to one particular former Salafi jihadi. Shaykh Tariq al-Fadhli, originally a southerner from Abyan (a former *mujahid* turned government ally), made a high-profile statement of support to the protesters at an independence rally on April 28. Fadhli fought with Usama Bin Laden and Gulbuddin Hekmatyar in Afghanistan and then allied himself with Saleh and the GPC for over 15 years. Al-Fadhli's switch exemplifies the fluidity of political alliances on the Yemeni scene, as well as the possibility that ideologically disparate elements may come together to promote GoY's further destabilization. See Elias Harfoush, "Between Yemen's Al-Qaeda and the Separatists," *al-Hayat* English, May 17, 2009.

divides—increase the future likelihood of rhetorical references, at the very least, to the Huthis among southern dissenters speaking against the GoY.[23]

Regional observers may be more concerned about a potential Huthi-AQAP relationship. Yet AQAP has persistently demonstrated a condemnatory attitude toward the Huthis—whom they lump with the Shi'a of the Arabian peninsula. The two groups are thus highly unlikely to join forces absent major ideological changes. Therefore, although al-Qa'ida writers lambaste the Saudis for calling anti-Huthi operations *jihad* while not permitting Muslims to combat U.S. forces in Iraq, they explicitly distance their own movement from the Huthis.[24] Indeed, AQAP's ideological disposition—in addition to Saleh's use of tribal paramilitaries and Salafis during the war—heightens the possibility of further Salafi-Zaydi sectarianization of the conflict. For example, in a January 2009 interview, AQAP's Amir Abu Basir asserted that "the war of Sa'da is an extension of the expansionist Iranian strategy to restore the Persian influence in Yemen."[25] While he did not call for violence against the Huthis, he blamed the GoY for the conflict and lamented the deaths of "5,000 military and other people in Sa'da," asserting that the *Rafidites*—a perjorative Sunni term for Shi'ites—are responsible for the deaths of innocent people in the north.[26] AQAP spokespeople have continued to assert Iranian support for the Huthis as part of a plan to take over Muslim lands by using the Huthis to infiltrate and establish control over Sunni areas in Sa'da.[27] Additionally, AQAP might in the future capitalize on the religious or revenge sentiment of tribes harmed by GoY or Huthi operations in the ungoverned and contested spaces

---

[23] Fadhli demonstrates the possibility for links between the Huthi and southern movements, despite their disparate ideologies and histories. In an interview with Sharq al-Awsat, when asked about his understanding of the Huthi war, Fadhli said, "Sa'da is a holocaust for the people of the south who do not understand its cause and the meaning and dimensions and why the system continues in its war against our brothers in Sa'da, and we have issued an appeal to the parents of our soldiers and officers in the southern Yemeni to return to their areas so there should not be this holocaust." See Arafat Mudabish, "Tariq al-Fadhli li-l-Sharq al-Awsat: al-Janub Yutalib bi-Huquqihi . . . wa Ana Musta'idd li-l-muhakama bi-Tahammat al-Irhab," *al-Sharq al-Awsat,* May 14, 2009.

[24] See Abi Yahya al-Libi, "Lasna Huthiyin: La Tadi' al-Jidh' wa Tubsir al-Qidha," *Markaz al-Fajr li-l-I'lam,* January 2010.

[25] Wuhayshi's full answer is the following: "The war of Sa'da is an extension of the expansionist Iranian strategy to restore the Persian influence in Yemen. It is an attempt to restore their kingdom and empire, which was defeated by the *mujahidin* at the time of Caliph 'Umar Ibn-al-Khattab, may God be pleased with him. This is why they hate and curse him . . . We are aware of the dangerous situation there. We are astonished at some people who claim to be scholars and preachers how they provide a political and media cover, through their party blocs, to justify the shedding of blood in Sa'da and other areas." See Abd al-Ilah Haydar Sha'i', "Akhbarani Abu Basir Annahu Qara'a Maqalati Awwal ma Kharaja min al-Sijin . . . wa Sa'id al-Shihri Sharaha li Hizamihi al-Nasifa," May 14, 2009; Abd al-Ilah Haydir Sha'i', "Abu Basir: Nansir Ghaza bi-Darb al-Masalih al-Gharbiya bi-l-Mintaqa," *al-Jazeera,* January 26, 2009.

[26] "Abu Basir: Nansir Ghaza bi-Darb al-Masalih al-Gharbiya bi-l-Mintaqa."

[27] See "al-Qa'ida Tattahimm Iran bi-Da'm al-Huthiyin li-l-Qada' 'ala Ahl al-Sunna," *MarebPress,* November 10, 2009; also see Abu al-Bara' al-San'ani, "al-Huthiyun Rawafid bi-Qana' Zaydi," *Sada al-Malahim,* Year 3, Issue 12, February 15, 2010.

of the north. Some journalists do imply that that AQAP wants to capitalize on both Huthi and southern grievances, but the Yemeni government minimizes the idea of this threat. Still, official GoY pronouncements tar the Huthis with the AQAP brush, at the same time delegitimating AQAP by speaking of "limited" AQAP efforts to link up with the Huthis.[28]

The Huthi Conflict and U.S. Interests

From one perspective, the Huthi conflict may appear less significant than other U.S. concerns regarding Yemen and region. The Huthis are not a transnational terrorist organization. They do not seek to agitate other regional countries' ethnic or religious minorities, and their linkages with other regional states or extremist groups have not been demonstrated. Further, in spite of anti-U.S. rhetoric, Huthi fighters have not yet targeted U.S. assets, and they share with the United States some of the same enemies in the region, such as intolerant expansionist Wahhabism and authoritarian state systems. In short, the Huthis are not AQAP, which does exhibit these characteristics, has targeted the American homeland, and has dominated the agenda of U.S.-Yemeni security cooperation since December 2009.

All the same, by 2010, the Huthi conflict had become the most physically destructive, militarily preoccupying, and economically draining threat confronted by San'a, also influencing domestic political alignments among Yemen's elites. Therefore, the Huthi conflict concerns the United States because of what it might do to the Yemeni state and its external relationships as the GoY seeks to deal with Sa'da. A Yemeni state stymied by Zaydi revivalists in asserting sovereign authority is unlikely to liberalize—though stalled liberalization has inhibited the sociopolitical integration of post-1994 Yemen. Further, a GoY locked in a struggle with the Huthis will likely respond uncooperatively to foreign interest in its domestic affairs or security policies. Of course, while the GoY will likely reject U.S. suggestions of moderation on the Huthi issue, the conflict's absorption of GoY attention will make the regime less capable of fully grasping and countering its other domestic threats, al-Qa'ida in particular—a clear concern for the United States.

At base, then, GoY focus on the Huthis lessens Yemen's ability to be a partner in confronting transnational terrorism. Furthermore, preoccupation with the Huthi conflict degrades capabilities and resources on a range of broader U.S. concerns, from piracy in the Gulf of Aden and the Arabian Sea to weapons proliferation in the Horn of Africa. In these cases, the Huthi conflict diminishes the returns on the post-2001 U.S. investment in Yemen's security forces.

The continuing Huthi conflict has other negative implications for U.S. interests. While Yemen might be a new U.S. partner in the region since 2001, Saudi Arabia has been a long-standing ally with whom the United States has a substantial secu-

---

[28] "YFM: Al-Qaeda's Elements in Yemen are Limited," *Yemen Post*, July 29, 2009.

rity relationship. The kingdom's entanglement in military operations on its southern border represents an unneeded escalation and geographical expansion of the conflict, regionalizing it both in fact and in the calculations of observers. More fundamentally, Saudi involvement may distract Riyadh—and thus Washington—from more important, enduring security issues in the region. Indeed, as Saudi Arabia and other countries learned in the 1960s, getting into a conflict in northern Yemen is much quicker and easier than getting out of one, and neither Saudi Arabia nor the United States can afford a drain on Riyadh's resources. Further, if the current regime-periphery conflict in northern Yemen cannot be solved militarily, it is of concern that Saudi involvement may render the kingdom a poor choice as a conflict mediator in the future.

On a broader regional level, if sustained warfare is renewed after the latest ceasefire and Yemen returns to accusing Iran of involvement, the latter might find it difficult to restrain itself solely to rhetoric as it responds to violence and Saudi intervention. However Iranian interest and regional aspirations express themselves, Iranian-Arab tension in southern Arabia and at the gateway to the Horn of Africa does not benefit the United States. Likewise, in order to sustain military operations, the GoY may pursue military aid relationships with countries the United States would want to keep out of the region—such as China or Russia. These governments may be willing to provide Yemen with weapons and other support on political terms preferable to ones the United States would offer. Thus, to deal with the Huthi threat, Saleh or his successor could choose partners unattractive to the United States.[29]

Additional problems may also attend a continuing GoY-Huthi conflict. As we have seen, Salafi elements in Yemen's government, military, and religious establishment have been interested parties to the conflict. Some, such as 'Ali Muhsin al-Ahmar, have been advocates of strong measures and military solutions. Others, among them *'ulama'* within and outside of the state apparatus, have legitimated the shedding of Yemeni blood through their *fatwas*. Additionally, the regime itself has cultivated Salafi-leaning elements, either as ideological defenders of the GoY approach or as volunteer fighters. This is not a positive development for the United States. It increases the influence of those who, unlike the Huthis, go beyond rhetoric in their anti-U.S. vehemence. Likewise, at a practical level, it may decrease U.S. influence in San'a as well as the quality of U.S.-Yemeni collaboration on a variety issues, from domestic security to regional cooperation. Even a Yemeni leader well-disposed to U.S. interests might be forced into obduracy by the need to preserve domestic political alliances as he conducts yet another anti-Huthi campaign.

Further, regardless of Yemeni or broader pan-Arab attitudes toward Zaydi revivalism and the Huthis, the image of a U.S.-supported authoritarian government killing its own citizens, destroying sacred Muslim sites, and violating traditional mores does great damage to America's standing. In this sense, the GoY anti-Huthi campaign presents a

---

[29] See "Yemen to Buy Russian Weapons," *New York Times,* December 7, 2008.

public diplomacy and strategic communications challenge for the United States itself. For example, just as Arabs saw images on television and the Internet of U.S.-supplied Israeli Apache helicopters firing on Palestinians, they have also encountered U.S.-supplied HMMWVs and APCs being destroyed by Huthi fighters. Therefore, while Saleh is vulnerable to Huthi (and Salafi) accusations of having become a U.S. lackey after 2001, the image of the United States might suffer among regional populations from the U.S. association with Saleh, particulary if the conflict continues unabated. Worrisome in this regard are recent Yemeni reports of high-profle U.S. visits to San'a and alleged U.S. statements of support for Yemen in its Huthi campaign.[30] A similar concern attends continued Saudi involvement in the fighting, since the kingdom is a U.S.-identified regional power employing American weapons in the conflict.[31]

Finally, the Huthi conflict is of concern to U.S. policy planners on a conceptual level. We have suggested that one of the reasons the GoY chose violent conflict in 2004 rather than cooptation or other neopatrimonial approaches was Saleh's estimate of his capabilities in light of U.S. support. If this is true, it suggests a conceptual dilemma attending foreign security aid and the building of partnership capacity. In this case, the United States chose to provide military aid and security capability enhancement to a weak country characterized by contested political cohesion. It did this to strengthen that state's internal security so that it could assist the United States in furthering American regional interests. Yet GoY elites prioritized their security concerns differently from the view of the United States, considering Sunni jihadist terrorism to be a less pressing threat than other matters. Against this backdrop of different priorities, U.S. support enabled certain calculations by regime elites about their capability to rearrange center-periphery relations and deal more aggressively with certain forms of domestic opposition. The actions resulting from these calculations have made the country less stable domestically, thus degrading it as a security partner. This chain of events suggests the need to carefully inform diplomatic and security assistance to other countries with a well-grounded assessment of how that aid may influence local leaders' perceptions of evolving threats and opportunities—and how those perceptions could enable policies and measures that are potentially inimical to U.S. interests.

---

[30] See "Ra'is al-Jumhuriya Yastaqbal Qa'id al-Qiyada al-'Askariya al-Amrikiya al-Markaziya: Bahatha ma'ahu al-Ta'awun al-'Askari wa Mukafahat al-Irhab," *26 September*, July 26, 2009; "Petraeus: US will Support Yemen anti-Terror Fight," Embassy of the Republic of Yemen Media Office Web site, July 27, 2009; Mohammed al-Kibsi, "US Supports Yemen's Security and Stability: McCain," *Yemen Observer*, August 17, 2009; "GCC and US Support Yemen's Unity and Stability," *Yemen Post*, September 27, 2009; "US Offers Yemen Help in 'Fight Against Terrorism,'" *al-Arabiya*, September 7, 2009.

[31] Saudi Arabia has reportedly employed U.S.-provided F-5 and F-15 aircraft to bomb Huthi targets—allegedly in Yemen—while some Saudi weapons captured by Huthis are of U.S. origin. See "Saudi Arabia: Satisfaction with the F-5 Performance," *Tactical Report*, December 4, 2009; for video of what appears to be an F-15 hitting Huthi targets, see "Al-Quwwat al-Jawwiya al-Su'udiya Taqsif Mawaqi' al-Huthiyin Jabal Dukhan," November 6, 2009; "Al-Quwwat al-Jawwiya al-Su'udiya wa Qasfuha l-Mawaqi' al-Huthiyin," November 11, 2009.

Factors in Future Conflict Trajectories

From 2004 onward, the main parameters and drivers of GoY-Huthi conflict have remained constant. Likewise, the protagonists' narratives have persisted intact. Huthi sources portray their activities as defensive, while insisting on their legitimate right to protect themselves, their families, and their areas and describing the thrust of their movement as cultural and religious. The GoY asserts that its operations are in defense of Yemen's sovereignty, law, and constitution, and the right of the government to exercise authority in all its territory as it seeks to protect innocent citizens. While President Saleh has vowed to crush northern resistance and has affirmed that he is ready to fight on for five or six more years, he and his spokesmen have also indicated a preference for peace and tranquility in the north.[32]

Still, the sixth phase of fighting and its immediate aftermath introduced some new factors. These include Saudi involvement, Iranian rhetorical attention, and the need for the GoY to demonstrate to the international community that it was taking serious and sustained measures to combat AQAP and reform its political-economic system. As such, the challenges San'a faces in its local conflict with the Huthis now interact more dynamically than before with national, regional, and global concerns. Therefore, although the details of the just-ended phase of conflict remain murky, it is important to ponder conflict evolution scenarios—not to predict the future, but to suggest developments to track.

Smoldering Violence and GoY-Benefiting Chaos

One possible future trajectory involves a level of smoldering violence, contained in Sa'da and the parts of 'Amran that have seen conflict up until now. After a sixth phase of GoY operations lasting six months or less, the region would see rumbling conflict at levels that we have characterized above as "interim." As seen subsequent to earlier ceasefires, this kind of scenario would prevent unfettered regime access to the region, absorb significant military attention, and result in a progressive destruction of the local means of existence. It could also diminish GoY enthusiasm for reconstruction, decrease residual confidence in the state among locals, and result in numbers of IDPs remaining displaced for longer periods of time. The GoY may perceive this situation as tolerable, as long as losses of materiel and deaths of GoY personnel remain below a certain threshold and allow it to demonstrate adequate focus on Sunni jihadism to outside observers. In the context of persistent Huthi recalcitrance, the GoY could plausibly appeal for regional support as it counters a local "Shi'a-inspired" threat and justify military operations that run contrary to the spirit of the February ceasefire. With increased U.S. economic and military aid, the GoY may over time come to feel newly empowered in such

---

[32] See "al-Ra'is Saleh: Lan Nataraji' Law Istamarrat al-Ma'raka fi Sa'da Khams aw Sitt Sanawat," *al-Mu'tammar.net*, September 28, 2009; Hakim al-Masmari, "President Saleh Losing," *Yemen Post*, September 27, 2009.

a course of action. Likewise, the GoY would likely continue to cultivate alliances with local tribal leaders, based on traditionally divisive and cooptative policies designed to exploit local opportunism. Finally, as Saleh prepares to transition rule to his son at a time when his tribal allies have shifted, persistent Huthi insurrection could provide an element of unity. This could be called "smoldering violence and GoY-benefiting chaos."

Huthi Persistence and GoY Capacity Exhaustion

Less-positive trajectories also exist. In one such scenario, GoY operations remain kinetic in focus though imprecise in execution. Seemingly indiscriminate and vindictive violence by the GoY would not be able to counter the core drivers of conflict related to identity assertion, material neglect, and an occluded political space. In this case, what we have referred to as GoY COIN could influence the evolution of the Huthi organism in the direction of insurgency. At the least, GoY actions would likely widen the geographic and social base of opposition to the regime, perhaps resulting in heretofore uninvolved groups supporting or condoning the Huthis, particularly as yet another ceasefire would have proven disappointing. These groups could include nominal Zaydis or even Shafi'is in conflict areas repelled by the regime's use of Salafi elements. In such a context, Huthi fighters are likely to acquire more sophisticated weapons and coordination capabilities, maturing into a self-sustaining organization with some transnational legitimacy. Continued Saudi involvement will also provide Huthi fighters with opportunities to acquire better weapons, at the same time permitting Huthi spokespeople to portray the movement as defending Yemeni sovereignty against foreign, Wahhabi-inspired invasion.

Conversely, a progressively contracting Yemeni economy—as oil prices falter and domestic oil production slows—would reduce the coercive and cooptative resources at the GoY's disposal. Foreign sponsors could then focus more on San'a's stalled democratization, economic mismanagement, disregard for human rights, and lackluster efforts against extremist Salafism. External powers might then push the GoY to accept more international mediation with more equitable terms—that is, less advantageous to the Yemeni regime. This may all negatively influence the internal cohesion of the GoY, as Saleh may be less able to practice neopatrimonial *mahsubiya* with fewer resources. Combined with lingering southern discontent and al-Qa'ida threats, this conjuncture of events would cast a new light on the Huthi insurrection and materially threaten the long-term viability of the Saleh regime, particularly if elements of the broader opposition (excluding al-Qa'ida) combine to remake the Yemeni political space. This scenario may be considered "Huthi persistence as a factor in GoY capacity exhaustion."

2007 All Over Again

A sustained offensive in the north reminiscent of the long fourth phase of 2007·is also possible, particularly if senior GoY leaders view the current ceasefire as a tactical move to gain a short breathing space for a move against AQAP while showing the international community good faith. This negative development would include renewed pressure on urban areas, perhaps to include mechanized assaults into cities and large towns and intensified aerial bombardments that might become sustained attacks with multiple aircraft. A Yemeni offensive demonstrating lessons learned from previous rounds of fighting would seek to avoid entanglement in small-scale yet continuous Huthi attacks on GoY units and instead would concentrate on major thrusts reminiscent of Falluja, attempting to get boots on the ground in outlying areas such as Naqʻa. Conflict in this case would likely spread to Jawf further into ʻAmran, and perhaps would result in terror attacks in the capital itself—because such an offensive would surely be accompanied by renewed arrest campaigns provoking revenge. In this case of "2007 all over again," a GoY campaign would last at least as long as the sixth phase of fighting.

In spite of increased military aid coming from Western countries, however, successful prosecution of "2007 all over again" would likely exceed the capabilities of the GoY military at the tactical, operational, and logistical levels—unless the regime deploys its Republican Guard and SOF in a sustained fashion, permitting them control of the campaign. This would have implications for regime security in confronting other threats and might alienate the regular army leadership. Thus, it is possible that the regime would get far enough into a shooting war to recognize that it had gone too far. But a slowdown reminiscent of 2007 would be quite costly. A "nonvictory" after a major campaign could jeopardize GoY cohesion, threaten the sustained political reliability of the army, and run the risk of alienating local pro-GoY elements. These elements may then turn to Huthis, providing them with a larger base of passive support, as well as fresh fighters, weapons, funds, and safe movement areas—a de facto Huthistan made of a patchwork quilt of "liberated" territory.[33] In this case, "2007 all over again" could roll into "GoY capacity exhaustion," particularly if it is accompanied by AQAP recrudescence and an empowered southern opposition. At that point, the Saudi government would have to determine the best way to secure its southern border and prevent other regional countries' encroachment in the area. Given the experiences of winter 2009–2010, a greater introduction of military force in the Yemeni-Saudi border region may be irresistible.

In such a context, the Huthis may, over time, convincingly portray GoY actions as oppressing all northern Yemenis who seek to live in peace, and they may successfully cast the Saudi presence as an affront to Yemeni sovereignty that the GoY is unable to answer. While diluting the sharpness of their cause, this portrayal could widen the Huthi base, permitting Huthi propagandists to appeal for outside support as a tyrannized ethnoregional minority. Additionally, more conflict, with greater Yemeni and Saudi military presence, would likely result in more heavy weapons coming into Huthi

---

[33] At the end of the first week of October 2009, the Huthist Web site *al-Menpar.net* claimed that the GoY had been ejected from the Munabbih district of Saʻda by locals sympathetic to the Huthis and opposed to government repression. Allegedly, Huthi leaders later took full control of the area. See "ʻAjil: al-Huthiyun Yuʻlinun al-Saytara al-Tamma ʻala Mudiriyat Munabbih al-Muhadda li-l-Suʻudiya," *al-Menpar.net*, October 7, 2009.

hands. And ongoing high-intensity conflict would retard development of a Huthi social welfare plank or a political wing inclined to in-system participation.

Thus, how this scenario unfolds will influence the way the Huthi entity moves from organism to organization. Transformation into a separatist movement seeking to secede from the Republic of Yemen would seem quite unlikely, given its potential to alienate local Zaydis or citizens from other regions—and because it runs against consistent Huthi ideological pronouncements. By contrast, aggravated conflict and greater kinetic capability may transform the Huthis into an insurgency, both organizationally and in terms of goals. Likewise, if the Huthi cause begins to be considered more of the cause of northern Yemenis as a whole, the Huthi leadership might posses the legitimacy and justification to reach out to other regional (Shi'ite) actors for support—though likely in not as acknowledged a fashion as was the case for Hizbullah in the 1980s–1990s. As suggested above, the latest round of fighting, featuring Saudi involvement and Iranian rhetorical condemnation of Saudi-Yemeni actions, points to a transnationalization and an increased sectarianization of the conflict. These developments, too, are contrary to the interests of the United States and its friends in the region. If allowed to continue, transnationalization and sectarianization of the Huthi conflict could be accompanied by an "*umma*-tization," whereby more Islamist groups in the Muslim world begin to take interest, evaluating both the GoY and their own regimes according to stances taken on the conflict. Hints of this development have begun to emerge in Egypt, Iraq, Lebanon, Bahrain, and Turkey, although the sociopolitical resonance of individual Islamist groups' statements is likely limited at present.[34]

More Carrots Than Sticks

Finally, the GoY and Huthi opposition could pursue a more positive course of "more carrots than sticks." For its part, the GoY could prioritize economic reconstruction in areas permitting it, thus earning credibility among elements of the population in regions under Huthi sway. In this scenario, the GoY would also permit the political and economic enfranchisement of those Huthist elements that demonstrate a willingness to transition into political advocacy. This could occur through traditional *mah-*

---

[34] See "Egypt Brotherhood Calls on Government, Rebels to Stop Fighting," *IkhwanWeb*, September 30, 2009. This is the Muslim Brotherhood's official English Web site. Also see "Sadrists do Not Back Houthis—MP," *Aswat al-Iraq*, September 12, 2009; and the *26 September* coverage of the Saudi cleric shaykh 'Ayidh al-Qurni's sermon on Yemeni unity: "al-Shaykh 'Ayidh al-Qurni Yad'u al-Muslimin ila al-Akhdh bi-Wahdat al-Yaman Tariqan ila Wahdatihim wa I'tilafihim," *26 September*, October 16, 2009. For comments by Hassan Nasrallah, General Secretary of Hizbullah, see "Da'a li-Taqarub Su'udi Irani . . . Nasrallah: Nahnu bi-Hajja li-Itfa'i Mukhlis fi Shamal al-Yaman," *Mareb Press*, November 12, 2009. For Bahrain, see "al-Huthi Yuqassim Barlaman al-Bahrayn," *Mareb Press*, November 11, 2009. For reference to Turkish protests outside the Yemeni Embassyi in Ankara against "massacres of Yemenis" by Saudi and Yemeni forces, see "Yemen Katliamlarına Büyük Tepki," *Velfecr*, November 23, 2009. *Velfecr*, associated with the Web site *Kudusyolu* and with possible links to the Islamist Anatolia Youth Organization (Anadolu Genç Derneği), is beyond mainstream Islam-inspired politics in Turkey. We thank Yurter Özcan and Soner Çağaptay of the Washington Institute for Near East Policy for insights on these and other Turkish Islamist groupings.

subiya or through negotiated inclusion into positions of local political and economic power, in effect bringing these Huthis into the Yemeni system while allowing them to retain their oppositionist identity. Such an approach would also garner regional support, likely improving Yemen's chances for accession to or association with the GCC. High-profile mediation would be less necessary, because local measures would diminish the impetus for large-scale insurrection. At the same time, if it permitted international mediation and monitoring by states or personalities not perceived as impartial by both sides, the GoY would be more likely to obtain foreign funding to implement reconstruction from both regional actors and global sponsors.

Such a development would be welcome and is suited to the post–February 2010 ceasefire climate. Yet, it would also require the regime to take the first steps toward conflict abatement. Still, the viability of "more carrots than sticks" would hinge upon certain indicators on the part of the Huthis. Statements by Huthi leaders conditionally condoning participation in the political process, or legitimating their followers' participation in GoY-sponsored reconstruction, would be important. Additionally, Huthi efforts to "outprovide" on the reconstruction and social welfare front, though seemingly an irritant to the GoY, would indicate a new emphasis for the movement. The regime itself, as well as outside partners, could cultivate this development. Of course, the durability of a "more carrots than sticks" initiative would be contingent on the Huthi leadership's exercising greater levels of control over its local area leaders, to the extent of firmly establishing a movement with organizational cohesion and operational discipline. Likewise, the GoY would have to ensure its own internal cohesion—between the army and civilians and between those with greater or lesser attachment to Salafism. This last issue, of internal cohesion among protagonists, could be the greatest impediment to a more positive scenario for the regime-periphery conflict in northern Yemen.[35]

---

[35] For discussion of Iran's foreign policy orientations and evolving regime dynamics, see Ray Takeyh, *Guardians of the Revolution: Iran and the World in the Age of the Ayatollahs* (New York: Oxford University Press, 2009). Also see Mohsen Milani, "Tehran's Take: Understanding Iran's U.S. Policy," *Foreign Affairs*, July/August 2009. For an examination of this issue subsequent to the June 2009 elections, see Henri Barkey, "Why America Should Play the Long Game in Iran," *The National*, August 13, 2009; Haleh Esfandiari, "Tehran's Self-Fulfilling Paranoia," *Washington Post*, August 21, 2009.

Population Characteristics of Sa'da Governorate

On the following pages, we reproduce population statistics from the 2004 Yemen Census.

Table A.1
Estimated Population of Yemen Governorates, by Age Groups and Gender

	Males 0–4	Males 5–15	Males 16–44	Males 45–59	Males 60+	Females 0–4	Females 5–15	Females 16–44	Females 45–59	Females 60+	Total Male Population	Total Female Population	Total Population
Abyan	42,951	67,314	86,383	15,649	8,870	39,677	62,483	84,375	16,837	9,196	221,220	212,561	433,787
Aden	60,855	95,359	122,307	22,190	12,623	51,488	81,039	109,368	21,777	11,981	313,334	275,610	588,934
Al Bayda	56,776	88,987	114,129	20,690	11,752	53,235	83,810	113,118	22,535	12,385	292,364	285,040	577,345
Al Dhale'e	46,808	73,345	94,088	17,014	9,634	42,786	67,449	91,012	18,082	9,903	241,103	229,369	470,512
Al Hudaydah	215,401	337,570	433,086	78,457	44,555	195,798	308,209	415,986	82,788	45,465	1,109,264	1,048,257	2,160,677
Al Jawf	24,382	87,457	109,768	16,579	6,458	27,420	70,984	90,520	13,337	3,047	241,101	202,648	450,030
Al Maharah	9,346	14,636	18,779	3,392	1,937	7,567	11,914	16,069	3,198	1,761	48,109	40,488	88,587
Al Mahwit	48,213	75,611	96,990	17,487	9,859	45,927	72,342	97,702	19,433	10,615	248,331	246,132	494,542
Amanat Al 'Asimah	171,259	268,380	344,299	62,438	35,535	134,009	210,901	284,646	56,674	31,172	881,979	717,354	1,599,321
'Amran	77,456	148,362	179,525	27,225	22,556	74,020	132,649	174,154	29,501	19,727	451,374	426,364	885,601
Dhamar	128,421	201,145	258,014	46,343	26,147	125,033	196,900	265,883	52,835	28,745	660,684	669,624	1,330,088
Hadramaut	102,957	161,345	207,005	37,475	21,237	93,034	146,476	197,759	39,385	21,567	530,151	498,308	1,028,632
Hajjah	149,708	234,679	301,070	54,404	30,765	132,237	208,282	281,194	56,046	30,541	771,099	708,391	1,479,443
Ibb	202,880	317,832	407,707	73,678	41,672	203,013	319,644	431,717	85,968	46,979	1,044,308	1,087,393	2,131,752
Lahj	70,101	109,869	140,933	25,471	14,459	67,494	106,305	143,582	28,599	15,688	360,981	361,662	722,582
Marib	17,297	42,277	55,864	7,478	4,402	16,769	37,167	46,660	7,015	3,444	127,386	111,119	238,503
Raymah	37,501	58,743	75,366	13,493	7,634	37,515	59,248	79,998	15,914	8,635	192,990	201,370	394,439
Sa'da	57,669	114,422	146,095	23,821	17,545	57,061	106,542	133,309	22,854	15,543	359,530	335,322	695,091
San'a	90,897	142,406	182,678	33,030	18,750	84,291	132,675	179,099	35,677	19,535	467,848	451,335	919,236
Shabwah	36,230	80,346	100,155	14,582	11,805	34,992	71,534	93,804	15,541	11,350	243,107	227,270	470,426
Taizz	223,381	350,231	449,115	80,887	45,783	232,104	365,530	493,411	98,095	53,657	1,150,242	1,243,170	2,393,325
Total	1,870,489	3,070,316	3,923,356	691,783	403,978	1,755,470	2,852,083	3,823,366	742,091	410,936	9,956,505	9,578,787	19,552,853

SOURCE: 2004 Yemen Census, 2007.

NOTE: Shaded cells indicate male populations between 16 and 44 years old in areas of most continuous Huthi-GoY fighting.

Table A.2
Population and Size of Sa'da Districts, and Population Densities Across Sa'da Governorate

District	Population	Percentage of Sa'da Population	Size of District (km^2)	Persons per km^2
Sahar	133,056	19.0	742.05	179
Majz	68,603	10.0	922.08	74
Razih	62,895	9.0	232.05	271
Haydan	60,329	8.6	568.51	106
Sa'da	58,692	8.4	27.13	2,163
Saqayn	52,523	7.6	533.78	98
Munabbih	51,843	7.5	439.28	118
al-Safra	50,848	7.3	1607.00	32
Kitaf wa al-Buq'a	43,028	6.0	5190.53	8
Baqim	22,976	3.3	1,072.06	21
Qatabir	22,660	3.0	192.75	118
al-Dhahir	22,438	3.0	209.09	107
Ghamr	19,721	2.8	135.12	146
al-Hashwa	14,281	2.0	427.01	33
Shada'a	11,287	1.6	67.98	166

Size of Sa'da Governorate: 12,366.42 km^2
Persons per km^2 over governorate: 56
Sa'da population density rank: 15 (out of 21 governorates)
Average number of persons per km^2 in Yemen: 334

Zaydism: Overview and Comparison to Other Versions of Shi'ism

Zaydism emerged in the 8th century among those early Muslims who felt that 'Ali should have followed the Prophet Muhammad as his first successor (caliph) in the spiritual and temporal leadership of Muslims. While Abu Bakr had become the first caliph in 632 CE, the partisans of 'Ali (*shi'at 'Ali*; hence Shi'a) felt that the latter's claim was more legitimate because of his reputed nomination by Muhammad and his family ties to the Prophet ('Ali was Muhammad's cousin and son-in-law). While Sunnis (or *ahl al-sunna*, meaning people of accepted tradition) recognized Abu Bakr and his successors as legitimate, partisans of 'Ali considered only those from the family of the Prophet, in the form of 'Ali's male descendants, to be worthy of rule. These male descendents became Imams, one in each generation—though on a few occasions, disagreement emerged over which descendent of 'Ali was to be considered Imam. This explains the emergence of Zaydism.

Zayd bin 'Ali, a grandson of 'Ali's son Husayn, was killed leading an unsuccessful rebellion against the Umayyads in 740. Whereas most Shi'ites regarded his brother, Muhammad al-Baqir, as the fifth Imam, some regarded Zayd as the fifth Imam. They became known as "Fivers" or Zaydis. Zaydism as a doctrine has emphasized philosophy and rationalism rather than textual literalism.[1] In practice, the later Zaydi Imamates demonstrated tolerance for Shafi'ism, the dominant Sunni school of thought in Yemen that is said to make up slightly over half the population.

Zaydi Political History in Yemen Up to 1962

Zaydi states have existed historically in two places, northern Iran and northwest Yemen. After several failed rebellions in Kufa, Hasan ibn Zayd founded a Zaydi state in historical Tabaristan, northern Iran, in 864. The Zaydis of Iran moved progressively

---

[1]   See Moojan Momen, *An Introduction to Shi'i Islam* (New Haven: Yale University Press, 1987). It is said that Zayd studied under Wasir Ibn 'Ata, the alleged founder of the *Mu'tazila*. The *Mu'tazila* are a rationalist theological school of Sunni thought with many parallels to *Shi'a* thought.

north, converting subjects in Daylam and Gilan. Zaydi communities remained near the Caspian Sea until their forced conversion in the 16th century to what is today the dominant form of Shi'ism ("Twelver" Shi'ism; see below) under the Safavid Empire.

The first Zaydi state in Yemen was established in 893 by Yahya bin al-Husayn (d. 911), who had originally been invited to Yemen to mediate between quarreling tribes. A Hijazi *sayyid* and scholar, he adopted the title al Hadi ila al-Haqq ("The Guide to the Truth") when he became political ruler of the Yemeni highlands and northern areas. Al-Hadi's theology (al-Hadawiya) forms the basis of the Zaydi *madhhab* in north Yemen,[2] the central tenet of which is that the spiritual leader of the Muslims should be a sayyid, a descendent of the Prophet through the lineage of 'Ali and Fatima. That spiritual leader—known as the Imam—should also be the leader of the state. Al-Hadi thus founded the first Zaydi Imamate in Yemen. Notably, his respect for *'urf* (tribal customary law) and use of tribal mediation practices facilitated a religiocultural melding between Hadawis and the tribes of the highlands, which persists to this day.[3]

Zaydi territorial claims beyond the northwest of Yemen, and various Imams' dominance over the tribes, ebbed and flowed as a number of al-Hadi's successors ruled from Sa'da city for the next seven centuries. These imams confronted internal sectarian strife and various opposing local dynasties in the south but eventually succeeded in Islamizing, though not subduing, the tribes under their domain. The first Ottoman invasion in the 16th century led to the rise of the Zaydi Imam Qasim the Great (r. 1597–1620), progenitor of the Qasimi hereditary dynasty. With the exception of a brief collapse and Ottoman interference in the late 19th century, the Qasimi and subsequent Hamid al-Din dynasties ruled more or less continuously from the mid-17th century until the republican revolution in 1962.[4] It should be noted that most scholars consider the Qasimi and Hamid al-Din dynastic periods legitimate "imamates," as the imams insisted that Hadawi law be applied to the regions under their aegis. However, a shift to dynastic, hereditary rule under the Qasimis no longer ensured that rulers had the merit-based qualifications necessary to be imams. These imamates abandoned some essential doctrines of Zaydi thought in favor of patronizing Sunni-oriented elites who would promote submission to their authority.

---

[2] The term *madhhab* refers to an Islamic school of thought or religious jurisprudence. While it is generally agreed that they do not constitute separate sects, the four Sunni *madhhabs* differ with respect to specific judgments and preferences for jurisprudential methods, stemming from the approaches of their originating scholars.

[3] Ira Lapidus, *A History of Islamic Societies*, 2nd ed. (Cambridge: Cambridge University Press, 2002), 53, 178, 565–572.

[4] See Bernard Haykel, "Rebellion, Migration or Consultative Democracy? Zaydis and their Detractors in Yemen," in Remy Leveau, Franck Mermier, and Udo Steinbach, eds., *Le Yemen Contemporain* (Paris: Editions Karthala, 1999), 194; Bernard Haykel, *Revival and Reform in Islam: The Legacy of Muhammad al-Shawkani* (Cambridge: Cambridge University Press, 2003).

Theology

At its core, Zaydi-Hadawi theology differs from other branches of Shi'ism regarding who is qualified to rule as imam and how the imamate may be established. Zaydis accept the Shi'a consensus that 'Ali, Hasan, and Husayn were the first three rightful imams. Most Zaydis are less vehement than other Shi'ites in their condemnation of the early Sunni caliphs, believing that while the latter were erroneous in their rejection of 'Ali, they were not essentially sinful. This belief permits tolerance of other interpretations of Islam, which are perceived as misguided rather than heretical in essence. Additionally, Zaydism does not consider imams after 'Ali, Hasan, and Husayn exempt from sin (infallible; *ma'sum*), as do the other Shi'ite traditions.

The Zaydi-Hadawi doctrine stipulates that the spiritual leader of the Muslim community should also be supreme ruler (*imam*) of the Muslim state, emphasizing the importance of an imam's scholarly credentials and descent. After the first three imams, Zaydis believe that the imamate is open to any learned and pious descendant (*sayyid*) who asserts his claim to the imamate publicly through *khuruj* (rebellion or uprising). In the case of an unjust ruler or a period of political transition, a qualified *sayyid* interested in a rebellion could publicly issue a call (*da'wa*) to allegiance and then had to win the support of the religious aristocracy made up of *sayyids* and *fuqaha'* (legal scholars), who are known as "the people who loosen and bind" (*ahl al-hall wa al-'aqd*).[5] Succession was theoretically based on acquired characteristics rather than birthright. To be eligible, an imam had to had to be "whole in mind and body, capable of leading the jihad or 'holy war' in person, and, by most readings, had to be a *mujtahid*—that is, capable of forming new law by extrapolation from scripture."[6] It is important to stress, however, that the imam was, of necessity, a *sayyid*, and all Zaydi imams have come from the *sayyid* social stratum. Yet, this is a broader pool than in other versions of Shi'ism. Additionally, Zaydism theologically reconciled itself to pragmatic politics through its doctrine that "the rule of the less preferred [but still qualified] [is accepted] over the rule of the preferred [but unavailable]."[7]

---

5   Shelagh Weir, *A Tribal Order: Politics and Law in the Mountains of Yemen* (Austin: University of Texas Press, 2007), 231.

6   Paul Dresch, *Tribes, Government, and History in Yemen* (New York: Oxford University Press, 1989), 161.

7   Translated as "hukm al-mafdul ma'a 'adam al-afdal," "hukm al-mafdul ma'a 'adam al-fadil," "taqdim al-mafdul 'ala al-fadil," and other variants. For more on this, see Muhammad Abu Zahrah, *al-Imam Zayd: Hayatuhu wa 'Asruhu Ara'uhu wa Fiquhu* (Cairo: Dar al-Fikr al-'Arabi, 1959); Muhsin Amin, *al-Shahid Zayd ibn 'Ali wa-l-Zaydiya* (Beirut, Dar Murtada, 2003); Naji Hassan, *Thawrat Zayd ibn 'Ali* (Beirut: al-Dar al-'Arabiya li-l-Mawsu'at, 2000). A late 18th century study recently edited and republished is Ahmad ibn Ahmad Sayyaghi, *al-Manhaj al-Munir Tatimmat al-Rawd al-Nadir*, ed. 'Abdullah ibn Hamud ibn Dirham al-'Izzi (San'a: Mu'assasat al-Imam Zayd ibn 'Ali al-Thaqafiya, 2005); for writings on this and other Zaydi issues by the early 17th century Zaydi ruler of Yemen, see *Majmu' Kutub wa Rasa'il al-Imam al-Mansur billah al-Qasim ibn Muhammad ibn 'Ali*, ed. 'Abd al-Salam 'Abbas al-Wajih (San'a: Mu'assasat al-Imam Zayd ibn 'Ali al-Thaqafiya, 2003). These are in addition to the works edited by Muhammad 'Izzan discussed in Chapter Three.

The Jarudi branch of Zaydism is a notable exception with respect to its views on the imamate. Jarudis constitute the earliest group of one of the three branches of Zaydism who were followers of Abu Jarud bin al-Mundhir al-'Abdi. They vehemently reject Abu Bakr and 'Umar for not recognizing the legitimacy of 'Ali's right to the imamate after the Prophet and believe in the return of Zayd as the *Mahdi*. The school of thought is important both historically and contemporaneously. While Imam al-Hadi adopted many Medinian legal views, he was a Jarudi in matters pertaining to the imamate.[8] Following Imam al-Hadi, the sect was active during the late Umayyad and early 'Abbasid period but has become mostly extinct due to similarities with the Twelvers. However, it is noteworthy that the Jarudis were royalists during the Yemen civil war (1962–1969) and proponents of an alleged coup in May 1987. Husayn al-Huthi and his father Badr al-Din have been called Jarudis by Arab analysts, journalists, and Yemeni sources.[9]

Practice and Interpretation

Zaydi practices are only marginally distinct from those of Sunnis. During prayer, hands are held at the side of one's body, differing from most Sunni hand placement but resembling that of the Maliki *madhhab*. Likewise, slight changes in the phrasing of the call to prayer and a few words' difference at the beginning of each prayer sequence are minor—and do not indicate a pro-'Ali bias or practices reminiscent of Twelver Shi'ites. Zaydis are theologically permitted to pray with Sunnis and behind a Sunni prayer-leader, and this has been the social reality in many parts of Yemen up to today (though likely not among hardcore Huthis). Zaydis also observe publicly recognized Muslim holidays in Yemen, such as Muharram and Ramadan, as well as the Prophet Muhammad's Birthday (*al-Mawlid al-Nabawi*), reviled by Wahhabis in Yemen. Historically, Zaydis do not celebrate the Shi'ite holiday of 'Ashura, which commemorates Husayn's martyrdom with nearly the same passion as among the Twelvers. Rather, like some Sunni Muslims, they observe the Tenth of Muharram as a muted fast day.

Additional Zaydi ritual differences from Sunnism are minor. In the call to prayer (*azzan*) for dawn prayer, Zaydis do not customarily include the Sunni formulation *al-salat khayr min al-nawm* ("prayer is better than sleep"). Further, after the usual *Hay 'ala al-salat, hay 'ala al-fallah* ("wake up to prayer, wake up to success"), Zaydis add *Hay 'ala khayri 'amal* ("rise for the best work"). More significantly, all Muslims say *Ashhadu inna Muhammad rasul Allah* ("I testify that Muhammad is the Messenger of Allah").

---

[8] Momen, *An Introduction to Shi'i Islam*, 50–51; Etan Kohlberg, "Some Zaydi Views on the Companions of the Prophet," Bulletin of the School of Oriental and African Studies 39:1 (1976), 91–98.

[9] Anwar al-Khidri, "al-Huthi wa-l-Waraqa al-Ta'ifiya al-Khasira," *Al-Bayyina*, May 6, 2006; Hassan abu Talib, "al-Huthiyun wa-l-Ma'raka ma Qabl al-Akhir fi-l-Yaman," al-Ahram Center for Strategic Studies, July 9, 2008.

While Twelver Shi'ites follow this with *Ashhadu an 'Ali wali Allah* ("I testify that 'Ali is the friend of Allah"), Zaydis do not add this clause, which distances them from Twelver Shi'ism. Prayers themselves begin with the Qur'anic chapter "al-Fatiha." Its initial phrase, *Bismillah al-rahman al-rahim* ("In the name of God the most merciful and compassionate"), is said aloud by many Muslims at prayer, including Zaydis—but not Salafis. Further, at the end of the Fatiha, while Sunnis say *amin* ("amen"), Zaydis do not.[10]

A significant, distinctive celebration for Zaydis has been 'Id al-Ghadir, the holiday commemorating the Prophet's designation of 'Ali as his successor. Officially recognized as a holiday prior to the 1962 revolution, al-Ghadir Day has become highly politicized in northwest Yemen. Zaydi revivalist ceremonies commemorating the date became contentious in the early 1990s. Most recently, the regime-Huthi conflict has provided an added impetus for tension on this matter.[11] Prohibited between 2004 and 2008, 'Id al-Ghadir was illicitly celebrated in Huthi areas and, after its 2008 relegalization, provided a venue for Huthi mobilization. In the last several decades Zaydis have also begun to revive other festivals abandoned after the revolution and to invent rituals commemorating religious figures. For example, the birthday of Imam Zayd bin 'Ali was first invoked as a holiday in 1660 but has been commemorated in the last two decades in particular in "an attempt to assert the legitimacy of the *zaydiya* in the face of the Sunni Islamist movement." This trend has benefited the Huthis.[12]

Zaydi Self-Definition

Zaydi interlocutors often invoke the history of the imamate to illustrate their doctrinal flexibility and tolerance for other forms of Islam, and in particular, their differences from other manifestations of Shi'ism. Some speak of a reliance on speculative philosophy more than jurisprudence.[13] This understanding of religion as a personal experience facilitates public acquiescence to the modern state. For example, a number of important Zaydi scholars publicly rejected the doctrine of *khuruj* in 1990 in an effort to show

---

[10] On these and other matters of traditional Zaydism, we acknowledge the generously given advice of Tarek al-Wazir, director of the Yemen Heritage and Research Center.

[11] Shelagh Weir, "A Clash of Fundamentalisms: Wahhabism in Yemen," *Middle East Report* 204 (July–September 1997), 23. In 2008, al-Ghadir Day was celebrated by Shafi'is and Isma'ilis in addition to Zaydis in San'a, al-Jawf, Marib, 'Amran, Lahj, Dhamar, and Sa'da.

[12] Vom Bruck, "Being a Zaydi in the Absence of an Imam: Doctrinal Revisions, Religious Instruction, and the (Re)invention of Ritual," in Remy Leveau, Franck Mermier, and Udo Steinbach, eds., *Le Yemen Contemporain* (Paris: Editions Karthala, 1999), 185–187.

[13] Vom Bruck, "Being a Zaydi in the Absence of an Imam," 188.

their deference to the state.[14] Additionally, some Zaydis emphasize how their legal approach has facilitated coexistence with Shafi'is and de-emphasized class inequalities throughout history.[15] Along with Zaydi-Hadawi doctrine and practice, Zaydi self-definition in the post-Imamate Yemen continues to evolve in relation to political power in the modern Yemeni state and as the Huthi rebellion continues. For instance, many prominent *sayyids* in the post-Imamate period have even attempted to accommodate republican political realities by rejecting the Hadawi stipulation that the imam must be a *sayyid*. In Chapter Three, we discussed this accommodation and also examined its pitfalls for the al-Haqq Party.[16]

Finally, Zaydis represent themselves as a fifth *madhhab* rather than a sect of Shi'ism.[17] As such, it is important to note their distinctions from the better-known Iraqi and Iranian version of Shi'ism (Twelver Shi'ism), both in doctrine and in practice. Theologically speaking, as we saw above, Zaydis do not consider Muhammad al-Baqir to have been the fifth Imam, nor do they consider the latter's descendents out to the twelfth post-Muhammad generation to be the proper line of imams. As such, Zaydis do not believe in a twelfth Imam who is in occultation (*ghayba*) since 874 and who will return as the *Mahdi* (messianic savior) at the end of days. Further, Zaydis place a premium on an esoteric, personal relationship with God, rather than on exoteric practices such as passion plays, fervent celebrations of Muharram, and shrine visits. They also oppose mystical folk Islam and Sufi practices. Thus there is no monopoly on esoteric knowledge because learned status is theoretically open to all. Notably, however, while the Zaydi doctrine does not advocate shrine visits, the historical territory of Sa'da—including the al-Hadi mosque, the tomb of Imam al-Hadi, and other associated tombs—gives the area religious significance in popular Zaydi consciousness. These and other areas important to sacred Zaydi history have been sites of visitation and prayer. (See Table B.1 for a comparison of versions of Shi'ism.)

In light of GoY and other Arab assertions of Huthi loyalty to the Islamic Republic of Iran, it is important to note a further point. Unlike Iran's policy of exporting its revolution since 1979, Zaydis have not been traditionally interested in proselytizing or propagating their beliefs. Likewise, neither Zaydi doctrine nor most Zaydis today are sympathetic to the Twelver Iranian theory of state called *wilayat al-faqih* (rule of the jurisconsult), championed by Khomeini during the Islamic revolution, which holds

---

[14]   Bernard Haykel, "Rebellion, Migration, or Consultative Democracy? The Zaydis and their detractors in Yemen," in Remy Leveau, Franck Mermier, and Udo Steinbach, eds., *Le Yemen Contemporain* (Paris: Editions Karthala, 1999).

[15]   Interviews during September–November 2008 with Zaydis long resident in the United States as well as Yemenis visiting the United States or residing in the United States after flight from the conflict zone.

[16]   See Vom Bruck, "Being a Zaydi in the Absence of an Imam."

[17]   Interview, Tarek and Zayd al-Wazir, November 18, 2008. Also see comment by Sayyid Muhammad al-Mansur in vom Bruck, "Being a Zaydi in the Absence of an Imam," 183.

Table B.1
Versions of Shi'ism Compared

Version of Shi'ism	Geography	Imam	History	Politics and Ideology	Practice	Contemporary Significance
Zaydi (Fiver) Subgroups: *Jarudiya,* *Sulaymaniya,* *Jaririya,* *Butriya,* *Salihiya*	Form an estimated 20 percent of Shi'ites worldwide. Initially spread to Caspian region in N. Iran. Modern communities located largely in Yemeni highlands. 50 percent of Yemeni population. Zaydi state established in Sa'da in 911. Sa'da has historically been the center of Zaydism and Zaydi practice in Yemen.	Ali, Hasan, Husayn first three rightful Imams; after them, imamate open to prepared/learned descendants (*ahl al-bayt*) claiming leadership through armed rebellion (*khuruj*). Accept Zayd ibn 'Ali as "Fifth Imam" instead of half-brother Muhammad al-Baqir, accepted by other Shi'a.	Zaydism is named after Zayd b. Ali, a grandson of Husayn, who led unsuccessful rebellion against Umayyad caliph Hisham in 740. Followers regard Zayd as fifth Imam, and are thus also known as "Fivers." Imamate until 1962 in northern Yemen.	Spiritual leader of Muslim community should also be ruler (imam) of Muslim state. Less emphasis on position of Imam; comparatively moderate; reject notion of hidden/infallible imam. Close to Sunni Shafi'i school and *mu'tazilis*, emphasizing free will, justice, rational thought. Accept *hukm al-mafdul 'ala hukm al-afdal* (leadership of less preferred [but qualified] over rule of more preferred [though unavailable]). Legitimizes existing leadership, even if there is a more preferred ruler.	Personal relationship w/ God emphasized, but textual knowledge superior to practice or ritual. Prominence of *sayyids* as descendants of Prophet and heirs to the Imamate. Prayer with arms extended at sides. Do not observe 'Ashura other than fasting. Celebrate birthdate of Prophet, but no birth and death dates of Imams. Flexibility allows for praying behind Sunni imam.	Leading Zaydi scholars in Yemen publicly renounced the institution of the imamate in 1990, arguing it is an obsolete historical construct. Revival in the 1990s leads to Huthi rebellion in 2004. Public acquiescence to republican regime, provided certain conditions are met, especially freedom of worship.

Table B.1—Continued

Version of Shi'ism	Geography	Imam	History	Politics and Ideology	Practice	Contemporary Significance
Jarudi	—	Consider companions of Prophet sinful by not recognizing legitimacy of 'Ali. Reject caliphs Abu Bakr and 'Umar. Also denounce Talha, Zubair.	Earliest, named for Abu' al-Jarud Ziyad ibn Abi Ziyad. Denied legitimacy of Abu Bakr, 'Umar, and 'Uthman. Denounced 'Aysha, Prophet's wife, Prophet's friends Talha and Zubayr. Active during the late Umayyad and early 'Abbasid period. Al-Hadi, leader of first Zaydi state in Yemen, was Jarudi on Imamate.	The Jarudis were Royalists during the civil war (1966–1969) and proponents of attempted coup in 1987.		It has become mostly extinct due to similarities with the Twelvers. Unsubstantiated rumors of Husayn al-Huthi's Jarudism in the Arab press. Huthi has been called Jarudi by Arab analysts, journalists, and some of our Yemeni contacts.
Sulaymani or *Jariri*	—	Imamate should be decided by consultation (*shura*). Abu Bakr and 'Umar erroneous, but not sinful. 'Uthman was an innovator (*mubtada'*).	Named after Sulayman ibn Jarir.	—		
Butri or *Salihi*	—	Nearly identical in belief to Sulaymanis.	Named for Kathir al-Nawa Al-Abtar and Hasan ibn Saleh.	—	Mu'tazila theology, Hanafi law, and, in some matters, agree with the Shafi'i and other Shi'a.	

Table B.1—Continued

Version of Shi'ism	Geography	Imam	History	Politics and Ideology	Practice	Contemporary Significance
Isma'ili (Seveners)	15 million, currently located in 25 countries around the world. Modern communities today in Central and South Asia, as well as Syria. The Sulaymani branch constitute the majority of Najran, Saudi Arabia.	Split with Shi'a in 765 over succession of sixth imam, Ja'far al-Sadiq. Believe in lineage and leadership of Musa al-Kazim's (seventh imam to the twelvers) older brother Isma'il. Isma'il and son Muhammad are said to have disappeared.	Split around turn of 10th century over the leadership of 'Ubayd Allah al-Mahdi as Imam. The Mahdi established the Fatimid dynasty in Egypt (909–1171). Split in early 12th century when Yemeni Isma'ilis took on the beliefs of the Fatimid dynasty. Najran, Saudi Arabia, is the seat of the religious leader of the Sulaimani Ismailis, al-Da'i al-Mutlaq (Absolute Guide) since 1640.	Imams believed to be of divine origin. Believe Imam succession continues. Two imams—the visible and the hidden. The identity of the hidden imam will one day return to lead.	Isma'ilis have their own legal system, essentially unmodified since the 11th century. Emphasis on exoteric and esoteric (i.e. mystical) practices. Emphasis on taqiyya or self-guarding or dissimulation to protect secret practices. Resemble Twelver Shi'ites in prayers, fasting, and Qur'anic instruction. Close to Sunnism in conservative practices. Do not observe the tenth of Muharram in manner of Twelvers.	Controversial presence in Najran province, Saudi Arabia located on the border with Yemen, approx. 60 miles from Sa'da City. Long discriminated against by the Saudi government. Isma'ilis in Najran belong to the Yam and Hamadan tribes which extend into Yemen. Najran's Zaydi community is about 2,000 today.

Table B.1—Continued

Version of Shi'ism	Geography	Imam	History	Politics and Ideology	Practice	Contemporary Significance
Ithna-'Ashari (Twelvers)	Approximately 80–85 percent of all Shi'ites. Found mostly in Iran, Bahrain, Iraq, and Azerbaijan. Minorities in Lebanon, Turkey, Kuwait, Saudi Arabia, Pakistan, and Afghanistan.	Attribute *ma'sumiya* (infallibility) to first twelve Imams. Followed Musa Kazim after J. al-Sadiq. Successor of Muhammad is an infallible human being who should rule community legally as well as interpret divine law. Twelfth Imam, Muhammad al-Mahdi, is still alive, exists in occultation since disappearance in 874. Twelfth Imam will return to earth as the *Mahdi* (messiah) in the end of days.	The Islamic Republic of Iran aims to propagate Twelver Shi'a Islam Leader of the revolution, Ayatollah Khomeini, championed *wilayat al-faqih*, that the state should be lead by the clerical leaders who would implement Islamic law.	Imam is political leader of Islam; modern governments without an Imam are illegitimate. Belief in *marja'*— a *marja'* in Shi'ism refers to a source to follow or emulate. Ayatollahs are *marjas*. Ayatollah Khomeini first advocated for *wilayat al-faqih* or rule of the jurists in 1969. The government formed after the revolution in 1979 has been based on this concept. The foreign policy of the state of Iran has aimed to "export" the Islamic revolution to other Shi'a.	Ja'fari school of law. Exoteric practice includes passion plays, saints, and tombs.	The GoY accused Hussein al-Huthi of having Twelver beliefs and has suggested the Huthi movement is aided by Iranian Twelver Shi'ites hoping to overturn the Yemeni government. The foreign policy of the state of Iran has aimed to "export" the Islamic revolution to other Shi'a communities.

that only Islamic jurists, as the embodiment of the hidden Twelfth Imam, are qualified to guard over the state and interpret its laws. While Zaydism long had a political imamate (and never felt the imam to have occulted), it was not called called *wilayat al-faqih*—nor was it tied to the Zayd family, much less to the imams of Twelver Shi'ism. And, whereas Twelver Shi'ism during the 1970s gradually moved *toward* the idea of a political imam in Iran, Zaydism has moved away from the imam as proper ruler of Yemen. Finally, Zaydis today are not subordinate to a clerical hierarchy or its jurists, as are Iranian Twelvers.

Major Huthist Ideological Tracts

Tracts from the Believing Youth Period, 1990s–2000

1. Title: *The Brief [Concise] Response [Reaction] to the Fatwas [Legal Rulings] Emerging from the Hijaz*
   Arabic: *al-Ijaz fi al-Radd ʿala Fatawa al-Hijaz*
   Author: Badr Din ibn Amir al-Din ibn al-Husayn al-Huthi
   Date: 1979
   Publication location: Sanʿa, Yemen (Maktabat al-Yaman al-Kubra, 1979)

   This is a response by Badr al-Din al-Huthi to anti-Zaydi statements, tracts, and rulings by Wahhabi clerics from Saudi Arabia, including Shaykh bin Baz, a monarchy-associated senior ʿalim for the Wahhabi establishment. Badr al-Din refutes bin Baz's accusations of inappropriate Muslim practices by Zaydis, also affirming that Zaydis can pray behind Sunnis and that Sunnis should feel legitimate praying behind and with Zaydis. Was reprinted and used in Zaydi revivalist circles in the 1990s.

2. Title: *Who Are the [Real] Rejectionists?*
   Arabic: *Man Hum al-Rafida*
   Author: Badr Din ibn Amir al-Din ibn al-Husayn al-Huthi; ed., Ibrahim al-ʾUbaydi
   Date: 2002
   Publication location: Sanʿa, Yemen (Muʾassasat al-Imam Zayd ibn ʿAli al-Thaqafiya)

   In this text, Badr al-Din refutes Sunni/Salafi claims that Zaydis are part of the larger community that rejects Sunnism (al-Rafida) and the basic monotheistic tenets of Islam. Indicating that Zaydism accepts much of Sunni ideas and law, he suggests that the true rejectionists are the Salafis, rejecting others from Islam.

3. Title: *The Key [Guide] to the Authoritative Sources of Zaydism*
    Arabic: *Miftah Asanid al-Zaydiya*
    Author: Badr Din ibn Amir al-Din ibn al-Husayn al-Huthi
    Date: Unknown
    Publication Location: Amman, Jordan

    The author lists the important authorities of Zaydi thought, theology, and law into the 20th century, as well as the chains of reporters (*Isnad/Asanid*) of Zaydism-supportive hadiths.

4. Title: *Liberation [Revision; Clarification] of Thoughts*
    Arabic: *Tahrir al-Afkar*
    Author: Badr Din ibn Amir al-Din ibn al-Husayn al-Huthi
    Date: 1997
    Publication location: Qum, Iran (al-Majma ʿal-ʿAlami li Ahl al-Bayt)

    A work of Zaydi thinking and revivalism, meant to provide guidance to emerging generations on proper Zaydi practices and beliefs. Published after Badr al-Din split from al-Haqq.

5. Title: *The Scholar al-Shami: Views and Positions*
    Arabic: *al-ʿAllama al-Shami: Araʾ wa Mawaqif*
    Author: Muhammad ʿIzzan
    Date: 1994
    Publication location: Amman, Jordan (Matabiʿ Sharikat al-Mawarid al-Sinaʿiya al-Urdiniya)

    A compilation of the ideas and views of Sayyid Ahmad bin Muhammad bin ʿAli al-Shami, a leading modern Zaydi thinker, supporter of early Believing Youth, and founder of al-Haqq. Focuses on views regarding modern Zaydism, integration with Yemeni state structures, the suspension of *khuruj* and historicity of the imamate, and the threats to Yemen and Zaydism of Wahhabism.

6. Title: *The Testimonial of the History of the Zaydi Imams*
    Arabic: *al-Ifada fi Taʾrikh Aʾimmat al-Zaydiya*
    Author: Muhammad ʿIzzan
    Date: 1996
    Publication location: Sanʿa, Yemen (Dar al-Hikma al-Yamaniya)

    This is an edited reissue of a work by Yahya ibn al-Husayn (d. 1032), covering, in classical Islamic literary form, the exploits, merits, and teachings of Zaydism's first imams and rulers of Yemen.

7. Title: *Imam Zayd ibn 'Ali: A Blazing Torch During the Night of Oppression*
Arabic: *al-Imam Zayd ibn 'Ali: Sha'la fi Layl al-Istibdad*
Author: Muhammad 'Izzan
Date: 1999
Publication location: San'a (Dar al-Hikma al-Yamaniya)

Praiseful biography, for modern audience, of Zayd ibn 'Ali, the half-brother of Muhammad al-Baqir. Zayd is seen by Zaydis as the true Imam of his generation (fifth after 'Ali ibn abi Talib), rather than Muhammad al-Baqir. Zayd is the progenitor of Zaydism, separating Zaydis from other Shi'a.

8. Title: *Anthology of Books and Letters by Imam Zayd ibn 'Ali*
Arabic: *Majmu' Kutub wa Rasa'il al-Imam Zayd ibn 'Ali*
Author: Muhammad 'Izzan
Date: 2001
Publication location: San'a (Dar al-Hikma al-Yamaniya)

Compilation intended to familiarize young Zaydis with the founder of the Zaydi *madhhab* and to instill pride in Zaydism.

Lectures by Husayn al-Huthi, 2002–2004, Reprinted 2004–2006

1. Title: "Imran Sura, 1st Lesson: 'If you obey a party from among those who have been given the Book, they will turn you back as unbelievers after you have believed.'"
Arabic: *Surat Al-'Imran al-Dars al-Awwal: In Tut'u Tariqan min alladhin Awthu al-Kitab Yaruddukum ba'd Imanikum Kafirin*
Author: Husayn Badr al-Din al-Huthi
Date, location delivered: January 8, 2002, Sa'da
Publication date: September 9, 2006

Husayn begins by noting that the "party" in the above quotation includes groups of Christians and Jews. These people of the book, as far as Husayn and his listeners are concerned, can be considered one party despite the history of hatred between them. He proceeds to discuss the interaction between the Arabian Jews and Islam during the early stages of the *umma,* noting that today's Jews look at the Arabian Jews (who accepted Islam) as backwards. He then examines anti-Jewish tracts, pointing to Qur'anic verses that highlight the importance of money to Jews, and how they use it "as a weapon." He goes on to point out that Jews today possess nuclear bombs, rockets, etc., and wish to divide the Muslim community. He also talks about the necessity of returning to Islam and the potential strength of Muslims. Both Islamic identity and Zaydi identity need to be asserted; Zaydis in particular are currently the weakest group among Muslims. He begins to list grievances (lack of political party, printers, a television channel, broadcast, newspaper, etc.) and concludes by noting that Isma'ilis, Twelvers, even Sufis are more loyal to Imam 'Ali than Zaydis are today.

2. Title: "'Imran Sura, 2nd Lesson: 'Hold Fast to the Rope of God.'"
    Arabic: *Surat al-'Imran, al-Dars al-Thani: wa I'tasimu bi-Habl Allah*
    Author: Husayn Badr al-Din al-Huthi
    Date, location delivered: January 9, 2002, Sa'da
    Publication date: September 23, 2006

Husayn begins by decrying the lack of religious consciousness (particularly the duty to battle enemies of God, including Jews, Christians, and their agents) in the Muslim world, noting that Zaydis are the worst with regards to this. He goes on to repeat his view that Muslims are under attack from those who seek to make them unbelievers. He argues that actions speak louder than words, and that there are even *'ulama'* who pray to Allah and then cooperate with His enemies. He decries Muslims who want to take the easy path, saying they face the danger of dying as an infidel. Indeed, real Muslims need to fight and kill the enemies of Allah. He further mentions that Jews want to turn the *umma* into an infidel *umma,* corrupting families and children. He mentions Iran and Hizbullah as good examples of standing up to America and Israel and delves into the tenets of Zaydism, which he sees as very important. He goes on to note that Muslims must be united, just as the infidel nations have united under America's lead to fight terrorism.

3. Title: "Lessons from the Qur'an: A Shriek in the Face of the Arrogant"
    Arabic: *Durus min al-Qur'an: al-Sarakha fi Wajh al-Mustakbirin*
    Author: Husayn Badr al-Din al-Huthi
    Date, location delivered: January 17, 2002, Sa'da
    Publication date: March 1, 2004

Husayn begins by discussing the fact that Muslims everywhere are being targeted by American and Israeli conspiracies. He goes on to point out the danger of the Jewish media and expresses his view that he and his followers are not afraid of Israel and America. He notes the current weakness of the Muslim world and the responsibility of Muslims to improve it, saying that each of his listeners has the ability to do so. He implies that American intelligence agents carried out the 9/11 attacks as an excuse for them to target the Shi'ites. He argues that Jews do not see Sunnis as a threat and chides contemporary *'ulama'* for telling Muslims not to speak out against America or Israel. Muslims should speak out, Husayn argues, and in doing so should chant "Death to America, Death to Israel, Curse Upon the Jews, Victory for Islam." He then mentions

Hizbullah as a proper form of resistance and martyrdom. He also argues that Usama bin Laden and the Taliban are currently safe, and that America is not truly targeting Wahhabis. Yet, the Wahhabis are the true terrorists because of their presence in local Yemeni towns, schools, and mosques. He further blames the Wahhabis for the divisions in contemporary Zaydism. He also stresses the importance of the Hajj in Islam as a tool to confront the enemies of Islam. This leads him to criticize Saudi Arabia, and he then goes on to criticize political parties who accepted Jews in their ranks. He concludes by pointing out the demonstrations that look place during American invasion of Iraq.

4. Title: "Lessons from the Qur'an: Allah's Knowledge–Allah's Sublimity, Lesson 7"
   Arabic: *Ma'rifat Allah–'Uzmat Allah*
   Author: Husayn Badr al-Din al-Huthi
   Date, location delivered: January 25, 2002, Sa'da
   Publication date: March 1, 2004

   Husayn begins by reciting a number of Qur'anic verses indicating Allah's greatness and all-knowing nature. He also discusses Allah's way of demonstrating the path to heaven as the *shari'a*, giving specific examples. Those who violate these rules are disbelievers who deserve damnation. Discussing the power of Allah, Husayn notes that his followers should not fear America's hegemony, given that its president is also under the rule of Allah. He then instructs governments seeking peace to look to Allah for strength, as peace will not accomplish anything unless an individual is coming from a position of strength and power. Noting that Islam is a religion of peace, Husayn suggests that Islamic peace must be a correct kind, not ruling out the possibility of war. (NB: This lecture does not end with the *shi'ar*.)

5. Title: "Lessons from the Qur'an: The Danger of America Entering Yemen"
   Arabic: *Durus min al-Qur'an: Khatir Dukhul Amrika al-Yaman*
   Author: Husayn Badr al-Din al-Huthi
   Date, location delivered: February 3, 2002, Sa'da
   Publication date: September 23, 2006

   Husayn begins by pointing out the existence of U.S. soldiers on Yemeni soil, lamenting that nobody has heeded his warnings. He cites Khomeini's warnings about the Great Satan, criticizing the country for allowing Americans to enter Yemeni territory. In his view, Yemen also opposed the Islamic revolution, despite the fact that Iran continues to be one of America's worst enemies today. He goes on to decry the Wahhabis' entrance into Yemen and the state's deception with regards to America's presence, which he feels could lead to a blockade. The Americans are going to use al-Qa'ida as an excuse to encroach on Yemen,

Husayn feels, and this needs to be resisted and fought by Yemenis. In doing so, they need to draw on the strength of Allah to fight America. He also notes the preferential treatment Wahhabis receive from 'Ali Muhsin al-Ahmar. Husayn concludes by arguing that Americans see the Shi'a as their primary concern.

6.   Title: "Lessons from the Qur'an: There Is No Excuse for Mankind in Front of Allah"
Arabic: *La 'Adhr l-il-Jumi' Amam Allah*
Author: Husayn Badr al-Din al-Huthi
Date, location delivered: March 6, 2002, Sa'da
Publication date: March 1, 2004
Husayn begins by noting that the Qur'an is not optional but rather should be seen as a mandatory guide to the right path. He then goes on to point out the presence of Christians and Jews in the *umma*, noting that Muslims have the responsibility to ensure that Islam prevails in the world. He calls on Muslims to fight the Christians and Jews. He then says all Muslims should support those who fight the enemies of Allah, and points out that Jews and Christians are currently oppressing Muslims. This actually puts Muslims below Jews and Christians in the eyes of Allah. Jews especially, as mentioned by the Qur'an, seek to corrupt the earth, Husayn says. Criticizing Arab and Muslim leaders, Husayn argues that present Islam, unlike historical Islam, has surrendered to its enemies. He reiterates that the true path in Islam is one of fighting and regrets that Muslims have become lazy. He then cites the significance of the Hajj as a tool to unite Muslims, which is why, in his view, Israel is seeking to control it.

7.   Title: "Lessons from the Qur'an: Terrorism and Peace"
Arabic: *Al-Irhab wa al-Salam*
Author: Husayn Badr al-Din al-Huthi
Date, location delivered: March 8, 2002, Sa'da
Publication date: September 23, 2002

The lecture starts with Badr al-Din talking about Islam being under attack by infidels. Ahmad bin Saleh al-Hadi then continues by reciting the slogan and introducing Husayn. Husayn instructs his listeners to remember their responsibility and ensure that Zaydism is preserved. He goes on to lament the current status of the Arab world, noting its current corruption and subjugation. He proceeds to address the fact that the terms *jihad* and *terrorism* (*irhab*) are used interchangeably by the West. He points out that *jihad* is a legitimate right to strike those who corrupt Muslims. He also points out that the Qur'anic definition of terrorism is one that is not used in the media, which instead uses the American version. He then criticizes President Saleh's support of America in the GWoT, while also claiming that Americans are the real terrorists. He reiterates the need for Muslims to be more religiously conscious, because in his view Islam is under attack. He then proceeds to call on his listeners to return to the Qur'an and expresses his fear that America will invade Yemen. He cites Hizbullah as an example of returning to the Qur'an and waging *jihad*, saying the Palestinians should use the Hizbullah model. He also criticizes Israel and America's stance toward Iran.

8. Title: "Lessons from the Qur'an: Lessons from the 'Ashura' Revelation"
   Arabic: *Durus min Wahi 'Ashura'*
   Author: Husayn Badr al-Din al-Huthi
   Date, location delivered: March 23, 2002, Sa'da
   Publication date: September 23, 2006

   In this lecture, Husayn compares the era of the martyred Imam 'Ali to the present, accusing Arab governments of having sold out to America's GWoT in order to stay in power. He continues to cite historical examples of this and notes that when people love power, they sacrifice their religion. He then ties in the Israeli/Palestinian conflict, calling on Arab leaders to support the Palestinians with weapons rather than calling for peace. He encourages his listeners not to be scared of America and to raise the slogan. He even calls on his followers to go to Palestine to fight, by way of President Saleh, who, Husayn claims, is not living up to his word. He further cites Hizbullah leader Nasrallah to support his arguments, concluding by calling for a reconnection with the Qur'an, a return to Muslims' true historical place.

9. Title: "Lessons from the Qur'an: Qur'anic Culture"
   Arabic: *Durus min al-Qur'an: al-Thaqafa al-Qur'aniya*
   Author: Husayn Badr al-Din al-Huthi
   Date, location delivered: August 4, 2002, Sa'da
   Publication date: March 3, 2004

   Husayn begins by discussing the evils of deviating from the true path or, even worse, attacking it. He then puts forth the idea allegedly promulgated by people of the book that Arabs have no culture. This causes him to move to the supremacy of the Qur'an as a basis for culture. He goes on to say that the Qur'an has guidelines for proper behavior but that many have lost sight of this Qur'anic wisdom. As evidence, Husayn points to the ability of America and Israel to succeed in their policies while Arabs stand by helpless. He points out that Jews lived among the Arabs for a long time and allied themselves with local Arab leaders because they were unable to make a home for themselves. This is intended to indicate that the Arabs have the capability to rule the Jews once again. He then proceeds to give reasons for the value of Qur'anic wisdom, including the guidelines it provides for confronting Allah's enemies. He goes on to praise

Hamas for its ability to provide to Muslims what no other force in Palestine can. Like many of his other lectures, this one concludes with Husayn speaking out against Israel and America, claiming that if the Arab people could vote, they would vote to confront the two countries.

10. Title: "ʿImran Chapter, from Verse 33 to Verse 91, the 13th Lesson"
    Arabic: *Surat ʿImran, min al-Ayyat 33 Ila al-Ayyat 91, al-Dars al-Thalith ʿashr*
    Author: Husayn Badr al-Din al-Huthi
    Date, location delivered: November 7, 2003, Saʿda
    Publication date: September 6, 2007

Taking his listeners, who in this case appear to be students, through a series of Qurʾanic verses, Husayn al-Huthi illustrates a number of key points. For one, he criticizes the tenets of the Christian and Jewish faiths. Furthermore, Husayn decries the lack of unity among his fellow Muslims, noting the vast control the Jews have over the media and world economy. In comparison, Muslims are in a weak position, given their sectarian squabbling.

Recent Media Since 2004

1. Title: "A Saʿda Child: A Poem Orally Giving an Account of the Status of Saʿda Children"
   Arabic: *Tifl Saʿda: Qasida Tahki Lisan Hal Atfal Saʿda*
   Author: Unknown
   Date: November 2007
   Format: Arabic poem, transmitted orally

Told from the first person perspective, this poem presents the story of a child experiencing a military attack presumably launched by GoY forces. It depicts the child's fear as a "land mine is on [his] right, and a rocket explodes to [his] left," while also accusing the GoY forces of doing America's work.

2. Title: "Badr al-Din al-Huthi to *al-Wasat*: The President Is Scared to Take [Husayn] from Him"
   Arabic: *Badr al-Din al-Huthi li-l-Wasat: al-Raʾis Khafa An Yaʾkhudh (Husayn) minhu*
   Author: *al-Wasat*
   Date: March 19, 2005
   Format: Interview, print

In this interview, Badr al-Din frames the conflict in religious terms. He also describes the BY as being concerned with resisting America's aggression on the Islamic world. He goes on to frame the conflict as the Huthis defending themselves from government encroachment. He also reveals that he fled to Iran during the conflict but claims he did not receive any aid from Tehran. Badr al-Din repeatedly states his opinion that Islam is under attack, and that defending it is the most important issue. He also appears hesitant to pledge his allegiance to the Saleh government.

3.   Title: "Interview with Sayyid 'Abd al-Malik Badr al-Din al-Huthi"
Arabic: *Hiwar ma'a Sayyid 'Abd al-Malik Badr al-Din al-Huthi*
Author: *al-Nas*
Date: April 26, 2006
Format: Interview, print

In this interview, 'Abd al-Malik says that within the government there is a group obstructing any peaceful resolutions. While he admits that the Huthis are using force, he says they are doing so in defense of their homes and that they have no ulterior motives or goals in the conflict. He also claims that the Huthis are stronger than ever and that any government encroachment will be met with heavy force.

4.   Title: "'Abd al-Malik al-Huthi from His Stronghold in Matra to al-Ahale: We Will Not Be a Political Party, and Rule of Ali and Husayn's Descendents Applies to Governments Today"
Arabic: *'Abd al-Malik al-Huthi min Ma'qilihi fi Matra li 'al-Ahali': Lan Nakun Hizban Siyasiyan, wa Walayat al-Batanin Tantabiq 'Ala Hukam al-Yawm*
Author: *al-Ahale*
Date: Undated
Format: Interview, print

In this interview, which took place just before the fifth war, 'Abd al-Malik portrays the Huthis' position as being primarily defensive. He argues that the Huthis are a cultural movement and that forming a political party is "not necessary." Furthermore, he denies having any connection with Iran or Libya. Finally, 'Abd al-Malik argues that current regimes are lacking religious legitimacy and claims that the issue is not whether or not rulers are descended from 'Ali and Husayn but rather the extent to which they rule with justice.

5.   Title: "The Yemen Government's Conflict with the Huthis"
Arabic: *Sira' al-Hukuma al-Yamaniya ma'a al-Huthiyin*
Author: *al-Jazeera*
Date: April 29, 2007
Format: Broadcast

In this broadcast, Yahya al-Huthi accuses the Yemeni government of wanting to completely wipe out both the Huthis and the Zaydis. He also states that the government has refused to allow the Huthis to undertake any peaceful activities. He goes on to deny that the government attempted anything but a military solution while also denying any external support.

6. Title: "So He Empowered Them"
    Arabic: *Fa-Amkana Minhum*
    Author: "The War Media Division" (Qism al-Iʿlam al-Harbi) of the Huthis
    Date: June 2008
    Format: Video, distributed via the Internet

    This hourlong video production contains a summary of events that occurred in the run-up to and during the fifth Saʿda war. It contains excerpts from a number of ʿAbd al-Malik and Husayn's speeches and also depicts the Saleh government as an agent of the United States that was launching an offensive against innocent civilians in the Saʿda governorate. The video further contains combat footage and images of Huthi fighters destroying GoY weaponry and driving along roads chanting the Huthi slogan. These images are accompanied by a number of *nashids*, or Islamic anthems, praising the *mujahidin*.

7. Title: "ʿAbd al-Malik al-Huthi Announces Their Adherence to International Human [Rights] Law and Welcomes All Human [Rights] Organizations"
    Arabic: *ʿAbd al-Malik al-Huthi Yuʿlin Iltazamahum bi-l-Qanun al-Duwali al-Insani wa Yurahhib bi-Kafat al-Munazzamat al-Insaniya*
    Author: ʿAbd al-Malik al-Huthi
    Date: June 23, 2009
    Format: Press release, distributed electronically via the al-Menpar Web site.

    ʿAbd al-Malik al-Huthi directly addresses recommendations made to the group by Human Rights Watch. He stresses the Huthis' adherence to human rights laws and emphasizes that the GoY, not the Huthis, are keeping human rights organizations from reaching Saʿda.

8. Title: "Eight Points Noting the Huthis' Stance on the War, Peace, Society, and the Regime"
    Arabic: *Thamaniyat Bunud Tudhakkir bi-Mawqif al-Huthiyin min al-Harb wa-l-Salam wa al-Mujtamaʿ wa al-Nizam*
    Author: ʿAbd al-Malik al-Huthi
    Date: August 17, 2009
    Format: Press release, distributed electronically via the al-Menpar Web site.

Articulates the group's stance by establishing the following:

- Huthis are Yemenis; the government is the one that has referred to them as a rebellion, refusing to recognize their religious, national, legal, and constitutional rights.
- Huthis have only used weapons out of self-defense.
- They have established proof that they are adhering to the regime, laws, and constitution; the government has initiated the conflict and attempted to draw in international actors.
- The government is responsible for the failure of the Doha agreement.
- The government has falsely accused the Huthis of many things, including the kidnapping of the German doctors, which the Huthis condemn, just as they condemn "shedding blood, money, honor, freedom, or dignity."
- Other political actors should live up to their responsibility to confront the regime about its crimes and protect civilians and IDPs.
- The government has not made an earnest effort toward solving the conflict.
- The Huthis will defend themselves due to the fact that the government insists on war.

9. Title: "'Abd al-Malik al-Huthi to *al-Khalij*: We don't receive support from Iran, the crisis is political and we don't want the return of the Imamate"
   Arabic: *al-Sayyid 'Abd al-Malik al-Huthi li-l-Khalij: La Natallaqi al-Da'm min Iran, wa al-Azma Siyasiya bi-Imtiyaz wa la Nurid' Awdat al-Imama*
   Author: 'Abd al-Malik al-Huthi
   Date: September 29, 2009
   Format: Interview, print

'Abd al-Malik al-Huthi argues that the GoY forces will not be able to achieve any important advances on the ground and insists that the Huthis maintain control over 65 military locations. Further, 'Abd al-Malik accuses the government of being responsible for the start of a sixth round of fighting. The Huthi leader also argues that the group is able to obtain weapons locally from weapons markets and from GoY military outposts. While denying that the Huthis receive money from Iran or strive for the return of the Imamate, he further points out that instances of tribal elements fighting alongside GoY units have been rare. Also, 'Abd al-Malik describes the "internationalization" of the conflict as to be "expected," and that the only link between the northern and southern discontent is the way in which the government deals with these two opposition movements.

10. Title: "'Abd al-Malik al-Huthi: We Are Not Betting on Any Regional Power and If the Government Stops Targeting Us, We Will End the Digging [of Trenches]"
Arabic: *'Abd al-Malik al-Huthi: La Nurahin 'ala Ayy Quwwa Iqlimiya wa Idha Awqafat al-Sulta Istihdafana, Sanantahi al-Tamtarus*
Author: 'Abd al-Malik al-Huthi
Date: September 20, 2009
Format: Interview, print

'Abd al-Malik claims to the pan-Arab *al-Sharq al-Awsat* that the government has not achieved any significant military advances in the sixth round of fighting. The Huthi leader further denies receiving any support from Iran, also pointing out that the Huthis have a number of means to break through the GoY's media blackout. He blames the government for the failure of the ceasefire. When asked about the announcements made by Hashid and Bakil tribal shaykhs expressing support of the GoY launching of a sixth war, 'Abd al-Malik points out that the Huthis maintain fighters from both of these tribes. Regarding the resolution of the fifth phase, 'Abd al-Malik argues that there was a verbal agreement between him and President Saleh. Regarding the GoY's conditions, 'Abd al-Malik argues that if the government stops aggression against them, they will stop firing on GoY forces. Further, 'Abd al-Malik points out that it is unreasonable for the GoY to expect Huthi cadres to come down from mountains, given that the regions they live in are mountainous. Finally, 'Abd al-Malik al-Huthi states that Badr al-Din al-Huthi is alive and well.

Important Personalities in the Huthi Conflict

Name	Tribe(s)	Profession	Orientation	Notes
Husayn al-Huthi		Former MP	Huthi	Huthi leader, deceased Sept. 2004
Badr al-Din al-Huthi			Huthi	Huthi family patriarch, ideologue
'Abd al-Malik al-Huthi			Huthi	Current Huthi leader
'Abdullah al-Razzami	Al-Razzam		Huthi	Huthi field commander
Muhammad al-Huthi			Huthi	Huthi leader, killed or arrested
'Abdullah al-Huthi			GoY	Son of Husayn; after imprisonment, came out against armed struggle
Yusuf al-Madani			Huthi	Huthi field commander, married to daughter of Husayn al-Huthi
Yahya al-Huthi		Former MP	Huthi	Huthi spokesman, currently residing abroad
Karim Jadban	Qabili	MP from GPC	Neutral	One of initial Believing Youth founders; knew Huthi family members but not part of Huthi armed movement; used by GoY as mediator in 2004–2005
Salah Falita	Hashimi	al-Haqq founder	Neutral	Zaydi elite, among early al-Haqq members, and was supportive of BY in mid-1990s. Used by GoY in 2004–2005 mediation efforts

Name	Tribe(s)	Profession	Orientation	Notes
Muhammad 'Izzan	'Izzan (?)	Runs GoY radio station in Sa'da	Neutral/ anti-Huthi	Non-Hashimi, early Zaydi revivalist in 1990s, edited works by Zaydi scholars, helped found BY in schools, and provided material to BY camps. Split from Huthis, condemns armed struggle as distorting Zaydism's image
Dirdah bin Ja'far	Sahar	Shaykh	GoY	Family targeted by Huthis
Hussein al-Surabi	Bani Mu'adh	Shaykh	Possibly passive Huthi	Expressed discontent for the environmental destruction of conflict
Uthman Mujalli	Rahban, al-Abdin, Ghuraz, Farwa	Security, former GPC MP	GoY	Family members killed by Huthis, including his brother. Resigned from GPC July 2009
Abdullah Hamis al-'Awjari (d)	Wa'ila (Hamdan Bakil)	Shaykh, former MP	GoY	Lost to Razzami in 1990 parliamentary elections. Family targetted by Huthis
Fa'iz 'Abdullah al-'Awjari	Wa'ila	Shaykh, former GPC MP	GoY	Resigned from GPC July 2009. 'Abdullah's son
Faysal 'Abdullah Man'a	Talh	MP of Talh area	GoY	Family repeatedly targeted by Huthis
Qa'id Shawit	Bani 'Uwayr	Former Islah MP	GoY	Wounded in Huthi ambush
'Abdullah Daris		Shaykh	GoY	Led tribesmen against Huthis in Wadi al-Ghil area
Hassan La'uj al-Jaradi (d)	Bani Dhwib	Shaykh	GoY	Killed by Huthis
Ibn Muqayt (d)	Khawlan bin 'Amr	Shaykh	GoY	Killed by Huthis
'Abd al-Muhsin al-Nimri (d)	Nimr	Shaykh	Huthi	Killed by GoY forces
Muhammad b. Mahdi al-Kubas	Kulayb	Shaykh	GoY	Tribesmen fought Huthis in Bani Mu'adh
	Al-'al'l		Huthi	Tribesmen in prison
Saghir bin 'Aziz		MP Harf Sufyan	GoY	Claimed his men would fight with GoY if there were to be a sixth war
Ahmad Habish (d)	Harf Sufyan	Shaykh	Huthi	Died fighting GoY
Ahmad Hindi Dughsan (d)			Huthi	Brother to MP Doghsan, who died under mysterious circumstances
	Bani Hushaysh		Huthi	

Name	Tribe(s)	Profession	Orientation	Notes
	Bukhtar		GoY	Fought Huthis in Al-Salim
	'Asimat (Hashid)		GoY	Fought with GoY in first round, Huthis killed their Shaykh
	Al-Hamid		Huthi	Fought against pro-GoY Mujali tribesmen
	Abqur, al-Qadami, Faris		Passive Huthi	GoY asked them not to allow Huthis to use their territory for transportation
	Elements of Baqim, Ghamr, Qatabir, Munabbih, Razih		GoY	Reported to have agreed to fight against Huthis
	Elements of Wa'ila		GoY	Permitted GoY to search their territory
	Qafir (Ibb governorate)		GoY	Pledged 400 men to GoY

Conflict Magnitude

	Phase 1 June–September 2004	Phase 2 March–April 2005	Interim 2 April – December 2005	Phase 3 December 2005–S February 2006	Interim 3 February 2006–February 2007	Phase 4 February 2007–January 2008	Interim 4 January–May 2008	Phase 5 May–July 2008
Duration (months)	3.5	2	6	3	10	11	5	2.5
No. of incidents	14	39	16	75	18	519	15	37
Average days between incidents	7.7	1.5	4.2	1.48	7.7	0.66	5.6	1.5
Casualties	480	500	75	270+	80+	3,035	65	200+
Huthi-initiated	4	12	11	33	12	140	5	6
GoY-initiated	6	14	2	14	2	166	8	12
High-level Huthi casualties	2	3		2		10		
High-level GoY casualties		10	9	6		16	2	

SOURCE: *al-Ayyam*, verified with English sources (*Yemen Times, Yemen Observer*) and *26 September*.

NOTES: Incident: Instance where source clearly indicates exchange of fire or use of GoY heavy platforms in offensive fashion. Does not include mere movement of troops or gear. Huthi-initiated: Instance where source clearly indicates that incident was begun by Huthi attack. Aggression, incitement, etc., or when nature of incident (ambush, etc.) is clearly an initiation. GoY-initiated: Instance where source clearly indicates that incident was begun by GoY attack, incursion, etc., or when nature of incident (artillery barrage, etc.,) is clearly an initiation.

Conflict Ceasefire Conditions

Doha Agreement, 2007–2008

Text of agreement produced by Qatari mediation, summer–fall 2007. GoY-Huthi representatives also met in Qatar in January–February 2008. The Doha agreement was signed on February 1, 2008.

1. Cessation of military operations; and adherence, of the Huthi and those with him, to the republican order [system], the constitution and the laws in force in the country.
2. Ending of the rebellion; implementation of the general amnesty decision; and the release of prisoners, except for those charged in cases turned over to the general prosecutor or under consideration by the courts; and search for [discovery of] the missing people and care for injured/wounded people; and release of corpses by whomever possesses them.
3. Life [should] return to normal in the regions [of conflict], and everyone [should] return to his area, and live as safe citizens, as all the other citizens in the regions of the republic.
4. Extension of the state's general order in the region, as in all other regions of the republic.
5. The relinquishment of medium weapons, along with their ammunition, to the state.
6. Respect for freedom of opinion, to include the right to establish a political party in accordance with the constitution and the laws in force in the country.
7. The arrival of 'Abd al-Malik al-Huthi, Yahya al-Huthi, 'Abd al-Karim al-Huthi, and 'Abdallah 'Izza al-Razzami to Qatar, without undertaking any political or media activity hostile to Yemen and without leaving Qatar except after the agreement of the Yemeni government.
8. Cessation of all matter of media campaigns and acts of provocative incitement.
9. The Yemeni government will undertake the reconstruction of what the war has destroyed and the treatment of its effects; the praiseworthy state of Qatar will undertake to contribute to a fund for the rebuilding of the affected areas and for

the compensation of those affected [by the fighting], and this fund will be open to the contributions of Arab and friendly states.

Source: "Waqf al-Qital fi Sa'da wa-l-I'lan 'an al-'Afu," *al-Ayyam*, June 17, 2007; International Crisis Group, "Yemen: Defusing the Saada Time Bomb," *Middle East Report* 86, May 27, 2009.

The GoY's Six Ceasefire Conditions, August 2009

These six conditions were originally enumerated by the GoY as the sixth round of fighting commenced. They were articulated by President Saleh in a speech delivered on the first night of Ramadan, Friday, August 21.

1. Withdraw from all of the districts and lift all roadblocks.
2. Descend from the mountains and trenches and stop "acts of sabotage."
3. Return stolen civilian and military property.
4. Reveal the fate of the six foreign kidnapping victims "which confirms information that the rebels were behind their kidnapping."
5. Return citizens who had been kidnapped by the group.
6. Do not interfere in the "local authorities' affairs."

Source: "fi Kalima Lahu Ila Abna' al-Sha'b al-Yamani bi-Munasiba Hulul Shahr Ramadan, Ra'is al-Jumhuriya Yamnah 'Anasir al-Takhrib bi-Sa'da Fursa Jadida li-l-Salam 'Ala Asas al-Iltizam bi-l-Sit al-Nuqat," *26 September*, August 21, 2009.

The GoY's Five Ceasefire Conditions, September 2009

These five conditions were established by the GoY on September 19, 2009, when it announced the implementation of a ceasefire arrangement. The following are the conditions of the ceasefire, which has essentially been nullified by continued clashes.

1. "Adhere to the ceasefire, opening roads, removing land mines, descending from mountains," and stop digging trenches.
2. "Withdraw from the districts and stop interfering in the local authorities' affairs."
3. Return stolen civilian and military property.
4. Free prisoners, including civilians and soldiers.
5. "Adhere to the constitution, regime, and laws."

Source: "al-Hukuma Tu'lin Ta'liq al-'Amaliyat al-'Askiriya fi al-Mantaqa al-Shamaliya al-Gharbiya bi-Munasiba 'Aid al-Fitr," *26 September*, September 19, 2009.

The Six-Point GoY-Huthi Agreement at the Ceasefire of February 12, 2010

The Huthis agree to

1. Adhere to the ceasefire, open the roads, remove land mines, descend from mountainous heights, and end the digging of trenches near military points and along roads
2. Withdraw from districts [occupied by Huthis] and not to interfere in the business of local authorities
3. Return captured Saudi and Yemeni weapons, ammunition, equipment, and civilian goods
4. Release Saudi and Yemeni civilian and military detainees
5. Adhere to the law and the constitution
6. Adhere to nonaggression against Saudi territory.

Source: 'Arafat Madabish, "al-Ra'is al-Yamani Yu'lin Waqf al-Harb fi Sa'da . . . Ba'd Muwafaqat al-Huthiyin 'ala Shurut al-Hukuma," *al-Sharq al-Awsat,* February 12, 2010.

Fifty-Five Huthi "Leaders" Wanted by the GoY, August 2009

These 55 wanted individuals were deemed by the GoY's attorney general to be Huthi commanders on August 18, 2009.

1. Badr al-Din al-Huthi
2. Ahmad Salah al-Hadi
3. 'Abd al-Rahman Qassim Mushahham
4. 'Abd al-Malik Badr al-Din al-Huthi
5. 'Abdullah 'Aidha al-Razzami
6. Amin Hassan al-Mu'ayyad
7. Qassim bin Qassim al-Hamran
8. Muhammad Badr al-Din Amir al-Din al-Huthi
9. Yahya Qassim Ahmad Abu 'Awwadah
10. Salih Ahmad Habra
11. Dayf Allah Qassim al-Shami
12. Yusuf 'Abdullah al-Ghayshi
13. Majid 'Ali 'Abdullah al-Matri
14. Muhsin Saleh al-Hamzi
15. Ahmad Yahya Muhammad Hamid
16. Yusuf Ahsan Isma'il al-Madani
17. 'Abdullah Yahya Khatir
18. Hassan Hamud 'Athaya
19. Salman Ahmad Hassan al-'Ayani
20. Ahmad Saleh Hindi Dughsan
21. Yahya 'Ali Yahya Muhsin Fawqa'
22. Saleh Ahmad Fadil
23. Hamd Dayf Allah Faris 'Aran
24. Mahdi 'Ali Shawban
25. 'Abdullah Yahya al-Hakim
26. 'Ali Muhammad Muhammad al-Mu'ayyad
27. Ahmad Husayn Salim Sarhah
28. Husayn Muhammad 'Ali a-Ghayli

29. Saleh Musfir Farhan
30. 'Abdullah Yahya Ahsan al-Majli
31. Muhammad 'Ali Muhammad al-'Awjari
32. Muhammad 'Abdullah 'Amr al-'Izzi
33. Ahmad 'Ali Husayn al-'Amri
34. Ahmad Jabir Sari'
35. Ahmad 'Ali Qassim al-Khatib
36. Jar Allah Muhammad Isma'il
37. 'Ali Husayn 'Abd al-Karim al-Qassimi
38. Salim 'Izah Jabal
39. 'Abd al-Latif Hamud al-Mahdi
40. Saleh 'Ali al-Samad
41. Yahya Nasir al-Yusufi
42. Ahmad Nasir al-Ba'dan
43. Husayn 'Ali Da'h
44. 'Abd al-Mushin Qassim Ta'us
45. Hazmal 'Ali Hazmal Shadhabah
46. Taha Ahsan Isma'il al-Madani
47. 'Abdullah Muhammad al-Hataf al-Hamzi
48. Yusuf Muhammad 'Abdullah Dahma
49. Najib al-Kashri
50. Husayn Yahya Ahmad Hanash
51. Salih Muhammad 'Ali Rahmah
52. al-'Asir 'Ali Munsir al-Ka'bi
53. 'Abd al-Basir 'Ali Ahmad al-Hadi
54. Ahmad Qassim al-Qassimi
55. 'Abd al-Ilah Yahya Qassim al-Husni

Source: "Tadman Qa'ima bi-Asma' 55 Shakhsan, al-Dakhiliya Tatlub min al-Niyaba al-'Amma Isdar Amr Qahari bi-l-Qabd 'ala Qiyyadat al-Tamarrud wa-l-Takhrib min al-Huthiyin bi-Sa'da," *26 September,* August 18, 2009.

Sources and Challenges in Understanding the Huthi Conflict

To understand the Huthi-regime conflict, one can use both Western-language material and Arabic sources. Western material of use in studying the Huthi conflict is both academic and policy-oriented. The academic literature examines governance, kin networks, and religion. While governance-focused work illuminates Yemen's political framework, a slightly larger body of writing on kin networks explains social structures and processes in the tribal north. It illuminates the hyper-local variability within Sa'da province and the regional divides that inform tribesmen's understanding of themselves, their surroundings, and their relationships to one another. Finally, work on religion highlights the Sunni and Zaydi revivals in the 1990s that catalyzed the socioreligious identities active in the Huthi conflict. Material in Arabic sheds light on protagonists' views, the background to the conflict, and the progression of the Sa'da wars. Arabic print and visual sources also illuminate efforts by the GoY and Huthis to portray the conflict in ways supportive to their claims.

Western Literature

Recent Western policy literature tends to focus on the confluence of problems facing Yemen, such as Islamic extremism and the abundance of arms, southern separatism, and a weak economy, in addition to the Huthi-regime conflict. Considering the conflict in a post–9/11 context from the perspective of U.S. interests, policy literature obscures the indigenous Yemeni sociopolitical and cultural context. Finally, NGO writing concentrates on the human costs of the war and the blockade on the north.

Political Technology and Governance

The Huthi-regime conflict is embedded in the wider context of Yemeni history and the GoY's cooptative political technologies—the practices and rationales of governance—under President Saleh. While autonomy and resistance to the state have remained central values for northern tribal communities, Sa'da in particular, the cooptation of certain shaykhs has remained a core modus operandi for Saleh. An account of Saleh's neopatrimonial strategies can be found in Sarah Phillips' *Yemen's Democracy Experi-*

ment in Regional Perspective. Phillips explains how informal loyalties completely permeate formal political institutions in Yemen, noting the selective nature of regime patronage (*mahsubiya*) in the north.[1] Phillips describes the state as "neo-tribal"—founded on personal and kinship relations but also on the "breakdown and reinterpretation of traditional tribal mechanisms."[2]

Neopatrimonialism in the north is evidenced by the manner in which the GoY has asserted itself during the Huthi conflict. Certain tribes have been drawn into battle due to their opposition to the military in places that traditionally saw weak central government presence, while others support the state security forces in the conflict.[3] Although the Yemeni government has been accused of favoring multiple protagonists, some writers consider institutionalized chaos to be a strategic calculation by the regime.[4] Yet, by strengthening certain tribal elements at the expense of others, the regime may have weakened its core and contributed to the decay of tribal norms that prohibit violence in certain areas and against certain "vulnerable" social groups.[5] Political scientists have speculated recently that the traditional grammar of mediated violence may have been altered in a way with which the regime is unprepared to cope.

Other comparative political studies offer further insight into the history of the various actors in Yemen's public space. Carapico's *Civil Society in Yemen* notes that, until unification in 1990, tribalism provided a decentralized sociopolitical alternative to the authority of the state, which "helped organize production, group protection, dispute management, and relations with non-tribal groups."[6]

Finally, introductory texts on Yemen provide the historical context for the current study. Paul Dresch's *A History of Modern Yemen* highlights the enduring dilemma of Yemeni identity, wherein "the wish for a single Yemeni state emerged in a context shaped by outside powers. Much of Yemen's history through the twentieth century connects with efforts to form that state, which was finally established in 1990."[7] By drawing attention to tribes, Islam, north-south tensions, and governance, Dresch helps the student of the Huthi conflict to see the fraught nature of center-periphery integration.

---

[1]   Sarah Phillips, *Yemen's Democracy Experiment in Regional Perspective* (London: Palgrave McMillan, 2008), 4.

[2]   Phillips, *Yemen's Democracy Experiment*, 91.

[3]   Phillips, *Yemen's Democracy Experiment*, 108.

[4]   For instance, see Lisa Wedeen, *Peripheral Visions: Publics, Power and Performance in Yemen* (Chicago: University of Chicago Press, 2008), 179.

[5]   Phillips, *Yemen's Democracy Experiment*, 110.

[6]   Sheila Carapico, *Civil Society in Yemen: The Political Economy of Activism in Modern Arabia* (London: Cambridge University Press, 1998), 64.

[7]   Paul Dresch, *A History of Modern Yemen* (Cambridge: Cambridge University Press, 2001), 1.

Tribes and Social Fabric in the North

Ethnographic accounts of the north focus on tribes, which have been central to the politics and patronage in the Yemeni highlands. These examine Yemeni tribalism as a form of social organization and system of justice. Dresch's preeminent *Tribes, Government and History in Yemen* analyzes tribal identity, social organization, economic ties, and political interaction.[8] He defines key terms for understanding northern tribal values and structures. Dresch notes the difficulty of mapping social structures within the tribes themselves, because individual tribal members and various subgroups perceive their role vis-à-vis the whole in different ways. The most comprehensive treatment of tribal definitions and cultural contexts can be found in Najwa Adra's 1982 dissertation based on research that began in 1979 in al-Ahjur.[9] She emphasizes the role of tribalism (*qabyala*) as a values complex, representing "all that is openly admired in tribal life. Honor, the fulfillment of one's obligations, generosity, and even beauty are described as *qabyala*."[10] The author also describes other northern social strata.

Shelagh Weir's 2007 *A Tribal Order* concentrates on the politics and law of one particular *mudiriya* (district) in Sa'da, Jabal Razih, an agricultural highland and important trade hub west of Sa'da city.[11] The study demonstrates how the society she observed has a "distinct geo-political identity, [where] the tribes are stable due to their small sizes and similar organizational structures."[12] By emphasizing the hyper-local conditions informing regional tribal identities and politics, Weir's narrative calls into question the Razih model's applicability to the rest of Sa'da *muhafaza* (governorate). Still, *A Tribal Order* demonstrates how Razih's tribal structures and norms provide stability in a particular context. Such order includes mechanisms for collecting taxes, solving disputes, and avoiding physical violence, and modes of cooperation with a state respectful of tribal norms.

Various authors also disaggregate the connotations of the word *qabili* (tribal) in Yemen, noting different normative portrayals.[13] Many political scientists consider tribal processes as impediments to state formation; people from the southern high-

---

[8]   Paul Dresch, *Tribes, Government, and History in Yemen* (New York: Oxford University Press, 1989).

[9]   Najwa Adra, "Qabyala: the Tribal Concept in the Central Highlands of the Yemen," unpublished Ph.D. dissertation, Temple University, 1982.

[10]   Adra, "Qabyala: the Tribal Concept," 17.

[11]   Shelagh Weir, *A Tribal Order: Politics and Law in the Mountains of Yemen* (Austin: University of Texas Press, 2007).

[12]   Additionally, Weir writes that each tribe in Razih "has a discrete and continuous territory (*ard, bilad*) with well-defined political borders (*hadd*, pl. *hudud*) and is bounded by several others—referred to as its 'neighbors' (*awthan*) or 'abroad' (*fil-kharij*)." See *A Tribal Order*, 14 and 67. Weir does note, however, that tribal structures allow for fluidity of loyalties, which evolve through defection or the alienation of shaykhs from their tribes. See pp. 114–115.

[13]   See also Stephen Day, "Power-Sharing and Hegemony: A Case Study of the United Republic of Yemen," Ph.D. dissertation, Georgetown University, 2001, 362; and Paul Dresch and Bernard Haykel, "Stereotypes and Political

lands and the former PDRY consider northerners behaviorally rough and tending toward violence;[14] and educated urban Yemenis may see *qabilis* as uneducated and impeding modernity.[15] The GoY attitude tends toward opportunism, forging relationships with shaykhs to afford the state access to peripheral regions when needed. This is the relationship on which we focus in this book because it illuminates the pattern of interaction between the regime and Sa'da. Broadly, recent research on state roles and tribal functions arrives at the unremarkable conclusion that "rather than *causing* the state to weaken, tribes *persist* when the state is weak." Views on tribal law, for example, remained favorable among both Yemeni Sunnis and Zaydis during 2004–2005,[16] implying the tribal inclination toward conflict resolution through nonstate legal modes as a basic social value. Literature in French has recently reexamined tribal law.[17]

The most recent depiction of the north can be found in Gerhard Lichtenthäler's 2003 book, *Political Ecology and the Role of Water,* which elucidates the "political sources, conditions, and ramifications of environmental change" in the Sa'da basin.[18] Based on fieldwork from 1996 to 1999, this book reinforces Weir's example of a variegated and hyper-locally constituted north, while providing more recent examples of how tribal norms evolve to face particular challenges. Lichtenthäler considers Sa'da a "highly politicized environment shaped by power relations and interests, expressed as control and resistance."[19] Describing the geography, ecology, and economy of the Sa'da basin, he also examines tribal and social aspects. The book gives the most comprehensive chart yet produced for the Khawlan bin 'Amr tribal confederation that predominates in the areas of Huthi-regime fighting, in addition to charts on the Bakil and Hashid confederations, also resident in the north.[20]

Styles: Islamists and Tribesfolk in Yemen," *International Journal of Middle East Studies,* 27: 4 (November 1995), 405–431.

[14] Dresch and Haykel, "Stereotypes and Political Styles," 408; Phillips, *Yemen's Democracy,* 80.

[15] Dresch and Haykel, "Stereotypes and Political Styles," 408; Phillips, *Yemen's Democracy,* 89.

[16] See Dan Corstange, "Tribes and the Rule of Law in Yemen," paper prepared for delivery at the 2008 Annual conference of the Middle East Studies Association, Washington, D.C., November, 22–25, 2008. The research for the article was based on public opinion poll data from Yemen in 2004–2005, excluding Sa'da because of security issues resulting from the conflict.

[17] See Baudouin Dupret and Francois Burgat, eds., *Le cheikh et le procureur: Systèmes coutoumiers et practiques juridiques au Yémen et en Égypte* (Cairo: CEDEJ, Egypte-Monde arab series 1:3, 2005), 323–335; Centre Français d'Archéologie et de Sciences Sociales de Sanaa (CEFAS), "Le règlement des conflits tribaux au Yémen," *Les Cahiers du CEFAS* (4:2003); Rashad al-Alimi et Baudoin Dupret, "Le droit coutumier dans la société yéménite: nature et développement," *Chroniques Yémenites* 9 (2001).

[18] Gerhard Lichtenthäler, *Political Ecology and the Role of Water: Environment, Society and Economy in Northern Yemen* (London: Ashgate Publishing, 2003), 1.

[19] Lichtenthäler, *Political Ecology and the Role of Water,* 3.

[20] Lichtenthäler, *Political Ecology and the Role of Water,* 41–44. It should also be noted that several articles discuss the remnants of north-south tensions and tribe-government relations on a regional basis throughout the historical

Religion and Revivalism

Tribalism has not been the only salient identity north of San'a. Although Zaydism remains under-studied in Western languages,[21] Sheila Carapico covers some roots of the Huthi conflict in the 1990s, such as the dual "reinvention of Islam and tribalism as political ideology" in the region.[22] Partly encouraged by the regime, the revival of Islam in the 1980s and 1990s featured the promotion of imported Wahhabi/Salafi thought, and thus galvanized a response by local Zaydis, in Sa'da in particular. The Zaydi revival's political manifestation was the al-Haqq party and the Union of Popular Forces.[23] As Shelagh Weir and Bernard Haykel show, the revival also featured the "emergence of a new generation of Zaydi *'ulema* with non-*sayyid*, tribal status" who zealously defended the Zaydi *madhhab* (religious school of thought). This group produced the BY under figureheads such as Badr al-Din al-Huthi. The literature on religion also addresses generational change and factionalism within the Zaydi community as it forged a more politicized identity.[24]

By examining the GoY's particular modes of rule, the diversity of tribal hierarchies, the hyper-locality of social organization within Sa'da itself, and the role of tribalism as a values complex, the academic literature provides an introduction to the topics a student of the Huthi rebellion will encounter. At the same time, the gaps revealed by the literature—particularly the anthropological writing for which the fieldwork was done in the 1970s and 1980s—necessitate consideration of change over time in the north and recognition of the hyper-local conflict context, even within Sa'da province itself.

Policy Writings

Policy-oriented literature provides a more contemporary perspective on the broader political struggles of the GoY. The first type of literature focuses on the confluence

---

development of the state. In particular, see Stephen Day, "Updating Yemeni National Unity: Could Lingering Regional Divisions Bring Down the Regime?" *Middle East Journal* 62:3 (Summer 2008).

[21] An exception is Wilferd Madelung, *Der Imam al-Qasim ibn Ibrahim und die Glaubenslehre der Zaiditen* (Berlin: Walter De Gruyter, 1965).

[22] Sheila Carapico, *Civil Society in Yemen: The Political Economy of Activism in Modern Arabia* (London: Cambridge University Press, 1998), 59.

[23] Carapico, *Civil Society in Yemen*, 145; Sarah Phillips, "Cracks in the Yemeni System," *Middle East Report*, July 28, 2005.

[24] See Samy Dorlian, "Zaydisme et modernization: émergence d'un nouvel universel politique?" *Chroniques Yéménites* 13:13 (2006), 93–98; Shelagh Weir, "A Clash of Fundamentalisms: Wahhabism in Yemen," *Middle East Report* 204 (July–September 1997); Bernard Haykel, "A Zaydi Revival?" *Yemen Update* 36 (1995): 20–21; Bernard Haykel, "Rebellion, Migration, or Consultative Democracy? The Zaydis and their Detractors in Yemen," in Remy Leveau, Franck Mermier, and Udo Steinbach, eds., *Le Yemen Contemporain* (Paris: Editions Karthala, 1999). Haykel has also written the biography of a prominent Zaydi convert to Salafism in the 17th and 18th centuries, Muhammad al-Shawkani. See Bernard Haykel, *Revival and Reform in Islam: The Legacy of Muhammad al-Shawkani* (Cambridge: Cambridge University Press, 2003).

of stresses facing the Saleh regime on multiple fronts. Other material focuses directly on the Huthi conflict, revealing diverging views about its genesis and protagonists' goals. Recent writing also covers the humanitarian challenges and issues generated by the rebellion and GoY COIN. Most recently, work by Stephen Day, Ginny Hill, and Christopher Boucek, as well as blog posts and articles by Gregory Johnsen and Brian O'Neill, lay out the current convergence of problems in Yemen, including the ongoing Huthi conflict and the threat Saleh faces from a southern separatist movement.[25] April Longley and 'Abdul Ghani al-Iryani emphasize the potential of the southern protests to cause further instability, recommending decentralization as the best option to preserve Yemeni unity.[26] The current-affairs literature, by Greg Johnsen in particular, also covers resurgent terrorist groups affiliated with al-Qa'ida,[27] economic instability,[28] references to a possible succession crisis, and regional threats from an increasingly lawless Horn of Africa that could eventually reach the Gulf of Aden.

In the context of increasing instability in the country, an examination of small arms in Yemen demonstrates how weapons possession in Yemen fits into the larger sociocultural context of tribal and community values. This research argues that rather than "rational calculations of differential power relations between groups . . . tribal rules of behaviour . . . are the main determinants of weapons possession, use, and the consequences of use."[29] As of 2001, tribesmen in Sa'da governorate (defined as males 15 years old and over) possessed an average of two guns each, with over 290,000 weapons total.[30] The environment was thus weapon-rich before the Huthi conflict began. Because the continuing war in the north affects tribal norms, the ubiquity of weapons is likely to hinder resolution of the Huthi-regime conflict.

Policy literature concentrating on the Huthi conflict itself demonstrated greater acuity early in the rebellion, when authors had greater access to the north. Some early

---

[25] Ginny Hill, "Yemen: Fear of Failure," Chatham House, November 2008; Owen Barron, "Things Fall Apart: Violence and Poverty in Yemen," *Harvard International Review* 30:2 (Summer 2008); Day, "Updating Yemeni National Unity; Christopher Boucek, "Yemen: Avoiding a Downward Spiral," Carnegie Endowment for International Peace, Middle East Program, Number 102, September 2009; Gregory Johnsen and Christopher Boucek, "The Well Runs Dry," *Foreign Policy*, February 2009; see also Gregory Johnsen and Brian O'Neill, "Waq al-Waq: Islam and Insurgency in Yemen," a wide-ranging blog also hosting or linking to articles by these two analysts.

[26] April Longley and Abdul Ghani al-Iryani, "Fighting Brushfires with Batons: An Analysis of the Political Crisis in South Yemen," *Middle East Institute Policy Briefing*, February 11, 2008.

[27] For example, see Greg Johnsen, "Borderlands," *The National*, September 4, 2009; Robert Worth, "For Yemen's Leader, a Balancing Act Grows Harder," *The International Herald Tribune*, June 23, 2008, 4.

[28] Hill, "Yemen: Fear of Failure."

[29] Derek Miller, "Demand, Stockpiles, and Social Controls: Small Arms in Yemen," *Small Arms Survey*, Occasional Paper No. 9, May 2003, vii.

[30] Miller, "Demand, Stockpiles, and Social Controls," 26. Also see Nicole Stracke, "Counter Terrorism and Weapon Smuggling: Success and Failure of Yemen-Saudi collaboration," *Insights*, Gulf Research Center, Issue 4, November 2006.

primers on the rebellion illustrate the lack of consensus on the origins and development of the rebellion—locating it within the context of an increasingly tumultuous international scene and pointing to possible GoY concerns that a sectarian conflict would expose its own weaknesses. This writing notes the GoY's association of the rebels with Hizbullah or Iran in order to emphasize Yemen's role in the "war on terrorism."[31] Other analysts have argued that the rebellion is but one symptom of the fragility of the Yemeni state and that the conflict base grew because the Huthi movement "struck a chord with segments of society extending beyond its own members simply because it is standing up to a regime seen as feckless and corrupt." Huthi recruitment has therefore benefited from the "increasing unpopularity of the government."[32] Terrorism and security analysts, as well as economists, have also covered the rebellion in Yemen. Starting in August 2004, several Jamestown Foundation articles surveyed the Huthi phenomenon, devoting much space to official allegations of Iranian support for the Sa'da uprising.[33] Demonstrating the extent to which the sixth war is making headlines in the Western press as of fall 2009, *The Economist* ran an insightful piece on the Huthi conflict in September 2009, noting, for instance, that "Much of the reason for their [Huthi] success lies with the army itself. Its aerial bombing and artillery fire have proved better at enraging locals than at subduing bands of guerrillas; and its induction of tribal allies has pushed their traditional rivals into the Houthis' arms."[34] Nevertheless, given the hurdles in reporting the facts as they evolve on the ground, it is unlikely that future reportage will add much to the surface nature of information on the conflict.

Authors examining the Huthi conflict beyond the prism of terrorism and security consider its human impact. In this regard, the Integrated Regional Information Networks (IRIN) news is perhaps the best English source for the Huthi conflict. IRIN has published a number of articles about the conflict, most recently covering such issues as displaced persons and child soldiers.[35] The site also brings Huthi leader statements to English-speaking audiences.[36]

---

[31] Iris Glosemeyer and Don Reneau, "Local Conflict, Global Spin: An Uprising in the Yemeni Highlands," *Middle East Report*, No. 232 (Autumn, 2004), 44-46.

[32] Phillips, "Cracks in the Yemeni System."

[33] See Stephen Ulph, "Yemen Facing Insurgency on Two Fronts," *Terrorism Focus* 2:8 (28 April 2005); Andrew McGregor, "Shi'ite Insurgency in Yemen: Iranian Intervention or Mountain Revolt?" *Terrorism Focus* 2:16 (12 August 2004); Brian O'Neill, "Yemen Downplays al-Huthi Rebellion," *Terrorism Focus* 4:25 (31 July 2007); Shaun Overton, "Understanding the Second Huthi Rebellion in Yemen," *Terrorism Focus* 3:12 (17 June 2005); Brian O'Neill, "Yemen's Three Rebellions," *Terrorism Focus* 6:10 (15 May 2008). McGregor does, however, note the problematic nature of Saleh's Iran-Huthi linkage, which "does not accurately reflect historical, social, linguistic, ethnic and even religious differences between the branches of Shi'ite Islam."

[34] "Strife in Yemen: The World's Next Failed State?" *The Economist*, September 10, 2009.

[35] "YEMEN: Humanitarian Situation Worsens After Short-Lived Truce," *IRIN*, September 6, 2008.

[36] "YEMEN: Rebel Leader Warns of More Conflict in Saada," *IRIN*, February 10, 2008.

The disappearance of civilians, arbitrary arrests of those identified with the Huthis, and challenges to humanitarian access in the north due to GoY COIN measures received focused treatment by Human Rights Watch (HRW) in 2008. HRW also has noted GoY targeting of Zaydi institutions, as the former conflates Zaydi revival with armed rebellion—while also addressing Huthi violations of human rights. Finally, HRW reporting reveals the extent to which the Huthi-regime conflict extends beyond the immediate areas of fighting to include regions to which internal displaced persons have fled.[37] Though not focused on the Huthi conflict or Sa'da, National Democratic Institute (NDI) reporting on their Tribal Conflict Management Program has revealed some overall trends in the north with respect to tribal mediation, emphasizing the effect of tribal conflict on impairing the government's reach in underdeveloped areas.[38] NDI has also noted the continuing centrality of mediation principles to the tribal groups observed.[39] Most recently, the International Crisis Group has issued a concise report skillfully bringing these themes together in the context of regime-Huthi conflict and reconciliation efforts.[40]

While useful, extant material does not provide a comprehensive picture of the Huthi movement. Although political scientists have conducted qualitative research, examining archives and conducting interviews, they must still contend with barriers to research in an autocratic society. Conversely, except for Lichtenthäler, ethnographic writing does not address regional change since the 1990s. Although Dresch examines the place of tribes and their values in a changing world, his ethnographic present refers to 1977–1983; Weir conducted fieldwork in 1977, 1979, 1980 and 1993. While illuminating structural features of tribalism, these authors cannot address social evolution over time across the Yemeni highlands. Furthermore, ethnographic literature cannot elucidate social changes resulting from the Huthi conflict. Finally, these authors traveled to Yemen for research in discrete regions. While conveying an understanding of

---

[37] See Human Rights Watch, "Disappearances and Arbitrary Arrests in the Armed Conflict with Huthi Rebels in Yemen," October 2008; Human Rights Watch, "Invisible Civilians: The Challenge of Humanitarian Access in Yemen's Forgotten War," November 19, 2008.

[38] National Democratic Institute, "Yemen: Tribal Conflict Management Program Research Report," March 2007.

[39] A final noteworthy English source for information on Yemen is Jane Novak, author of the blog "Armies of Liberation." Known in Yemen for supporting the cause of various human rights and pro-democracy organizations, Ms. Novak has been extremely helpful to us in our work. She makes no claim to be an expert but aggregates the majority of English information on Yemen in one place, including an archive devoted entirely to news on Sa'da. See Jane Novak, "Armies of Liberation—Saada War File." Further, Novak occasionally publishes her own articles, which emphasize important points about the conflict, such as the repression of Hashimis, the human cost of war, and the internal schisms in Yemen's politics between an increasingly Salafi-oriented military and the civilian government. See, for example, Jane Novak, "Yemen's Internal Shia Jihad," *Global Politician*, March 21, 2007.

[40] International Crisis Group, "Yemen: Defusing the Saada Time Bomb," *Middle East Report*, No. 86, May 27, 2009.

the hyper-local nature of identities in the north, they are not focused on the Saʿda *muhafaza* as a whole.

Additionally, policy-oriented literature gives only a spotty understanding of the type of campaigns that both sides are pursuing against one another. This literature tends to be written with U.S. interests in mind rather than developed with an understanding of the sociocultural mechanisms that lay the framework for the conflict in the north. In particular, policy-oriented literature in English either exaggerates the direct line from the Believing Youth of the 1990s to the Huthi opposition of today, or obscures the role of social change and Zaydi activism in the 1990s in preparing the ground for post-2001 Huthi emergence. Further, Western analyses tend to portray Huthi actions as "insurgency," in the absence of data aligned with current definitions of insurgency used in the U.S. military doctrine.[41]

Ultimately, Western literature provides some idea of the context, roots, and proximate causes of the Huthi conflict, with the aforementioned caveats. In aggregate, it suggests that a curiously disproportionate regime reaction to Huthi opposition represents a departure in the approach to the northern periphery, and thus generates more violence. Particularly in the current international political context and dangerous regional climate, the attempt to insert the state into the periphery has yet to demonstrate success.

Arabic-Language Coverage

The media environment in Yemen is heavily monitored, and at times directly controlled, by the GoY. Indeed, journalists and editors often face court cases that result in fines, suspensions, or incarceration. Intentionally vague laws governing journalist conduct and the potentially negative repercussions of media "transgressions" lead many to engage in self-censorship, avoiding open criticism of the Saleh regime. Additionally, while independent newspapers technically exist in Yemen, journalists employed by them often simultaneously work for state-run newspapers or receive subsidies from the GoY, leading to clear conflicts of interest.[42] Such an environment complicates the Yemeni media's portrayal of the Huthi conflict.

Beyond state methods of control and cooptation that are typical across the broader Middle East, the particular sociocultural fabric of Yemen creates a context in which information is not only biased but incomplete as well. Indeed, Yemenis' knowledge of the geography, societies, and political trends outside of their immediate surroundings is severely limited, yielding highly localized reporting in which news outlets must rely

---

[41]   See, for example, Jack Freeman, "The al Houthi Insurgency in the North of Yemen: An Analysis of the Shabab al Moumineen," *Studies in Conflict and Terrorism* 32:11 (November 2009), 1008-1019; also see Ken Silverstein, "Six Questions for Gregory Johnsen on Yemen," *Harpers Magazine*, January 7, 2010, question 5 in particular.

[42]   Daniel Corstange, "Drawing Dissent: Political Cartoons in Yemen," *Political Science and Politics* 40:2: 293–296, Cambridge University Press, 2007.

on local *masadir* (sources) for information. Indeed, journalists working in San'a likely have little knowledge of the geography of the north unless they have resided there previously.

At the same time, the Yemeni media environment has been inundated with transnational news coverage from the pan-Arab press that hastily attempts to place local Yemeni events and developments in what is perceived to be their broader regional and global contexts. Such reporting tends to oversimplify local Yemeni phenomena, repeating old platitudes about the country while ignoring its idiosyncrasies. Compounded with GoY control mechanisms and the media blackout imposed on the north, the simultaneous localization and transnationalization of the Yemeni media environment yields a context in which portrayals of the conflict are opaque or incomplete at best, contradictory or nonexistent at worst.

Table H.1 demonstrates the various affiliations, biases, and methods and frequency of distribution of Arabic resources that cover the Huthi conflict, illuminating the extent to which certain sources can be utilized in understanding various dimensions of the topic. These sources are naturally rife with biases, contradictions, and varied methods of distribution, which are indicative of both the controversial nature of the subject matter and internal factors unique to Yemen.

Yemeni news outlets run the gamut from being directly affiliated with state institutions or the ruling party to being nominally independent or affiliated with opposition parties. These orientations inform the biases in their reporting. Huthi-affiliated Web pages as well as locally composed literature delineate both the Huthi narrative and local responses to the pre- and postconflict context. On top of this, many Yemenis access pan-Arab media outlets, which typically place the conflict into its broader regional context, reflecting Sunni fears of a resurgent Iran.

Government-Affiliated Newspapers

Government-affiliated outlets disseminate the regime's narrative on the Huthi conflict by highlighting different dimensions of the GoY's information strategy. Predictably, these papers reproduce both transcripts and summaries of statements delivered by government officials and nominally independent analysts. These newspapers also uniformly carry reports of government measures taken toward rebuilding the Sa'da province and compensating the Sa'da residents,[43] while highlighting GoY military victories and denying the use of heavy-handed or indiscriminate tactics.[44] The government-

---

[43] See "Ra'is al-Jumhuriya Yuwajih bi-Sur'a Mu'alajat Athar Fitnat al-Huthi fi Marran Ta'wid al-Mutadarrarin," *26 September*, October 9, 2006.

[44] See "Al-Irhabiyun Qat'u Atraf Jundi wa Isab'ahu wa Udhunihu: al-Yemen Yanfi Istikhdam al-Tiran wa al-Aslaha al-Kimawiya Did al-Huthin," *26 September*, February 14, 2007.

Table H.1
Arabic Resources Related to the Sa'da Wars

	Government of Yemen	Independent	Political Party	Huthi	Pan-Arab
	26 September / Saba' News Agency / al-Motamar / 14 October (Aden) — al-Thawra / al-Mithaq / 22 May	al-Ayyam / Mareb Press — al-Wasat / al-Ahale / al-Ghad / al-Nida'	al-Ishtiraki / al-Thawry — al-Sahwa	al-Menpar / al-Ommaal-Balagh — Qasa'id [Poems] / Khutab [Sermons]	al-Hayat / al-Sharq / al-Awsat / al-Arabiya / al-Jazeera / al-Bayana / al-Ahram Center for Strategic Studies
Daily					
Weekly					
Interview/statement					
Combat narrative					
Economic/human impact					
Regional context					
Web					
Print					
Broadcast					
Cassette tape/oral					

NOTE: The darkness of the cell indicates the means of distribution within each source category or the extent to which the topic is covered.

funded dailies, *Saba' News*, *26 September*, and *al-Mu'tammar*, thus serve as the most useful resources in cataloguing official government rhetoric and perspectives on the events of the Sa'da wars. Less useful in this regard is the Aden-based daily *14 October*, which, given its southern focus, likely has little to no access to the north. As such, *14 October* and government weeklies such as *22 May, al-Mithaq*, and *al-Thawra* primarily disseminate pro-GoY editorials demonizing the GoY's opponents.

Party-Affiliated Newspapers

The Yemeni media scene also features a number of news outlets affiliated with specific Yemeni political parties. These include, but are not limited to, *al-Thawry* and *al-Ishtiraki.net* (the Socialist party) and *al-Sahwa* (the Islah party). These report almost exclusively on day-to-day events throughout the conflict, with both antigovernment and anti-Huthi tendencies. For instance, *al-Sahwa*, which is distributed weekly in print form, can be viewed via mobile phones, and has events added daily to its Web page, has reported widely on the conflict. In one case the paper revealed that the government requested support from Salafi-leaning Dammaj institutes, likely in an attempt to draw attention to the inadequacy of GoY tactics.[45] While copies of *al-Thawry* are not available online, *Al-Ishtiraki.net* covers daily events, has conducted interviews with Huthi leaders, and was one of the first news outlets to deny the government's claim that Badr al-Din al-Huthi had been killed in 2005.[46] These party-affiliated newspapers, while certainly slanted against the government and in some cases the Huthis, remain of great utility. Ultimately, they have to balance their desire to use the Sa'da conflict to criticize the government against the fear of appearing too supportive of the Huthis.

Independent Media

While the notion of truly independent news sources in Yemen is clouded by state intrusion and subsidization of nearly all media, nominally independent Yemeni newspapers are important resources in researching the conflict. The Yemeni daily *al-Ayyam* and news Web site *Mareb Press* have been the most comprehensive in their coverage, reporting daily events and developments, including both Huthi and government casualties. *Al-Ayyam*, for instance, not only reports instances of violence but their aftereffects as well.[47] It must be noted that the GoY's frequent attempts to shut down independent Web sites is an impediment to tracking the conflict and its daily evolution. Following

---

[45] "Ithr Tasa'ud Hajimat 'Ansar al-Huthi fi al-Muhafaza . . . al-Sulta al-Mahalliya fi Sa'da Tatlub al-Musanada min Zu'ama' al-Qaba'il wa Khutaba' al-Masajid wa Mashayikh Dammaj," *al-Sahwa*, December 27, 2005.

[46] See, for example, "Badr al-Din al-Huthi Bakhir wa La Sihha li Ma Qalahu Mudir Mudiriyat Haydan Hawl Maqtalihi," *al-Ishtiraki*, October 12, 2006.

[47] "Al-Alaf Yashi'aun Dahyan Haditha al-Masjid bi Sa'da wa al-Muhafaza Yatawa'id bi-l-Iqtisas li-hum min al-Huthiyin," *al-Ayyam*, May 5, 2008.

increased unrest in the south, the *Al-Ayyam* Web site was down for most of the summer of 2009, right at the height of the run-up to the sixth war.

Independent weeklies, such as *al-Ahale, al-Wasat, al-Ghad*, and *al-Nida'*, provide less coverage of specific events during the war, instead focusing on interviews with the conflict's actors, summaries of its developments, and editorials critical of both government and Huthi supporters. For example, *al-Ahale* printed a report in which the Islah founder accused the Iranian ambassador of visiting Dahyan,[48] while another article highlights the Saudi role in driving the conflict.[49] From an event-reporting perspective, these papers focus on specific areas within Sa'da—for example, *al-Nida'* published a lengthy report on the expanding nature of the conflict.[50] Despite the total information blackout on the Sa'da governorate, *al-Ahale* is one of the few newspapers whose reporters obtained access to the Sa'da area, permitting rare, firsthand reports from the conflict zone.[51] Thus, while perhaps not as comprehensive in their covering of specific outbreaks of violence, *al-Ahale, al-Wasat, al-Nida'*, and *al-Ghad* are useful in understanding local perspectives, actors, and event summaries of the conflict.

Pan-Arab Media

Pan-Arab broadcast and print news coverage has ranged from interviews and discussions with Huthi leaders to editorials that emphasize foreign involvement in the Sa'da wars. Qatari-owned *al-Jazeera*, for example, has run a number of broadcast segments covering the conflict, including an April 2007 interview with Yahya al-Huthi.[52] Similarly, the Saudi-owned *al-Arabiya* news network has broadcast interviews with Huthi leaders,[53] while the *al-Hayat* newspaper has attempted to draw connections between Huthi and Khomeinist ideology.[54] The Saudi-owned *al-Sharq al-Awsat*, as well as pan-Arab think tanks and Web sites, reveals a clear Sunni Arab bias, popularizing a por-

---

[48] 'Abd al-Bassat Al-Qa'di, "al-Shaykh al-Razihi 'Sulayman al-Farah': al-Safir al-Irani Yazur Dahyan min ba'd al-Wahda," *al-Ahale*, undated.

[49] See "Al-Nufudh al-Su'udi Yatasaddir al-Qa'im . . . al-Yaman Saha Sira'at Jadida," *al-Ahale*, undated.

[50] "Jughrafiyat al-Harb al-Khamisa," *al-Nida'*, June 5, 2009.

[51] See 'Abd al-Mahadhri, "'Abd al-Malik al-Huthi min Ma'aqalihi fi Matra li-l-Ahali': Lan Nakun Hizban Siyasiyan, wa Walayat al-Batinin Tantabiq 'ala Hukam al-Yawm," *al-Ahale*, undated.

[52] Khadija Bin Qina (hostess), "Ma Wara' al-Khabr: Sira' al-Hukuma al-Yamaniya ma'a al-Huthiyin," al-Jazeera, April 29, 2007.

[53] Hassan Ma'ud, "Nuqtat al-Nizam: ma'a Yahya al-Huthi," *Al-Arabiya*, May 20, 2005.

[54] Faysal Makram, "Harb Sa'da . . . min al-Tahaluf ma'a al-Sulta Wasulan Ila al-Harb al-Khamisa (1 min 2) . . . al-Huthiyin Basharu al-Tamarud bi-Inqillab 'ala Hulafa'ihum wa awsaluhu Ila Hamla 'Khomeyniya' 'ala al-Mujtama'," al-Hayat, July 11, 2008; Faysal Makram, "Harb Sa'da . . . Bad'an min al-Thalif ma'a al-Sulta Wasulan Ila al-Harb al-Khamisa (2 min 2) . . . al-Huthi Fawada al-Sulta min Tehran . . . wa Libya Awqafat Da'muhu b'ad Ali Salih," al-Hayat, July 12, 2008.

trayal of the Huthis as Khomeini-inspired revolutionaries.[55] Finally, the Iranian Arabic broadcast channel *al-Alam* covered the conflict in a manner that was supportive of the Huthis' goals and critical of GoY measures.[56] Pan-Arab reporting on the conflict thus gives a regional perspective on the Sa'da wars, highlighting the role of foreign actors.

Huthi-Affiliated Web Pages

While the Huthis lack an official press, they electronically distribute their narrative via the *al-Menpar* Web page and, to a lesser degree, *New Omma* Web page affiliated with the Haqq party. Launched in May 2007, *Al-Menpar* serves as the mouthpiece of Huthi leaders, disseminating anti-GoY editorials, propaganda pamphlets, and Huthi leaders' interviews and media statements. The site is useful in gaining the Huthis' combat narrative, which is delineated in the *Basha'ir al-Nasir* (Omens of Victory) series summarizing Huthi military gains. *Al-Menpar* also contains reports on the human toll of the conflict, as well as documentation of the alleged "steps they [the Huthis] took toward supporting peace and carrying out the items of the Doha agreement," which was brokered by Qatar in 2007–2008.[57] Most recently, the Huthis have added a new Web site, *Sada Online*. Huthi propaganda is also ubiquitous, popular, and growing on several YouTube channels (including *Sada Online*), which use videos as an alternative means of exploiting violence despite the information blackout, particularly in the sixth war. These run the gamut from portions of speeches by Husayn al-Huthi and 'Abd al-Malik al-Huthi to videos demonstrating the group's military strength and the weapons they have captured. The Huthi Web pages thus serve as a vital resource for understanding the group's ideological propagation and conflict narrative.

The Zaydi-connected Web page *New Omma*, affiliated with the al-Haqq party, while not extensively reporting on the events of the conflict itself, contains a considerable amount of Zaydi *fiqh* (jurisprudential) literature, biographical information on the Huthi family, and pro-Huthi editorials. Not surprisingly, the Haqq party Web page has cautiously supported the Huthis. For instance, Hassan Muhammad Zayd delicately condemned both Huthi attacks on government forces and government escalation of the conflict.[58] Similarly, in a piece entitled "The Prestige of the State and the Wisdom of the President," religious scholar Muhammad Muftah simultaneously affirms the state's monopoly over the use of force and expresses his desire for the con-

---

[55] See "al-Yaman, al-Huthiya w-al-Hajis al-Iraniya," *al-Sharq al-Awsat*, May 15, 2008; Anwar Qassim al-Khidri, "al-Huthi wa-l-Waraqa al-Ta'ifiya al-Khasira," *al-Bayina*, May 6, 2006; Hassan abu Talib, "al-Huthiyun wa-l-Ma'raka ma Qabl al-Akhir fi-l-Yaman," al-Ahram Center for Strategic and Political Studies, July 9, 2008.

[56] "Taht al-Du': Harb Sa'da al-Khamisa!" *al-'Alam*, January 11, 2008.

[57] See "al-Huthiyun Yakshifun 'an al-Khatawat allati Qamu biha fi Sabil Da'm al-Salam wa Tanfidhan li-Bunud Ittifaq al-Doha," *al-Menpar*, October 8, 2008.

[58] "Ra'is al-Da'ira al-Siyasiya: Haml al-Silah fi Wajh al-Sulta Karitha wa la Ijad li-l-Harb wa al-Tasa'ud Ayy Mubarar," *NewOmma.net*, January 29, 2007.

flict to end.[59] While constrained by what are sure to be government suspicions of Hizb al-Haqq endorsement of the Huthi movement, the material on *New Omma* is useful in gaining a pro-Huthi perspective that is less contentious than that which is propagated on *al-Menpar*.

Given the considerable range of biases that inform Yemeni reportage, contradictions permeate the Arabic-language resources. For example, as alluded to previously, Ministry of Defense–affiliated *26 September*'s claim that Badr al-Din al-Huthi had been killed was later denied by *al-Ishtiraki*. Similarly, *al-Menpar* denied claims made by both *al-Sahwa* and official government news sources that the Huthis were removing teachers and students from a school in Haydan.[60] The Huthis again found themselves at odds with *al-Sahwa* when the latter published a report that the group attacked a military checkpoint in Marran, with *al-Ishtiraki* printing the Huthi claim that the report was intended to "cover the crimes of bombing civilian villages in the region."[61] Furthermore, *26 September* also has found itself in disagreement with *al-Ishtiraki*, accusing its report of the killing of civilians in Dahyan as being based on "false allegations."[62] These are just a few of the many examples that demonstrate the naturally conflicting dimensions of the Yemeni media environment.

Qasa'id and Khutab

Arabic resources related to the conflict also include a number of written *qasa'id* (poems; sing. *qasida*) and *khutab* (sermons; sing. *khutba*) related to both Islamic revivalism in general and the conflict specifically. These materials are significant insomuch as they can reach illiterate populations in the north and, given the methods of distribution, are virtually impossible to monitor, regulate, or censor. *Al-Menpar* contains a number of locally composed *qasa'id*, some of which are of the laudatory (*madih*) category, praising the martyr (*shahid*) Husayn al-Huthi.[63] Another *qasida* entitled "A Sa'da Child" (*Tifl Sa'da*) focuses on the negative humanitarian repercussions of the conflict, in which a child tells of the "mines to my right, and rockets exploding to my left."[64]

While some Huthi lectures are available on *al-Menpar,* a number of them also circulate among Yemenis within the conflict zone via cassette tapes and printed manuscripts. The lectures, many of which were delivered by Husayn al-Huthi in 2002, cover

---

[59] Muhammad Muftah, "Haybat al-Dawla wa Hikmat al-Ra'is," *NewOmma.net,* March 13, 2007.

[60] "Masdar Muqarib min al-Sayyid 'Abd al-Malik Yunafi ma Nushira bi-Khusus Tard al-Tulab," *al-Menpar,* March 15, 2008.

[61] "Anba' 'an Maqtal Jundiyayn bi-Sa'da wa al-Huthi Yunafi," *al-Ayyam,* November 7, 2007.

[62] "Masdar Mahali fi Sa'da Yukdhib Muz'am (al-Ishtiriki net) Hawl al-Ahdath fi Dahyan," *26 September,* March 24, 2007.

[63] 'Abd al-Muhsin Husayn al-Nimri al-Hamdani, "Qasida fi-l-Sayyid al-'Allama Husayn al-Huthi," *al-Menpar,* October 3, 2007.

[64] "Tifl Sa'da: Qasida Tahki Lisan Hal Atfal Sa'da," *al-Menpar,* November 20, 2007.

a wide range of topics. Some, such as "Surat 'Amran: First Lesson," include anti-Jewish tracts in which Husayn al-Huthi highlights the need for an Islamic (specifically Zaydi) revival.[65] Others decry the lack of religious consciousness among Zaydis,[66] while others deride American foreign policy and the U.S. relationship with the GoY.[67] *Qasa'id* and *khutab* related to the conflict are significant, given that their method of distribution makes them universally accessible to Sa'da residents, regardless of their socioeconomic background or literacy. Furthermore, the existence of *qasa'id*, which are a long-held universal means of cultural propagation in northern Yemen and are disseminated via mechanisms outside the GoY's control,[68] could reflect a growing pro-Huthi sentiment in the region.

The wide range of biases, means, and frequency of distribution associated with Arabic-language material related to the Huthi conflict thus produces an environment in which contradicting claims and reports are the norm. Indeed, gaining a unitary narrative on even a single event across these sources is virtually impossible given their various biases and local sources.[69] There is utility, however, in using these sources as archives to trace the evolution of combat methods, rhetoric, and other dimensions of the conflict as they relate to specific actors and audiences. The goal of examining such contradictory claims, reports, and depictions of the conflict should not be establishing whose interpretation is "correct" but rather noting the fact that such differences highlight the complexity, localized nature, and numerous narratives of the conflict itself.

Although a cease-fire has now been declared in the conflict, the international community will likely continue to concentrate on issues that may lead to increased instability in Yemen. In addition to the Huthi issue, these include al-Qa'idist violence, southern separatism, and any fragmentation of the ruling elite. These latter issues, therefore, will provide the basis for Western journalistic or policy writing's consid-

---

[65] Husayn al-Huthi, "Surat 'Imran: al-Dars al-Awwal: In Tuti'u Fariqan min aladhin Awthu al-Kitab Yaruddukum ba'd Imanikum Kafirin," delivered by Husayn Badr Al-Din Al-Huthi, January 8, 2002.

[66] Husayn al-Huthi, "Surat Al-'Imran: al-Dars al-Thani: wa I'tsamu bi-Habl Allah," delivered by Husayn Badr Al-Din Al-Huthi, January 9, 2002.

[67] Husayn al-Huthi, "Durus min Hadi al-Qur'an al-Karim: Khatir Dukhul Amrika al-Yaman," delivered by Husayn Badr Al-Din Al-Huthi, February 3, 2002, printed September 23, 2006.

[68] See Flagg W. Miller, "Metaphors of Commerce: Trans-Valuing Tribalism in Yemeni Audiocassette Poetry," *International Journal of Middle East Studies,* 34:1 (2002), 29–57; also see Steven Caton, *"Peaks of Yemen I Summon": Poetry as Cultural Practice in a North Yemeni Tribe* (Berkeley, Calif.: University of California Press, 1992).

[69] A very helpful basic source for understanding the human geography of northern Yemen—affiliated neither with the Huthis nor the GoY—is Ibrahim Ahmad al-Maqhafi, *Mu'jam Buldan wa Qaba'il al-Yamaniya (Dictionary of Yemeni Villages and Tribes)*, (San'a: Dar al-Kalima Center for Printing, Publishing and Distribution, 1422–2002). Although only a portion was available to this study's authors, it lists tribes, locations, and their interrelationships, also providing correct voweling according to MSA. It will be of use to researchers examining the region in the future, provided they compare the information in the *Mu'jam* to what ethnographic fieldwork has determined through close observation and interpretation of local interlocutors' understandings.

eration of the Huthi conflict. Given the barriers to obtaining information about the day-to-day happenings in the Huthi-regime conflict, therefore, as well as the growing tendency of the media to view it in terms of a Shi'ite "proxy war," analysts will need to approach writing from inside and out of the region with an increasingly critical eye.

Bibliography: Western Sources

"18 Houthi Terrorists Killed in Separate Areas," Almotamar.net, September 28, 2009. As of January 19, 2010:
http://www.almotamar.net/en/6718.htm

2004 Yemen Census, April 2007. As of March 21, 2010:
http://www.mophp-ye.org/docs/Data/2004%20Yemen%20Population%20Estimates.pdf

"Abd Al Malik Al-Houthi: Yahya Represents the Ruling Party and Wasn't in Our Resistance Movement Against America," *Al-Wasat*, August 30, 2005.

"About 140,000 Weapons Confiscated in Yemen," *Bernama.com,* June 30, 2008. As of January 19, 2010:
http://www.bernama.com/bernama/v5/newsindex.php?id=342819

Adams, Michael, "One Yemen or Two?" in I. R. Nettod, ed., *Arabia and the Gulf: from Traditional Society to Modern States: Essays in Honour of M.A. Shaban's 60th Birthday,* London: Croom Helm Ltd., 1986.

Adra, Najwa, "Qabyala: The Tribal Concept in the Central Highlands of the Yemen," unpublished Ph.D. dissertation, Temple University, 1982.

———, "Dance and Glance: Visualizing Tribal Identity in Highland Yemen," *Visual Anthropology* 11, 1998, pp. 55–103.

———, "The Tribal Concept in the Central Highlands of the Yemen Arab Republic," in Saad Eddin Ibrahim and Nichols S. Hopkins, eds., *Arab Society: Social Science Perspectives*, Cairo: The American University in Cairo Press, 1985, pp. 275–285.

'Ālá Difā', Shūrā-yi, *The Imposed War: Defence vs. Aggression*, Tehran: Supreme Iran Defense Council, 1985.

Alaini, Mohsin A., *50 Years in Shifting Sands: Personal Experience in the Building of a Modern State in Yemen*, trans. Hassan al-Haifi, Beirut: Dar An-Nahar, 2004.

al-Alimi, Rashad, and Baudoin Dupret, "Le droit coutumier dans la société yéménite: nature et développement," *Chroniques Yéménites* 9, 2001. As of January 20, 2010:
http://cy.revues.org/document.html?id=71

al-'Amri, Husayn 'Abdullah, *Yemen in the 18th and 19th Centuries: A Political and Intellectual History,* London: Ithaca Press, 1985.

Anderson, Benedict, *Imagined Communities*, new ed., London: Verso, 2006.

Ariqi, Amel, "Editor disappears after publishing critical material," *Yemen Times*, September 27, 2009. As of March 17, 2010:
http://www.yementimes.com/article.shtml?i=1298&p=local&a=1

Arrabyee, Nasser, "Interpol Agrees to Extradite al-Houthi, Government Says," *Yemen Observer*, April 14, 2007. As of October 14, 2008:
http://www.yobserver.com/editorials/printer-10012077.html

————, "Yemen's Rebels Undefeated," *al-Ahram Weekly* No. 838, April 4, 2007. As of January 21, 2010:
http://weekly.ahram.org.eg/2007/838/re8.htm

al-Asaadi, Mohammed, "Yemen Strives to Stop Firearms Proliferation," *Yemen Times*, July 30, 2008. As of February 17, 2010:
http://www.yementimes.com/defaultdet.aspx?SUB_ID=26028

al-Asbahi, Essedine Saeed, "Arms in Yemen (Part I of II): A Source of Pride or Instability," *Yemen Times*, Issue 634, December 8, 2009. As of February 17, 2010:
http://www.yementimes.com/defaultdet.aspx?SUB_ID=30699

————, "Arms in Yemen (Part II of II): A Source of Pride or Instability," *Yemen Times*, Issue 635, December 9, 2009. As of February 17, 2010:
http://www.yementimes.com/defaultdet.aspx?SUB_ID=30730

Asfaruddin, Asma, *Excellence and Precedence: Medieval Islamic Discourse on Legitimate Leadership*, Leiden: Brill, 2002.

"At Least 34 Killed in North Yemen Clashes," *AFP*, October 3, 2009. As of January 19, 2010:
http://www.google.com/hostednews/afp/article/ALeqM5jig7uQL_6Ix-nJWSsoHCgs8iKYGg

Auchterlonie, Paul, and G. Rex Smith, *Yemen*, 2nd ed., Santa Barbara: ABC-CLIO, Inc., 1998.

Barfi, Barak, "Yemen's Schizoid Take on Terror," *The Jerusalem Report*, Vol. 18, No. 10, August 20, 2007, pp. 21–25.

Barkey, Henri, "Why America Should Play the Long Game in Iran," *National*, August 13, 2009.

Barron, Owen, "Things Fall Apart: Violence and Poverty in Yemen," *Harvard International Review* 30:2, Summer 2008. As of January 21, 2010:
http://www.harvardir.org/index.php?page=article&id=1763&p=

Bedoucha, G., and G. Albergoni, "Hierarchie, mediation et tribalisme en Arabie du sud: la *hijra* Yemenite," *L'Homme*, Vol. 118, 1991, pp. 7–36.

Bidwell, Robin, *The Two Yemens*, Harlow, Essex: Longman; Boulder, Colo.: Westview Press, 1983.

Biedermann, Ferry, "Disquiet Over Rise of Yemeni Moral Police," *The Financial Times*, September 1, 2008. As of December 2, 2008:
http://www.ft.com/cms/s/0/fe1d5f30-7843-11dd-acc3-0000779fd18c.html

Bisharat, Mary, "Yemeni Farm Workers in California," *Arab Workers: Middle East Report*, Vol. 34, Washington, D.C.: The Middle East Research and Information Project, 1975, pp. 22–26.

Black, Ian, "Yemen: Soft Approach to Jihadists Starts to Backfire as Poverty Fuels Extremism: Ministers Say That Limited Resources Forced a Dialogue Between State and Terrorists," *The Guardian*, July 30, 2008.

Blanche, Ed, "Yemen Cracks Down on Militant Groups," *Jane's Intelligence Review*, August 1, 2004. As of November 20, 2008:
http://www.janes.com/articles/Janes-Intelligence-Review-2004/Yemen-cracks-down-on-militant-groups.html

Bonnefoy, Laurent, "Entre pressions extérieures et tensions internes, un équilibre instable au Yémen," *Le Monde diplomatique*, October 2006. As of November 2, 2008: http://www.monde-diplomatique.fr/2006/10/BONNEFOY/14054

———, "L'illusion apolitique: adaptations, évolutions et instrumentalisations du salafisme yéménite," in Bernard Rougier, ed., *Qu'est ce que le salafisme?* Paris: Presses Universitaires de France, 2008.

———, "How Transnational is Salafism in Yemen?" in Roel Meijer, ed., *Global Salafism: Islam's New Religious Movement*, London: C. Hurst and Company, New York: Columbia University Press, 2009.

———, "Deconstructing Salafism in Yemen," *CTC Sentinel*, 2:2, February 2009.

———, "La nation yéménite: entre fondements historiques anciens et remises en cause continues," in Joao Medeiros, ed., *La question nationale*, Paris: Institut de recherche pour le développment, 2010.

———, "Le Yémen," *L'état du monde*, Paris: La Découverte, all, annually since 2004.

———, "Les identités religieuses contemporaines au Yémen: convergence, résistances et instrumentalisations," *Revue du monde musulman et de la Méditerranée*, No. 121–122, 2008, pp. 201–215.

———, "Public Institutions and Islam: A New Stigmatization?" *Institute for the Study of Islam in the Modern World (ISIM) Newsletter*, No. 13, December 2003, pp. 22–23.

———, "Salafism in Yemen: A 'Saudisation'?" in Madawi al-Rasheed, ed., *Kingdom Without Borders: Saudi Expansion in the World*, London: C. Hurst and Company, 2009, pp. 245–263.

———, "Yemen" in Barry Rubin, ed., *Global Survey of Islamism*, New York: M. E. Sharpe, Inc., February 2009.

Bonnefoy, Laurent, and Fayçal Ibn Cheikh, "Le Rassemblement Yéménite pour la Réforme (al-Islâh) face à la crise du 11 septembre et la guerre en Afghanistan," *Chroniques yéménites*, No. 9, 2002, pp. 169–176.

Bonnefoy, Laurent, and Renaud Detalle, "The Security Paradox and Development in Unified Yemen (1990–2005)," in Michael Lund and Necla Tschirgi, eds., *The Security/Development Nexus*, Boulder, Colo.: Lynne Rienner Publishers, Inc., 2009.

Bonte, P., E. Conte, and P. Dresch, eds., *Tribus, parentele, etat en pays d'islam* [Tribe, Kindred and State in the Muslim World], presented at the Institute of Social and Cultural Anthropology et Maison Française Colloquium, Oxford University, Oxford, Great Britain, September 18–19, 1997.

Bouagga, Jalel, ed., *Voyage en Arabie Heureuse: Le Yemen*, Paris: Peuples du Monde Itinerance, 1988.

Boucek, Christopher, "Yemen: Avoiding a Downward Spiral," Carnegie Endowment for International Peace, Middle East Program, Number 102, September 2009. As of September 30, 2009: http://www.carnegieendowment.org/files/yemen_downward_spiral.pdf

Boustany, Nora, "Yemeni Proclaims His Nation's Solidarity with US in Fight against Terrorism," *Washington Post,* November 27, 2002, p. A13.

Brandon, James, "Yemen Attempts to Rein in Outlaw Tribes," *Christian Science Monitor,* January 24, 2006: http://www.csmonitor.com/2006/0124/p06s02-wome.html

Bratton, Michael, and Nicolas van de Walle, *Democratic Experiments in Africa: Regime Transitions in Comparative Perspective*, Cambridge: Cambridge University Press, 1997.

"British, French Killed and Algerian Wounded in Saada," *Al-Sahwa*, March 26, 2007.

Bruck, Gabriele vom, *Ethnographic Atlas of 'Asir: Preliminary Report*, Vienna: Austrian Academy of Sciences Press, 1983.

————, *Descent and Religious Knowledge: 'Houses of Learning' Modern Sana'a, Yemen Arab Republic*, Ph.D. dissertation, London School of Economics, 1991.

————, "Enacting Tradition: The Legitimation of Marriage Practices Amongst Yemeni Sadah," *Cambridge Anthropology* 16:2, 1992/3, pp. 54–68.

————, "Disputing Descent-Based Authority in the Idiom of Religion: The Case of the Republic of Yemen," *Die Welt des Islams, New Series* 38:2, July 1998, pp. 150–191.

————, "Being a Zaydi in the Absence of an Imam: Doctrinal Revisions, Religious Instruction, and the (Re-) Invention of Ritual," in Remy Leveau, Frannck Mermier, and Udo Steinbach, eds., *Le Yemen Contemporain*, Paris: Editions Karthala, 1999, pp. 169–192.

————, *Islam, Memory, and Morality in Yemen: Ruling Families in Transition*, New York: Palgrave Macmillan, 2005.

Bruwer, Johannes, "Yemen: War and Water Woes," ICRC Interview, December 9, 2008.

Burgoit, François, and Muhammad Sbitli, "Les Salafis au Yémen ou . . . La modernisation malgré tout," *Chroniques Yéménites* 10:2, 2002. As of January 21, 2010: http://cy.revues.org/document137.html

Burrowes, Robert D., *The Yemen Arab Republic: The Politics of Development, 1962–86*, Boulder, Colo.: Westview Press, 1987.

————, "Oil Strikes and Leadership Struggle in South Yemen: 1986 and Beyond," *Middle East Journal*, 43:3, 1989, pp. 437–453.

————, *The Other Side of the Red Sea and a Little More: The Horn of Africa and the Two Yemens*, Washington, D.C.: Middle East Institute, 1990.

————, *Historical Dictionary of Yemen*, Lanham, Md.: The Scarecrow Press, Inc., 1995.

Byman, Daniel "Understanding Proto-Insurgencies," Santa Monica, Calif.: RAND Corporation, OP-178, 2007. As of March 17, 2010: http://www.rand.org/pubs/occasional_papers/OP178

Cammann, Schuyler V.R., "The Cult of the Jambiya: Dagger Wearing in Yemen," *Expedition Magazine*, 19:2, 1977, pp. 27–34.

Carapico, Sheila, *The Political Economy of Self-Help: Development Cooperatives in the Yemen Arab Republic*, dissertation, Binghamton, N.Y.: State University of New York at Binghamton, 1984.

————, "Self-Help and Development Planning in the Yemen Arab Republic," in Jean-Claude Garcia-Zamor, ed., *Public Participation in Development Planning and Management*, Boulder, Colo.: Westview Press, 1985, pp. 203–234.

————, "Yemeni Agriculture in Transition," in Keith McLachlan and Peter Beaumont, eds., *The Agricultural Development of the Middle East*, London: Wiley Press, 1986.

————, "Autonomy and Secondhand Oil Dependency of the Yemen Arab Republic," *Arab Studies Quarterly*, 10:2, Spring 1988, pp. 193–213.

————, "Women and Participation in Yemen," *Middle East Report* 173, Vol. 26, No. 6, November/December 1991, p. 15.

————, "Yemen: Unification and the Gulf War," *Middle East Report* 170, 21:3, May/June 1991.

————, "Campaign Politics and Coalition-Building: The 1993 Parliamentary Elections," *Yemen Update*, No. 33, Summer/Fall 1993.

————, "The Economic Dimension of Yemen Unity," *Middle East Report* 184, 23:5, September/October 1993, pp. 9–14.

————, "Elections and Mass Politics in Yemen," *Middle East Report* 185, 26:6, November/December 1993, pp. 2–6.

————, "Pluralism and Polarization: Yemen's Democratic Experiment," in Rex Brynen, Bahgat Korany, and Paul Noble, eds., *Political Liberalization and Democratization in the Arab World: Arab Experiences*, Boulder, Colo.: Lynne Rienner Publishers, 1995–1998.

————, "Yemen Between Civility and Civil War," in Augustus Richard Norton, ed., *Civil Society in the Middle East*, Vol. II, New York: E.J. Brill, 1996, pp. 287–316.

————, "Gender and Status Inequalities in Yemen: Honor, Economics, and Politics," in Valentine Moghadam, ed., *Trajectories of Patriarchy and Development*, Oxford: Clarendon Press, 1996, pp. 80–98.

————, "Mission: Democracy," *Middle East Report* 28:4, Winter 1998, pp. 17–20.

————, *Civil Society in Yemen: The Political Economy of Activism in Modern Arabia*, London: Cambridge University Press, 1998.

Carapico, Sheila, and Cynthia Myntti, "A Tale of Two Families: Change in North Yemen 1977–1989," *Middle East Report* 170 21:3, May/June 1991, pp. 24–29

Carapico, Sheila, and Richard Tutwiler, *Yemeni Agriculture and Economic Change*, Milwaukee: American Institute for Yemeni Studies, 1981.

Carapico, Sheila, Tjip Walker, and John Cohen, *Emerging Rural Patterns in the Yemen Arab Republic: Results of a 21-Community Cross Sectional Study*, Ithaca: Cornell University Center for International Studies, Yemen Research Program, March 1983.

Carlson, Alvar W. "A Map Analysis of Middle East Immigrants in Detroit and Suburbs, 1961–1973," *International Migration* 14:4, 1976, pp. 283–298.

Caton, Steven C., "Power, Persuasion, and Language: A Critique of the Segmentary Model in the Middle East," *International Journal of Middle East Studies* 19, 1987, pp. 77–102.

————, "Salam Tahiyah: Greetings from the Highland of Yemen," *American Ethnologist* 13, 1986, pp. 290–308.

————, *"Peaks of Yemen I Summon": Poetry as Cultural Practice in a North Yemeni Tribe*, Berkeley, Calif.: University of California Press, 1992.

————, *Yemen Chronicle: An Anthropology of War and Mediation*, New York: Hill and Wang, 2005.

"CC Says Annulling Yahya al-Houthi's Immunity Legal Request," *NewsYemen.net,* February 27, 2007.

Center for Defense Information, "Yemen," backgrounder on U.S. military assistance, 2007. As of January 21, 2010:
http://www.cdi.org/pdfs/yemen.pdf

Center for Defense Information Terrorism Project, "U.S. Foreign Military Training: A Shift in Focus," April 8, 2002. As of January 21, 2010:
http://www.cdi.org/terrorism/miltraining-pr.cfm

Centre Français d'Archéologie et de Sciences Sociales de Sanaa (CEFAS), "Le règlement des conflits tribaux au Yémen," *Les Cahiers du CEFAS* 4:2003. As of March 20, 2010:
http://cy.revues.org/document138.html

Chaise, Christian, "One Yemeni Paper Facing Government Wrath," *Middle East Online*, June 5, 2009. As of June 10, 2009:
http://www.middle-east-online.com/english/?id=32520

Chelhod, Joseph, *L'Arabie du Sud: Histoire et Civilisation, Col 3: Culture et Institutions du Yemen*, Paris: G. P. Maisonneuve et Larose, 1985.

"Chronology: News in Brief," *Contemporary Arab Affairs*, July–October 2007, pp. 111–135. As of November 15, 2008:
http://dx.doi.org/10.1080/17550910701812305

Cigar, Norman, "Local and National Loyalties in the People's Republic of Yemen," *Journal of Arab Affairs* 8, 1989, pp. 136–140.

———, "South Yemen and the USSR: Prospects for a Relationship," *Middle East Journal* 39:4, 1985, pp. 775–795.

Colburn, Marta, *The Republic of Yemen: Development Challenges in the 21st Century*, London: Stacey International Publishers, 2002.

Collier, Robert, "U.S.-Yemen Relationship in Spotlight: Few Answers About Who Did What in Killing of al Qaeda Operative," *San Francisco Chronicle*, November 6, 2002. As of January 21, 2010:
http://www.sfgate.com/cgi-bin/article.cgi?file=/chronicle/archive/2002/11/06/MN134110.DTL

Corstange, Daniel M., "Yemen (1962–1970)," in Karl DeRouen and Uk Heo, eds., *Civil Wars of the World: Major Conflicts Since World War II*, Santa Barbara: ABC-CLIO Inc., 2007, pp. 809–827.

———, "Drawing Dissent: Political Cartoons in Yemen," *PS: Political Science and Politics* 40:2, April 2007, pp. 293–296.

———, "Tribes and the Rule of Law in Yemen," paper prepared for delivery at the 2008 Annual conference of the Middle East Studies Association, Washington, D.C., November 22–25, 2008.

Crouch, M., *An Element of Luck: to South Arabia and Beyond*, New York: Radcliffe Press, 1993.

"Cutting Off Communication Confounds al-Houthi Fighters," *NewsYemen.net*, February 15, 2007.

Daragahi, Borzou, "Blast Just One Sign of Yemen's Strife," *Los Angeles Times*, July 6, 2008, p. 3.

Davis-Packard, Kent, "Antiterror Measures Incite Sectarianism in Yemen," *Christian Science Monitor*, August 29, 2008. As of September 30, 2008:
http://www.csmonitor.com/2008/0829/p04s01-wome.html

Day, Stephen, "Power-Sharing and Hegemony: A Case Study of the United Republic of Yemen," Ph.D. dissertation, Georgetown University, 2001.

———, "Updating Yemeni National Unity: Could Lingering Regional Divisions Bring Down the Regime?" *Middle East Journal* 62:3, Summer 2008, pp. 413–436.

Deffarge, Claude, and Gordian Troeller, *Yémen 62–69: De La Révolution Sauvage à La Trêve Des Guerriers,* Paris: Robert Laffort, 1969.

DeLong-Bas, Natana, *Wahhabi Islam: From Revival and Reform to Global Jihad,* London: Oxford University Press, 2004.

Detalle, Renaud, ed., *Tensions in Arabia: The Saudi-Yemeni Fault Line,* Baden-Baden: Nomos Verlagsgesellschaft, 2000.

Dorlian, Samy, "Zaydisme et modernization: émergence d'un nouvel universel politique?" *Chroniques Yéménites* 13:13, 2006, pp. 93–98. As of January 21, 2010: http://cy.revues.org/docannexe1405.html

Dorsky, Susan J., *Women of 'Amran: A Middle Eastern Ethnographic Study*, Salt Lake City, Utah: University of Utah Press, 1986.

———, *Women's Lives in a North Yemeni Highlands Town*, dissertation, Cleveland, Ohio: Case Western Reserve University, 1989.

Dresch, Paul, *The Northern Tribes of Yemen: Their Origins and Their Place in the Yemen Arab Republic*, dissertation, Oxford: Oxford University, 1981.

———, "Tribal Relations and Political History in Upper Yemen," in Brian Pridham, ed., *Contemporary Yemen: Politics and Historical Background,* London: Croom Helm, 1984.

———, "The Position of Shaykhs Among the Northern Tribes of Yemen," *Man, New Series* 19:1, March 1984, pp. 31–49.

———, "The Significance of the Course Events Take in Segmentary Systems," *American Ethnologist* 13:2, 1986, pp. 309–324.

———, *Tribes, Government and History in Yemen*, New York: Oxford University Press, 1989.

———, "The Tribes of Hashid-wa-Bakil as Historical and Geographical Entities," in Jones, ed., *Arabicus Felix, Luminosus Britannicus: Essays in Honour of A. F. L. Beeston on His Eightieth Birthday*, 1991, pp. 8–24.

———, "The Tribal Factor in the Yemeni Crisis," in Jamal S. Al-Suwaidi, ed., *Yemeni War of 1994: Causes and Consequences*, Abu Dhabi: The Emirates Center for Strategic Studies and Research, 1995, pp. 33–55.

———, *A History of Modern Yemen*, Cambridge: Cambridge University Press, 2001.

Dresch, Paul, and Bernard Haykel, "Stereotypes and Political Styles: Islamists and Tribesfolk in Yemen," *International Journal of Middle East Studies* 27:4, November 1995, pp. 405–431.

Dupret, Baudouin, and Francois Burgat, eds., *Le cheikh et le procureur: Systèmes coutoumiers et practiques juridiques au Yémen et en Égypte*, Cairo: CEDEJ, Egypte-Monde arab series 1:3, 2005, pp. 323–335.

Dweik, Badr, *The Yemenites of Lackawanna, New York: A Community Profile*, Special Studies Series No. 130, Buffalo: Council on International Studies, State University of New York Press, 1980.

"Egypt Brotherhood Calls on Government, Rebels to Stop Fighting," *IkhwanWeb*, September 30, 2009. As of January 20, 2010: http://www.ikhwanweb.com/article.php?id=21156

Eickelman, Dale F., and James Piscatori, *Muslim Politics,* Princeton, N.J.: Princeton University Press, 1996.

Eisenstadt, Michael, "Tribal Engagement Lessons Learned," *U.S. Army Military Review,* September–October 2007, pp. 16–31.

Engel, Richard, "Yemen's Weapon Culture," *BBC News*, January 22, 2002. As of January 20, 2010: http://news.bbc.co.uk/2/hi/middle_east/1775938.stm

Esfandiari, Haleh, "Tehran's Self-Fulfilling Paranoia," *Washington Post*, August 21, 2009.

Fargues, Phillipe, "Presentation demographique des pays de la peninsula Arabique," in Paul Bonnenfant, ed., *La Peninsule Arabique D'Aujourd'hui*, Paris: Editions du Centre National de la Recherche Scientifique, pp. 155–190.

"FM: Tehran Concerned about Shiites Condition in Yemen," *Fars News Agency*, August 27, 2009. As of January 19, 2010: http://english.farsnews.com/newstext.php?nn=8806050534

"Four Killed in Sanaa Protest," *Yemen Times* 13:627, March 17, 2003.

Freeman, Jack, "The al Houthi Insurgency in the North of Yemen: An Analysis of the Shahab al Moumineen," *Studies in Conflict and Terrorism* 32:11, November 2009, pp. 1008–1019.

Freitag, U., and G. Clarence-Smith, *Hadrami Traders, Scholars and Statesmen in the Indian Ocean 1750s-1960s*, Leiden, The Netherlands: Brill Academic Publishers, 1997.

Gaffney, Patrick, *The Prophet's Pulpit: Islamic Preaching in Contemporary Egypt*, Berkeley, Calif.: University of California Press, 1994.

Gause, F. Gregory, III, *Saudi-Yemeni Relations: Domestic Structure and Foreign Influence*, New York: Columbia University Press, 1990.

———, "Gulf Regional Politics, Revolution, War, and Rivalry," in William Howard Wiggins, T. P. Lyons, and F. Gregory Gause, *Dynamics of Regional Politics: Four Systems on the Indian Ocean Rim*, New York: Columbia University Press, 1992.

GCC and US Support Yemen's Unity and Stability," *Yemen Post*, September 27, 2009. As of January 21, 2010: http://www.yemenpost.net/Detail123456789.aspx?ID=3&SubID=1323

Gerholm, Tomas, "Aspects of Inheritance and Marriage Payment in North Yemen," in Ann Elizabeth Mayer, ed., *Property, Social Structure and Law in the Modern Middle East*, Albany, N.Y.: State University of New York Press, 1985, pp. 129–151.

———, "Provincial Cosmopolitans: The Impact of World Events on a Small Yemeni Town," *Peuples Mediterraneens* 9, October–December 1979, pp. 53–72.

Gingrich, Andre, "How the Chiefs' Daughters Marry: Tribes, Marriage Patterns and Hierarchies in Northwest Yemen," in *Kinship, Social Change and Evolution: Proceedings of the Symposium Held on the Occasion of Walter Dostal's 60th Birthday in Vienna, 7th and 8th April 1988,* Andre Gingrich, Siegried Haas, Sylvia Haas, and Gabriele Palczek, eds., Vienna Contributions to Ethnology and Anthropology, Volume 5. Horn-Wien: Verlag Ferdinand Berger & Sohne, 1989.

———, "Les Munebbih du Yemen percus par leur voisins: Description d'une societe par le corps et sa parure," *Techniques et culture* 13, 1988, pp. 127–139.

Glatzer, Bernt, "Center and Periphery in Afghanistan: New Identities in a Broken State," *Sociologus* 52:1, 2002, pp. 107–125.

Glosemeyer, Iris, and Don Reneau, "Local Conflict, Global Spin: An Uprising in the Yemeni Highlands," *Middle East Report,* No. 232, Autumn 2004, pp. 44–46. As of January 20, 2010: http://www.jstor.org/stable/1559484

Gochenour, D. Thomas, "Towards a Sociology of the Islamisation of Yemen," in B. R. Pridham, ed., *Contemporary Yemen: Politics and Historical Background*, pp. 1–19, London: Croom Helm, 1984.

Golden, Tim, "Mideast Turmoil: Demonstrations: At Least 2 Killed in Egypt and Yemen as Protests Mount," *New York Times,* April 10, 2002. As of January 21, 2010: http://www.nytimes.com/2002/04/10/world/mideast-turmoil-demonstrations-least-2-killed-egypt-yemen-protests-mount.html

Greenslade, Roy, "Al-Khaiwani a 'Very Special Journalist,'" *Guardian, Greenslade Blog,* May 18, 2009. As of May 19, 2009: http://www.guardian.co.uk/media/greenslade/2009/mar/18/press-freedom-yemen

Gregg, Gary S., *The Middle East: A Cultural Psychology,* New York: Oxford University Press, 2005.

al-Haifi, Hassan, "Standing up to the Culture of Violence," *Yemen Times* 13:747, June 17, 2004.

al-Haj, Ahmed, "Yemen, Saudis Join to Stem Weapons Trade," *Yemen Times* 13:679, October 23, 2003.

al-Hajjri, Ibrahim, "The New Middle East Security Threat: The Case of Yemen and the GCC," Thesis, Naval Postgraduate School, Monterey, California, June 2007.

Hales, Gavin, "Guns in Yemen: Culture, Violence and Realpolitik," paper presented at *Guns, Crime, and Social Order: An International Workshop*, York University, May 14, 2008. As of March 21, 2010: http://www.osgoode.yorku.ca/conferences/documents/2008-05-1416NC.pdf

Halliday, Fred, "Labor Migration in the Middle East," *MERIP Reports* 10:56, 1977.

———, "Labor Migration in the Arab World," *MERIP Reports* 14:4, 1984.

———, *Revolution and Foreign Policy: The Case of South Yemen*, Cambridge: Cambridge University Press, 1990.

———, *Arabs in Exile: Yemeni Migrants in Urban Britain*, London: I. B. Tauris & Co Ltd, 1992.

Harfoush, Elias, "Between Yemen's Al-Qaeda and the Separatists," *al-Hayat* English, May 17, 2009. As of March 21, 2010: http://www.daralhayat.com/portalarticlendah/17469

Hart, David M., *Tribe and Society in Rural Morocco,* London: Routledge, 2000.

Haweidi, Fahmi, "Yemen's Ignored Issues Should Have Place in Media," *Yemen Times,* September 4, 2008. As of November 2, 2008: http://yementimes.com/article.shtml?i=1187&p=opinion&a=2

Haykel, Bernard, "A Zaydi Revival?" *Yemen Update* 36, 1995. As of October 1, 2009: http://www.aiys.org/webdate/hayk.html

———, "Hizb al-Haqq and the Doctrine of the Imamate," paper presented to the Middle East Studies Association annual meeting, Washington, D.C., November 1996.

———, "Rebellion, Migration or Consultative Democracy? The Zaydis and Their Detractors in Yemen," in Remy Leveau, Frannck Mermier, and Udo Steinbach, eds., *Le Yemen Contemporain*, Paris: Editions Karthala, 1999.

———, "Recent Publishing Activity by the Zaydis in Yemen: A Select Bibliography," *Chroniques Yéménites* 9, 2001, pp. 225–230.

———, "The Salafis in Yemen at a Crossroads: An Obituary of Shaykh Muqbil al-Wâdi'î of Dammâj (d. 1422/2001)," *Jemen Report,* October 2002, pp. 28–31.

———, *Revival and Reform in Islam: The Legacy of Muhammad al-Shawkani*, Cambridge: Cambridge University Press, 2003.

Headquarters, Department of the Army, *FM 3-24: Counterinsurgency*, Washington, D.C.: December 2006.

Hear, Nicholas Van, "The Socio-Economic Impacts of the Involuntary Mass Return to Yemen in 1990," *Journal of Refugee Studies* 7:1, 1994, pp. 18–38.

Hegghammer, Thomas, "Terrorist Recruitment and Radicalization in Saudi Arabia," *Middle East Policy* 13:4, 2006, pp. 39–60.

———, "Islamist Violence and Regime Stability in Saudi Arabia," *International Affairs* 84:4, 2008.

Heiss, Johann, "War and Mediation for Peace in a Tribal Society," in *Kinship, Social Change and Evolution: Proceedings of the Symposium Held on the Occasion of Walter Dostal's 60th Birthday in Vienna, 7th and 8th April 1988,* Andre Gingrich, Siegried Haas, Sylvia Haas, and Gabriele Palczek, eds., Vienna Contributions to Ethnology and Anthropology, Volume 5, Horn-Wien: Verlag Ferdinand Berger & Sohne, 1989.

Heper, Metin, "Center and Periphery in the Ottoman Empire," *International Political Science Review* 1:1, 1980, pp. 81–104.

Hill, Ginny, "Yemen's Fight Against Resurgent Al Qaeda," *Christian Science Monitor*, August 29, 2008, p. 4.

———, "Yemen: Fear of Failure," Chatham House Briefing Paper, Middle East Programme, MEP BP 08/03, November 2008.

"History of Huthist Rebellion in Yemen, Part One," BBC Worldwide Monitoring, August 3, 2008.

Ho, Engseng, "Yemenis on Mars: The End of Mahjar (Diaspora)?" *Middle East Report,* No. 211, Trafficking and Transiting: New Perspectives on Labor Migration, Summer 1999.

"al-Houthi Calls Foul (Savagery Behavior) of Authorities in Saada," *NewsYemen.net,* August 19, 2006.

"al-Houthi: It Is Unjustified War. Official Statement: al-Houthis Started Attacking Military Locations," *NewsYemen.net,* February 2, 2007.

"al-Houthi Welcomes America's Refusal to Classify Houthis as Terrorist," *Mareb Press*, July 6, 2008. As of March 21, 2010:
http://marebpress.net/news_details.php?lng=english&sid=12108

Human Rights Watch, "Disappearances and Arbitrary Arrests in the Armed Conflict with Huthi Rebels in Yemen," Report 1-56432-392-7, October 2008.

———, "Invisible Civilians: The Challenge of Humanitarian Access in Yemen's Forgotten War," Report 1-56432-396-X, November 19, 2008.

Hundreds of Rebels Killed in North Yemen," *UPI.com,* September 21, 2009. As of January 20, 2010: http://www.upi.com/Emerging_Threats/2009/09/21/Hundreds-of-rebels-killed-in-north-Yemen/UPI-56681253566875/

Hunter, F. M., and C. W. Sealey, *Arab Tribes in the Vicinity of Aden,* London: Darf Publishers, 1909 (reprinted 1986).

Integrated Regional Information Network (IRIN), *Guns Out of Control: The Continuing Threat of Small Arms,* New York: United Nations, 2006.

———, *Yemen: The Conflict in Saada Governorate—Analysis*, July 24, 2008. As of January 21, 2010: http://www.unhcr.org/refworld/docid/488f180d1e.html

International Crisis Group, "Yemen: Coping with Terrorism and Violence in a Fragile State," *Middle East Report*, No. 8, January 8, 2003. As of November 15, 2008:
http://www.crisisgroup.org/home/index.cfm?id=1675&l=1

———, "Yemen: Defusing the Saada Time Bomb," *Middle East Report* 86 (13), May 27, 2009. As of January 21, 2010:
http://www.crisisgroup.org/home/index.cfm?id=6113&l=1

International Monetary Fund, World Economic Outlook Database, October 2009. As of January 21, 2010:
http://imf.org/external/pubs/ft/weo/2009/02/weodata/index.aspx

"Iran Points to Saudi Terrorism in Yemen," *UPI*, November 18, 2009. As of January 21, 2010:
http://www.upi.com/Top_News/Special/2009/11/18/Iran-points-to-Saudi-terrorism-in-Yemen/UPI-54301258575310/

"Iran Ready to Solve Crisis in Yemen," *Fars News Agency,* October 29, 2009. As of January 20, 2009:
http://english.farsnews.com/newstext.php?nn=8808070460

al-Iryani, Abd al-Karim, "Yemen: the Role of the State in a Traditional Society," speech delivered at the Center for Arab Gulf Studies the University of Exeter Conference on Yemen: The Challenge of Social, Economic and Democratic Development, Exeter, England, April 1, 1998. As of October 14, 2008:
http://www.al-bab.com/yemen/gov/iryani1.htm

The Islamic Imagery Project, Combating Terrorism Center at West Point, March 2006. As of January 20, 2010:
http://ctc.usma.edu/imagery/imagery_nature.asp#sunfig

"Islamist Violence and Regime Stability in Saudi Arabia," *International Affairs* 84:4, 2008.

Ismael, Tareq Y., and Jacqueline Ismael, *The People's Democratic Republic of Yemen: Politics, Economics, and Society,* Boulder, Colo.: Lynne Rienner Publishers, 1984.

Jamjoom, Mohammed, "State-Run Media: Yemeni Military Kills 150 Rebels," *CNN*, September 21, 2009. As of January 21, 2010:
http://www.cnn.com/2009/WORLD/meast/09/20/yemen.violence/index.html#cnnSTCText

Jane's Islamic Affairs Analysis, Fearing Multiple Insurgencies in Yemen, August 18, 2008. As of May 1, 2009:
http://www4.janes.com/subscribe/jiaa/doc_view.jsp?K2DocKey=/content1/janesdata/mags/jiaa/history/jiaa2008/jiaa5152.htm@current&Prod_Name=JIAA&QueryText=

Johnsen, Gregory, "Yemen's al-Iman University: A Pipeline for Fundamentalists?" *Jamestown Foundation Terrorism Monitor* 4:22, November 16, 2006. As of January 21, 2010:
http://www.jamestown.org/programs/gta/single/?tx_ttnews[tt_news]=970&tx_ttnews[backPid]=181&no_cache=1

———, "Borderlands," *The National*, September 4, 2009. As of September 30, 2009:
http://www.thenational.ae/apps/pbcs.dll/article?AID=/20090904/REVIEW/709039984/1192

———, "The Sixth War," *The National*, November 12, 2009. As of March 21, 2010:
http://www.thenational.ae/apps/pbcs.dll/article?AID=/20091112/REVIEW/711129992/1008/ART

Johnsen, Gregory, and Christopher Boucek, "The Well Runs Dry," *Foreign Policy*, February 2009. As of September 30, 2009:
http://www.foreignpolicy.com/story/cms.php?story_id=4717&page=1

Johnsen, Gregory, and Brian O'Neill, "Waq-al-Waq: Islam and Insurgency in Yemen," As of March 21, 2010:
http://islamandinsurgencyinyemen.blogspot.com/

Kalantari, Hashem, Fredrik Dahl, and Samia Nakhoul, "Iran Military Denounces Saudi 'Killing' in Yemen," *Reuters*, November 17, 2009. As of January 21, 2010:
http://www.reuters.com/article/idUSDAH749814

al-Kasir, Ahmed, "The Impact of Emigration on Social Structure in the Yemen Arab Republic," in B. R. Pridham, ed., *Economy, Society and Culture in Contemporary Yemen*, London: Croom Helm Ltd, 1985, pp. 122–131.

Katz, Mark, "External Powers and the Yemeni Civil War," in Jamal S. al-Suwaidi, ed., *The Yemeni War of 1994*, 1995, pp. 81–93.

———, "U.S.-Yemen Relations and the War on Terror: A Portrait of Yemeni President Ali Abdullah Saleh," *Jamestown Foundation Terrorism Monitor* 2:7, May 19, 2005. As of February 17, 2010:
http://www.jamestown.org/single/?no_cache=1&tx_ttnews%5Btt_news%5D=404

Kaye, Alan S., "Review of Social Issues in Popular Yemeni Culture by Janet C. E. Watson," *Journal of the American Oriental Society*, 123:2, April–June 2003.

Keddie, Nikki R., "The Yemen Arab Republic (North Yemen): History and Society," in Jonathan Friedlander, ed., *Sojourners and Settlers: The Yemeni Immigration Experience*, Salt Lake City, Utah: University of Utah Press, 1988, pp. 1–16.

Kelley, Ron, "Yemeni Farmworkers in California," in Jonathan Friedlander, ed., *Sojourners and Settlers: The Yemeni Immigrant Experience*. Salt Lake City, Utah: University of Utah Press, 1988, pp. 69–97.

Kent, Davis, "Anti-Terror Measures Incite Sectarianism in Yemen," *Christian Science Monitor*, August 29, 2008, p. 4.

Kenyon, Peter, "Yemen Tries to Shut Down Shiite Insurgency," Morning Edition, National Public Radio, August 26, 2009. As of January 21, 2010:
http://www.npr.org/templates/story/story.php?storyId=112234278

Kepel, Gilles, *Jihad: The Trail of Political Islam*, London: I.B. Taurus, 2002.

Khalid, Shaker, "Yemeni Jews . . . From Creation to the Magic Carpet Operation," *Yemen Post*, January 5, 2009. As of May 28, 2009:
http://www.yemenpost.net/62/Reports/20082.htm

Khalidi, Omar, "Consequences of Hadrami Migration to India: The Arab Presence in Haydarabad," *Ad-Darah* 10, 1984, pp. 5–29.

al-Khameri, Shakib M., "Characteristics of Yemeni Migrant Workers," *Dirasat Yamaniyyah* 5, 1980, pp. 1–16

al-Kibsi, Mohammed, "US Supports Yemen's Security and Stability: McCain," *Yemen Observer*, August 17, 2009. As of March 21, 2010:
http://www.yobserver.com/front-page/10017099.html

Knights, Michael, "Jihadist Paradise—Yemen's Terrorist Threat Re-emerges," *Jane's Intelligence Review*, May 15, 2008. As of September 15, 2008:
http://www4.janes.com/subscribe/jir/doc_view.jsp?K2DocKey=/content1/janesdata/mags/jir/history/jir2008/jir10395.htm@current&Prod_Name=JIR&QueryText=

———, "U.S. Embassy Bombing in Yemen: Counterterrorism Challenges in Weak States," *PolicyWatch #1404*, The Washington Institute for Near East Policy, September 24, 2008.

Knysh, A., "The Cult of Saints in Hadramawt: an Overview," *New Arabian Studies I*, 1993, pp. 37–152.

Kohlberg, Etan, "Some Zaydi Views on the Companions of the Prophet," *Bulletin of the School of Oriental and African Studies* 39:1, 1976, pp. 91–98.

Kostiner, J., *The Struggle for South Yemen*, London: Croom Helm, 1984.

Kruse, Hans, "Tribal Systems and Social Stratification: The Case of North Yemen," *Indian Journal of Political Science*, 40:3, 1979, pp. 380–394.

Labaune, Patrick, "Democratie tribale et systeme politique en Republique Arabe du Yemen," *L'Afrique et l'Asie Modernes* 129, 1981, pp. 12–32.

Lackey, Sue A., "Yemen After the *Cole:* Volatile Nation Remains a Strategically Important Ally, But Experts Worry About Its Intrinsic Vulnerabilities," *Seapower Magazine*, March 2005. As of January 21, 2010:
http://www.navyleague.org/sea_power/mar_05_28.php

Lalani, Arzina R., *Early Shi'i Thought: The Teachings of Imam Muhammad al-Baqir*. London: I.B. Tauris, 2000.

Lapidus, Ira, *A History of Islamic Societies*, 2nd ed., Cambridge: Cambridge University Press, 2002.

Leupp, Gary, "The 'War on Terrorism' in Yemen," *CounterPunch*, May 20, 2002. As of January 21, 2010:
http://www.counterpunch.org/leupp0520.html

Lichtenthäler, Gerhard, *Political Ecology and the Role of Water: Environment, Society and Economy in Northern Yemen*, Surrey, UK: Ashgate Publishing, 2003.

Lichtenthäler, Gerhard, and A. R. Turton, "Water Demand Management, Natural Resource Reconstruction and Traditional Value Systems: A Case Study from Yemen," Occasional Paper No. 14, Water Issues Study Group, School of Oriental and African Studies (SOAS), University of London, 1999.

Longley, April, "The High Water Mark of Islamist Politics? The Case of Yemen," *Middle East Journal*, Spring 2007, pp. 240–260.

Longley, April, and Abdul Ghani al-Iryani, "Fighting Brushfires with Batons: An Analysis of the Political Crisis in South Yemen," Middle East Institute Policy Briefing, February 11, 2008.

Lumpe, Lora, "U.S. Foreign Military Training: Global Reach, Global Power, and Oversight Issues," *Foreign Policy in Focus,* Special Report, May 2002.

Luqman, 'Ali Hamzah, "Education and the press in South Arabia," in D. Hopwood, ed., *The Arabian Peninsula: society and politics*, Melbourne, Australia: Allen and Unwin Book Publishers, 1972, pp. 255–268.

MacDonald, Eileen, *Brides for Sale? Human Trade in North Yemen*, Edinburgh: Mainstream Publishing, 1988.

Mackintosh-Smith, Tim, *Yemen: Travels in Dictionary Land*, London: John Murray Publishers Ltd., 1997.

al-Madaghi, Ahmed Noman Kassim, *Yemen and the United States: A Study of a Small Power and Super-State Relationship, 1962–1994,* London: IB Tauris, 1994.

Madayash, Arafat, "The Arms Trade in Yemen," *al-Sharq al-Awsat English*, January 9, 2007. As of February 17, 2010:
http://www.aawsat.com/english/news.asp?section=3&id=7594

Madelung, Wilferd, *Der Imam al-Qasim ibn Ibrahim und die Glaubenslehre der Zaiditen*, Berlin: Walter De Gruyter, 1965.

Mahdi, Kamil, Anna Wurth, and Helen Lackner, eds., *Yemen into the Twenty-First Century: Continuity and Change*, Berkshire, UK: Ithaca Press, 2007.

Manea, Elham M., "Yemen, the Tribe and the State," paper presented to the International Colloquium on Islam and Social Change, University of Lausanne, on October 10–11, 1996.

———, "La tribu et l'Etat au Yemen," in Mondher Kilani, ed., *Islam et changement social,* Lausanne: Editions Payot, 1998, pp. 205–218.

"Many Killed' in Yemen Air Raid," *BBC News,* September 17, 2009. As of January 20, 2009: http://news.bbc.co.uk/2/hi/8260414.stm

Mardin, Serif, "Center-Periphery Relations: A Key to Turkish Politics?" *Daedalus* 102:1, 1973, pp. 169–191.

Marechaux, Pascal, *Arabia Felix: Images of Yemen and its People*, Woodbury, N.Y.: Barron's, 1980.

Masmari, Hakim, "President Saleh Losing," *Yemen Post*, September 27, 2009. As of March 21, 2010: http://www.yemenpost.net/Detail123456789.aspx?ID=1&SubID=1327

al-Mawry, Munir, "Yemeni MP: Clashes May Spread Beyond Northern Yemen," *Asharq al-Awsat*, February 26, 2007. As of October 14, 2008: http://aawsat.com/english/news.asp?section=1&id=8131

al-Maytami, Muhammad, "Le marche du travail Yemenite après l'unification," *Revue du Monde Musulman et de la Mediterranee* 67, 1993, pp. 121–129.

McGregor, Andrew, "Shi'ite Insurgency in Yemen: Iranian Intervention or Mountain Revolt?" *Jamestown Foundation Terrorism Monitor* 2:16, May 10, 2005. As of January 21, 2010: http://www.jamestown.org/single/?no_cache=1&tx_ttnews%5Btt_news%5D=367

———, "Yemen and the U.S.: Different Approaches to the War on Terrorism," *Jamestown Foundation Terrorism Monitor* 5:9, May 10, 2007. As of January 21, 2010: http://www.jamestown.org/programs/gta/ single/?tx_ttnews[tt_news]=4146&tx_ttnews[backPid]=182&no_cache=1

Meissner, Jeffrey R., "Tribes at the Core Legitimacy, Structure and Power in Zaydi Yemen." Ph.D. dissertation, Columbia University, Ann Arbor: University Microfilms International, 1987.

Meneley, Anne, *Tournaments of Value: Sociability and Hierarchy in a Yemeni Town*, Toronto: University of Toronto Press, 1996.

Mermier, Franck, "L'Islam politique au yemen ou la 'tradition' contre les traditions?" *Monde Arabe Maghreb-Machrek* 155, 1997, pp. 6–19.

———, "Yémen: le Sud sur la voie de la sécession?" *EchoGéo, Sur le vif 2008*, July 18, 2008. As of November 1, 2008: http://echogeo.revues.org/index5603.html

Messick, Brinkley M., "Transactions in Ibb: Society and Economy in a Yemeni Highlands Town," Ph.D. dissertation, Princeton University, Ann Arbor: University Microfilms International, 1978.

———, "The Mufti, the Text and the World: Legal Interpretation in Yemen," *Man, New Series* 21:1, 1986, Royal Anthropological Institute of Great Britain and Ireland, pp. 102–119.

Migdal, Joel S., *Strong Societies and Weak States: State-Society Relations and State Capabilities in the Third World*, Princeton: Princeton University Press, 1988.

Milani, Mohsen, "Tehran's Take: Understanding Iran's U.S. Policy," *Foreign Affairs*, July/August 2009.

Miller, Derek B., "Demand, Stockpiles, and Social Controls: Small Arms in Yemen," *Small Arms Survey*, Occasional Paper No. 9, May 2003.

Miller, W. Flagg, "Metaphors of Commerce: Trans-Valuing Tribalism in Yemeni Audiocassette Poetry," *International Journal of Middle East Studies* 34:1, 2002, pp. 29–57.

Moghram, Mohamed Abdo, "Political Culture of Corruption and State of Corruption in Yemen," Sana'a University, Yemen Republic. As of January 4, 2009:
http://www.u4.no/training/incountry-open/yemen-docs/political-culture-corruption-yemen-abdomoghram.pdf

Mojali, Almigdad, "Tribal Norms Protecting Women Are Diminishing," *Yemen Times*, September 2, 2007.

———, "When Cultural Norms Undermine Tribal Rules," *Yemen Times*, November 1–3, 2007. As of January 21, 2010:
http://www.yementimes.com/defaultdet.aspx?SUB_ID=26440

———, "Rehabilitation Program for Young Victims of Sa'ada war," *Yemen Times*, March 30, 2008. As of May 28, 2009:
http://www.yementimes.com/article.shtml?i=1142&p=local&a=2

Molyneux, Maxine, "Women's Rights and Political Contingency: The Case of Yemen 1990–1994," *Middle East Journal* 49:3, 1995, pp. 418–431.

———, "The Law, the State and Socialist Policies with Regard to Women: The Case of the PDRY, 1967–1990," in D. Kandiyoti, ed., *Women, Islam and the State*, Philadelphia: Temple University Press, 1991.

Momen, Moojan, *An Introduction to Shi'i Islam,* New Haven: Yale University Press, 1987.

Moran, Dominic, "Yemen: Discontent Challenges Government," ISN Security Watch, April 18, 2008. As of January 4, 2009:
http://www.isn.ethz.ch/isn/Current-Affairs/Security-Watch/
Detail/?ots591=4888CAA0-B3DB-1461-98B9-E20E7B9C13D4&lng=en&id=88695

"More al-Houthi Insurgents Surrender," al-Motamar.net, July 16, 2008. As of January 4, 2009:
www.almotamar.net/en/5074.htm

Mundy, Martha, *Domestic Government: Kinship, Community and Polity in North Yemen (Society and Culture in the Modern Middle East)*, London: IB Tauris & Co Ltd., 1995.

Mutahhar, Abd al-Rahman, *Social Issues in Popular Yemeni Culture*, Arabic text, plus translation into English, edited and annotated by Janet C.E. Watson, Sana'a: Social Fund for Development, 2002.

Myntti, Cynthia, "Yemeni Workers Abroad: The Impact on Women," MERIP Reports No. 124, 14:5, 1984, pp. 11–16.

———, "Hegemony and Healing in Rural North Yemen," *Social Science and Medicine* 27:5, 1988, pp. 515–520.

Nakash, Yitzhak, *The Shi'is of Iraq,* Princeton: Princeton University Press, 1994.

———, *Reaching for Power: the Shi'a in the Modern Arab World,* Princeton: Princeton University Press, 2006.

National Democratic Institute for International Affairs, *Yemen: Tribal Conflict Management Program Research Report*, Washington, D.C., NDI, March 2007. As of January 21, 2010:
http://www.ndi.org/files/2368_ye_report_engpdf_09122008.pdf

"New Reinforcements by Army, Al-Houthi Prepared for Guerrilla War," *Yemen Post,* Saa'da War Weekly, January 28, 2008. As of November 15, 2008:
http://www.yemenpost.net/SadaWeeklyReview/2.htm

"Northern Yemen: Population Faces Increasingly Cold Winter," International Committee of the Red Cross, February 2, 2009. As of January 20, 2009:
http://www.icrc.org/web/eng/siteeng0.nsf/htmlall/
yemen-update-010109?OpenDocument&style=custo_print

"North Yemen Calm After Truce," *al-Jazeera.net*, February 12, 2010. As of February 15, 2010:
http://english.aljazeera.net/news/middleeast/2010/02/2010211183014399724.html

Novak, Jane, "Yemen's Internal Shia Jihad," *Global Politician*, March 21, 2007. As of March 21, 2010:
http://www.genocidewatch.org/images/Yemen_07_03_21_Yemen_s_Internal_Shia_Jihad.doc

———, "Ali Abdullah Saleh Family in Yemen Govt. and Business," Armies of Liberation, April 8, 2006. As of May 18, 2009:
http://armiesofliberation.com/archives/2006/04/08/
ali-abdullah-saleh-family-in-yemen-govt-and-business/

———, "Saada War File," Armies of Liberation. As of January 20, 2010:
http://armiesofliberation.com/archives/category/yemen/a-security/saada-war/

———, "Yemen Strikes Multi-Faceted Deals with al-Qaeda," *The Long War Journal*, February 11, 2009. As of January 21, 2010:
http://janenovak.wordpress.com/2009/02/13/yemen-strikes-multi-faceted-deals-with-al-qaeda/

O'Neill, Brian, "Yemen Downplays al-Huthi Rebellion," *Terrorism Focus* 4:25, July 31, 2007.

———, "Yemen's Three Rebellions," *Terrorism Focus* 6:10, May 15, 2008.

Obermeyer, G., "al-Iman and al-Imam: Ideology and State in the Yemen, 1900–1948," in Marwan R. Buheiry, ed., *Intellectual Life in the Arab East 1890–1939*, Beirut: American University, 1981.

"Official Statistics Show 750,000 African Refugees in Yemen," *Yemen Observer*, September 9, 2008. As of May 15, 2009:
http://www.yobserver.com/local-news/10014898.html

Oudah, Abdul-Aziz, "Al-Jawf Citizens Prepare to Resort to KSA," *Yemen Observer*, April 7, 2009. As of January 21, 2010:
http://www.yobserver.com/local-news/10016109.html

———, "BHS Works to Secure Health Care for Poorest Areas," *Yemen Observer,* March 31, 2007. As of May 26, 2009:
http://www.yobserver.com/reports/10011985.html

Overton, Shaun, "The Yemeni Arms Trade: Still a Concern for Terrorism and Regional Security," *Jamestown Foundation Terrorism Monitor* 3:9, May 6, 2005.

———, "Understanding the Second Houthi Rebellion in Yemen," *Jamestown Foundation Terrorism Monitor* 3:12, June 17, 2005.

Peterson, J. E., "The al-Huthi Conflict in Yemen," Arabian Peninsula Background Note, APBN-006, published on www.JEPeterson.net, August 2008. As of January 21, 2010:

http://www.jepeterson.net/sitebuildercontent/sitebuilderfiles/APBN-006_Yemen_al-Huthi_Conflict.pdf

———, "Tribes and Politics in Yemen," Arabian Peninsula Background Note, APBN-007, published on www.JEPeterson.net, December 2008. As of May 1, 2009: http://www.jepeterson.net/sitebuildercontent/sitebuilderfiles/APBN-007_Tribes_and_Politics_in_Yemen.pdf

"Petraeus: US will Support Yemen Anti-Terror Fight," Embassy of the Republic of Yemen Media Office Web site, July 27, 2009. As of January 20, 2009: http://www.yemenembassy.org/pressrel/medianews/index.php?id=view&fn_mode=fullnews&fn_id=37

Phillips, Sarah, "Cracks in the Yemeni System," *Middle East Report*, July 28, 2005. As of February 19, 2009: http://www.merip.org/mero/mero072805.html

———, *Yemen's Democracy Experiment in Regional Perspective: Patronage & Pluralized Authoritarianism*, New York: Palgrave McMillan, 2008.

Piscatori, James, ed., *Islamic Fundamentalisms and the Gulf Crisis*, Chicago: University of Chicago Press, 1991.

"Pity Those Caught in the Middle," *Economist*, November 19, 2009. As of January 20, 2009: http://www.economist.com/world/middleeast-africa/displaystory.cfm?story_id=14920092

Plaut, Martin, "Yemen & Eritrea: Friends Once More?" *Review of African Political Economy* 25:78, December 1998, pp. 659–661.

"PM Approves Saada Reconstruction Fund's 2009 Budget," *Saba News Agency*, March 23, 2009. As of May 26, 2009: http://www.sabanews.net/en/news179106.htm

Prados, Alfred B., and Jeremy M. Sharp, "Yemen: Current Conditions and U.S. Relations," *CRS Report for Congress,* January 4, 2007.

Pradhan, Prasanta Kumar, "Houthis and External Intervention in Yemen," *IDSA Comment*, Institute for Defence Studies and Analyses, November 25, 2009. As of January 21, 2010: http://www.idsa.in/idsacomments/HouthisandexternalinterventioninYemen_pkpradhan_251109

"Pre-empting Terrorism in Yemen: U.S. Special Forces are in Osama bin Laden's Home Ground Assisting Local Soldiers to Hunt al Qaeda Terrorists," *Veterans of Foreign Wars Magazine,* August 2002. As of January 20, 2010: http://www.vfw.org/resources/levelxmagazine/0208_Soldiers%20Hunt%20al%20Qaeda.pdf

"President Saleh Says Conflict in Sa'ada Is 'Over,' al-Houthi Demands Doha Deal Implementation," *NewsYemen.net*, July 19, 2008.

Pridham, B. R., ed., *Economy, Society and Culture in Contemporary Yemen*, London: Croom Helm, 1985.

Puin, G. R., "The Yemenite *hijrah* concept of tribal protection," in T. Khalidi, ed., *Land Reform and Social Transformation in the Middle East*, Beirut: American University, 1984.

Putz, Ulrike, "Hezbollah Exhibit Celebrates War and 'Martyrs,'" *Spiegel Online*, September 4, 2008. As of January 21, 2010: http://www.spiegel.de/international/world/0,1518,576267,00.html

al-Rasheed, Madawi, *Politics in an Arabian Oasis: The Rashidis of Saudi Arabia*, London: IB Tauris, 1997.

al-Rasheed, Madawi, and Robert Vitalis, eds., *Counter-Narratives: History, Contemporary Society, and Politics in Saudi Arabia and Yemen*, New York: Palgrave Macmillan, 2004.

Raum, Tom, "Cheney Promises Help to Yemen in War on Terror," Seattlepi.com, March 15, 2002. As of March 21, 2010:
http://www.seattlepi.com/national/62370_dick15.shtml

———, "Cheney Discusses Terror War in Yemen," *BBC News*, March 14, 2002. As of March 21, 2010:
http://news.bbc.co.uk/2/hi/middle_east/1872648.stm

"Rebellion in Yemen: Sa'dah Conflict 2004–2007," BIPPI.org, March 2007. As of January 15, 2009:
http://www.bippi.org/bippi/menu_left/conflicts/Yemen/Yemen.htm

"Rebels Kill Battalion in Harf Sufyan, Spokesman Claims," *Yemen Post*, September 27, 2009. As of March 21, 2010:
http://www.yemenpost.net/Detail123456789.aspx?ID=100&SubID=1321&MainCat=3

Republic of Yemen Central Statistics Organization, 2004 Census Data Release. As of January 21, 2010:
http://www.cso-yemen.org/content.php?lng=english&pcat=234

Reuters AlertNet—Yemen. As of September 30 2008:
http//www.alertnet.org/thefacts/countryprofiles/221859.htm

Robinson, Glenn E., "Palestinian Tribes, Clans, and Notable Families," *Strategic Insights*, Fall 2008. As of January 21, 2010:
http://www.nps.edu/Academics/centers/ccc/publications/OnlineJournal/2008/Sep/robinsonSep08.html/

Rodionov, M., "Poetry and Power in Hadramawt," *New Arabian Studies* 3, 1996, pp. 118–133.

Ronfeldt, David, *In Search of How Societies Work: Tribes—The First and Forever Form,* Santa Monica, Calif.: RAND Corporation, WR-433-RPC, 2006. As of January 18, 2009:
http://www.rand.org/pubs/working_papers/WR433/

Rosefsky-Wickham, Carrie, *Mobilizing Islam: Religion, Activism, and Political Change in Egypt,* New York: Columbia University Press, 2002.

Rosen, Lawrence, *The Culture of Islam: Changing Aspects of Contemporary Muslim Life,* Chicago: University of Chicago Press, 2002.

"The Saada War in Yemen," *Jane's Intelligence Digest*, April 27, 2007. As of May 13, 2009:
http://www.janes.com/articles/Janes-Intelligence-Digest-2007/The-Saada-war-in-Yemen.html

"Sadrists Do Not Back Houthis–MP," *Aswat al-Iraq*, September 12, 2009. As of January 20, 2010:
http://en.aswataliraq.info/?p=118912

"Sahwa Net Correspondent Wounded in Sa'da," *al-Sahwa.net*, September 28, 2009. As of January 20, 2010:
http://www.alsahwanet.net/view_nnews.asp?sub_no=401_2009_09_28_73151

Saif, Abdelkareem, "Yemen: State Weakness and Society Alienation," *al-Masar Journal* 1:2, 2000, pp. 1–15. As of January 21, 2010:
http://www.al-bab.com/yemen/pol/saifstate.htm

Sallam, Mohammed bin, "200 Killed or Wounded: Al-Hothy Appeals," *Yemen Times*, June 30, 2004.

———, "Houthis Seize Four Sa'ada Districts," *Yemen Times*, April 29, 2007.

———, "Yemen Recalls its Ambassador to Iran and Libya," *Yemen Times,* May 16, 2007.

————, "Dozens Killed as Sa'ada Clashes Become Fierce," *Yemen Times,* June 29, 2008.

————, "Sa'ada Security Situation Relatively Calm," *Yemen Times*, August 17, 2008.

————, "Blaming the Government for Only Being Interested in Upcoming Election Houthis Claim YR 300 Billion in Compensation for War-Related Damage," *Yemen Times,* September 24, 2008. As of May 26, 2009:
http://www.yementimes.com/article.shtml?i=1193&p=local&a=1

————, "Four Killed, Six Injured in Shia Ghadir Day Celebrations," *Yemen Times*, December 17, 2008. As of May 26, 2009:
http://www.yementimes.com/article.shtml?i=1217&p=local&a=2

Salmoni, Barak, "Islamization and American Policy," in James A. Russell, ed., *Critical Issues Facing the Middle East,* London: Palgrave Macmillan, 2006.

Salzman, Philip Carl, *Culture and Conflict in the Middle East,* New York: Humanity Books, 2008.

"Saudi Arabia: Satisfaction with the F-5 Performance," *Tactical Report*, December 4, 2009. As of January 20, 2010:
http://tacticalreport.com/view_news/Saudi_Arabia:_Satisfaction_with_the_F-5_performance/942

"Saudis and Yemenis Versus Jihadists: A Bloody Border," *Economist*, November 5, 2009. As of January 21, 2010:
http://www.economist.com/world/middleeast-africa/displaystory.cfm?story_id=14816827

"Saudis Taking Lead in Battling Houthi Rebels," *Peninsula*, December 2, 2009. As of January 20, 2010:
http://www.gulfinthemedia.com/index.php?m=politics&id=497556&lim=20&lang=en&tblpost=2009_12&PHPSESSID=8

Sayigh, Yezid, *Armed Struggle and the Search for State: The Palestinian National Movement 1949–1993*, Oxford, UK: Clarendon Press, 1997.

Schmitz, Charles, "Book Review of Political Ecology and the Role of Water: Environment, Society, and Economy in Northern Yemen, by Gerhard Lichtenthäler," *Journal of Political Ecology,* 11, 2004, pp. 14–17.

Schwedler, Jillian, "Yemen's Aborted Opening," *Journal of Democracy* 13:4, 2002, pp. 33–44.

Scott, Hugh, *In the High Yemen*, London: Macmillan, 1942.

Serjeant, R. B., "Historian and Historiography of Hadramaut," *Bulletin of the School of Oriental and African Studies*, London, 15, 1962, pp. 239–261.

————, "The Zaydī Tribes of the Yemen: A New Field Study," *Bulletin of the School of Oriental and African Studies,* University of London, 55:1, Cambridge University Press on behalf of School of Oriental and African Studies, 1992.

Serjeant, R. B., ed., "Dawlah, Tribal Shaykhs, the Mansab of the Waliyyah Sa'idah, *Qasamah* in the Fadli Sultanate, South Arabian Federation," in Ibrahim Mooawiyah, *Arabian Studies in Honour of Mahmoud Ghul,* Wiesbaden: Harassowitz, 1989.

Shadhili, Wafeq, "Wheat or Qat!" *Yemen Times,* 15:1133, February 28, 2008. As of January 21, 2010:
http://www.yementimes.com/article.shtml?i=1133&p=opinion&a=3

Sharif, Abdu H., "Weak Institutions and Democracy: The Case of the Yemeni Parliament, 1993–1997," *Middle East Policy* 9:1, 2002, pp. 82–93.

Sharp, Jeremy M., "Yemen: Background and U.S. Relations," Congressional Research Service, January 22, 2009.

al-Shawthabi, Abdul Rahim, "Government Investigates with 70 Rebel Soldiers," *Yemen Post,* February 9, 2009. As of January 21, 2010:
http://www.yemenpost.net/67/LocalNews/20086.htm

———, "Jambiya: Deep-Rooted Tradition," *Yemen Post,* March 12, 2009. As of January 21, 2010:
http://www.yemenpost.net/Detail123456789.aspx?ID=3&SubID=170&MainCat=5

"Shia Fighters 'Capture Another Gov't Position,'" *PressTV* (Iran), October 3, 2009: As of January 20, 2010:
http://www.presstv.ir/detail.aspx?id=107725&sectionid=351020206

Silverstein, Ken, "Six Questions for Gregory Johnsen on Yemen," *Harpers Magazine,* January 7, 2010.

Solnick, Steven, "Will Russia Survive?" in Barnett R. Rubin and Jack Snyder, eds., *Post-Soviet Political Order: Conflict and State Building,* London: Routledge, 1998.

Stark, Freya, *The Southern Gates of Arabia: A Journey in the Hadramaut,* London: John Murray, 1936.

"State-Run Media: Yemeni Military Kills 150 Rebels," *CNN.com,* September 21, 2009. As of March 21, 2010:
http://edition.cnn.com/2009/WORLD/meast/09/20/yemen.violence/index.html

Stevenson, Thomas, "Yemeni Workers Come Home: Reabsorbing One Million Migrants," *Middle East Report* 23:2, March–April 1993.

Stracke, Nicole, "Counter-Terrorism and Weapon Smuggling: Success and Failure of Yemeni-Saudi Collaboration," Gulf Research Center Security and Terrorism Research Bulletin, Issue 4, November 2006, p. 10. As of March 21, 2010:
http://edoc.bibliothek.uni-halle.de/servlets/MCRFileNodeServlet/HALCoRe_derivate_00002730/Security%20&%20Terrorism.pdf;jsessionid=lhev6w0l43h0?hosts=

"Strife in Yemen: The World's Next Failed State?" *Economist,* September 10, 2009.

Swagman, Charles F., "Tribe and Politics: An Example from Highland Yemen," *Journal of Anthropological Research* 44:3, 1988.

———, *Development and Social Change in Highland Yemen,* Salt Lake City: University of Utah Press, 1988.

Takeyh, Ray, *Guardians of the Revolution: Iran and the World in the Age of the Ayatollahs,* New York: Oxford University Press, 2009.

Taminian, Lucine, "Persuading the Monarchs: Poetry and Politics in Yemen, 1920–50," in R. Leveau, F. Mermier, and U. Steinbach, eds., *Le Yemen contemporain,* Paris: Editions Karthala, 1999.

Taminian, Lucine, ed., *Challenging the Familiar: Anthropological and Historical Studies of Yemen,* Tucson, Ariz.: American Institute for Yemen Studies, MESA Secretariat, 2006.

"Three of the Insurgency Leaders Killed," *Almotamar.net,* September 4, 2009. As of January 20, 2010:
http://www.almotamar.net/en/6637.htm

Toumi, Habib, "Yemen Security High on the GCC Agenda Summit," *Gulf News,* November 17, 2009. As of March 21, 2010:
http://gulfnews.com/news/gulf/kuwait/yemen-security-high-on-the-gcc-agenda-summit-1.528709

Tutwiler, R., "Tribe, Tribute and Trade: Social Class Formation in Highland Yemen," unpublished Ph.D. thesis, SUNY Binghamton, 1987.

"Two Dead in New Clashes in Troubled South Yemen," *Reuters*, June 8, 2009.

Tyler, Patrick E., "Yemen, an Uneasy Ally, Proves Adept at Playing off Old Rivals," *New York Times*, December 19, 2002, p. A1. As of January 21, 2010:
http://www.nytimes.com/2002/12/19/world/threats-responses-mideast-yemen-uneasy-ally-proves-adept-playing-off-old-rivals.html

Ulph, Stephen, "Yemen Facing Insurgency on Two Fronts," *Terrorism Focus* 2:8, April 28, 2005. As of January 21, 2010:
http://www.jamestown.org/programs/gta/single/?tx_ttnews%5Btt_news%5D=30319&tx_ttnews%5BbackPid%5D=238&no_cache=1

———, "UN Agency Fears 30 Somali Boat People Dead in Tragedy Off the Coast of Yemen," *UN News Center*, April 7, 2009. As of June 10, 2009:
http://www.un.org/apps/news/story.asp?NewsID=30414&Cr=gulf+of+aden&Cr1=

United Nations Children's Fund, *UNICEF Humanitarian Action Report 2009*, New York: UNICEF, 2009. As of January 21, 2010:
http://www.unicef.org/har09/files/HAR_2009_FULL_Report_English.pdf

United Nations Security Council, "Report of the Monitoring Group on Somalia Pursuant to Security Council Resolution 1811 (2008)," S/2008/768, December 10, 2008.

———, "Report of the Panel of Experts on Somalia Pursuant to Security Council Resolution 1474 (2003)," S/2003/1035, November 4, 2003.

"United States Provided 121 Million Dollars as Assistance to Yemen; Yahya Al-Houthi Rejects," *Yemen Post*, September 17, 2009.

U.S. State Department Bureau of Democracy, Human Rights and Labor, "Yemen: International Religious Freedom Report," 2007. As of May 26, 2009:
http://www.state.gov/g/drl/rls/irf/2007/90224.htm

"US Offers Yemen Help in 'Fight Against Terrorism,'" *al-Arabiya,* September 7, 2009. As of January 20, 2010:
 http://www.alarabiya.net/articles/2009/09/07/84190.html

Van Hear, N., "The Socio-Economic Impact of the Involuntary Mass Return to Yemen in 1990," *Journal of Refugee Studies* 7:1, 1994, pp. 18–38.

"War Continues, Government Warns About Media Coverage," *Yemen Times*, March 11, 2007.

"Weapons in Yemen," *IRIN Films* (United Nations), November 8, 2007. As of May 21, 2009:
http://www.youtube.com/watch?v=aI_AGXb1-Ec

Weber, Max, *The Theory of Social and Economic Organization*, New York: Free Press, 1947.

Wedeen, Lisa, *Peripheral Visions: Publics, Power and Performance in Yemen,* Chicago: University of Chicago Press, 2008.

Weir, Shelagh, "A Clash of Fundamentalisms: Wahhabism in Yemen," *Middle East Report* 204, July–September 1997.

———, *A Tribal Order: Politics and Law in the Mountains of Yemen*, Austin: University of Texas Press, 2007.

———, "Qat in Yemen: Consumption and Social Change," London: British Museum, 1985.

———, "Trade and Tribal Structures in North West Yemen," *Cahiers du GREMAMO* 10, 1991, pp. 87–101.

Worth, Robert, "Yemen's Instability Grows as One of 3 Insurgencies Heats Up," *New York Times,* August 10, 2009. As of January 21, 2010:
http://www.nytimes.com/2009/08/11/world/middleeast/11yemen.html

Worth, Robert F., "Yemen's Government Agrees to a Cease-Fire with Rebel Forces," *New York Times,* February 11, 2010. As of February 15, 2010:
http://www.nytimes.com/2010/02/12/world/middleeast/12yemen.html?scp=1&sq=houthi&st=cse

———, "Yemen Seems to Reject Cease-Fire with Rebels," *New York Times,* January 31, 2010. As of February 15, 2010:
http://www.nytimes.com/2010/02/01/world/middleeast/01houthis.html?scp=3&sq=houthi&st=cse

———, "For Yemen's Leader, a Balancing Act Grows Harder," *International Herald Tribune,* June 23, 2008, p. 4.

———, "Gunman Kills 8 Worshipers at Mosque in Yemen," *New York Times,* May 31, 2008, p. A1.

Wurth, A., "A Sanaa Court: The Family and the Ability to Negotiate," *Islamic Law and Society* 2–3, 1995, pp. 320–340.

Yamani, Mai, "The Two Faces of Saudi Arabia," Survival 50:1, February–March 2008, pp. 143–156.

"Yemen Army Air Raid Kills 80 Civilians: Witnesses," *al-Arabiya.net,* September 17, 2009. As of January 20, 2010:
http://www.alarabiya.net/articles/2009/09/17/85222.html

"Yemen Blames Sadrists for Rebel Support," *UPI.com,* September 10, 2009. As of January 20, 2010:
http://www.upi.com/Emerging_Threats/2009/09/10/Yemen-blames-Sadrists-for-rebel-support/UPI-75331252602463/

"Yemen to Buy Russian Weapons," *New York Times,* December 7, 2008: As of January 20, 2010:
http://www.nytimes.com/2009/02/27/world/africa/27iht-27yemen.20489549.html

Yemen Central Statistics Organization 2004 census data release, 2004. As of May 27, 2009:
http://www.cso-yemen.org/content.php?lng=english&pcat=234

"YEMEN: Children in Clash-Prone North Highly Traumatized—Aid Workers," *IRIN News,* February 18, 2008. As of January 20, 2010:
http://www.irinnews.org/Report.aspx?ReportId=76801

"Yemen Clashes: Northern Mountain Rebellion," *Alertnet,* Thomson Reuters Foundation, May 30, 2008. As of January 20, 2010: http://www.alertnet.org/db/crisisprofiles/YE_CLA.htm

"Yemen Conflict Inflaming Saudi-Iranian Rivalry," *CBS News,* November 24, 2009.

"Yemen: The Conflict in Saada Governorate—Analysis," *IRIN*—UN Office for the Coordination of Humanitarian Affairs, July 24, 2008. As of May 26, 2009:
http://www.irinnews.org/Report.aspx?ReportId=79410

"Yemen: Coping with Terrorism and Violence in a Fragile State," *Middle East Report* 8, January 8, 2003. As of November 15, 2008:
http://www.crisisgroup.org/home/index.cfm?id=1675&l=1

"Yemen: Despite Ban on Arms, Activists Warn of Increasing Violence," *IRIN News,* July 8, 2007. As of January 20, 2010:
http://www.irinnews.org/Report.aspx?ReportId=73130

"Yemen to Establish Coast Guard with U.S. Assistance," *MarineLink.com,* October 18, 2002. As of January 20, 2010:
http://marinelink.com/Story/Yemen+to+Establish+Coast+Guard+with+U.S.+Assistance-9687.html

"Yemen to Fight Rebels for 'Years,'" *BBC News,* September 26, 2009: As of January 20, 2010: http://news.bbc.co.uk/2/hi/middle_east/8276438.stm

"YEMEN: Government Calls for International Support to Reconstruct War-Affected Areas," *IRIN,* September 18, 2008. As of May 26, 2009: http://www.alertnet.org/thenews/newsdesk/IRIN/938a2c6ab46e2dd62bdda1719e772a18.htm

"Yemen: Human Rights Defender and Journalist Abdul-Karim al-Khaiwani Sentenced to Six Years Imprisonment," *Front Line,* June 10, 2008. As of February 19, 2009: http://www.frontlinedefenders.org/node/1463

"YEMEN: Humanitarian Situation Worsens After Short-Lived Truce," *IRIN,* September 6, 2008. As of January 20, 2010: http://www.irinnews.org/Report.aspx?ReportId=86022

"Yemen: Investigate Aerial Bomb Attacks," Human Rights Watch, September 16, 2009. As of January 20, 2010: http://www.hrw.org/en/news/2009/09/16/yemen-investigate-aerial-bomb-attacks

"Yemen Protests to Iran over Shi'ite Rebels," *Reuters,* August 31, 2009. As of January 20, 2010: http://www.reuters.com/article/worldNews/idUSTRE57U2MY20090831

"Yemen Rejects Houthi Truce Offer," *al-Jazeera English*, January 31, 2010. As of February 15, 2010: http://english.aljazeera.net/news/middleeast/2010/01/2010131947582572.html

"YEMEN: Saada City Residents Most Affected by Fighting," *IRIN,* September 24, 2009. As of January 20, 2010: http://www.irinnews.org/Report.aspx?ReportId=86129

"Yemen: Spotlight on IDPs in Amran," *IRIN News*, August 18, 2008. As of May 26, 2009: http://www.irinnews.org/Report.aspx?ReportId=79860.

"YEMEN: Rebel Leader Warns of More Conflict in Saada," *IRIN,* February 10, 2008. As of January 20, 2010: http://www.alertnet.org/thenews/newsdesk/IRIN/249972bf301e3a07ac833945b8252212.htm

"Yemen Troops Pound Northern Rebels with Artillery," *al-Arabiya TV, Mosaic News,* September 29, 2009. As of January 20, 2010: http://www.linktv.org/scripts/episode_transcript.php?episode=mosaic20090929

"Yemen: Weapons Ban Declared in Capital," *Almotamar.net*, August 24, 2007. As of February 17, 2010: http://www.almotamar.net/en/3264.htm

"Yemeni Forces Kill 28 Houthis in North," *Press TV* (Iran), September 30, 2009. As of March 21, 2010: http://www.presstv.ir/detail.aspx?id=107531&sectionid=351020206

"Yemeni Leader Blames Sa'dah Rebellion on Deposed Traditional Rulers," *BBC Worldwide Monitoring,* June 23, 2008.

"Yemeni Public Opinion Pressure Forced Government to End Saada Insurgency," *Almotamar.net*, August 20, 2009. As of March 21, 2010: http://almotamar.net/en/6588.htm

al-Yemeni, Maryam, and Nadia Al-Sakkaf, "Relative Optimism As Humanitarian Aid Slowly Finds Its Way to Sa'da," *Yemen Times,* July 30, 2008.

"Yemen's Elusive Peace Deal: A Bloody Blame Game," *Economist*, February 4, 2010. As of February 15, 2010:
http://www.economist.com/world/middleeast-africa/displaystory.cfm?story_id=15464505

"Yemen's Jews Uneasy as Muslim Hostility Grows," *Jerusalem Post*, April 27, 2009. As of May 28, 2009:
http://abcnews.go.com/International/wireStory?id=7433925

"YFM: Al-Qaeda's Elements in Yemen are Limited," *Yemen Post*, July 29, 2009. As of January 21, 2010:
http://www.yemenpost.net/Detail123456789.aspx?ID=3&SubID=1059

al-Zaidi, Hasan, "Fierce Clashes in Sa'ada after Ceasefire," *Yemen Post*, February 4, 2008. As of October 14, 2008:
http://www.yemenpost.net/SadaWeeklyReview/3.htm

al-Zaidi, Hasan, "Interior Ministry Orders Lifting Tribal Road Blockade; Diesel Still Unavailable in Some Gas Stations," *Yemen Post*, July 21, 2008. As of May 26, 2009:
http://www.yemenpost.net/39/LocalNews/20083.htm

al-Zwaini, Laila, "Mediating Between Custom and Code: Dar al-Salam, an NGO for Tribal Arbitration in San'a," in Baudouin Dupret and Francois Burgat, eds., *Le cheikh et le procureur: Systèmes coutoumiers et practiques juridiques au Yémen et en Égypte,* Cairo: CEDEJ, Egypte-Monde Arab Series 1:3, 2005.

―――, "State and Non-State Justice in Yemen," paper presented at conference: The Relationship Between State and Non-State Justice Systems in Afghanistan, December 10–14, 2006, United States Institute for Peace, Kabul, Afghanistan.

"23 Qatilan wa 33 Jarihan fi Muwajahat bayn Atba' al-Huthi wa Al al-Hamati," *al-Ayyam*, December 4, 2008. As of February 17, 2010:
http://www.al-ayyam.info/Default.aspx?NewsID=cfe5bac3-9901-4230-93e7-c5436a772404

"26 Septembernet Tunshir Nass Muhadarat 'al-Huthi' allati kashafat Ab'ad al-Mukhattat al-Ta'ammurri," *26 September*, May 16, 2005.

"30 Qatilan wa Jarihan fi Ma'arik bi-Sa'da wa Kamin Akhar Yanju minhu Na'ib al-Muhafiz," *al-Ayyam,* April 7, 2005. As of February 17, 2010:
 http://www.al-ayyam.info/Default.aspx?NewsID=f4d673b3-9d63-44b6-9db2-0a0aab1312f8

"48 Sa'a Mahla li-l-Huthi wa Munasirihi li-Taslim Anfusihum" *al-Ayyam*, April 3, 2005. As of February 17, 2010:
http://www.al-ayyam.info/Default.aspx?NewsID=678e76ef-1220-4401-b3c4-c9e952a6f9a8

'Abd al-Ilah, Haydar Sha'i', "Akhbarani Abu Basir Annahu Qara'a Maqalati Awwal ma Kharaja min al-Sijin . . . wa Sa'id al-Shihri Sharaha li Hizamahu al-Nasifa," May 14, 2009.

———, "Abu Basir: Nansir Ghaza bi-Darb al-Masalih al-Gharbiya bi-l-Mintaqa," *al-Jazeera*, January 26, 2009.

" 'Abd al-Malik al-Huthi min Ma'qilihi fi Matra li 'al-Ahali': Lan Nakun Hizban Siyasiyan, wa Walayat al-Batanin 'Ala Hukam al-Yawm," *al-Ahale,* n.d. As of January 22, 2010:
http://alahale.net/details.asp?id=1984&catid=1&keyword=%DA%C7%C8%CF%20%C7%E1%E3%E5%D0%D1%ED

" 'Abd al-Malik al-Huthi: La Nurahin 'ala Ayy Quwwa Iqlimiya wa Idha Awqafat al-Sulta Istihdafana, Sanantahi al-Tamtarus," *al-Sharq al-Awsat*, September 20, 2009. As of January 22, 2010:
http://www.aawsat.com/details.asp?section=4&article=536701&issueno=11254

" 'Abd al-Malik al-Huthi: Lam Nabda' al-Harb al-Fi'liya Ba'd," *al-Akhbar*, July 3, 2008. As of January 22, 2010:
http://www.al-akhbar.com/ar/node/79547

'Abd al-Rabb, Nabil, "Fusul Qissat Muntahiya . . . 'al-Shabab al-Mu'min' min Mukhayyamat Dahyan ila 'Fallal' al-Doha," *al-Mithaqnet*, June 25, 2007. As of January 22, 2010:
http://www.almethaq.net/news/news-3614.htm

'Abd al-Salam, Muhammad, "Sa'da . . . Harban Sadisatan Taluh fi-l-Ufuq," *al-Menpar,* January 8, 2009. As of January 21, 2010:
http://www.almenpar.net/news.php?action=view&id=1128

Abu Bakr, 'Abdullah, "'Abd al-Malik al-Huthi li-l-'Nahar': al-Nizaman al-Su'udi wa-l-Yamani Tajawwaza Masalih Sha'biha Ila Hisabat Ukhra," *al-Menpar*, November 12, 2009. As of January 22,

2010:
http://www.almenpar.net/news.php?action=view&id=1758

Abu Gahnem, Fathel, and Ali Ahmad, *al Qabila wa-l-Dawla fi-l-Yaman*. Cairo: Dar Almanar, 1990.

Abu Shusha', Yassir, "al-Su'udiya: Ihtilal al-Yaman wa Tadlil I'lami," *al-Menpar*, November 25, 2009. As of January 23, 2010:
http://www.almenpar.com/news.php?action=view&id=1806

Abu Talib, Hassan, "al-Huthiyun wa-l-Ma'raka ma Qabl al-Akhir fi-l-Yaman," al-Ahram Center for Strategic Studies, July 9, 2008. As of January 23, 2010:
http://www.alzoa.com/docView.php?con=25&docID=52868

Abu Zahrah, Muhammad, *al-Imam Zayd: Hayatuhu wa 'Asruhu Ara'uhu wa Fiquhu*. Cairo: Dar al-Fikr al-'Arabi, 1959.

"Ahamm al-Mu'shirat fi Muhafazat Sa'da," n.d. As of January 21, 2010:
http://www.yemen-nic.info/gover/saedaa/service/

"Ahdath al-Masa': Inkisar al-Zahf al-Su'udi 'ala Jabal al-Ramih wa Tadmir (3) Malalat wa (18) Ghara Jawiya 'ala Qarya Yamaniya," *al-Menpar*, December 7, 2009. As of January 21, 2010:
http://www.almenpar.com/news.php?action=view&id=1881

al-Ahmadi, Muhammad, "Min Ab'ad Fitnat Husayn al-Huthi – 2: al-Huthi, Ara'uhu wa Mu'taqadatuhu," *Al al-Bayt*, May 30, 2005. As of March 21, 2010:
http://www.alalbayt.com/index.php?option=com_content&task=view&id=1834&itemid=200

" 'Ajil: al-Huthiyun Yu'linun al-Saytara al-Tama 'ala Mudiriyat Munabbih al-Muhadda li-l-Su'udiya," *al-Menpar*, October 7, 2009. As of January 22, 2010:
http://www.almenpar.com/news.php?action=view&id=1630

" 'Ajil: al-Saytara al-Kamila 'ala (Mudiriyat Qatabir) al-Muhadda li-l-Su'udiya," *al-Menpar*, November 10, 2009. As of January 22, 2010:
 http://www.almenpar.com/news.php?action=view&id=1753

" 'Ajil: al-Sayyid 'Abd al-Malik al-Huthi Yuwwajih bi-Iqaf Itlaq al-Nar," *al-Menpar*, February 12, 2010. As of February 15, 2010:
http://www.almenpar.com/news.php?action=view&id=2076.

" 'Ajil: al-Su'udiya Taqsif Mantaqat al-Malahit bi-l-Tiran," *al-Menpar.net*, August 27, 2009. As of January 22, 2010:
http://www.almenpar.com/news.php?action=view&id=1498

"Akkada al-Ta'amul ma'a al-Fi'at al-Dala al-Kharija 'an al-Qanun bi-Mas'uliya Wataniya, Ra'is al-Jumhuriya: Al-Quwwat al-Musallaha wa al-Amn Satuwasil 'Amaliyatiha hatta al-Qada' Niha'iyan 'ala Fitnat al-Tamarrud bi-Sa'da," *26 September*, August 19, 2009. As of January 22, 2010:
http://www.26sep.net/news_details.php?lng=arabic&sid=56507

"Akkada Haqq al-Dawla fi Ijtithath man Yakhraj 'an al-Dustur wa-l-Qanun al-Shaykh al-Sadiq al-Ahmar: Qabilat Hashid Satakun Ila Janib al-Quwwat al-Musallaha al-Amn al-Mulahiqqa al-Huthi wa 'Asabatahu," *26 September*, August 19, 2009. As of January 22, 2010:
http://www.26sep.net/news_details.php?lng=.0a1rabic&sid=56515

al-Akwa', *Hijar al-'Ilm wa-Ma'aqiluhu fi-l-Yaman*, Vols. 1-5, Beirut: Dar al-Fikr al-Mu'asir, Damascus: Dar al Fikr, 1995.

"al-Alaf Yashi'un Dahyan Haditha al-Masjid bi Sa'da wa al-Muhafiza Yatawa'ad bi-l-Iqtisas li Hum min al-Huthiyin," *al-Ayyam*, May 5, 2008. As of January 22, 2010:
http://www.al-ayyam.info/Default.aspx?NewsID=3bdd61b0-a039-4f38-b441-15190de85b44

"al-'Alam: al-Yaman Tuwasil 'Amaliyat 'al-Ard al-Mahruqa' fi Ma'arikiha ma'a al-Huthiyin," *al-Sabah* (Iraqi), September 17, 2009. As of January 21, 2010:
http://www.alsabaah.com/paper.php?source=akbar&mlf=interpage&sid=89825

" 'Ali 'Abdullah Salih: al-Tansiq al-Yamani–al-Su'udi Mumtaz I'dam Saddam Intiqaman wa Tahawwul al-Bashir Matluban Lidha Ansah al-Akhirin An Yasta'du," *al-Hayat,* March 28, 2008. As of January 21, 2010:
http://international.daralhayat.com/internationalarticle/2801

al-'Allama al-Shami: Ara' wa Mawaqif, Amman, Jordan: Matabi' Sharikat al-Mawarid al-Sina'iya al-Urdiniya, 1994.

al-Alwa', Muhammad 'Ali, *Safha min Ta'rikh al-Yaman al-Ijtima'i wa-Qissat Hayati.* Damascus: Matba'at al-Katib al-'Arabi, 1980.

Amin, Muhsin, *al-Shahid Zayd ibn 'Ali wa-l-Zaydiya*, Beirut, Dar Murtada, 2003.

" 'An Akhbar al-Yawm al-'Id: al-Huthi Yunafi ma Tud'ihi I'lamiyat al-Sulta min Qittal fi Madinat Sa'da," *al-Menpar*, September 20, 2009.

"al-A'mal al-Irhabiya wa al-Khuruqat Allati Qamat bi-ha al-'Anasir al-Irhabiya al-Safawiya min ba'd I'lan Waqf al-Harb fi 17 July 2008," *26 September*, August 13, 2009. As of January 22, 2010:
http://www.26sep.net/news_details.php?lng=arabic&sid=56359

" 'Anasir al-Huthi Tantaqil fi Manatiq Bani Mu'adh wa Sahar wa Safra' 'abr al-Mazari' al-Kabira," *al-Ayyam*, April 18, 2007. As of January 21, 2010:
http://www.al-ayyam.info/Default.aspx?NewsID=abd4ccac-b3d4-4b5e-bef2-7385ec941db8

" 'Anasir al-Huthi Yufajjirun Mabna Mahattat Kahraba' Qatabir bi-Sa'da," *al-Ayyam*, April 19 2007. As of January 21, 2010:
http://www.al-ayyam.info/Default.aspx?NewsID=67f71049-49d1-4316-9225-53327be6379c

"Anba' 'an Maqtal Jundiyaynn bi-Sa'da wa-l-Huthi Yunafi," *al-Ayyam*, November 7, 2007. As of February 2009:
http://www.al-ayyam.info/Default.aspx?NewsID=40fba28a-b4ea-4dd8-b795-0168d0519914

"Anba' 'an Saytarat al-Huthiyin 'ala Liwa' Yamani fi Sa'da," *Ilaf*, August 6, 2009. As of January 21, 2010:
http://www.elaph.com/Web/Politics/2009/8/469089.htm

Ansar al-Haqq Web site. As of February 18, 2010:
http://ansaar.yoo7.com

"Anshuda Hajim al-'Askariya li-Ansar al-Huthi," video posted to Youtube.com, December 30, 2009. As of February 15, 2010:
http://www.youtube.com/watch?v=as3lUb7vwrk

" 'Arabistan Qabayil-o-'Ashayir-e Yaman-ra Baraye Moqabele ba Huthiha Bassij Mi-Konad," *Farsnews*, December 7, 2009. As of January 21, 2010:
http://www.farsnews.net/newstext.php?nn=8809160177

al-'Arjli, 'Amar Husayn, "al-Su'udiya Taza'za' Amn al-Yaman wa Tantahik Siyadatahu, wa Qara' Tabul al-Hurub fi-l-Yaman Tabda' min al-Riyad," *al-Menpar*, April 3, 2009.

Artesh-e 'Arabistan az Bambha-ye Khushe'i 'alayhi Mardom-e Yaman Estefade mi-Konad," *FarsNews,* December 7, 2009. As of January 22, 2010:
http://www.farsnews.net/newstext.php?nn=8809160350

" 'Asharat al-Algham Tanfajir fi-l-Huthiyin wa Dahyan Muhawir al-Ma'raka al-Ra'is," *al-Ayyam*, March 31, 2007. As of January 22, 2010:
 http://www.al-ayyam.info/Default.aspx?NewsID=1ac08ec8-6e0d-4609-9820-d348bf589c72

" 'Asharat al-Jarha min Ataba' al-Huthi wa Afrad al-Jaysh Yunaqilun Ila Mustashfa al-Salam bi-Sa'da," *al-Ayyam*, January 4, 2006. As of January 22, 2010:
 http://www.al-ayyam.info/Default.aspx?NewsID=84b0e948-6ee9-4f29-91a8-4f0f29f34a9f

"As'ila Muwajjaha li-l-Huthiyin Ansar al-Haqq," *Ansar al-Haqq Forum*, December 27, 2008. As of January 22, 2010:
http://ansaar.yoo7.com/montada-f3/topic-t55.htm

"Astawilu 'ala Qura ba'd Ishtibakat Adat Ila Suqut 12 Qatilan min Abna' al-Mintaqa," *al-Ayyam*, July 3, 2007. As of January 22, 2010:
http://www.al-ayyam.info/Default.aspx?NewsID=536623c6-3c4f-4a01-9b3c-746df82553be

"Atlaqa 'ala Nafsihi Amir al-Mu'minin wa Za'ama annahu al-Mahdi al-Muntazar," *26 September*, June 24, 2004. As of January 21, 2010:
http://www.26sep.net/narticle.php?sid=1440

"Ba'd al-Ghana'im min al-Dhakha'ir wa-l-Asliha allati Tamm al-Saytara 'alayha khilal Shahr Wahid," video posted to 4shared.com, October 17, 2009. As of February 15, 2010:
http://www.4shared.com/file/141526301/9b84a2dd/_____.html

"Ba'd al-Ghana'im min al-Jaysh al-Su'udi wa Qasf al-Su'udi 'ala al-Aradi al-Yamaniya, wa Asra min al-Jaysh al-Yamani, wa li-Nazihin Madaniyin," *al-Menpar*, November 13, 2009.

"Ba'd al-Ifraj 'anhu . . . Muftah: Sujintu dun Mubarrir wa Utalib bi-Itlaq Jami' al-Sujuna' wa Ta'widihum," *al-Ayyam*, September 8, 2009. As of January 22, 2010:
http://www.al-ayyam.info/Default.aspx?NewsID=f1ddd2df-5583-4dc3-8e7b-6d7c8c475f05

"Ba'd Intiha' al-Mahla li-Taslim Aslihatihum . . . Istimrar al-Muwajahat bayn al-Jaysh wa Atba' al-Huthi aladhin Yuwasilun Hajamatahum," *al-Ayyam*, February 3, 2007. As of January 22, 2010:
http://www.al-ayyam.info/Default.aspx?NewsID=607590d1-d247-4cb3-ae71-a34c2487d21c

"Badr al-Din al-Huthi Bakhir wa La Sihha li Ma Qalahu Mudir Mudiriyat Haydan Hawl Maqtalihi," *al-Ishtiraki,* October 12, 2006. As of January 21, 2010:
 http://www.aleshteraki.net/news_details.php?lng=arabic&sid=1295

"Badr al-Din al-Huthi li-l-Wasat: al-Ra'is Khafa An Ya'khudh (Husayn) minhu," *al-Wasat,* March 19, 2005.

"Ba'd Usbu' min Iktishaf Muqatilin Sumaliyin fi Sufuf al-Tamarrud bi-Sa'da . . . al-Jiza'iya Tabda' al-Yawm Jalsataha bi-Muhaktmat 12 Qursanan Sumaliyan," *Akhbar al-Yawm*, September 29, 2009. As of January 21, 2010:
http://www.alshomoa.net/todaynews/index.php?action=showNews&;id=7885

"Ba'd Yawmayn li-Maqtal 10 Ashkhass bi-Khilaf 'ala Masjid bi-l-Jawf Maqtal al-'Aqid 'Idrus al-Yafa'i wa Ithnayn min Harasihi, fi Kamin Musallah bi-Mahadhir Sa'da," *Mareb Press*, July 21, 2009.

"al-Barlamani Yahya al-Huthi Yuwajjih Risala Ila Ahzab al-Liqa' al-Mushtarak," *al-Menpar,* July 5, 2008.

"Bayan min Maktab al-Sayyid 'Abd al-Malik al-Huthi Hawl Ikhtitaf 9 Ajanib fi Madinat Sa'da," *al-Menpar*, June 14, 2009.

"Bayyan Sadir min Qibal Mashayikh Muhafazat al-Jawf Yudinun fihi A'mal Khalid al-Sharif," *al-Menpar*, July 30, 2009. As of January 22, 2010:
http://www.almenpar.com/news.php?action=view&id=1401&spell=0&highlight=%CC%E6%DD

"al-Bayyan al-'Askari al-Sadir min al-Quwwat al-Musallaha: Quwwatina al-Musallaha Tu'min al-Qura al-Su'udiya al-Muhita bi-Jabal Dukhan wa-l-Dawd wa-l-Ramih wa Tadhar al-Mutasallilin," *Saudi Ministry of Defense*, undated a. As of January 21, 2010: http://www.moda.gov.sa/Detail.asp?InSectionID=21&InNewsItemID=1865

"Da'a li-Taqarub Su'udi Irani . . . Nasrallah: Nahnu bi-Hajja li-Itfa'i Mukhlis fi Shamal al-Yaman," *Mareb Press*, November 12, 2009. As of January 21, 2010: http://marebpress.net/news_details.php?lng=arabic&sid=20034

"Dabt 3 Shahinat Asliha wa-l-Huthiyin Yatahatifun 'Abr al-Aqmar al-Istina'iya," *al-Ayyam*, May 30, 2007. As of January 21, 2010: http://www.al-ayyam.info/Default.aspx?NewsID=711a197d-5482-4cda-b6b6-f4ae17bc30d4

"Damn al-Majmu'a 4 li-'saba Qatl wa A'mal Takhrib fi Bani Hushaysh, al-Jaza'iya al-Mutakhassisa Tuqadi bi-I'dam Sab'a wa Sijin Sab'a Akhirin min 12 Ila 15 'am," *Mareb Press*, July 6, 2009.

"Dar Khwast-e Tehran az Hamas Baraye Komak beh al-Huthiha Tekdhib Shod," *FarsNews*, December 1, 2009. As of January 21, 2010: http://www.farsnews.net/newstext.php?nn=8809111917

"Darba Qawwiya Murtaqiba li-Hasm al-Ma'raka fi Sa'da bi-Aqall Waqtin," *al-Ayyam*, February 12, 2007. As of January 21, 2010: http://www.al-ayyam.info/Default.aspx?NewsID=c2a96634-121e-4add-9b10-81f441a00d81

"Dowlat-e Iran Bayed Sazemanha-ye Mokhtallef-e Islami-ra Darbareh Havadeth-e Yaman Fo'al Konad," *FarsNews*, November 23, 2009. As of January 21, 2010: http://www.farsnews.net/newstext.php?nn=8809020152

"Dr. Abu Bakr al-Qirbi: Ajhizat al-Amn Mustamirra fi al-Taharri 'an Ayy Da'm Khariji Yasl ila Jama'at al-Huthi," *al-Ayyam,* June 11, 2005.

"Dr. al-Qirbi, Ziyarati li-Iran li-Sharh Tatawwurat Tamarrud al-Huthi wa Man' Istighlaliha li-l-Waqi'a," *al-Ayyam,* May 26, 2005.

"Dubat Asra Yansahun al-Sulta bi-Iqaf al-Harb," posted to Youtube.com, September 2, 2009. As of February 15, 2010: http://www.youtube.com/watch?v=ENK22Kd7Cqc&feature=related

al-Dughshi, Ahmad Muhammad, "al-Zahira al-Huthiya: Dirasa Manhajiya fi Tab'iyat al-Nash'a wa Jadaliyat al-'Alaqa bi-l-Ta'rikh," *Nashwan News*, April 20, 2009. As of February 17, 2010: http://www.nashwannews.com/news.php?action=view&id=1034

"Fa Amkana Minhum," Huthi video, *Qism al-I'lam al-Harbi*, June 2008. Hosted at Internet Archive as "The Islamic Shia Revolution in Yemen: New Realise." As of February 5, 2010: http://www.archive.org/details/TheIslamicShiaRevolutionInYemennewRealise

al-Faqih, Ahmad Salih, "al-Istratijiya al-'Askariya li-l-Dawla wa-l-Huthiyin fi Harb Sa'da al-Haliya," *al-Taghyir*, October 1, 2009. As of January 21, 2010: http://www.al-tagheer.com/arts.php?id=3098

"Faris Mana': al-Huthi Yasa'i Ila Ta'zim al-Awda' wa Nasf Juhud al-Salam," *26 September,* May 30, 2009.

"Fidiyu min Maktab al-Huthi: Yuzhir fihi al-'Inaya al-Tibbiya wa-l-Sakaniya li-l-Asra al-Su'udiyin," *al-Menpar*, November 9, 2009.

"Fi-l-Ard al-Mahruqa bi-l-Yaman . . . Junud Murhaqun wa Nazihun Ghadibun min al-Huthiyin," *al-Sharq al-Awsat*, September 18, 2009. As of January 21, 2010: http://www.aawsat.com/details.asp?section=1&issueno=11252&article=536492

"Fi Kalima Lahu Ila Abna' al-Sha'b al-Yamani bi-Munasiba Hulul Shahr Ramadan, Ra'is al-Jumhuriya Yamnah 'Anasir al-Takhrib bi-Sa'da Fursa Jadida li-l-Salam 'Ala Asas al-Iltizam bi-l-Sit al-Nuqat," *26 September*, August 21, 2009. As of January 21, 2010: http://www.26sep.net/news_details.php?lng=arabic&sid=56567

"Fima Lajnat al-Ishraf 'ala Tanfidh Ittifaqiyat al-Htkuma wa-l-Huthiyin Tuwasil 'Amalha . . . Maqtal Ahad al-Mashayikh fi Muwajahat 'Anifa ma'a al-Huthiyin," *al-Ayyam*, June 20, 2005.

"Fima Qaba'il Bakil Tad'u Ila Tahkim al-'Aql wa Iqaf al-Harb . . . Masra' Habish wa Isabat Akharin bi-Harf Sufyan fi 'Amran," *al-Ayyam*, May 17, 2008.

"Fima Batat Nihayatuhum Qariba fi Zull Tadyiq al-Khinaq 'alayhim: Ajhizat al-Amn Tulqi al-Qibd 'ala Irhabiyin fi Sa'da bi-Sharashif Nisa'iya," *26 September*, March 22, 2007. As of January 21, 2010: http://www.26sep.net/narticle.php?sid=24870

"Fi Muhadara Muhimma Alqaha bi-l-Kulliya al-Harbiya bi-San'a': Fakhamat Ra'is al-Jumhuriya: Alladhin Yarfa'un Shi'ar al-Mawt li-Amrika al-Mawt li-Isra'il Kidhban wa Zawran Hum Yarfa'un Shi'ar Mawt li-l-Watan," *al-Ayyam*, No. 4649, November 30, 2005.

Ghalab, Najib, "al-Yaman wa-l-Huthiya wa-l-Hajis al-Irani," *al-Sharq al-Awsat*, May 15, 2008. As of January 22, 2010: http://www.asharqalawsat.com/leader.asp?section=3&issueno=10761&article=470852

"Ghana'im Su'udiya Khilal al-Zahf al-Akhir," November 3, 2009. As of January 21, 2010: http://www.youtube.com/watch?v=sNH9ZDL7Y3g

"Ghana'im Su'udiya min Mawqa' al-Ramih," video posted to YouTube, November 27, 2009.

"Ghara Jari'a 'ala Awkar al-Huthiyin fi Sa'da," September 16, 2009. As of January 23, 2010: http://www.youtube.com/watch?v=3pEjHdTfaGw

"al-Hadath al-'Arabi wa-l-'Alam: San'a Tatlub Rasmiyan Min Libiya Taslimaha al-Huthi," *al-Mada*, n.d. As of January 21, 2010: http://almadapaper.net/paper.php?source=akbar&mlf=interpag&sid=15431

al-Hadirmi, 'Ali, "Jum' Muhadarat wa Durus Husayn Badr al-Din al-Huthi," *Majalis al-Muhammad*, May 9, 2006. As of January 22, 2010: http://al-majalis.com/forums/viewtopic.php?t=4330

"Hajamat li-Marawhiyat 'ala Mawaqi' li-l-Huthiyin bi-Sa'da," *al-Ayyam*, May 6, 2008. As of January 23, 2010: http://www.al-ayyam.info/default.aspx?newsID=d4fa48e2-d44b-422a-8311-9ebf61ee7e20

"Hal Yushakkil al-Huthiyun Tanziman Siyasiyan bi Ism 'Hizb al-Shuhada'?" *al-Ayyam*, August 4, 2007. As of January 21, 2010: http://www.al-ayyam.info/Default.aspx?NewsID=8c38db7b-bf8d-48c4-8678-0b04fdc5be55

"Hamdasti-ye Niruha-ye al-Qa'ida ba Dowlat-e San'a dar Sarkub-e Shi'iyan-e al-Huthi," *Farsnews* December 2, 2009. As of January 21, 2010: http://www.farsnews.net/newstext.php?nn=8809110755

"al-Haraka Tashall bi-Sa'da Ba'd Ghurub al-Shams wa Raqaba Mafruda 'ala Madakhil al-Madina," *al-Ayyam*, April 10, 2005. As of January 21, 2010: http://www.al-ayyam.info/Default.aspx?NewsID=29d04da6-127c-4ed1-af98-0dd6a8f42abf

"Harb I'lamiya Maqru'a wa Masmu'a bayn al-Jaysh wa al-Huthiyin bi-Sa'da," *al-Ayyam,* May 29, 2007.

Hassan, Naji, *Thawrat Zayd ibn 'Ali*, Beirut: al-Dar al-'Arabiya li-l-Mawsu'at, 2000.

Hizb al-Haqq Web site. As of March 21, 2010:
http://www.newomma.net

"Hudu' Jabhat al-Qital fi Saʻda Naharan wa Ishtiʻaluha Laylan" *al-Ayyam,* March 3, 2007. As of January 21, 2010:
http://www.al-ayyam.info/Default.aspx?NewsID=3c7e86ec-0ada-497c-a32d-713573ace27f

"al-Hudu' Yasud Saʻda baʻd Wusul al-Muhafiz Ila Maʻqal al-Huthi," *al-Ayyam*, February 22, 2006. As of January 22, 2010:
http://www.al-ayyam.info/Default.aspx?NewsID=fa883506-f091-462b-ba34-acaf72b4c95f

"al-Hukuma Tuʻlin Taʻliq al-ʻAmaliyat al-ʻAskiriya fi al-Mantaqa al-Shamaliya al-Gharbiya bi-Munasiba ʻId al-Fitr," *26 September*, September 19, 2009. As of January 22, 2010:
http://www.26sep.net/news_details.php?lng=arabic&sid=57175

"Hujum ʻAnif li-Marwahiyatin ʻala Atbaʻ al-Huthi bi-Kitaf," *al-Ayyam*, April 21, 2005.

"Hujum Barri wa Jawwi Wasiʻ ʻala Mawaqiʻ al-Huthiyin wa-l-ʻUthur ʻala Juthath Madaniyin," *al-Ayyam,* May 22, 2007.

"Hushud ʻAskariya Kabira li-Ijtiyah Dahyan wa al-Saytara ʻalayha," *al-Ayyam*, March 19, 2007.

al-Huthi, Badr Din ibn Amir al-Din ibn al-Husayn, *al-Ijaz fi al-Radd ʻala Fatawa al-Hijaz,* Sanʻa: Maktabat al-Yaman al-Kubra, 1979.

al-Huthi, Badr Din ibn Amir al-Din ibn al-Husayn, *Man Hum al-Rafida*, ed. Ibrahim ibn Muhammad al-ʻUbaydi, Sanʻa: Muʻassasat al-Imam Zayd ibn ʻAli al-Thaqafiya, 2002.

al-Huthi, Badr Din ibn Amir al-Din ibn al-Husayn, *Miftah Asanid al-Zaydiya,* Amman, Jordan, n.d.

al-Huthi, Badr Din ibn Amir al-Din ibn al-Husayn, *Tahrir al-Afkar*, Qum, Iran: al-Majmaʻ al-ʻAlami li Ahl al-Bayt, 1997.

"al-Huthi: Itlaq Sirah 24 Asiran min ʻAskar a-Nizam Taʻkidan li-Khiyar al-Salam," *al-Menpar,* August 8, 2009.

al-Huthi, Yahya, "Al-Quwwat al-Dawliya fi-l-Yaman min Ajl Himayat al-Diktaturiya," *al-Menpar,* March 10, 2009.

"al-Huthiyun Yakshifun ʻan al-Khatawat allati Qamu biha fi Sabil Daʻm al-Salam wa Tanfidhan li-Bunud Ittifaq al-Duha," *al-Menpar,* October 8 2008. As of January 22, 2010:
http://www.almenpar.net/news.php?action=view&id=1020

"al-Huthi Yuqassim Barlaman al-Bahrayn," *Mareb Press*, November 11, 2009. As of January 21, 2010:
http://www.marebpress.net/news_details.php?sid=20027&lng=arabic

"al-Huthi Yurid al-Khilafa li-Nafsihi: Sahifat Watan Tunshir (Wajh al-Iman) wa bi-l-Wathaʼiq Haqiqat Ahdaf al-Fitna fi Saʻda," *26 September*, June 2, 2007. As of January 22, 2010:
http://www.26sep.net/narticle.php?sid=28301

"al-Huthi Yuwassi bi-Qatʻ Raʼsihi idha Mat Hatta La Yuʻraf," *26 September*, September 3, 2004. As of January 22, 2010:
http://www.26sep.net/narticle.php?sid=2514

"al-Huthiyun Yudammirun Manzalan Yatamarkaz bi-Dakhilihi Junud al-Jaysh," *al-Ayyam,* January 14, 2008. As of January 22, 2010:
http://www.al-ayyam.info/Default.aspx?NewsID=a99ec7c8-d6fd-433b-9d39-ad16bf5c00b3

"Huwa al-Sayyid al-ʻAllama al-Wali al-Wariʻ al-Zahid al-Sabir al-Mufassir Badr al-Din bin Amir al-Din bin al-Husayn bin Muhammad al-Huthi," undated document provided by Yemeni immigrant. Originally hosted at www.alhothi.com.

"Ihtijaz Majmuʻa min Al-ʻUzam bisabab Mutalabatihum bi-Tariq Farʻi Ila Mintaqatihum," *al-Ayyam*, April 30, 2006.

"Ihtiraq al-Taʾira," posted to 4shared.com, October 5, 2009. As of February 15, 2010: http://www.4shared.com/file/137861962/e49c60b3/__online.html

"Indilaʻ al-Qital Mujaddadan bayna al-Jaysh wa al-Ansar al-Huthi bi-Saʻda," *al-Ayyam,* March 29, 2005. As of January 22, 2010: http://www.al-ayyam.info/default.aspx?newsID=47954621-850d-4542-9faf-9491c0e163d8

"Infijar ʻAnif Yahazz Madinat Baqim bi-Muhafazat Saʻda," *al-Ayyam*, December 10, 2006.

"Infijar Taʾira ʻumudiya wa Suqutuha fi Haydan baʻd Isabatiha bi-Niran al-Huthiyin," *al-Ayyam*, February 4, 2008.

"Insihab al-Liwaʾ 105 al-Mutamarkaz fi Mawaqiʻ Asfal Marran," video posted to YouTube.com, September 2, 2009. As of February 15, 2010: http://www.youtube.com/watch?v=2CJF6R4JZaA

"al-Irhab al-Huthi Wathaiʾiq Khatira Tunshar li-Awwal Marra": pt. 1 (3:15–7:15), video hosted at 26 September.net's devoted Web page.

"al-Irhabiyun Qatʻu Atraf Jundi wa Isabʻahu wa Udhunihu: al-Yaman Yanfi Istikhdam al-Tiran wa-l-Asliha al-Kimawiya Did al-Huthin," *26 September*, February 14, 2007. As of January 21, 2010: http://www.26sep.net/narticle.php?sid=23172

"Isaba Baligha li-Walidatihi wa Hiyya Tuhawil Himayatahu bi-Jasadiha Wa Masdar Mahalli Yuʻakkid innaha Tuʻakkis Inhiyarahum," *26 September*, June 16, 2008. As of January 21, 2010: http://www.26sep.net/narticle.php?sid=42855

"Ishtibakat bayn Junud al-Amn al-Markazi wa al-Huthiyin bi-Saʻda," *al-Ayyam*, February 28, 2009.

"Ishtibakat Musallaha maʻa Ansar al-Huthi wast Madinat Saʻda," *al-Ayyam*, March 20, 2005. As of January 21, 2010: http://www.al-ayyam.info/Default.aspx?NewsID=7a851b2a-a370-4a22-b2f5-728d90e03f80

"Isthibakat ʻAnifa bayn al-Huthiyin wa Rijal Ihda al-Qabaʾil wa Suqut Thamaniyat ʻAshir Qatilan min al-Janibayn," *al-Ayyam*, April 7, 2008.

"Istimrar al-Hisar ʻala Katibat al-Jaysh bi-Haydan wa Inkhifad al-Hajamat al-Mutabadila bayna al-Janibayn," *al-Ayyam* January 24, 2008. As of January 21, 2010: http://www.al-ayyam.info/Default.aspx?NewsID=0754beee-733e-4b8d-8be1-ea7eb6e9050b

"Istimrar al-Muwajahat fi Saʻda wa Maqtal Arbaʻa min al-Mutatawwaʻin," *al-Ayyam*, February 3, 2008. As of January 21, 2010: http://www.al-ayyam.info/Default.aspx?NewsID=f1eadf1f-84e6-4588-a71c-e4a1f872193d

"Istimrar al-Qital al-ʻAnif fi Dahyan wa Taʻzizat ʻAskariya Murtaqiba li-l-Jaysh," *al-Ayyam*, April 7, 2007. As of January 21, 2010: http://www.al-ayyam.info/Default.aspx?NewsID=3c2a3fa1-debb-403d-96d4-a553fea20cfe

"Istimrar Tabadul al-Hajamat bayn Atbaʻ al-Huthi wa Wahdat al-Jaysh," *al-Ayyam*, December 25, 2005.

"Istimrar Tabadul Itlaq al-Nar bayn al-Huthiyin wa Junud al-Jaysh," *al-Ayyam*, August 8, 2007. As of January 21, 2010: http://www.al-ayyam.info/Default.aspx?NewsID=ca4873dc-570b-47d2-9590-75287615a499

"Istimrar Tashdid al-Ijraʾat al-Amniya bi-Madinat Saʻda Wasat Tasaʻud li-l-Muwajihat," *al-Ayyam*, May 8, 2007.

"al-Isti'nafiya Kanat qad Qadat bi-Habasihi Khamas Sanawat: al-Ra'is Ya'mur bi-l-Ifraj 'an al-Qadi Luqman fi Itar 'Afuhi 'an Atba' al-Huthi," *26 September*, August 7, 2006. As of January 21, 2010: http://www.26sep.net/narticle.php?sid=17395

"Istishhad Qa'id Katiba wa Masra' 6 min Atba' al-Huthi bi-Sa'da," *al-Ayyam* , February 13, 2007.

"Ithr Tasa'ud Hajimat 'Ansar al-Huthi fi-l-Muhafaza…al-Sulta al-Mahalliya fi Sa'da Tatlub al-Musanada min Zu'ama' al-Qaba'il wa al-Khutaba' al-Musajid wa Mashayikh Dammaj," *al-Sahwa* December 27, 2005. As of January 23, 2010:
 http://www.alsahwa-yemen.net/view_sub.asp?s_no=11283&c_no=1

"Itihamat Hukumiya Li-l-Huthiyin bi Takdis al-Asliha al-Haditha Isti'dadan li Jawla Jadida," *Al-Ayyam,* April 24, 2009.

"Itlaq Nar wa Qanabil Musila al-Dumu' li-Muwajahat 'Isiyan fi Sijin Sa'da," *al-Ayyam*, December 19, 2006.

"Ittisa' Ruq'at al-Muwajahat bayn al-Jaysh wa-l-Huthiyin," *al-Ayyam*, April 17, 2007.

'Izzan, Muhammad, *al-'Allama al-Shami: Ara' wa Mawaqif,* Amman, Jordan: Matabi' Sharikat al-Mawarid al-Sina'iya al-Urduniya, 1994.

———, *al-Imam Zayd ibn 'Ali: Sha'la fi Layl al-Istibdad,* San'a: Dar al-Hikma al-Yamaniya 1999.

'Izzan, Muhammad, ed., *al-Ifada fi Ta'rikh A'immat al-Zaydiya* (original author Yahya ibn al-Husayn, d. 1032), San'a: Dar al-Hikma al-Yamaniya, 1996.

———, *Majmu' Kutub wa Rasa'il al-Imam Zayd ibn 'Ali,* San'a: Dar al-Hikma al-Yamaniya, 2001.

" 'Izzan Mukhatiban al-Huthiyin: Intum Shawwahatum al-Madhhab al-Zaydi fa-Alqu bi-Aslihatikum wa Salamu Anfusakum li-l-Dawla," *26 September,* June 17, 2008. As of January 22, 2010:
http://www.26sep.net/narticle.php?sid=42859

"Jama'at al-Huthi Shirdhima Irhabiya Tastahdif al-Wahda wa-l-Jumhuriya wa Yajib Hasmha: 26 Sebtember net Tunshir Nass Taqrir al-Aman al-Qawmi al-Muqaddam Ila Majlis al-Nuwwab wa al-Shura Hawl Ahdath al-Fitna fi Sa'da," *26 September*, February 15, 2007. As of January 21, 2010:
http://www.26sep.net/narticle.php?sid=23234

al-Jarbani, Husayn, "al-Yaman: Al-Qabdh 'ala 7 Sumaliyin Yuqatilun ma'a al-Huthiyin wa-Tawaqqu'at bi-Silatihum bi-Jama'at Jihadiya," *al-Sharq al-Awsat*, September 27, 2009. As of January 22, 2010:
http://www.aawsat.com/details.asp?section=4&article=537636&issueno=11261

———, "al-Yaman: Najl al-Huthi Yasif al-Huthiyin bi-'al-Kharijin 'an al-Nizam'.. wa Yarfud Taza"um tamarrudihim," *al-Sharq al-Awsat,* July 14, 2008. As of January 22, 2010:
http://www.aawsat.com/details.asp?section=4&article=478717&issueno=10821

"al-Jaysh wa 'Anasir al-Huthi Yujriyan Taharrukat wa Isti'dadat Kabira bi Sa'da ba'd Ma'rik Ghamr," *al-Ayyam*, April 5, 2009. As of January 22, 2010:
http://www.al-ayyam.info/Default.aspx?NewsID=da7c30a4-b7a3-47c8-b96d-fb40e929a3bf

"al-Jaysh Yadkhul Madinat al-Nazir li al-Marra al-Thaniya wa 'Awdat ba 'd al-Sukkan li Madinat al-Talh," al-Ayyam May 14, 2007. As of January 22, 2010:
http://www.al-ayyam.info/default.aspx?newsID=9c098bc2-4a24-46c5-a08d-cc584812e5da

"al-Jaysh Yaktashif Nisa' Muqatilat fi Sufuf al-Huthiyin," *al-Ayyam*, June 7, 2007: As of January 21, 2010:
http://www.al-ayyam.info/Default.aspx?NewsID=7b06a952-84dd-4a99-a0b8-14e1c379ec6c

"al-Jaysh Yamnah Fursa Akhira li-l-Ahali fi-l-Talh li-Ikhraj Atba' al-Huthi min Mintaqatihim," *al-Ayyam*, February 19, 2006. As of January 22, 2010: http://www.al-ayyam.info/Default.aspx?NewsID=d2230f8e-a0bc-4c04-a9c7-45606bbeee29

"al-Jaysh Yatamakkan min al-Saytara 'ala Mu'azzam Ajza' Jabal Gharaba bi-Sa'da," *al-Ayyam*, April 24, 2007. As of January 21, 2010: http://www.al-ayyam.info/Default.aspx?NewsID=6ba17cf8-788a-4e69-b95e-42d49adf8fc4

"al-Jaysh Yatamakkan min Dukhul Madinat al-Nazir bi-Sa'da," *al-Ayyam*, May 9, 2007. As of January 21, 2010: http://www.al-ayyam.info/Default.aspx?NewsID=0287c40b-c785-4212-9356-7e4a51d21016

"al-Jaysh Yatamakkan min Dukhul Suq al-Talh wa Yudammir Mahattat Wuqud bi-Dahyan Yashtabih bi-Tazwidiha al-Huthiyin bi-l-Banzin," *al-Ayyam*, March 24, 2007. As of January 21, 2010: http://www.al-ayyam.info/Default.aspx?NewsID=5769faa3-d2b2-43b6-ac7c-1706bb7417e8

"al-Jaysh Yataqqadam fi 'Iddat Mawaqi ' wa Yahkum al-Saytara 'ala Dahyan," *al-Ayyam*, April 22, 2007. As of January 22, 2010: http://www.al-ayyam.info/Default.aspx?NewsID=6a3b1b6e-99f4-4f8b-b8cc-36f2ac2d33f9

"al-Jaysh Yudammir Manzilayn Tabi'ayn li Qa'id Jumu' al-Huthi wa Marwahiya Taqsif Mawaqi' fi Bani Mu'adh," *al-Ayyam*, March 1, 2006. As of January 21, 2010: http://www.al-ayyam.info/Default.aspx?NewsID=615fba8c-025f-4c46-b19c-213a8da6553a

"al-Jaysh Yuhajim Manatiq Matra bi-l-Sawarikh wa Ta'zizat 'Askariya Satasul Sa'da Qariban," *al-Ayyam*, January 18, 2008. As of January 22, 2010: http://www.al-ayyam.info/Default.aspx?NewsID=6ff92b69-2277-47a2-9060-75779a40e486

"al-Jaysh Yuhaqqiq Saytara Shibha Kamila 'ala Bani Mu'adh wa Al 'Ammar Ba 'd Khaluha min al-Huthiyin," *al-Ayyam*, March 20, 2007. As of January 21, 2010: http://www.al-ayyam.info/Default.aspx?NewsID=fe896f05-3eda-49ed-bd50-18fbc5175e50

"al-Jaysh Yuhaqqiq Ba'd Tadmir 5 Manazil li-l-Muwatinin bi-Qadhai'ifihi," *al-Ayyam*, May 31, 2007. As of January 21, 2010: http://www.al-ayyam.info/Default.aspx?NewsID=263d5bac-5c43-4708-a366-669ff24beaf7

"al-Jaysh Yuwajjih Darbat li-Kull min Tasul lahu nafsuhu Musa'adat al-Huthiyin," *al-Ayyam*, June 5, 2007. As of January 22, 2010: http://www.al-ayyam.info/Default.aspx?NewsID=2e8d3407-9bb6-4e13-bf38-9222ed769b39

"al-Jaysh Yuzhir Jumi' al-Jabal al-Mushrifa 'ala Madinat al-Nazir," *al-Ayyam*, May 27, 2007. As of January 22, 2010: http://www.al-ayyam.info/Default.aspx?NewsID=203d87ce-3ef1-493a-867b-42964d2ccb11

"Jughrafiyat al-Harb al-Khamisa," *al-Nida'*, June 5, 2009. As of March 2009: http://www.alnedaa.net/index.php?action=showNews&id=1846

"Jundi Yunashid Wazir al-Difa' Inha' Harmanihi Ratibihi Mundhu 17 Shahran," *al-Ayyam*, September 2, 2009. As of January 21, 2010: http://www.al-ayyam.info/Default.aspx?NewsID=d046e7f2-813a-4bfd-aecc-3db69d7afcf1

"Junud Tamm Asruhum min qabl al-Muqatilin al-Huthiyin," posted to Youtube.com, August 31, 2009. As of February 15, 2010: http://www.youtube.com/watch?v=WZBraUQL4-Q&feature=related

"Kamin Thalith Yanju minhu Na'ib Muhafiz Sa'da wa Rami Qanbulatayn 'ala Taqim 'Askari," *al-Ayyam*, May 3, 2005. As of February 17, 2010: http://www.al-ayyam.info/Default.aspx?NewsID=c0882b89-52e6-4af8-8f00-cd606272bdb8

"Khasa'ir Fadiha li-l-Janibayn fi Sa'da wa Taghyirat 'Askariya wa Amniya Murtaqiba," *al-Ayyam*, April 25, 2007.

"Khasa'ir Fadiha li-l-Janibayn fi Sa'da wa Taghyirat 'Askariya wa Amniya Murtaqiba," *al-Ayyam*, April 25, 2007.

"Khasa'ir al-Ma'rak bi-Dahyan Faqat Khasa'ir Harb 2005," *al-Ayyam*, April 10, 2007.

al-Khidri, Anwar, "al-Huthi wa-l-Waraqa al-Ta'ifiya al-Khasira," *Al-Bayyina,* May 6, 2006. As of January 22, 2010:
http://www.albainah.net/index.aspx?function=Item&id=11168&highlight=%25D8%25A7%25D9%2584%25D8%25AD%25D9%2588%25D8%25AB%25D9%258A%20&lang=AR

"al-Lajna al-Amniya: al-Huthi Najaha fi Farar min al-Juhr aladhi Akhtaba'a fihi," *al-Ayyam*, April 14, 2005. As of January 22, 2010:
http://www.al-ayyam.info/Default.aspx?NewsID=5e3a58c9-f46e-4b47-99b7-1d1d6021dc68

al-Libi, Abi Yahya, "Lasna Huthiyin: La Tadi' al-Jidh' wa Tubsir al-Qidha," *Markaz al-Fajr li-l-I'lam,* January 2010.

al-Lisani, 'Abd al-Hamid, "Mudakhala Hadi'a Ma'a 'Zayd' . . . 'An al-Huthiya wa-l-Zaydiya wa-l-Hashimiya wa-l-Futun al-Ukhra," *al-Mithaq.net,* July 16, 2007. As of January 23, 2010:
http://www.almethaq.net/news/news-3866.htm

Luqman, 'Ali Hamzah, *Tarikh al-qaba'il al-yamaniya*, San'a: Dar al-Kalimah, 1985.

"Ma'arak Dariya fi 'Iddat Mawaqi' bi-Sa'da," *al-Ayyam*, December 28, 2005.

"Ma'arik bayn al-Jaysh wa-l-Huthiyin bi-Harf Sufyan wa 'Ummal a-Nazafa Yantashilun al-Juthath min al-Shawari'," *al-Ayyam*, May 29, 2008. As of January 22, 2010:
http://www.al-ayyam.info/Default.aspx?NewsID=21e2cab4-7d9c-4335-bf8b-b2055b865696

Madabish, 'Arafat, "al-Ra'is al-Yamani Yu'lin Waqf al-Harb fi Sa'da . . . Ba'd Muwafaqat al-Huthiyin 'ala Shurut al-Hukuma," *al-Sharq al-Awsat*, February 12, 2010. As of February 15, 2010:
http://www.aawsat.com/details.asp?section=4&issueno=11399&article=556890&search=اليمن &state=true

al-Mahadhri, 'Abd, "'Abd al-Malik al-Huthi min Ma'qlihi fi Matra li al-Ahale': Lan Nakun Hizban Siyasan, wa Walayat al-Batanin Tantabaq 'ala Hukam al-Yum," *al-Ahale*, n.d. As of February 2009:
http://www.alahale.net/details.asp?id=1984&catid=20&keyword=%E3%DA%DE%E1%E5%20 %DD%ED%20%E3%D8%D1%C9

Mahjub, Tayyib, "al-Tamarrud al-Zaydi fi Shimal al-Yamanj: Haraka Siyasiya wa 'Askariya," *al-Sabah al-Jadid* (Iraq), October 2, 2009. As of January 23, 2010:
http://www.newsabah.com/look/article.tpl?IdLanguage=17&IdPublication=2&NrArticle=32705&Nr Issue=1537&NrSection=5

"Mahrajan al-Intisar," n.d. As of January 23, 2010:
http://sh.g4z4.com/uploads/g4z4-com-12434497210.3gp

"al-Majlis al-Yamani," May 18, 2007. As of January 22, 2010:
http://www.al-yemen.org/vb/showthread.php?p=2876906

"Majmu'a min Shuban Ibb Yutalibun bi-Radd al-I'tibar li-Min Ahtajazahum al-Amn al-Siyasi bi-Tahma Munasirat al-Huthi," *al-Ayyam*, February 28, 2007.

"Makram, Faisal, "Harb Sa'da . . . min al-Tahalif ma' al-Sulta Wasulan Ila al-Harb al-Khamisa (1 min 2) . . . al-Huthin Bashiru al-Tamarud bi-Inqlab a'la Halfa'hum wa Iwsluihi Ila Hamla 'Khomeniya' 'ala al-Mujtama'," *al-Hayat,* July 11, 2008.

————, "Harb Sa'da . . . Bad'an min al-Thalif ma' al-Sulta Wasulan Ila al-Harb al-Khamisa (2 min 2) . . . al-Huthi Fawuda al-Sulta min Tehran . . . wa Libya Iwqafat d'amuhu b'ad Ali Saleh,"*al-Hayat*, July 12, 2008. As of January 23, 2010:
http://www.daralhayat.com/special/features/07-2008/Article-20080711-12d4e911-c0a8-10ed-0007-ae6da3af9241/story.html

"Maktab al-Huthi: Fidiyu li-Qat' al-Ittisalat fi al-Jabal al-Ahmar, wa Fawda Dakhil al-Jaysh wa al-Sulta," *al-Menpar*, September 10, 2009.

"al-Manbar Yu'id Nashr Hiwar al-Sayyid 'Abd al-Malik al-Huthi ma' Sahifat al-Diyar," *al-Menpar*, January 20, 2009. As of January 22, 2010:
http://www.almenpar.com/news.php?action=view&id=1146

"Maqati' min Khutab al-Sayyid 'Abd al-Malik Badr al-Din al-Huthi Hafazuhu Allah" Posted to Youtube.com, August 31, 2009. As of February 15, 2010:
http://www.youtube.com/watch?v=lzidq2Hguj8&feature=related

"Maqta' Fiydiyu Yuwwadih Haqiqat al-Tamwin al-'askari al-Sa'udi Did al-Huthiyin," *al-Menpar,* 3 September 3, 2009. As of February 18, 2010:
http://www.almenpar.com/news.php?action=view&id=1517&spell=0&highlight=%D3%DA%E6%CF%ED

al-Maqhafi, Ibrahim Ahmad, *Mu'jam Buldan wa Qaba'il al-Yamaniya*, San'a: Dar al-Kalima Center for Printing, Publishing and Distribution, pp. 1422–2002.

"Marhale-ye Jadid-e Hamlat-e 'Arabistan-o-Yaman beh Shi'iyan-e Huthi," *Hamshahri,* December 10, 2009. As of February 17, 2010:
http://www.hamshahrionline.ir/News/?id=102424

"Marwahiya 'Askariya Tuhajim Ma'qalan Jabaliyan Yushakkil Khuturatan 'ala Tanaqqulat Wahdat al-Jaysh," *al-Ayyam*, January 1, 2006. As of January 21, 2010:
http://www.al-ayyam.info/Default.aspx?NewsID=6181c46f-b4ed-412e-abe8-f9512fdc13f3

"Marwahiya 'Askariya Tulqi Munasharat Tad'u 'Ansar al-Huthi li-l-Istislam," *al-Ayyam*, April 11, 2005.

"Masadir Mahalliya Tu'akkid Tamakkun al-Huthiyin min al-Saytara 'ala Jisr Khaniq al-Wasil bayna Harf Sufyan wa San'a," *al-Hadath,* October 3, 2009. As of January 21, 2010:
http://www.alhadath-yemen.com/index.php?news_id=4834

"al-Masajid Masrah li-l-Qatl, Sa'at min al-Harb bayn al-Ma'zin wa al-Huthiyin wa al-Islah Hal Yadkhal al-Muwajaha," *Mareb Press*, July 20, 2009. As of January 22, 2010:
http://marebpress.net/news_details.php?lng=arabic&sid=17659

 "Masdar Mahali fi Sa'da Yukdhib Muz'am (al-Ishtiriki net) Hawul al-Ahdath fi Dahyan Dahyan," *26 September*, March 24, 2007. As of March 2009:
http://www.26sep.net/news_details.php?lng=arabic&sid=24989

"Masdar Muqarib min al-Sayyid 'Ab al-Malik Yunafi ma Nushira bi-Khusus Tard al-Tulab," *al-Menpar*, March 15, 2008. As of February 2009:
http://www.almenpar.com/news.php?action=view&id=537&spell=0&highlight=%C7%E1%D5%CD%E6%C9+%E3%E6%C8%C7%ED%E1

"Mashhad al-Siyasi fi al-Yemen," *al-Jazeera*, August 5, 2009.

"Masra' 3 'Askariyin fi Ishtibakat Musallaha wast San'a," *al-Ayyam,* April 16, 2007. As of January 23, 2010:
http://www.al-ayyam.info/Default.aspx?NewsID=4c787a52-4aa1-4226-be3c-8de6aec64a21

"Masra' Arba'a min Qiyadat 'Anasir al-Irhab wa-l-Tamarrud," *26 September*, September 28, 2009. As of January 23, 2010:
http://www.26sep.net/news_details.php?lang=arabic&sid=57415

"Masra' Mudir li-l-Bahath al-Jina'i wa 3 Murafiqin lahu wa Naja Mas'ul Akhar bi-Sa'da," *al-Ayyam*, January 28, 2006.

"Masra' Thalatha min Qiyyadat al-Tamarrud al-Matlubin Dimn Qa'ima al-55," *26 September*, September 26, 2009.

"Masra' wa Isaba 75 min Atba'ihi: al-Huthi Yalja' ila Istikhdam al-Muwatinin ka-Duru' Bashariya," *26 September*, July 10, 2004. As of January 23, 2010:
http://www.26sep.net/narticle.php?sid=1672

Ma'ud, Hassan, "Nuqtat al-Nizam: ma'a Yahya al-Huthi," *Al-Arabiya,* May 20, 2005. As of January 23, 2010:
http://www.alarabiya.net/programs/2005/05/22/13273.html

al-Menpar Web site. As of March 21, 2010:
http://www.almenpar.com

"Min Isdarat Atba' al-Sayyid Husayn al-Huthi, Muzahir Intisaratihum," video posted to YouTube.com, March 17, 2008. As of February 19, 2010:
http://www.youtube.com/watch?v=FzevuazQazs Junud Tamm Asirhum

"al-Minbar.net Yu'id Nashr Hiwar al-Sayyid 'Abd al-Malik al-Huthi ma'a Sahifat al-Diyyar," *al-Menpar*, January 20, 2009.

"Mobarezan–e al-Huthi Seh Dastegah-e Tank-e Artesh-e 'Arabistan-ra Monheddem Kardand," *Farsnews,* December 4, 2009.
As of January 23, 2010: http://www.farsnews.net/newstext.php?nn=8809130720

"Mu'assasat al-Salih Qaddamat Musa'adat Ghadha'iya li-Khamsat Alaf Usra Mutadarrara min Fitnat al-Huthi," *26 September*, October 31, 2004. As of January 23, 2010:
http://www.26sep.net/narticle.php?sid=3279

"Mubarak Yu'lin Da'mahu li-l-Yaman wa-l-Su'udiya Tanfi Qasf Mawaqi' li-l-Huthiyin," *al-Akhbar* (Lebanon), October 3, 2009. As of March 21, 2010:
http://al-akhbar.com/ar/node/159590

Mudabish, Arafat, "Tariq al-Fadhli li-l-Sharq al-Awsat: al-Janub Yutalib bi-Huquqihi . . . wa Ana Musta'idd li-l-muhakama bi-Tahammat al-Irhab," *al-Sharq al-Awsat,* May 14, 2009. As of January 23, 2010:
http://www.aawsat.com/leader.asp?section=4&issueno=11125&article=519131

"Mudarra'at Su'udiya Tamma al-Istila' 'alayha Khilal al-Muwajahat," November 29, 2009: As of March 21, 2010:
http://www.youtube.com/watch?v=V9PMnjC114o&feature=related

"Mudiriyat Ghamar fi Sa'da Tashhad Ma'arik 'Anifa," *al-Ayyam*, April 12, 2007. As of January 23, 2010:
http://www.al-ayyam.info/Default.aspx?NewsID=cb6a7ffc-3ada-4632-b037-f17c4ac76e52

Muftah, Muhammad, *"Hibat al-Dawla wa Hikmat al-Ra'is, NewOmma.net,* March 13, 2007. As of February 2009:
http://www.newomma.net/index.php?action=showDetails&id=11

"Muhafiz Sa'da al-Jadid Yubashir Muhamihu fi Aqqal min 24 Sa'a," *al-Ayyam*, April 21, 2007. As of January 23, 2010:
http://www.al-ayyam.info/Default.aspx?NewsID=711aad89-ad1c-418f-a6f9-643fda35c8b0

"Muhafiz Sa'da li-26 Sabtambir: al-Ma'raka al-Hasima Lam Tabda' Ba'd min Janib al-Dawla," *26 September*, February 15, 2007.
As of January 23, 2010: http://www.26sep.net/narticle.php?sid=23214

al-Muhsin, 'Abd Husayn al-Nimri al-Hamdani, "Qasida fi-l-Sayyid al-'Allama Husayn al-Huthi," *al-Menpar*, October 3, 2007. As of January 22, 2010:
http://almenpar.net/news.php?action=view&id=178&spell=0&highlight=%DE%D5%ED%CF%C9

"Mukhayyamat al-Yaman . . . Furas Badila li-Himayat al-Shabab," *al-Moheet.com*, August 27, 2008.
As of January 21, 2010:
http://www.moheet.com/show_news.aspx?nid=160177

"Muqabalat al-Sayyid 'Abd al-Malik al-Huthi ma' Sahifat al-Nas," originally printed in *Al-Naas*, April 26, 2006. As of January 22, 2010:
http://www.al-majalis.com/forum/viewtopic.php?t=8749

"Musa Yu'akkid Rafdahu al-Massas bi-Siyadat al-Su'udiya wa-l-Yaman," League of Arab States Website, November 10, 2009. As of January 21, 2010:
http://www.arableagueonline.org/las/arabic/details_ar.jsp?art_id=6373&level_id=944

"Musadamat 'Anifa bi-Sa'da wa-l-Huthiyin Yaqta'un Tariq Sa'da-San'a," *al-Ayyam*, May 10, 2008. As of January 22, 2010:
http://www.al-ayyam.info/Default.aspx?NewsID=6dcb393b-e25e-42e5-b34b-9aba3b1be850

"Musadamat 'Anifa bi-Shawari' Sa'da bayn al-Amn wa 'Anasir al-Huthi," *al-Ayyam*, April 9, 2005. As of January 21, 2010:
http://www.al-ayyam.info/Default.aspx?NewsID=a2f991c3-b880-480e-8394-5fd965409bea

"Mutalaba Urubiya li Idraj Tanzim al-Huthi Dimn al-Munazzamat al-Irhabiya," *26 September*, February 7, 2007. As of January 21, 2010:
http://www.26sep.net/narticle.php?sid=22902

al-Mu'tammar Web site. As of January 23, 2010:
http://www.almotamar.net/news/60084.htm

"Muwajihat bayn Qabilatayn Ahadahuma Mawaliya li-l-Hukuma wa Ukhra li-l-Huthi," al-Ayyam, April 5, 2005.

"Muwatinin min Haydan: al-Huthi Farada 'ala Atba'ihi Dafa' Nasab min Amwalihim ka Atawat Ba'dama Atlaqa 'ala Nafsihi Siffat Amir al-Mu'minin," *26 September,* June 25, 2004. As of January 22, 2010:
http://www.26sep.net/narticle.php?sid=1453

"Nabdha Ta'rifiya 'an Muhafazat Sa'da" (Informative Section about the Sa'da Governorate), *Yemeni National Information Center*, n.d. As of January 23, 2010:
http://www.yemen-nic.info/gover/saedaa/brife/

"Na'ib Muhafiz Sa'da wa Mudir Amnuha Yata'arradan li-Kamin Musallah," *al-Ayyam*, April 4, 2005.

"Naja Ra'is al-Istikhbarat al-'Askariya min Muhawalat al-Ightiyal," *al-Ayyam*, April 27, 2005: As of January 23, 2010:
http://www.al-ayyam.info/Default.aspx?NewsID=e6f3b797-b891-4833-9954-d0fe103f106f

"Najl Husayn al-Huthi; Ad'u 'Anasir al-Tamarrud fi Sa'da li-Taslim Anfusihim li-l-Dawla Dun Shurut," *26 September.net*, July 13, 2008. As of January 23, 2010:
http://www.26sep.net/narticle.php?sid=43754

Na'man, Jamal, "Al-Tahaluf al-Jadid bayn 'Ali Salih wa al-Qa'ida fi-l-Yaman," *al-Menpar*, January 28, 2009.

"al-Nashat al-Iqtisadiya li Muhafazat Sa'da" (Economic Activity for the Sa'da Governorate), undated. As of January 21, 2010:
http://www.yemen-nic.info/gover/saedaa/actionecnom/

"Nass Hiwar Sahifat al-'Arab al-Qatariya ma'a al-Sayyid 'Abd al-Malik al-Huthi," *al-Menpar*, June 2, 2008. As of January 23, 2010:
http://www.almenpar.com/news.php?action=view&id=457

"al-Nufudh al-Su'udi Yatasaddir al-Qa'ima . . . al-Yaman Saha Sira'at Jadida," *al-Ahale*, undated. As of February 2009:
http://www.alahale.net/details.asp?id=1505&catid=4&keyword=%C7%E1%CD%E6%CB%ED

al-Qa'di, 'Abd al-Bassat, "al-Shaykh al-Razihi 'Suleman al-Farah': al-Safir al-Irani Yazur Dahyan min ba'd al-Wahda," *al-Ahale*, undated. As of February 2009:
http://www.alahale.net/details.asp?id=1540&catid=20&keyword=%C7%E1%CD%E6%CB%ED

"Al-Qa'ida Tattahimm Iran bi-Da'm al-Huthiyin li-l-Qada' 'ala Ahl al-Sunna," *Mareb Press*, November 10, 2009. As of January 22, 2010:
http://marebpress.net/news_details.php?lng=arabic&sid=19999

"Qal Inna Tamarrud 'Anasir al-Irhab bi-Sa'da Sina'a Istikhbariya . . . Wazir al-Awqaf yatahmm Duwal wa Mu'assasat Shi'iya bi-Istihdaf al-Yaman," *26 September*, February 18, 2007. As of January 23, 2010:
http://www.26sep.net/narticle.php?sid=23375

"Qalu Anna al-Sulta Tata'amal ma'a Shurafa' al-Muhafaza wa kannahum Majami' Murtaziqa: Arba'a min Nuwwab Sa'da 'an al-Mu'tammar al-Hakim Yuqaddimun Istiqalatahum min al-Mu'tammar li-Rai'is al-Jumhuriya," *Mareb Press*, July 12, 2009. As of January 23, 2010:
http://www.marebpress.net/news_details.php?lng=arabic&sid=17491

"al-Qibd 'ala Majami' Kabira min Atba' al-Huthi," *26 September*, June 19, 2008. As of January 22, 2010:
http://www.26sep.net/narticle.php?sid=42926

Qina, Khadija bin (hostess), "Ma Wara' al-Khabr: Sira' al-Hukuma al-Yamaniya ma'a al-Huthiyin," *al-Jazeera*, April 29, 2007. As of February 2009:
http://www.aljazeera.net/NR/exeres/CC38FEF3-FAD9-4B2F-9895-4526FFBBE3D5.htm

"al-Qissa al-Kamila lil Huthi wa al-Zaydiya fi al-Yemen," *al-Arabiya*, July 10, 2004. As of May 2009:
http://www.alarabiya.net/articles/2004/07/10/4917.htm

"al-Qurbi Yu'akkid: Yumkin bi-l-Irada al-Siyasiya Tajawuz 'Amil al-Zaman li-Indimam al-Yaman li Majlis al-Ta'awun al-Khaliji," *26 September*, October 10, 2008. As of January 21, 2010:
http://www.26sep.net/narticle.php?sid=38215

"al-Qurbi: La Wasata bayn al-Yaman wa Iran wa Milaf al-Huthi Sayughlaq Qariban," *26 September*, August 4, 2007. As of January 21, 2010:
http://www.26sep.net/narticle.php?sid=30989

"Al-Quwwat al-Jawwiya al-Su'udiya Taqsif Mawaqi' al-Huthiyin Jabal Dukhan, November 6, 2009. As of January 21, 2010:
http://www.youtube.com/watch?v=vbQuN9qViWA&feature=related

"Al-Quwwat al-Jawwiya al-Su'udiya wa Qasfuha l-Mawaqi' al-Huthiyin," November 11, 2009. As of January 21, 2010:
http://www.youtube.com/watch?v=p4l1IeZM46A&NR=1

"Quwwat al-Jaysh Ta'thur 'ala Makhzan Silah fi Ihda Manatiq Mudiriyat Sahar bi-Sa'da," *al-Ayyam*, March 22, 2007. As of January 23, 2010:
http://www.al-ayyam.info/Default.aspx?NewsID=fb7dd6f0-923c-406b-bb03-188c6be4ebdb

"al-Quwwat al-Musallaha Taqtal 'Adadan min al-Mutamarridin fi Ishtibakat Qaryat al-'Ayn al-Hara," *Saudi Ministry of Defense*, undated. As of January 21, 2010:
http://www.moda.gov.sa/Detail.asp?InSectionID=21&InNewsItemID=1845

al-Ram'i, Ahmad, "al-Khilafat al-Jalliya li-l-Huthi ma'a Madhhab al-Zaydiya," *al-Mithaq.net*, May 21, 2007. As of January 22, 2010:
http://www.almethaq.net/news/news-3192.htm

"Ra'is al-Da'ira al-Siyasiya: Haml al-Silah fi Wajih al-Sulta Karitha wa la Ijd li-al-Harb wa al-Tasa'id Ayy Mubarar," NewOmma.net, January 29, 2007. As of February 2009:
http://www.newomma.net/index.php?action=showNews&id=5

"Ra'is al-Jumhuriya Ya'mur bi-Iqaf Tanfidh al-Ahkam al-Qada'iya fi Haqq al-Daylami wa Miftah wa-l-Ifraj 'Anhuma," *26 September*, May 20, 2006. As of January 23, 2010:
http://www.26sep.net/narticle.php?sid=15138

"Ra'is al-Jumhuriya Yar'as Ijtima'an li-l-Lajna al-Wataniya Iqaf al-'Amaliyat al-'Askariya fi al-Mintaqa al-Shamaliya al-Gharbiya" *26 September*, February 11, 2010. As of February 15, 2010:
http://www.26sep.net/news_details.php?sid=61153

"Ra'is al-Jumhuriya Yastaqbal Qa'id al-Qiyada al-'Askariya al-Amrikiya al-Markaziya: Bahatha ma'ahu al-Ta'awun al-'Askari wa Mukafahat al-Irhab," *26 September*, July 26, 2009. As of January 23, 2010:
http://www.26sep.net/news_details.php?lng=arabic&sid=55796

"Ra'is al-Jumhuriya Yuwajih bi-Sur'a Mu'alajat Athar Fitnat al-Huthi fi Marran Ta'wid al-Mutadarrarin," *26 September*, October 9, 2006. As of January 23, 2010:
http://www.26sep.net/narticle.php?sid=19206

"al-Ra'is Saleh: Lan Nataraji' Law Istamarrat al-Ma'raka fi Sa'da Khams aw Sitt Sanawat," *al-Mu'tammar.net*, September 28, 2009. As of January 21, 2010:
http://www.almotamar.net/news/74074.htm

"al-Ra'is Yufaddil al-Hall al-Silmi Kay La Tuthar al-Na'arat al-Madhhabiya wa-l-'Ulama' Yarfudun Ihtikar al-Wilaya li-Sallala Mu'ayyana," *26 September*, June 2, 2007. As of January 21, 2010:
http://www.26sep.net/narticle.php?sid=28301

"Al-Ra'is: Sana'rad Usrat Al Hamid al-Din 'an Mumtalakatihum," *al-Ayyam*, September 26, 2005. As of January 21, 2010:
http://www.al-ayyam.info/Default.aspx?NewsID=51a6eb98-09b3-4e83-963d-dadc86386980

Sabi', Nabil, "Tard al-Shuhud min al-Yaman wa Ighlaq al-Bilad 'ala Hurub Ghayr Mahduda," *al-Nida'*, April 30, 2009. As of January 23, 2010:
http://www.alnedaa.net/index.php?action=showNews&id=2539

Sa'da Now Web site. As of March 21, 2010:
http://www.sadahnow.com

Sa'da Online Web site. As of March 21, 2010:
http://www.sadahonline.org

Salam, 'Abd al-Karim, "Man Huwwa al-Shaykh Badr al-Din al-Huthi," April 7, 2005. As of January 23, 2010:
http://www.swissinfo.ch/ara/front/detail.html?siteSect=105&sid=5663639&cKey=1112857971000

"Salih Habra Yawajjih Khutabahu Ila al-Ra'is wa Yatasa''al In Kanat Tasrihat al-Jundi Tansalan Rasmiyan min Ittifaq al-Doha," *al-Menpar*, April 15, 2008. As of January 23, 2010: http://almenpar.net/news.php?action=view&id=607

al-San'ani, Abu al-Bara', "al-Huthiyun Rawafid bi-Qana' Zaydi," *Sada al-Malahim*, Year 3, Issue 12, February 15, 2010.

Sayyaghi, Ahmad ibn Ahmad, *al-Manhaj al-Munir Tatimmat al-Rawd al-Nadir*, ed. 'Abdullah ibn Hamud ibn Dirham al-'Izzi, San'a: Mu'assasat al-Imam Zayd ibn 'Ali al-Thaqafiya, 2005.

"al-Sayyid 'Abd al-Malik al-Huthi fi Hiwar Jadid ma'a Sahifat al-Nas," *al-Menpar*, June 21, 2008. As of January 21, 2010: http://www.almenpar.com/news.php?action=view&id=850

"al-Sayyid 'Abd al-Malik al-Huthi li-l-Khalij: La Natallaqi al-Da'm min Iran, wa al-Azma al-Siyasiya bi-Imtiyaz wa la Nurid 'auda al-Imama," originally printed in *al-Khalij*, September 29, 2009. As of January 22, 2010: http://www.almenpar.com/news.php?action=view&id=1614

Shahrastani, Muhammad ibn 'Abd al-Karim, *Kitab al-Milal wa-l-Nahl,* Leipzig: Harassofitas, 1923.

al-Sha'lan, Zafir, "Mufti al-Su'udiya: al-Mutasallilun Da'at Fasad wa Dalal . . . wa Afrad al-Jaysh 'Mujahidun'," *Elaf,* November 11, 2009. As of January 22, 2010: http://www.elaph.com/Web/NewsPapers/2009/11/502060.htm

"al-Shami: al-Silat bayn al-Huthiyin wa-l-Qa'ida wa-l-Infisaliyin Mawjuda mundhu Fitra," *al-Mu'tammar Net*, September 30, 2009. As of January 23, 2010: http://www.almotamar.net/news/74120.htm

"al-Shami Yu'akkid anna Fitnat al-Huthi Tamm Mu'alajatuha Niha'iyan," *26 September*, October 13, 2006. As of January 22, 2010: http://www.26sep.net/narticle.php?sid=19314

Sharbil, Ghassan, " 'Ali 'Abdullah Salih li-l-Hayat: La 'Ilm Li bi-Muhawalat li-Ightiyali wa-l-Safqa al-Iraniya al-Amrikiya Mawjuda," *al-Hayat*, March 28, 2009. As of January 23, 2010: http://www.daralhayat.com/internationalarticle/2844

Sharbil, Ghassan, "'Ali 'Abdullah Salih: al-Tansiq al-Yamani-al-Su'udi Mumtaz," *al-Hayat*, March 28, 2009. As of January 23, 2010: http://www.daralhayat.com/internationalarticle/2801

al-Sharjabi, Qa'd, *al-Qarya wa-l-Dawla fi-l-Mujtama' al-Yamani,* Beirut: Dar al-Tadamun, 1990.

"al-Shaykh 'Ayidh al-Qurni Yad'u al-Muslimin ila al-Akhdh bi-Wahdat al-Yaman Tariqan ila Wahdatihim wa I'tilafihim," *26 September*, October 16, 2009. As of January 21, 2010: http://www.26sep.net/news_details.php?lng=arabic&sid=57905

"al-Shurta al-Nisa'iya Tusharik fi Ta'aqqub 'Anasir al-Fitna wa-l-Irhab," *26 September*, June 22, 2008. As of January 21, 2010: http://www.26sep.net/narticle.php?sid=43029

"Silah al-Hudud bi-Sa'da wa Masra' Najlihi wa Shaqiqihi fi Kamin Musallah," *al-Ayyam*, May 14, 2005.

"al-Silah al-Jawwi Yughar 'ala Mawaqi' al-Huthiyin fi-l-Talh wa-l-Madfa'iya Taqsuf Tahsinatahum fi Nushur," *al-Ayyam*, February 28, 2007. As of January 22, 2010: http://www.al-ayyam.info/Default.aspx?NewsID=8836c10d-b9d4-4a23-84b8-f044794dc86f

al-Silmi, Sadiq, "al-Yaman Ya'tamidd Siyasat 'al-Ard al-Mahruqa' li-l-Qada' 'ala al-Huthiyin,"
al-Watan, August 20, 2009. As of January 22, 2010:
http://www.alwatan.com.sa/news/newsdetail.asp?issueno=3247&id=114724

Subhi, Ahmad Mahmud, *Fi 'Ilm al-Kalam: Dirasa Falsafiya li-Ara' al-Furuq al-Islamiya fi Usul
al-Din,* 3rd ed. Beirut, Dar al-Nahda al-'Arabiya, 1991.

———, *al-Zaydiya*, Cairo: al-Zahra li-l-I'lam al-'Arabi, 1984.

"Sudur al-'Addad al-Awwal min Nashrat Basha'ir al-Nasr fi al-Harb al-Sadisa," *al-Menpar*,
September 14, 2009.

al-Sulwi, 'Adil, "Shabakat al-Ta'awun al-Duwali Tuhaqqiq Ziyada Naw'iya fi 'Adad al-Manihin
bi-Miqdar al-Du'f Khilal Sanawat al-Wahda," *SabaNet,* May 18, 2009. As of January 22, 2010:
http://www.sabanews.net/ar/news183857.htm

al-Suri, Abu Mus'ab, "Mas'uliya Ahl al-Yaman tujjah Muqaddasat al-Muslimin wa-Tharwatihum,"
Sada al-Malahim, AQAP, Year 2, Issue 8, p. 21.

"Tadman Qa'ima bi-Asma' 55 Shakhsan: al-Dakhiliya Tatlub min al-Niyaba al-'Amma Isdar Amr
Qahari bi-l-Qabd 'ala Qiyadat al-Tamarrud wa-l-Takhrib min al-Huthiyin bi-Sa'da," *26 September*,
August 18, 2009. As of January 23, 2010:
http://www.26sep.net/news_details.php?lng=arabic&sid=56466

"Taht al-Du': Harb Sa'da al-Khamisa!" *al-'Alam*, January 11, 2008. As of February 2009:
http://71.18.61.110/archive/video/sadah10108.wmv

"Tajaddada al-Ishtibakat bayn Wahdat al-Jaysh wa Atba' al-Huthi bi-Sa'da," *al-Ayyam*, December 21,
2005. As of January 23, 2010:
http://www.al-ayyam.info/Default.aspx?NewsID=1b1a25e8-126b-40b9-8d9c-c21b6fedc862

"Tajaddud al-Ishtibakat bayn Quwwat al-Amn wa-l-Jaysh wa-l-Huthi," *al-Ayyam*, June 7, 2006. As of
March 21, 2010:
http://www.al-ayyam.info/Default.aspx?NewsID=91188ad8-a937-4ccb-805e-3bd2a3c2bb59

"Tajawaban ma'a Ruh al-Wataniya li-l-Muwatinin: al-Mu'askarat Tastaqbil A'dad al-Mutatawa'in
min Abna' al-Qaba'il al-Yamaniya li-l-Tasadi li-D'at al-Fitna wa al-Tamarrud," *26 September*, August
19, 2009. As of January 23, 2010:
http://www.26sep.net/news_details.php?lng=arabic&sid=56505

"Taqrir 'an Harb Sa'da 2004–2005 wa Tabi'atuha," *al-Menpar*, 2006. As of January 23, 2010:
http://www.almenpar.com/id2.php#_Toc148908625.5

"al-Taqrir al-Hukumi Yukashif Tadmir al-Huthiyin 10 Alf Mansha'a fi 11 Mudiriya," *26 September*,
August 16, 2009. As of February 17, 2010:
http://www.26sep.net/news_details.php?lng=arabic&sid=56419

"al-Taqrir al-Khitami li-l-Dhikra al-Sanawiya al-Ula li-l-Shuhada' wa-l-Mafqudin," *al-Menpar*, May
14, 2009. As of February 17, 2010:
http://www.almenpar.com/news.php?action=view&id=1280

"Taqallus Mawaqi' Atba' al-Huthi wa Masadir Tufid bi-annihum Yuqatilun bi-Sharasa," *al-Ayyam,*
January 2, 2006. As of January 23, 2010:
http://www.al-ayyam.info/Default.aspx?NewsID=13591581-a34f-46ef-9c60-7b298bf967e4

"Tasjil al-Sawti li-l-Sayyid 'Abd al-Malik Badr al-Din al-Huthi Yuwwadih fihi ba'd al-Nuqat
al-Muhimma Jidan," *al-Menpar,* November 10, 2009. As of January 23, 2010:
http://www.almenpar.com/news.php?action=view&id=1754;%20

"Ta'zizat 'Askariya Dakhma li-Yasl Ta'dad al-Quwwat Nahu 20 Alf Jundi. . . , al-Jaysh Yuhasir Thani Akbar Madina bi-Sa'da Isti'dadan li-Muhajamat al-Huthiyin," *al-Ayyam*, March 8, 2007. As of January 21, 2010:
http://www.al-ayyam.info/Default.aspx?NewsID=55f1f0b7-d110-4eb3-bf1e-5977d0b6d730

"Thamaniya Bunud Tudhakkir bi-Mawqif al-Huthiyin min al-Harb wa al-Salam wa al-Mujtama' wa al-Nizam," *al-Menpar*, August 17, 2009.

al-Thulaya, Yahya, "Harf Sufyan: Kayf Ahtaraqat Maqqarat al-Ahzab wa Hallat Mahalha al-Huthiya!? Al-Shabab al-Mu'min, min Awwal al-Ghadir Ila Akhir Talaqa . . . Wafa' wa Salsabil wa Haykal . . . Yudhakirun Bila Aml fi Akhtabarat!!" *al-Ahale*, n.d. As of January 22, 2010:
http://www.alahale.net/details.asp?id=2736&catid=3

———, "Jami'at al-Mutanaqidat . . . Dammaj al-Salafiyin, wa Dahyan al-Huthiyin, wa Sa'da al-Mu'tammar al-Sha'bi," *al-Ahale.net*, n.d. As of January 22, 2010:
http://www.alahale.net/details.asp?id=2952&catid=3

———, "Sa'da Ta'rikh Mutamarrid," *al-Ahale*, August 12, 2008. As of January 22, 2010:
http://www.alahale.net/details.asp?id=2936&catid=3

"Tifl Sa'da: Qasida Tahki Lisan Hal Atfal Sa'da," *al-Menpar*, November 20, 2007. As of February 2009:
http://almenpar.net/news.php?action=view&id=273

"Tunshir Nass Taqrir al-Aman al-Qawmi al-Muqaddam Ila Majlis al-Nuwwab wa al-Shura Hawl Ahdath al-Fitna fi Sa'da," *26 September*, February 15, 2007. As of March 21, 2010:
http://www.26sep.net/narticle.php?sid=23234

"al-Ustadh Salih Habra li-l-Manbar: Nutalib al-Sulta bi-l-Iltizam bi-Ittifaq al-Doha Aw An Tukshif Rafdha lahu 'Alnan," *al-Menpar*, November 22, 2008.

"al-'Uthur 'ala Adilla Tathbut Tawarrut Jihat Iqlimiya wa Mahalliya Fi Da'm al-Tamarrud alladhi Qadahu," *26 September,* September 16, 2004. As of January 21, 2010:
http://www.26sep.net/narticle.php?sid=2699

"Wad'u Shurutan Jadida fi Muqabil Tanfidh Ittifaq Waqf al-Tamarrud: 'Huthiyin' Yushakkilun Qiyadat Jadida Munawwa'a li-l-Ittifaq al-Mawqa' ma'a al-Yemen," *al-Arabiya*, June 24, 2007. As of January 23, 2010:
http://www.alarabiya.net/articles/2007/06/24/35847.html

al-Wajih, Abd al-Salam 'Abbas, ed., *Majmu' Kutub wa Rasa'il al-Imam al-Mansur billah al-Qasim ibn Muhammad ibn 'Ali*, San'a: Mu'assasat al-Imam Zayd ibn 'Ali al-Thaqafiya, 2003.

"Waqf al-Qital fi Sa'da wa-l-I'lan 'an al-'Afu," *al-Ayyam*, June 17, 2007. As of January 23, 2010:
http://www.al-ayyam.info/Default.aspx?NewsID=c4611e46-76f5-4008-b34e-6db8af743a93

"Waqfat Amam Tatawwurat bi-Sa'da wa Munashida al-Sulta al-Mahalliya li-l-Dawla Himayat al-Muwatinin: al-Lajna al-Amaniya al-'Uliya Tujaddid Tahdhiraha li-'Anasir al-Tamarrud min Maghbat al-Istimrar fi A'maliha al-Irhabiya wa Tu'akkid Idtirar al-Dawla li-l-Qiyyam bi-Mas'uliyatiha Tibqan li-l-Dustur wa al-Qawanin," *26 September*, August 11, 2009. As of January 23, 2010:
http://www.26sep.net/news_details.php?lng=arabic&sid=56324

"Wasata Qabaliya Tatawassal Ila Rafa' Nuqta Mustahditha Aqamuha Musalahun bi-Tariq 'Amran-Sa'da," *al-Ayyam*, July 22, 2006. As of January 23, 2010:
http://www.al-ayyam.info/Default.aspx?NewsID=36a33004-784d-4a54-9af1-01230002e14c

"Wijhat Nazr al-Akh Yahya al-Huthi Hawla Mawdu' al-Infisal wa Qadiyat al-Janub," *al-Menpar*, May 24, 2009.

"al-Yaman: al-Huthiyun Yaksibun al-Ma'raka al-I'lamiya wa Ihkam bi-I'dam Dubat Muwatinin ma'a al-Huthiyin," *al-Quds al-Arabi*, November 18, 2009. As of January 22, 2010:
http://www.moltaqaa.com/?act=artc&id=4233

"al-Yaman al-Kubra… Tarwi Fusul al-Qissa al-Kamila li-Khanadiq al-Muwajahat fi Sa'da," *al-Yaman al-Kubra*, n.d. As of January 22, 2010:
http://yemenonline.org/makalt/2007/7/makalt5.html

"al-Yaman min Janubihi ila Shimalihi Ma'raka Maftuha 'ala Kull al-Ihtimalat," *Ilaf*, October 1, 2009. As of January 21, 2010:
http://www.elaph.com/Web/Politics/2009/10/488786.htm

"al-Yaman Tastad'i Safiraha bi-Libiya wa-l-Akhira Tanfi Mughadaratahu," *al-Ayyam*, May 12, 2007. As of January 21, 2010:
http://www.al-ayyam.info/default.aspx?NewsID=2012a5ef-5a78-4e66-9c00-bd183b64c792

"al-Yaman Tatlub al-Interbol al-Duwali bi-Taslimiha al-Irhabi Yahya Badr al-Din al-Huthi," *26 September*, February 10, 2007. As of January 21, 2010:
http://www.26sep.net/narticle.php?sid=23013

"al-Yaman, al-Huthiya wa al-Hajis al-Iraniya," *al-Sharq al-Awsat*, May 15, 2008. As of January 21, 2010:
http://www.asharqalawsat.com/leader.asp?section=3&issueno=10761&article=470852&search=%C7%E1%CD%E6%CB%ED%C9&state=true

al-Yamani, 'Ali, "Al-Tahaluf al-Thulayi fi Mu'amarat al-'Udwan al-Sadis…Da'm Mali Su'udi…wa Lujisti wa Fini Amriki. Wa Tanfidh Yamani," *al-Menpar*, April 20, 2009. As of January 22, 2010:
http://www.almenpar.com/news.php?action=view&id=1230&spell=0&highlight=%C7%E1%D3%DA%E6%CF%ED

"Yemen Katliamlarına Büyük Tepki," *Velfecr*, November 23, 2009. As of January 23, 2010:
http://www.thememriblog.org/turkey/blog_personal/en/6369.htm

Yemeni National Information Council 2004, "Nabdha Ta'rifiya 'an Muhafazat Sa'da, *Yemeni National Information Center*, n.d. As of January 23, 2010:
http://www.yemen-nic.info/gover/saedaa/brife/

al-Yemen.org, Web site.

al-Zafiri, 'Ali (host), "Sira' bayn Jama'at al-Huthi wa al-Hukuma al-Yamaniya," *al-Jazeera*, January 2, 2007. As of January 22, 2010:
http://www.aljazeera.net/NR/exeres/58F82D43-51B9-408C-AE6A-AA450B6B27B2.htm